AF479121

This volume is published on the occasion of Corin Hewitt's exhibition *The Hedge* at the Museum of Contemporary Art Cleveland, and documents seven of the artist's installation-performances. Beginning with *Toad in a Hole* (2007) at Bard College, which became a foundational model for future projects, and moving forward through *Weavings* (2007) at Small A Projects, a commercial gallery in Portland, OR; *Seed Stage* (2008–9) at the Whitney Museum of American Art in New York; *Wall* (2010) at Western Bridge in Seattle; *Drying Flowers with Microwaves* (2010) at Dorsch Gallery in Miami; and *The Grey Flame and the Brown Light* (2010) at BCA Center in Burlington, VT.

The following texts examine Hewitt's projects as a continuum of interconnected actions and materializations; instances of generative discovery and contextual play. My interview with Hewitt took place over several months and, much like his work, circles the edges of a generous practice, formed through expansive thinking and pragmatic rigor. Judith Rodenbeck offers an in-depth reading of Hewitt's use of the places of production, connecting him to a lineage of artists who have opened their studios up to viewers. Tina Kukielski considers Hewitt's practice through the genre of still life, the history of photography, and the medium's pliable nature. Finally, Rose Bouthillier leaves us with an epilogue on the visual memory-impression of Hewitt's work. Together with these texts, the extensive collection of images herein—including preparatory sketches, process shots, exhibition documentation, and discrete photographic works—constitute a rich, comprehensive resource that can be returned to for ongoing reflection on Hewitt's practice.

Interview

David Norr: Typically, the place where artists create their work (the studio) is separate from the site of presentation (the museum or gallery). Over the past seven years, you've produced a series of installations for exhibitions that merge the two. Can you describe the parameters of these projects?

Corin Hewitt: In various ways, each of these installations dealt with that anxious relationship between the site of making and the site of viewership. They all consisted of a partially visible enclosed space where I made a body of work over a certain period of time. The installations function like theatrical sets, designed to push a series of site-specific issues forward. The sets are simultaneously photographic, sculptural, architectural, and theatrical. Once I begin working, the elements contained within the set are transformed, synthesized, and reconstituted, all in the service of image making. Five of the projects were geared toward producing a body of photographs, one toward a video, and the most recent, *The Hedge* (2013), toward a group of sunken reliefs.

DN: The sets you construct for the performances create very specific physical constraints for yourself and viewers. What informs the physicality of the structures?

CH: Each set takes on a different group of questions. The sets for *Toad in a Hole* (2007), *Weavings* (2007), and *Seed Stage* (2008-9) were all adapted photo studios inside of white cubes, designed as environments within which I could create a body of still life photographs. Viewers could peer into the space through vertical corner slits in the exterior walls, which created a wide-angle view.

The interior architecture of each of these sets also helped guide the work. For example, for *Seed Stage* I created a series of interrelated structures and systems that utilized decay and preservation as a way to generate images. There were stocks of food, organic and digital composting systems, computers, printers, kitchen equipment, and shop tools that were used to create and process the images. I generated the photographs in the interior space, and after they were framed by the museum, they were hung on the walls surrounding the installation. Over the duration of the show, I removed photographs from the exterior walls and used them as elements for new images that I was making inside.

While conceiving the work, I became interested in using the Whitney Museum's upturned ziggurat shape, designed by Marcel Breuer, as an opportunity to explore a process of image making. The ziggurat was the form of many ancient temples in Mesopotamia. In the 20th century, the inverted or upended ziggurat became a common form for architecture and sculpture. Breuer's Whitney, planned and built between 1963–6, followed Constantin Brancusi's sculpture *Prodigal Son* (1915) and Frank Lloyd Wright's building for the Guggenheim Museum (1959), among several other examples. I was particularly interested in the visual and metaphoric similarity between Brancusi's use of the inverted ziggurat as a base form in *Prodigal Son* and Breuer's design for the Whitney. Brancusi was known for upturning and cycling the relationship between object and base. Breuer's museum seemed to me to be a great space to think about the cycling of materials and upturning of figure and ground.

DN: How was the interior of *Seed Stage* organized?

CH: The space was divided into a front and back by an elevated stage and a row of large, black, inverted ziggurat-shaped storage units. Underneath the stage there was a root cellar and worm bins that were used to compost both photographs and food. The front space was a synthesis of a workshop, photo studio, and kitchen. The rear space was the "historical" area where things were stored and slowly processed, while the front area contained the computers and printer that moved the images through a digital "composting" process.

DN: And the other projects?

CH: The structures of the next four projects were all different. *Wall* (2010) was a fragmented cube; *Drying Flowers with Microwaves* (2010) was a single high wall with mirrors protruding above it; *The Grey Flame and the Brown Light* (2010) was an excised section of Vermont forest floor with a wooden gymnasium floor laid on top; and lastly, *The Hedge* involved a workspace entirely concealed behind false gallery walls. The interiors for the first three white cube projects, along with *Drying Flowers with Micro-waves*, combined elements of a photo studio set up for still life photography with site-specific investiga-tions. *Wall, The Grey Flame and the Brown Light,* and *The Hedge* all contained workspaces that were not photo-centric per se, but were still structured around different image-making processes.

DN: So, the set becomes the system, and the system directs you. The entire enterprise seems to strive for methods of production that are auto-generative.

CH: I am interested in the freedom that limits can create in systems, particularly limits that allow for expansion, mutation, and change. In each of these projects, I tried to allow that freedom to unfold within a structure, a specific architecture, set of tools, and set of materials that I would then manipulate to make images over a given length of time. The digital and analog tools I use to process images in these works are an important part of the system. As I mentioned, in *Seed Stage,* I wanted to use both digital and analog composting systems to transform the images I was shooting. For the analog part, I made a series of worm compost bins where I decayed photographic prints along with food. The compost was another way to "process" the photographs. After they had spent several days in the worm bin, I would take the prints out and reuse them as backdrops or as parts of new images. For the digital component, I asked artist Siebren Versteeg to help me make an algorithm that would transform, or "compost," digital photographs into plaid patterns. This program, *Ouikiltit,* creates a digital loom out of an image, where the colors are averaged and arranged in a grid. I was able to go in and change the "thread count" and scale, and could use an eyedropper tool to reintroduce colors culled from the image back into the loom. These plaids were then printed out and incorporated into future images.

DN: In the 60s, your father, Francis Hewitt, along with Ernst Benkert and Ed Mieczkowski, started the Anonima Group in Cleveland, an influential arts collective focused on perceptual psychology. You have done a lot of the historiography around Anonima's work, and there are moments in your own practice when you directly reference their projects. Can you talk about this influence?

CH: Growing up, I perceived the work done by the Anonima Group to be academic, didactic, and impersonal. I didn't really understand that their work actually created a productive tension between the mechanics of perception and a subjective exploration of seeing. In 1965 they made a four-year plan, which said that each year they would make paintings about a different perceptual "cue"—size change,

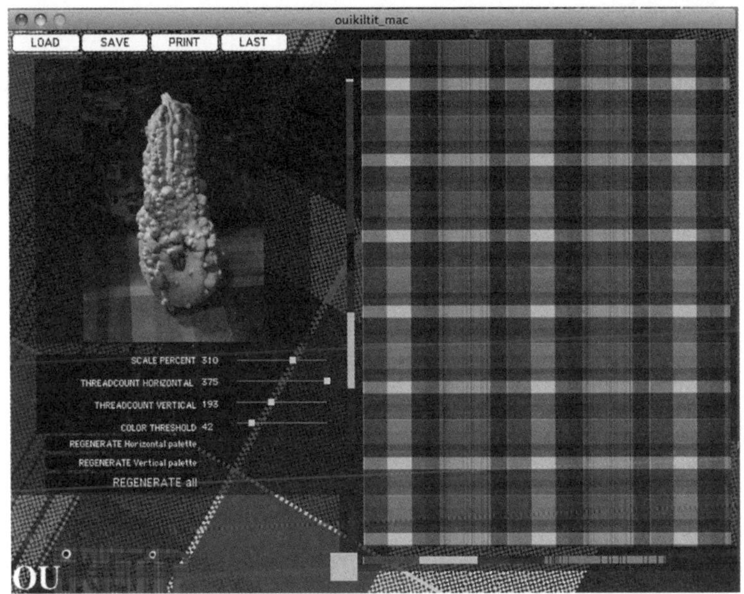

Corin Hewitt, screen capture of Ouikiltit application, 2008. Courtesy of the artist and Laurel Gitlen, New York.

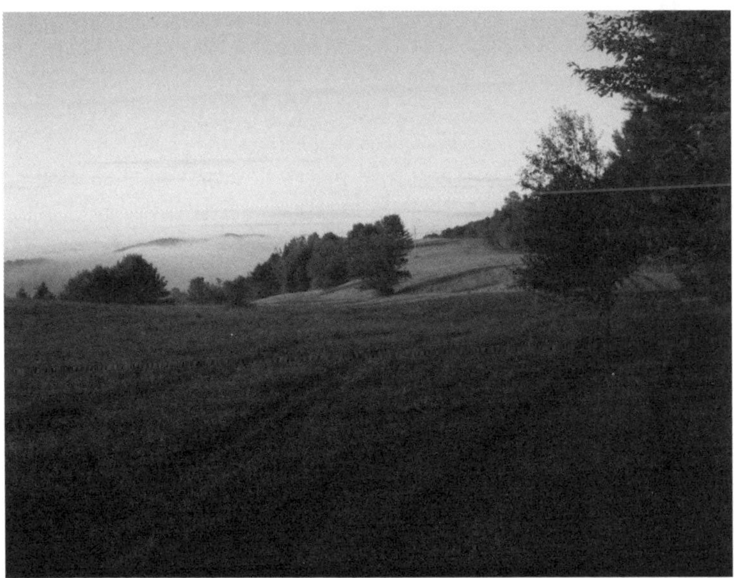

The Hewitt family land in East Corinth, Vermont. Photo: Corin Hewitt, 2011.

overlap, brightness, light and shade—that gave the illusion of depth on a two-dimensional surface. That structured annual system remains interesting to me.

One connection I feel with Anonima's approach is a focus on the perceptual process itself, and an interest in systems. That famous late-sixties Jack Burnham essay "Systems Esthetics" is provocative to think about in relation to what they were doing. Like several other writers and artists at the time, Burnham championed an art of "stable, ongoing relationships between organic and non-organic systems." Also within this context, Richard Brautigan wrote his great poem "All Watched Over by Machines of Loving Grace" where he talks about the fantasy of a "cybernetic meadow" of perfect harmony. This fantasy of a steady-state ecology was deeply connected to other hopes of finding systems that, if maintained, would support a truly democratic utopian society. Like the inspirations for Anonima, this impulse stretches back in art to the socialist and constructivist programs of the early twentieth century in Europe. I think that my father really wanted to find a stable system where the group could keep producing indefinitely, but in the end, ambition and individual style created fissures and eventually broke up the group.

Also, my mother, Karen Hewitt, was very involved with Anonima as an artist early on. She ended up becoming a toy designer and educator, focusing on open-ended systems. She designed a wide array of block sets where kids are allowed to create meaning as they play. This freedom to respond to work as it progresses feels connected to the way I look at systems in my installations.

DN: There are also tools within these systems, such as cameras, which equally direct your activities. I am thinking about *Double Room* (2009), the collaboration you did with Molly McFadden, and how the format of the Polaroid shaped the entire project.

CH: For *Toad in a Hole*, I used a variety of cameras, in part because I knew very little about photography and hoped that a wide arsenal of tools would result in something, anything, happening. It was similar with lighting—I initially got a bunch of lights and just started playing around. Throughout the projects, I became increasingly aware of the potential of different image formats, and the setup and processing that each requires. I discovered that many of the image-making processes could be seen as analogous to the ways in which I was processing food. The slow processing of the 4x5 started to feel like the process of the freezer, the 35mm more like the fridge, the digital like an electric cooktop, and the Polaroid like the microwave oven. Cool and hot cameras.

For *Double Room*, Molly and I exclusively used Polaroid cameras. I liked how they provided an instant image that is often difficult to interpret. For this work, we constructed two identical rooms that viewers could see into through large cutouts. These rooms were about 35 feet long, quite narrow, and had a mirror at the far wall. The walls and floors narrowed as they extended away from the audience, creating the effect that as we moved further away from the audience, our bodies appeared to stay the same size. Each morning, we would enter separate rooms and begin making an alteration to the room. At noon, we would each take two Polaroids of the alteration and exchange them under a door connecting the rooms. Using these two Polaroids, we would do our best to reproduce the alteration that the other had done. The next morning, we would switch rooms and start again. Over the course of three months these two rooms grew like uneasy twins, blurring the lines between original and reproduction. It was really interesting to see how fidelity of reproduction played out in relation to different images, different actions, and different materials.

DN: When did performance first enter your work?

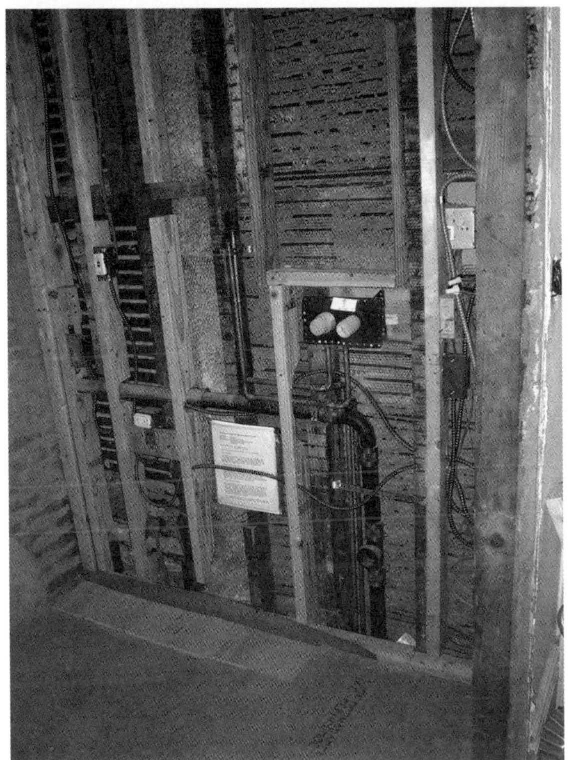

Packet left by Corin Hewitt in an interior wall after a plumbing job, 1998.

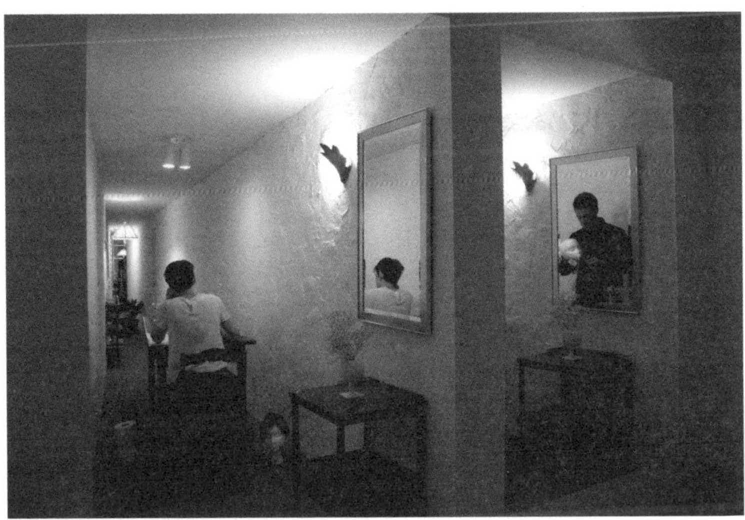

Corin Hewitt and Molly McFadden, *Double Room*, 2009, performative installation, 8 x 45 x 20 feet.
Photo: Nick Johnson. Recess Activities, New York. Courtesy of the artists.

CH: The performative elements go back to when I was a student at Oberlin College. In 1992, I did a performance where I was hidden behind a long wall and drew the audience using a marker held in my mouth. The wall had two monitors in it that showed the audience partial views of me working, and a camera that sent a live feed of the audience back to me. I remember feeling a particular kind of energy, or charge, while I was doing that piece. Because I was only visible from controlled views, I felt somehow freer than I had in performances where I was in the same space as the audience.

I didn't return to working this way for another 14 years, when I was in graduate school at Bard College. For my thesis show, I had taken over a provisional kitchen in the grad studio to make a body of still life photographs of food. I started using a refrigerator, freezer, microwave, and stove to alter the food I was photographing. I also brought in all sorts of cameras. I had a 4x5, a 35mm, a bunch of drugstore disposables, and a few digital cameras. I was sculpting with Plasticine, and casting some of the food I was including in the images. Over the course of the summer, the space became extraordinarily alive and dense, and I came to feel that I was just another element in a room that was in a state of movement and change. I felt like a fly on the surface of things, but also like a worm moving through them. This was really exciting to me, and I decided I wanted to open the room up and somehow make it visible to an audience, to turn it into an image. One day, after a productive talk with the artist Taylor Davis, I decided to cut a thin vertical section out of the corner of the room for viewers to peer through, creating an effect similar to looking through a wide-angle lens. So, as I was making photographs on the contained set within, the whole room also existed as a mutable image. I wasn't working with any kind of plan. The action of the performance was the action of making images.

I had a great feeling in that space, being in the midst of making something as it was being interpreted. I also liked that my moment-to-moment actions were of minor importance compared to the larger image. It reminded me of the immersed feeling of playing basketball. Your individual actions are being observed, but you are part of a game that has a larger flow.

DN: How do live audiences influence your work?

CH: I've found that I make the most interesting decisions when an audience is close by, but not looking directly at me. Being a part of the work gives me a different kind of freedom, to act in ways more intuitive and improvisational than I had previously experienced alone in the studio. The audience provides a constant, yet low-level, sense of pressure.

Although I experience this generalized pressure due to the audience's presence, I have rarely been conscious of any one individual. I don't speak to any of the viewers and I try not to make eye contact. I imagine it's similar for actors or musicians on a stage. In the installations with the corner apertures, I could often hear people incredibly clearly if they were close to the openings and talking to each other. Their voices projected inside, but I don't think they realized that I could hear them. This running commentary served as a low-volume feedback loop that I could occasionally tune into.

DN: Despite this potential for interactivity, I find your work deeply hermetic. Which is something you really pushed in *The Hedge*, where your workspace was entirely invisible to the audience.

CH: All of my installations have been tightly contained and physically inaccessible to the audience, but in *The Hedge* I was completely removed from view. Separation from the audience has been important to me throughout these projects; I want the installations to have autonomy and be primarily visual

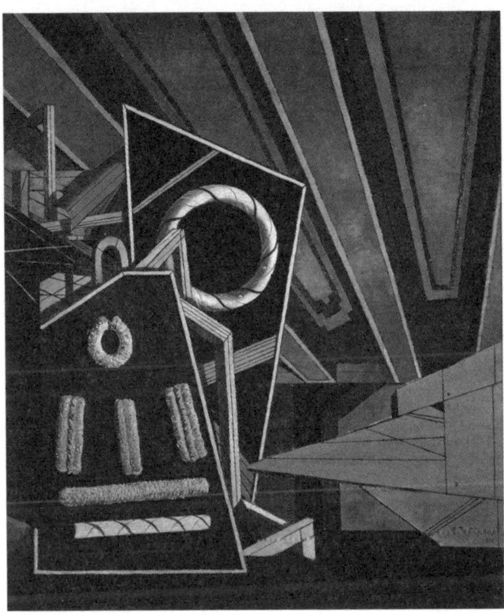

Giorgio de Chirico, *The Revolt of the Sage*, 1916, oil on canvas. Image courtesy of Estorick Collection, London, UK / The Bridgeman Art Library. © 2013 Artists Rights Society (ARS), New York / SAE, Rome

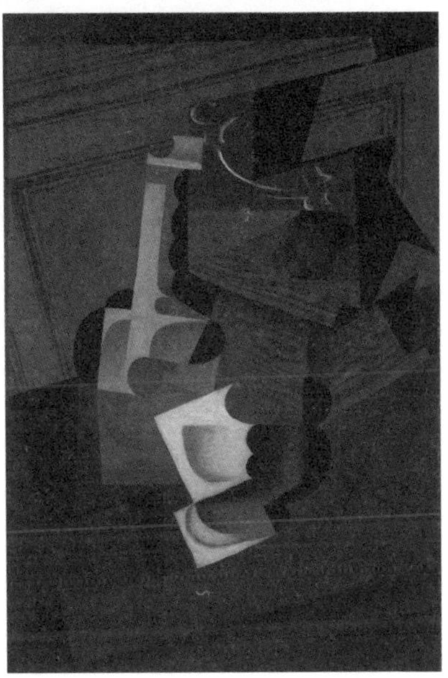

Juan Gris, *The Coffee Mill*, 1916, oil on canvas, 21 5/8 x 14 15/16 inches, unframed. Cleveland Museum of Art. Purchase from the J. H. Wade Fund 1980.8.

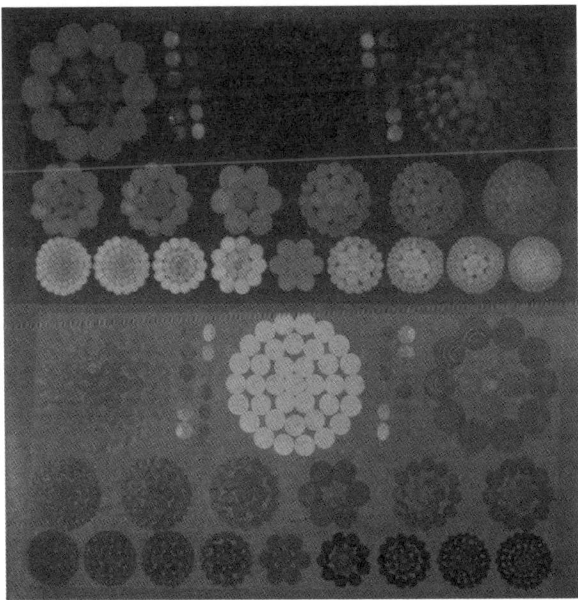

Francis Hewitt, *Altered by Judgment EVEN*, 1964, acrylic on canvas, 62 x 62 inches. Collection of Karen and Corin Hewitt. Reproduction Photo: Corin Hewitt, © Karen and Corin Hewitt.

experiences. I am rarely interested in participatory or relational artworks, where the audience becomes an integral part of the work.

I am also drawn to various hermits throughout history. In my early 20s, I began reading the writing of Thomas Merton, a mid-20th-century monk, mystic, and activist. He wrote strangely and beautifully about hermetic mysticism. After a bohemian life in the 1920s, where he became close with writers and artists such as Ad Reinhardt, he went to a seminary and joined the Trappist order, remaining there for most of the rest of his life. His spiritual practice was searching and expansive, within the limits of Catholicism. He also loved the disciplined and structured improvisation of jazz, and you could feel that in his descriptions of spiritual practice. His form of hermeticism was really appealing to me—structured and ecstatic.

DN: That is interesting, as the title, *The Hedge*, leads me to think about personal space, but also growth.

CH: For *The Hedge*, I wanted to create ambiguity about what it means to have an installation be "live." We generally consider art to be "live" when it is in an active state of change and incorporates the presence of a human actor. I wanted to have this work create uncertainty around that idea—the audience could hear me working inside the walls, but it was intentionally unclear whether the sounds were live or recorded. I wanted there to be a sense of constant and ongoing labor, but for only the results of that labor to be visible.

I also tried to capture this tension when I titled the work. As a kid, I used to play baseball in a park that was bordered by a tall hedge that separated it from a parking lot. That hedge was like a wall but it was alive and kept absorbing things—we lost so many balls in that hedge. It was both a wall and a living, growing space. That hedge fascinated and scared me.

Later, working as a plumber and electrician in New York during the 90s, I spent a lot of time working inside of walls. I became more aware of the fact that although walls appear to most people as flat, two-dimensional surfaces, they actually hold the collected evidence of a multitude of laborers. They are hidden receptacles for action over time, storing and recording history. When I was working on a job at the Knickerbocker Club in New York, I spent months hidden in the specially designed service walls and between the floors of the building. It was a strange feeling—again, I kind of felt like a worm, reworking things underneath and behind the walls' surfaces.

DN: You told me once about the packages you used to leave inside the walls.

CH: I often wished that I knew who the workers were and what their thoughts were as they labored inside these confined spaces. I started making packages in which I included descriptions of the job I was doing, my thoughts on the work, and photographs of myself working in the space. I put these notes and images, along with my contact information, inside ziploc bags. I left these bags where I felt my repair work was weakest and most likely to require re-entry into the wall. I left about 15 of these packages in buildings around New York City. No word yet.

DN: I wanted to ask you about dirt, which makes its way into many of your projects. When did you first begin working with it?

CH: I've used dirt collected from under our cabin in Vermont since the late 90s, when I cast an elaborate doorway and pediment to frame the first version of my Willard Scott installations, which were built

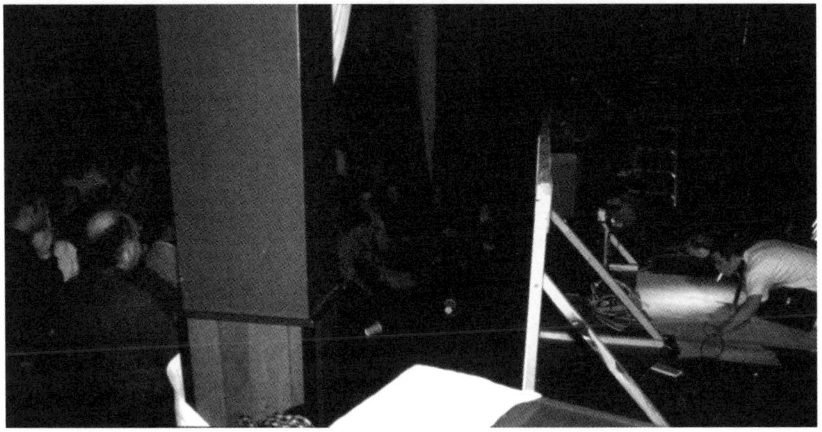

Corin Hewitt, *Drawing From Behind a Wall*, 1992, performance view, Oberlin College. Courtesy of the artist.

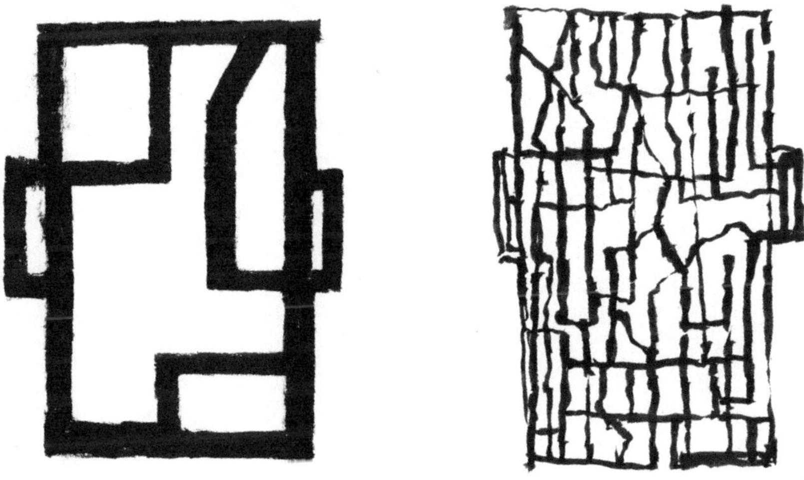

Ernst Benkert, selections from *109 Stackheads*, undated, ink on paper. © Ernst Benkert Estate, and used with kind permission of the artist's family.

around an oversized cast marble sculpture I had made of Scott, an iconic weatherman. The final realization of that work ended up with him buried in the earth on our land. I was also making a lot of cast dirt picture frames around this time, to hold my drawings of this project. I continued to mix this same dirt with resin, which I used to make *85 Union Street* (2004), a sculpture of the Skylab space station. I've been using dirt as a casting medium in a variety of projects since then.

DN: The dirt must also be personal. Your father was a seventh-generation Vermonter. After living in Cleveland and New York, your parents bought a large piece of land in Vermont, and you spent your summers there growing up. Since your father's death, you and your mother have continued caring for the land.

CH: Growing up, I moved dirt around all the time, and got comfortable being dirty. To the dismay of many who are close to me, I'm actually most at ease when I have some grime on me…it helps me know where I've been.

Something my father thought a lot about in his painting is how dirt is simultaneously a color and a location. Different soils have different compositions, and therefore different colors. Different soils cause things to rot differently, or alternately, help to preserve them. I really thought about the preservation aspect of soil when I saw these amazing exhumed mummies in Guanajuato, Mexico. They were disinterred because the graveyard in this hilltop town got filled up and the local government started requiring relatives to pay taxes to keep the bodies in the ground. As they were removed, they found that many of the bodies had been preserved by the chemical composition of the soil. I think a lot about that unintended suspension of decay.

DN: Then there is the little compressed ball of dirt in *The Hedge*. It was sitting on one of the exposed studs within the wall and looked like it had been rolled in mineral pigments. It also had what looked like makeup pads half buried within it. It was this rich little ball of material data that held together a lot of clues.

CH: For years, I have made these balls using the leftover dirt from the casting process. After filling molds with the resin mixed dirt, I take the leftovers and mix it with stuff around the studio. They are small accretions that didn't enter the larger system. Like hairballs thrown up by a cat.

I like to think about the mysterious depth of the generations of life contained within soil. Darwin was also interested in soil and felt that it contained secrets forever hidden from scientific understanding. He had this wonderful idea about the earthworm's role that I like to think about. He posited that the weather will never be truly predictable because of the unpredictable way that worms move moisture and material around in the soil. We will never be able to determine exactly where evaporation will occur. According to him, we are in a kind of unstable sandwich between the shifting earth below and the shifting sky above. Funny to give the earthworm so much credit. This was, of course, before we knew about plate tectonics.

Working on our land in Vermont, we have to deal with endless amounts of glacial rock that keep rising up in the soil. Each year the cycle of freeze and thaw lifts bigger rocks up, like quarters in a jar of change. The building of stone walls across the state helps get these stones out of the fields, while also serving as fencing and property dividers. I was thinking about this in *The Grey Flame and the Brown Light*, where I was scanning rocks and topsoil and then using Photoshop to compress the scanned images into a single color. I would then make a print of this color and let it fall back into the soil on the floor of the install-ation. Over the duration of the show, the soil started decomposing and reabsorbing these monochromes.

DN: It is interesting to relate soil to collage, as a layering of histories atop histories.

CH: I think about how things overlap in time. Although time may go only in one direction, history is not merely sequential. I like how materials and actions rest on top of one another, but rarely does sequencing alone feel like progress. Collage and its history are very present in my mind, especially in the most recent projects.

Back in a high school art class, I copied one of Juan Gris's synthetic cubist paintings for an assignment. This exercise left a strong impression on me; I still appreciate Gris's sophisticated way of using *trompe l'oeil* and collage to visually collapse arrangements on café tabletops. Even though the objects (cups, plates, cutlery, newspapers, tables, etc.) and their environments (windows, rooms, exterior views) inherently overlap each other, various parts oddly bleed through and assert themselves. Gris's paintings evoke the complex, layered, and familiar experience of watching things pass over a surface. The ways that objects dissolve into each other in these paintings reminds me of materials composting into dirt. When I'm working, I like to think about soil, walls, and computer screens in a similar way.

DN: In *The Hedge*, viewers look at compositions recessed into the walls. Everything "on view" is actually behind the walls, which is not exactly what viewers expect when they walk into a museum.

CH: I wanted to have the viewers enter the installation and initially think they were looking at a series of photographic images on the walls. Then, as they moved into the room, they would see that these "images" were actually spaces between two strangely close walls. With this relationship between image and space, you could also consider this installation as a series of relief sculptures.

During the time I worked as a plumber, I encountered these things called "truth windows," which are openings in walls that reveal the layers or materials inside. They usually exist as a way to show a special material or historic aspect of the building. I like thinking about this in reference to how a surface often contains a complex history.

DN: There were also large images that you inserted within the walls, which functioned much like backdrops. The actual images were shots of the walls in your studio in Richmond. I was interested in the tension or confusion over what I was seeing, whether I was looking at real space or image space. It is actually a combination of both.

CH: The photographic backgrounds that slid behind cutouts in the second wall proposed a kind of third wall. These low saturation, nearly monochromatic images of walls were taken from my studio, printed on vinyl, and mounted. Over the course of the exhibition, I manipulated versions of these images, and then put them back into the installation. I cut them, and applied spackle, paint, and other materials in order to give them a greater physical presence.

DN: Though the backgrounds are presented vertically, you often lay them flat, like a table surface, to work on them. Some elements sink into the ground and others "stand out," if you will. I am wondering if this perspective shift alters the way you place and layer images?

CH: I worked on the backgrounds both horizontally and vertically. Working with liquid materials is obviously very different when working horizontally, just like suspending things on the wall is different than setting things on a tabletop. I like thinking about the differences between the work of 19th-century painter William Harnett, who made these great trompe l'oeil paintings of vertical surfaces, versus, say, Gris, Pablo Picasso, or Georges Braque, who mostly focused on tabletops. Another favorite series of paintings is Giorgio de Chirico's *Metaphysical Interiors*, which he made in a tiny apartment in Ferrara, Italy, in 1917. They are magical and full of beautifully strange inventions. These paintings also have a lot of back and forth between the horizontal and the vertical. Part of the intention of my work is to keep the vertical/horizontal and figure/ground relationships in states of change. Each installation begins with a certain set of ideas that have the potential to develop those endlessly mutable relationships.

DN: In addition to the photographic backdrops, *The Hedge* incorporated unusual sculptural elements that reference the 2x4 studs used to frame walls. These elements are abstract and seem structural, but are also quite figurative. Can you talk about how they were generated?

CH: The sculptures were made to fit between studs in standard wall framing. They are cast with Structo-Lite, a material that is generally used as a base coat for plaster. The shapes of the sculptures themselves were influenced by two main sources: the unusual stud formations I have seen inside of walls, often created by years of repair, and a wonderful series of drawings called *Stackheads* by Ernst Benkert, who continued to be a close family friend after the breakup of Anonima. *Stackheads* was a large series of rectangular abstract ink drawings (onto which Benkert often added square ears). These drawings appear as heads filled with geometric arrangements that avoid representation at all costs— containers for meandering Cartesian thoughts. Some of my sculptures directly quote the forms of Benkert's drawings.

DN: What about the very particular types of objects—toast and rubber gloves, for example—that lay atop these sculptural formations?

CH: These objects are very specific for me: they all share personal and idiosyncratic relationships to different kinds of surfaces. Toast is like a blank canvas or blank wall to hang things on. Each slice offers a kind of fresh promise cut from a larger loaf. Crackers are similar, but not as big of a commitment. Foundation makeup is used to "put on a new face" and reminds me how much people love to resurface themselves. Rubber gloves and work boots are functional separations between the body and the world. They both create temporary protective surfaces that accumulate wear. Flash drives are memory storage devices that are hard to truly wipe clean. This tension between origins and history is an ongoing theme in my work. With all these objects there is a conversation between freshness/newness and material histories that accrete over time.

DN: This conversation seems to be the crux of your work: it's an integral aspect of reproducibility, both artistic and biological. Matter, images, and forms in constant oscillation.

CH: I want to pursue systems that assume an endlessness that moves between deep absurdity and hope.

Still Life in Plaid:
Corin Hewitt's environments

by Judith Rodenbeck

The studio is a complex refuge, a place of retreat from the world but also the setting for its production. Picture Saint Jerome, whose monumental translation of the Bible into the Latin Vulgate arguably consolidated the medieval European world view: locked away in his study, accompanied by creatures (a lion, a mouse) and some musty tomes, he hunches over a blank book, shifting his attention from its surface to the spare materiality of his environment to the abstract space of the Word. At the dawn of the Modern era this image of world-making was encoded in one of the tropes of humanism's noble architecture in the form of the *studiolo*, a special room devoted to literature, music, and the arts. Decorated with objects and emblems of natural and cultural realms, these chambers were insignias of knowledge and of its increasingly categorical and, quite literally, architectural indexing; it is from such private cabinets of curiosities that our modern public museums evolved. For artists, the studio itself has posed as topos and problem since at least the 17th century, serving as both site and subject of representation.

The conceit of the studio space as a stage set within the larger theater of the museum has been one signal of Modernism's historical self-consciousness. When Jacques-Louis David first displayed his history painting *The Intervention of the Sabine Women* (1799) in his atelier at the Louvre, the installation included a very large mirror placed in such a way that viewers would find themselves visually incorporated into the massive painting.[1] Twenty years later, while completing his painting *The Raft of the Medusa* (1819), Théodore Géricault crammed his workspace with a model of the raft and a miscellany of rotting body parts from which he executed extensive preparatory drawings; for the final "object study" he shaved his own head to keep himself from going out into the social world. As art historian Svetlana Alpers writes, "The studio is, in an almost primordial sense, a place where things are introduced in the interest of being experienced."[2]

Critic Brian O'Doherty, writes that

Studio time is defined by [a] mobile cluster of tenses, quotas of past embodied in completed works, some abandoned, others waiting for resurrection, at least one in process occupying a nervous present, through which, as James Joyce said, future plunges into past, a future exerting on the present the pressure of unborn ideas. Time is reversed, revised, discarded, used up. It is always subjective, that is, elastic, stretching, falling into pools of reflection, tumbling in urgent waterfalls.[3]

1) See Frédérique Desbuissons, "A Ruin: Jacques-Louis David's Sabine Women," *Art History* 20:3 (September 1997), 432-448.
2) Svetlana Alpers, "The Studio, the Laboratory, and the Vexations of Art," *Picturing Science, Producing Art*, eds. Caroline Jones and Peter Galison (New York: Routledge, 1998), 401-417; quote appears on 408.
3) Brian O'Doherty, *Studio and Cube: On the relationship between where art is made and where art is displayed* (New York: Temple Hoyne Buell Center for the Study of American Architecture at Columbia University and Princeton Architectural Press, 2007), 18.

Gustave Courbet took up this temporal problem of the atelier in his monumental image, *The Artist's Studio, a real allegory summing up seven years of my artistic and moral life* (1854-5), representing the past while also showing, as he famously put it, "the whole world coming to me to be painted."[4] The moment of the great picture is thus both summation and potentiality, and in that very equation, implicative— even as the painter depicts himself splayed back to regard the tip of his brush in what Alpers calls the "forward, probing lean" of in-studio representation. Experientially, then, world-making takes place in the artist's studio, and for much of the history of Modern art that dynamic process has found an awkward ontological corkage in the fixed space of the museum.

In 1960, the American artist Allan Kaprow installed what he described as an "environmental maze of chicken-wire, colored lights, bunched-up newspaper, straw, cloth, fake and real apples, and much litter" in a small basement gallery in New York's Greenwich Village.[5] Visitors to *An Apple Shrine* entered a chambered maze, passing into a darkened inner sanctum where an arrangement of apples awaited their delectation. For the symbolically inclined, the fruit, as well as the act of choice, might evoke the biblical Fall or the judgment of Paris; in the context of early 1960s New York, enfolded by newsprint and fencing, the new Pop "nature" of commercial reproduction and the gesture of mimicry and con- sumption would also ring familiar. Just as surely, for the artist himself the apples would have evoked Paul Cézanne's deceptively simple and architectonic still life motifs, which he had studied in depth.[6] In rethinking the still life as both presentation and representation, and expanding "painting" into the spatial and temporal real, Kaprow's environmentally scaled work is a key reworking of the quintessential studio project, "representing the perception of a thing, and representing it for viewers, in such a way as to encourage the mind to dwell on perceiving it as a process."[7]

The still life is a mode of depiction for which the absence of the human figure is crucial, art historian Norman Bryson has argued.[8] Devoted to the unimportant, the transient, the banal—what Bryson dubs "rhodopography" (versus "megalography," the depiction of great things)—the still life releases depiction from straightforward teleological narrativity, and in its very embrace of the quotidian has the potential to resist hierarchy. It is the studio form *par excellence*. What happens, though, when the artist in the studio—think of Courbet, indubitably "megalo-," smack-dab in the center of his picture—becomes an increasingly dominant focus of attention? According to O'Doherty, part of the narrative of artistic Mod- ernism is that eventually the studio itself draws that attention as the index of the live creature that is its inhabitant: "The studio," he writes, "has become the artist *manqué*."[9] The studio retains the vestiges, the maculae, of the artist's process, "what we might call para-creations, footnotes to the departed painting."[10]

The labor is constant though its rhythms are not, temporalities overlap, interweave; studio time is emphatically non-linear. "As one work is worked on," O'Doherty explains, "the others, finished and unfin- ished, are detained in a waiting zone, one over the other, in what you might call a collage of compressed tenses. They—and the studio itself—exist under the sign of process…"[11] In 1961, just a few blocks away from the gallery where *An Apple Shrine* had been installed, Claes Oldenburg began a two-month

4) From a letter Courbet sent to Champfleury (Jules François Felix Fleury-Husson) in 1854, see Karen Hosack Janes, *Great Paintings: The World's Master- pieces Explored and Explained* (New York: DK Publishing, 2011), 157.
5) Allan Kaprow in *Remembering Judson House*, eds. Elly Dickason and Jerry Dickason (New York: Judson Memorial Church, 2000): 286. See also Jeff Kelley's exhaustive description of this work in *Child's Play: The Art of Allan Kaprow* (Berkeley: University of California Press, 2004), 52-55.
6) Kaprow had been a student of Meyer Schapiro, whose writings on Cézanne's apples is lapidary, among them *Paul Cézanne* (New York: Harry N. Abrams, 1952) and "The Apples of Cézanne: An Essay on the Meaning of Still-life," *Art News Annual* 36 (1968), 35-53. For an interesting discussion of Schapiro and Cézanne, see: David Trotter, *Cooking with Mud: The Idea of Mess in Nineteenth-Century Art and Fiction* (Oxford: Oxford University Press, 2000).
7) Alpers, 408.
8) Norman Bryson, *Looking at the Overlooked: Four Essays on Still Life* (London: Reaktion Books, 1990).
9) O'Doherty, 13.
10) Ibid.
11) Ibid., 18

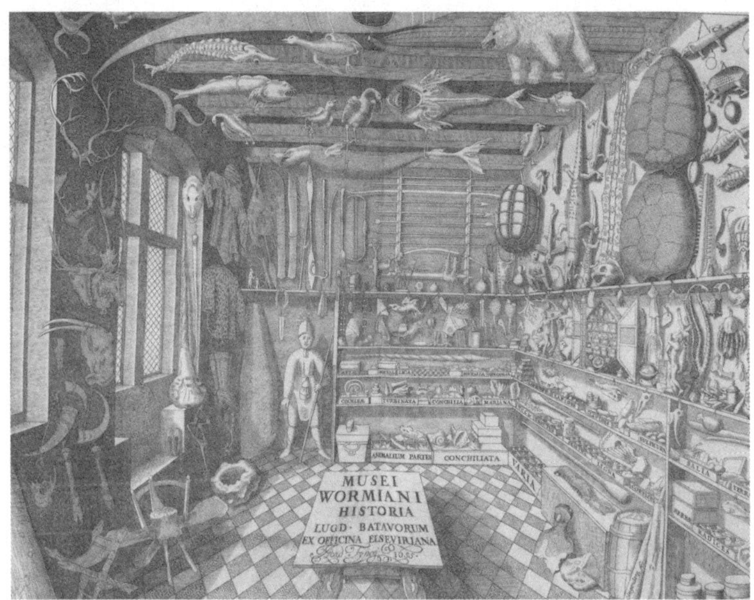

Ole Worm, *Museum Wormianum...* , 1655, engraved title page. Courtesy of Smithsonian Institution Libraries, Washington D.C.

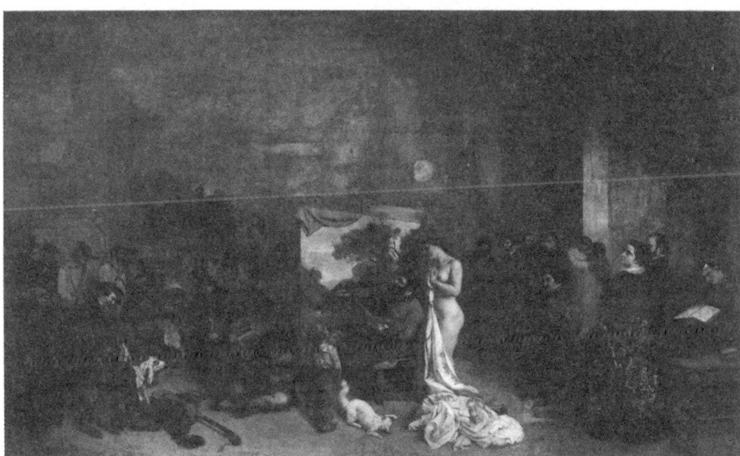

Gustave Courbet, *The Artist's Studio, a real allegory summing up seven years of my artistic and moral life*, 1854/1855, oil on canvas, 142 1/8 x 235 7/16 inches. Reproduction Photo: Gerard/Herve Lewandowski. Musée d'Orsay, Paris, France. © RMN-Grand Palais/Art Resource, NY.

durational project called *The Store*. Renting a storefront in a decaying neighborhood of Mom-and-Pop emporia, Oldenburg set up a space in the back area and spent his days there working with chicken wire, plaster, kapok, and paint, producing and displaying outsized cognates of dresses, stockings, candy bars, and pieces of cake. Visitors could watch the artist at work and purchase items, which would be rung up at the cash register. In Oldenburg's hands, and typical of his transformative representational and scalar vocabulary, these imitations of simple commodities took on uncanny, even fetishistic, bodily aspects. The artist, slathered in plaster and paint, became harder and harder to spot among the faux dry goods. Oldenburg and Kaprow were part of a developing scene of performance done by studio artists, putting acts of material transformation on view, and in doing so, revealing the temporal aspects of production.

Corin Hewitt has taken up the performative legacies of these Pop-inflected environments in a suite of remarkable projects executed since 2007.[12] Hewitt also draws from earlier 20th-century examples including the *Merzbau* of Kurt Schwitters, the self-curated Paris atelier of Constantin Brancusi, and the many studios translated by Piet Mondrian into models of his paintings.[13] Hewitt cuts these with the more proximal punning alchemies of Post-Minimalism—one thinks of Bruce Nauman's *Flour Arrangements* (1967), Vito Acconci's *Seed Bed* (1971), Gordon Matta-Clark's experimental restaurant *Food* (1971, with Carol Goodden), or Mierle Laderman Ukeles's Maintenance Art (1969–ongoing). Each of these projects radically reconfigured labor, production, and consumption via the double-edged critique afforded by old-fashioned studio practice and its complicated attachment to both locale and the dislocated medium of photography.

Hewitt's projects present viewers with a sequence of unusual inversions in the relations between the studio, artist, and gallery. Inside what might be thought of as the architectural core of each project, the artist carries out a myriad of activities: eating, reading, moving objects about, storing them or retrieving them, growing things or canning them, copying things as three-dimensional models or photographs, making prints or analogs and producing what are, in a sense, "seeds" that scatter centrifugally from the workspace to its perimeter. Sequences of complex and gnomic images result—color photographs (such as those generated during *Seed Stage*, many of which have since been used as conceptual mulch for later projects), mirror reflections (*Drying Flowers with Microwaves*), digital projections from an otherwise inaccessible space (*The Grey Flame and the Brown Light*), or deep picture planes embedded in walls (*The Hedge*)—details from a collaged, poetic world itself composed of many shifting details.

Hewitt conceives of these projects in quasi-theatrical terms, and the set designs draw on site-specific details, a private store of spatial memories, and skills garnered over many years working as a contractor. The language of construction is integrated into the range of techniques deployed during each "performance," whether the delicacies of flower arranging or the indelicacies of turning compost. In *Seed Stage*, for instance, the rectangular enclosure contained about ten feet of workshop space, at the end of which was a kitchen counter that also marked the beginning of the "stage" proper. A root cellar and water system occupied the space beneath the stage while shelves above were stacked with canned and dried

12) The projects are: *Toad in a Hole* (2007), Bard College, Annandale-on-Hudson, NY; *Weavings* (2007), Small A Projects, Portland, OR; *Seed Stage* (2008-9), Whitney Museum of American Art, New York; *Weavings: Performance #2* (2009, Seattle Art Museum); *Double Room* (2009) with Molly McFadden, Recess Activities, New York; *Drying Flowers with Microwaves* (2010), Dorsch Gallery, Miami; *The Grey Flame and the Brown Light* (2010), BCA Center, Burlington, VT; *Wall* (2010), Western Bridge, Seattle; and *The Hedge* (2013), Museum of Contemporary Art Cleveland.
13) Hans Ulrich Obrist describes the *Merzbau* as "a series of intensities" that are "less like an envelope and more like a gradual process of sedimentation, a process which is never stabilized," in "Installations Are The Answer, What Is The Question?" *Oxford Art Journal* 24:2 (2001): 95-101. On the *Merzbau*, see Dorothea Dietrich, "The Fragment Reframed: Kurt Schwitters's 'Merz-Column,'" *Assemblage* 14 (April 1991): 82-92; on Brancusi's studio, see the marvelous atmospheric account by Beatrice Wood, "Visit to Brancusi," *Archives of American Art Journal*, 32:4 (1992): 19-24; most useful on Mondrian and architecture is Yve-Alain Bois, "Mondrian and the Theory of Architecture," *Assemblage* 4 (October 1987): 102-130.

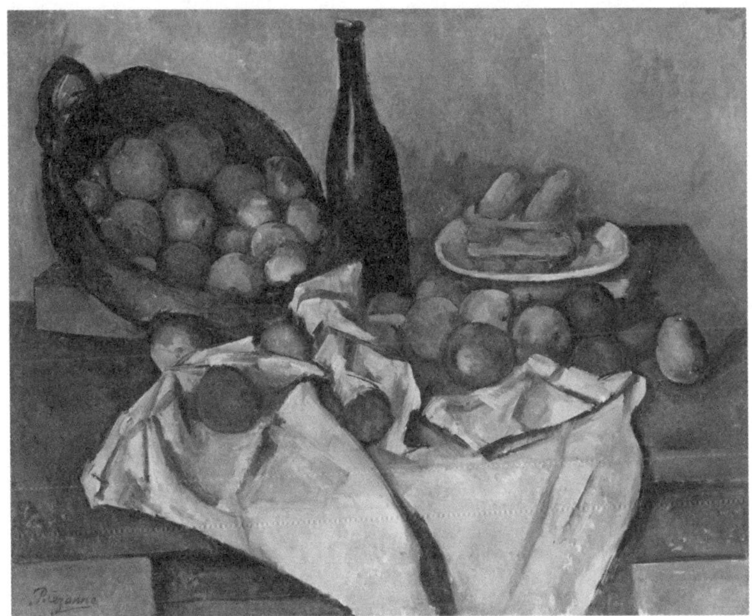

Paul Cézanne, *The Basket of Apples*, c. 1893, oil on canvas, 25 7/16 x 31 1/2 inches. Helen Birch Bartlett Memorial Collection, 1926.252, The Art Institute of Chicago. Photography © The Art Institute of Chicago.

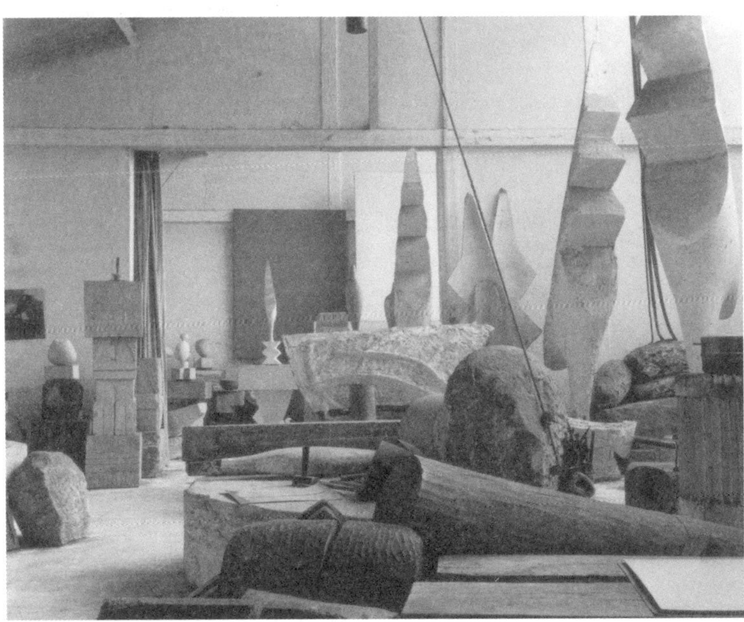

Alexander Liberman, *Constantin Brancusi (studio)*, 1955, photograph. The Getty Research Institute, Los Angeles (2000.R.19). © J. Paul Getty Trust.

goods. Behind the stage, what Hewitt called the "historic" storage held preserved stuff, including older photographs. (Hewitt's studio verb list includes, alongside "cutting, casting, heating, cooling," the word "holding.") As with nearly every dimension of the piece, these built elements were generated through a form of retooling, in this instance taking the profile of the Whitney's iconic Marcel Breuer building, mutating it at scalar and planar levels, and then rendering it horizontally (as flooring/stage) and vertically (as shelving), effectively recycling the building's architectural design elements.

The performed dimension of Hewitt's projects most immediately seems to reward Romantic notions of solitary artistic mystery and the inaccessibility of the creative impulse—a retort of sorts to the contemporary genre of spectacular, but often alienating, participatory artworks.[14] Yet as performances these projects do not *represent* everyday studio activity; if anything, they are anti-heroic, being straightforwardly comprised of that activity. That is to say, they are a kind of rhodopography-in-process. What Hewitt refers to as the "set" is a place of productive and perceptual mobility, addressed, he says, to "the very open relational possibilities between things, but also to the limits of reproduction and the anxieties of reproduction."[15] The activity is potentially infinite, though the artist isn't the "star."

Each of Hewitt's inhabited environments present the artist in a complex kinetic relationship to the set as both object and image. Visually yet only fractionally accessible to viewers, the sets tend to optically flatten under the constraints of radically limited perspectives. But this is not straightforward. In perhaps the most visually available of Hewitt's performance projects, *Double Room* (2009), a collaborative work with Molly McFadden, two parallel shotgun chambers extended like narrow and spare motel rooms towards the back of the gallery, each inhabited by one of the artists. The spaces were constructed in a *trompe l'oeil* fashion to produce the effect of recession into relatively deep space while the binocularity was both confirmed and utterly undermined by the performance. The artists worked steadily in their respective spaces making things, photographing them, and passing the photographs to each other through a small portal, each effectively giving the other artist an assignment to make the thing in the photograph. *Double Room* projected *iterability*, sequentiality, and difference, versus absolute if parallactic synchrony.

This understanding of the studio/laboratory and its performative processes as mediated by the camera is also an understanding of the studio/chamber itself as a camera, a consistent analogy in Hewitt's work. The peculiar game of telephone yielded by procedural homology and duplication performs a looping series of translations: the formal shifts that result when mass is re-presented in two dimensions, when color is approximated by chemistry, when form is translated from the register of the real to that of the virtual. Critic David Joselit has identified the performative aspects of a similar kind of movement in contemporary abstract painting, noting "a form of transmission where passage consists of the passage of an image (a quantum of visual content) from one site, which may be virtual or actual, to another; and/or the passage of the viewer from one painting to another within a site-specific installation."[16] For Joselit, contemporary painting has become what he thinks of as a "broadcast medium," enacting "the dislocation or transfer of populations of images."[17] For Hewitt, a

14) On such projects, see Robert Atkins et al, *The Art of Participation* (London: Thames & Hudson, 2008) and Claire Bishop, *Artificial Hells: Participatory Art and the Politics of Spectatorship* (London: Verso, 2012).
15) Corin Hewitt, conversation with the author, December 10, 2008.
16) David Joselit, "Signal Processing: Abstraction Then and Now," *Artforum* 49:10 (Summer 2011): 356-361, 430.
17) Ibid.

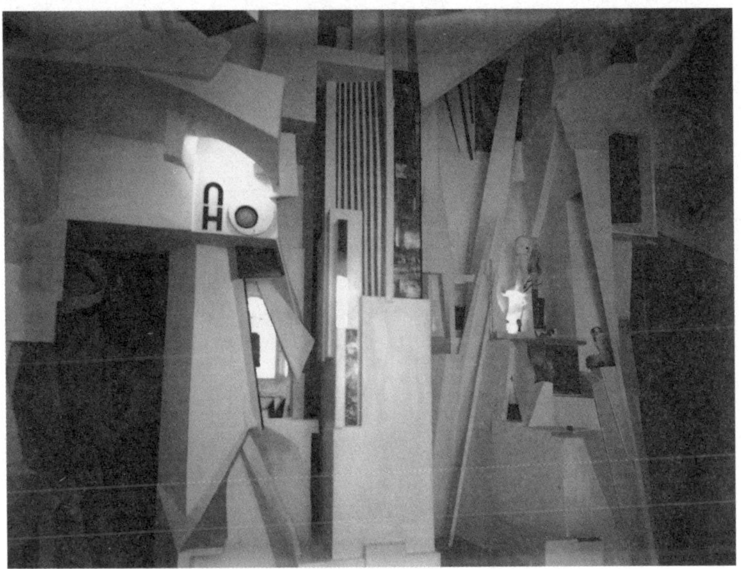

Kurt Schwitters, *Merzbau in Hanover* [view: Staircase entrance page], 1933. Photo: bpk, Berlin/Sprengel Museum Hanover/ Wilhelm Redemann/Art Resource, NY. © 2013 Artists Rights Society (ARS), New York / VG Bild-Kunst, Bonn.

similar concern mobilizes the process of making. "I became interested in the way that photography holds three-dimensional objects that no longer exist," Hewitt says, "especially now that, with such ready access to two-dimensional representations of three-dimensional things, more and more people are experiencing the three-dimensional world in two dimensions."[18] One result of this interest has been the development of a complex conceptual architecture around the idea (and the actuality) of plaid: Hewitt has collaborated with Siebren Versteeg on Ouikiltit, a software program that samples images at a variety of scales to generate plaid patterns. This effectively "composts" the digital data, rendering it into a fertile soil used to form new elements on shelves, in photographs, and in deteriorating mulch. It's a completely crazy idea, but one that brings the conjunction of abstraction and Hewitt's ecstatic materiality into view. A short list of "plaid artists" would surely include not only Schwitters, Brancusi, and Mondrian, but also Ad Reinhardt, Sol LeWitt, Dieter Roth, Phyllida Barlow, Judy Pfaff, Allan McCollum, and R. H. Quaytman—and seen through this lens the "image population" presented by those artists shifts our own gaze back to the studio. The intense material scrutiny exercised in Hewitt's work acknowledges the problem of mediation: the image ecology being explored is quite literally one of proliferation, dislocation, and transfer. Crucially, it is an ecology that has, at its core, a model of generation.

18) Corin Hewitt, conversation with the author, December 10, 2008.

Free Association by Tina Kukielski

"Just at the point where the eye thinks it knows the form and can afford to skip, the image proves that in fact the eye had not understood at all what it was about to discard."[1]
– Norman Bryson

For artist Corin Hewitt, photography persists between poles: the original and the copy, the real and the artificial, parent and child, disappearance and remembrance, the photograph and its reproduction, what we can see in an image and what we cannot. An intentional struggle to conflate the beginning of things with the end of things directs Hewitt's work, which subsumes the modes of sculpture, performance, video, and photography, each in constant cyclical motion. His process is grounded in a series of self-designed, often site-referential systems, which produce new ways of looking at the everyday.

Hewitt's photographs are copies of copies—they collapse distance and close range. They show elevated, or otherwise oblique, views of identifiable and unidentifiable subjects, inviting ambiguity between structure and space, background and foreground, high and low. Both a lack of discrimination in what is being photographed, and a freeing relationship to subject, lead Hewitt to create dense images with heavily-textured layers; sometimes photographs are physically stacked on top of other photographs. What was once on the surface disappears out of the frame, until it is resurrected and reappears later in a new form.

Hewitt had his own distancing experience with a set of photographs when he was just 21 years old. They were the photographs from his father's autopsy. In an interview with critic Michael Brenson, Hewitt explains: "Those photographs, and perhaps also the fact of his death, instantly changed him from a subject in my life to a sort of object."[2] Hewitt's father, the painter Francis Hewitt, died during his son's last year at Oberlin College (also Hewitt senior's alma mater). Since then, Hewitt has assimilated a series of inherited questions as part of the process of asserting his own voice as an artist. This anxiety about origin permeates his work and propels projects that are as equally invested in beginnings, as they are in endings.

Photography made guest appearances in Hewitt's work starting in 1993, before becoming an integral fixture and indispensable tool in his work across different mediums. Early on, it was typical for Hewitt to make a work of sculpture—sometimes realistic, sometimes more abstract—then take a picture of that sculpture, and hang it beside its original. This began in a student exhibition at Oberlin,

1) Norman Bryson, *Looking at the Overlooked: Four Essays on Still Life Painting* (Cambridge, MA: Harvard University Press, 1990), 65.
2) "Corin Hewitt and Michael Brenson in Conversation," in *Corin Hewitt, Weavings: Performance #2* (Atlanta: J&L Books, Inc., 2009), unpaginated.

where Hewitt made an object out of beeswax which resembled a human organ, and hung it hidden within a rectangle of blue curtains. Although there were several viewing holes cut into the curtains (at the relative heights and positions of orifices in the body), allowing partially obstructed views inside, one view of the interior could be seen in a single photograph placed on the wall a few feet away. In 2004, Hewitt completed *85 Union Street*, a sculptural homage to his grandmother as seen through the collapsing of two distinct, historic sites built in replica: the fallen Skylab space station after it crashed to Earth, and two rooms of his grandmother's home, re-constructed from photographs taken immediately after her death. The miniature kitchen and living room could be seen either by looking through various cracks through Skylab's surface, or alternately, in two photographs hanging nearby. The work was meant to provoke an experience of partial views, of looking without entering, playing with what is visible and what is not.

That the original and its photographic copy were so frequently paired in Hewitt's earliest work is perhaps an indication of the importance of both to his perspective on the world. He has said: "I wanted to close the gap between the history of the object and the history of the image of the object."[3] It was this desire to collapse time in the interest of immediacy that led Hewitt to reengage with performative work in graduate school at Bard College, culminating in his thesis project, *Toad in a Hole* (2007).[4] Turning a kitchen into his on-campus studio, Hewitt engaged in a series of activities centered on the making of still life photographs. This first performative installation laid the groundwork for those to come over the next five years: *Weavings* (2007), *Seed Stage* (2008–9), *Wall* (2010), *Drying Flowers with Microwaves* (2010), *The Grey Flame and the Brown Light* (2010), and *The Hedge* (2013). In all iterations of Hewitt's installations, one aspect remains constant: a fixed aperture through which the public experiences the work. This is often a narrow cut in a wall or a slit through the corner of an enclosure that enhances the voyeuristic aspect of looking. For *Drying Flowers with Microwaves*, mirrors suspended overhead created an elevated viewing plane high above Hewitt's production and performance space. In *Wall*, viewing could also take place via a real-time camera, directed downward at a lightbox table where the artist was working; the live feed was projected on a wall just outside of the performance space. By creating a controlled viewing experience, Hewitt insists on a singularity of perspective through a clear separation of performer and viewer, performance space and gallery. Looking through a slit in a wall mimics the view through the aperture of a camera; it forms an image in the mind's eye in reduced and delimited space. It precipitates, as Hewitt intends, "an image-based relationship to a physical space," as if collapsing three dimensions into two.[5] Such strategies for conflation recur often in Hewitt's single photographs, as much as they direct the sometimes *trompe l'oeil* designs for his installation environments.

If our eyes see one thing, then Hewitt's camera sees something else entirely. Whether we are looking in real time at an event, or piecing it together later via photographic reproductions, Hewitt's work invites confusion between premeditated and improvised actions. Consider sculptor-photographer Bruce Nauman's *Finger trick with mirror*, from the series *Eleven Color Photographs* (1967/1970).

3) Quoted in T.J. Carlin, "Food for Thought: Artist Corin Hewitt creates a gesamtkunstwerk for still lifes," *Time Out: New York* (October 2-8, 2008), 61.
4) Performance was not entirely new to Hewitt at the time. While at Oberlin, Hewitt launched the first in a series of performances in which he was hidden from view. The tension between what is seen or not seen has been a basic tenet of Hewitt's practice since.
5) Interview with the author, January 5, 2012.

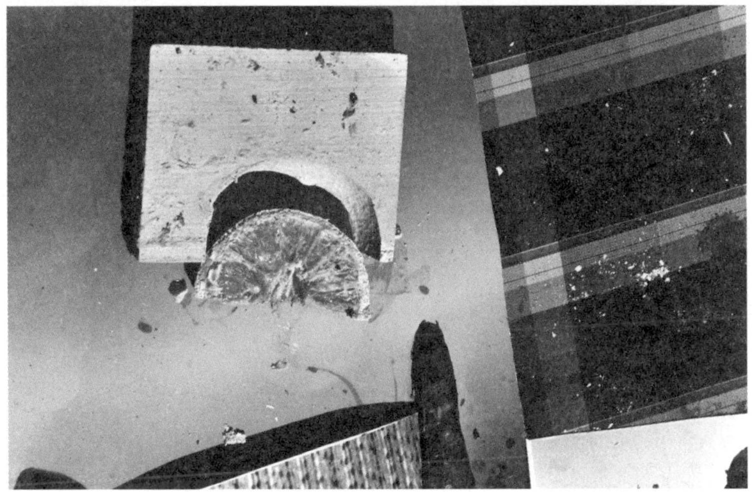

Corin Hewitt, *Untitled #33, November 9, 2008*, 2008, from *Seed Stage*, pigment print, 17 x 21 1/4 inches. Collection of the Whitney Museum of American Art, New York; purchase, with funds from the Photography Committee and Henry Nias Foundation, 2009.28.33. Courtesy of the artist and Laurel Gitlen, New York.

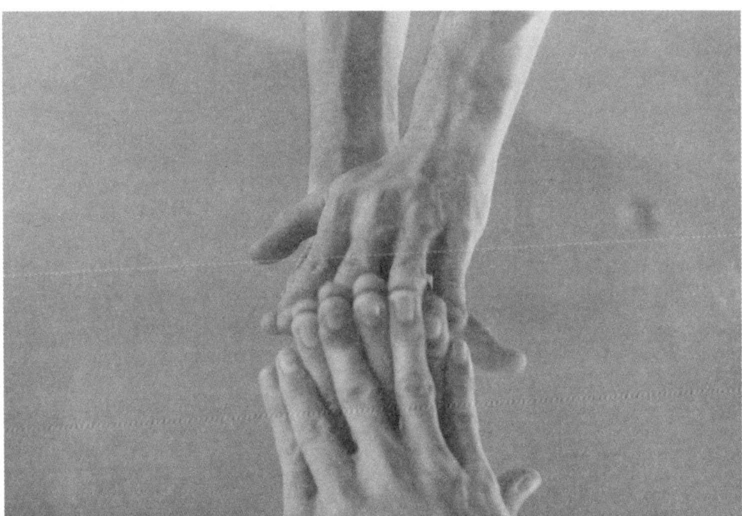

Bruce Nauman, *Finger trick with mirror*, 1967, color photograph, 15 3/4 x 23 10/16 inches. National Gallery of Australia, Canberra, purchased 1978. © 2013 Bruce Nauman / Artists Rights Society (ARS), New York.

In this image, Nauman creates the illusion of hands touching; in fact, there is only one hand (the artist's), reflected in a mirrored surface.[6] This photograph, like a number of works in Nauman's series, is a visual pun.[7] In a similar manner, Hewitt's photograph *Untitled #60*, from *Weavings*, tricks the eye. Here, the viewer might assume a reflective surface has been used to capture a portrait of Hewitt sculpting an apple. In fact, what we see is a photograph of two cropped paint cans onto which Hewitt adhered photographic print-outs. By cropping *Untitled #60*, he distorts the original shape of the cans so they read as false mirrored images of the same scene from slightly different angles; on the left the artist is present at the table, on the right his chair is empty. Such visual trompe l'oeil is furthered in Hewitt's *The Hedge*, where large photographs taken of various banal surfaces in Hewitt's studio (for instance brick walls or air vents) are seamlessly applied to the inner walls behind large cut-outs in the gallery space, confusing the distinction between Hewitt's production set and the innards of the museum. Hewitt's installations embody critic and theorist Boris Groys's description of the place of contemporary art production as a "finite, closed space that becomes the space of open conflict and unavoidable decision between original and reproduction, between presence and representation, between unconcealed and concealed."[8] It is in this space of conflict that Hewitt's photographs break open and expand.

If Hewitt has a plan when he is actively engaged in picture making, it is an agenda of transmutation guided by a commitment to the metamorphosis of materials, both natural and man-made. Like the "artist-alchemists" of the Arte Povera movement, Swiss artist Dieter Roth, with his obsession with the abjectness and beauty of decaying food, or the serious-yet-playful experimental artists associated with Surrealism, Hewitt is interested in the potential to transform our experience of the world with an embrace of the unglamorous materials of the everyday. In this way, some of his photographs recall Brassaï's 1933 photographic series *Sculptures Involontaires*, which first appeared in *Minotaure*, a Surrealist journal. The "sculptures" were tiny found objects, exemplifying the most banal of things, including bits of paper, bread, lint, and soap—motifs that are also rampant in a Hewitt installation.

In the late 1960s, concurrent with the expanding field of sculptural practice, the photograph became crucial, opening up new relationships between space, architecture, nature, and the body. Artists like Robert Smithson, Gordon Matta-Clark, Dóra Maurer, and Nauman adopted the medium's techniques, making it their own. Similarly, Hewitt's treatment of photographs transforms what could be mistaken as a document, a simple record of what took place, into a collagist vision of the world. Decades before Hewitt or his post-minimalist forbearers, Cubist collage first tested expectations of the world of physical objects. Writing about the Cubists in 1965, Hewitt's father saw the work through the psychology of visual perception, and his text reads like a manifesto for Hewitt the younger:

The Cubists, at least in their early, analytical stage, also explored the perceptual process as an event of sequential seeing. Their aim was the dissolution of the constancy of things, and when they succeeded, objects became subject to our normative and conceptual applications. The disintegration of the object

6) This motif recurs throughout Nauman's oeuvre finding its way into sculptures like *Fifteen Pairs of Hands* (1996) and *Untitled (Hand Circle)* (1996).
7) The series also includes *Eating My Words*, a photograph of the artist at a table, applying jelly to white bread cut into the shapes of letters.
8) Boris Groys, "The Topology of Contemporary Art," *Antimonies of Art and Culture: Modernity, Postmodernity, Contemporaneity*, eds. Terry Smith, Okwui Enwezor, and Nancy Condee (Durham and London: Duke University Press, 2008), 80.

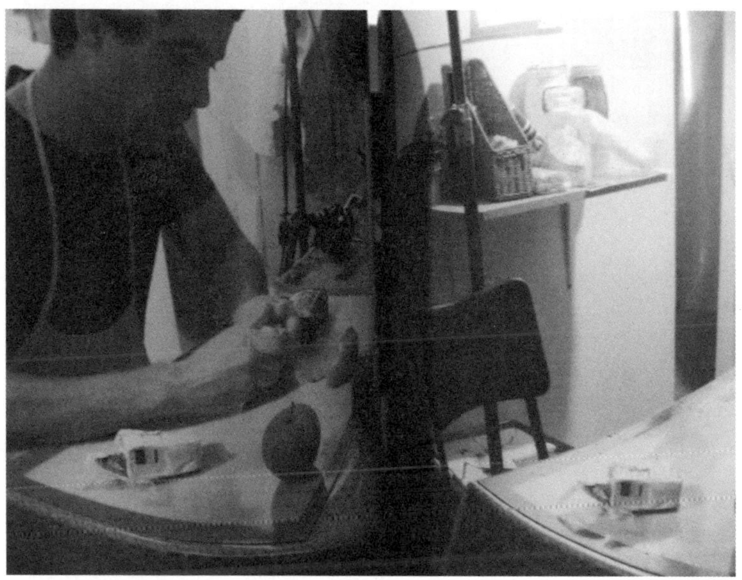

Corin Hewitt, *Untitled #60*, 2007, from *Weavings*, pigment print, 10 1/2 x 14 inches. Miller Meigs Collection.
Courtesy of the artist and Laurel Gitlen, New York.

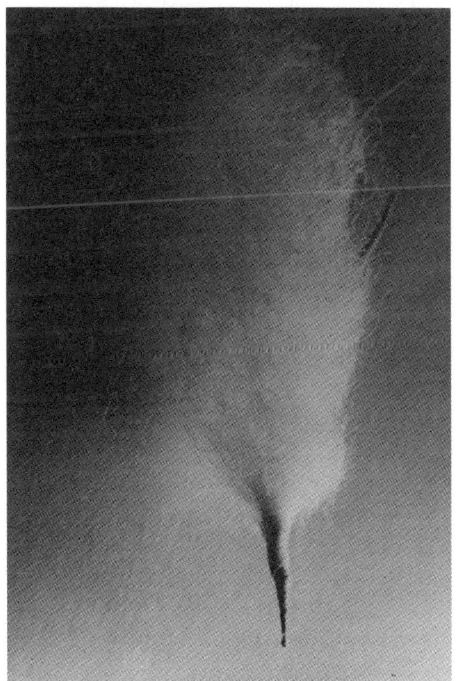

Brassaï, *Sculptures Involontaires*, 1932, gelatin silver print, 9 1/8 x 6 1/2
inches. Musee National d'Art Moderne, Georges Pompidou, Paris, France.
Reproduction photo: Georges Meguerdictchian. CANC/MNAM/Dist.
RMN-Grand Palais /Art Resource, NY. © The Brassaï Estate – RMN.

opened the possibility for new perceptual experience—a new attitude toward the older mistaken view of the finality of substance.[9]

Seed Stage, Hewitt's most extensive performative project to date, offers a case study for the potential of the photograph to disintegrate the object. Take any image from this project—for instance, *Untitled #42, November 21, 2008*—and the inconstancy of things becomes readily apparent. In the collapsing of figure and ground, a thin rock-like material, perhaps stone, perhaps molded plasticine, sits atop a pile of photographs and fabric. In Hewitt's images, we find new relationships to things only after they have abandoned their assumed function, when they separate from the practical world: gloves become canvases, fruits become sculptures, photographs become composted material. Old assumptions die. New beginnings emerge.

Following on the heels of Cubism, in the spirit of Surrealism, and influenced by the photographic school of Neue Sachlichkeit ("New Objectivity"), is the work of German artist Wols. Though primarily known for his paintings, Wols was experimenting with photography as early as the 1930s, creating images that offer what art historian Christine Mehring has characterized as a "defamiliarizing assault on the real."[10] Wols made a series of photographic still lifes in his kitchen laboratory, using fresh meat, cheese, fruits, and vegetables in odd and unrecognizable arrangements—the resemblance to Hewitt's style is uncanny.[11] In reversing the visual hierarchies of what was useful or not, what was incidental rather than primary, Wols's black-and-white photographs suggest a haunting world of beauty and its decay.

Hewitt's work, like Wols's, resonates with works by 17th-century Spanish still life painters, including Juan Sánchez Cotán and Francisco de Zurbarán, who, unlike Wols, are both acknowledged influences on Hewitt's style.[12] This is best exemplified in a work like *Untitled #32, November 9, 2008* from *Seed Stage*, where Hewitt adopts Cotán's anachronistic way of hanging vegetables from string for preservation, in this case both a cabbage and measuring cup. Here, Hewitt boosts the artificial light, casting deep shadows onto a collage of photographs and fabric that engulfs the shallow background. Called *bodegónes*, Cotán's style of still life was composed mostly of fruits and vegetables, some hanging, some sitting, painted in direct sunlight against an impenetrable darkness. The technique has a tendency to flatten narrative impulse, giving preference to the depiction of things which otherwise lacked importance. Such flatness recurs in Hewitt's *Untitled #33, November 9, 2008*, also from *Seed* Stage, inviting curiosity and close inspection. Looking down upon a range of subjects, blasted with high contrast light, Hewitt creates a disturbed still life with a petrified slice of orange and cropped root vegetable. The photograph encourages a sense of familiarity, but is nonetheless destabilizing in its peculiarity.

In life, and in work, Hewitt questions permanence. "I have been thinking about the promise and impossibility of ownership and how photography can navigate this by acting as a steward of material over time," he wrote in 2008.[13] He continues, albeit one year later, "Photography [...] grabs at something that is passing, but it also becomes a foundation to build things on top of."[14] His words resign to the

9) Francis R. Hewitt, "The Mind's Eye or the Eye's Mind," *New Tendencies 3* (Zagreb: Gallery for Contemporary Art, Museum for Art and Work, 1965), unpaginated.
10) Christine Mehring, *Wols Photographs* (Cambridge, MA: Busch-Reisinger Museum, Harvard University Art Museums, 1999), 22.
11) As Mehring writes: "Looking at Wols's still lifes, we experience not simply a strange, dissolving reality, but a profound lack of control over a world of human subjects," ibid., 25.
12) Mehring also explores Wols's relationship to these painters in her book, ibid.
13) Quoted from written notes in one of Hewitt's notebooks, 2008, unpaginated.
14) Podcast artist interview with Jen Graves, "In/Visible: Corin Hewitt: The Desire and Anxiety of Reproduction and Decay," *The Stranger* (Seattle) online, posted April 22, 2009, accessed on December 15, 2012.

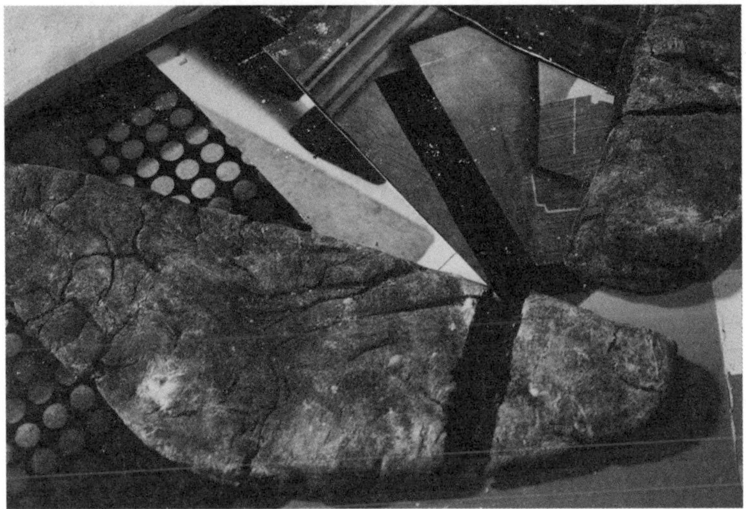

Corin Hewitt, *Untitled # 42, November 21, 2008*, 2008, from *Seed Stage*, pigment print, 11 x 17 inches. Collection of the Whitney Museum of American Art, New York; purchase, with funds from the Photography Committee and Henry Nias Foundation, 2009.28.42. Courtesy of the artist and Laurel Gitlen, New York.

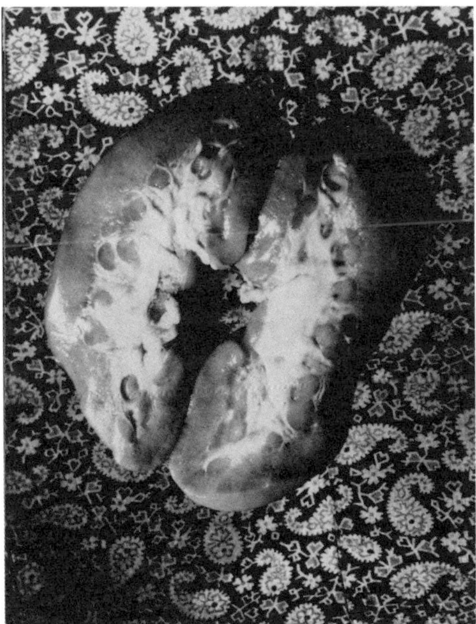

Wols, *Untitled (Pork Kidneys)*, 1938, vintage gelatin silver print, 8 1/2 x 6 5/16 inches. Reproduction photo: Phillippe Migeat. Musee National d'Art Moderne, Centre Georges Pompidou, Paris, France. CNAC/MNAM/Dist. RMN-Grand Palais/Art Resource, NY. © 2013 Artists Rights Society (ARS), New York / ADAGP, Paris.

fleetingness of everything—experience, ownership, family, art, and time—while acknowledging, with hope and curiosity, the unflinching qualities of the photograph as a sometimes wayward, yet obedient, steward. Encountering an installation by Hewitt, we see the makings of the original; all of the tools and ingredients are there. Yet, as quickly as we think we know what we are looking at, Hewitt upends the mental equation. Original does not lead to copy. We cannot jump ahead to those assumptions.
In a panoply of images, there is nothing here to discard, all is active, all is in play. And associations are nothing but free.

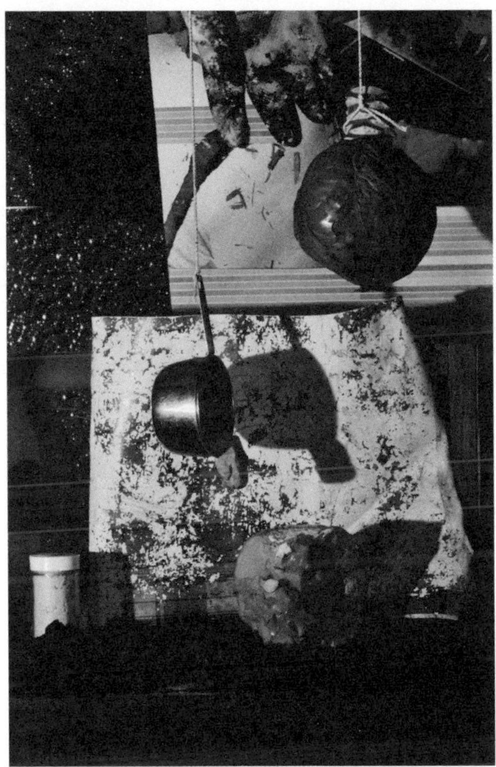

Corin Hewitt, *Untitled #32, November 9, 2008*, 2008, from *Seed Stage*, pigment print, 22 x 15 15/16 inches. Collection of the Whitney Museum of American Art, New York; purchase, with funds from the Photography Committee and Henry Nias Foundation, 2009.28.32. Courtesy of the artist and Laurel Gitlen, New York.

by Rose Bouthillier

The Rubik's cube catches your eye. Solid, standing out against all of that softness, all of that accumulation. A structure of 43,252,003,274,489,856,000 permutations bound within one form, forever mid-configuration, its complexity seemingly irreconcilable with its simplicity. Gridded with charts, graphs, fades, algorithms for perception, each side appears as a code to be broken up, dispersed, but always discrete. Later, you remember it as a cipher for all that you saw here.

You begin to sort the information, and this proves to be a confounding and pleasurable task. What is central, peripheral, genuine, forged, meaningful, or indifferent. Memory and place seep into material facts; walls are topsoil.

One image keeps rushing to your mind: peas, carrots, and corn spilling out of an image of peas, carrots, and corn. The vegetables are like spongy crystals, fuzzy with cold, their likeness is wrinkled, warm. Yet, they intend to be the same thing, or, they reveal how all things are really compilations. You try to focus, but the surface is hard to hold in place; there is something pushing through it, exhausting it: a haziness, a thickness, transposition. You think: all objects are wrapped in images of themselves.

There enters your mind a notion of *compositional force*: at once physical, perceptual, and psychological. The coming together of materials, how they fit, layer, slip across; the optical reflex to classify and arrange; the affect of material: comfort, absurdity, repulsion, strangeness. A force seen always at work, in every picture, arrangement, recollection, and glance.

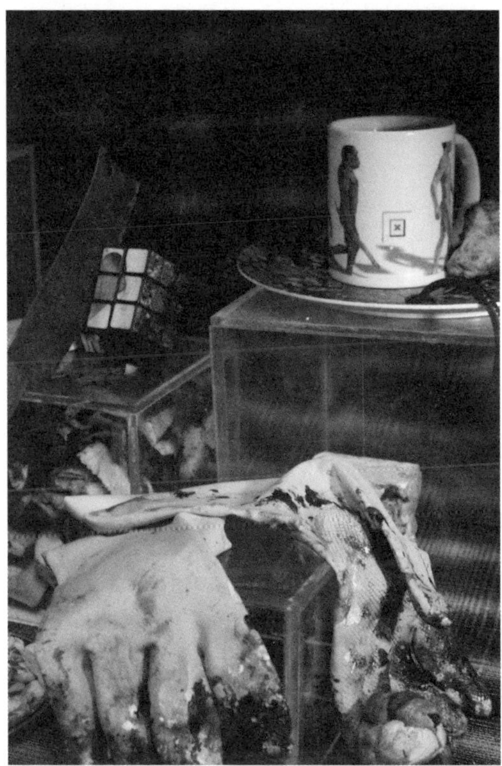

Corin Hewitt, working image from *Seed Stage*, 2008–9. Courtesy of the artist.

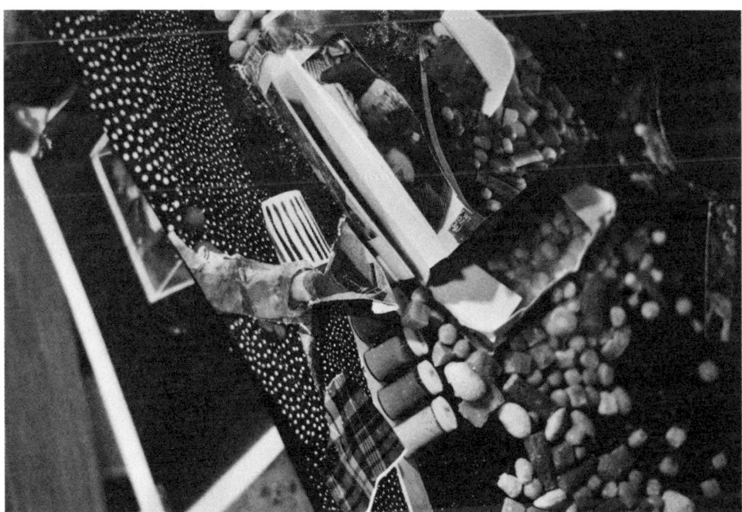

Corin Hewitt, working image from *Seed Stage*, 2008–9. Courtesy of the artist.

Chapter 1, **Toad in a Hole**

Chapter 1, **Toad in a Hole**

Toad in a Hole
Bard College, Annandale-on-Hudson, NY
August 2007

Toad in a Hole was Hewitt's first performance-installation, produced for his MFA thesis show at Bard College's Milton Avery Graduate School of the Arts. He developed the installation over the course of the summer, and a final four-day performance took place in August. The installation occupied a makeshift kitchen that had been used by previous students, and was visible through a vertical cutout in a corner wall, which allowed a wide-angle view of the interior. The room was full of real and replica foodstuffs, cooking devices, sculpting materials, and different types of cameras, which Hewitt used to produce a final set of 22 photographs.

Captions

1, 31, 41: *Toad in a Hole*, 2007. Installation view, Milton Avery Graduate School of the Arts, Bard College. Photo: Dani Leventhal. Courtesy of the artist.
4, 5, 7, 9, 11, 12, 14, 16–18, 22, 23, 25, 26, 30, 32, 43: Working image from *Toad in a Hole*, 2007. Courtesy of the artist.
6, 10, 38–40, 44, 46, 47: *Toad in a Hole*, 2007. Performance documentation. Photo: Dani Leventhal. Courtesy of the artist.
21, 28, 29, 33: Set documentation of *Toad in a Hole*, 2007. Courtesy of the artist.
34: *Toad in a Hole*, 2007. Performance documentation. Photo: Peter Mauney. Courtesy of the artist.

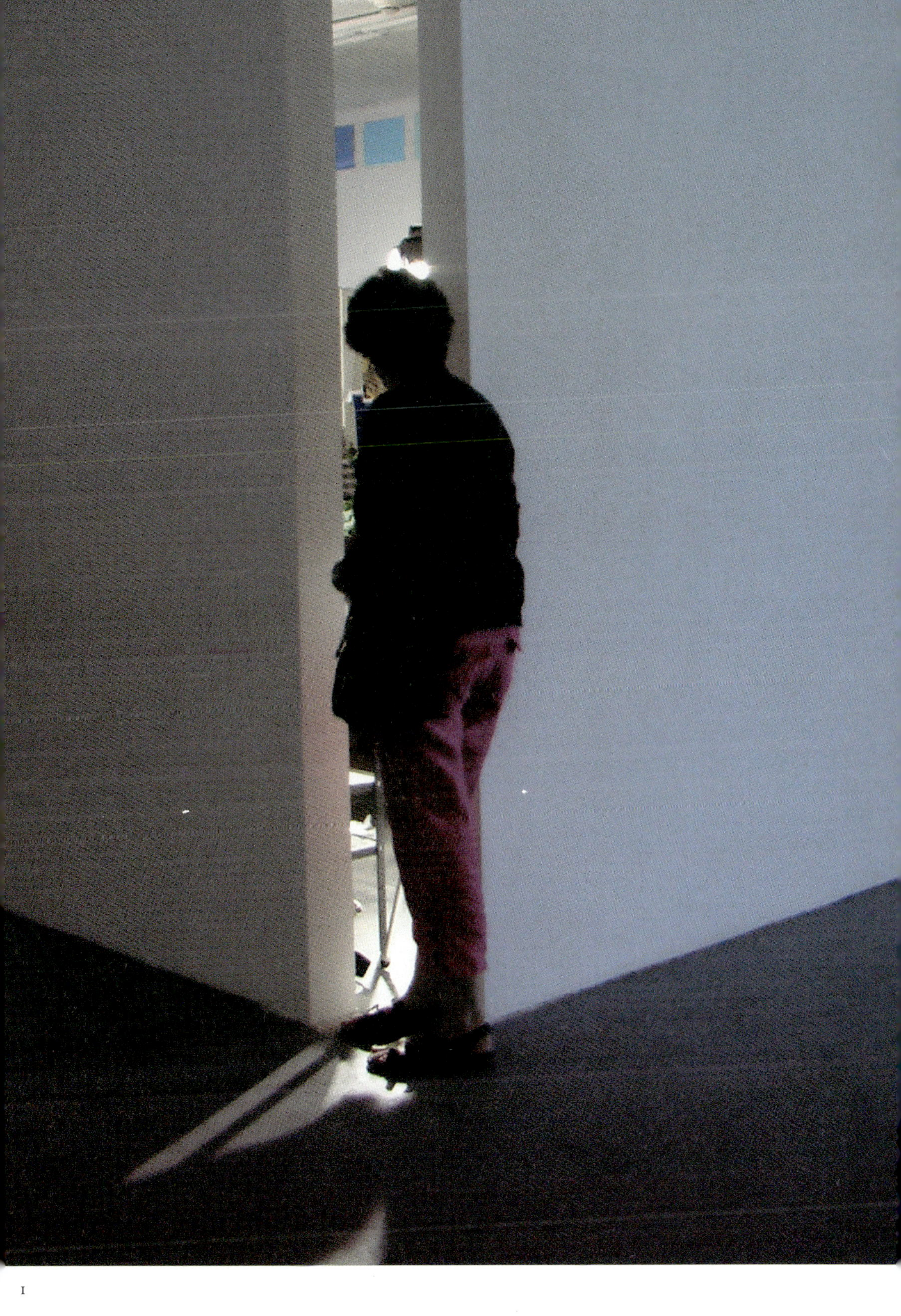

I

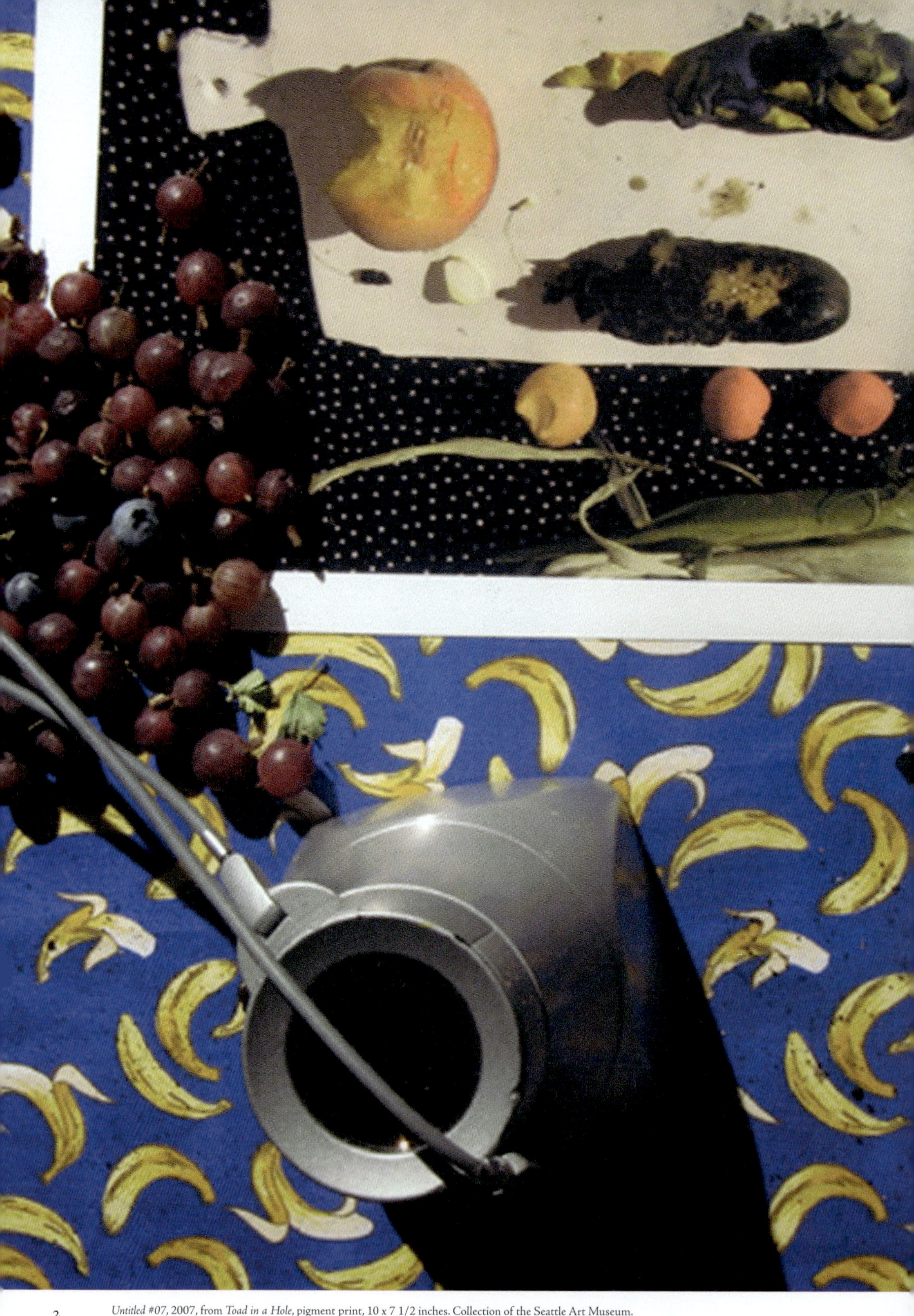

Untitled #07, 2007, from *Toad in a Hole*, pigment print, 10 x 7 1/2 inches. Collection of the Seattle Art Museum.
Gift of Rebecca and Alexander Stewart in honor of Mimi Gardner Gates. Courtesy of the artist and Laurel Gitlen, New York.

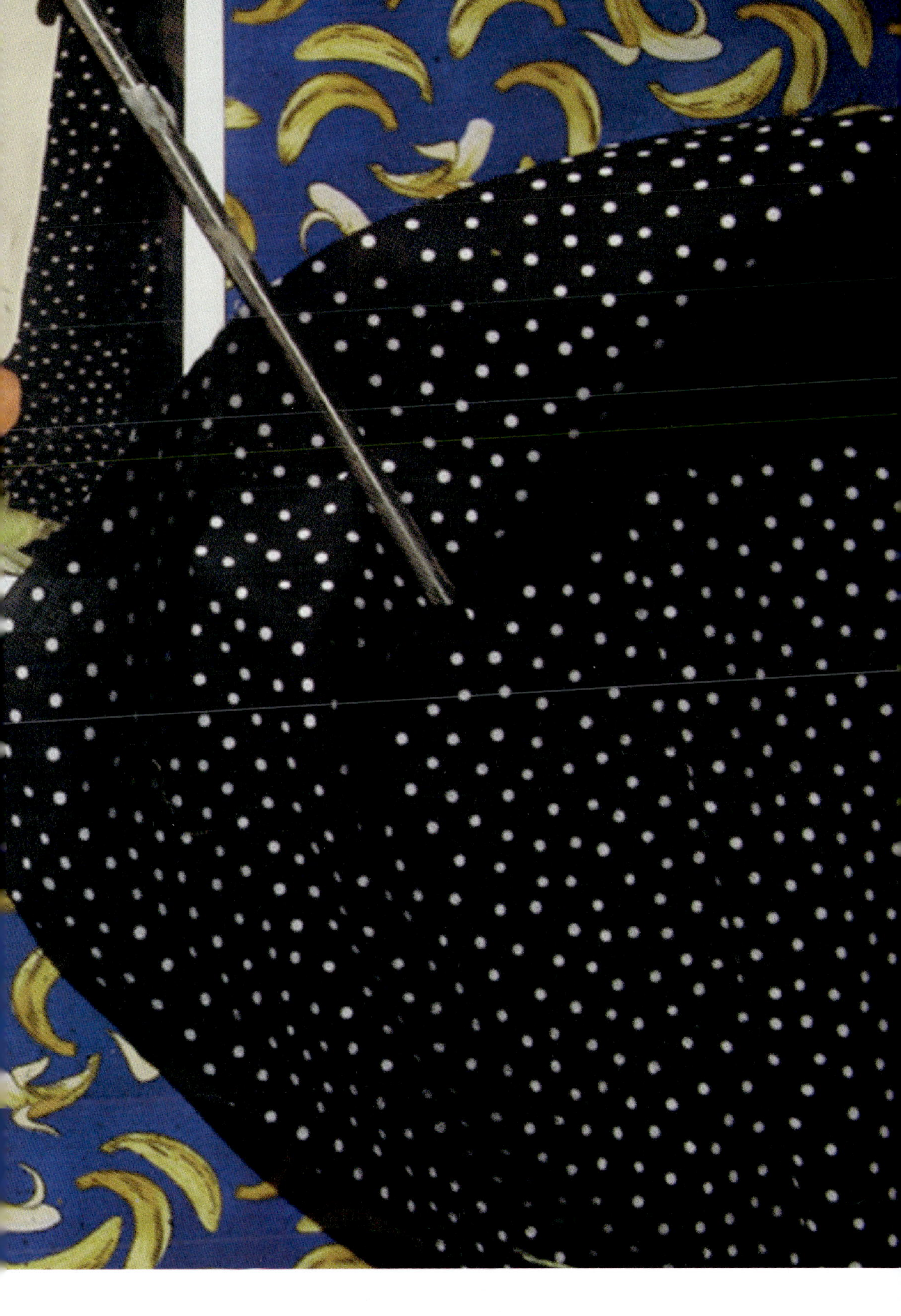

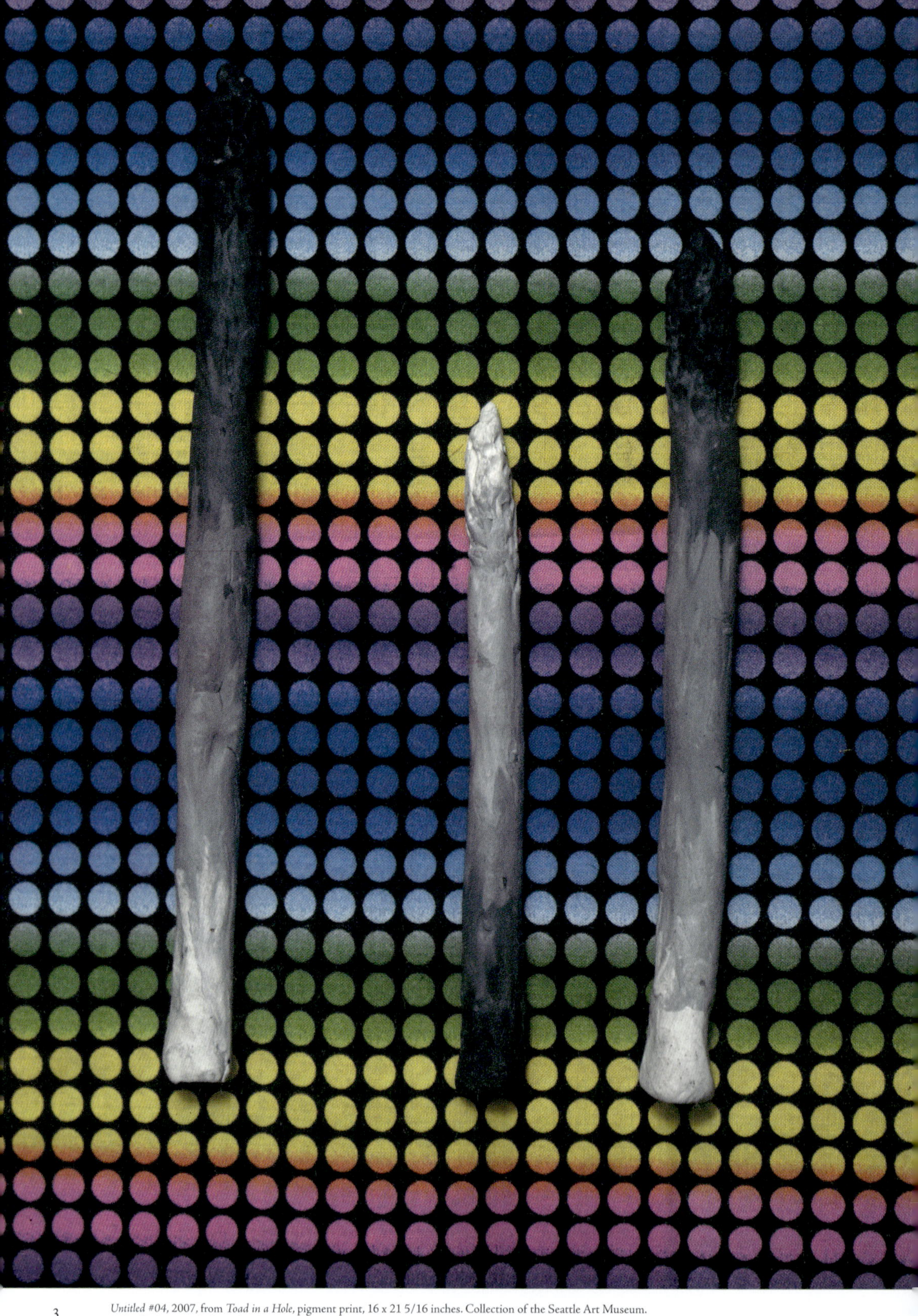

Untitled #04, 2007, from *Toad in a Hole*, pigment print, 16 x 21 5/16 inches. Collection of the Seattle Art Museum.
Gift of Rebecca and Alexander Stewart in honor of Mimi Gardner Gates. Courtesy of the artist and Laurel Gitlen, New York.

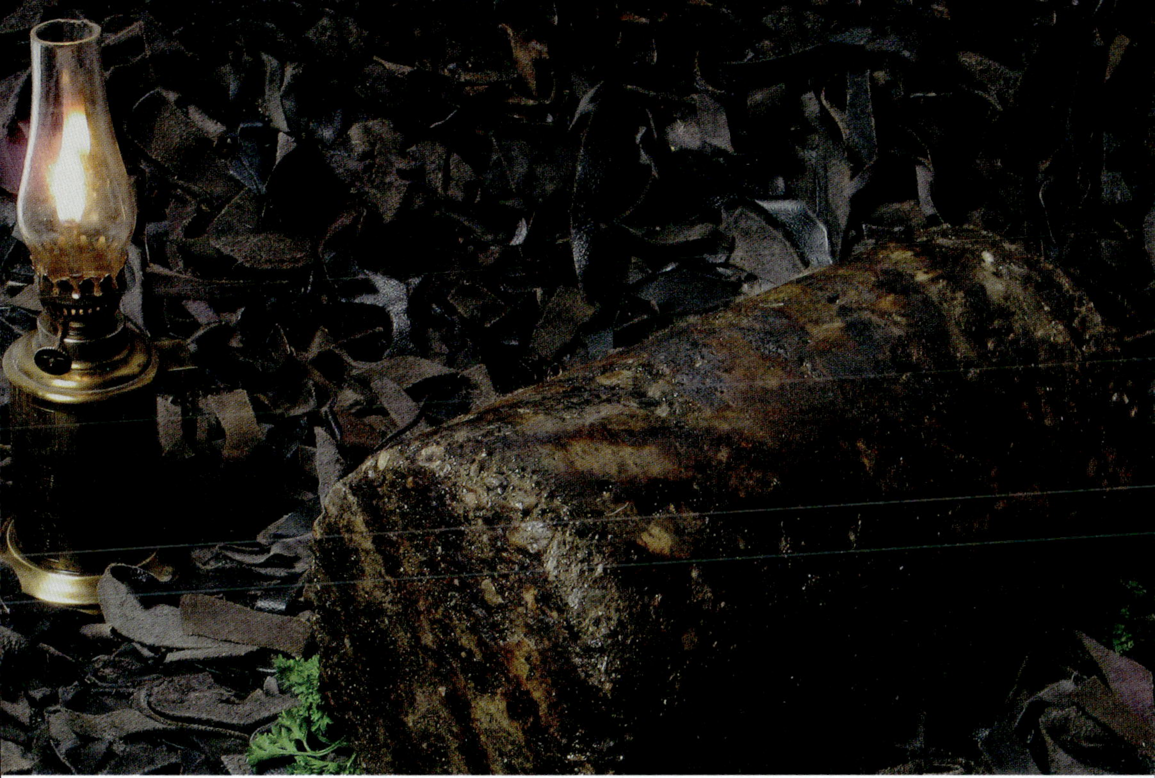

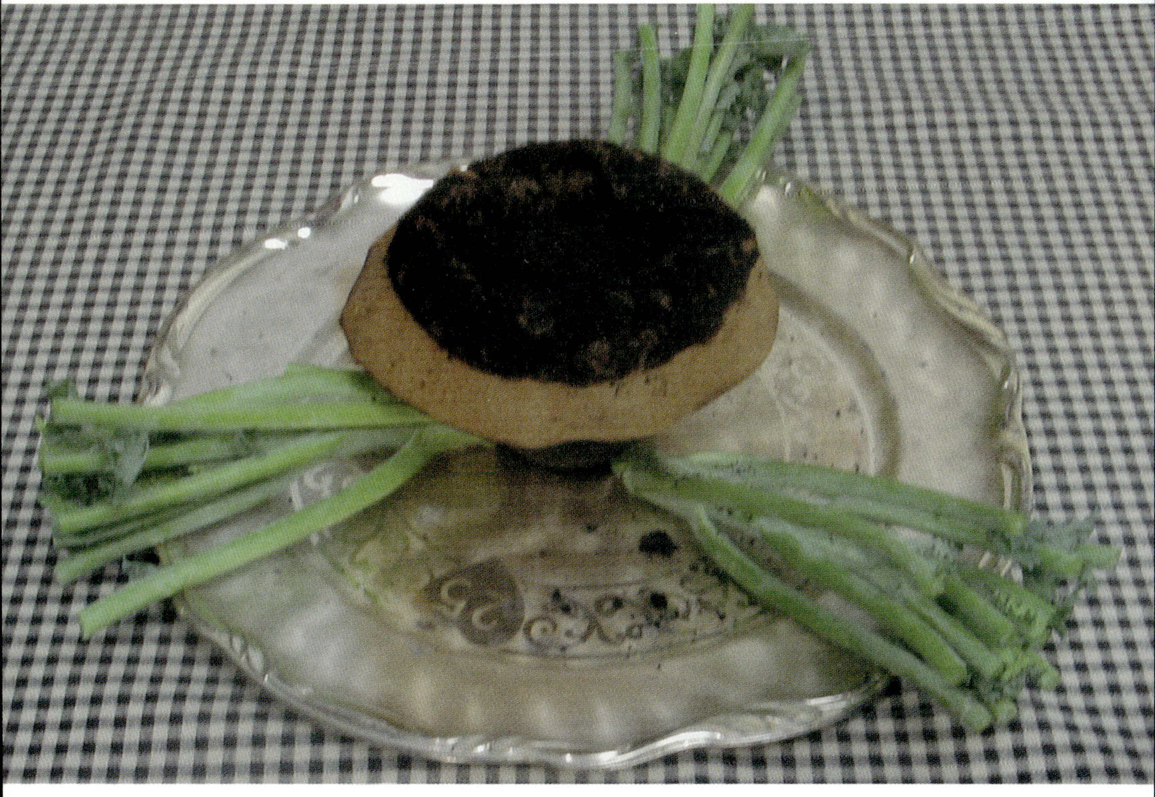

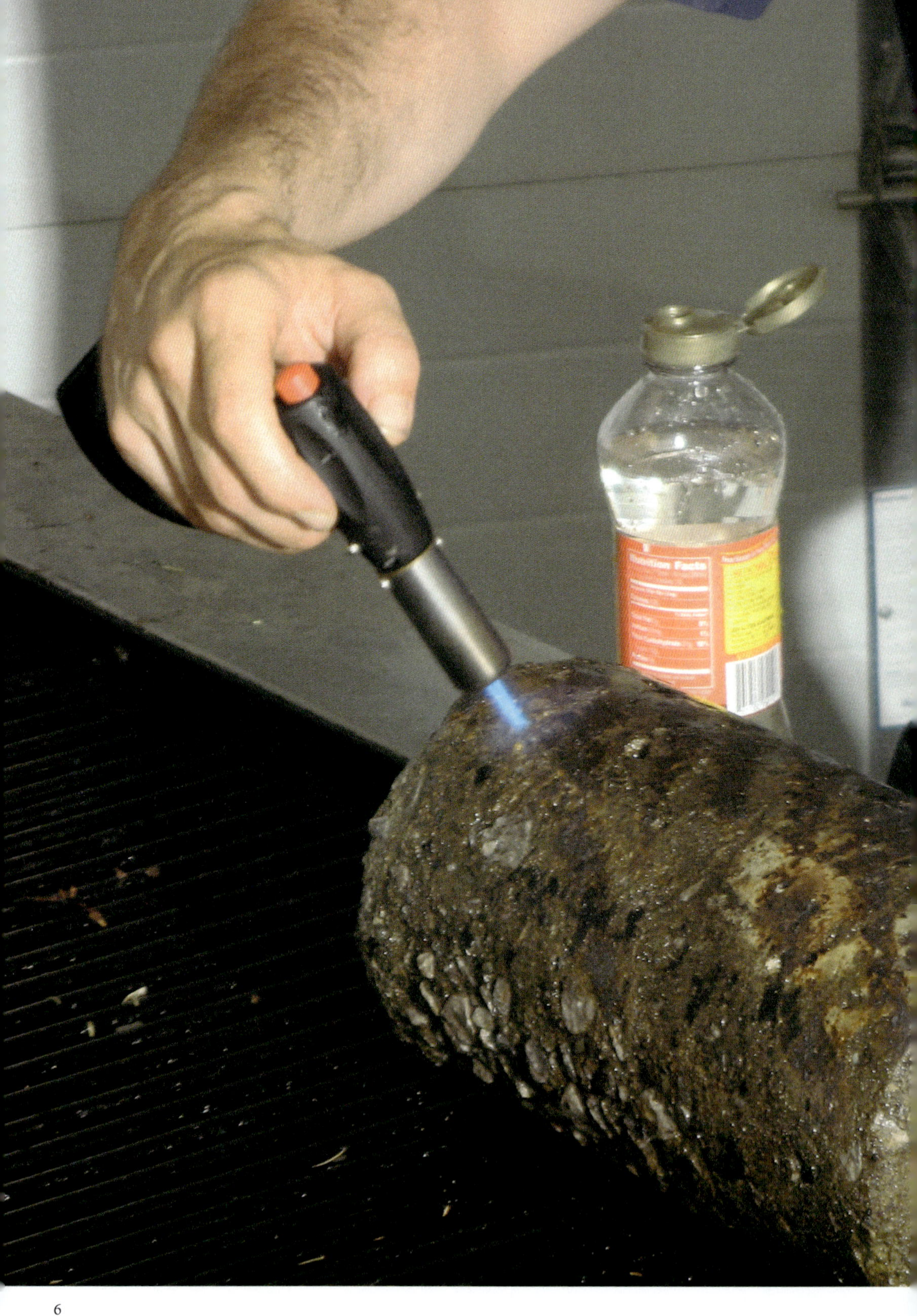

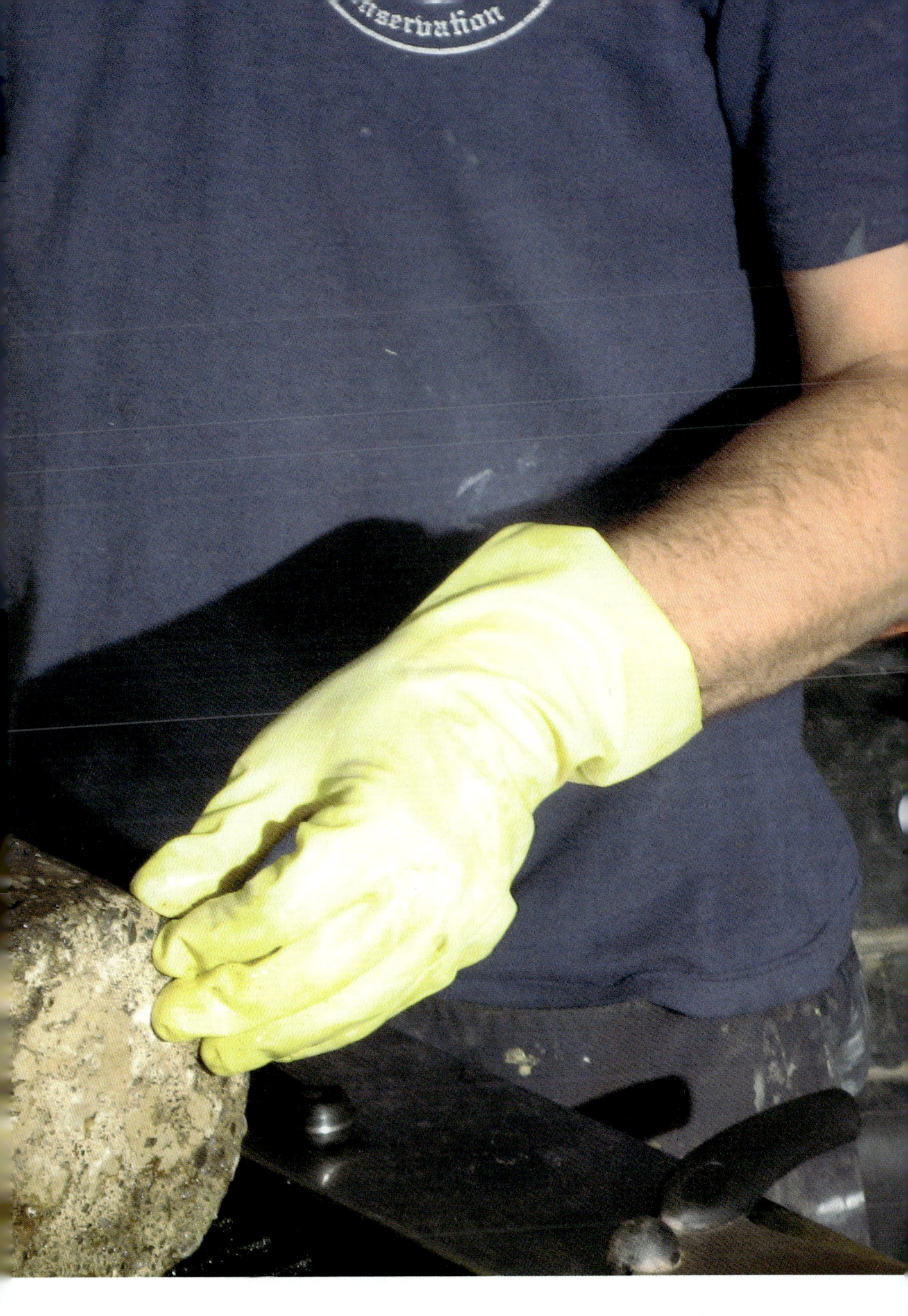

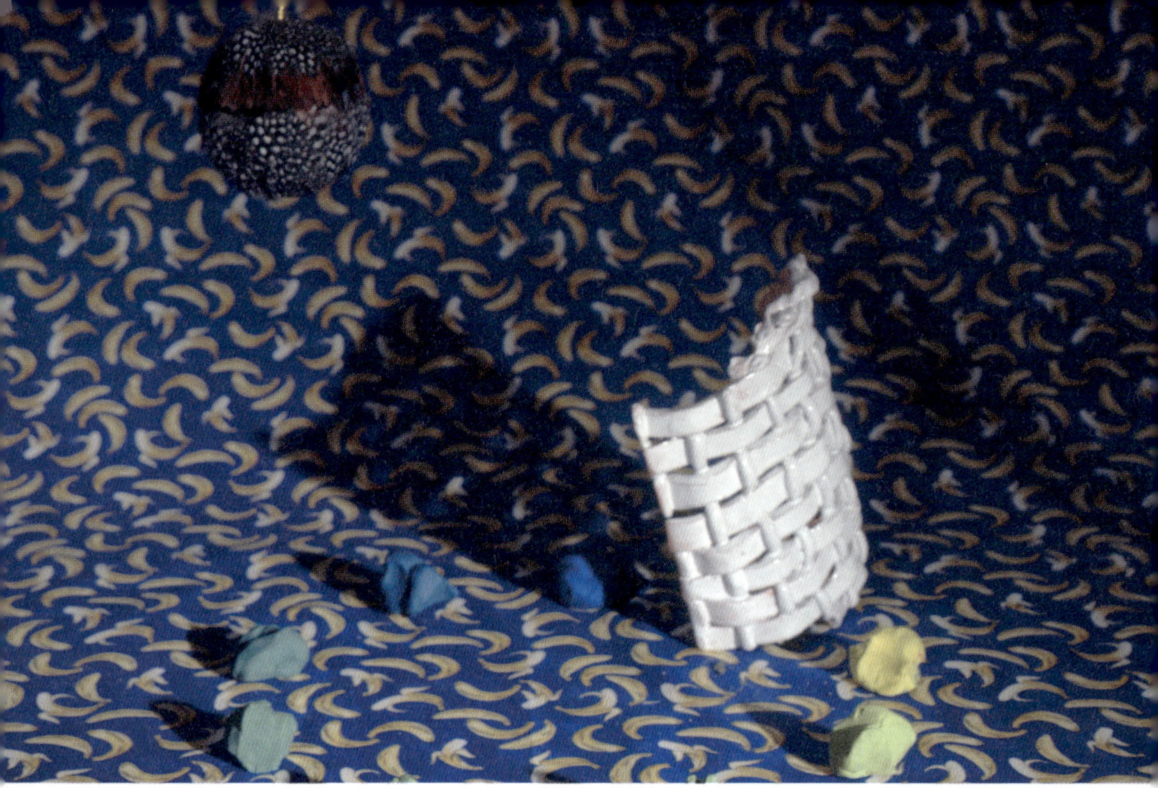

7

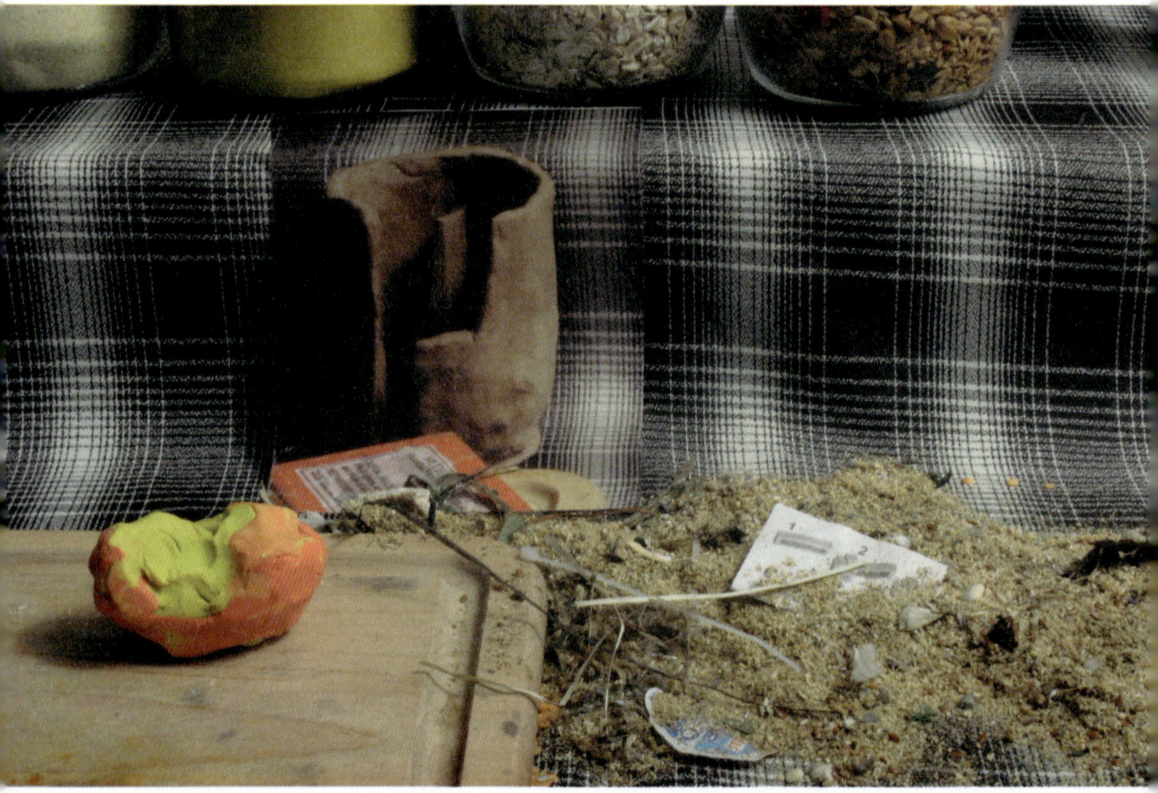

8   *Untitled #20*, 2007, from *Toad in a Hole*, pigment print, 12 x 16 inches. Collection of the Seattle Art Museum.
Gift of Rebecca and Alexander Stewart in honor of Mimi Gardner Gates. Courtesy of the artist and Laurel Gitlen, New York.

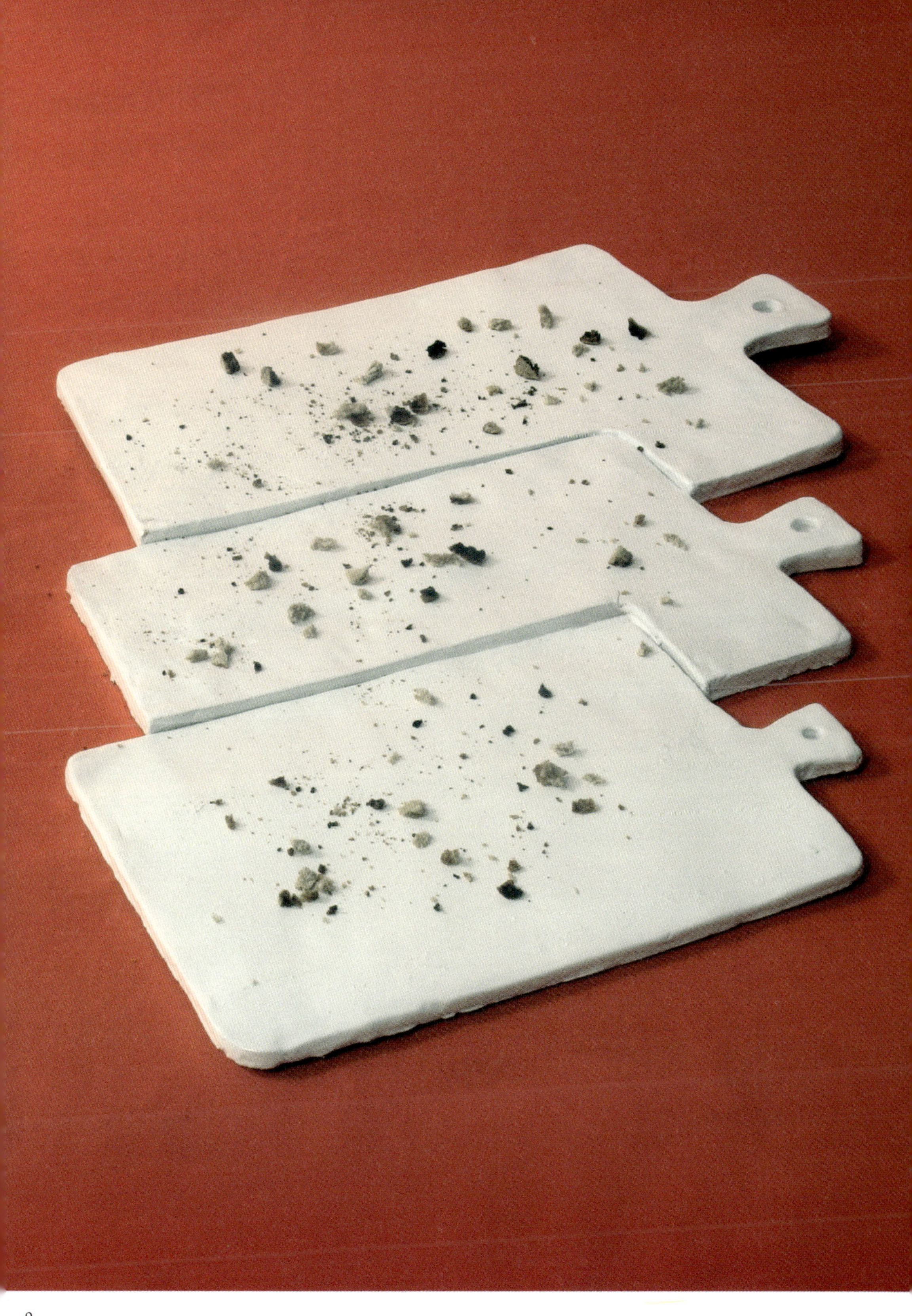

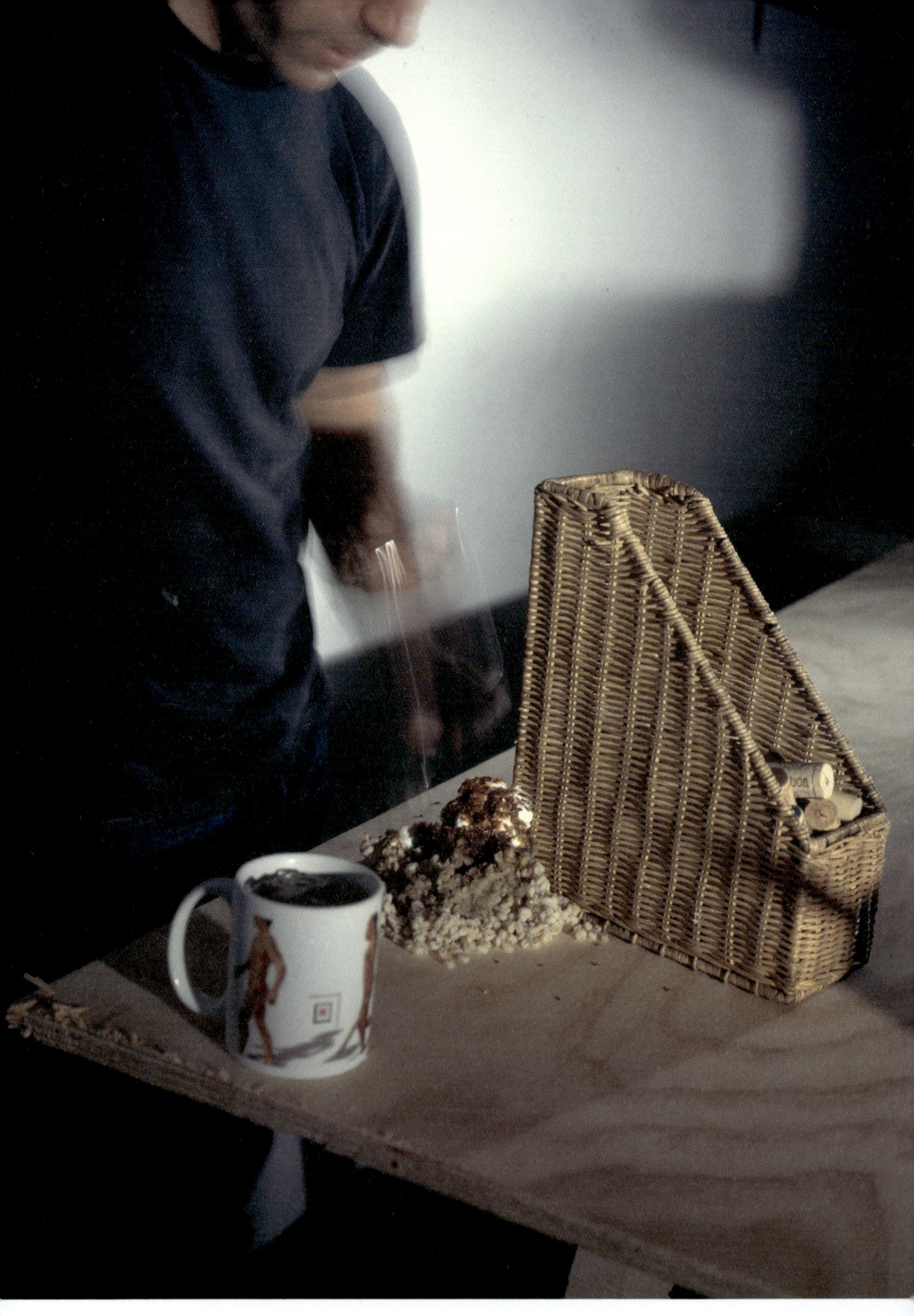

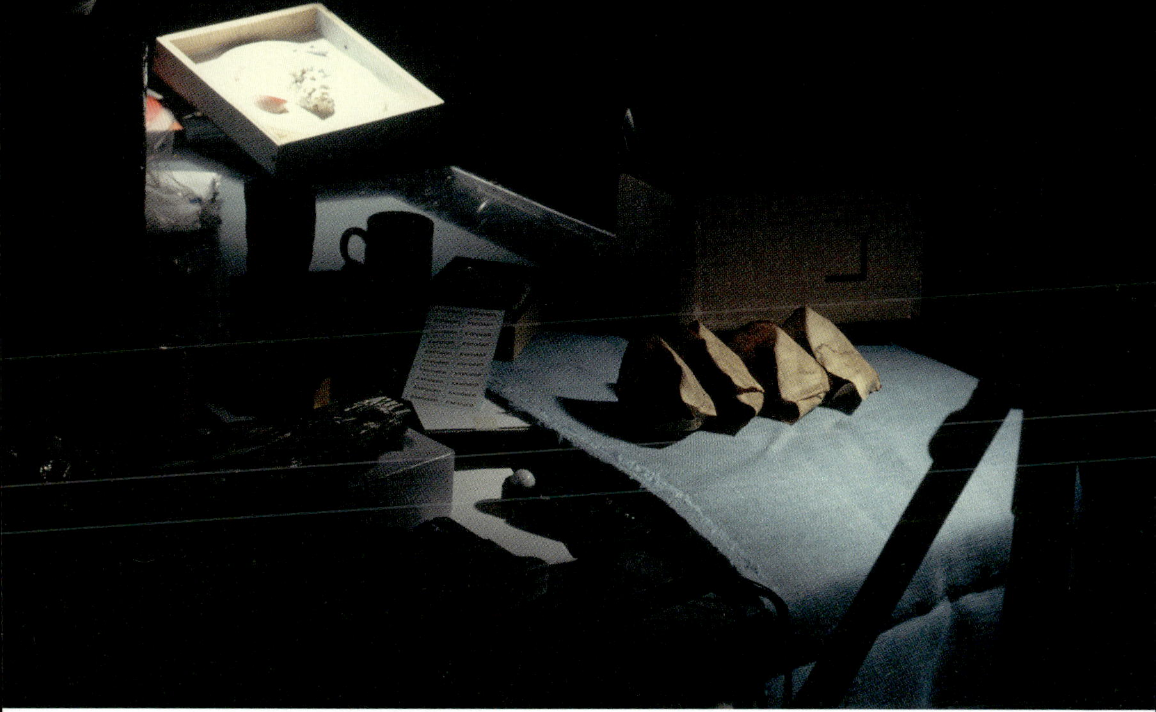

11

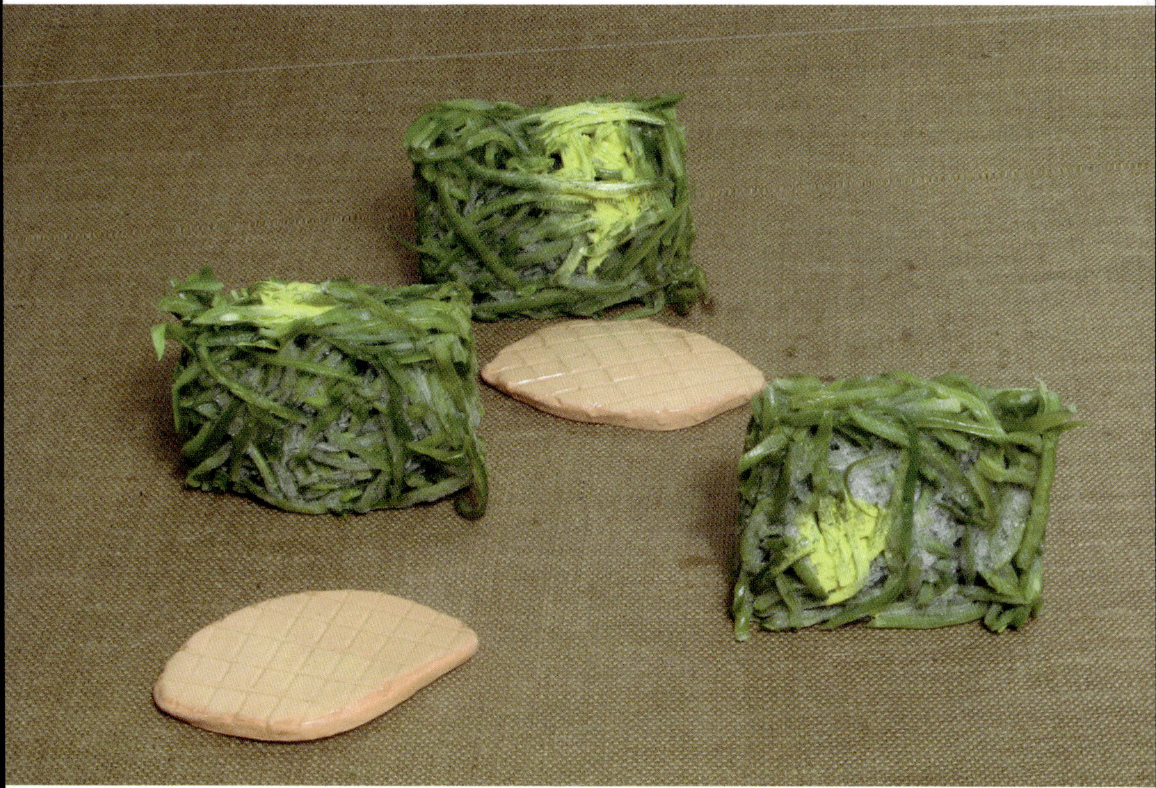

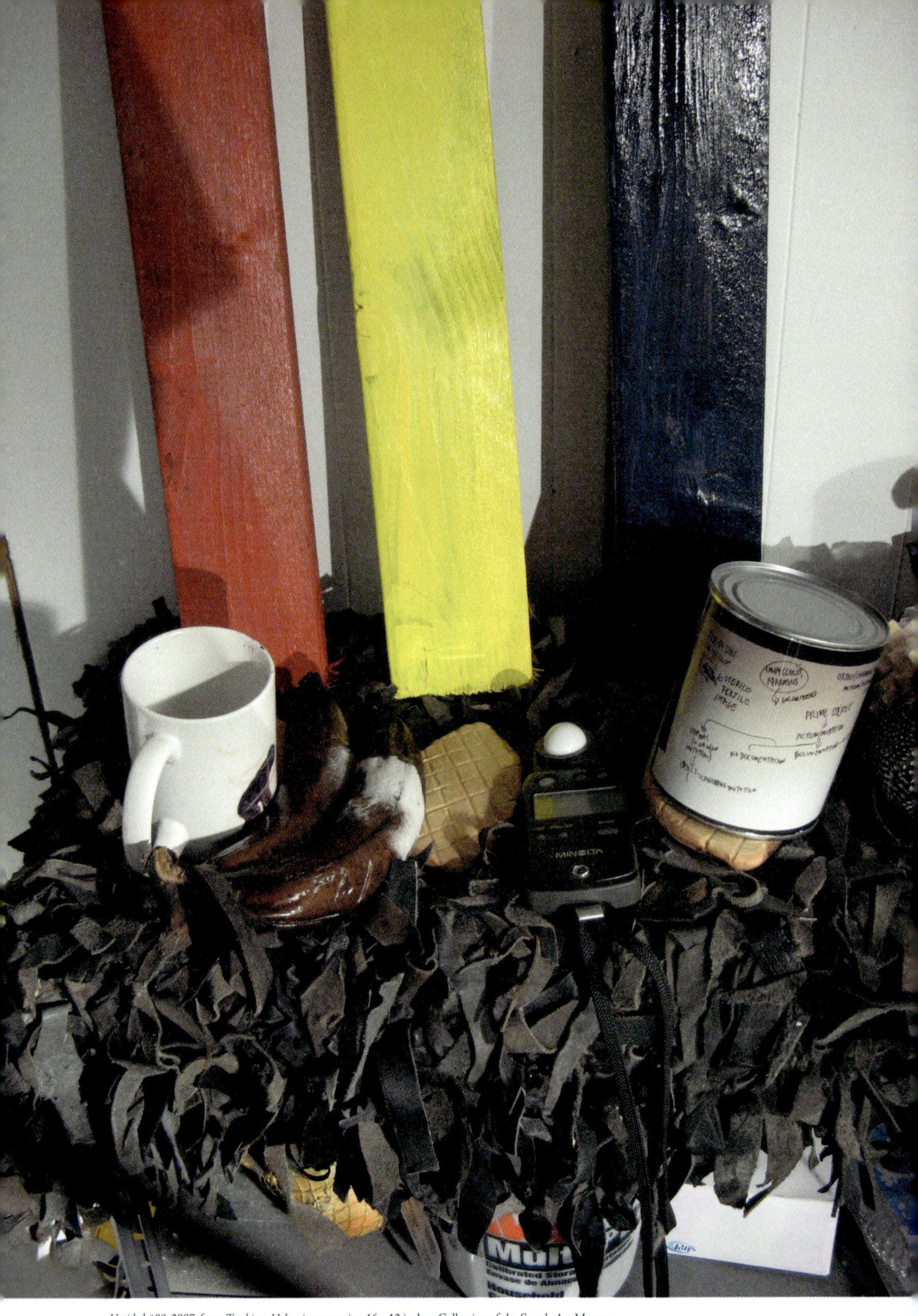

13   *Untitled #09*, 2007, from *Toad in a Hole*, pigment print, 16 x 12 inches. Collection of the Seattle Art Museum.
Gift of Rebecca and Alexander Stewart in honor of Mimi Gardner Gates. Courtesy of the artist and Laurel Gitlen, New York.

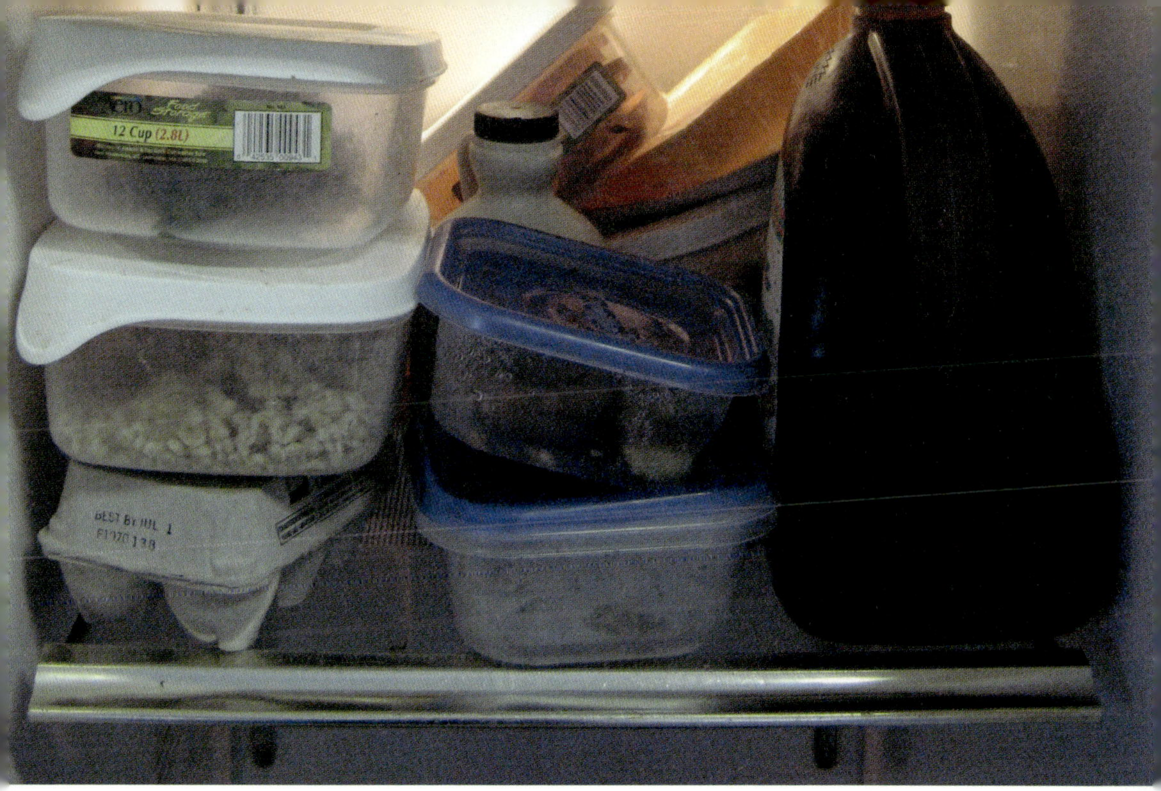

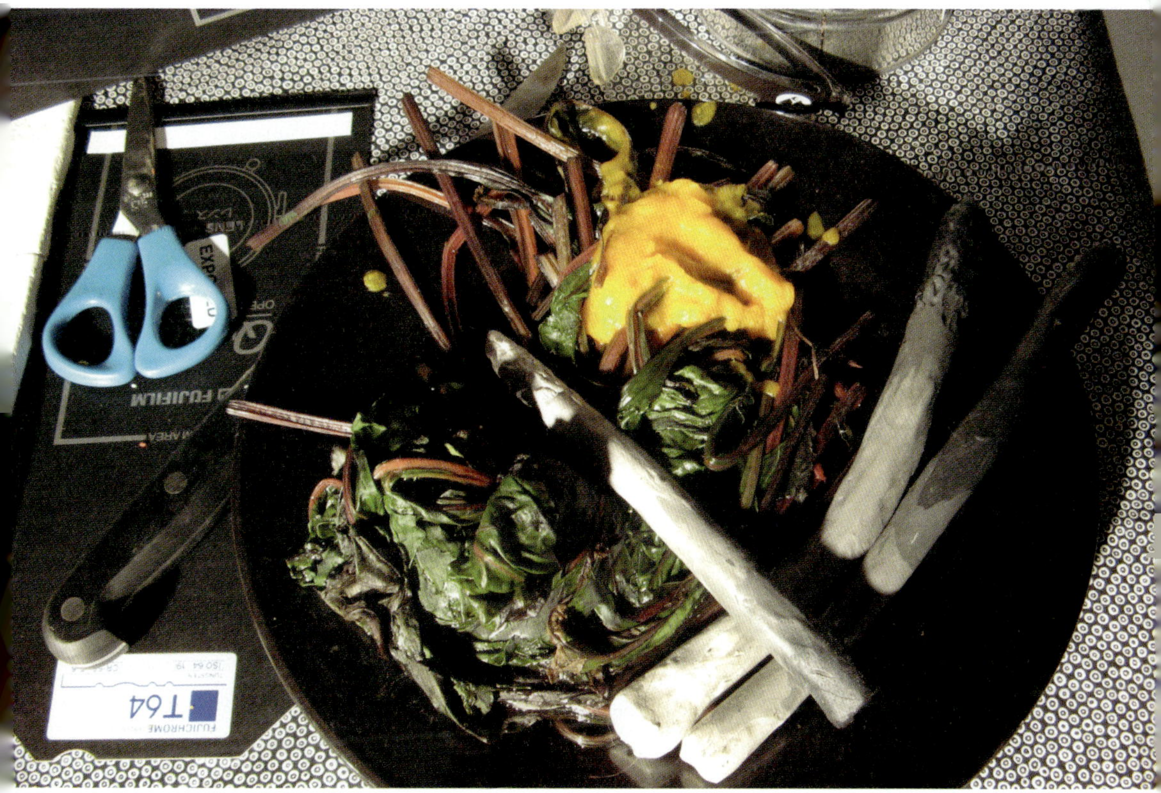

15 *Untitled #10*, 2007, from *Toad in a Hole*, pigment print, 12 x 16 inches. Collection of the Seattle Art Museum.
Gift of Rebecca and Alexander Stewart in honor of Mimi Gardner Gates. Courtesy of the artist and Laurel Gitlen, New York.

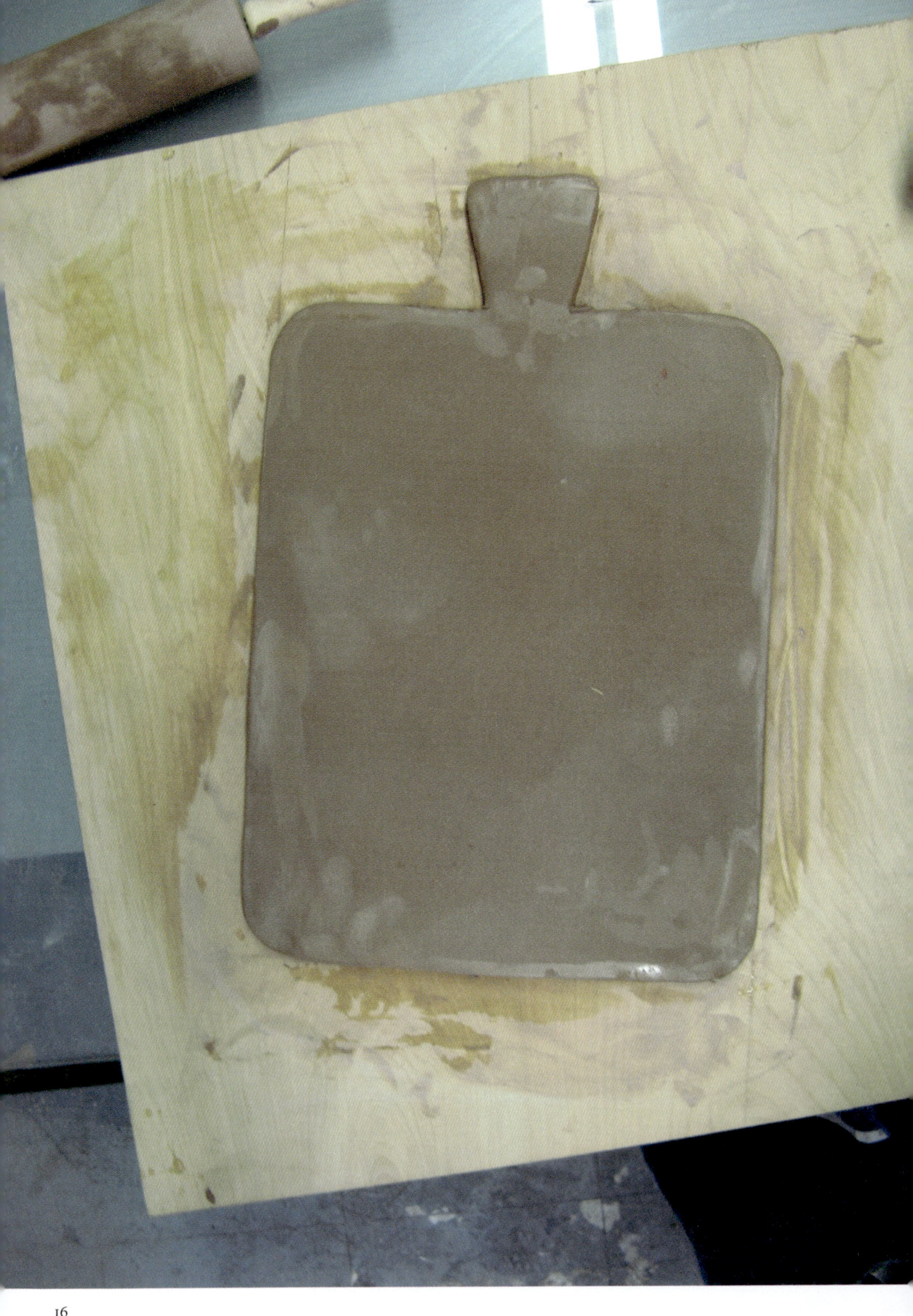

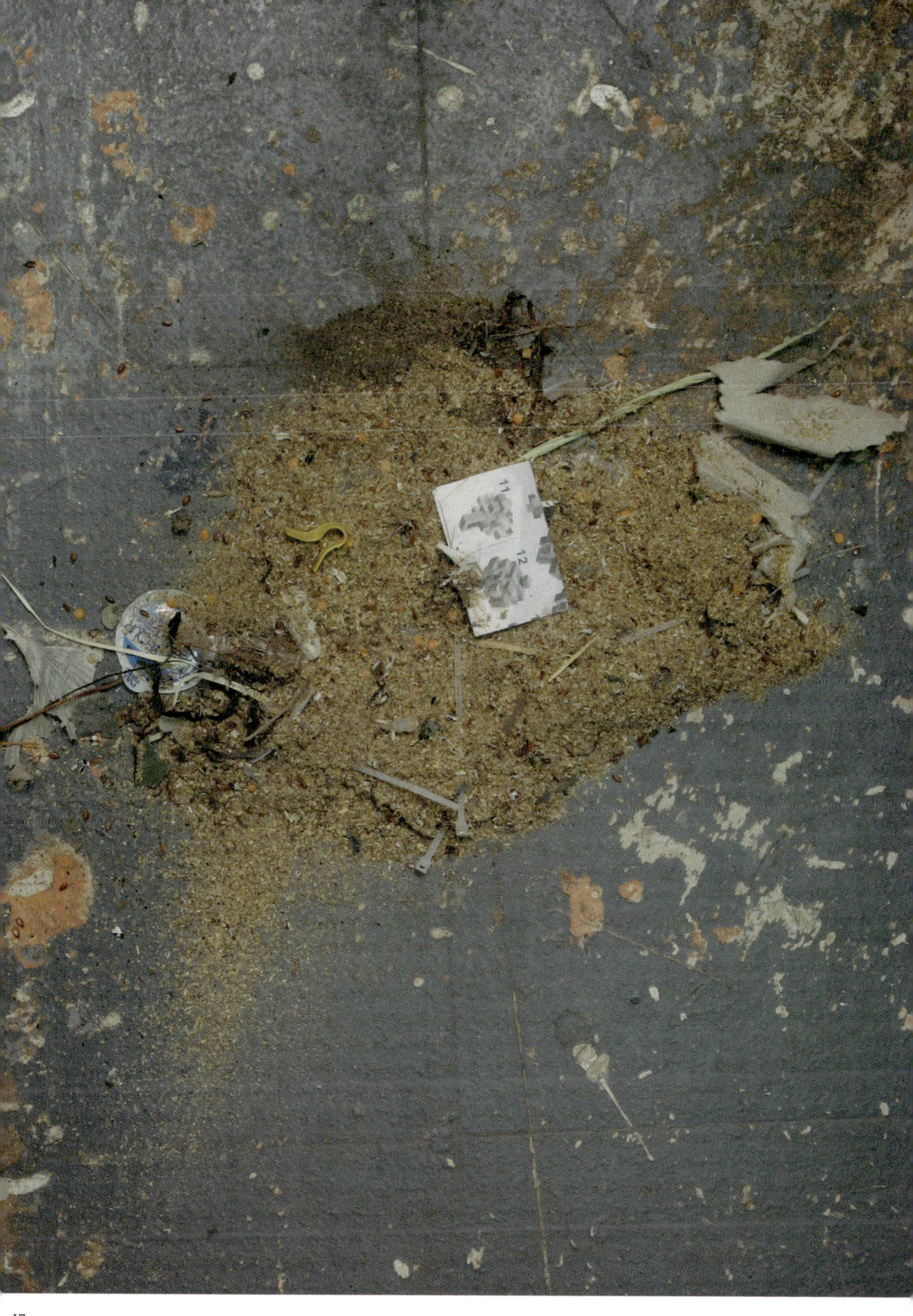

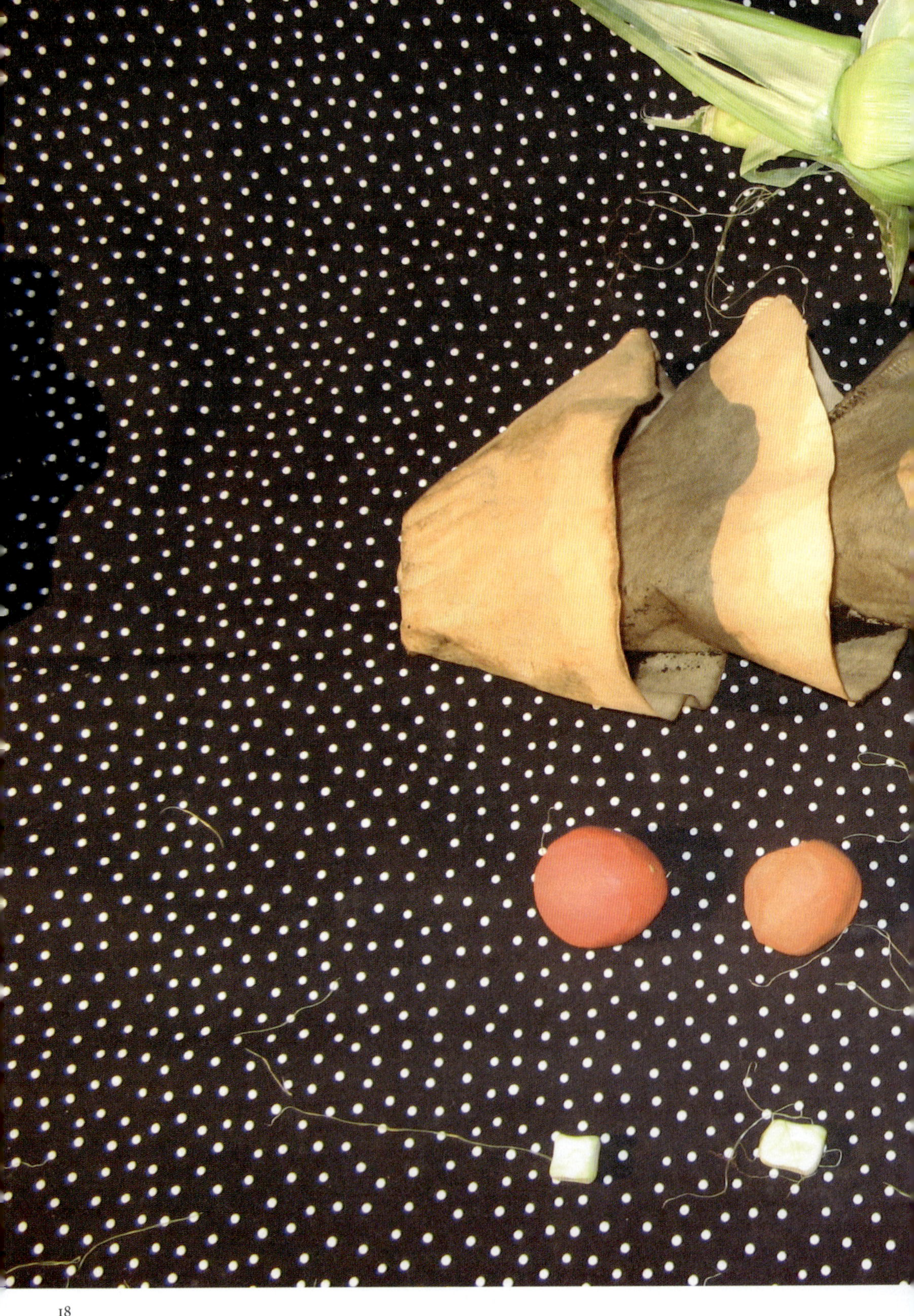

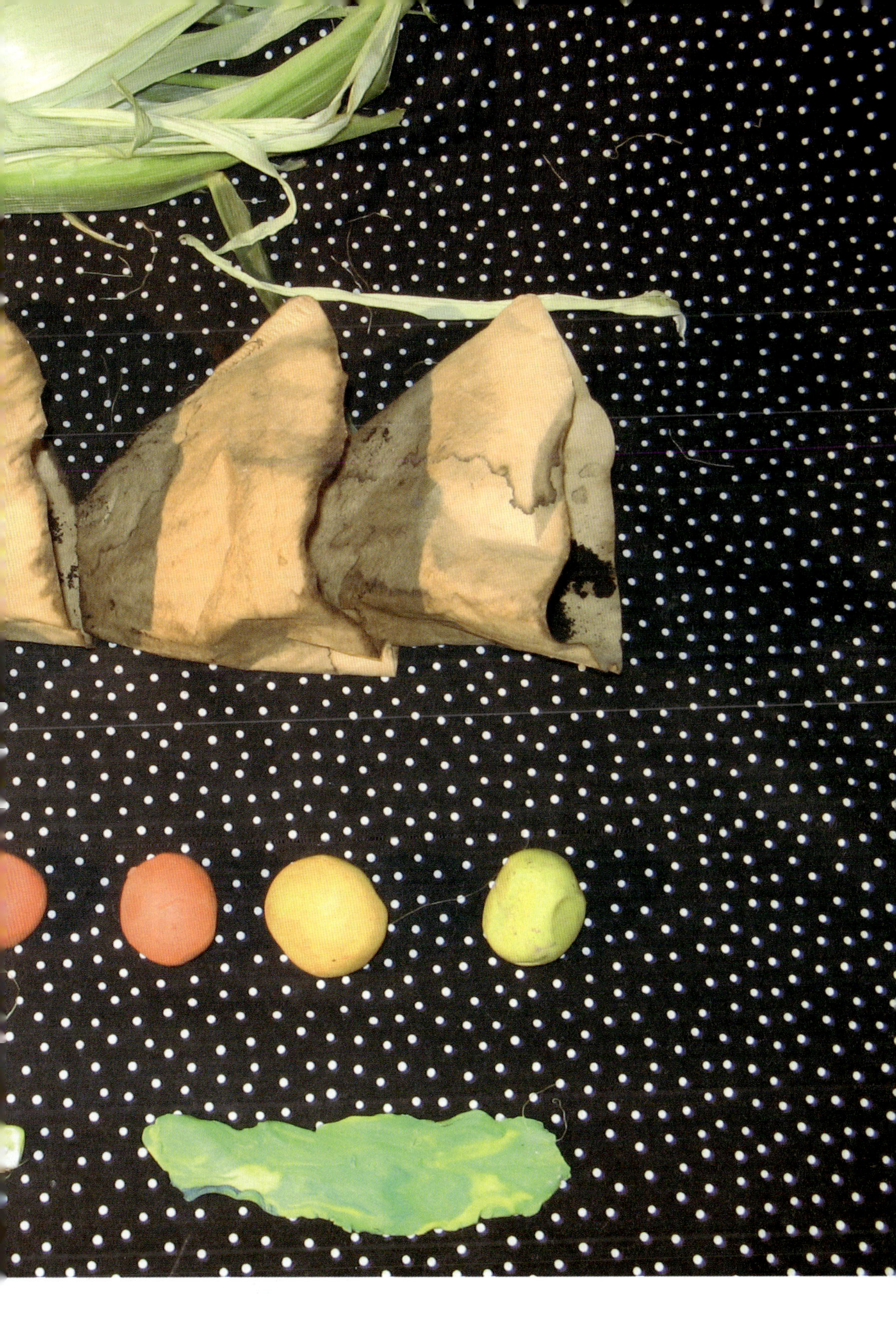

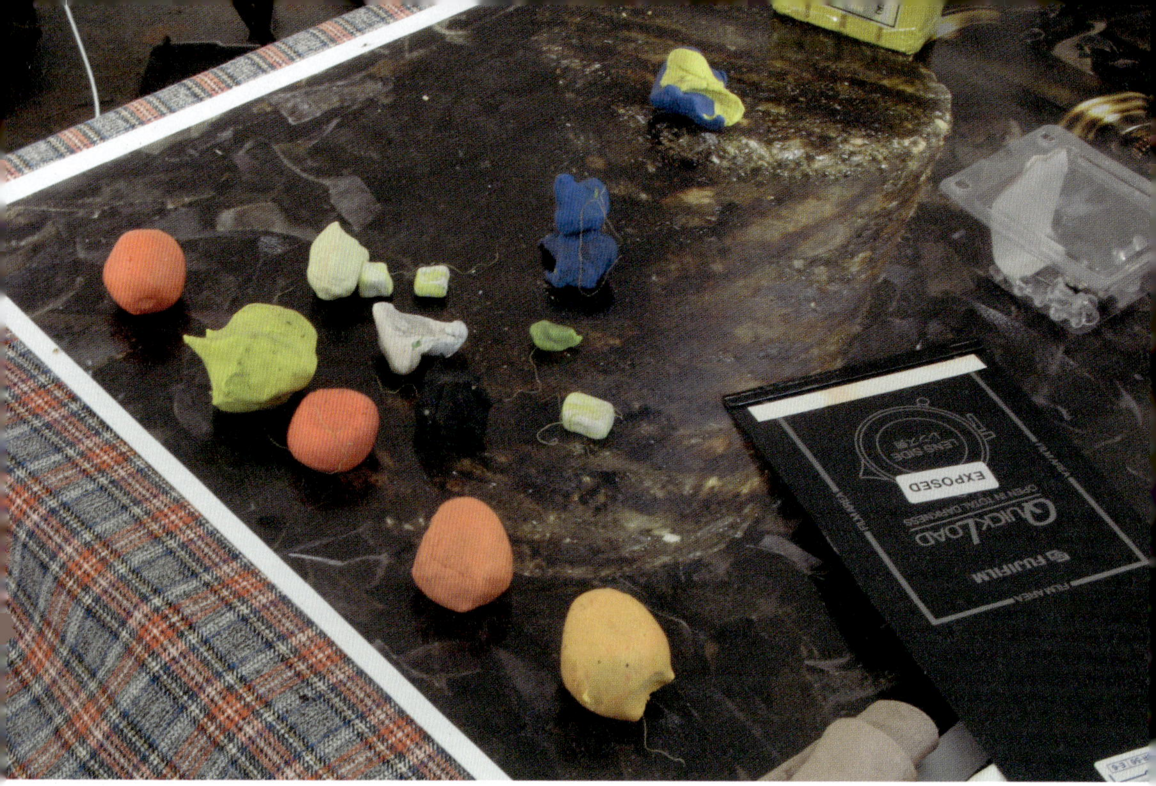

19   *Untitled #18*, 2007, from *Toad in a Hole*, pigment print, 12 x 16 inches. Collection of the Seattle Art Museum.
Gift of Rebecca and Alexander Stewart in honor of Mimi Gardner Gates. Courtesy of the artist and Laurel Gitlen, New York.

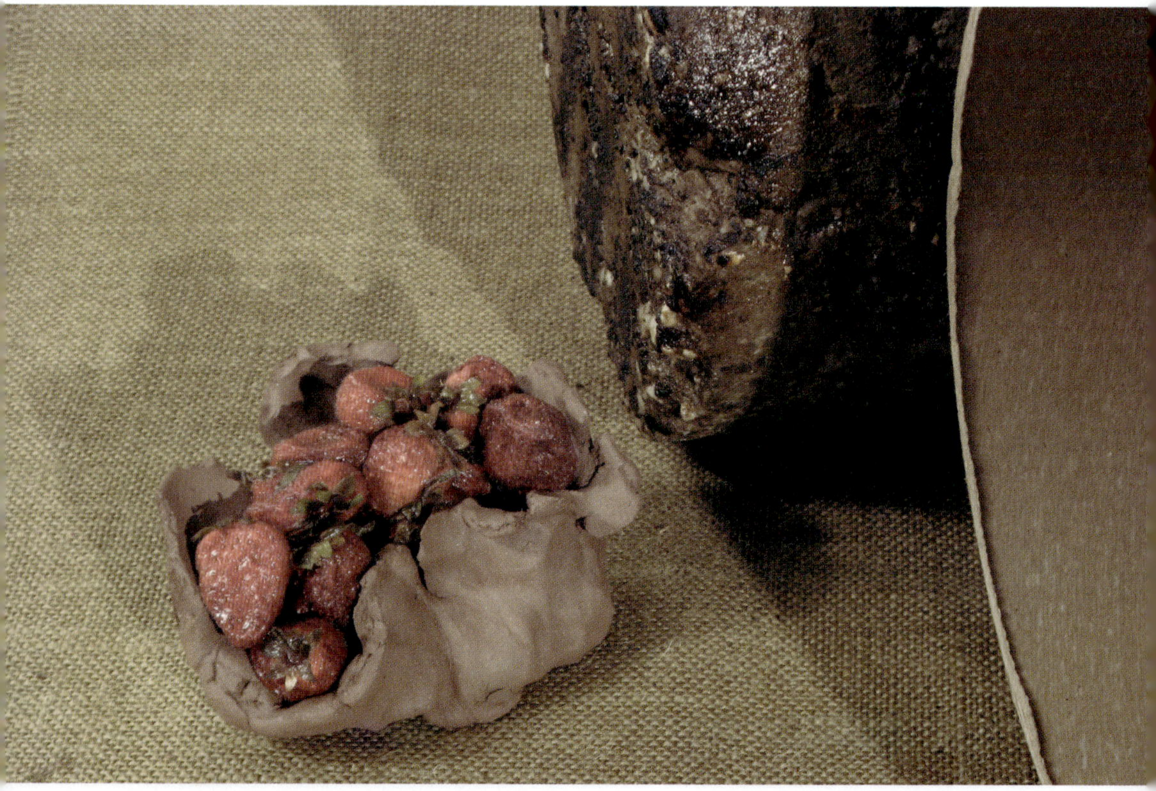

20   *Untitled #19*, 2007, from *Toad in a Hole*, pigment print, 16 x 21 5/16 inches. Collection of the Seattle Art Museum.
Gift of Rebecca and Alexander Stewart in honor of Mimi Gardner Gates. Courtesy of the artist and Laurel Gitlen, New York.

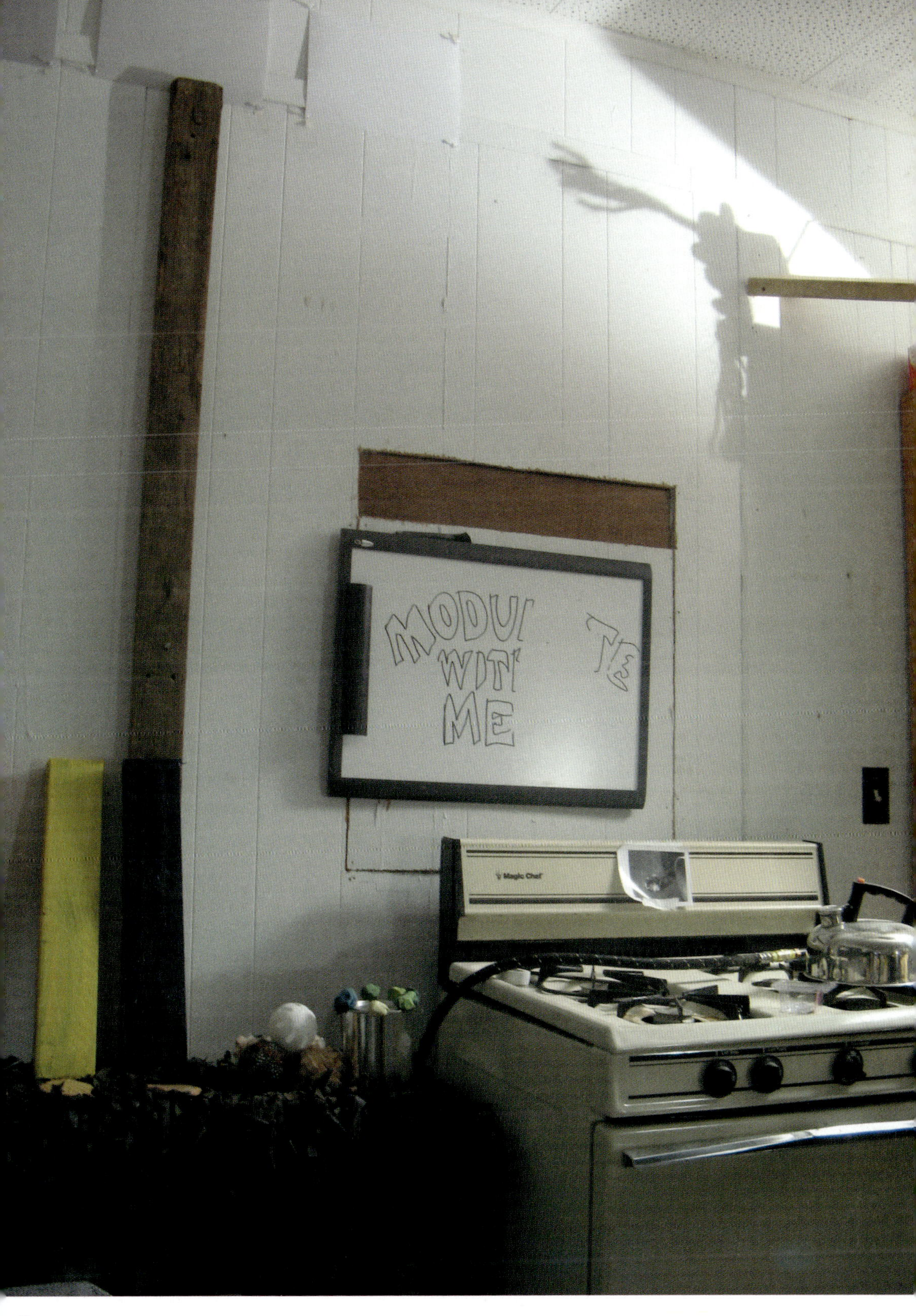

MODUI
WITI
ME
Magic Chef

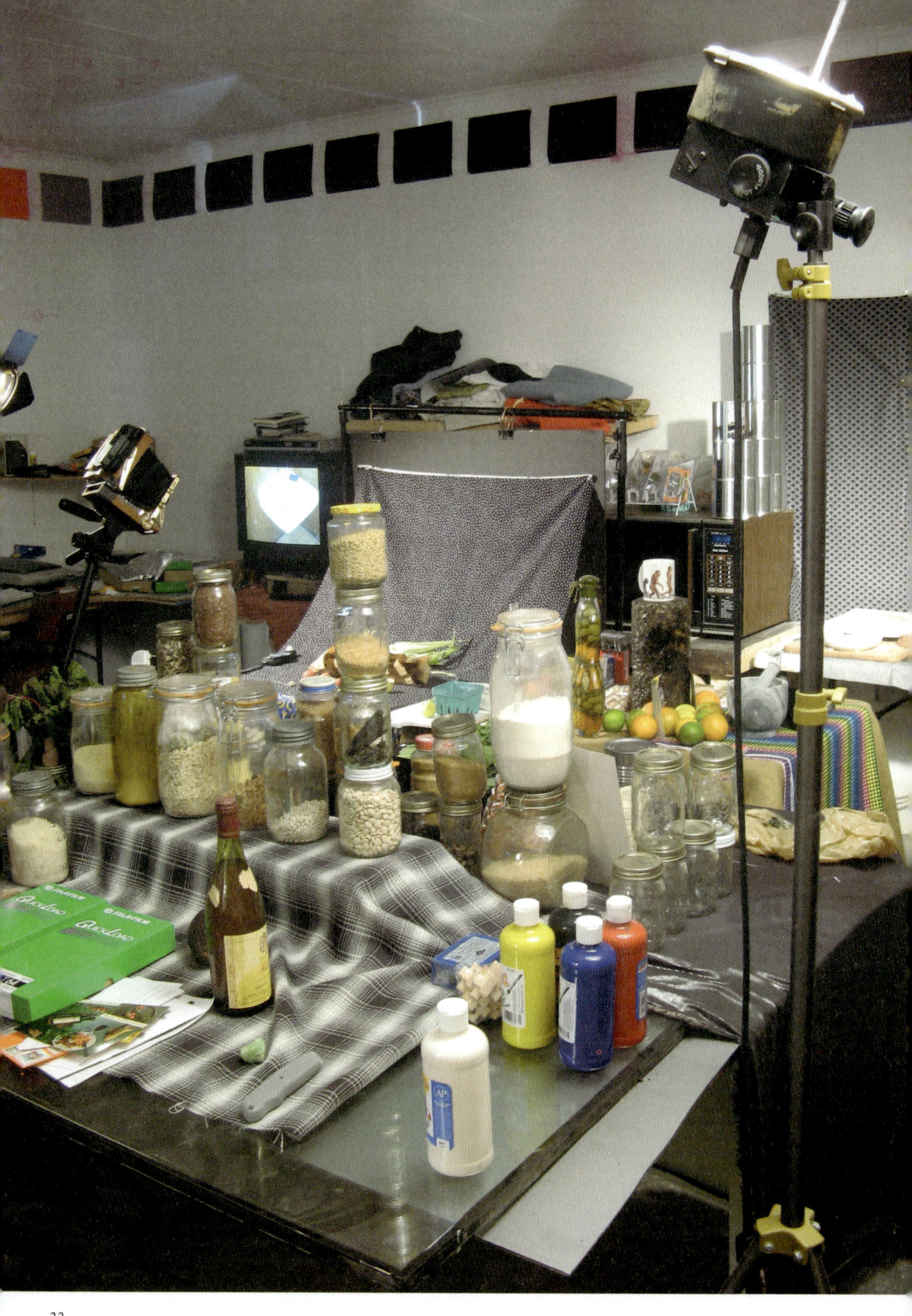

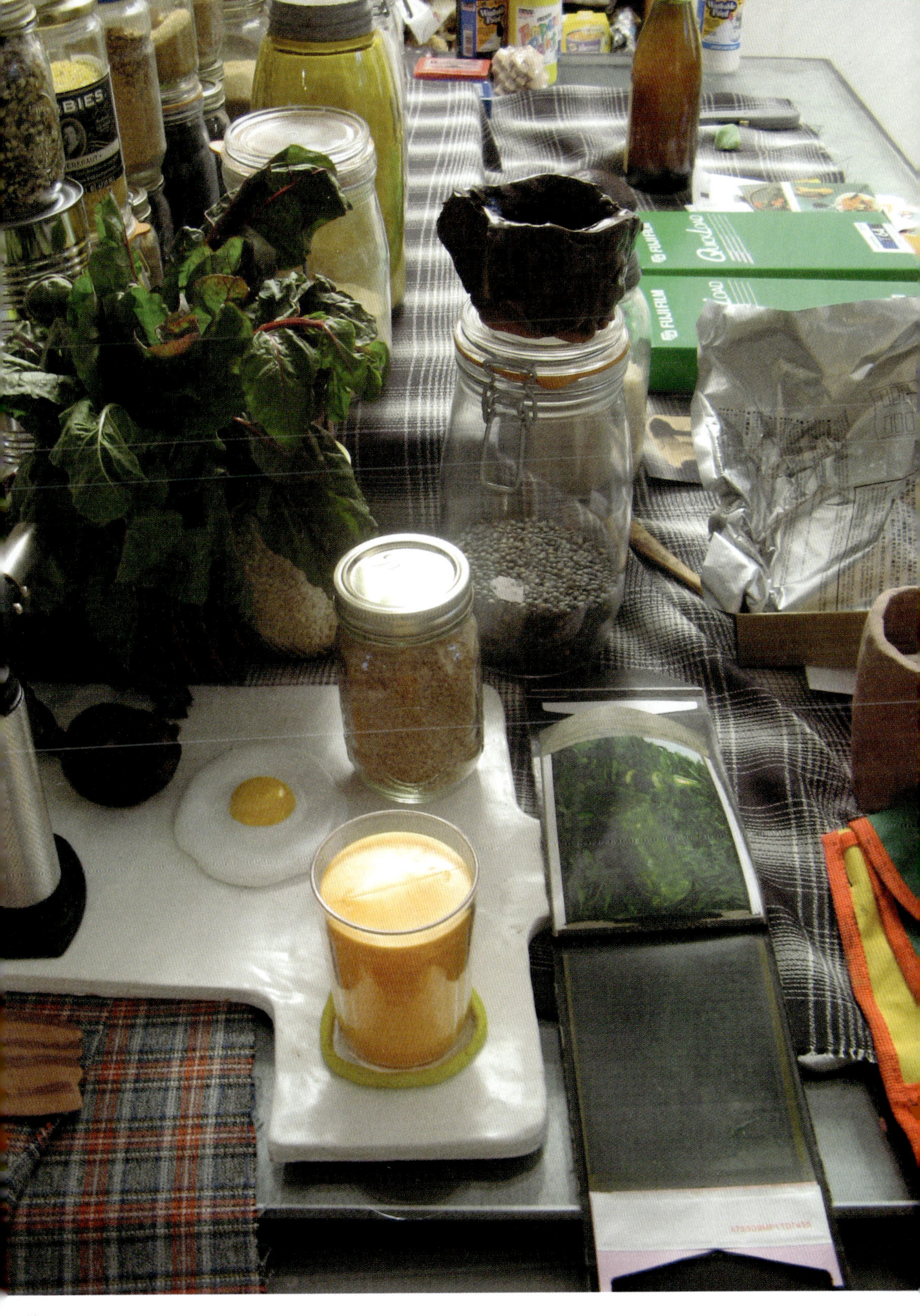

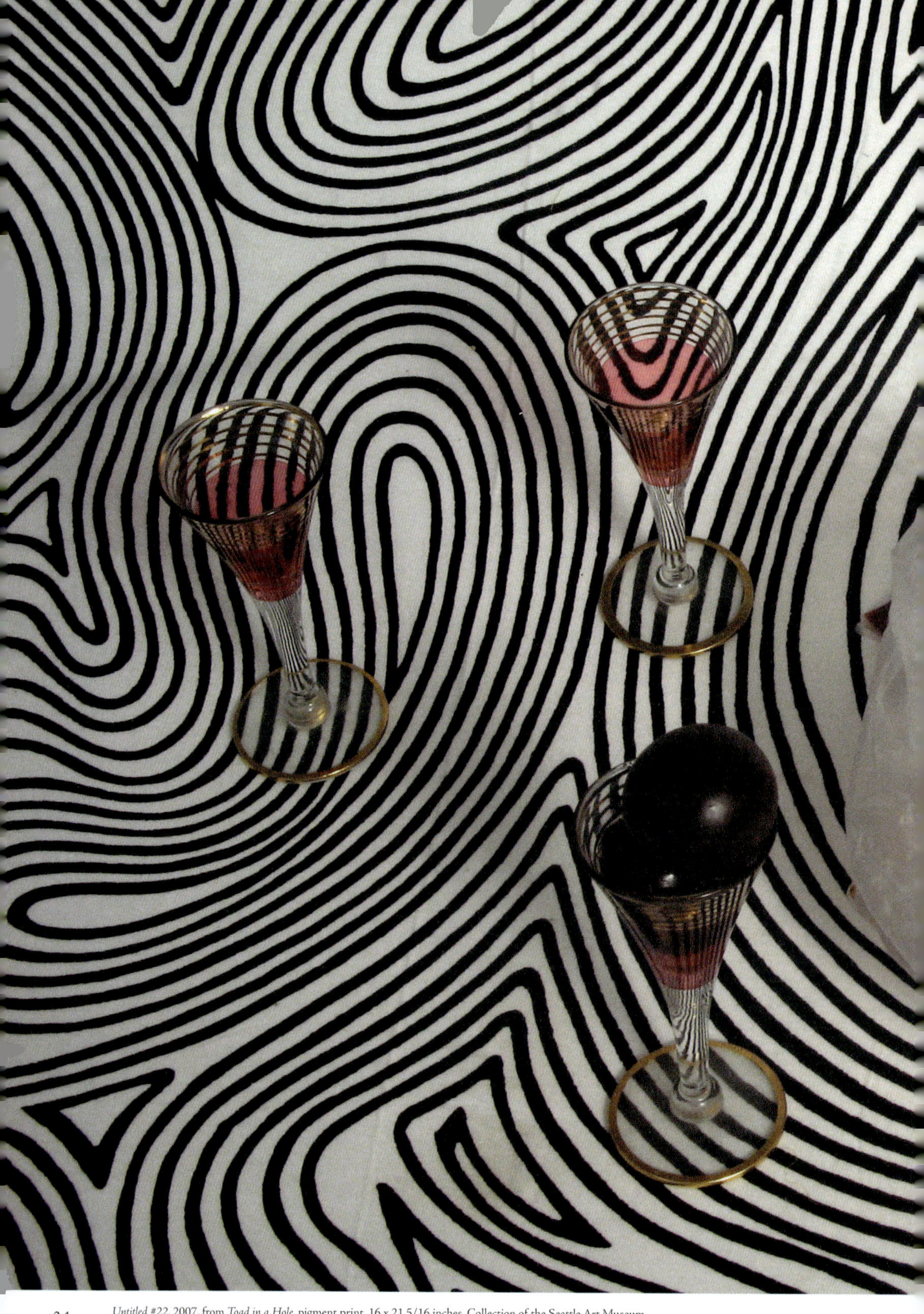

 Untitled #22, 2007, from *Toad in a Hole*, pigment print, 16 x 21 5/16 inches. Collection of the Seattle Art Museum. Gift of Rebecca and Alexander Stewart in honor of Mimi Gardner Gates. Courtesy of the artist and Laurel Gitlen, New York.

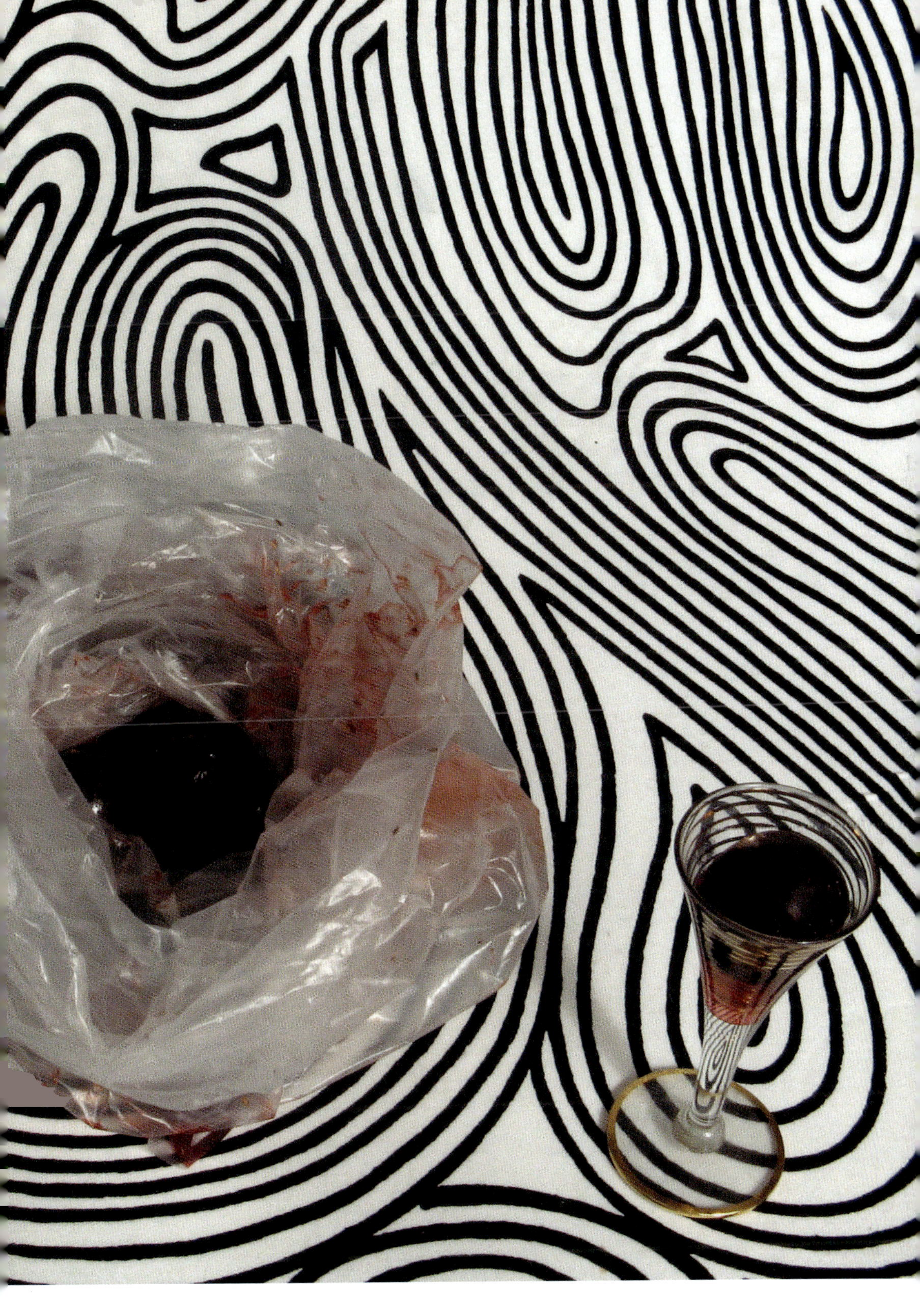

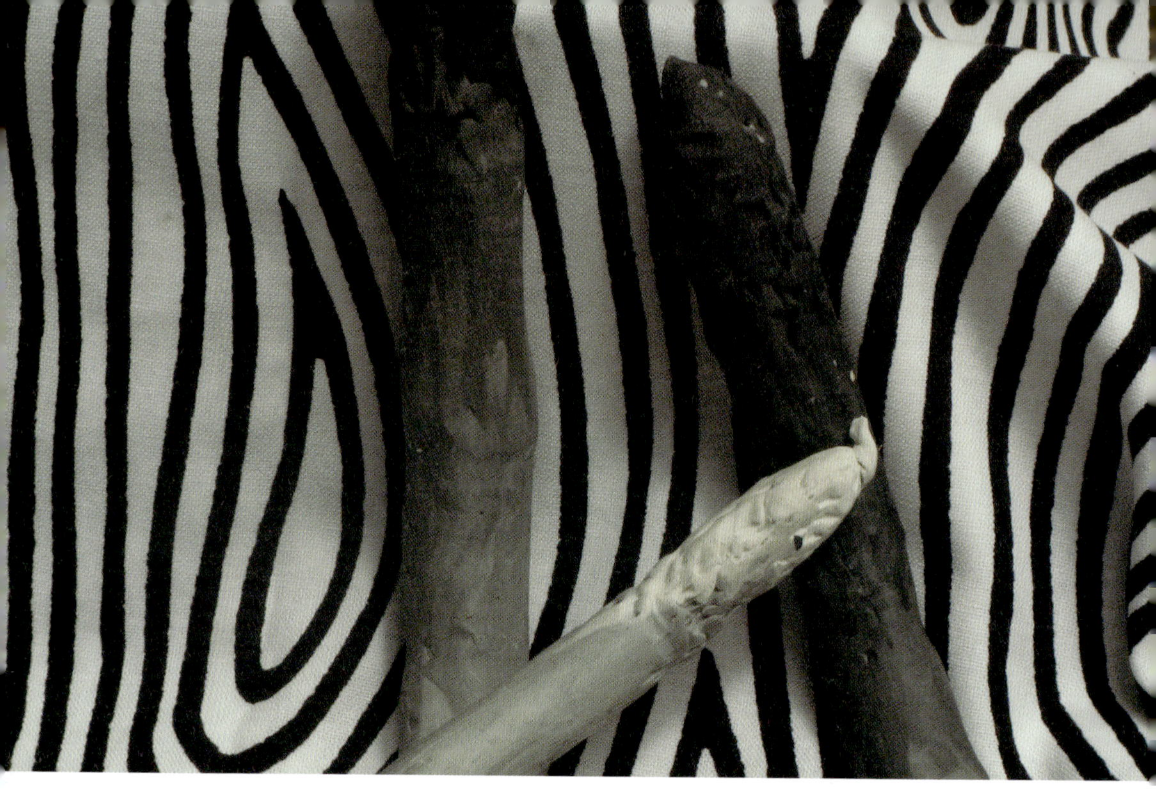

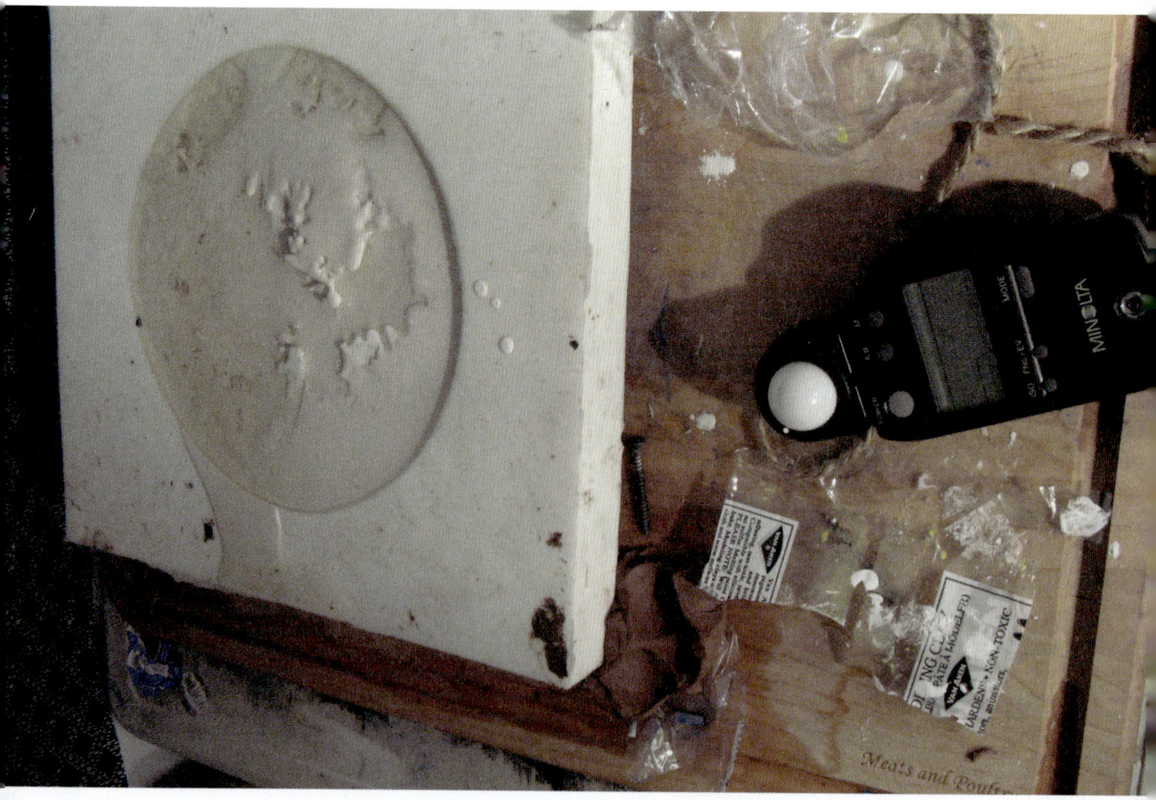

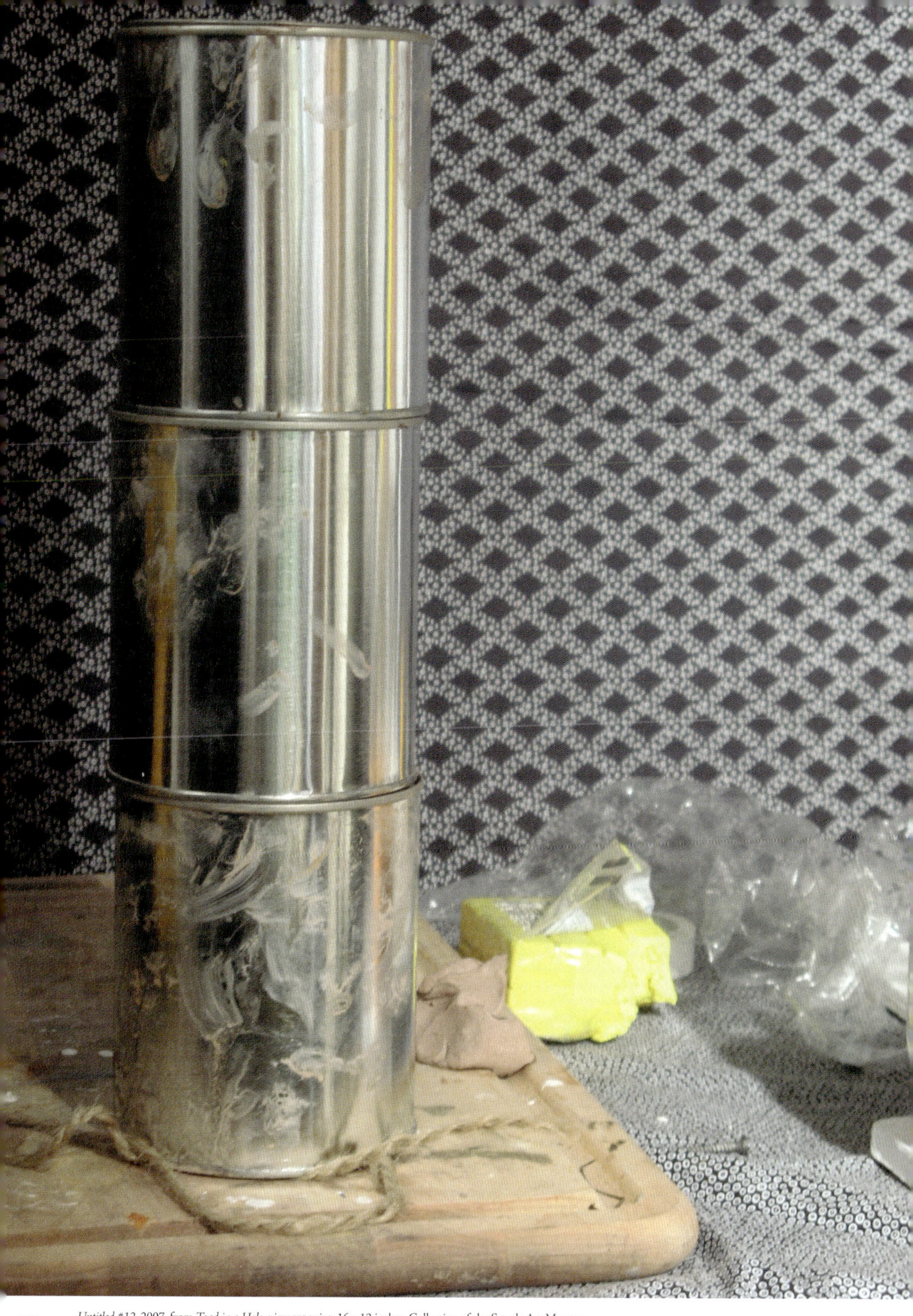

Untitled #12, 2007, from *Toad in a Hole*, pigment print, 16 x 12 inches. Collection of the Seattle Art Museum.
Gift of Rebecca and Alexander Stewart in honor of Mimi Gardner Gates. Courtesy of the artist and Laurel Gitlen, New York.

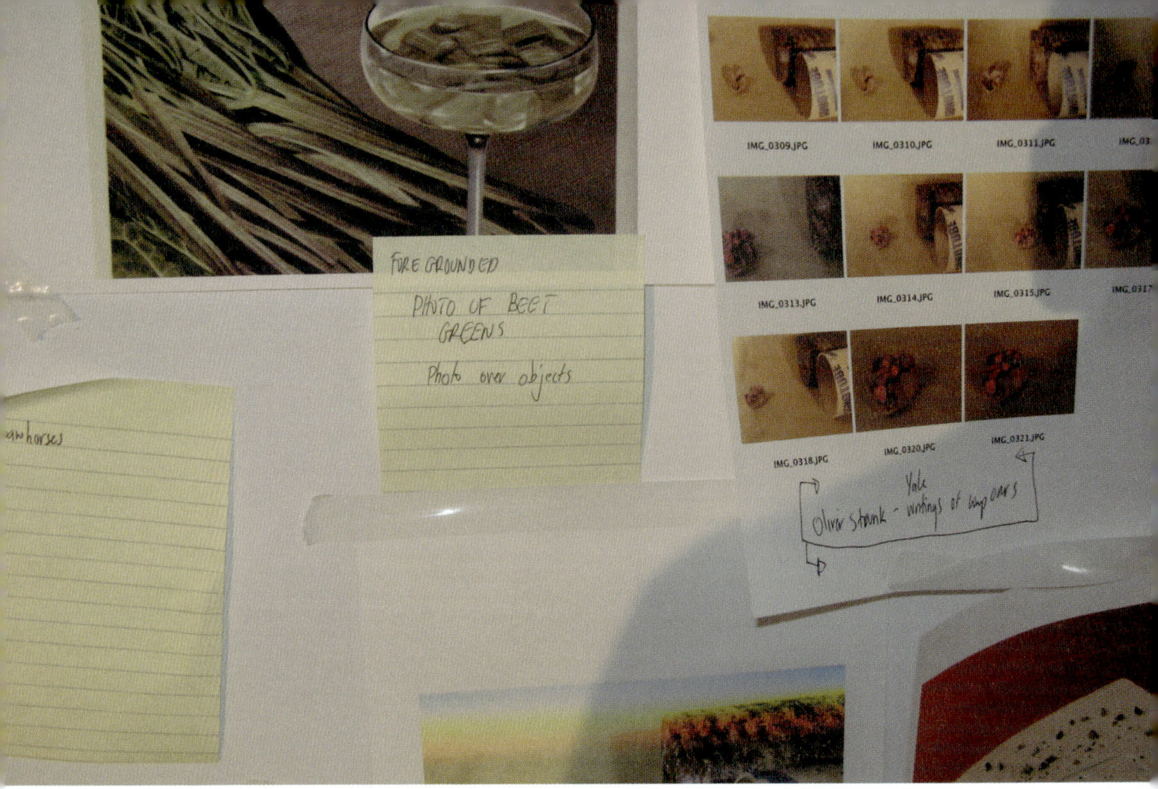

FORE GROUNDED

PHOTO OF BEET
GREENS

Photo over objects

an horses

IMG_0309.JPG   IMG_0310.JPG   IMG_0311.JPG   IMG_03
IMG_0313.JPG   IMG_0314.JPG   IMG_0315.JPG   IMG_0317
IMG_0318.JPG   IMG_0320.JPG   IMG_0321.JPG

Yale
Oliver Strunk – writings of composers

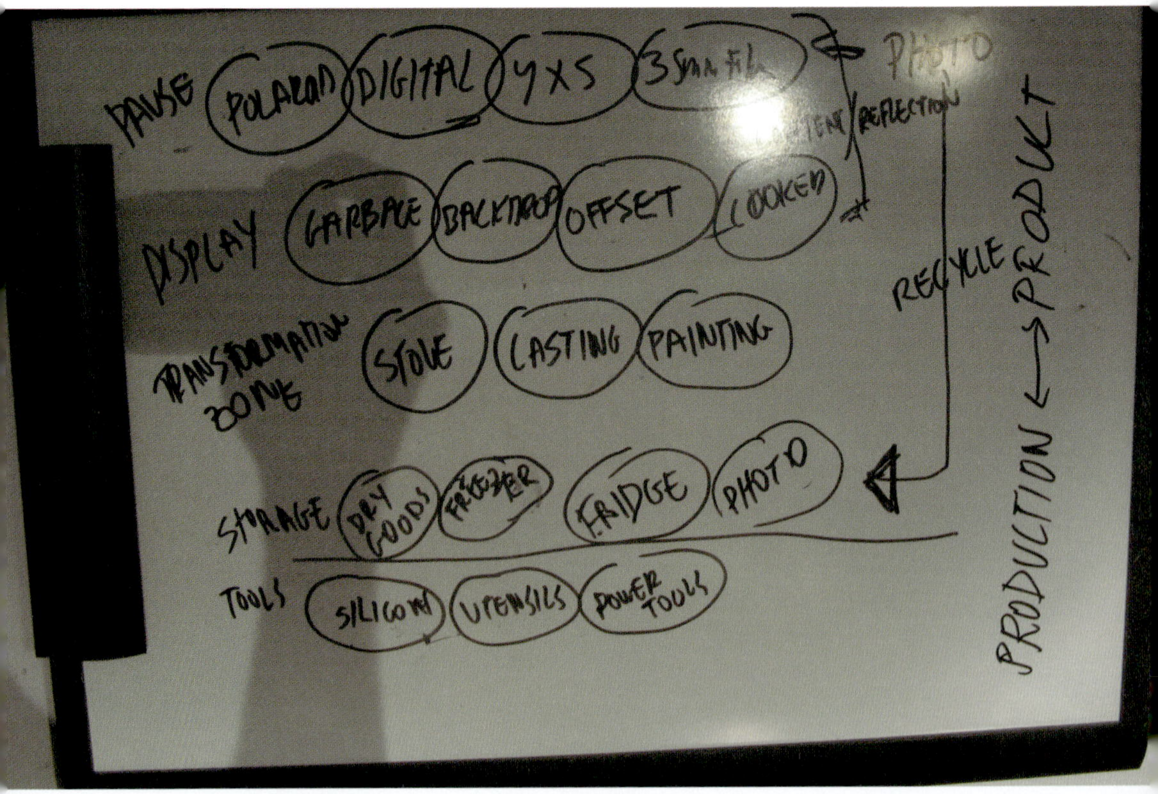

PAUSE (POLAROID) (DIGITAL) (4 X 5) (35mm film) PHOTO
REFLECTION

DISPLAY (GARBAGE) (BACKDROP) (OFFSET) (COOKED)

TRANSFORMATION ZONE (STOVE) (CASTING) (PAINTING)

RECYCLE

STORAGE (DRY GOODS) (FREEZER) (FRIDGE) (PHOTO)

TOOLS (SILICON) (UTENSILS) (POWER TOOLS)

PRODUCTION ↔ PRODUCT

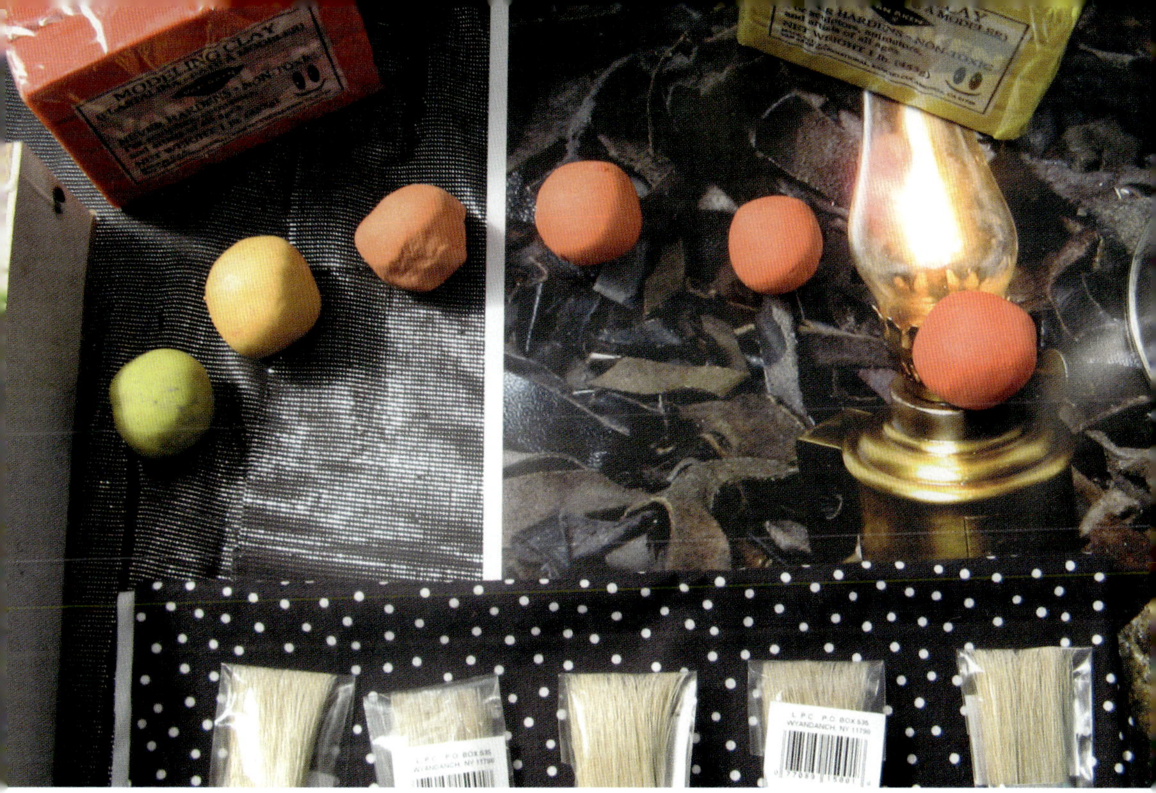

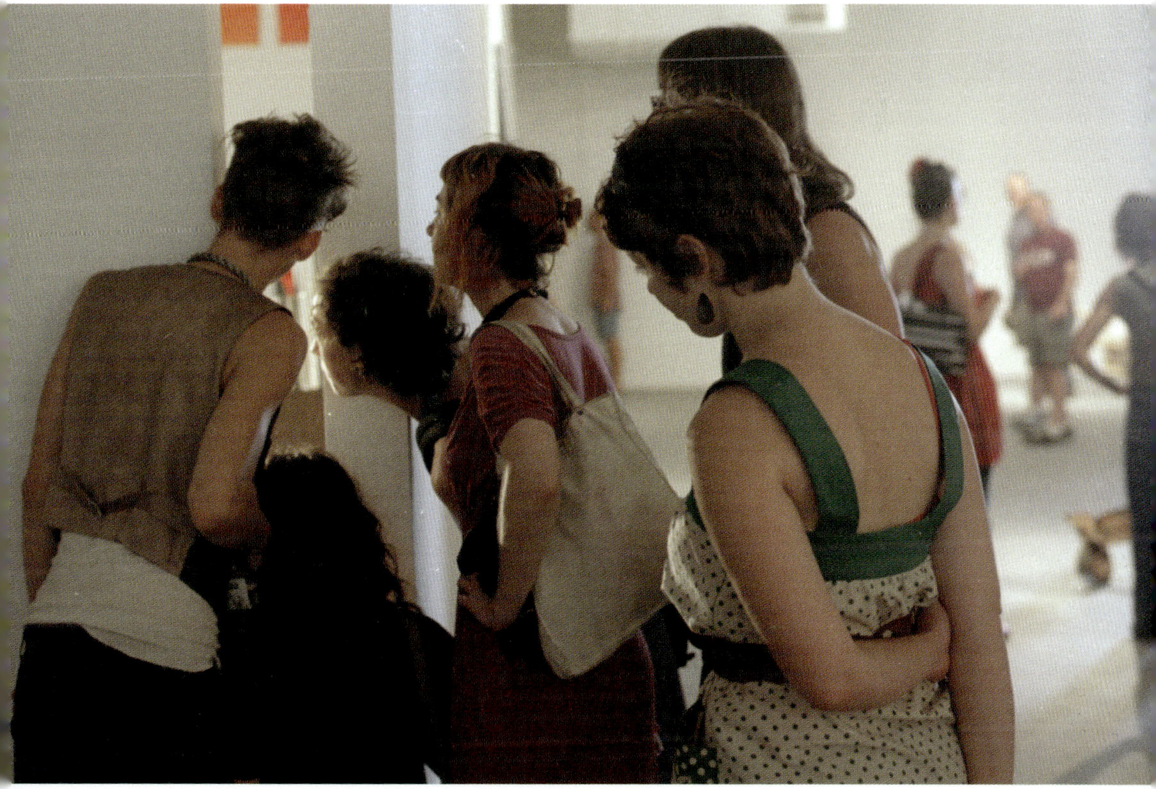

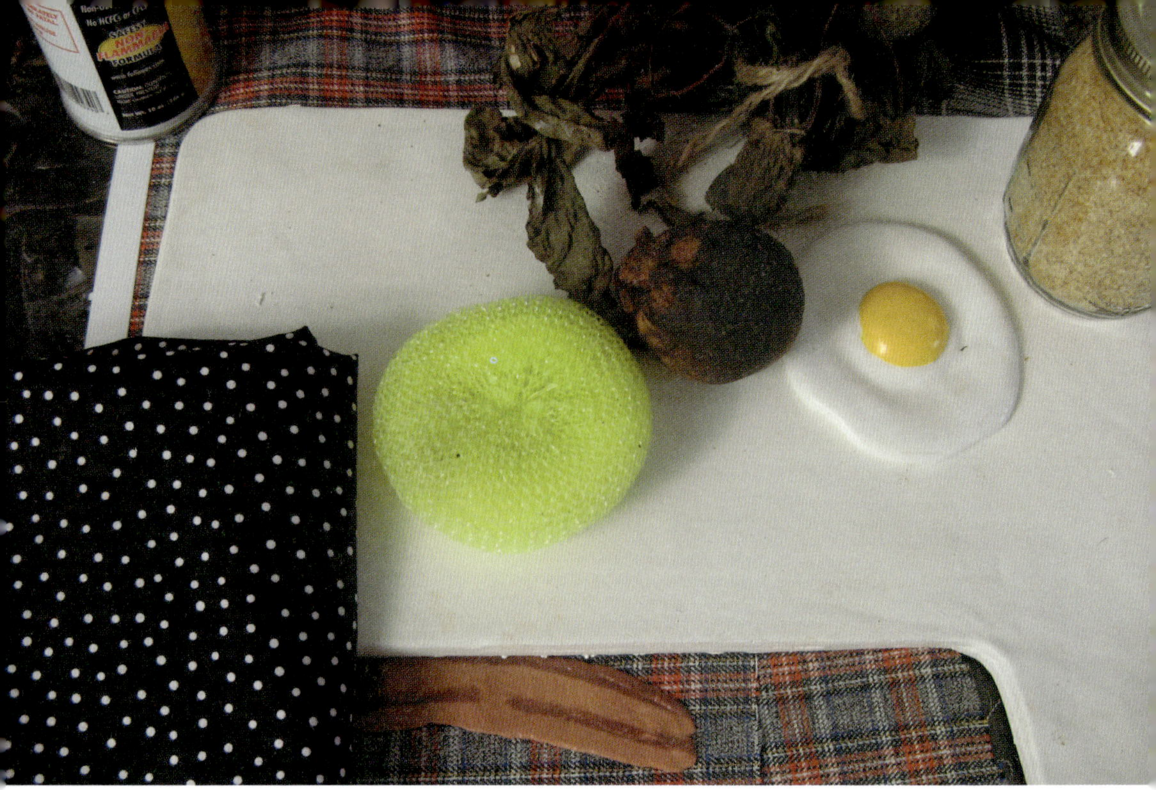

MODULATE
ME
WITH ME

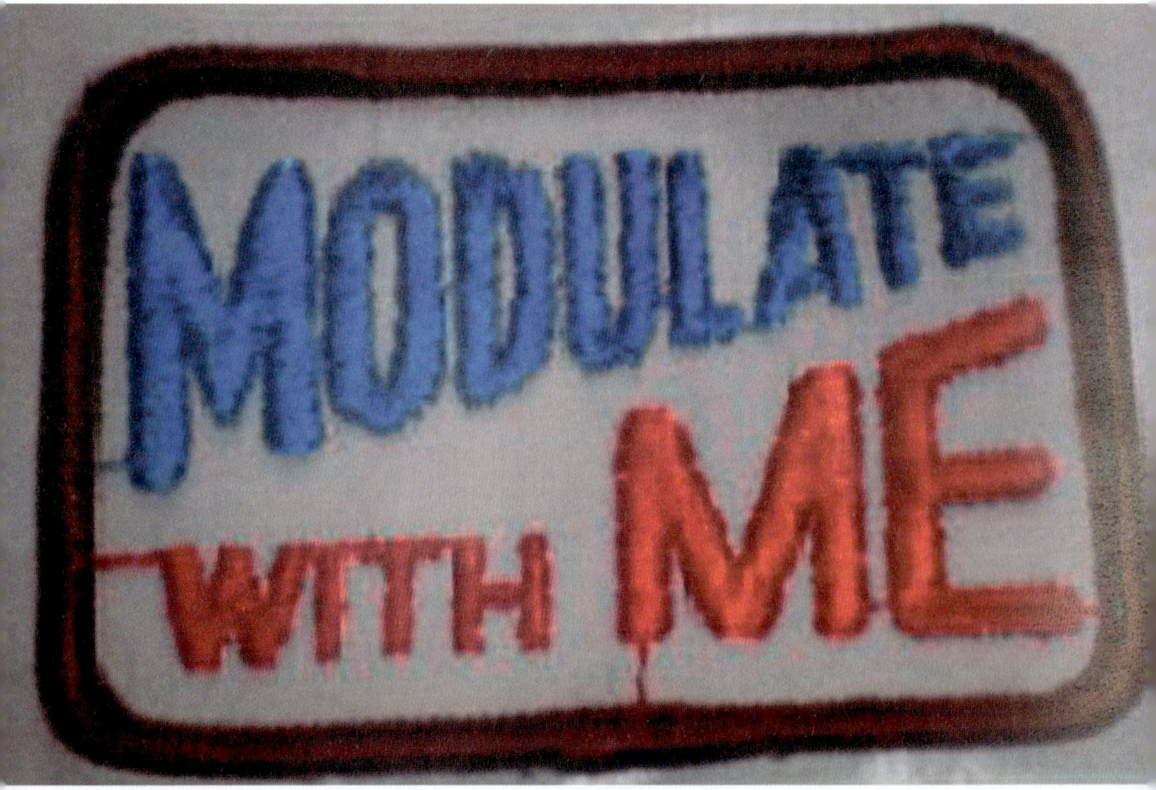

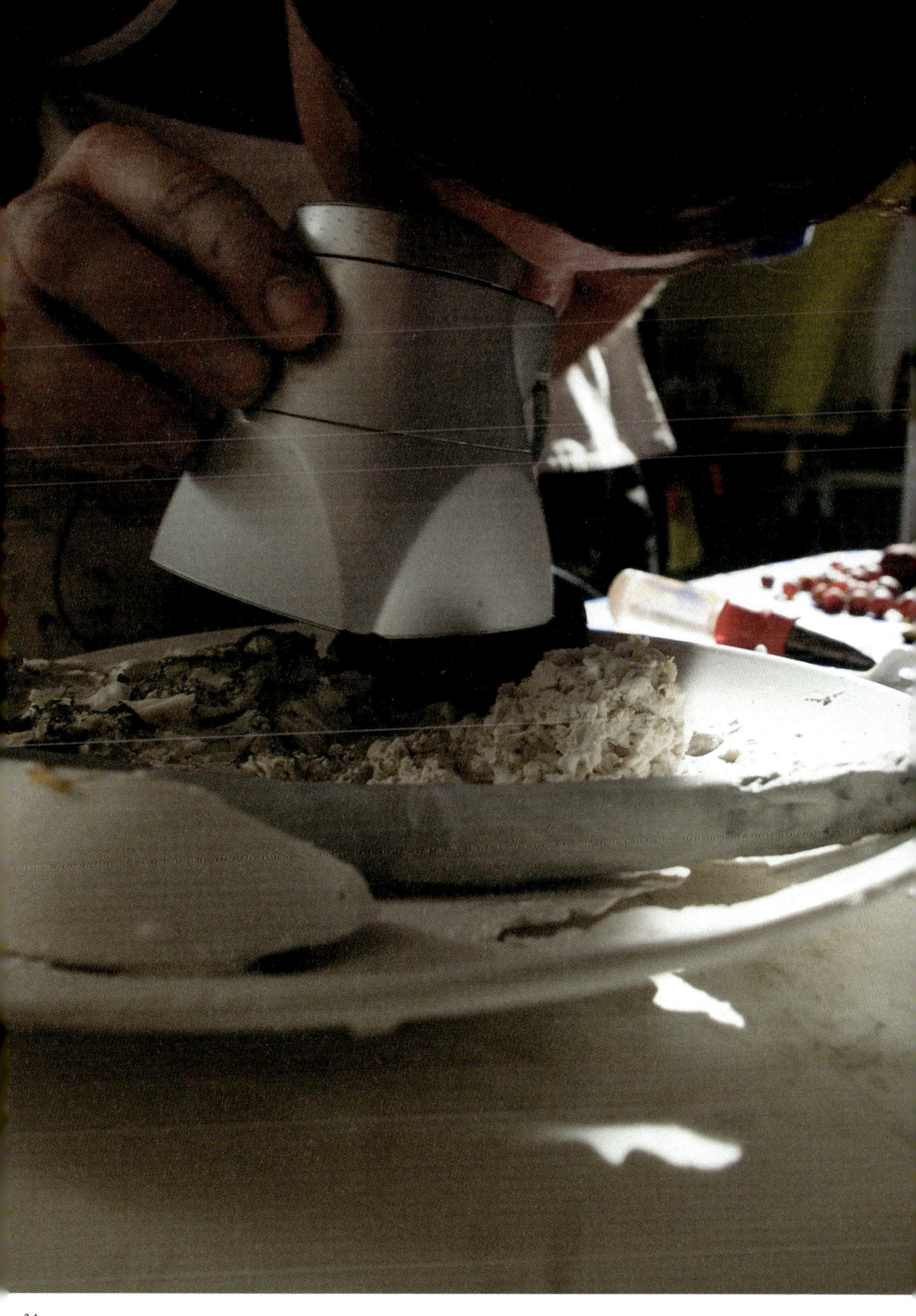

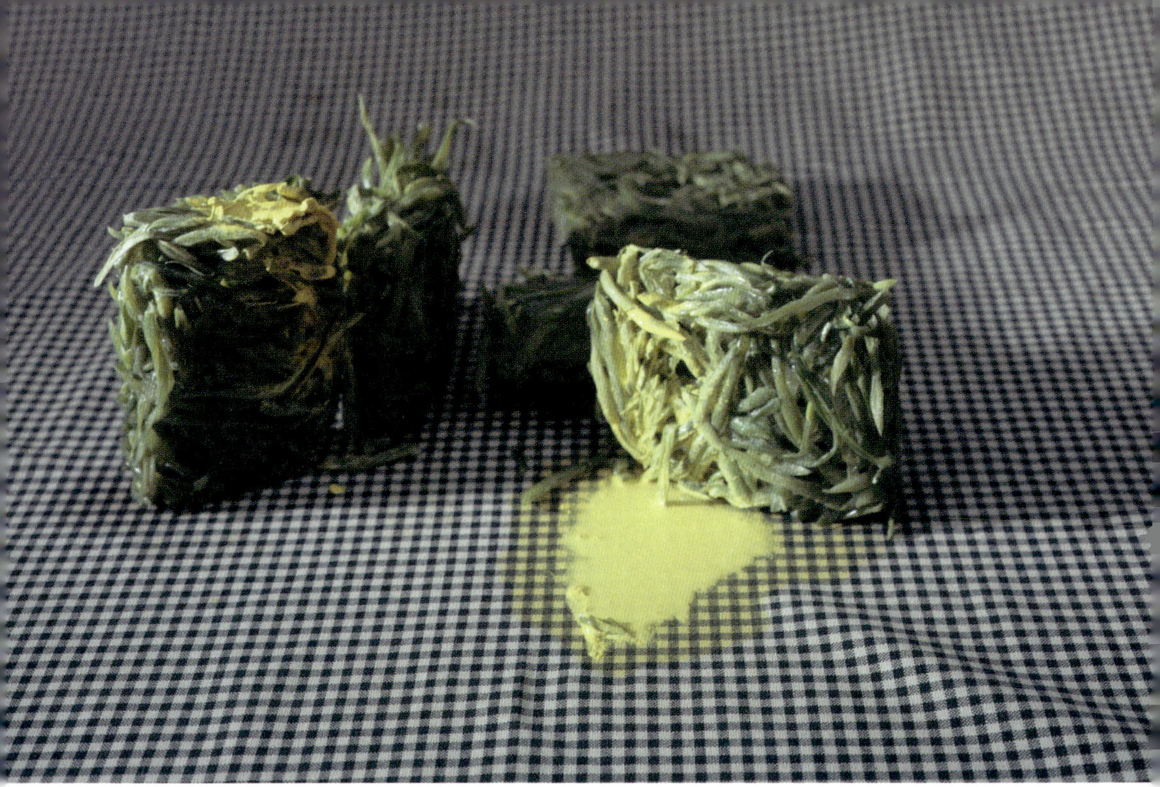

  Untitled #17, 2007, from *Toad in a Hole*, pigment print, 16 x 21 5/16 inches. Collection of the Seattle Art Museum.
Gift of Rebecca and Alexander Stewart in honor of Mimi Gardner Gates. Courtesy of the artist and Laurel Gitlen, New York.

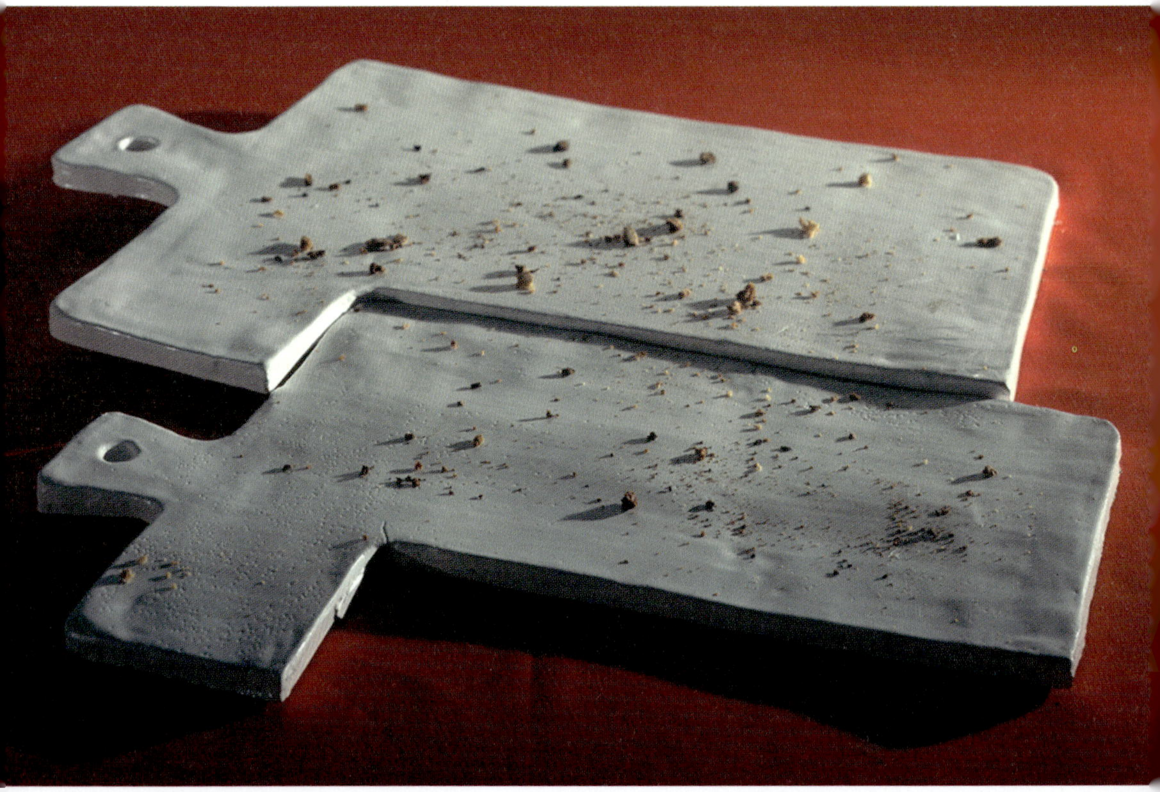

  Untitled #13, 2007, from *Toad in a Hole*, pigment print, 16 x 21 5/16 inches. Collection of the Seattle Art Museum.
Gift of Rebecca and Alexander Stewart in honor of Mimi Gardner Gates. Courtesy of the artist and Laurel Gitlen, New York.

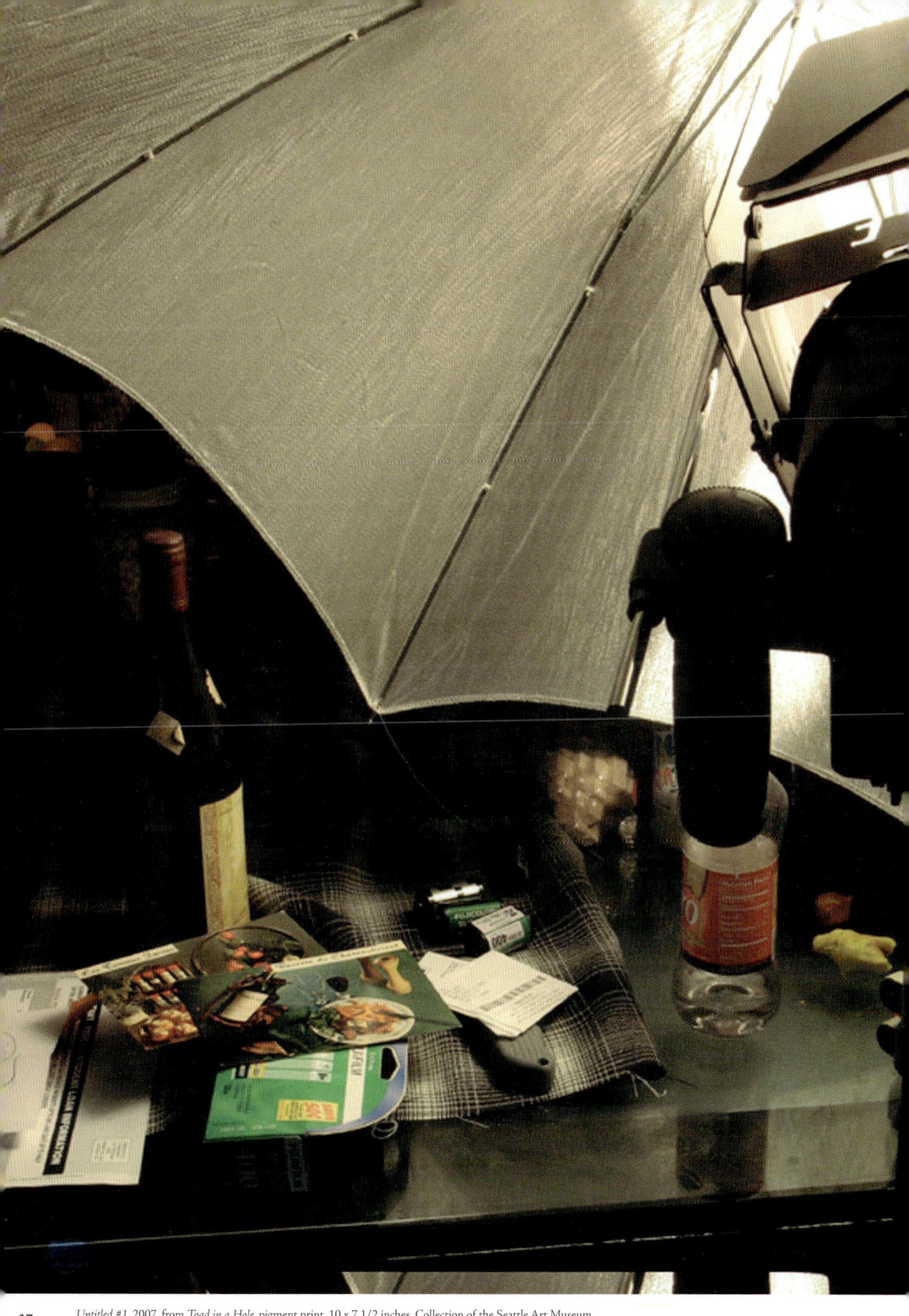

 Untitled #1, 2007, from *Toad in a Hole*, pigment print, 10 x 7 1/2 inches. Collection of the Seattle Art Museum.
Gift of Rebecca and Alexander Stewart in honor of Mimi Gardner Gates. Courtesy of the artist and Laurel Gitlen, New York.

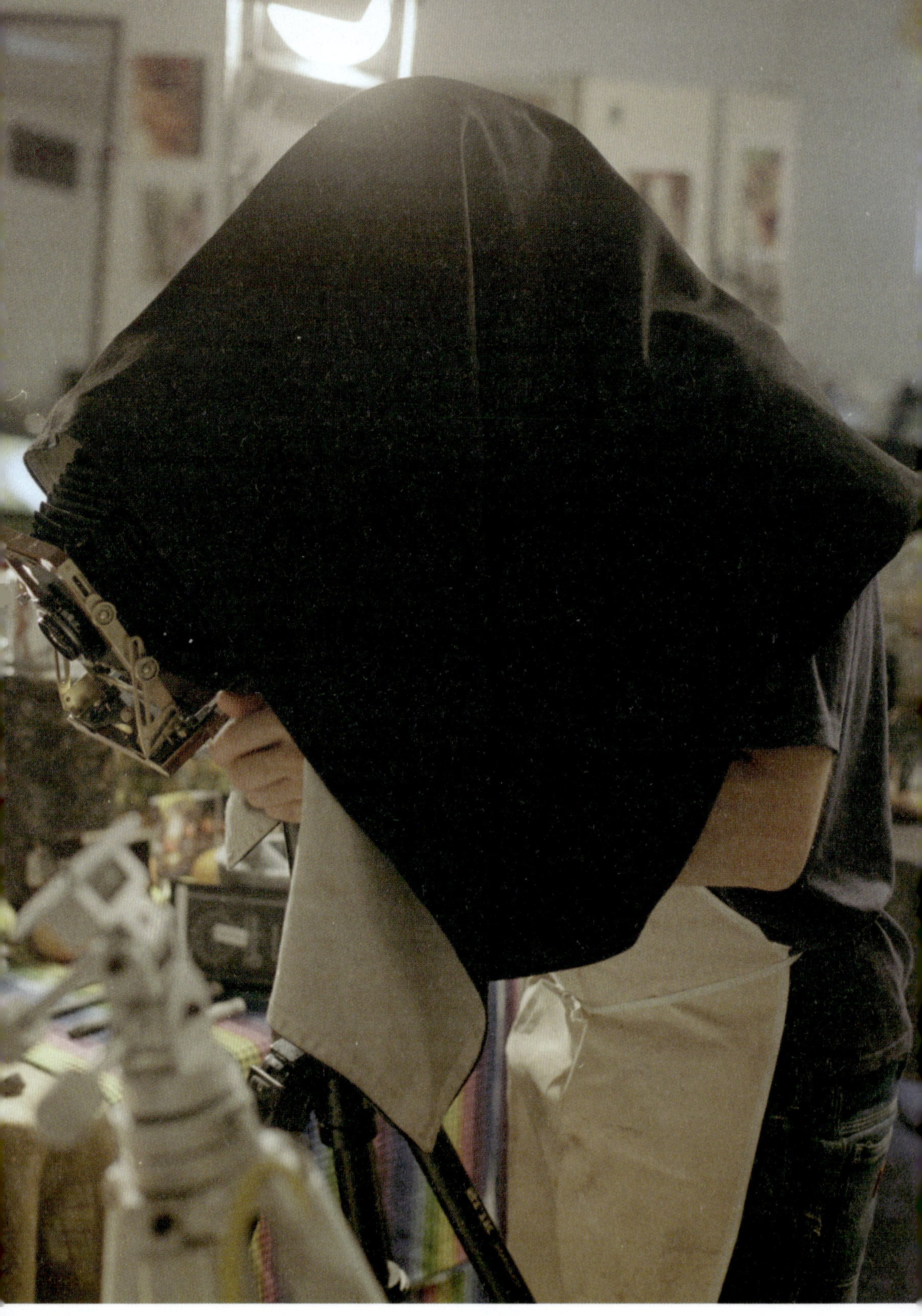

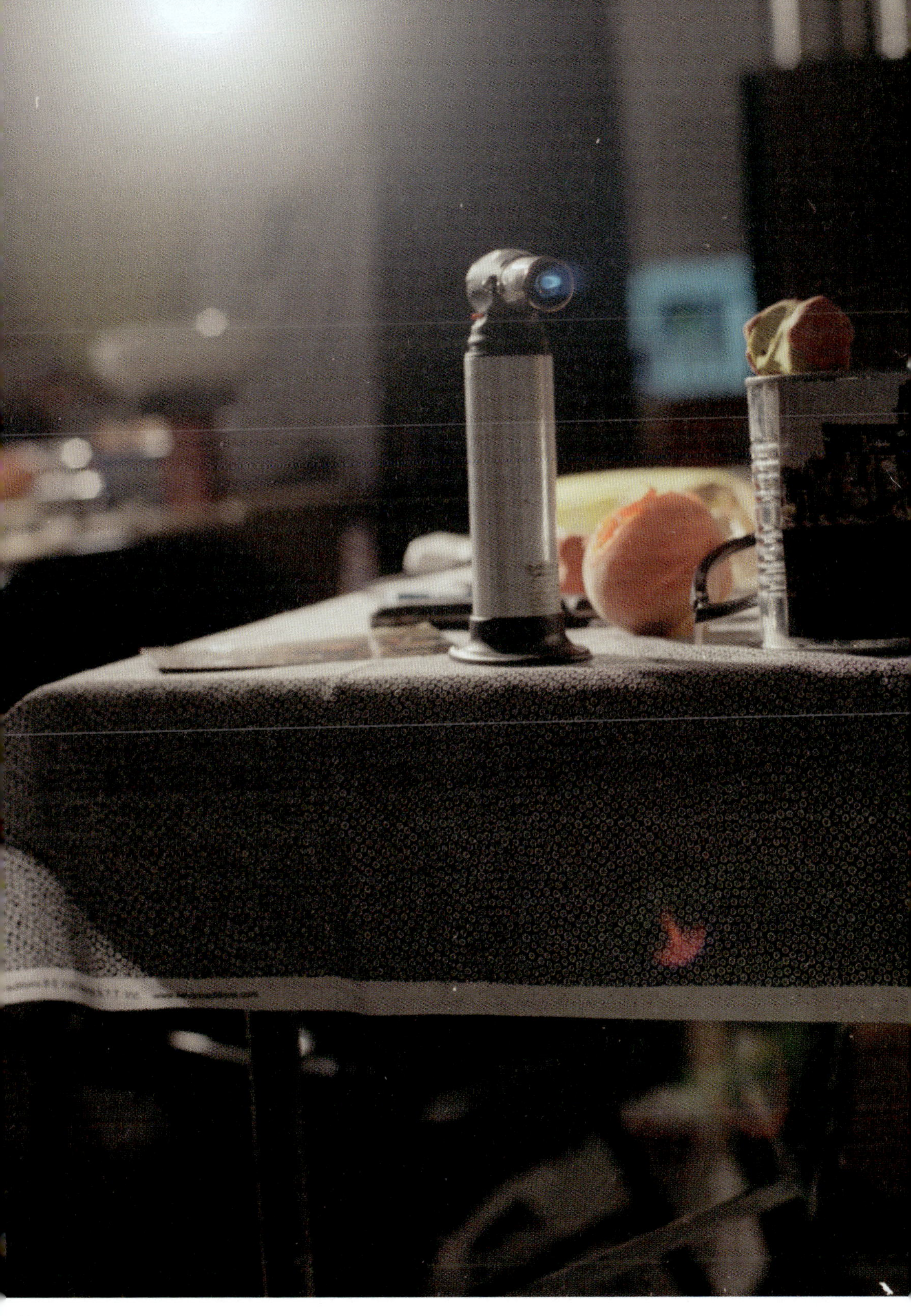

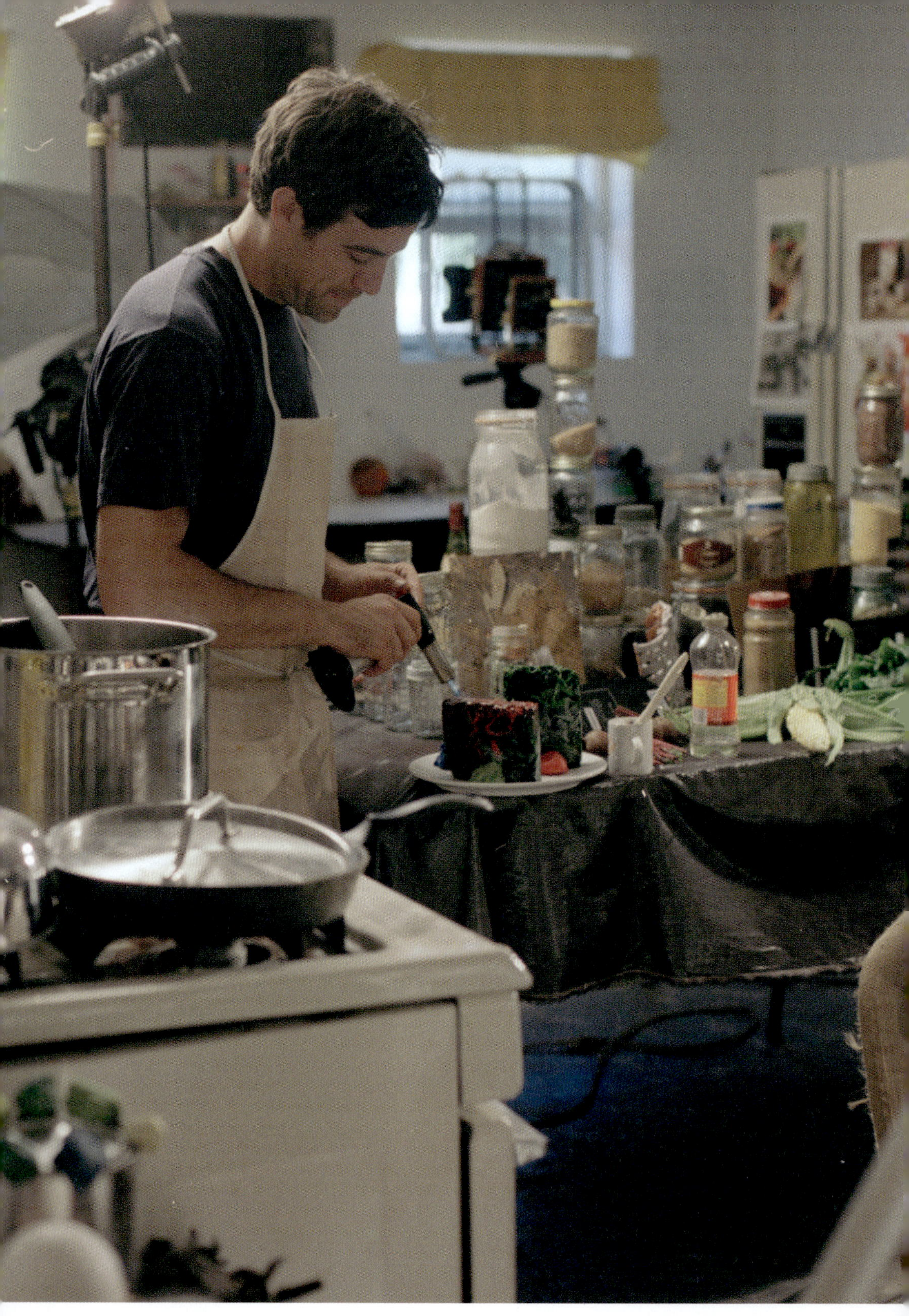

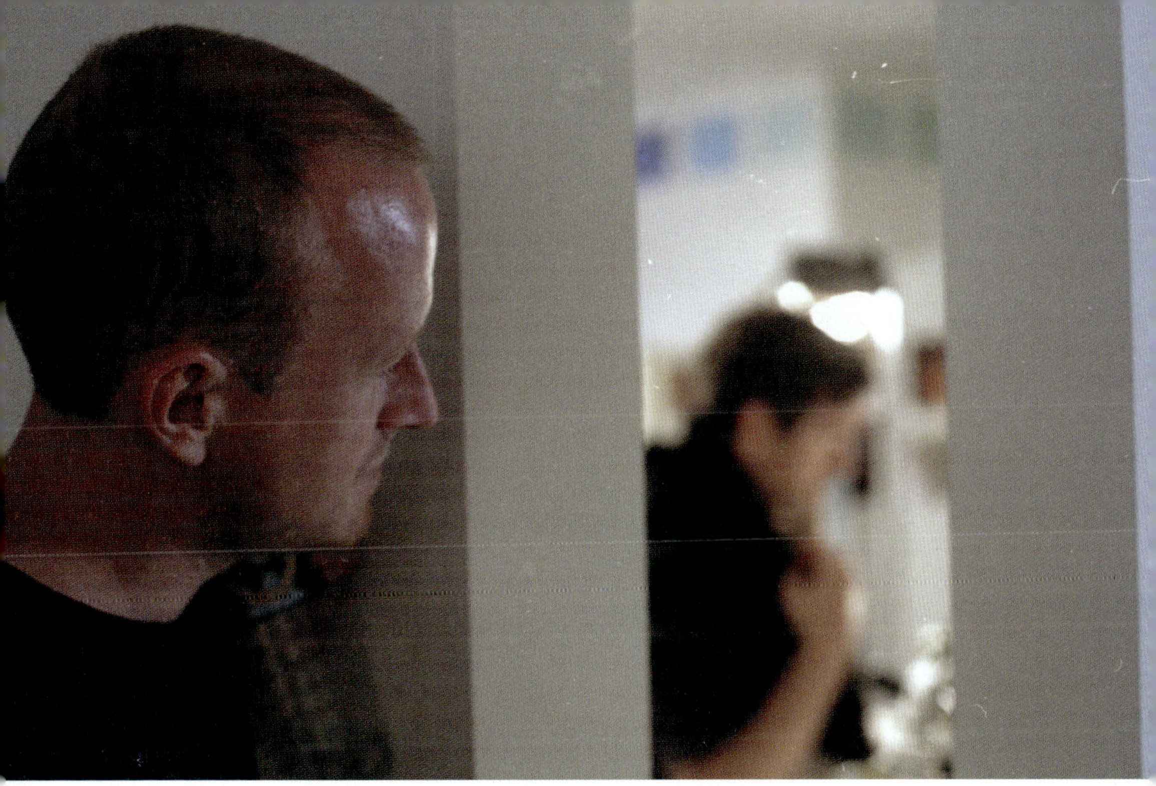

Untitled #14, 2007, from *Toad in a Hole*, pigment print, 10 x 7 1/2 inches. Collection of the Seattle Art Museum.
Gift of Rebecca and Alexander Stewart in honor of Mimi Gardner Gates. Courtesy of the artist and Laurel Gitlen, New York.

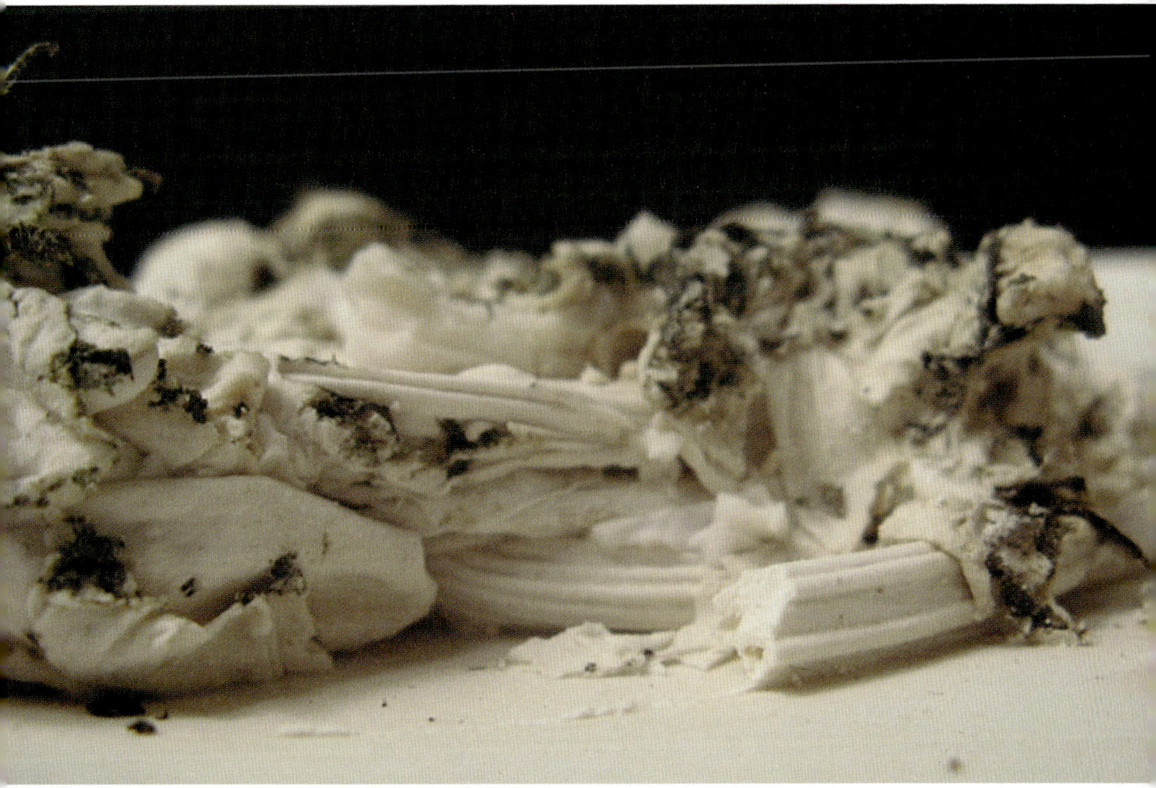

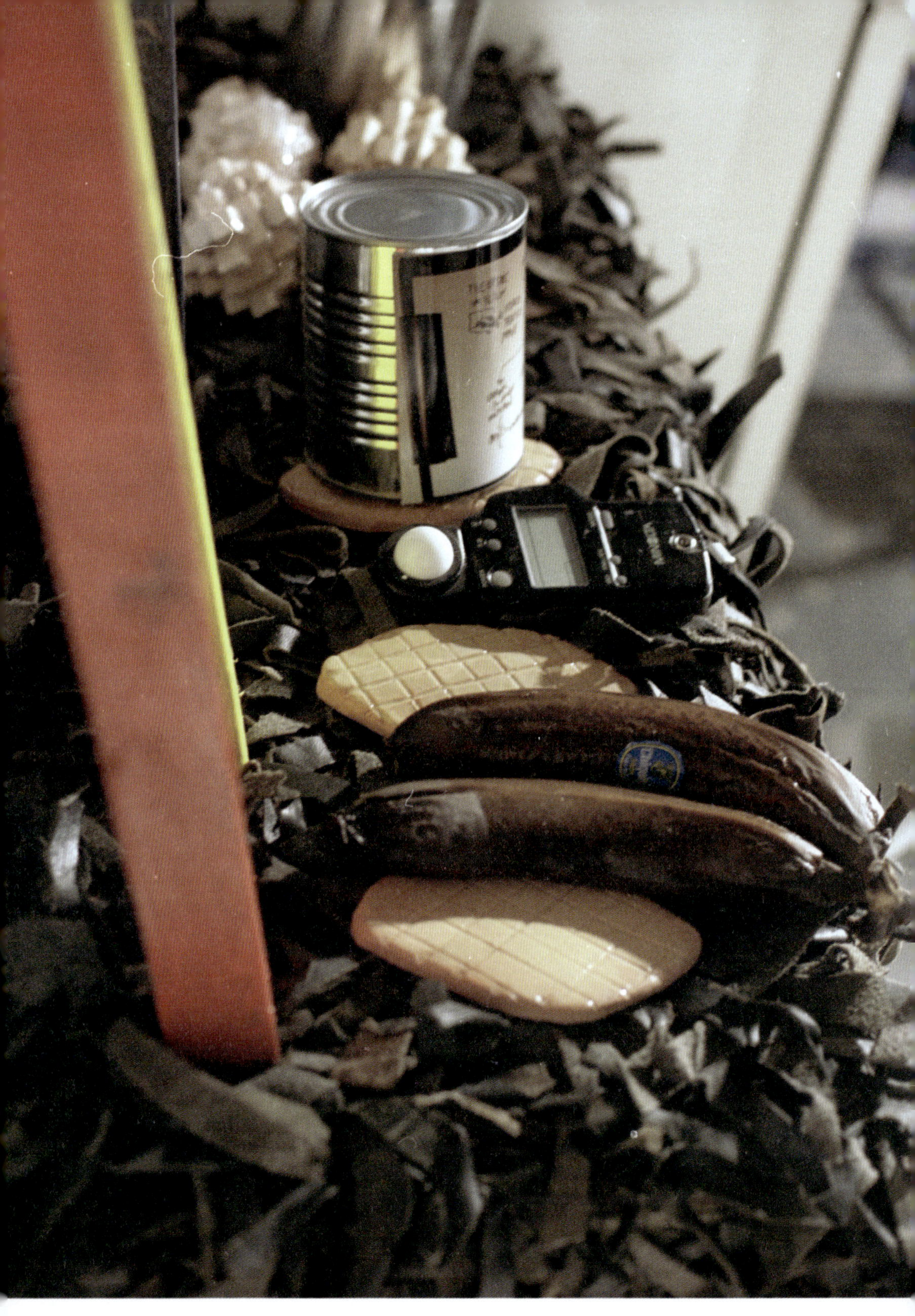

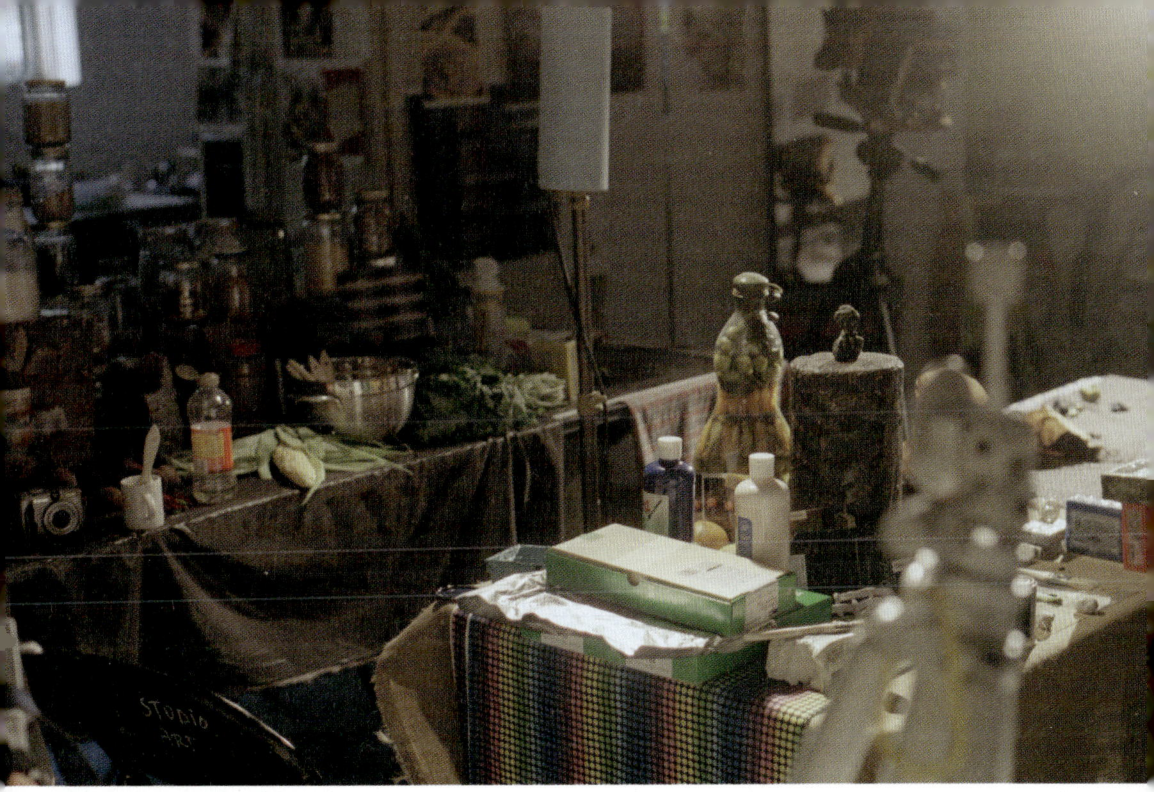

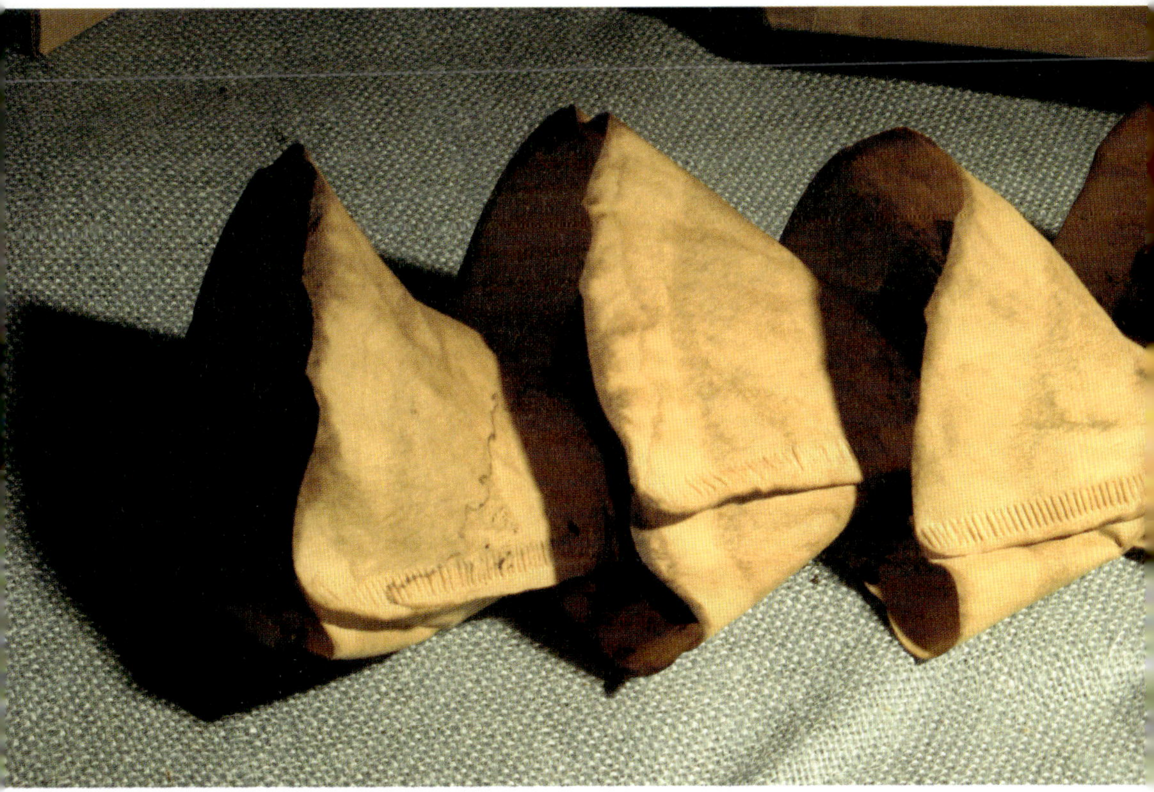

45 *Untitled #16*, 2007, from *Toad in a Hole*, pigment print, 12 x 16 inches. Collection of the Seattle Art Museum.
Gift of Rebecca and Alexander Stewart in honor of Mimi Gardner Gates. Courtesy of the artist and Laurel Gitlen, New York.

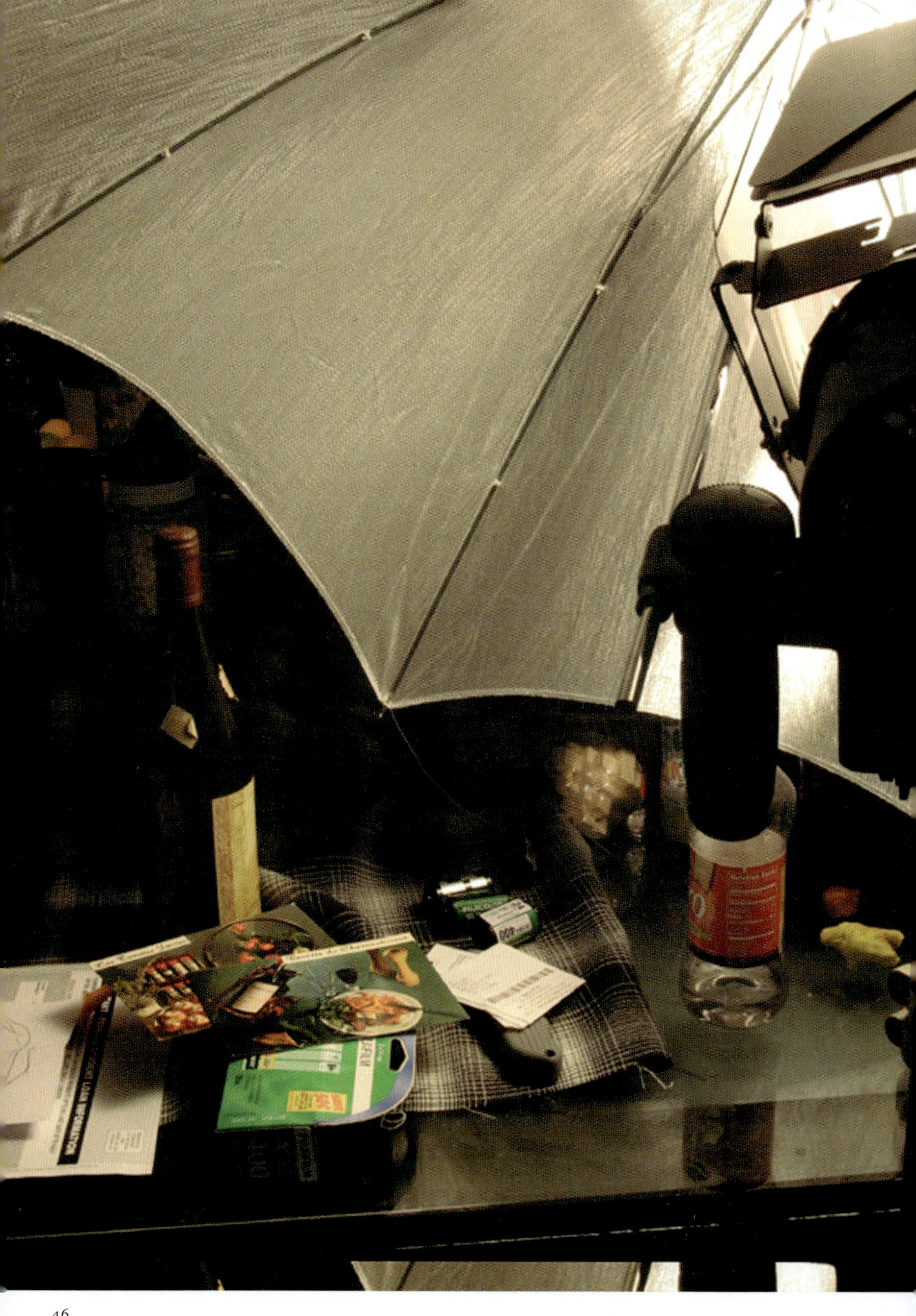

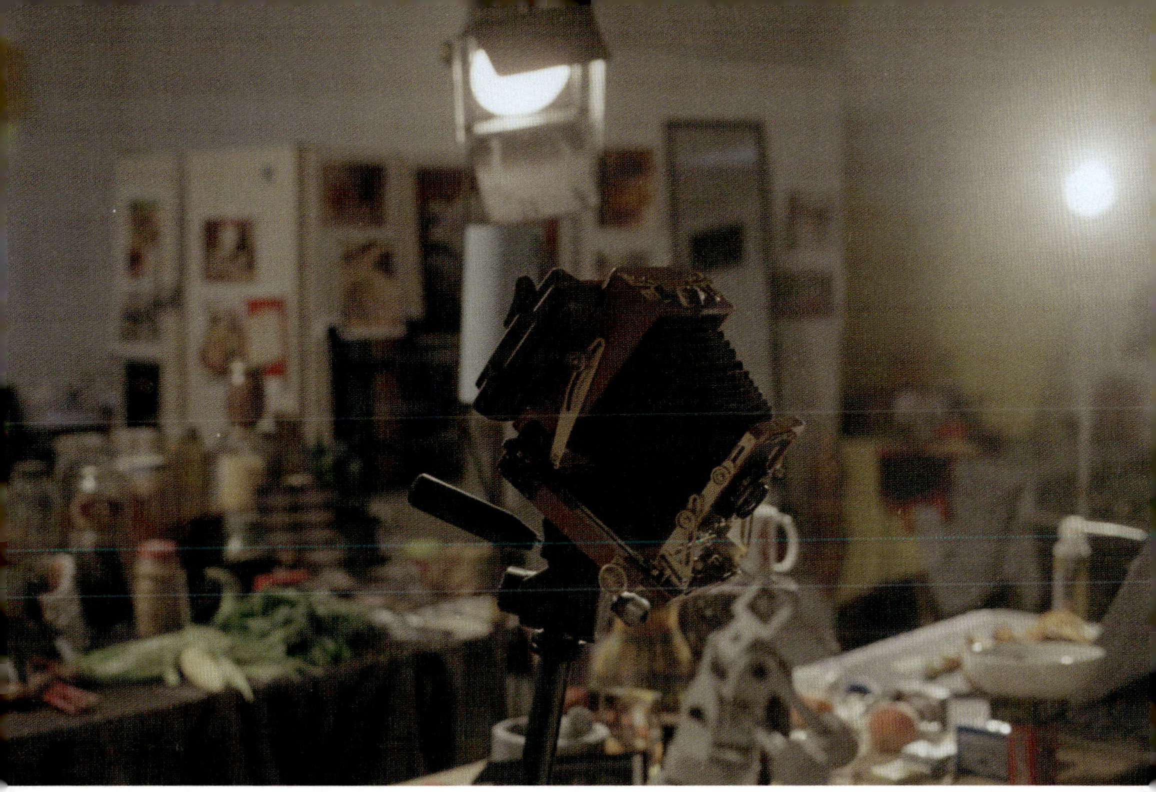

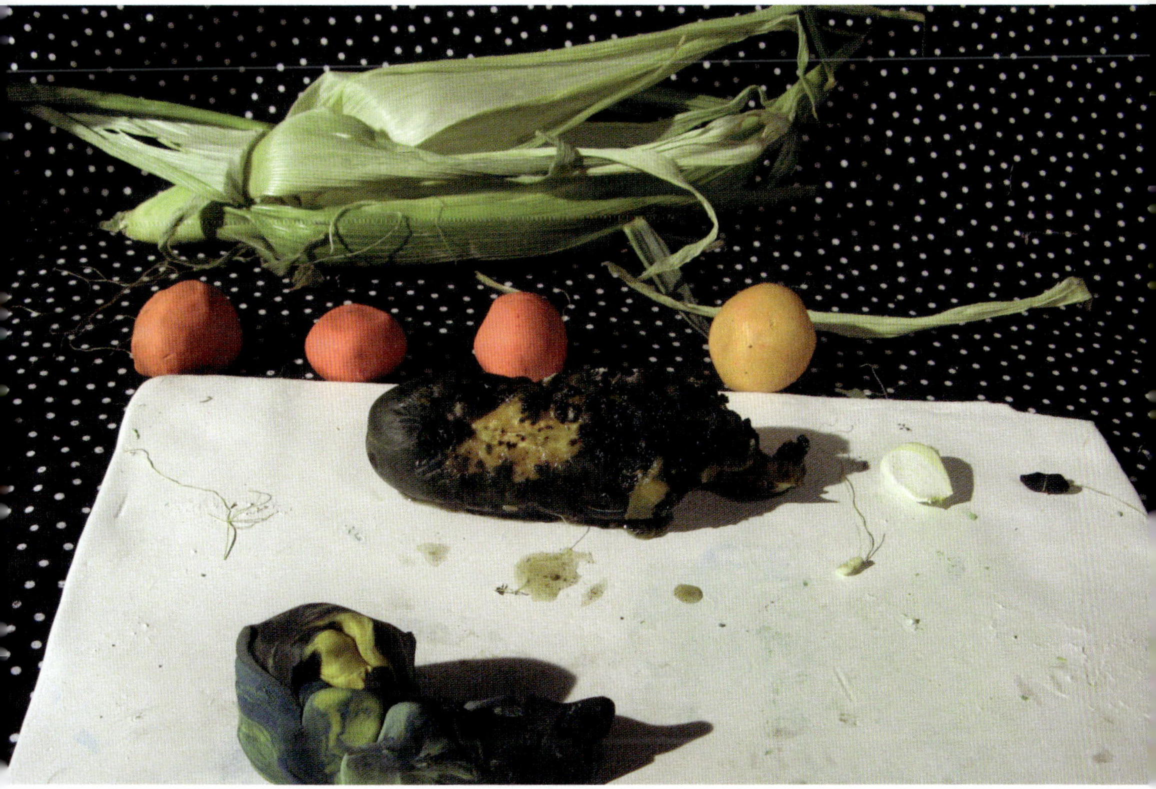

Untitled #6, 2007, from *Toad in a Hole*, pigment print, 16 x 21 5/16 inches. Collection of the Seattle Art Museum.
Gift of Rebecca and Alexander Stewart in honor of Mimi Gardner Gates. Courtesy of the artist and Laurel Gitlen, New York.

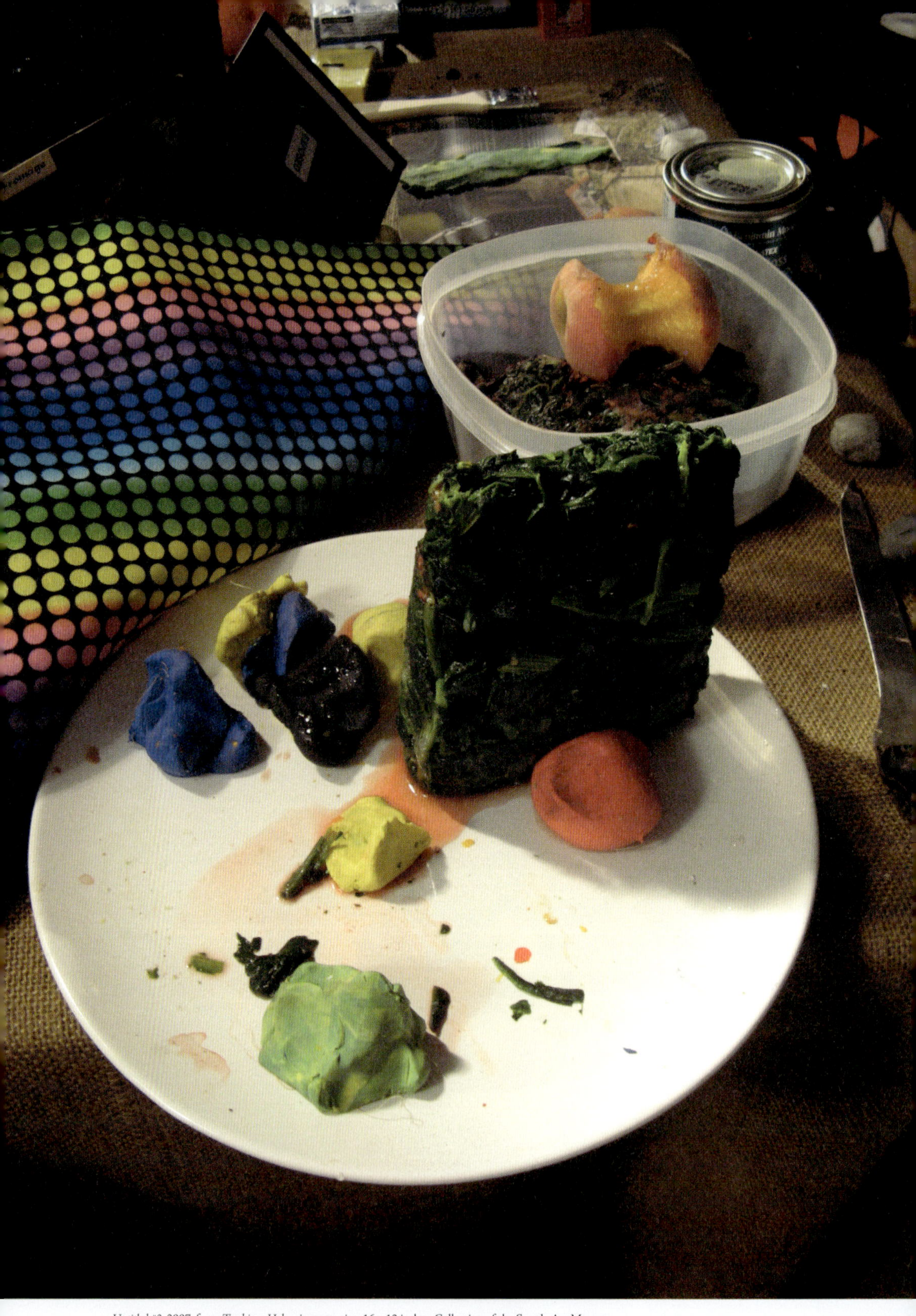

Untitled #2, 2007, from *Toad in a Hole*, pigment print, 16 x 12 inches. Collection of the Seattle Art Museum.
Gift of Rebecca and Alexander Stewart in honor of Mimi Gardner Gates. Courtesy of the artist and Laurel Gitlen, New York.

Chapter 2, **Weavings**

Weavings
Small A Projects, Portland, OR
September 14–October 20, 2007
Curated by Laurel Gitlen

For *Weavings*, Hewitt reformulated the structure of *Toad in a Hole* (2007) and made a freestanding set
with an open ceiling inside the gallery. Viewers were able to peer in through a vertical cutout in a corner
of the structure. Over a period of 10 days, Hewitt worked inside the set using a variety of materials and
processes, including cooking and sculpting, to produce subjects for a series of photographs. This work
developed through an engagement with, and synthesis of, various modes of "weaving" found in Portland:
the regional history of indigenous basketry, lumberjack/grunge plaids, and homemade pasta.

Captions

52–54, 57, 58, 61, 62, 92, 93, 98, 99, 103: Working image from *Weavings*, 2007. Courtesy of the artist.
59: *Weavings*, 2007. Installation view, Small A Projects, Portland, OR. Photo: Dan Kvitka. Courtesy of the artist and Laurel Gitlen, New York.
95: Notes for *Weavings*, 2007. Courtesy of the artist.

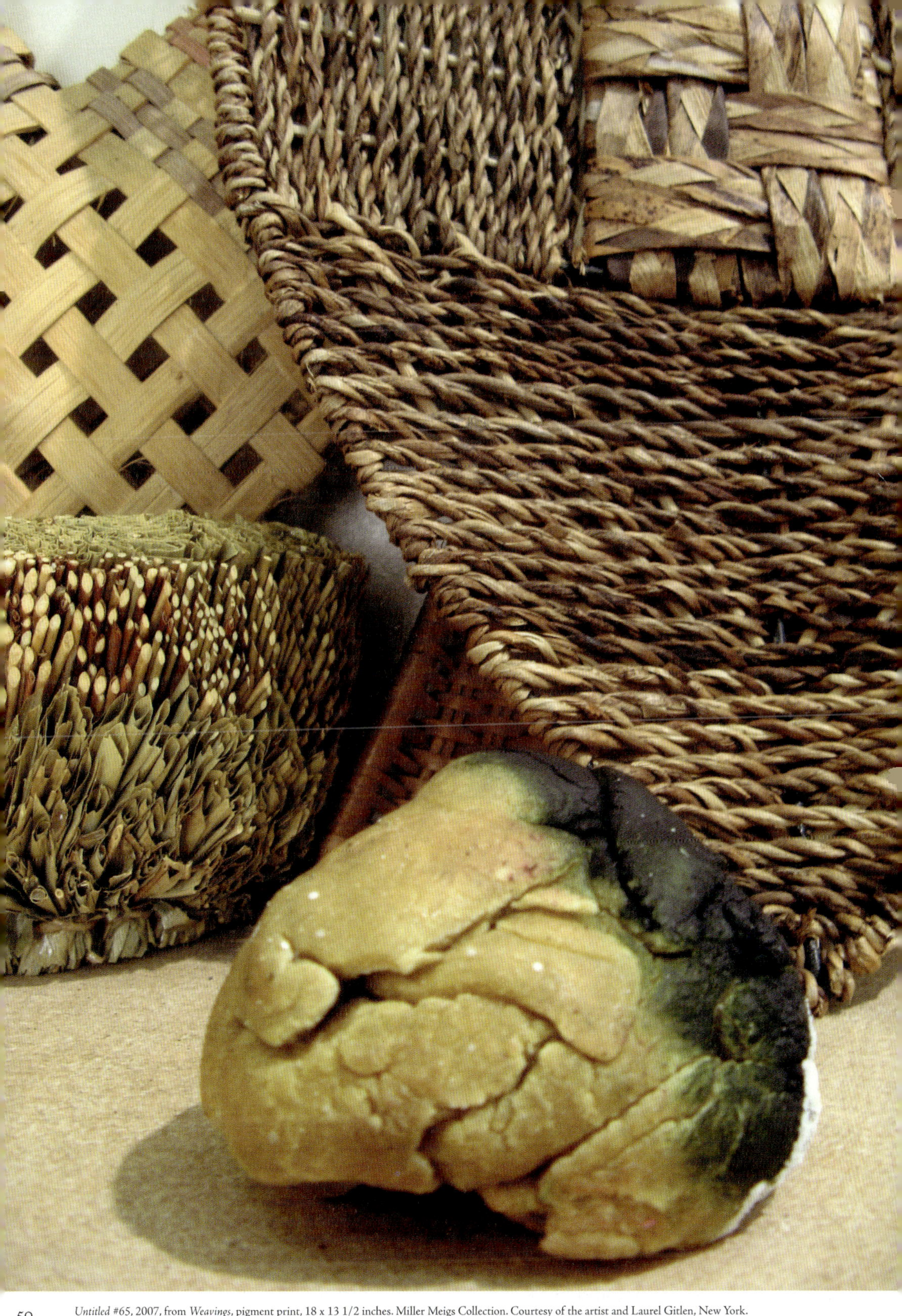

 Untitled #65, 2007, from *Weavings*, pigment print, 18 x 13 1/2 inches. Miller Meigs Collection. Courtesy of the artist and Laurel Gitlen, New York.

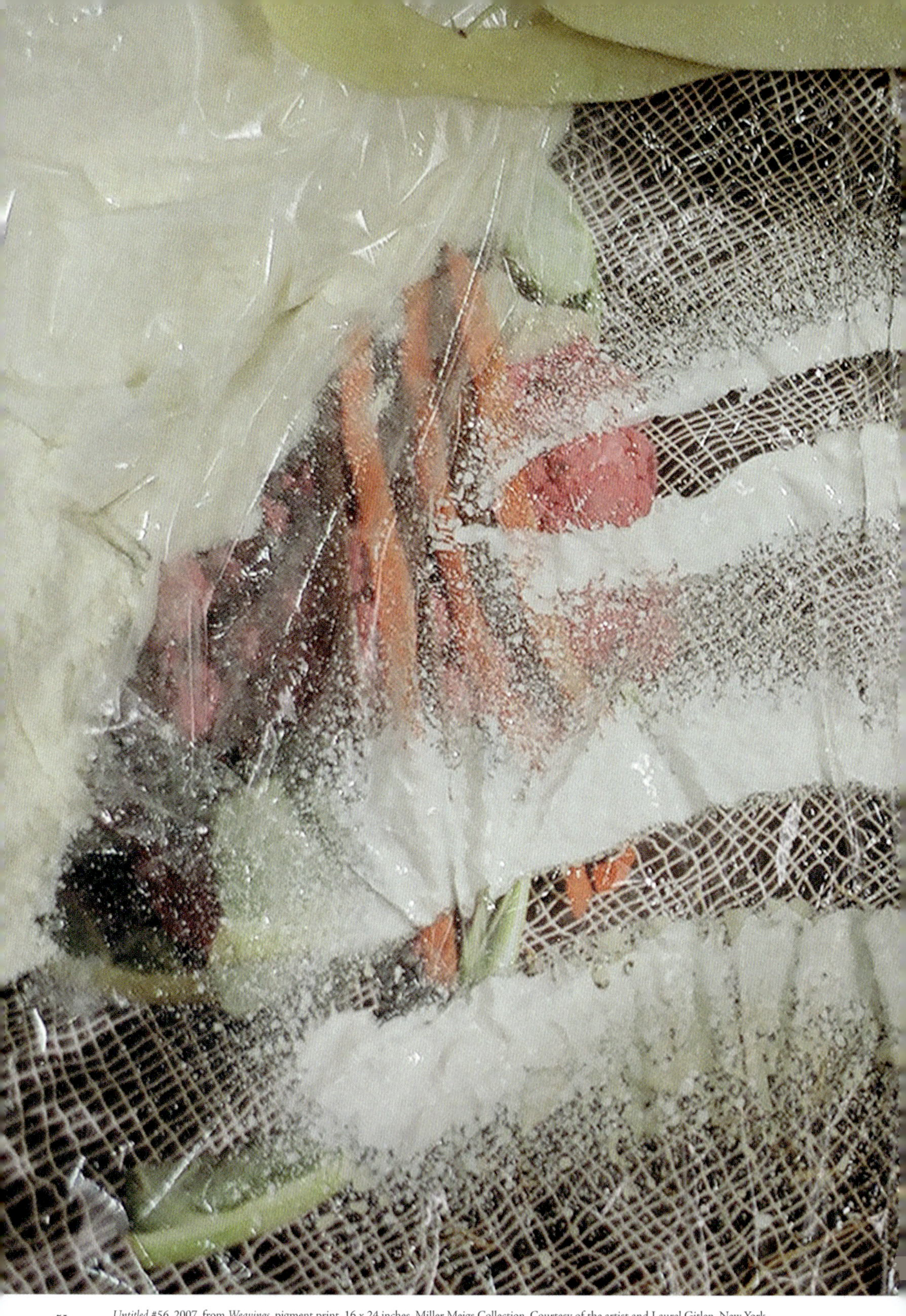

  Untitled #56, 2007, from *Weavings*, pigment print, 16 x 24 inches. Miller Meigs Collection. Courtesy of the artist and Laurel Gitlen, New York.

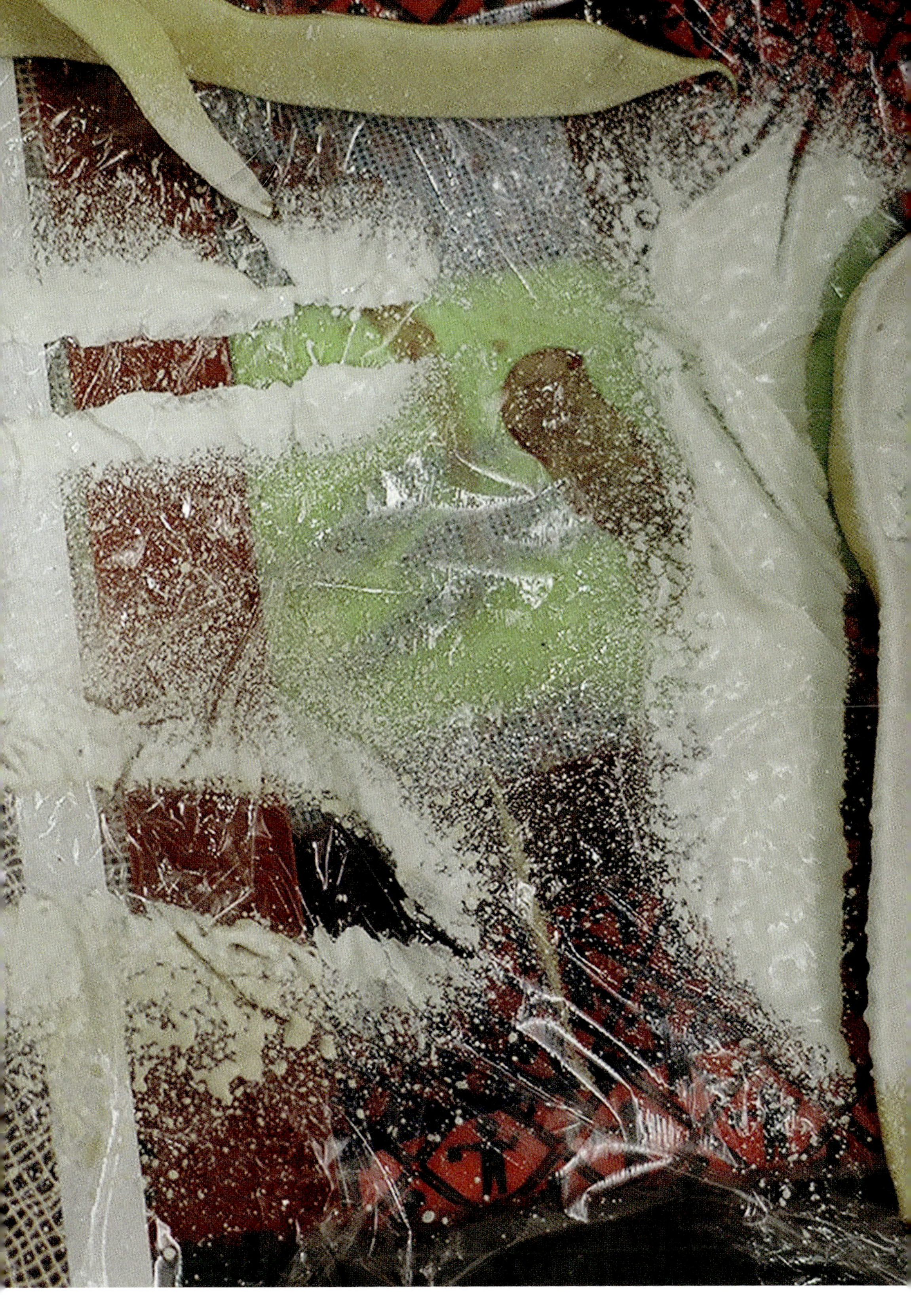

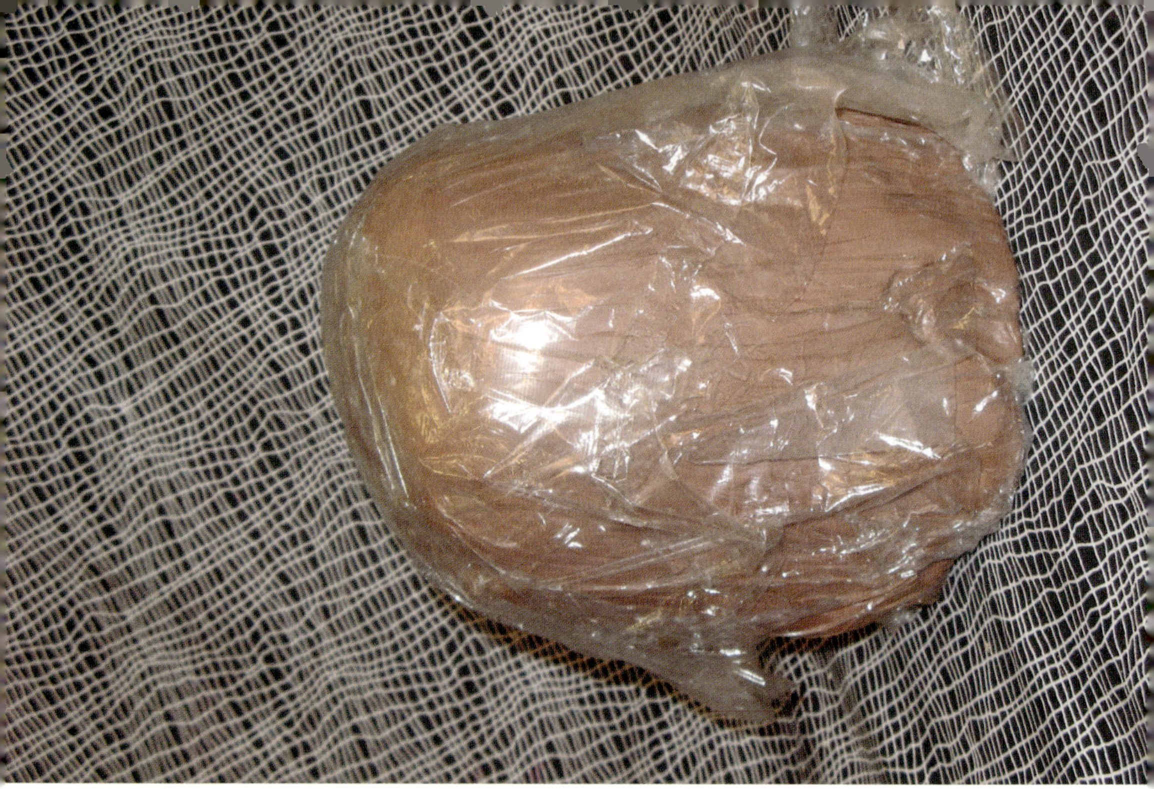

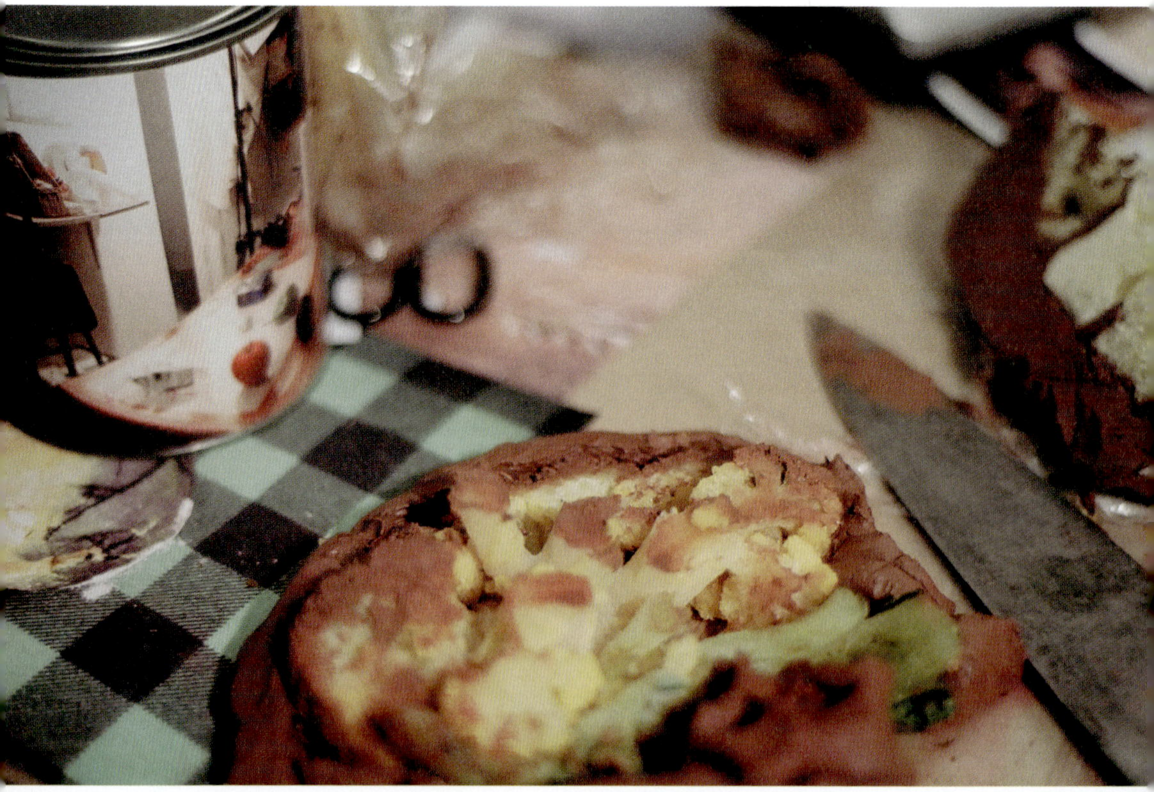

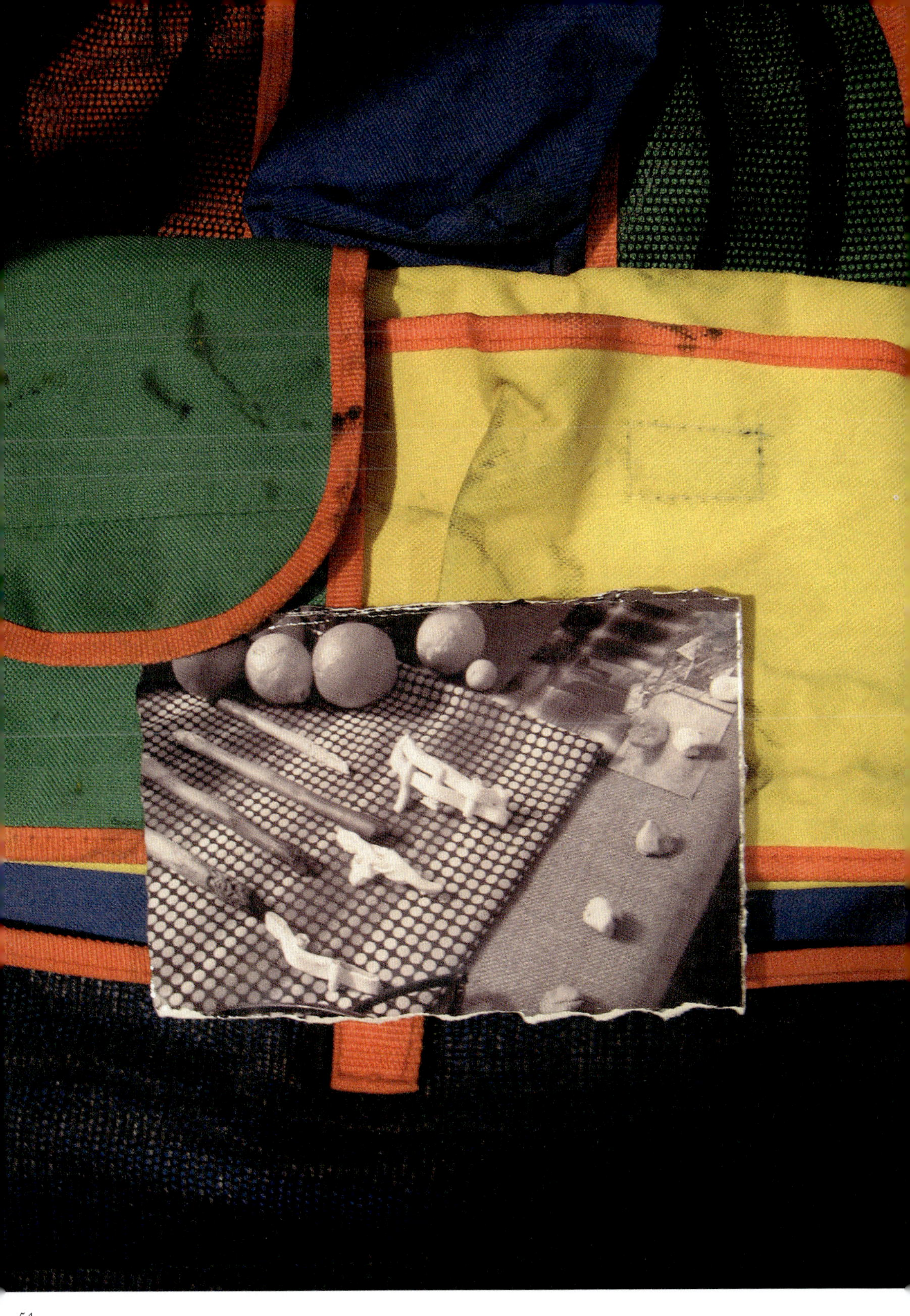

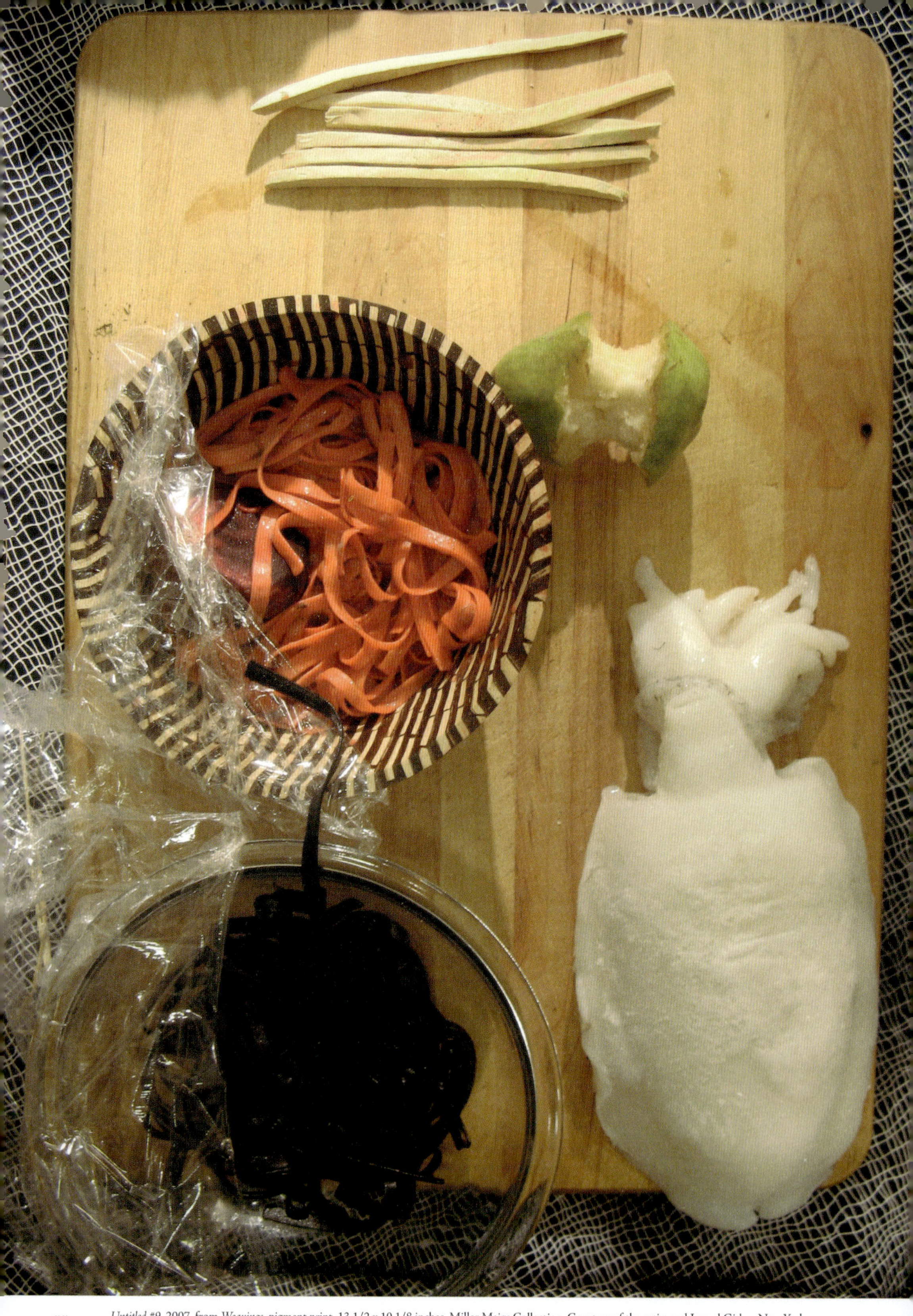

55   *Untitled #9*, 2007, from *Weavings*, pigment print, 13 1/2 x 10 1/8 inches. Miller Meigs Collection. Courtesy of the artist and Laurel Gitlen, New York.

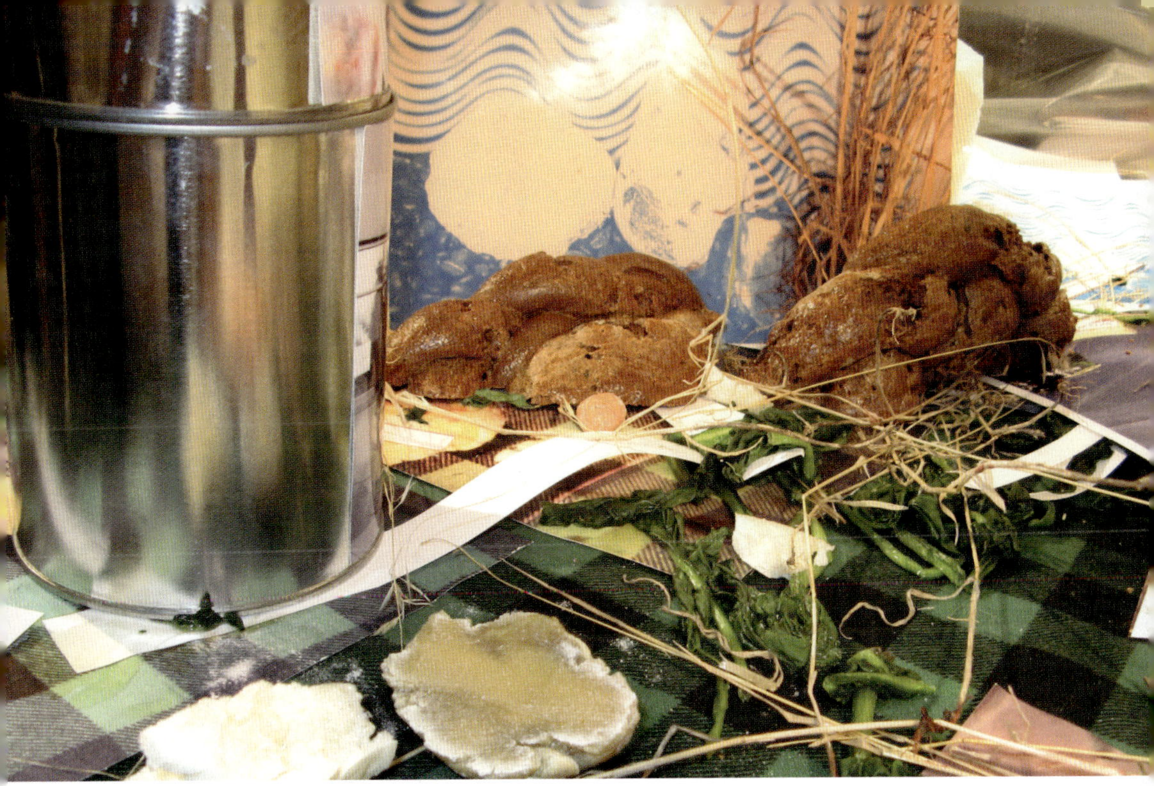

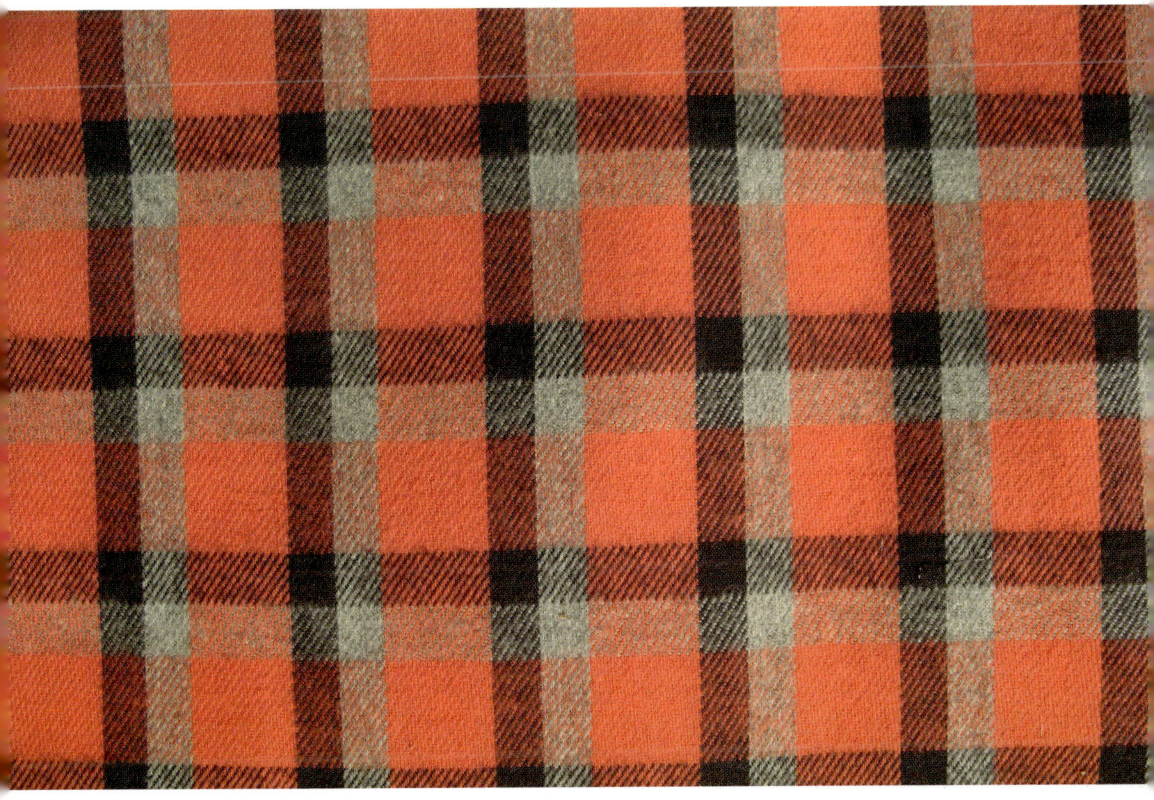

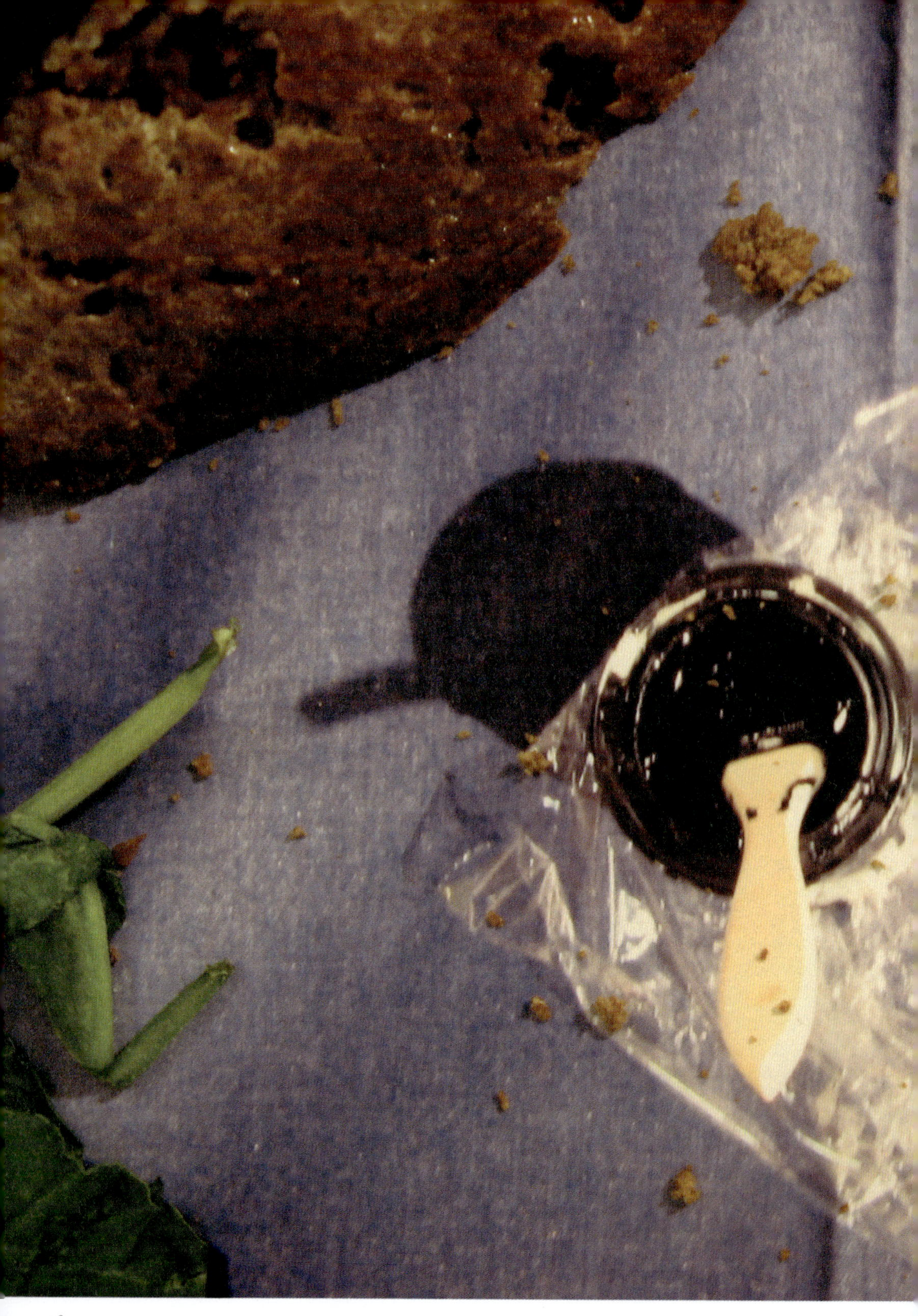

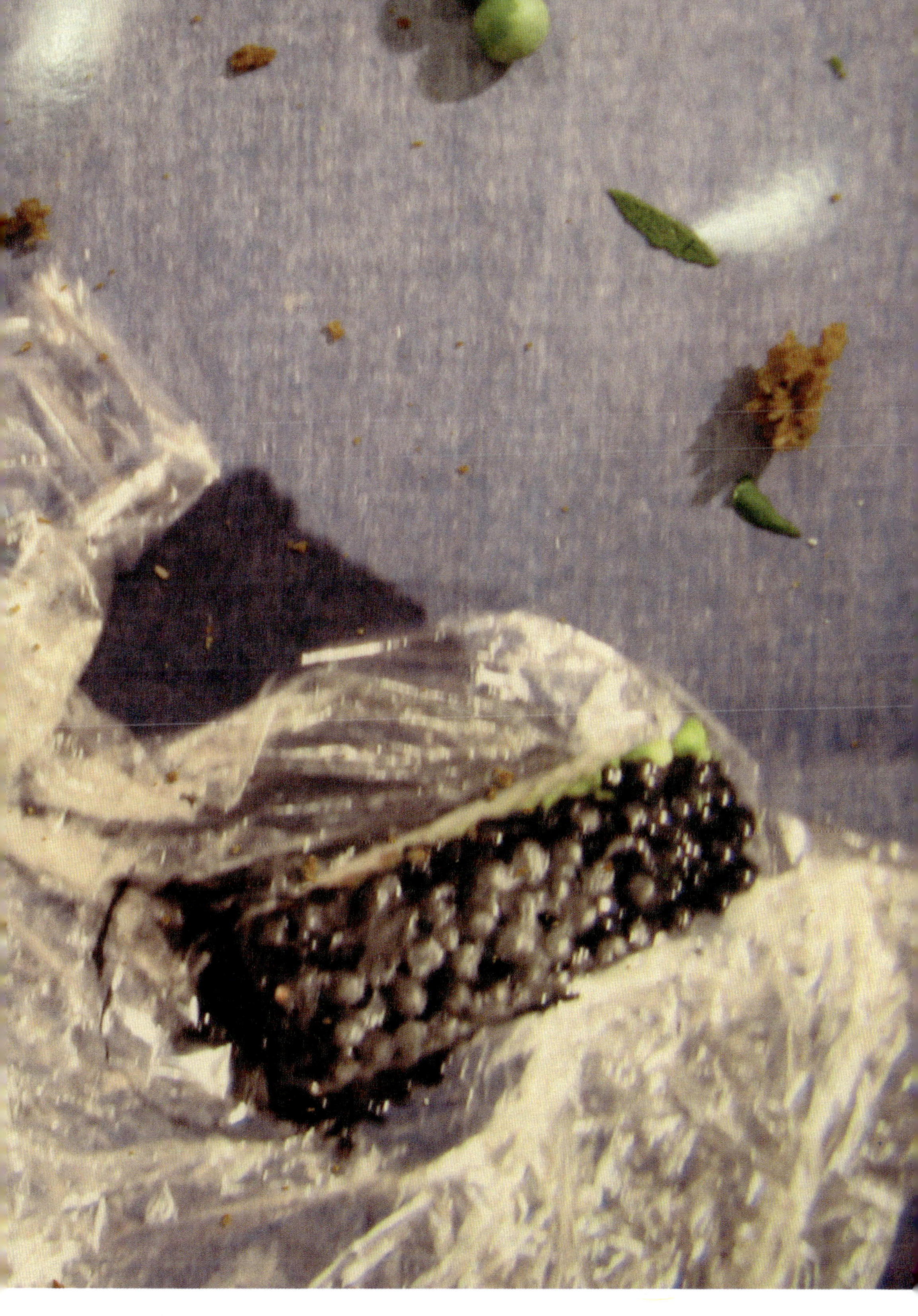

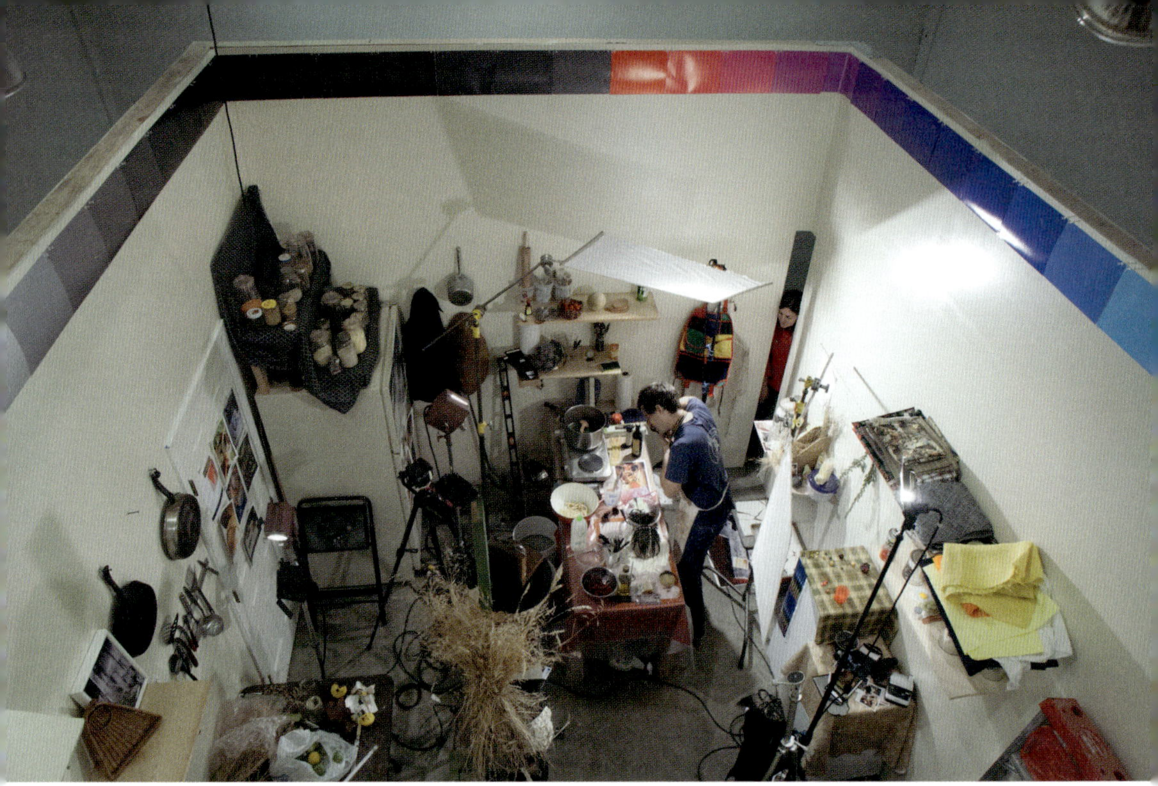

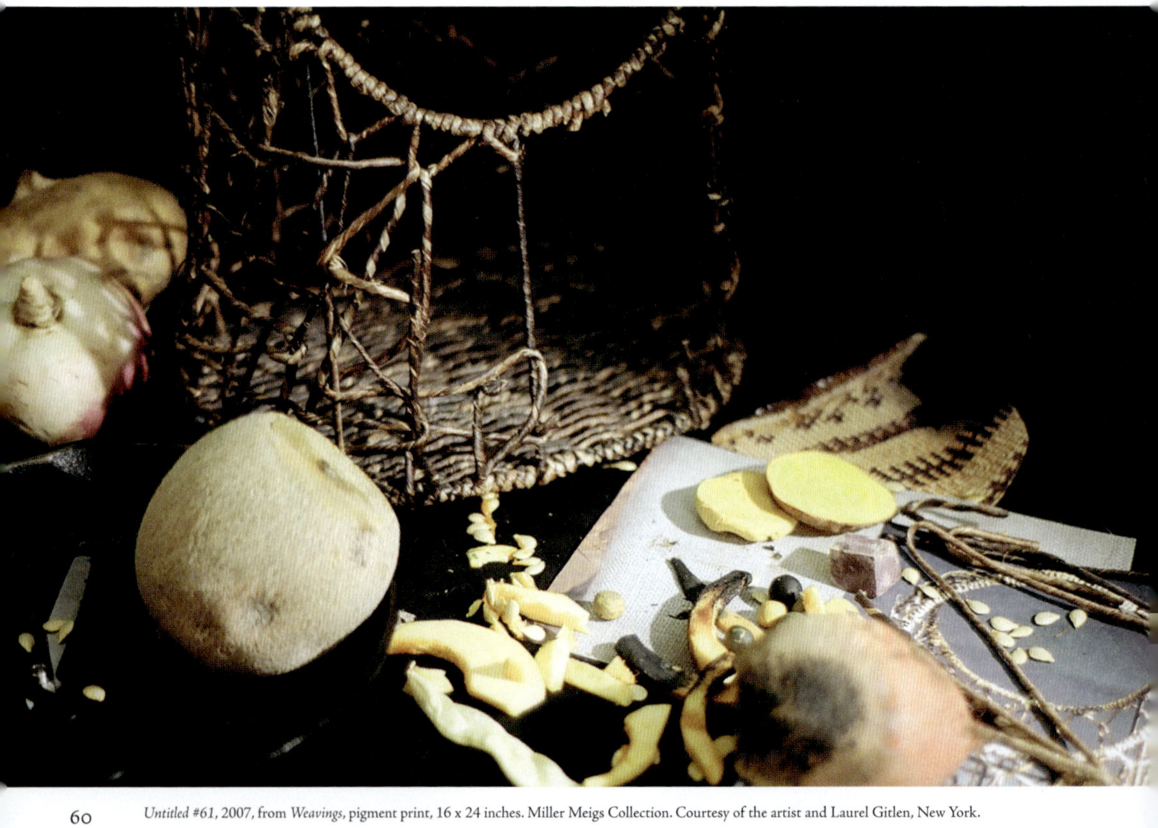

  Untitled #61, 2007, from *Weavings*, pigment print, 16 x 24 inches. Miller Meigs Collection. Courtesy of the artist and Laurel Gitlen, New York.

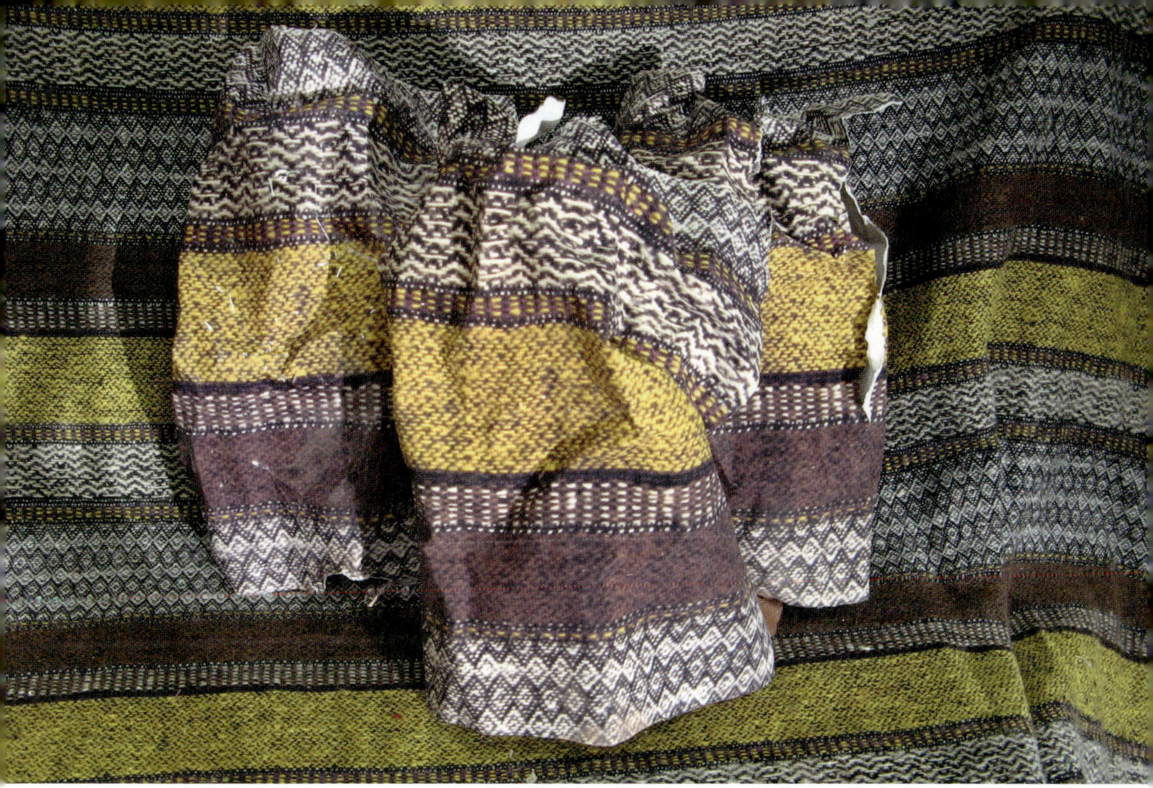

61

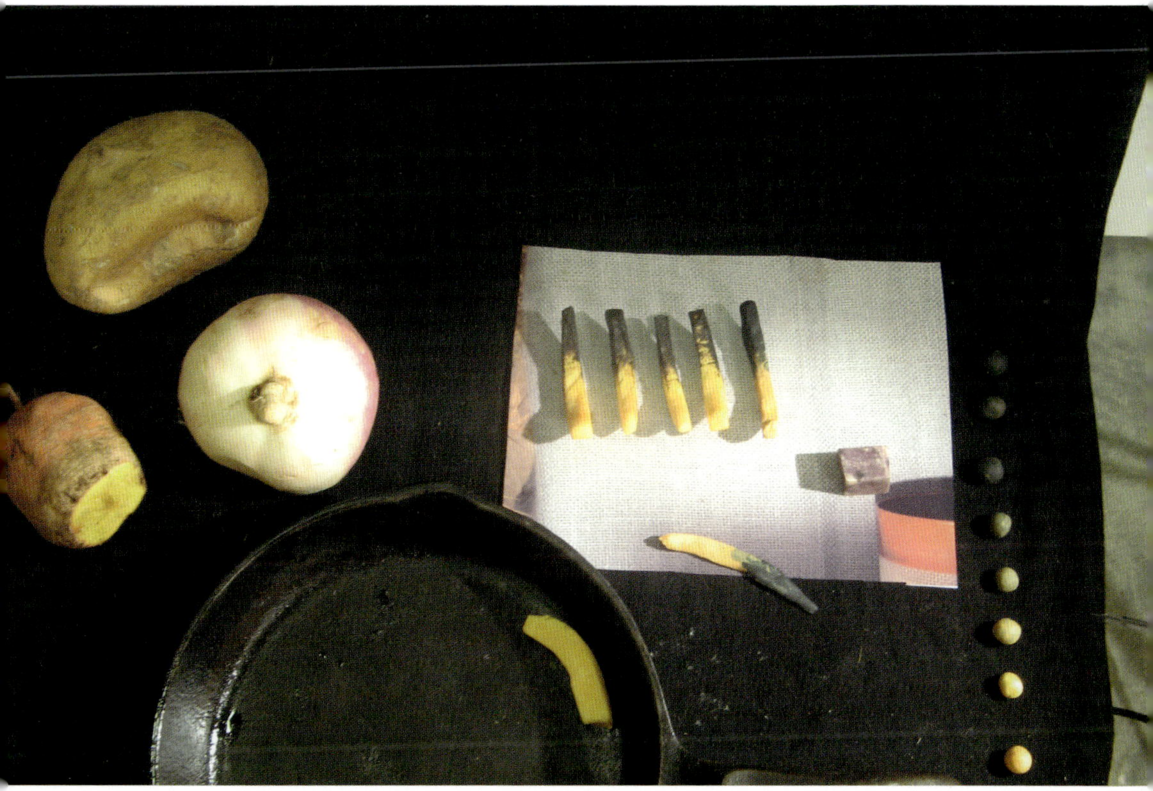

62

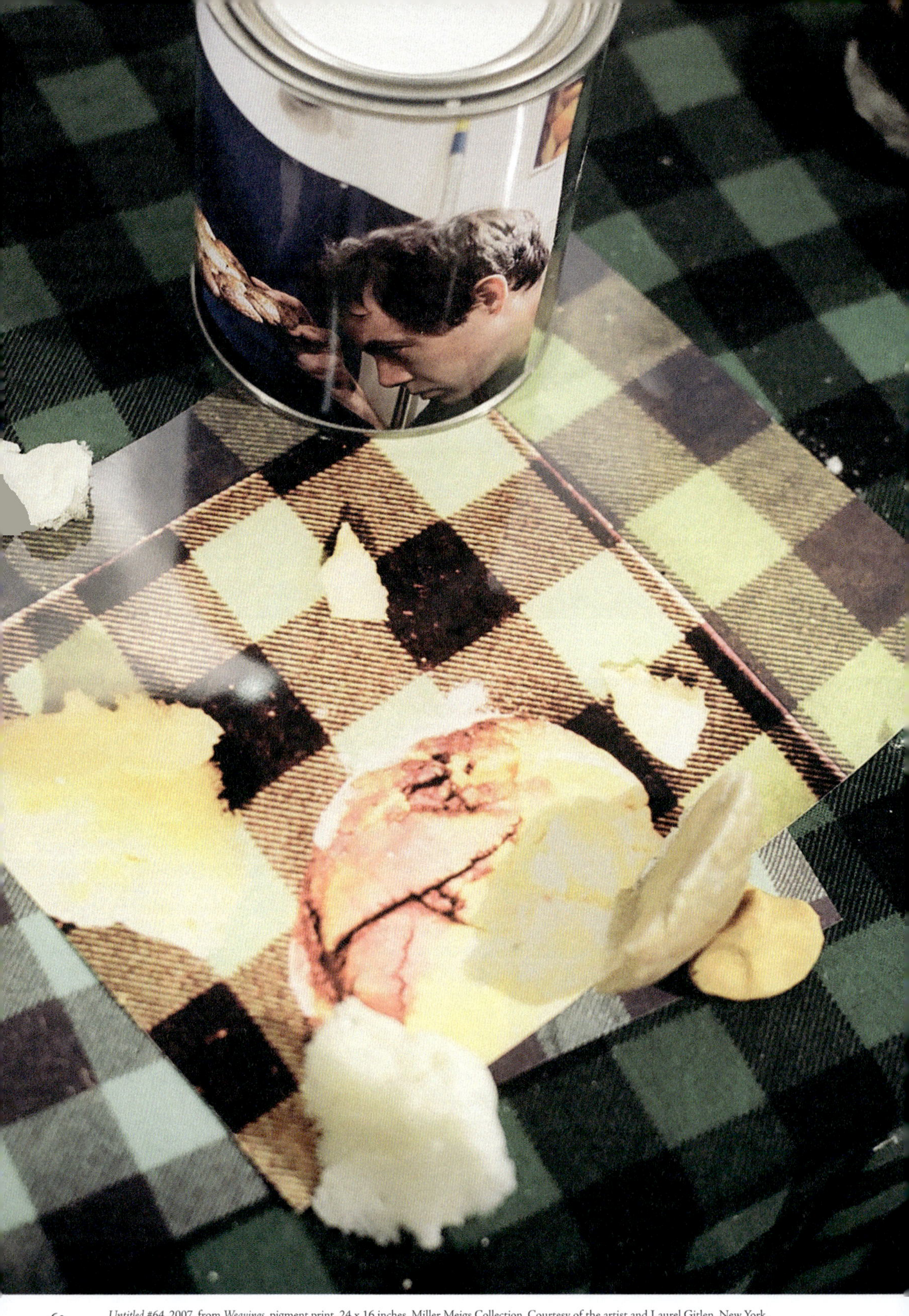

  Untitled #64, 2007, from *Weavings*, pigment print, 24 x 16 inches. Miller Meigs Collection. Courtesy of the artist and Laurel Gitlen, New York.

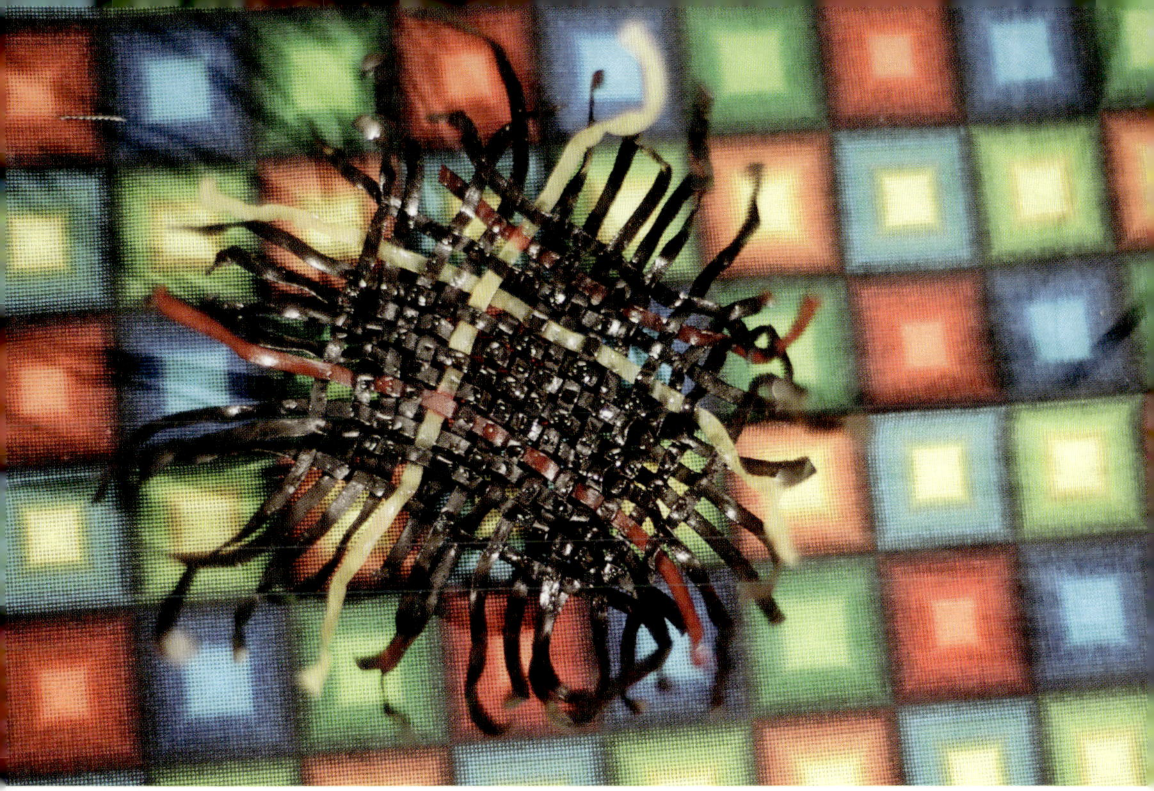

Untitled #54, 2007, from *Weavings*, pigment print, 16 x 24 inches. Miller Meigs Collection. Courtesy of the artist and Laurel Gitlen, New York.

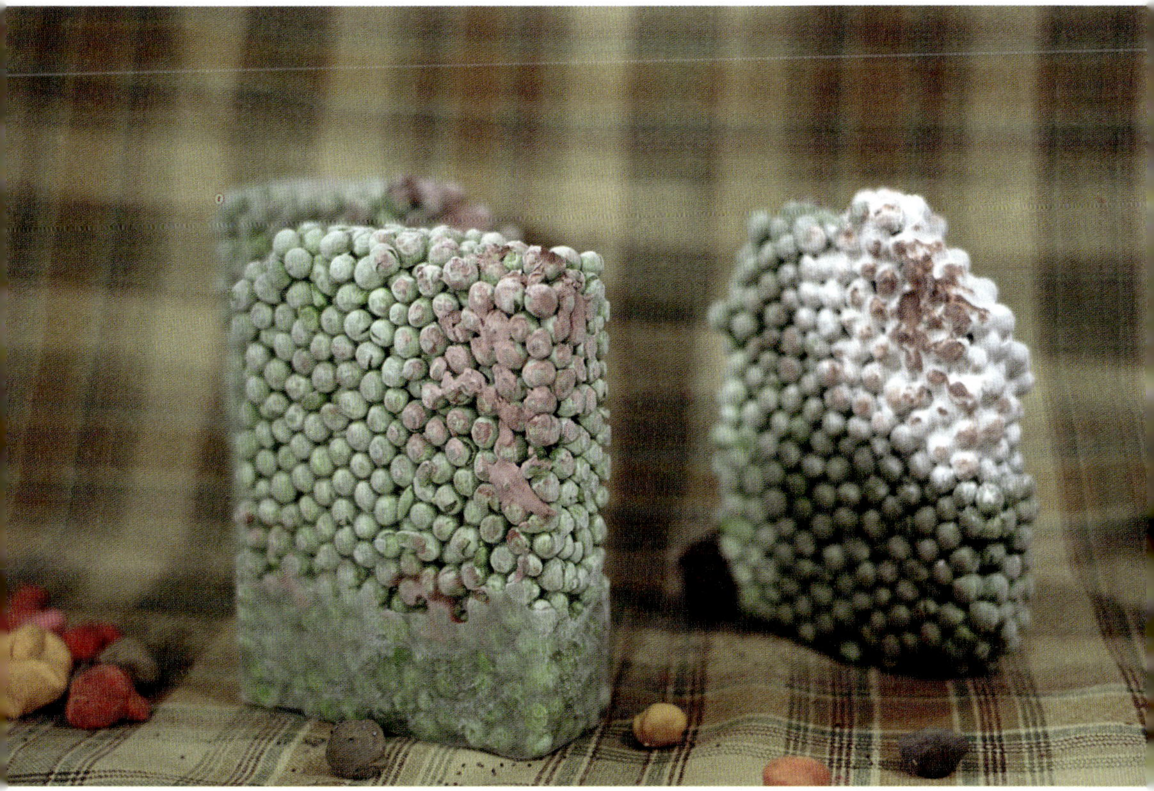

Untitled #53, 2007, from *Weavings*, pigment print, 16 x 24 inches. Miller Meigs Collection. Courtesy of the artist and Laurel Gitlen, New York.

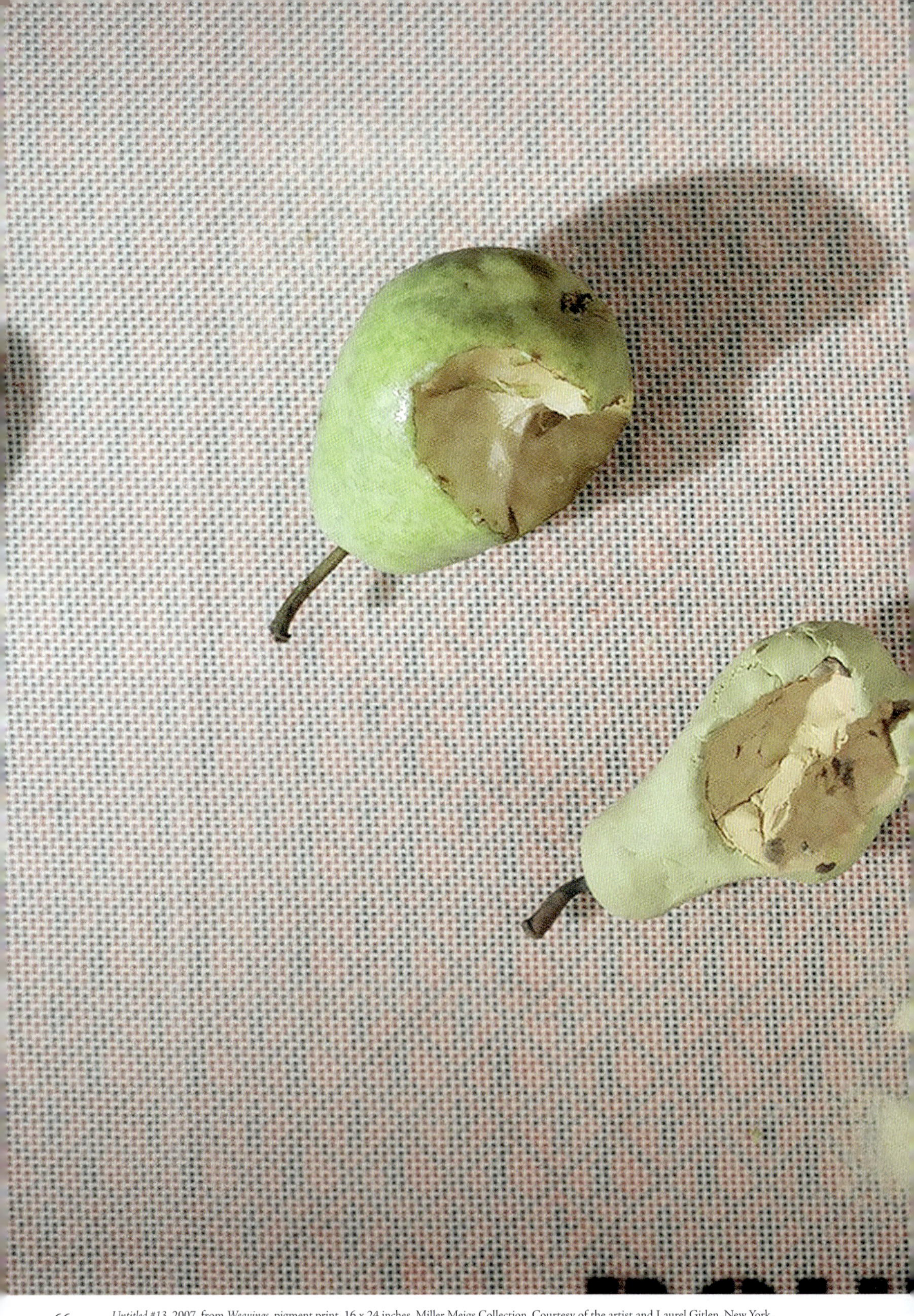

 Untitled #13, 2007, from *Weavings*, pigment print, 16 x 24 inches. Miller Meigs Collection. Courtesy of the artist and Laurel Gitlen, New York.

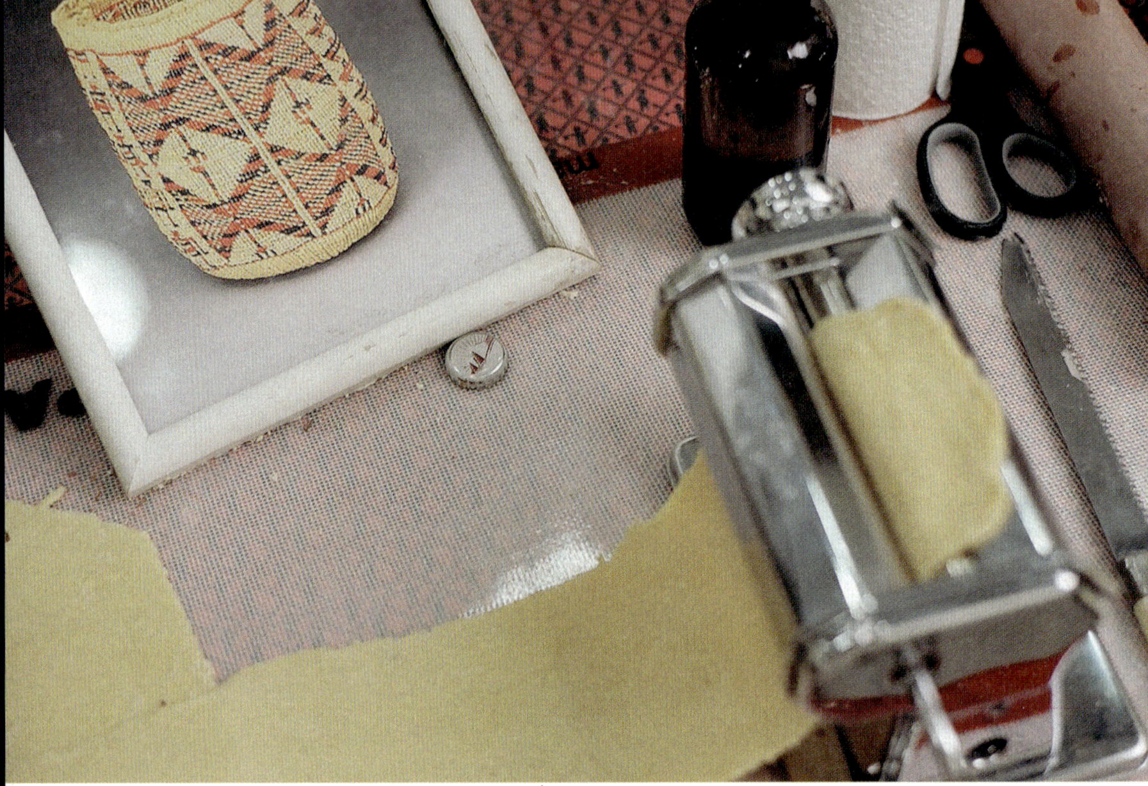

  Untitled #1, 2007, from *Weavings*, pigment print, 16 x 24 inches. Miller Meigs Collection. Courtesy of the artist and Laurel Gitlen, New York.

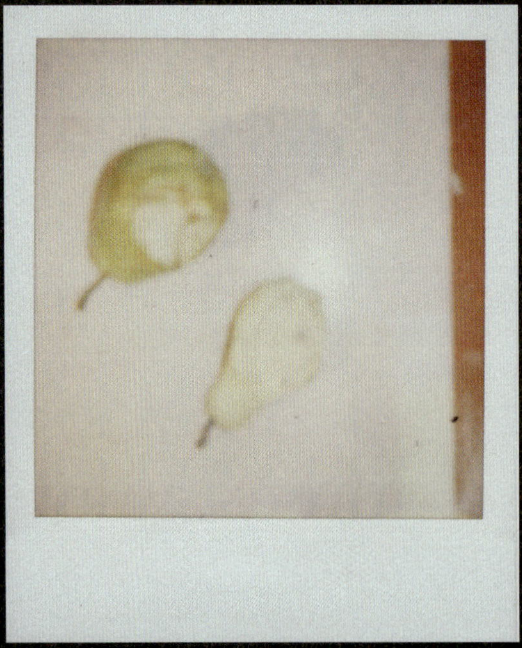

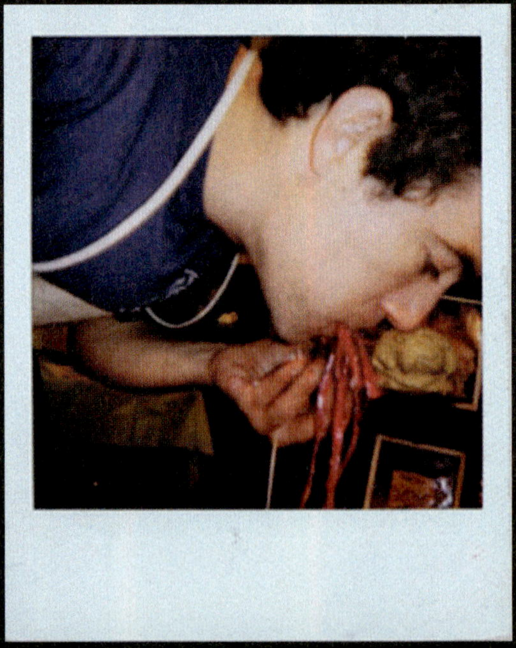

  (left) *Untitled #17*, 2007, from *Weavings*, Polaroid photograph, 4 1/4 x 3 1/2 inches; (right) *Untitled #14*, 2007, from *Weavings*, Polaroid photograph, 4 1/4 x 3 1/2 inches. Miller Meigs Collection. Courtesy of the artist and Laurel Gitlen, New York.

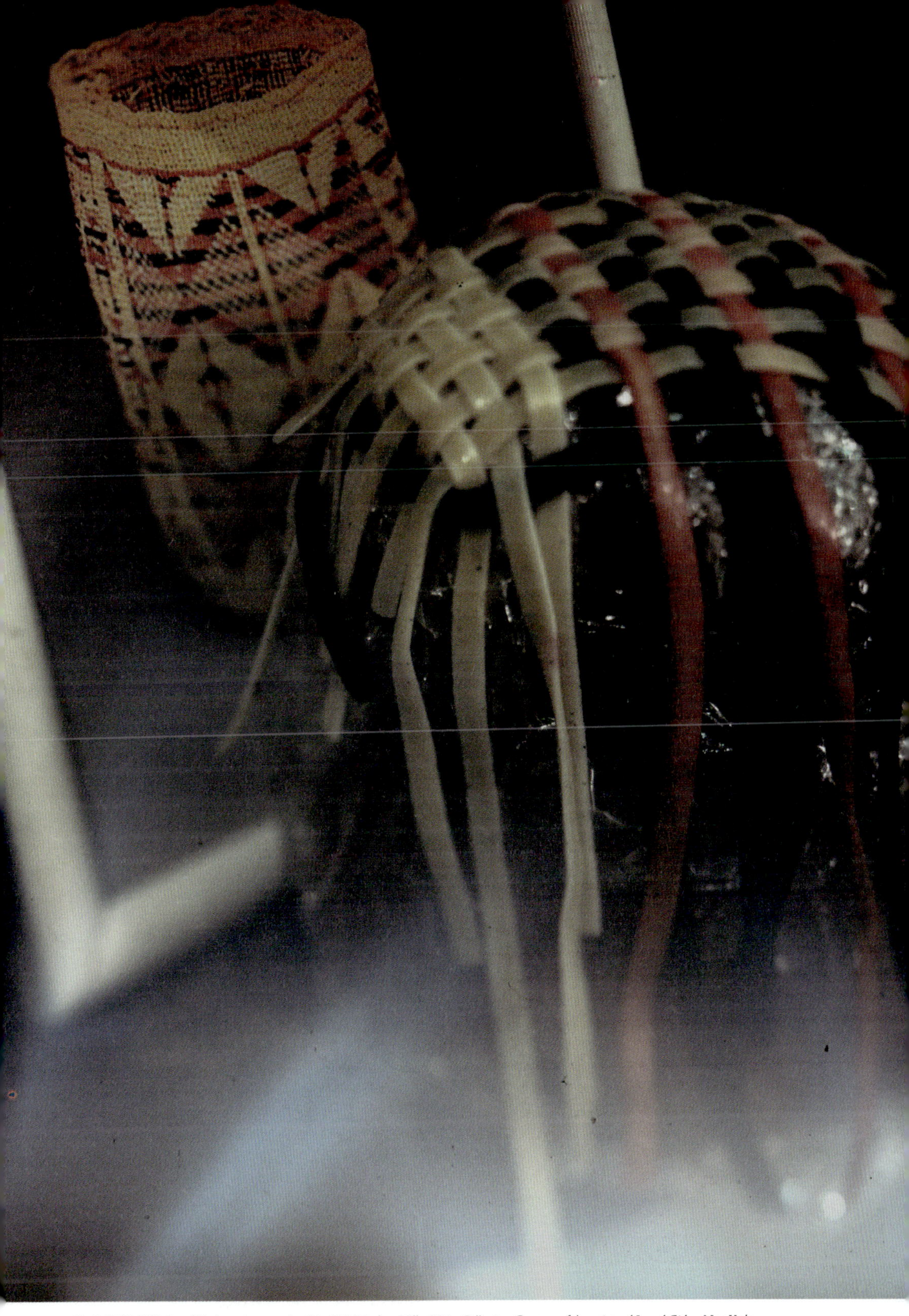

   Untitled #11, 2007, from *Weavings*, pigment print, 36 x 29 1/2 inches. Miller Meigs Collection. Courtesy of the artist and Laurel Gitlen, New York.

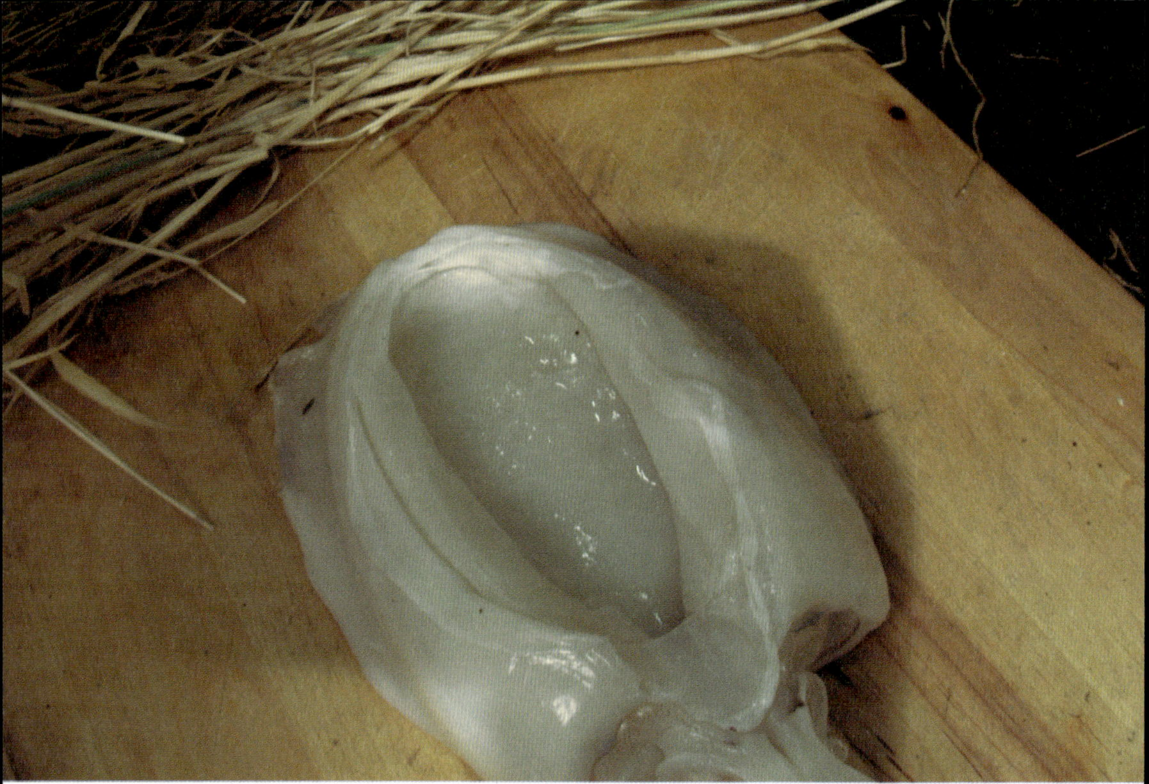

70   *Untitled #8*, 2007, from *Weavings*, pigment print, 12 x 16 inches. Miller Meigs Collection. Courtesy of the artist and Laurel Gitlen, New York.

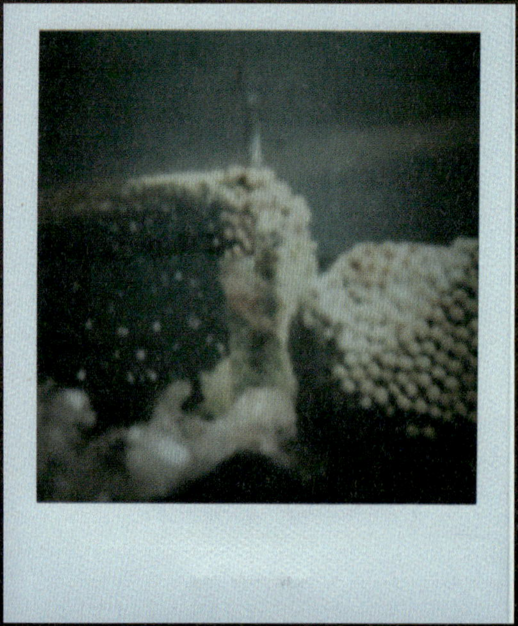

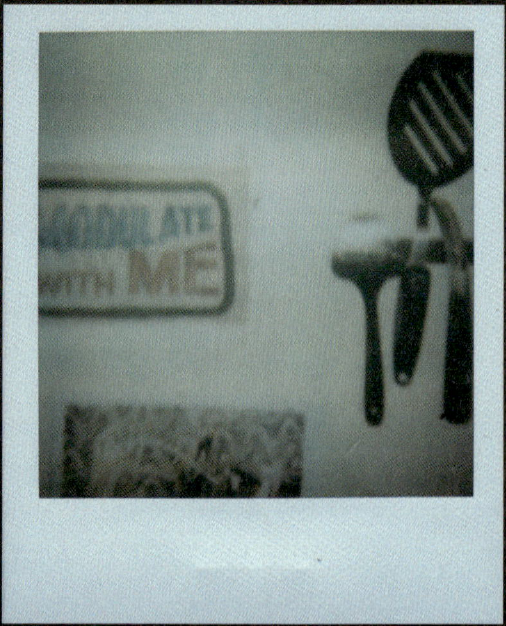

71   (left) *Untitled #59*, 2007, from *Weavings*, Polaroid photograph, 4 1/4 x 3 1/2 inches; (right) *Untitled #58*, 2007, from *Weavings*, Polaroid photograph, 4 1/4 x 3 1/2 inches. Miller Meigs Collection. Courtesy of the artist and Laurel Gitlen, New York.

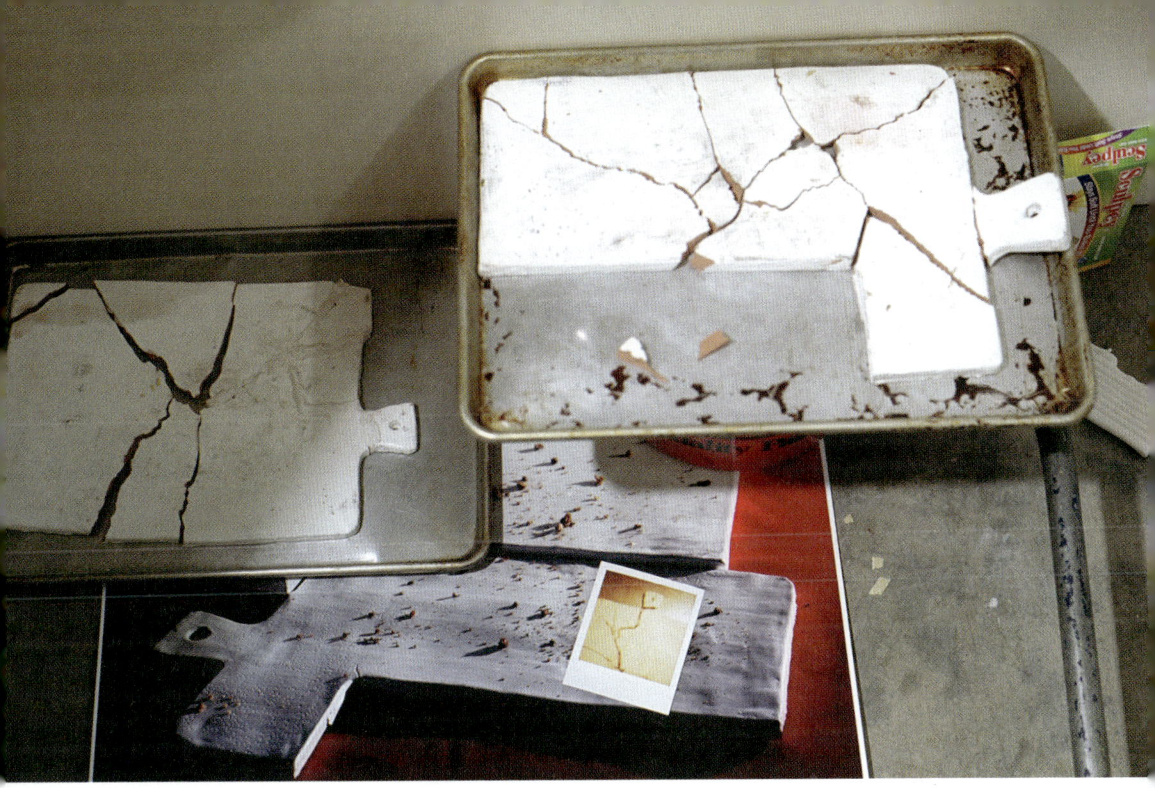

Untitled #21, 2007, from *Weavings*, pigment print, 24 x 16 inches. Miller Meigs Collection. Courtesy of the artist and Laurel Gitlen, New York.

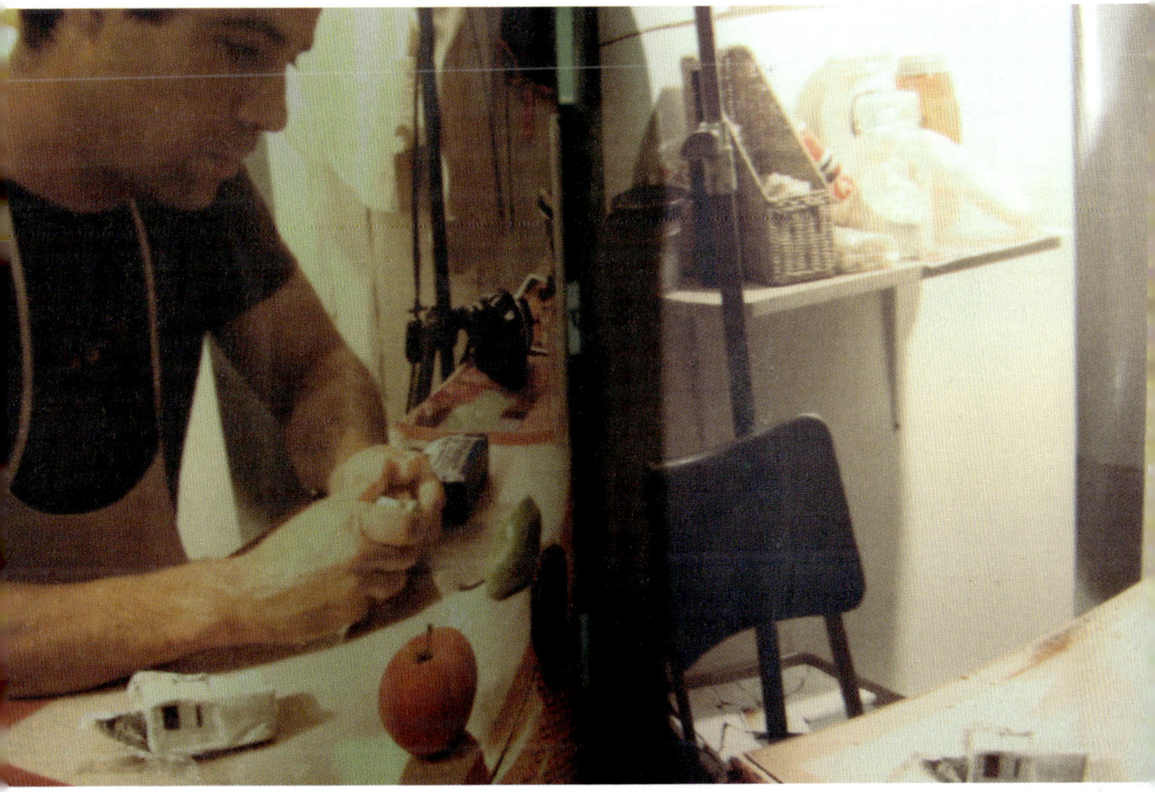

Untitled #60, 2007, from *Weavings*, pigment print, 10 1/2 x 14 inches. Miller Meigs Collection. Courtesy of the artist and Laurel Gitlen, New York.

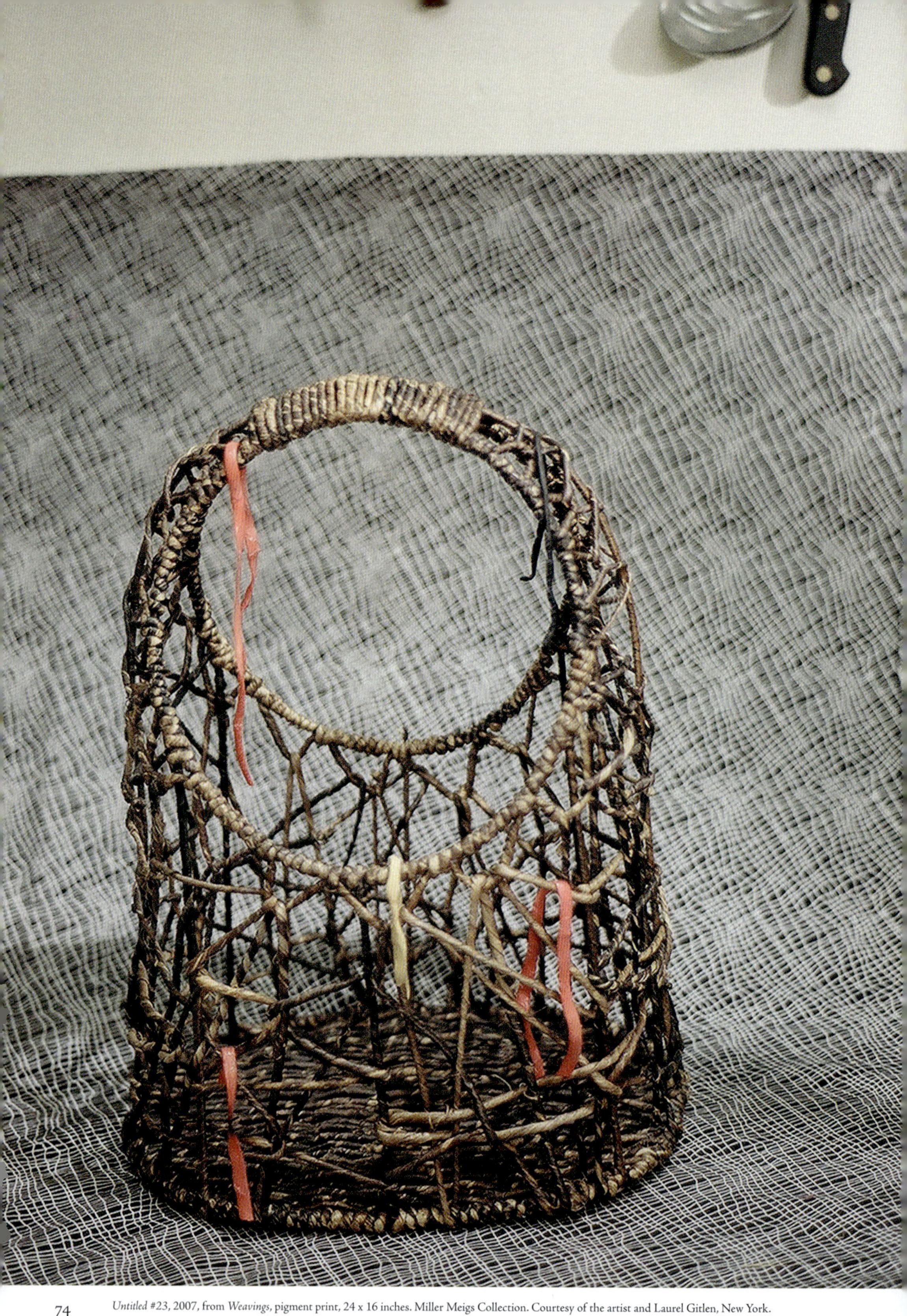

74 *Untitled #23*, 2007, from *Weavings*, pigment print, 24 x 16 inches. Miller Meigs Collection. Courtesy of the artist and Laurel Gitlen, New York.

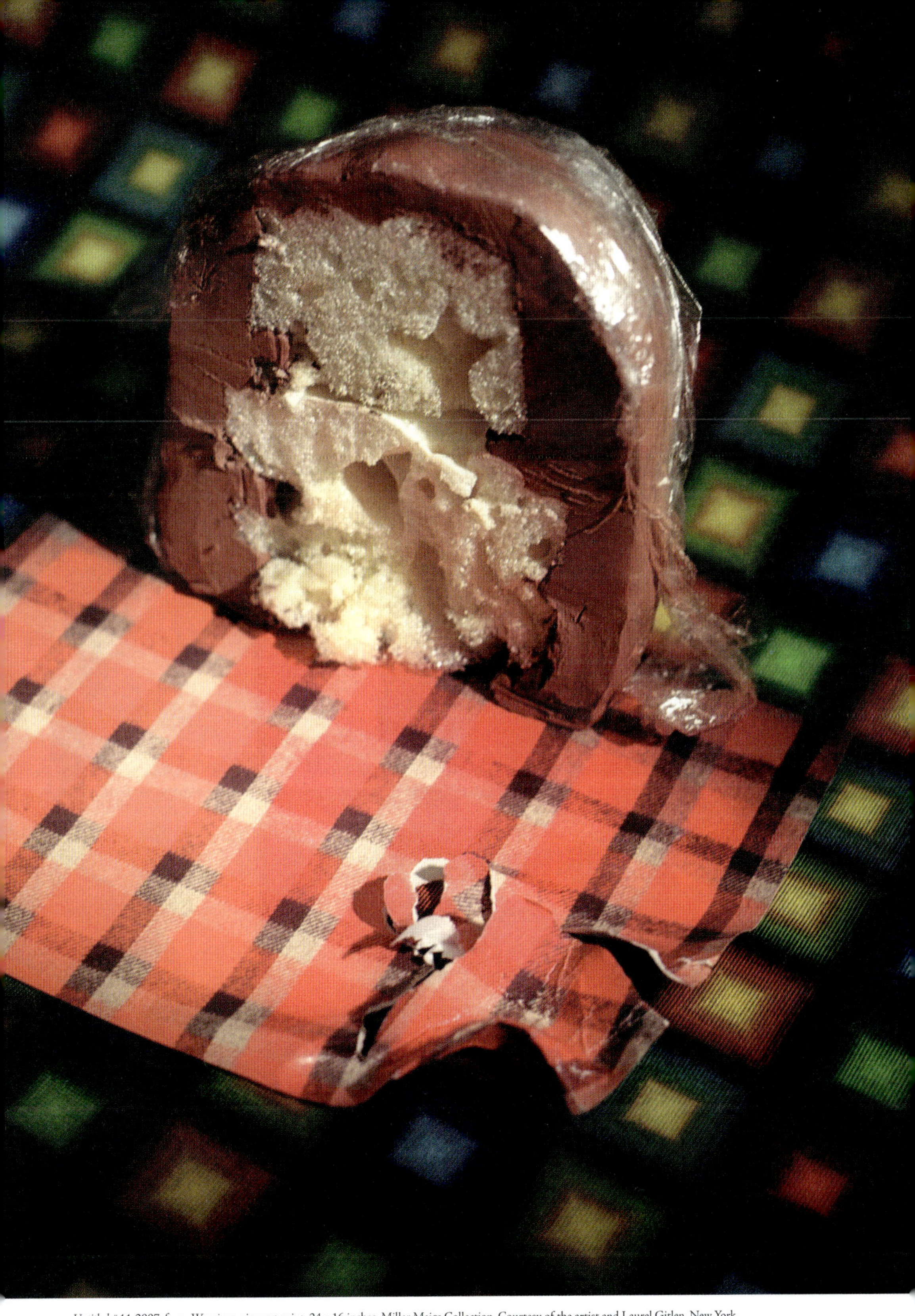

Untitled #44, 2007, from *Weavings*, pigment print, 24 x 16 inches. Miller Meigs Collection. Courtesy of the artist and Laurel Gitlen, New York.

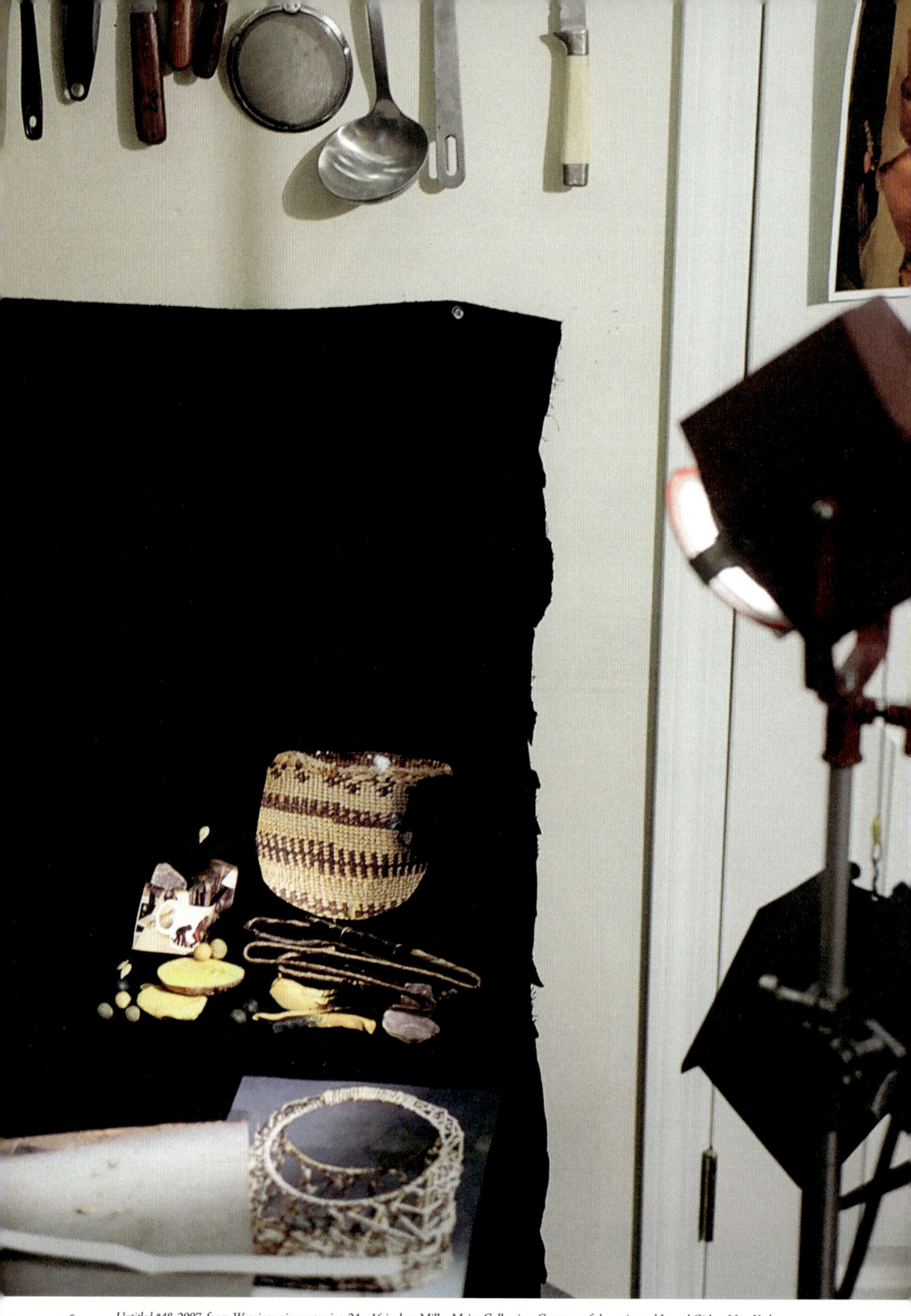

Untitled #48, 2007, from *Weavings*, pigment print, 24 x 16 inches. Miller Meigs Collection. Courtesy of the artist and Laurel Gitlen, New York.

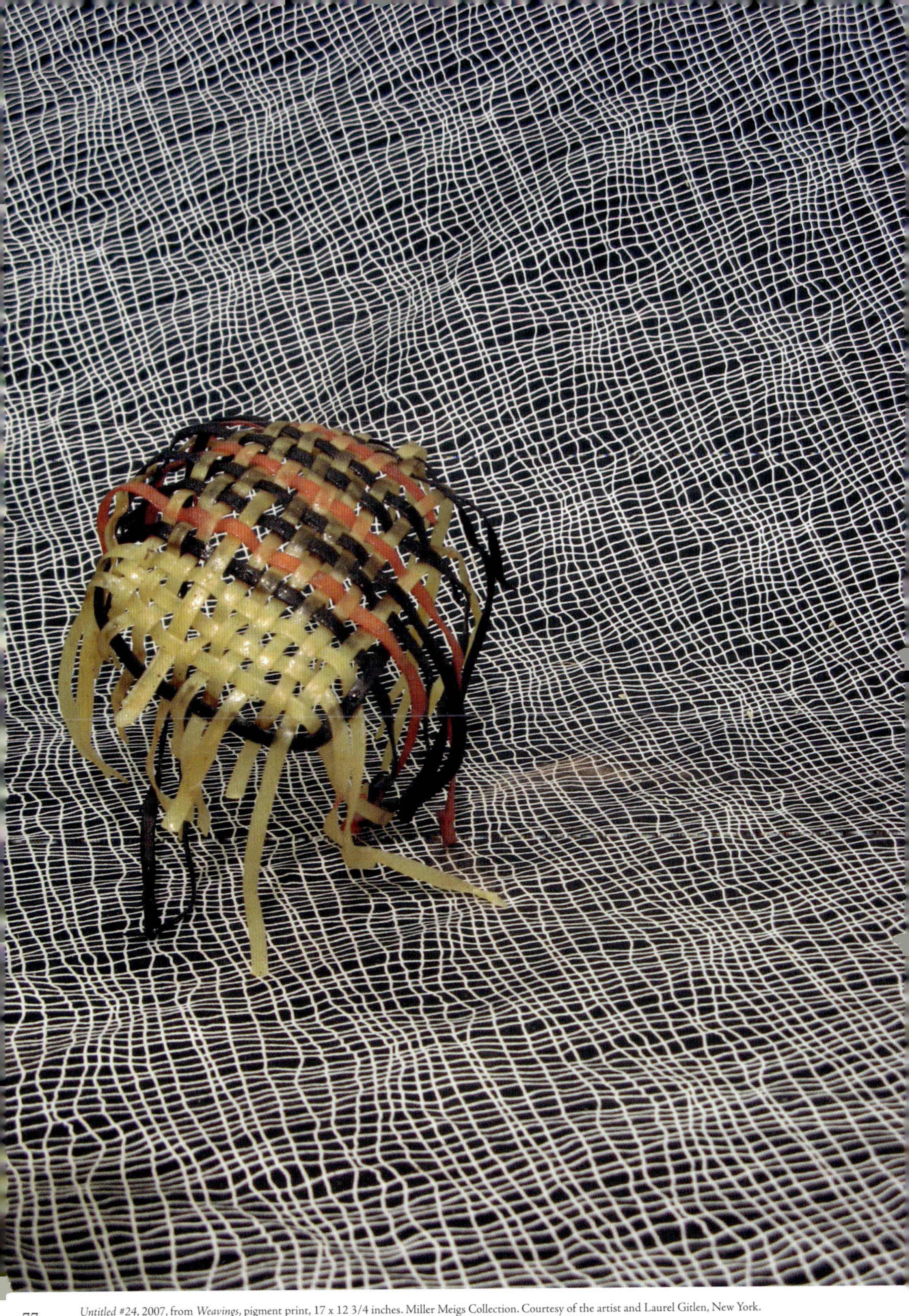

Untitled #24, 2007, from *Weavings*, pigment print, 17 x 12 3/4 inches. Miller Meigs Collection. Courtesy of the artist and Laurel Gitlen, New York.

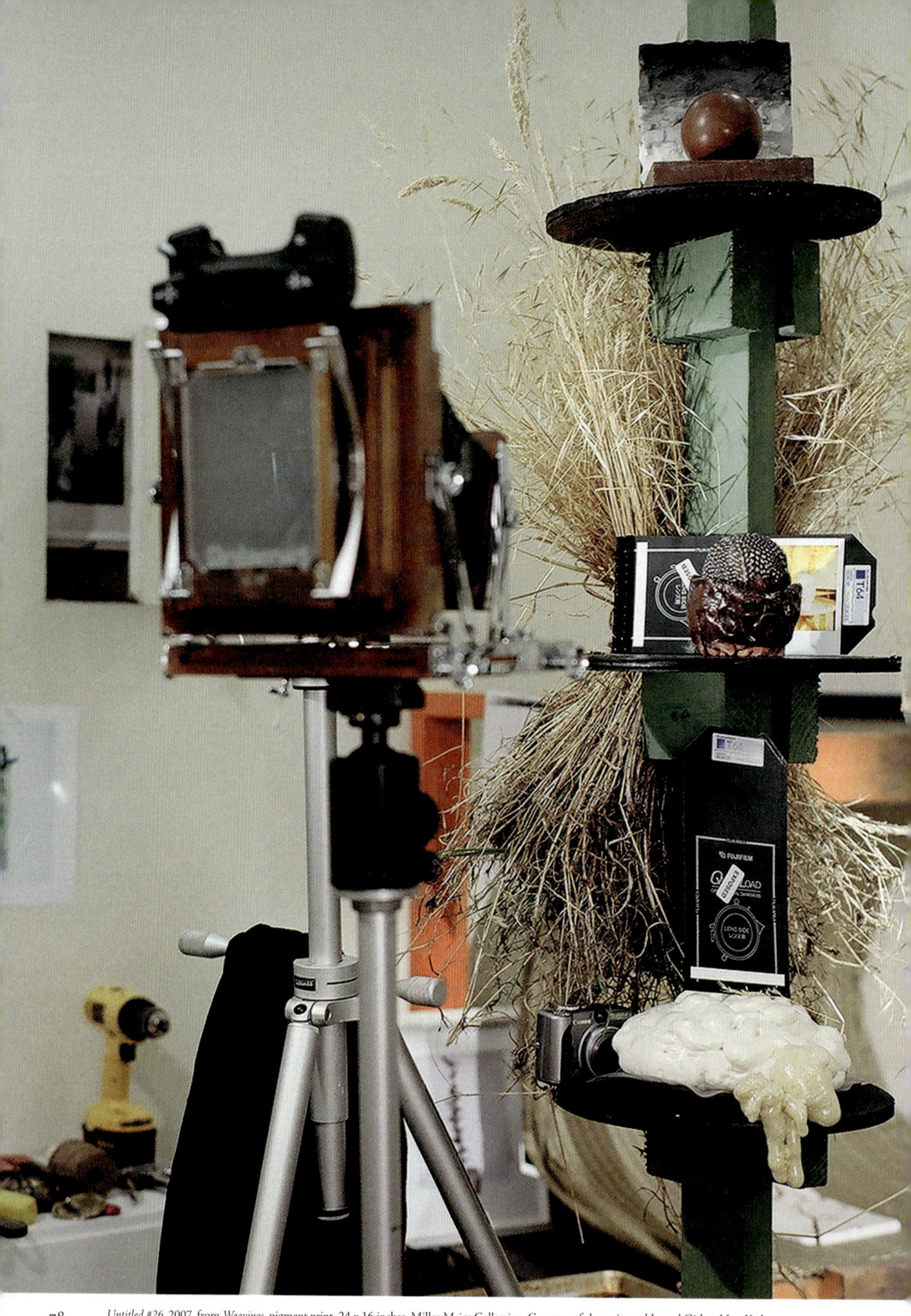

  Untitled #26, 2007, from *Weavings*, pigment print, 24 x 16 inches. Miller Meigs Collection. Courtesy of the artist and Laurel Gitlen, New York.

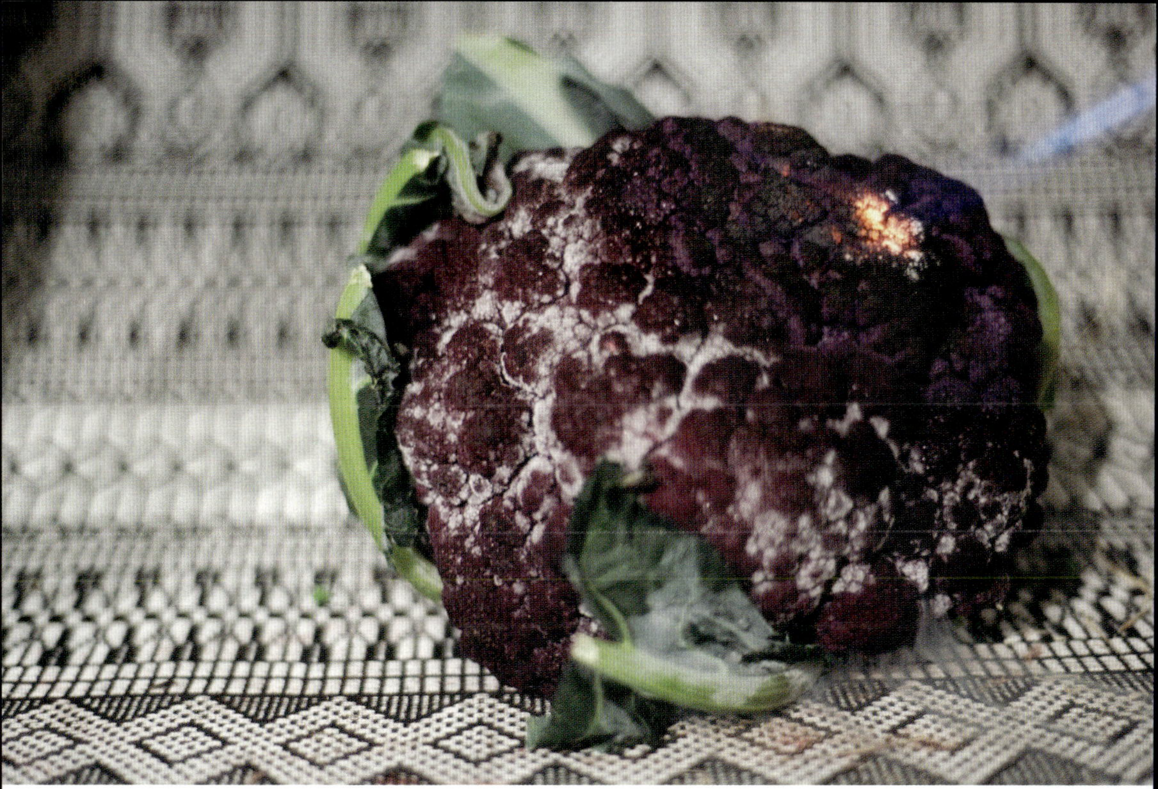

79   *Untitled #33*, 2007, from *Weavings*, pigment print, 16 x 24 inches. Miller Meigs Collection. Courtesy of the artist and Laurel Gitlen, New York.

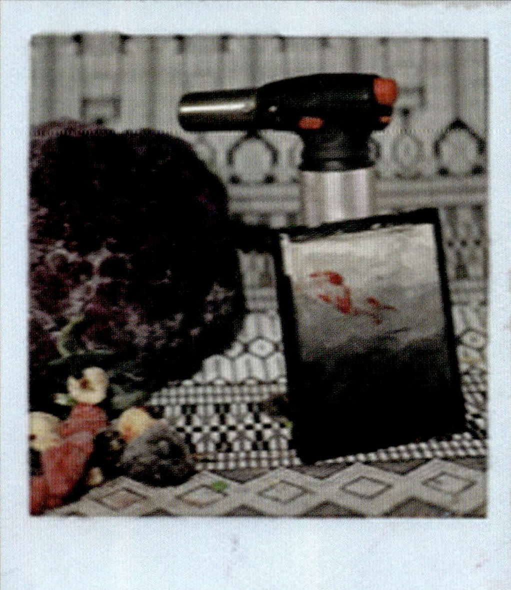
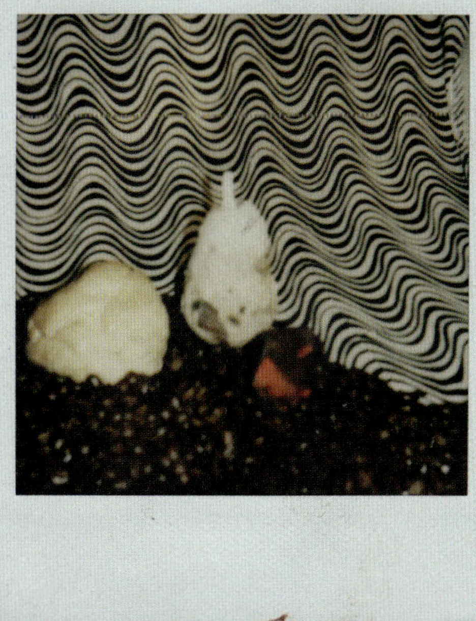

80   (left) *Untitled #34*, 2007, from *Weavings*, Polaroid photograph, 4 1/4 x 3 1/2 inches; (right) *Untitled #36*, 2007, from *Weavings*, Polaroid photograph, 4 1/4 x 3 1/2 inches. Miller Meigs Collection. Courtesy of the artist and Laurel Gitlen, New York.

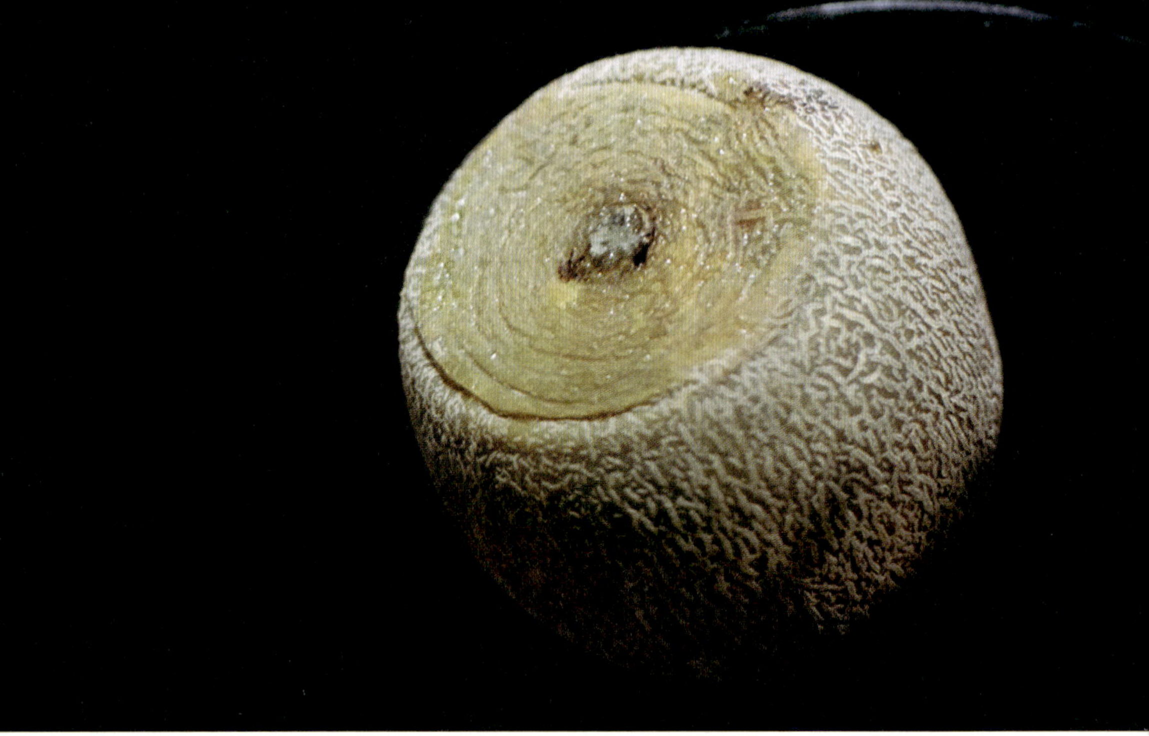

    Untitled #63, 2007, from *Weavings*, pigment print, 16 x 24 inches. Miller Meigs Collection. Courtesy of the artist and Laurel Gitlen, New York.

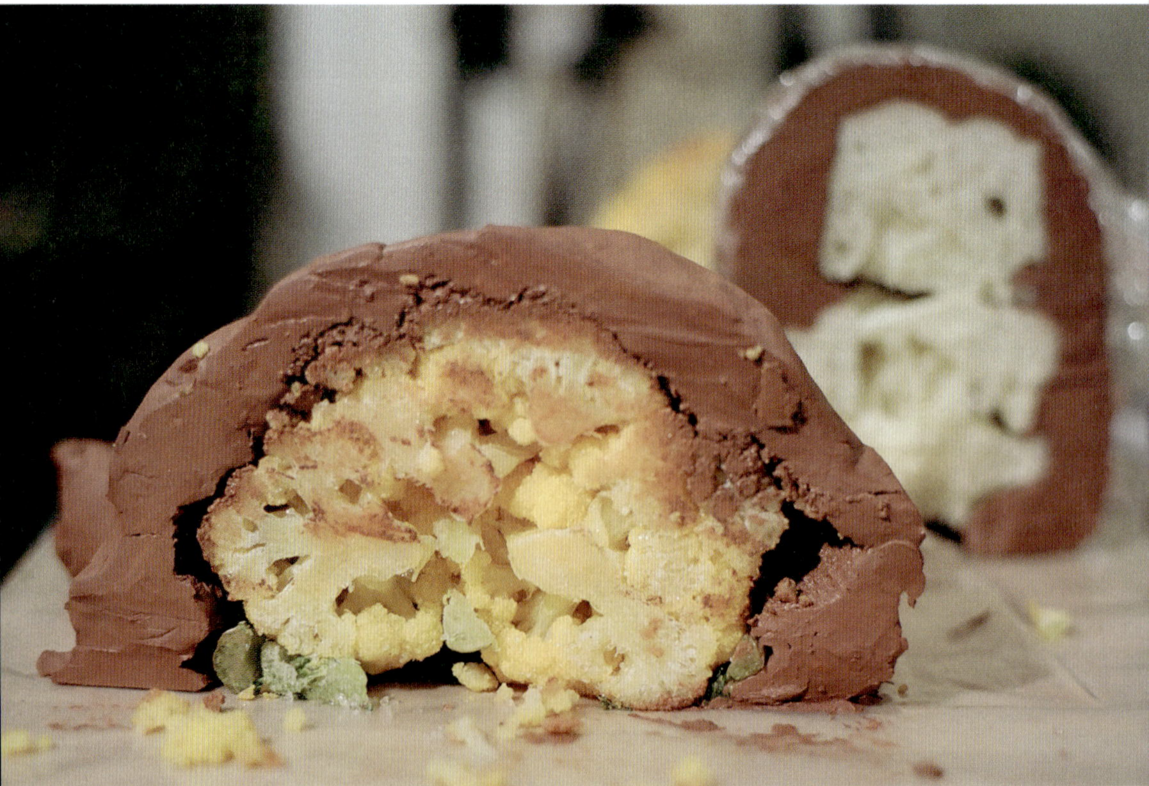

    Untitled #42, 2007, from *Weavings*, pigment print, 16 x 24 inches. Miller Meigs Collection. Courtesy of the artist and Laurel Gitlen, New York.

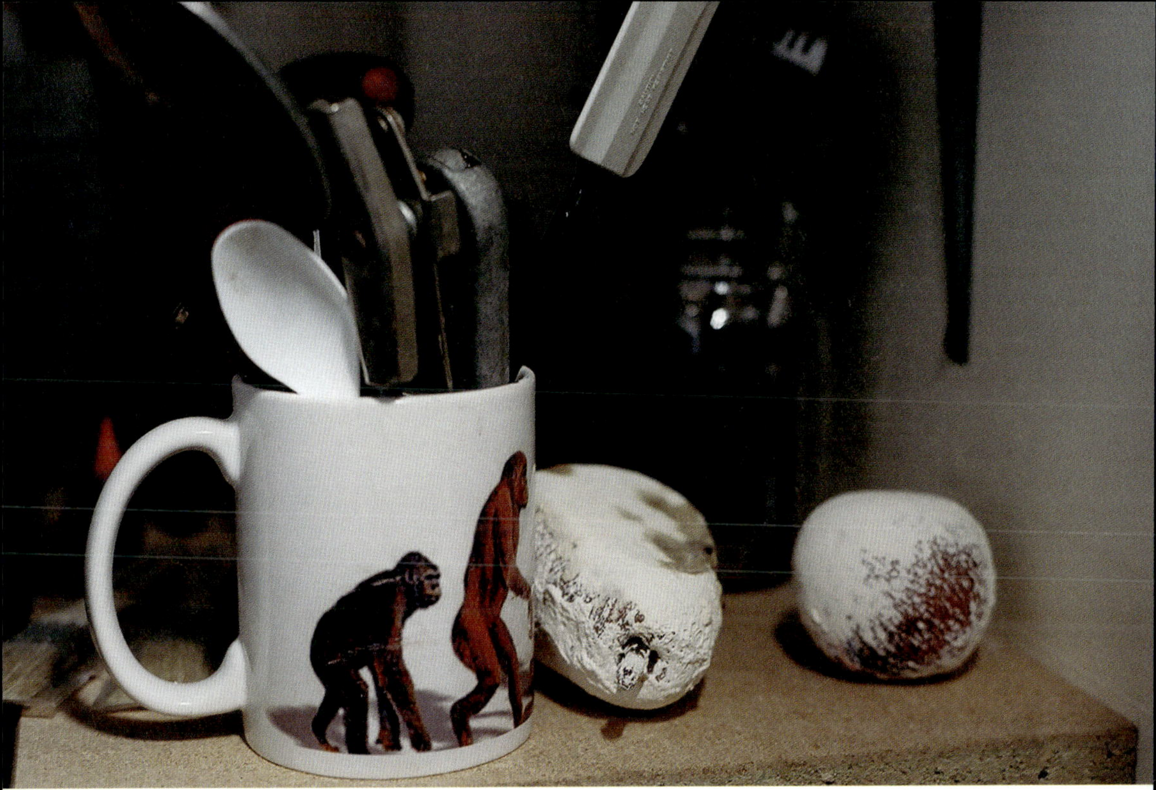

 Untitled #39, 2007, from *Weavings*, pigment print, 16 x 24 inches. Miller Meigs Collection. Courtesy of the artist and Laurel Gitlen, New York.

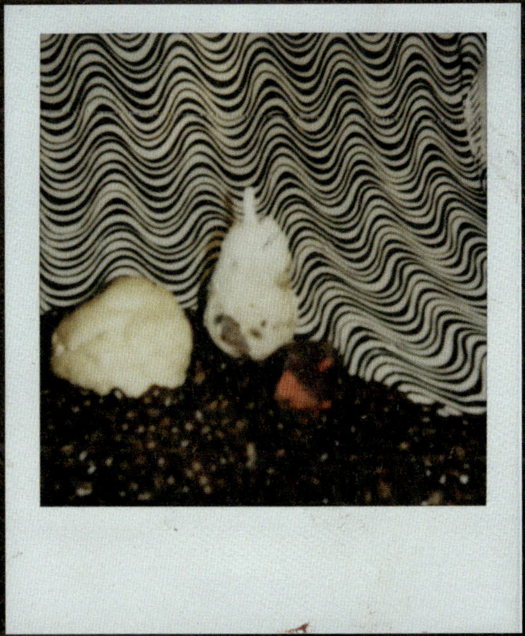

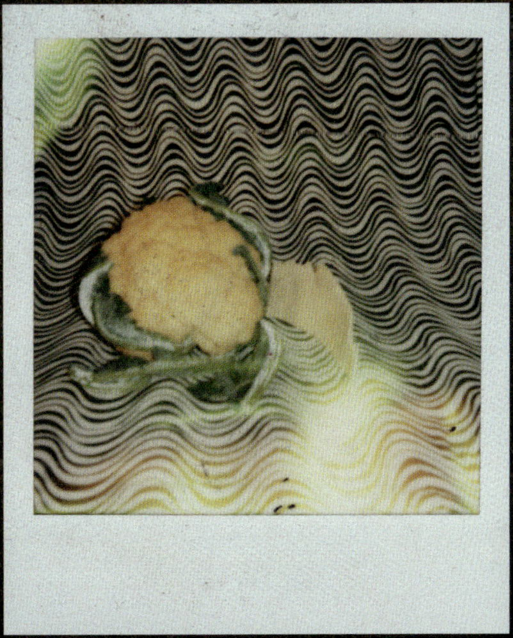

 (left) *Untitled #36*, 2007, from *Weavings*, Polaroid photograph, 4 1/4 x 3 1/2 inches; (right) *Untitled #41*, 2007, from *Weavings*, Polaroid photograph, 4 1/4 x 3 1/2 inches. Miller Meigs Collection. Courtesy of the artist and Laurel Gitlen, New York.

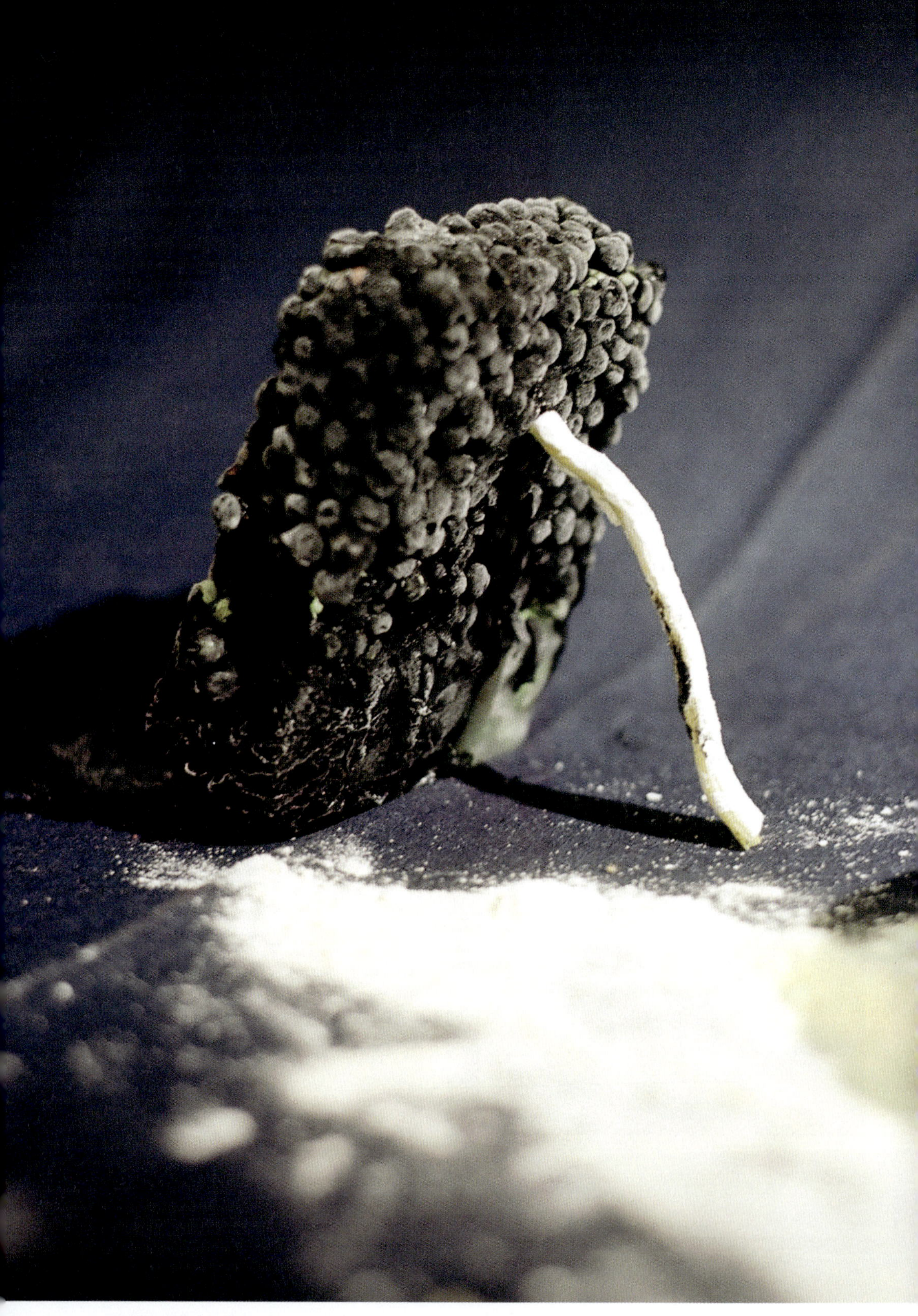

 Untitled #57, 2007, from *Weavings*, pigment print, 24 x 16 inches. Miller Meigs Collection. Courtesy of the artist and Laurel Gitlen, New York.

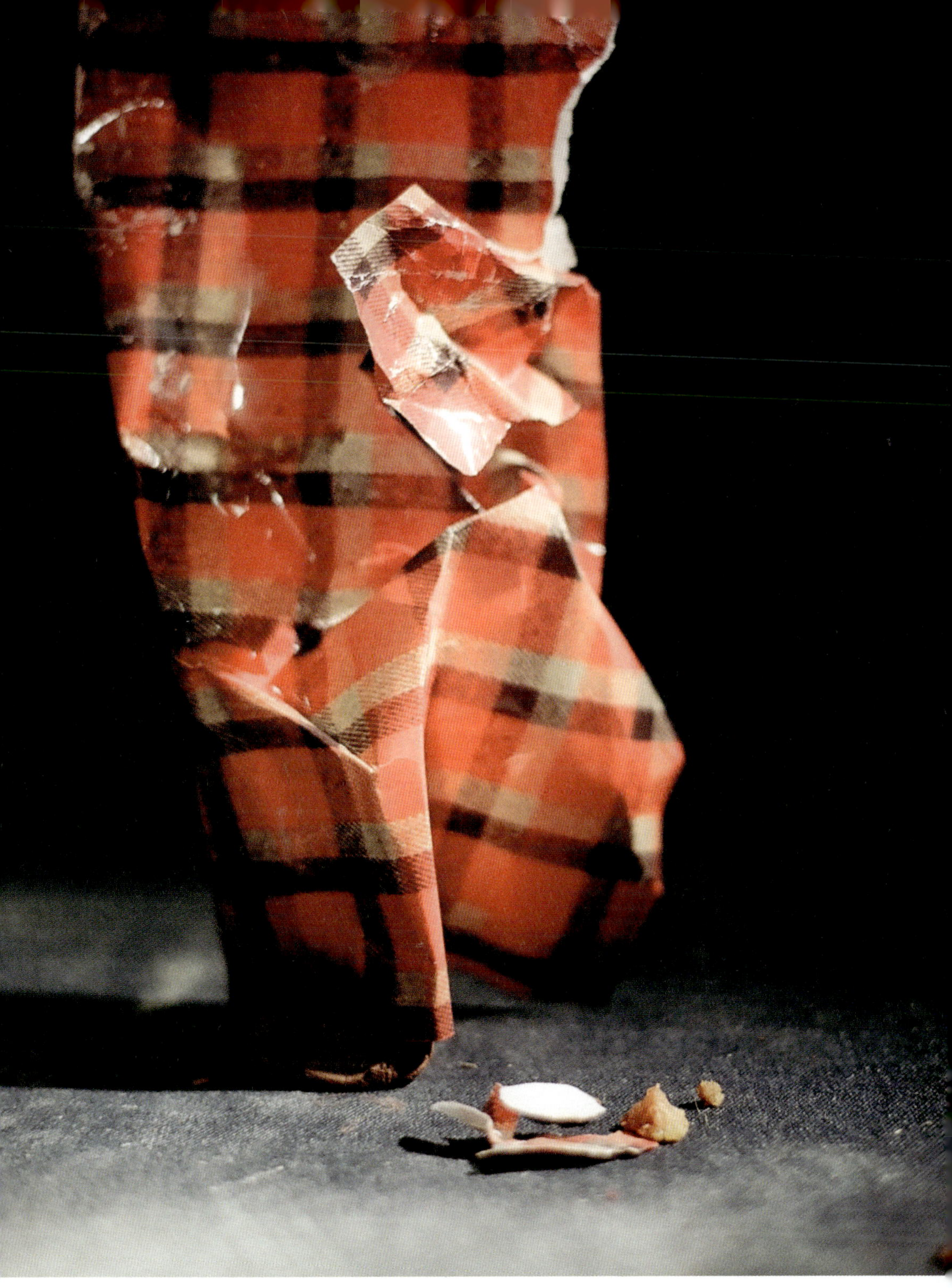

 Untitled #72, 2007, from *Weavings*, pigment print, 24 x 16 inches. Miller Meigs Collection. Courtesy of the artist and Laurel Gitlen, New York.

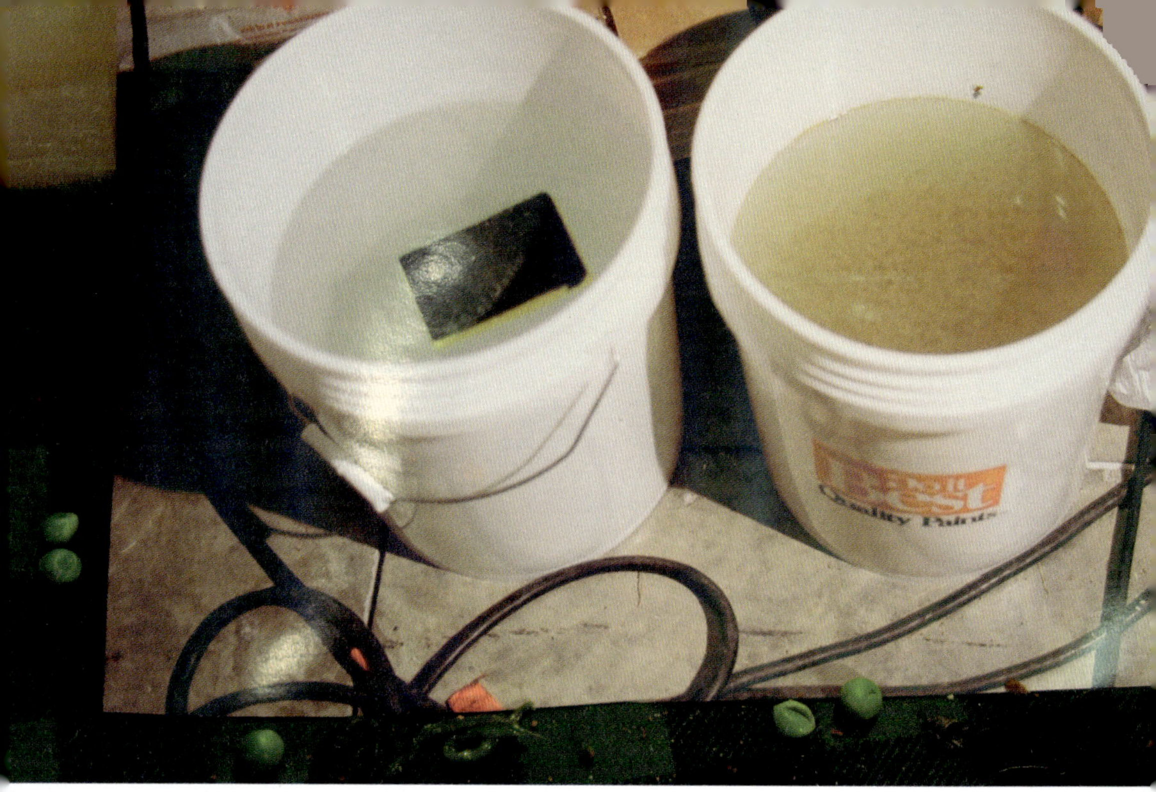

 Untitled #67, 2007, from *Weavings*, pigment print, 24 x 16 inches. Miller Meigs Collection. Courtesy of the artist and Laurel Gitlen, New York.

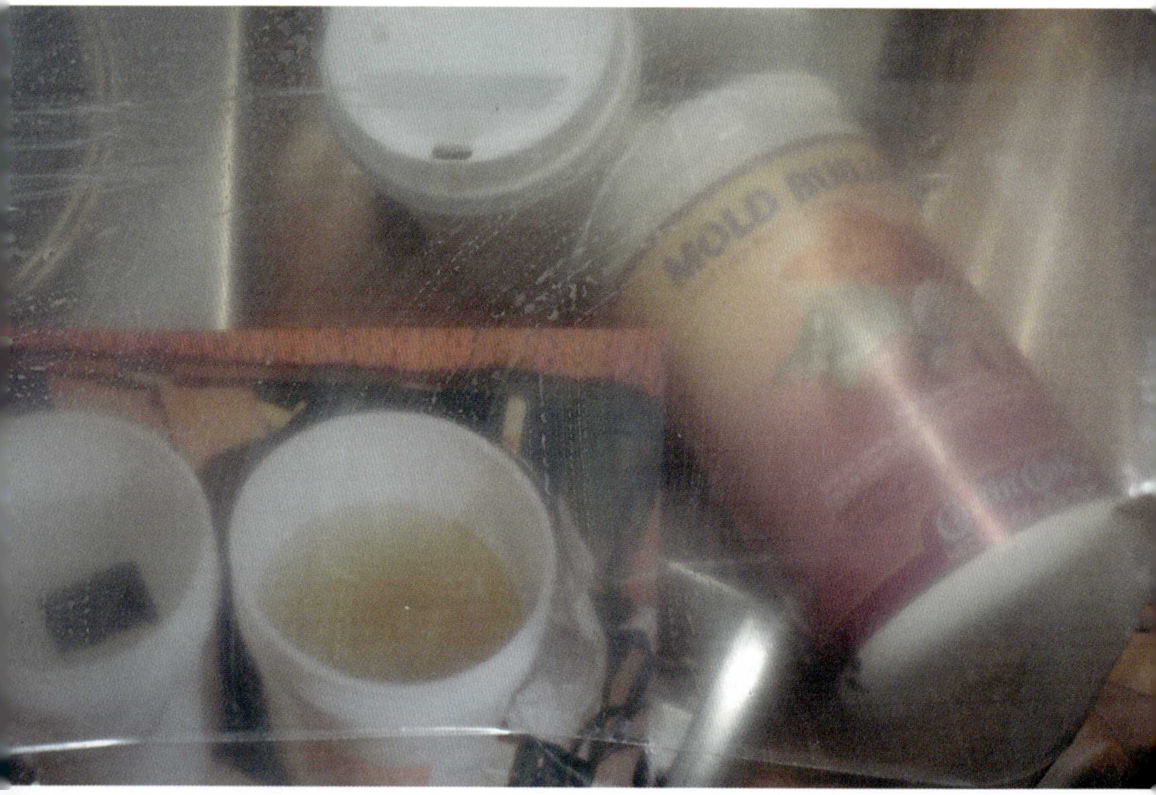

 Untitled #68, 2007, from *Weavings*, pigment print, 16 x 24 inches. Miller Meigs Collection. Courtesy of the artist and Laurel Gitlen, New York.

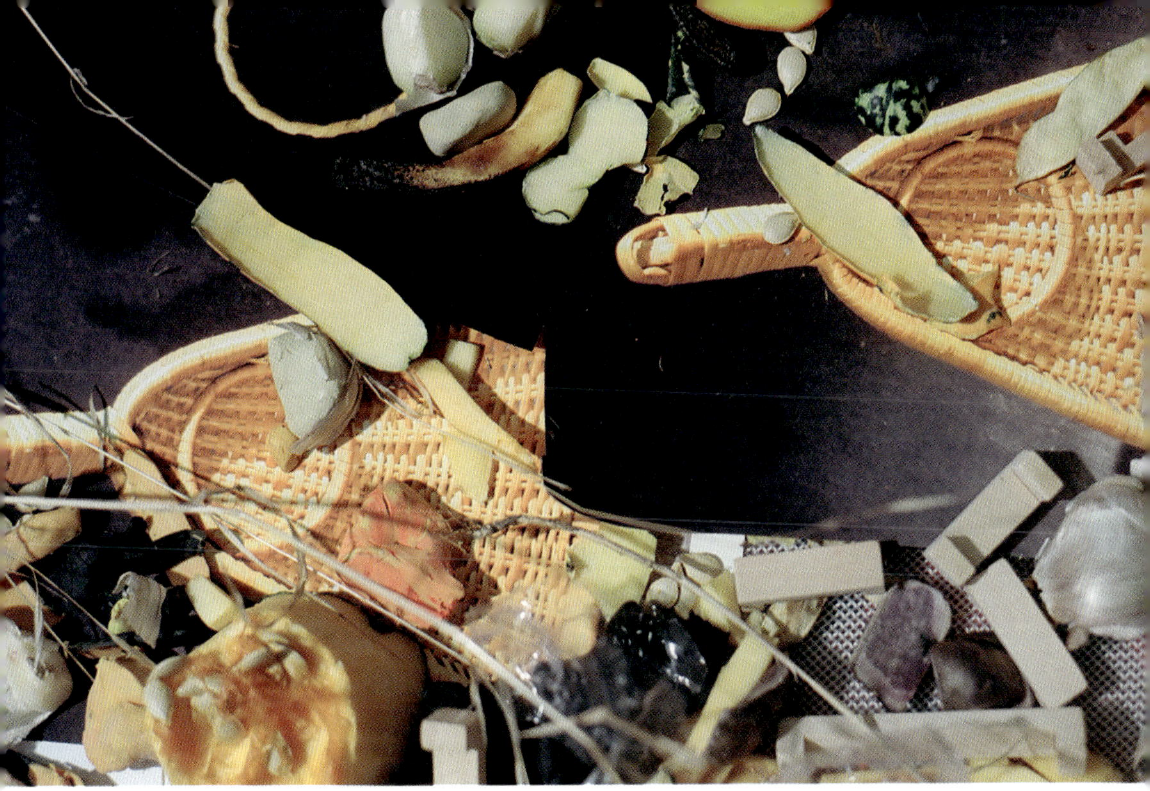

Untitled #70, 2007, from *Weavings*, pigment print, 16 x 24 inches. Miller Meigs Collection. Courtesy of the artist and Laurel Gitlen, New York.

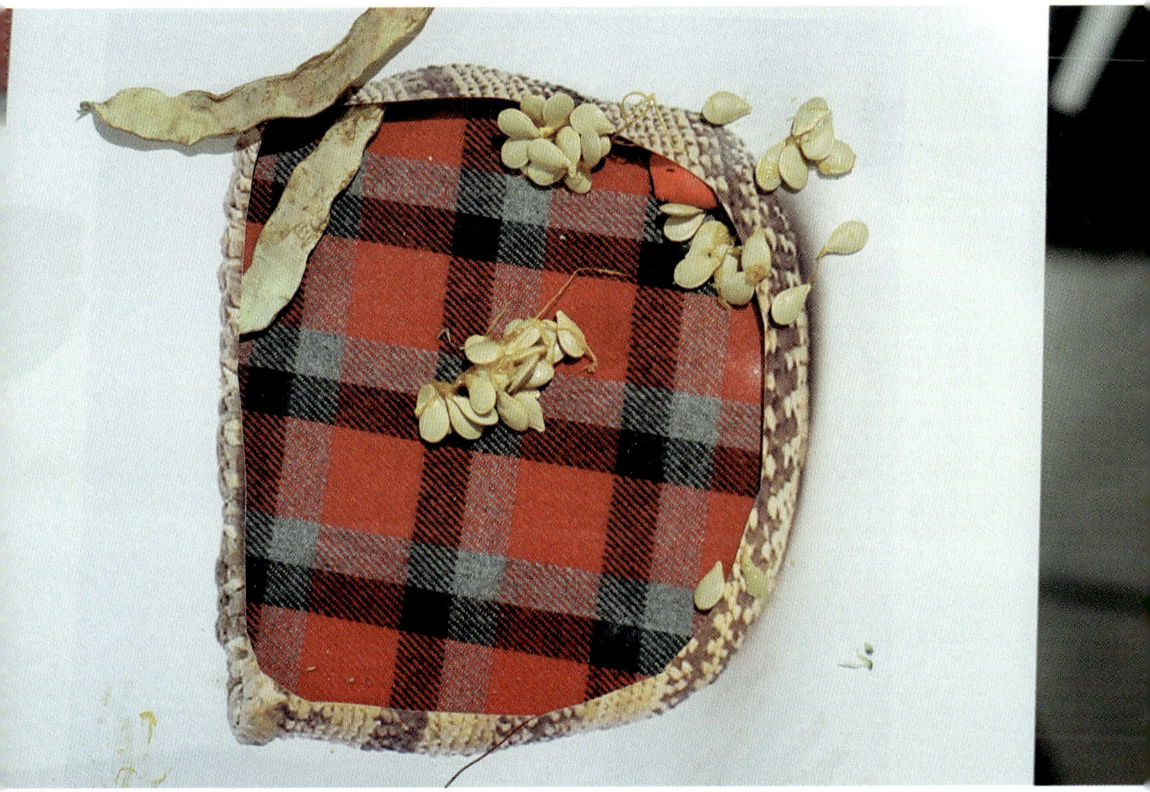

Untitled #71, 2007, from *Weavings*, pigment print, 16 x 24 inches. Miller Meigs Collection. Courtesy of the artist and Laurel Gitlen, New York.

 Untitled #74, 2007, from *Weavings*, pigment print, 36 x 29 1/2inches. Miller Meigs Collection. Courtesy of the artist and Laurel Gitlen, New York.

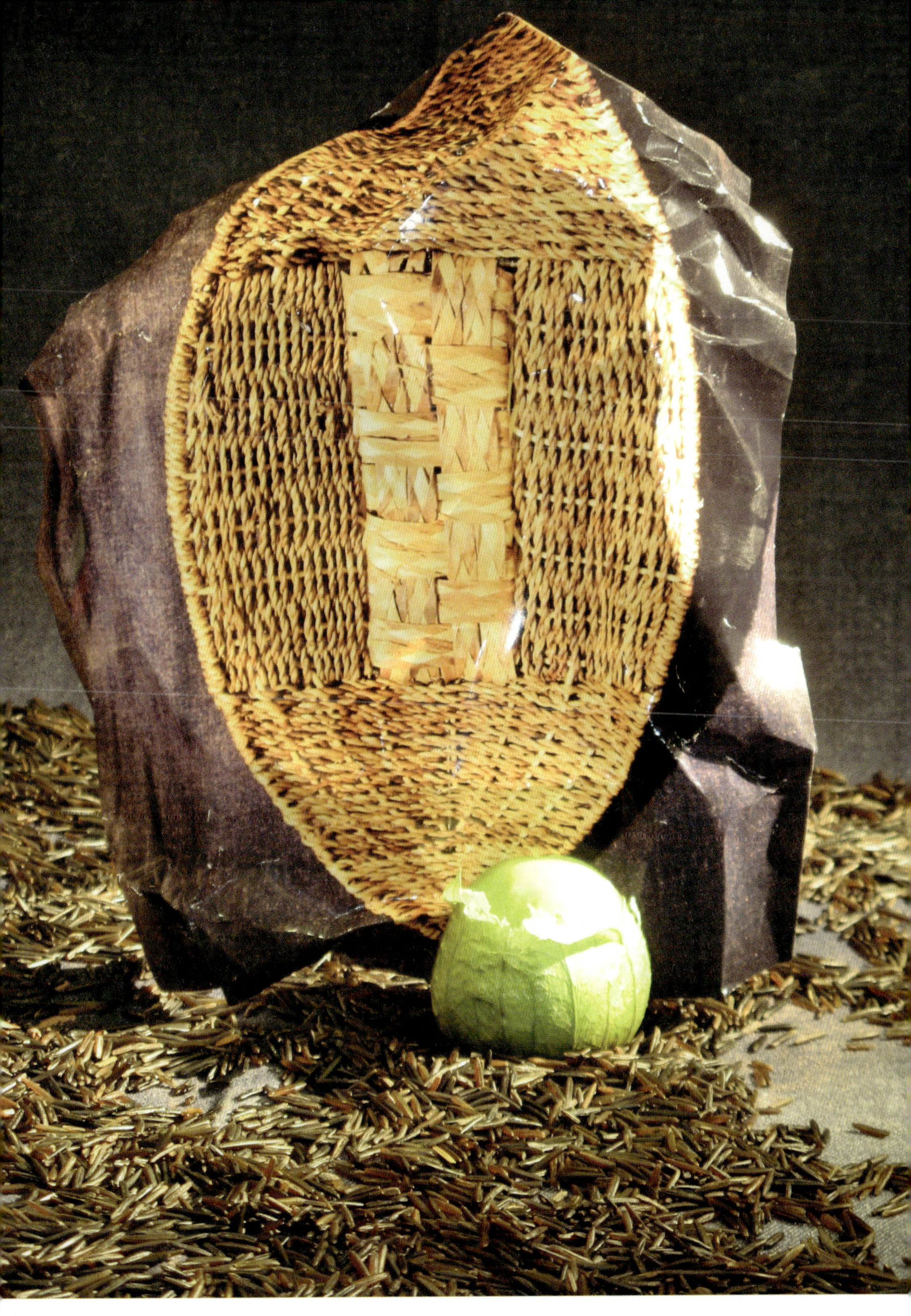

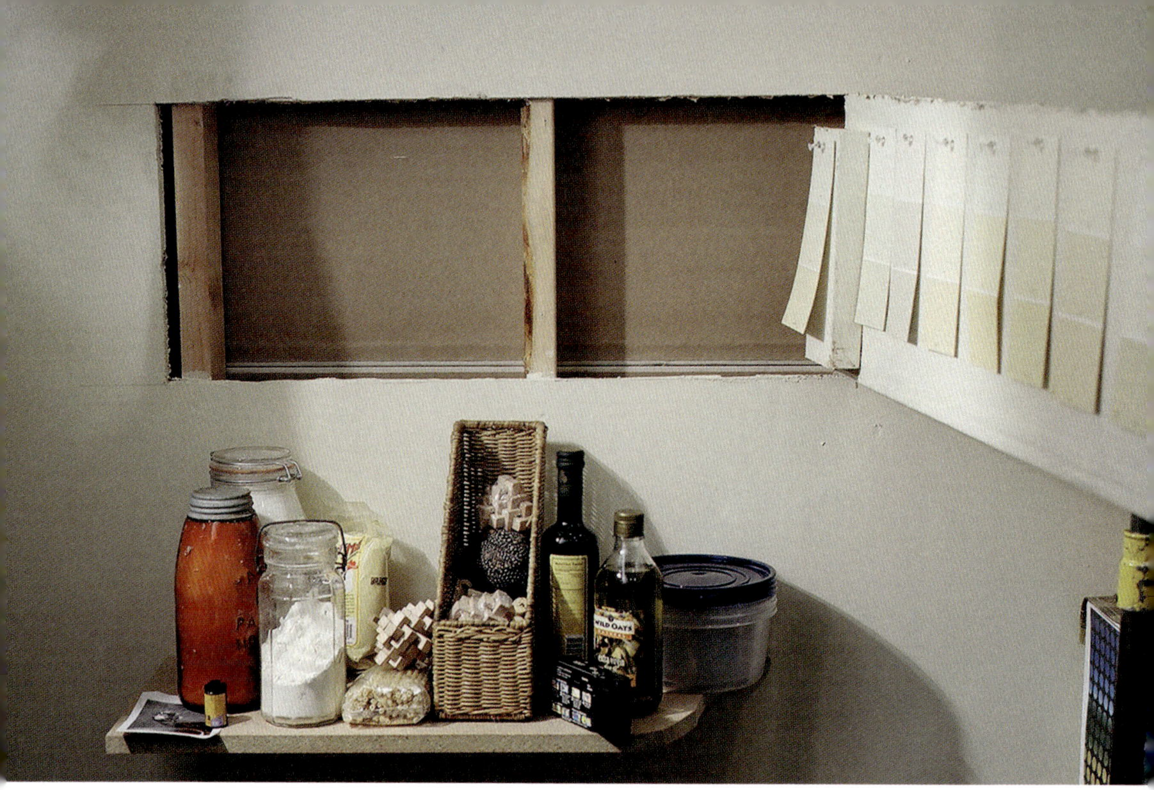

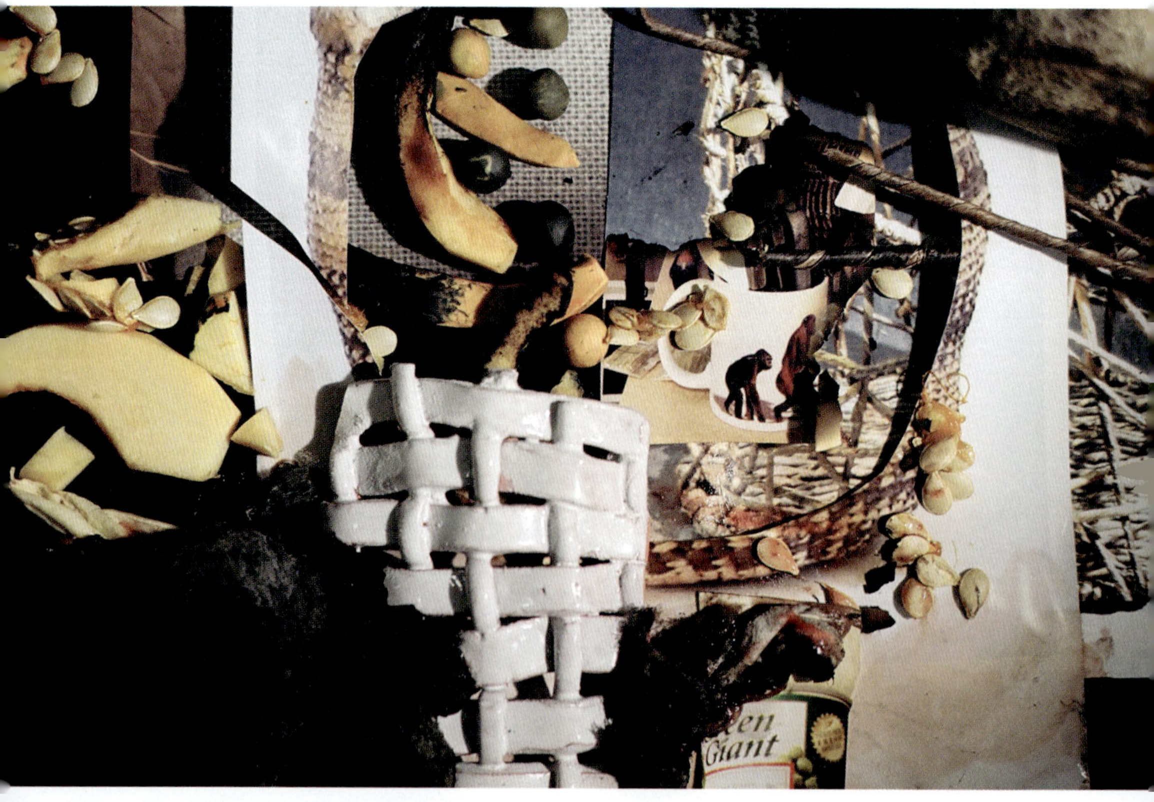

94   *Untitled #75*, 2007, from *Weavings*, pigment print, 16 x 24 inches. Miller Meigs Collection. Courtesy of the artist and Laurel Gitlen, New York.

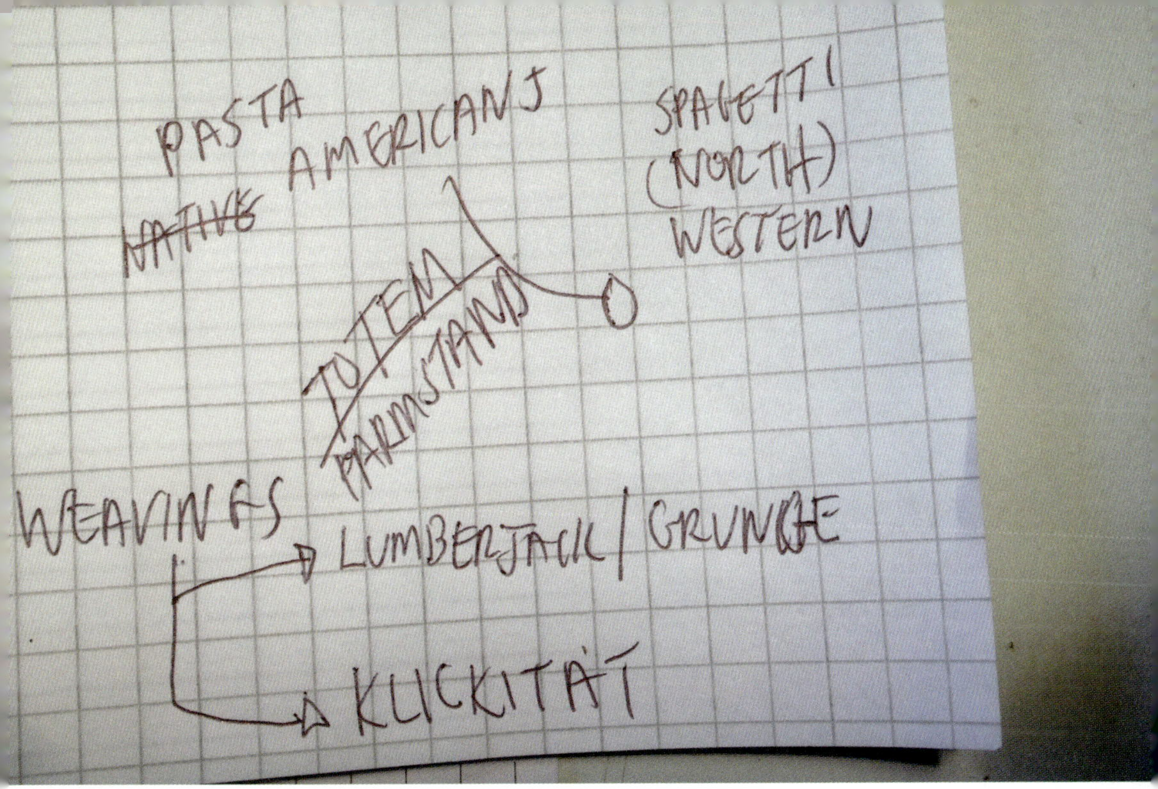

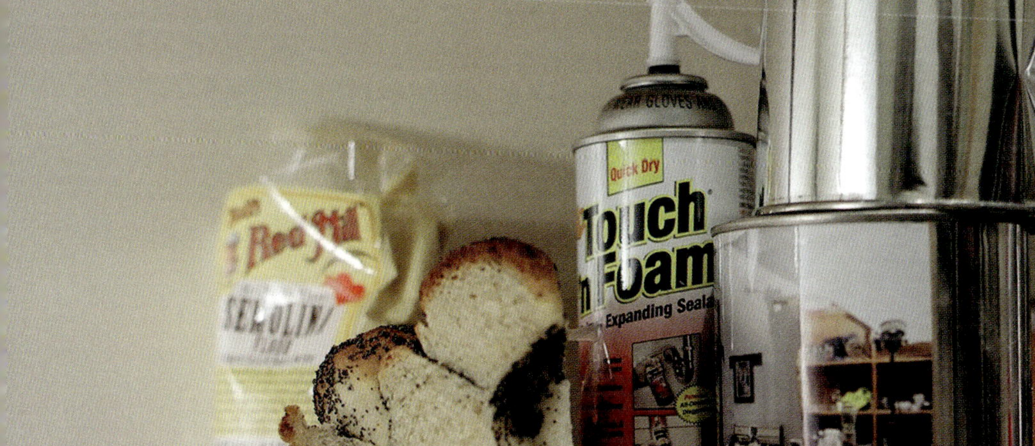

Untitled #49, 2007, from *Weavings*, pigment print, 16 x 24 inches. Miller Meigs Collection. Courtesy of the artist and Laurel Gitlen, New York.

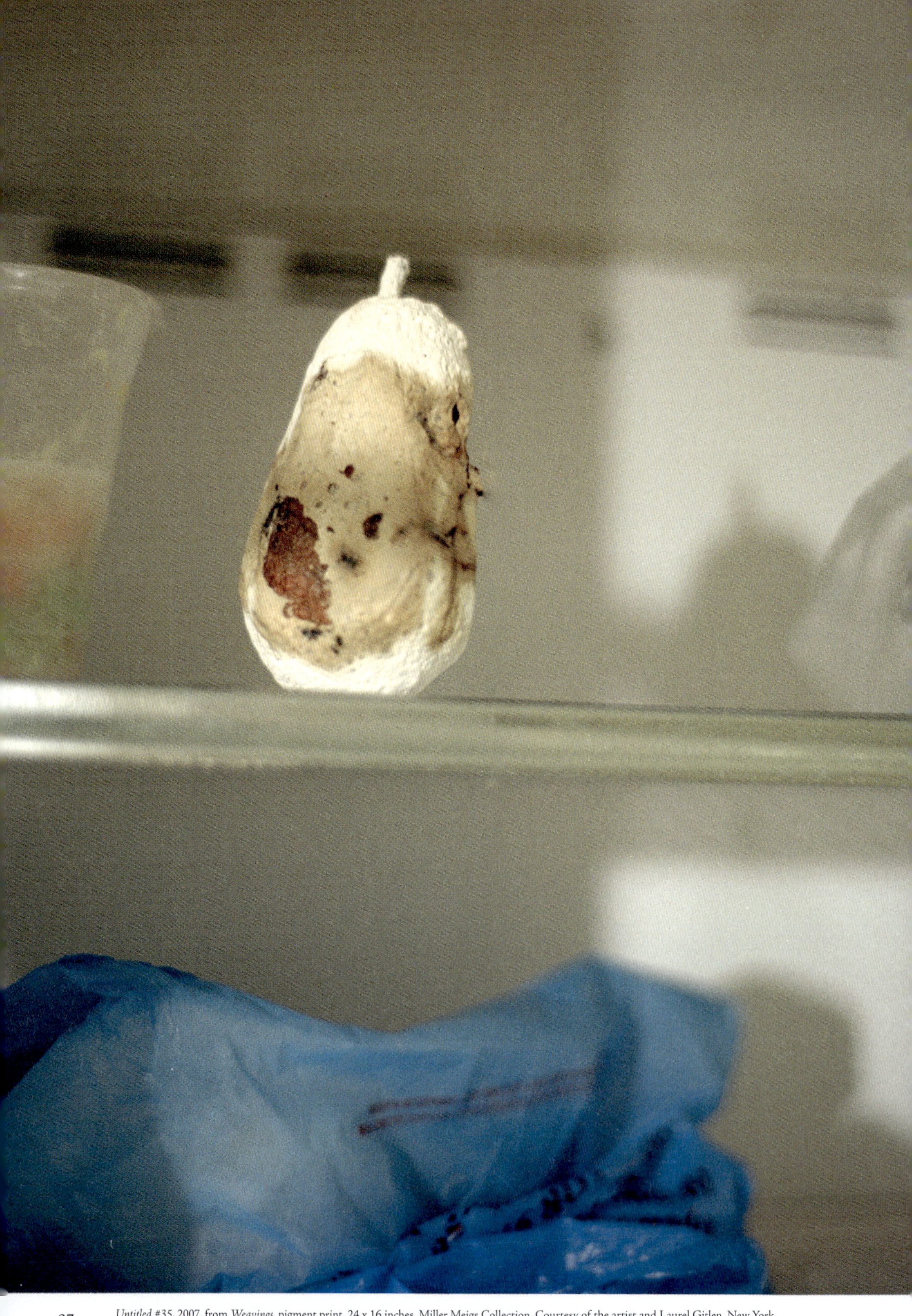

    Untitled #35, 2007, from *Weavings*, pigment print, 24 x 16 inches. Miller Meigs Collection. Courtesy of the artist and Laurel Gitlen, New York.

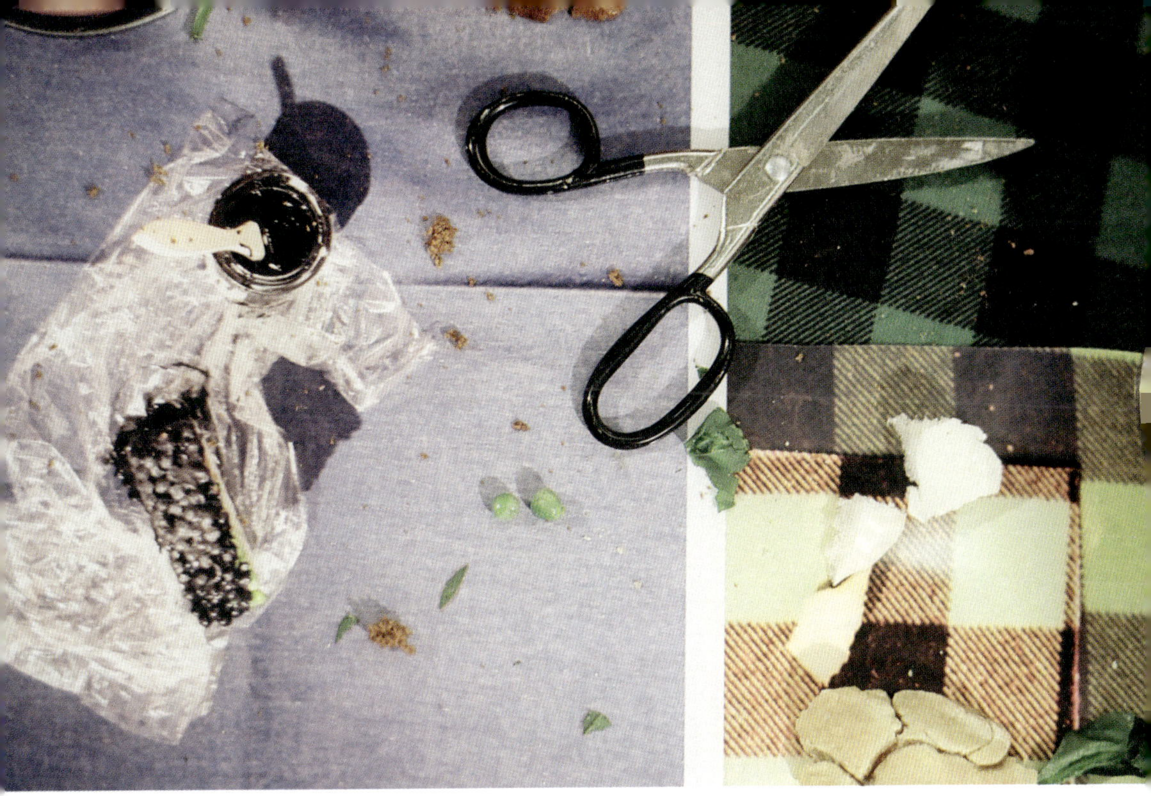

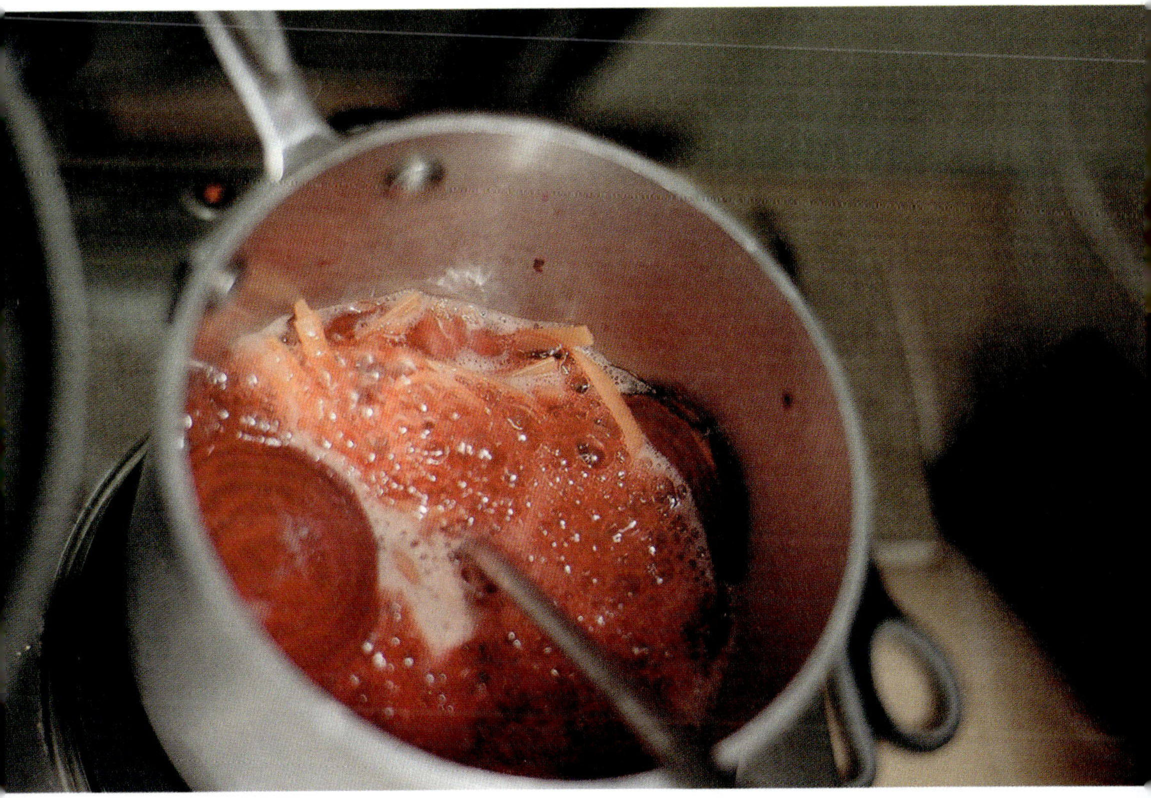

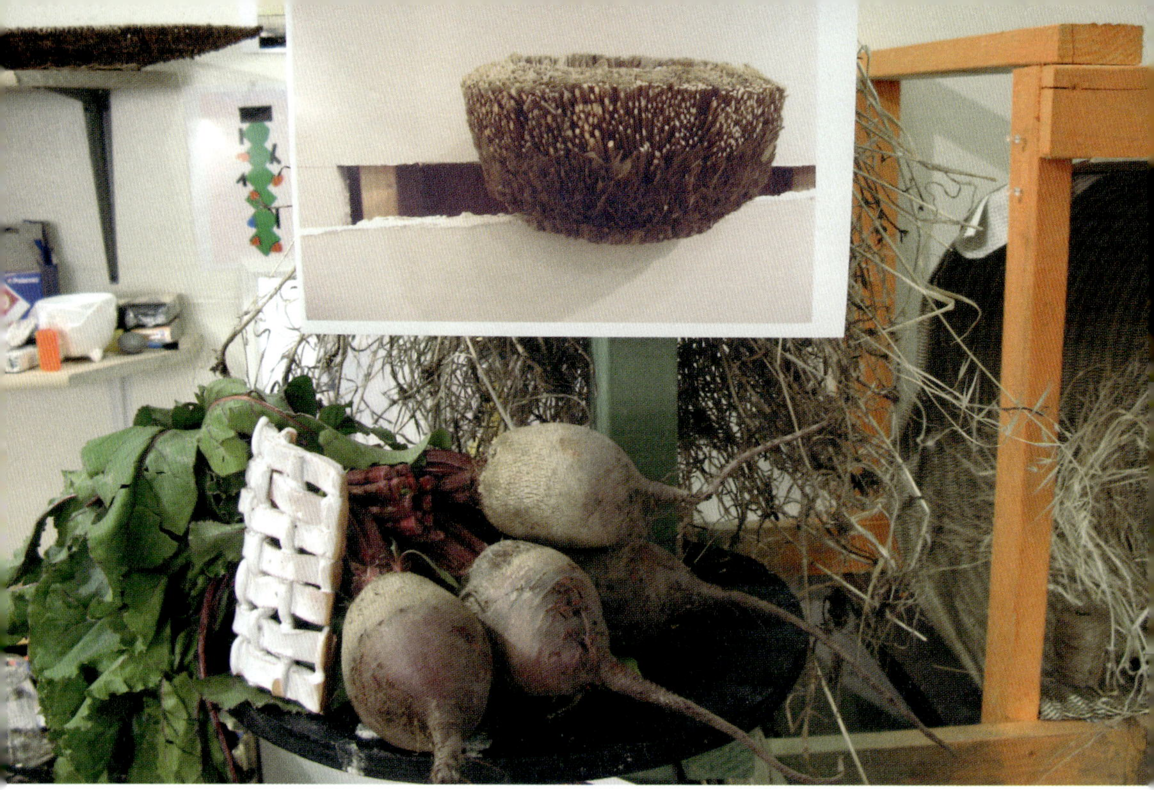

 Untitled #5, 2007, from *Weavings*, pigment print, 10 1/8 x 13 1/2 inches. Miller Meigs Collection. Courtesy of the artist and Laurel Gitlen, New York.

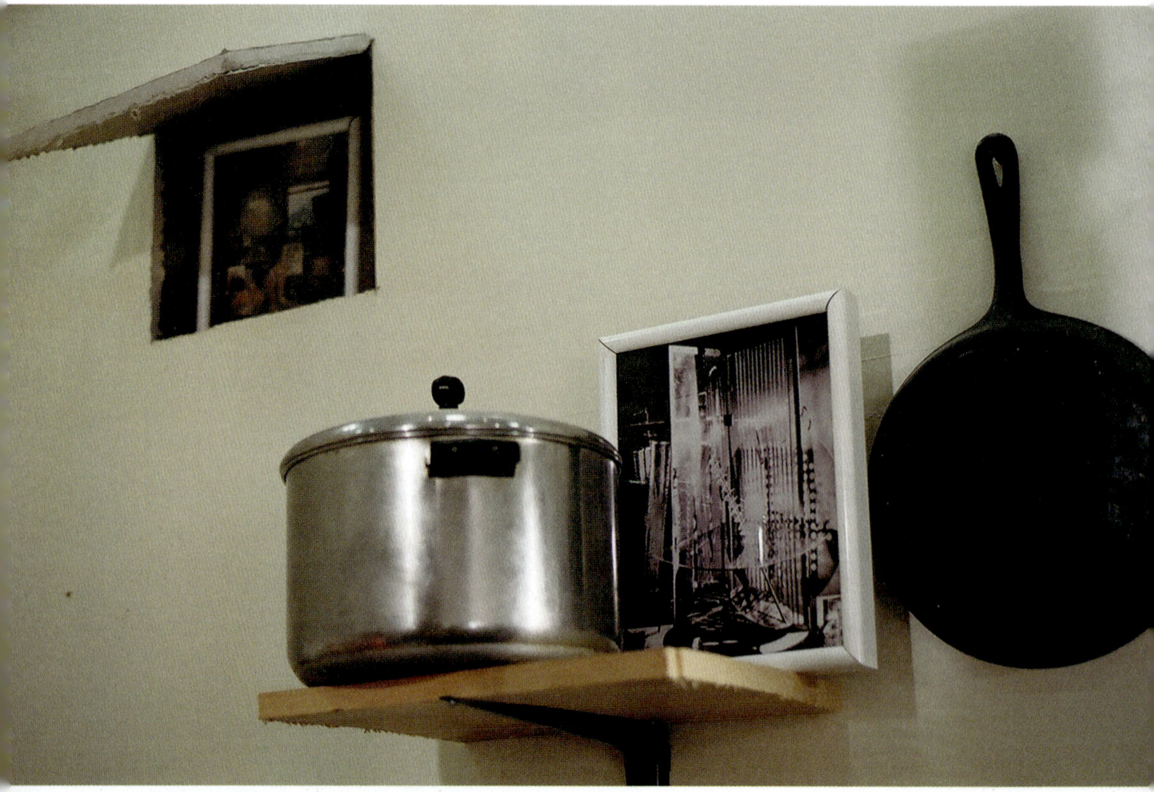

 Untitled #45, 2007, from *Weavings*, pigment print, 16 x 24 inches. Miller Meigs Collection. Courtesy of the artist and Laurel Gitlen, New York.

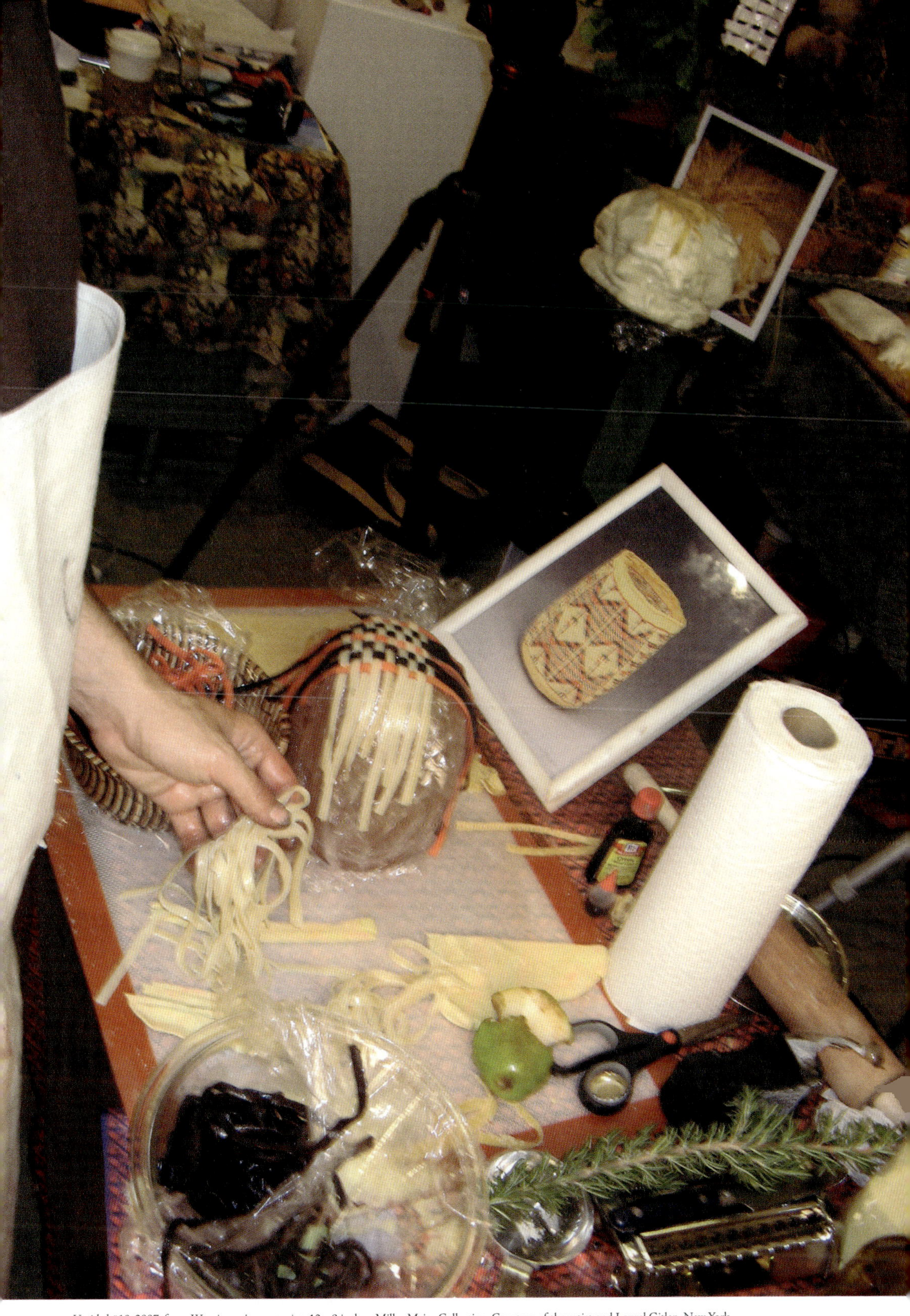

Untitled #10, 2007, from *Weavings*, pigment print, 12 x 9 inches. Miller Meigs Collection. Courtesy of the artist and Laurel Gitlen, New York.

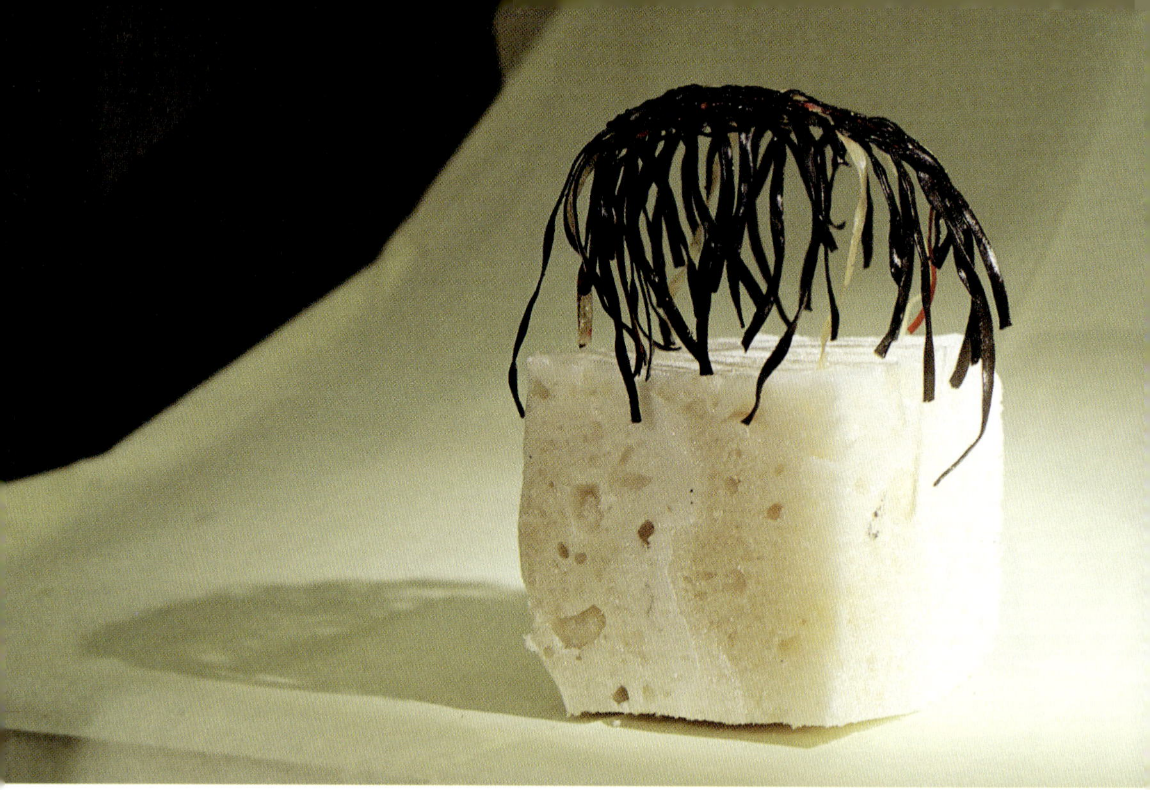

  Untitled #2, 2007, from *Weavings*, pigment print, 16 x 24 inches. Miller Meigs Collection. Courtesy of the artist and Laurel Gitlen, New York.

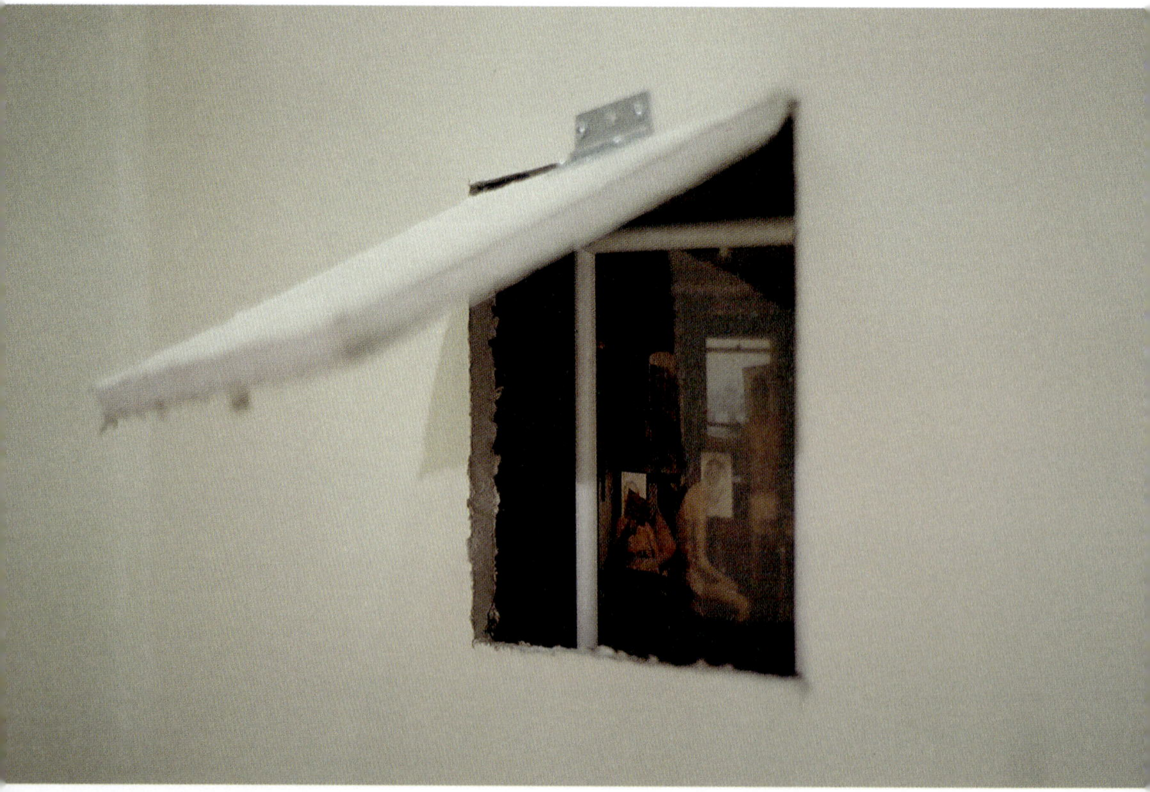

Seed Stage
Whitney Museum of American Art, New York, NY
October 3, 2008–January 4, 2009
Curated by Tina Kukielski

Seed Stage expanded upon the freestanding set of *Weavings* (2007), with vertical cutouts in all four of the room's corners. The set contained a complex arrangement of interior spaces, which were inspired by Marcel Breuer's upturned-ziggurat design for the Whitney Museum. Hewitt synthesized architectural motifs with image-making processes to investigate notions of "composting," through an inorganic digital system (an algorithm that compressed images into colored grids or "plaids"), as well as an organic system (a worm compost that physically decayed photographic prints).

Hewitt worked in the space for three days a week over a period of three months. Over the course of the exhibition, selected photographs were framed and hung on the gallery walls, however these were often returned to the system for reprocessing. Through this constant flux, *Seed Stage* explored the role of preservation and decay in both the genre of still life and art-making in general.

Captions

105, 110, 115, 118, 124, 125, 128, 133, 136, 138, 139, 141, 143, 150–152, 154, 155, 164, 166: Working image from *Seed Stage*, 2008-9. Courtesy of the artist.
106–108, 117, 122: Preparatory work for *Seed Stage*, 2008. Courtesy of the artist.
109: Preparatory construction for *Seed Stage*, 2008. Courtesy of the artist.
111, 116, 127, 131: *Seed Stage*, 2008-9. Performance documentation. Photo: Sheldan C. Collins. Courtesy of the artist.
113: Plaid pattern generated from Ouikiltit program. Courtesy of the artist.
121, 149, 159: Set documentation of *Seed Stage*, 2008-9. Courtesy of the artist.
134, 160, 161: *Seed Stage*, 2008-9. Installation view, Whitney Museum of American Art, New York. Photo: Sheldan C. Collins. Courtesy of the artist.
137: Research material for *Seed Stage*, 2008-9. Courtesy of the artist.

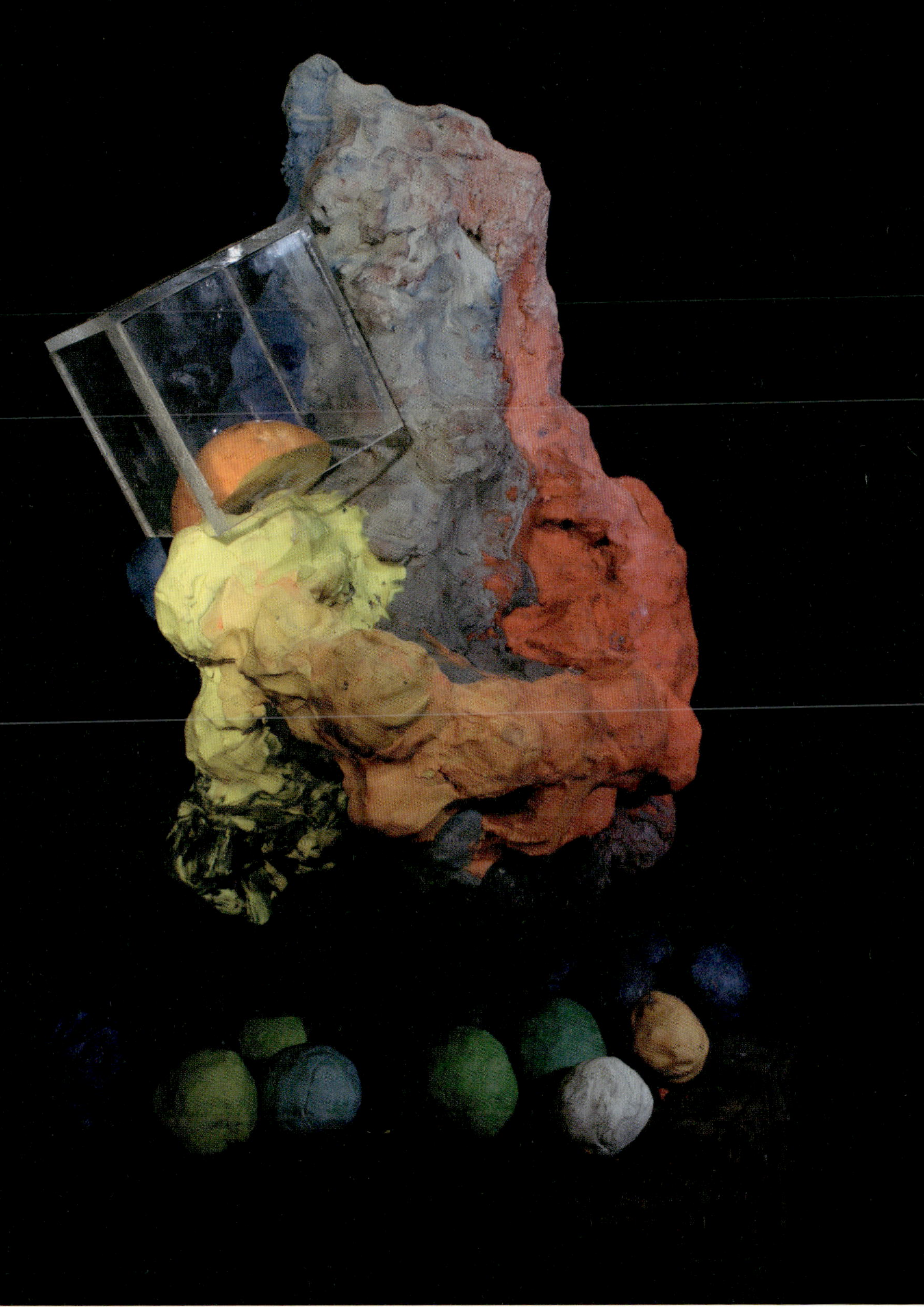

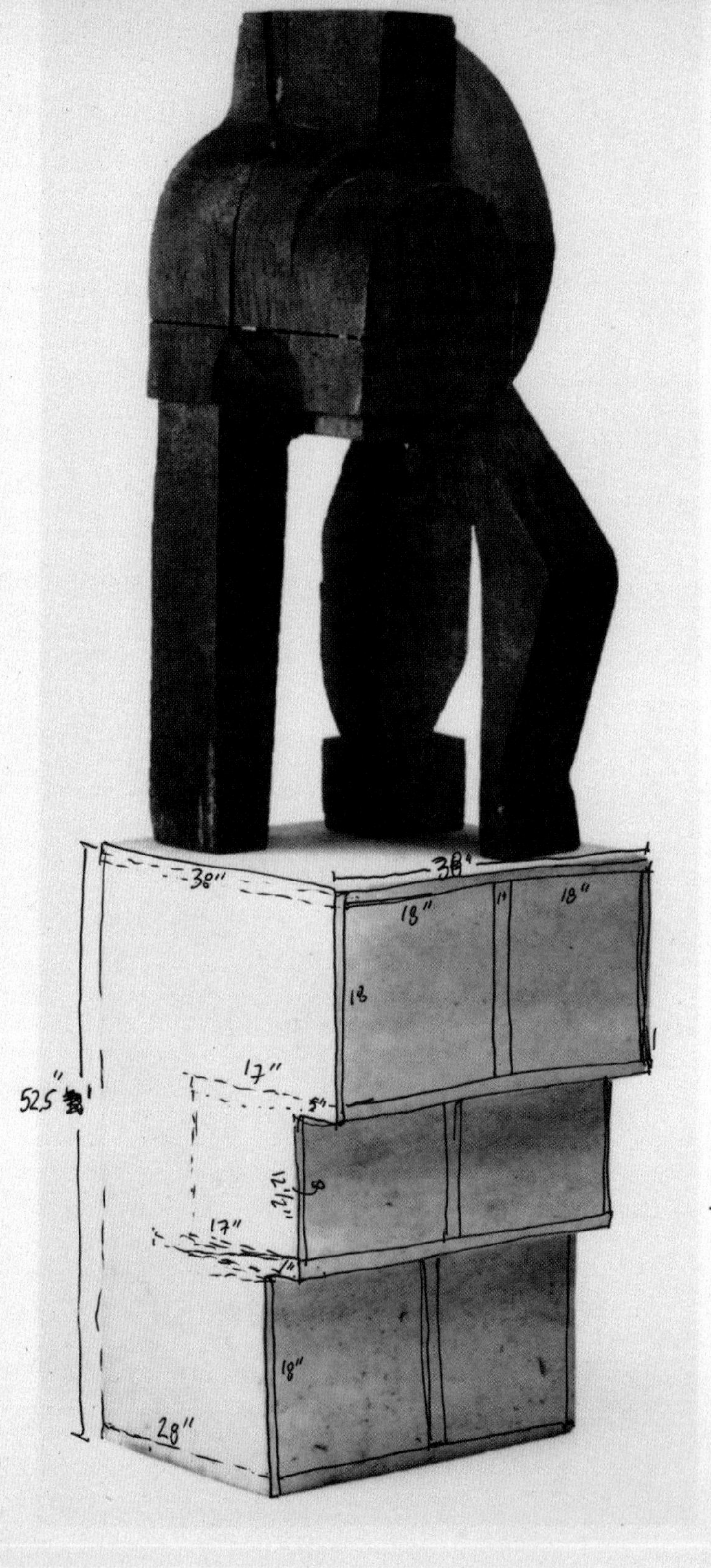

30"
38"
18"
1"
18"
18
52.5"
17"
5"
12 1/2"
17"
1"
18"
28"

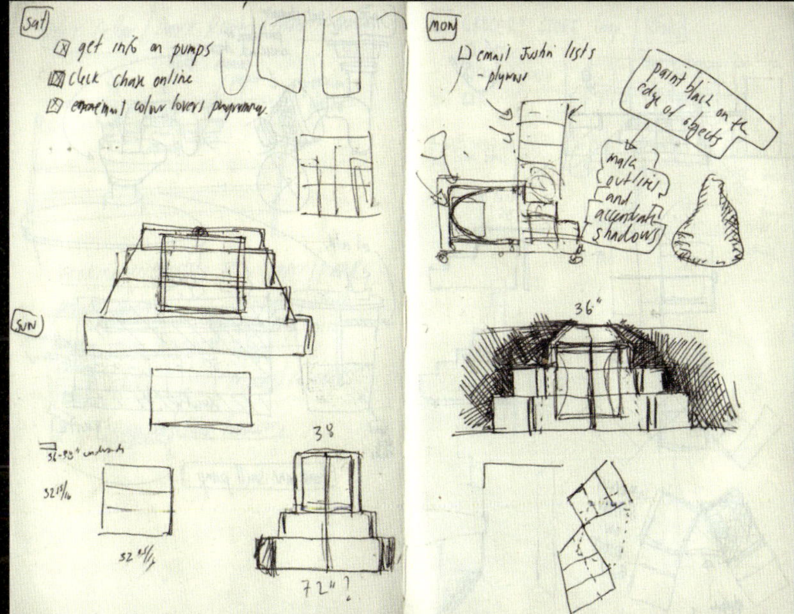

sat
get info on pumps
Check chain online
email colour lovers playmemory.
SUN
MON
email Justin lists
- plywood
paint black on the edge of objects
make outlines and accidental shadows
36"
38
72"?

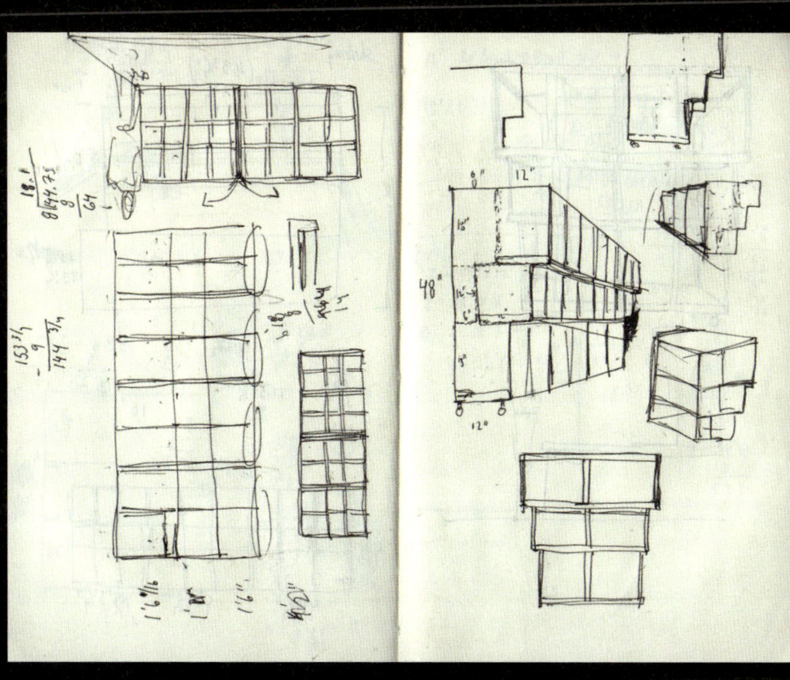

6"   12"
48"
12"

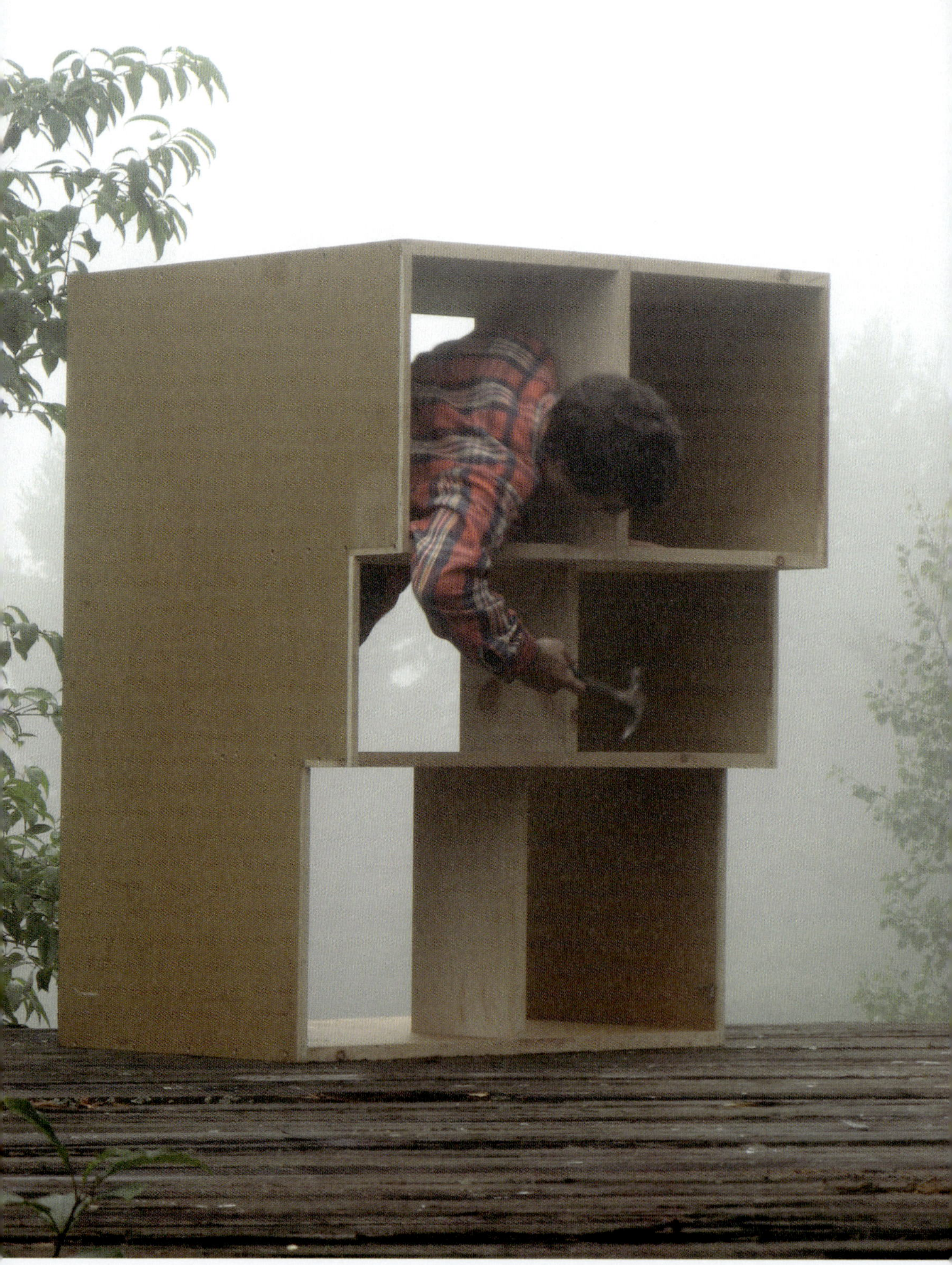

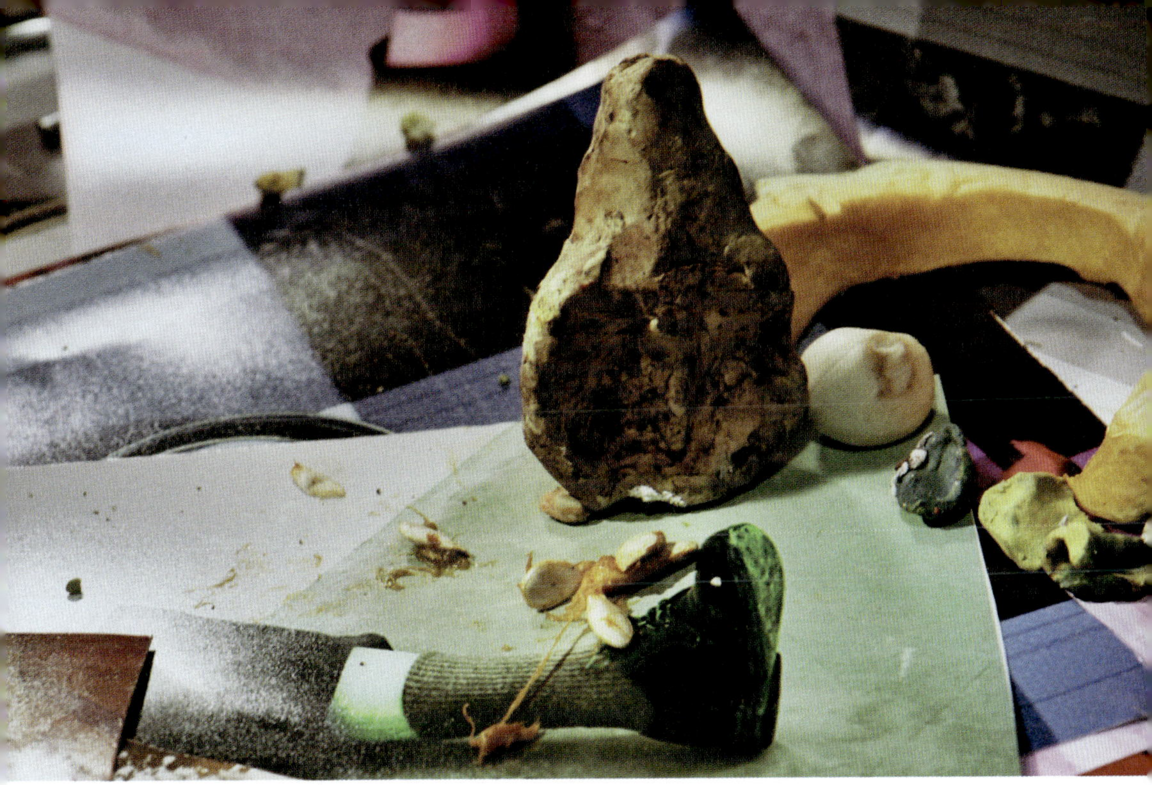

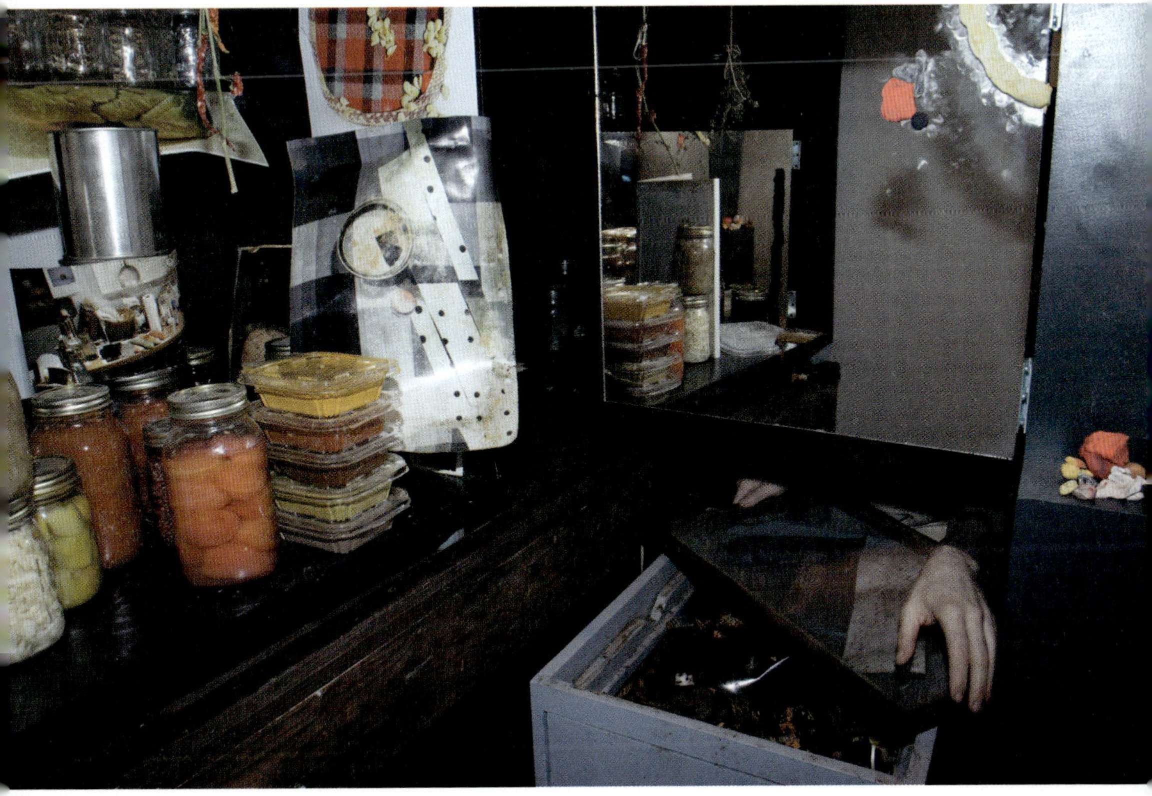

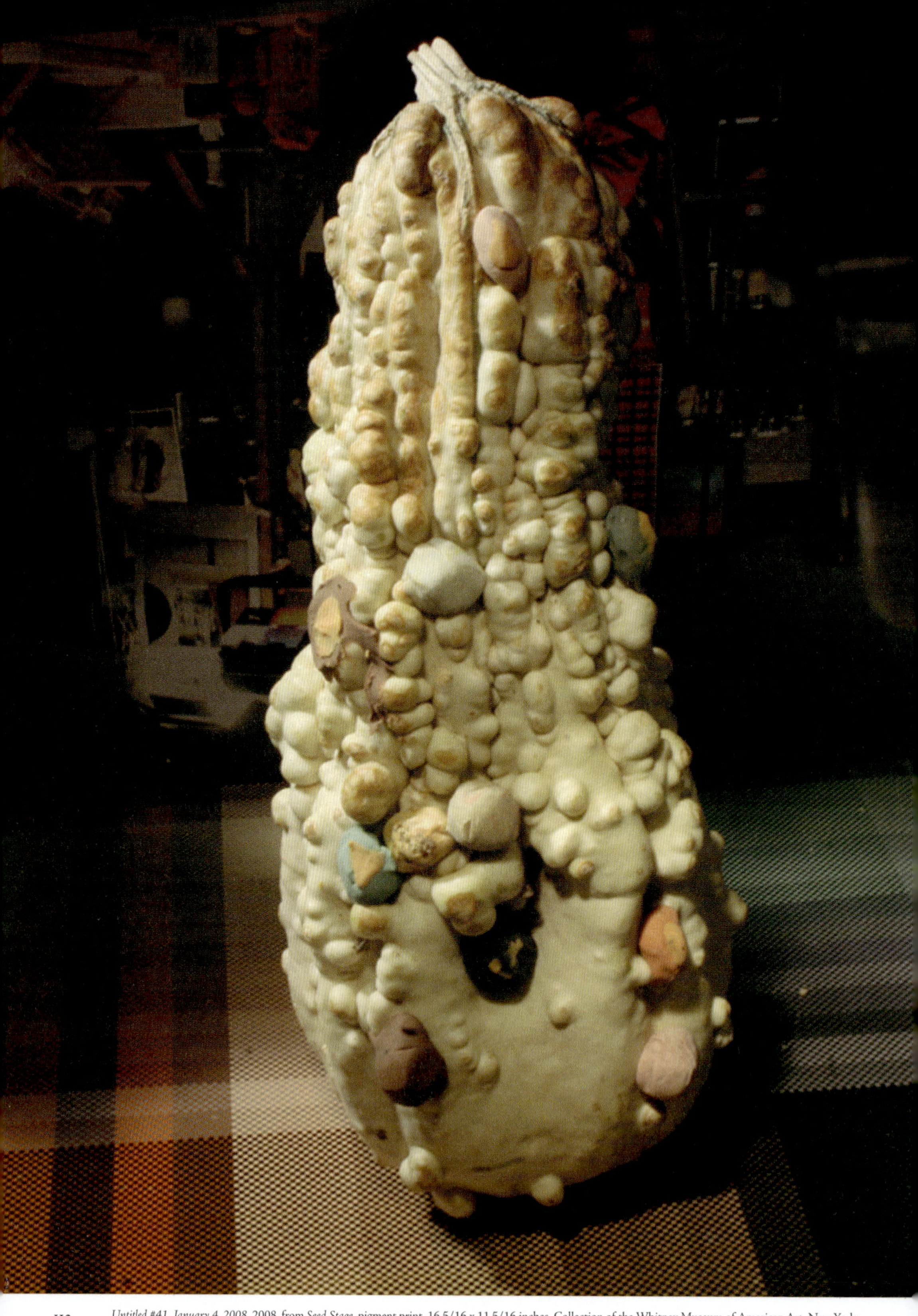

112   *Untitled #41, January 4, 2008*, 2008, from *Seed Stage*, pigment print, 16 5/16 x 11 5/16 inches. Collection of the Whitney Museum of American Art, New York; purchase, with funds from the Photography Committee and Henry Nias Foundation, 2009.28.41. Courtesy of the artist and Laurel Gitlen, New York.

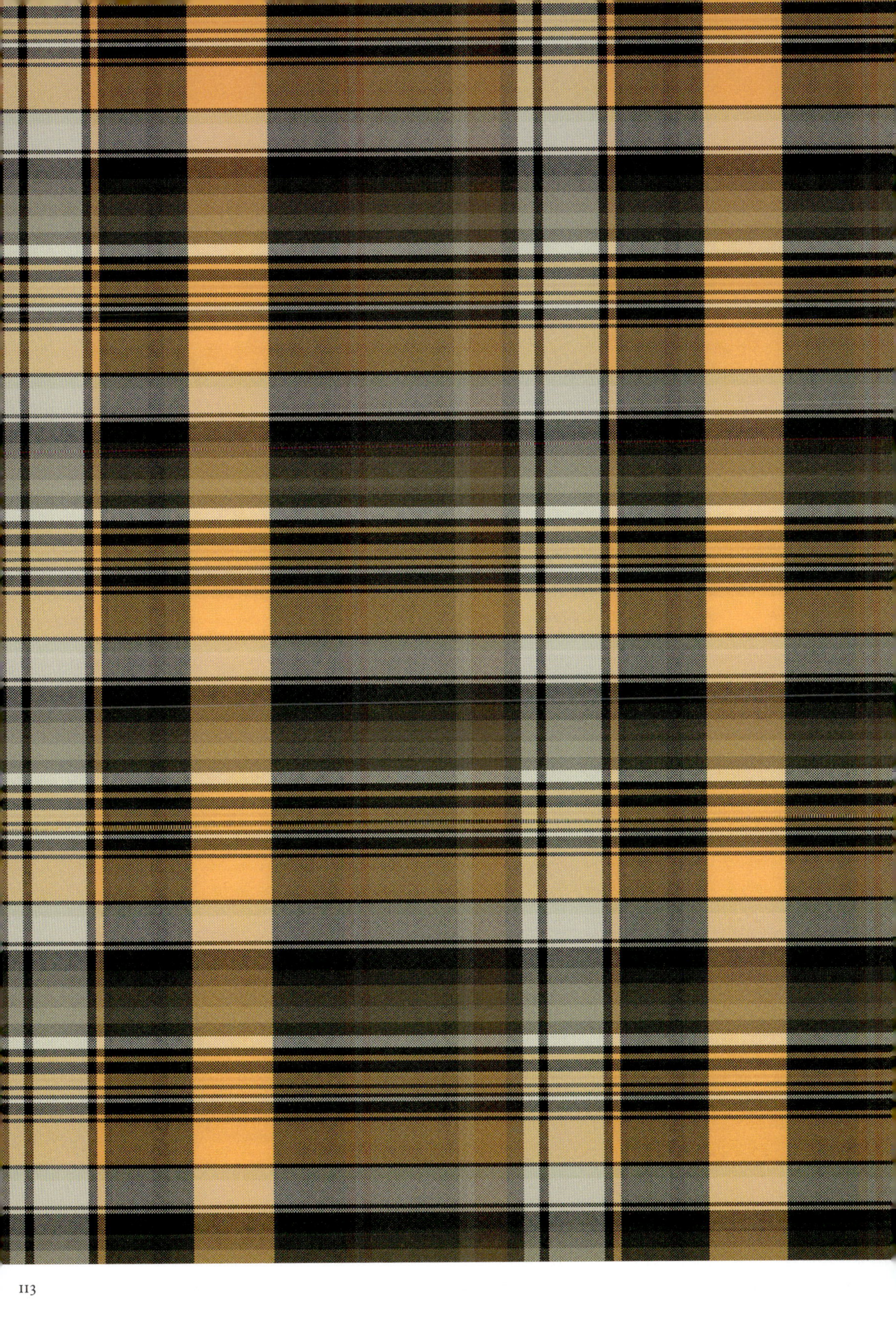

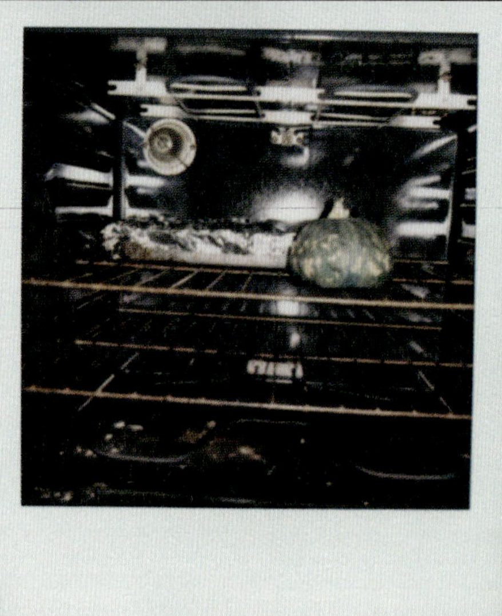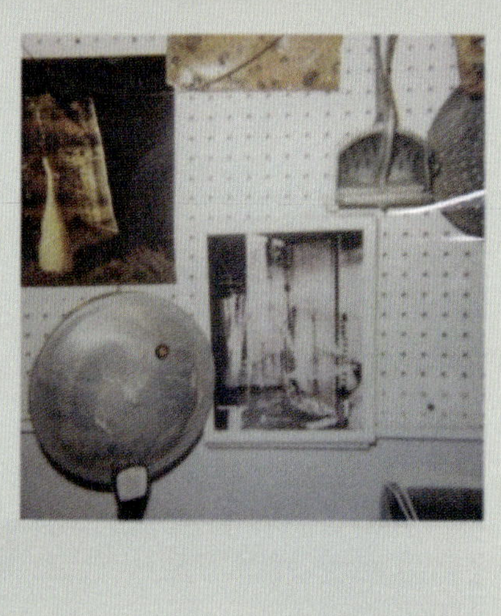

(left) *Untitled #35, November 14, 2008,* 2008, (right) *Untitled #64, January 4, 2009,* 2009, from *Seed Stage,* Polaroid photographs, 4 1/4 x 3 1/2 inches each; Collection of the Whitney Museum of American Art, New York, purchase, with funds from the Photography Committee and Henry Nias Foundation, 2009.28.35 and 2009.28.64.

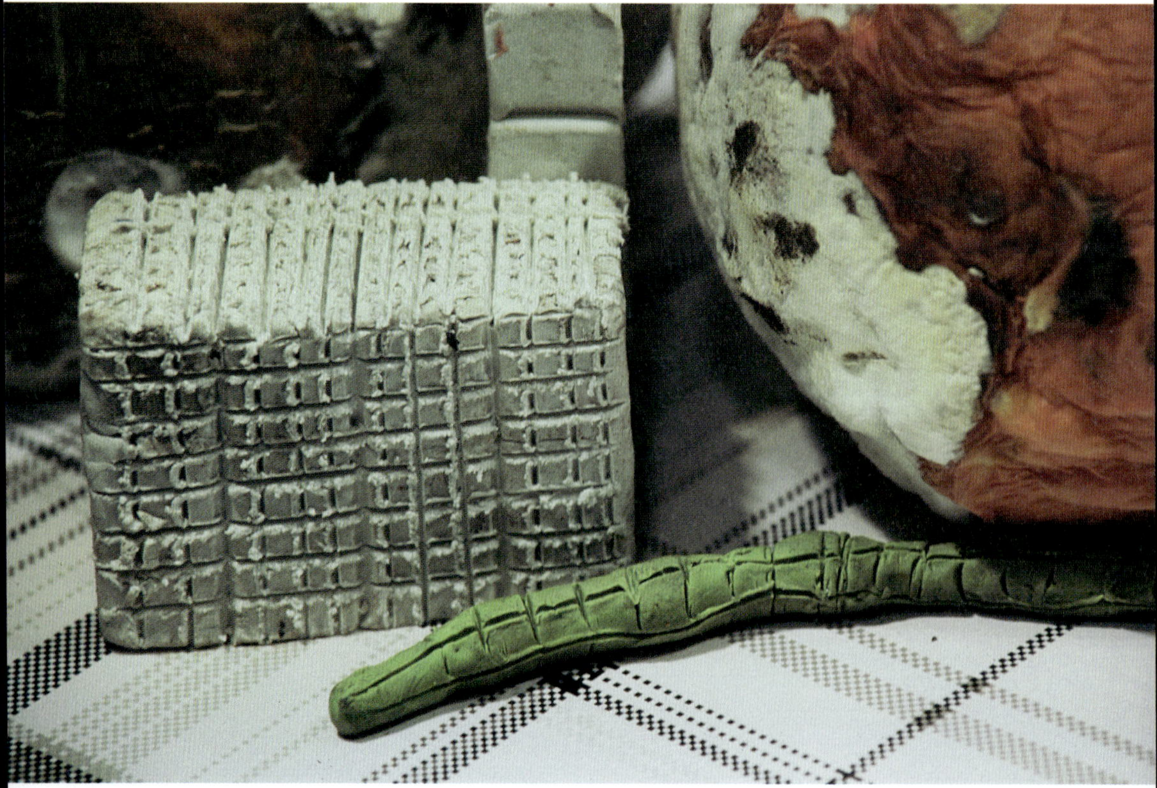

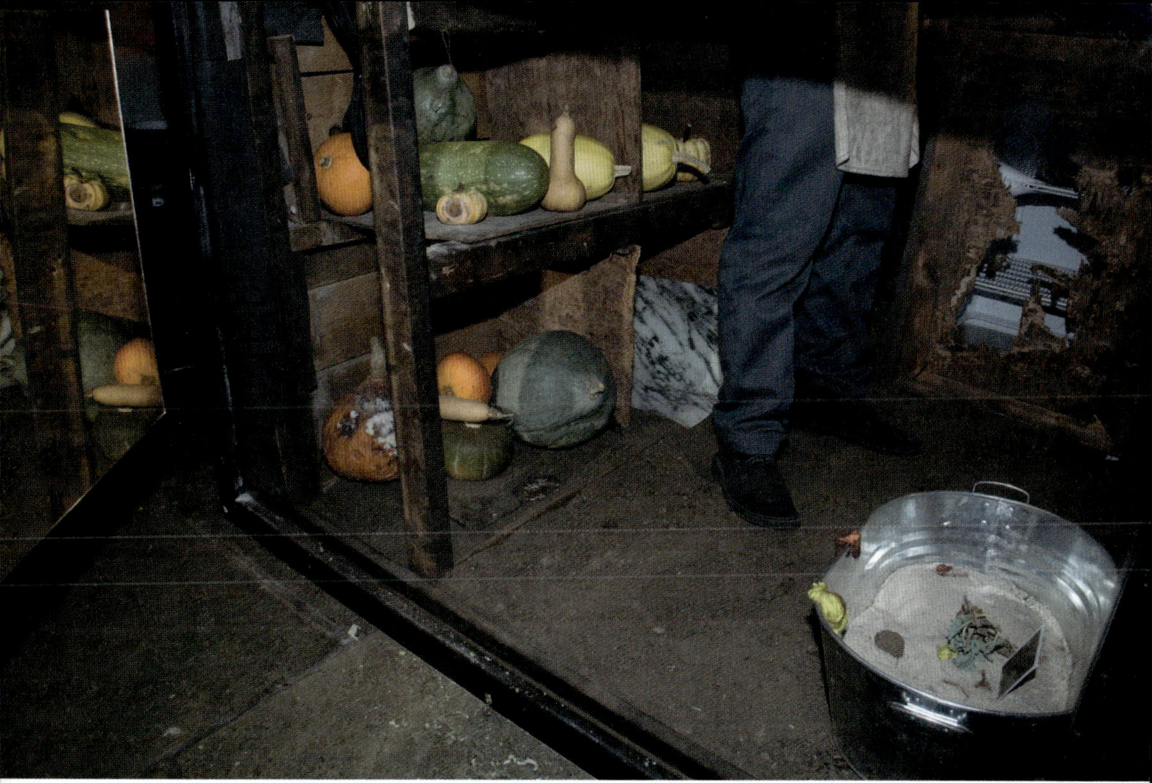

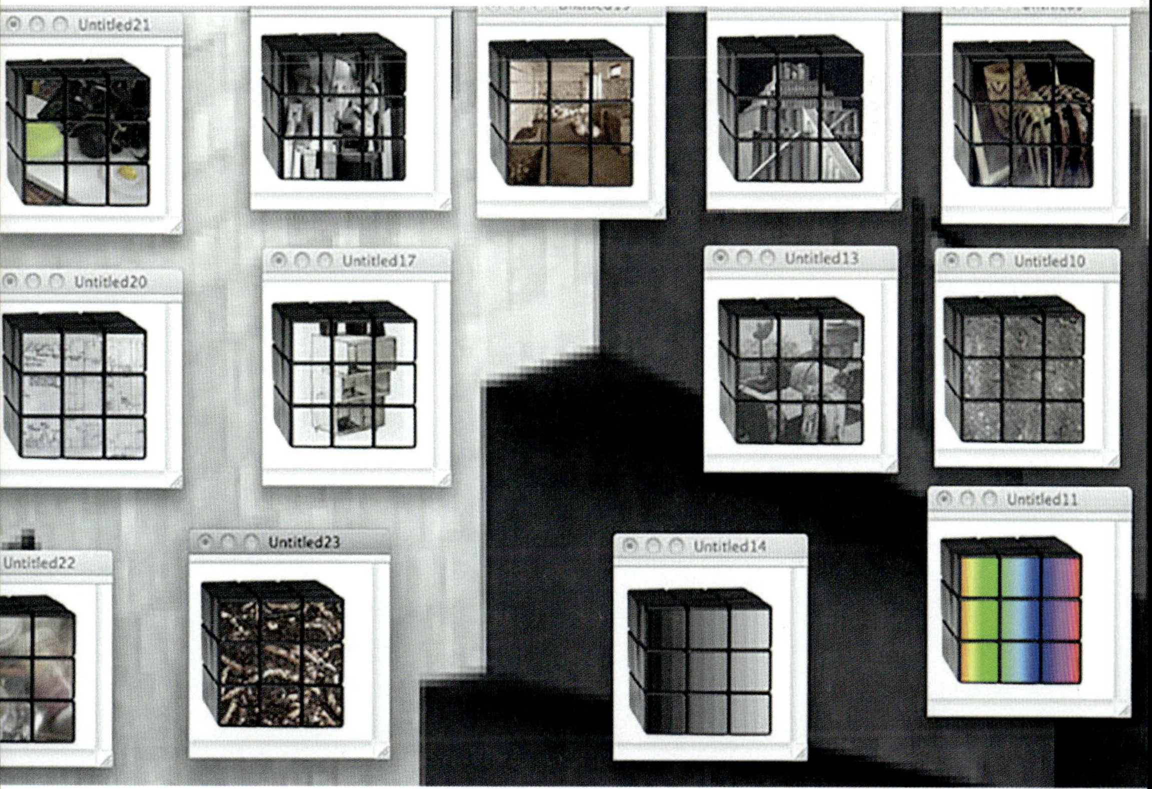

Untitled21
Untitled20
Untitled17
Untitled13
Untitled10
Untitled22
Untitled23
Untitled14
Untitled11

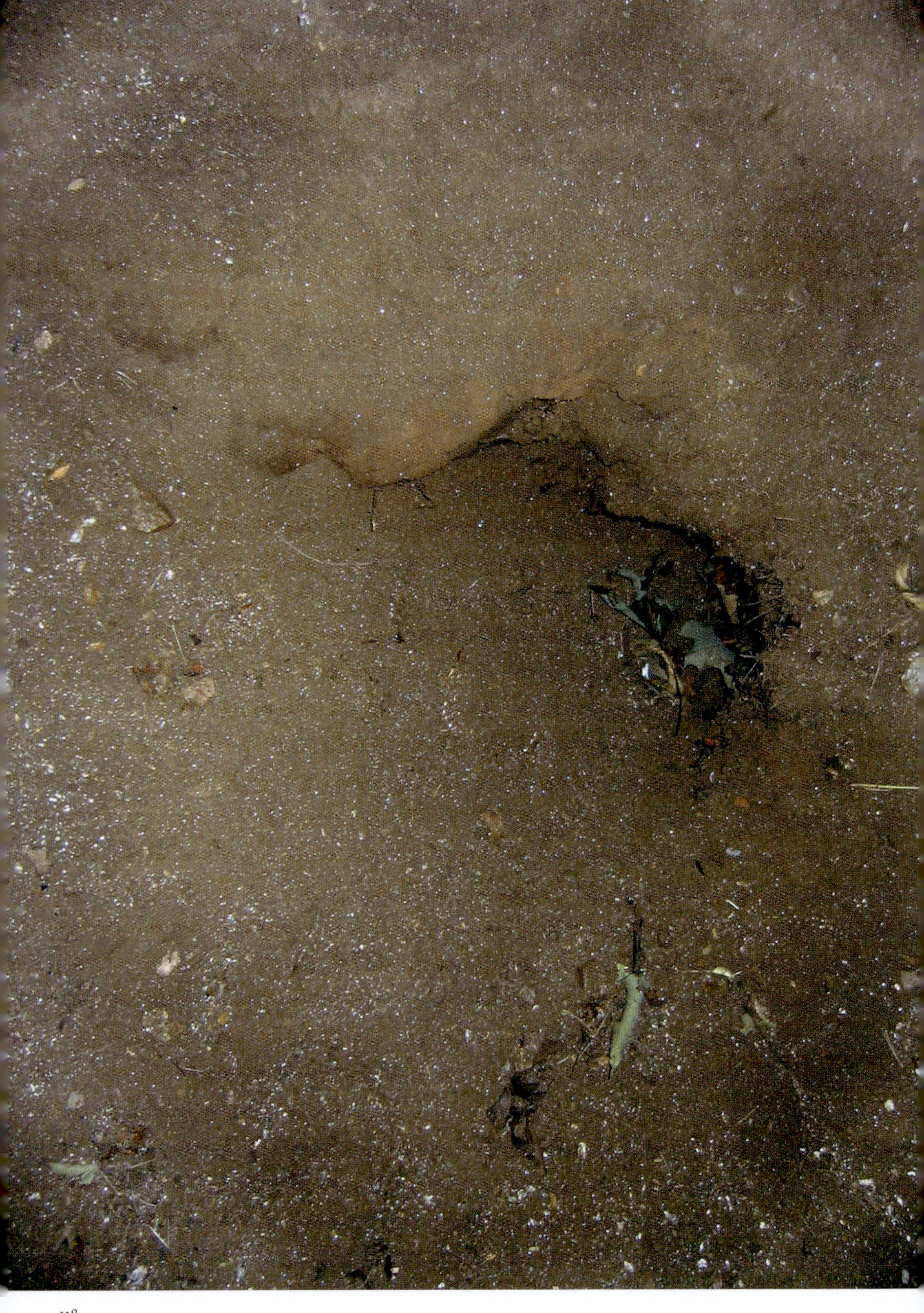

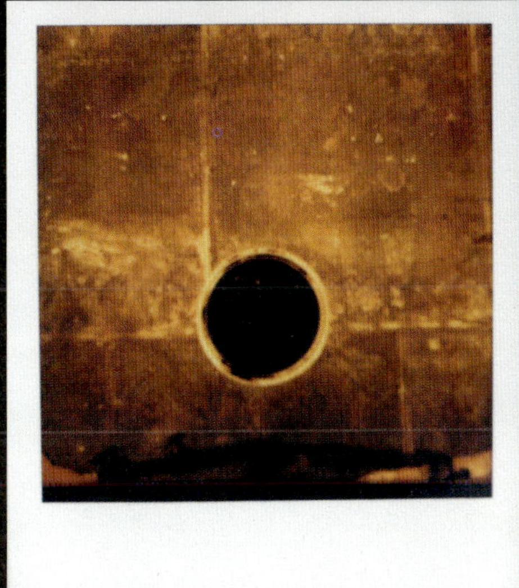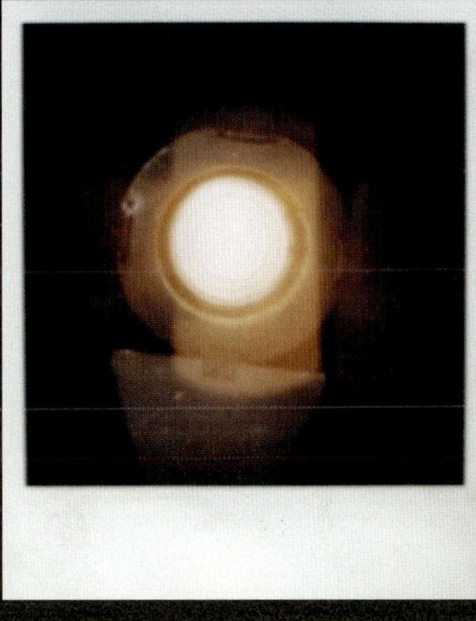

 (left) *Untitled #3, October 1, 2008*, 2008; (right) *Untitled #27, November 2, 2008*, 2008, from *Seed Stage*, Polaroid photographs, 4 1/4 x 3 1/2 inches each. Collection of the Whitney Museum of American Art, New York, purchase, with funds from the Photography Committee and Henry Nias Foundation, 2009.28.3 and 2009.28.27.

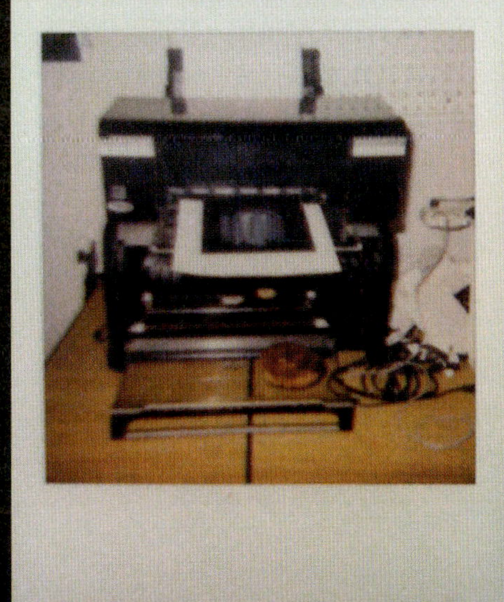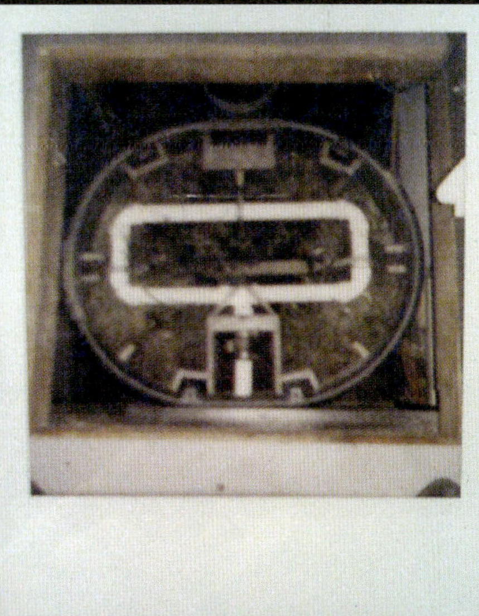

 (left) *Untitled #36, November 14, 2008*, 2008; (right) *Untitled #5, October 4, 2008*, 2008, from *Seed Stage*, Polaroid photographs, 4 1/4 x 3 1/2 inches each. Collection of the Whitney Museum of American Art, New York, purchase, with funds from the Photography Committee and Henry Nias Foundation, 2009.28.36 and 2009.28.5.

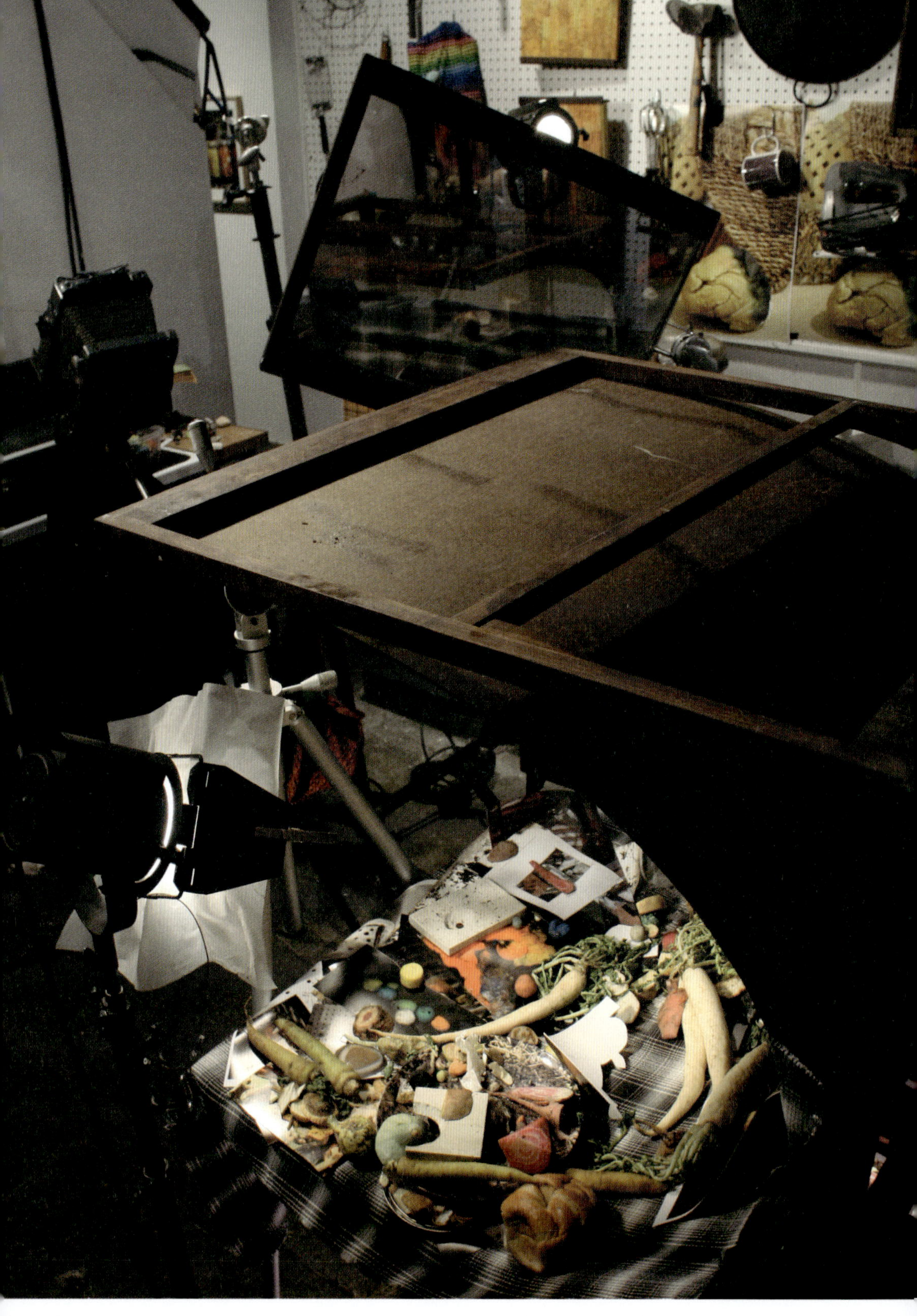

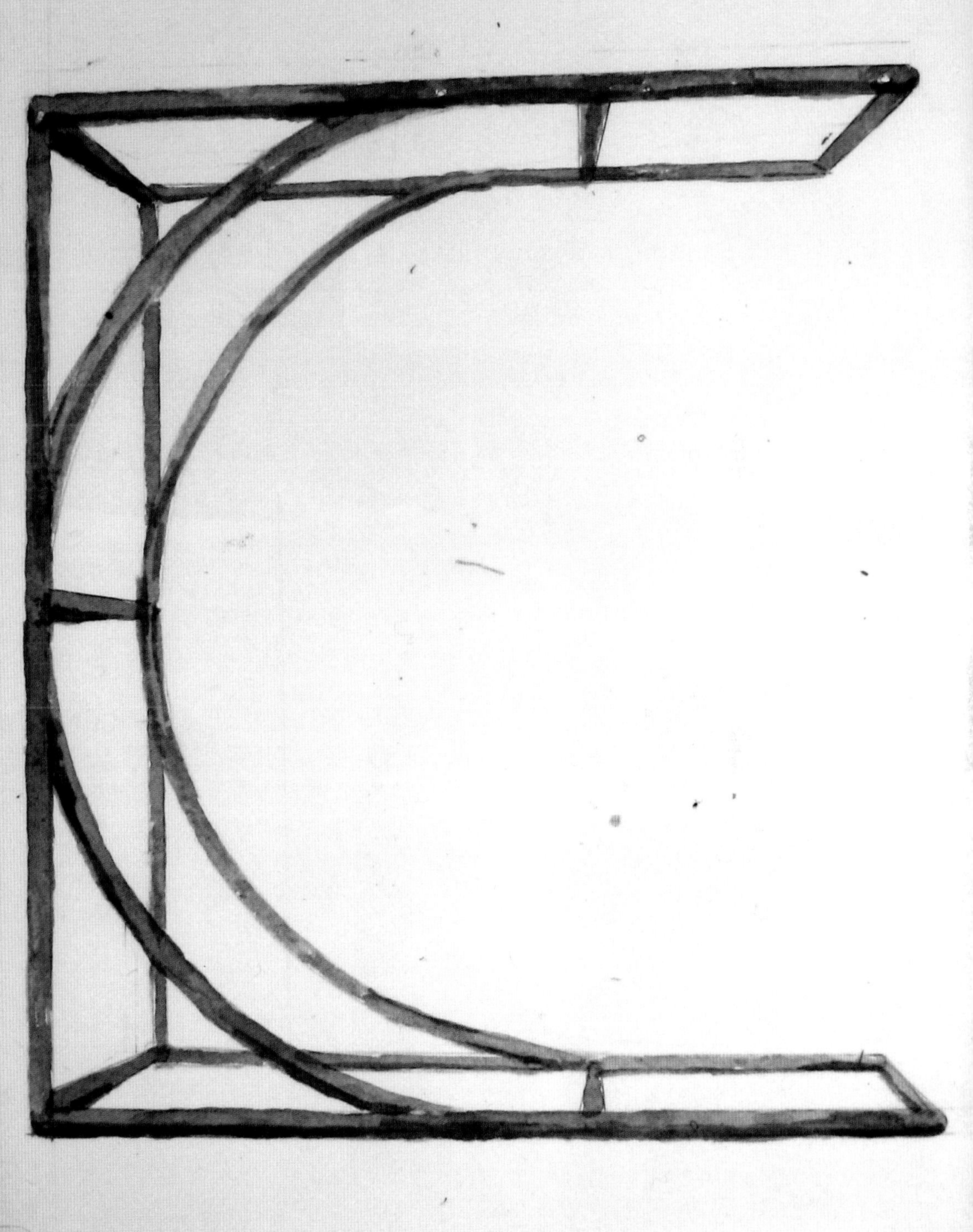

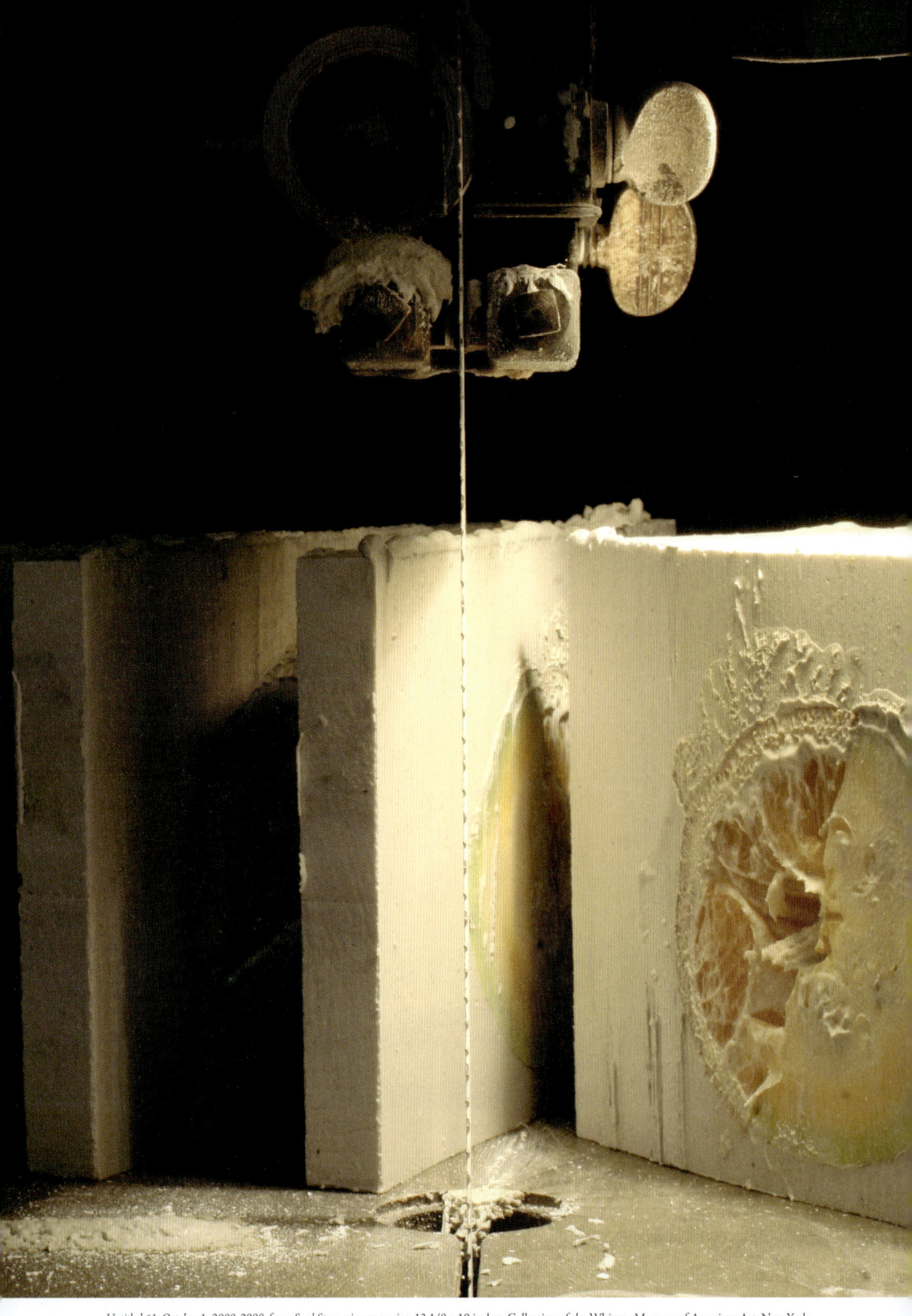

123   *Untitled #1, October 1, 2008*, 2008, from *Seed Stage*, pigment print, 13 1/8 x 10 inches. Collection of the Whitney Museum of American Art, New York; purchase, with funds from the Photography Committee and Henry Nias Foundation, 2009.28.1. Courtesy of the artist and Laurel Gitlen, New York.

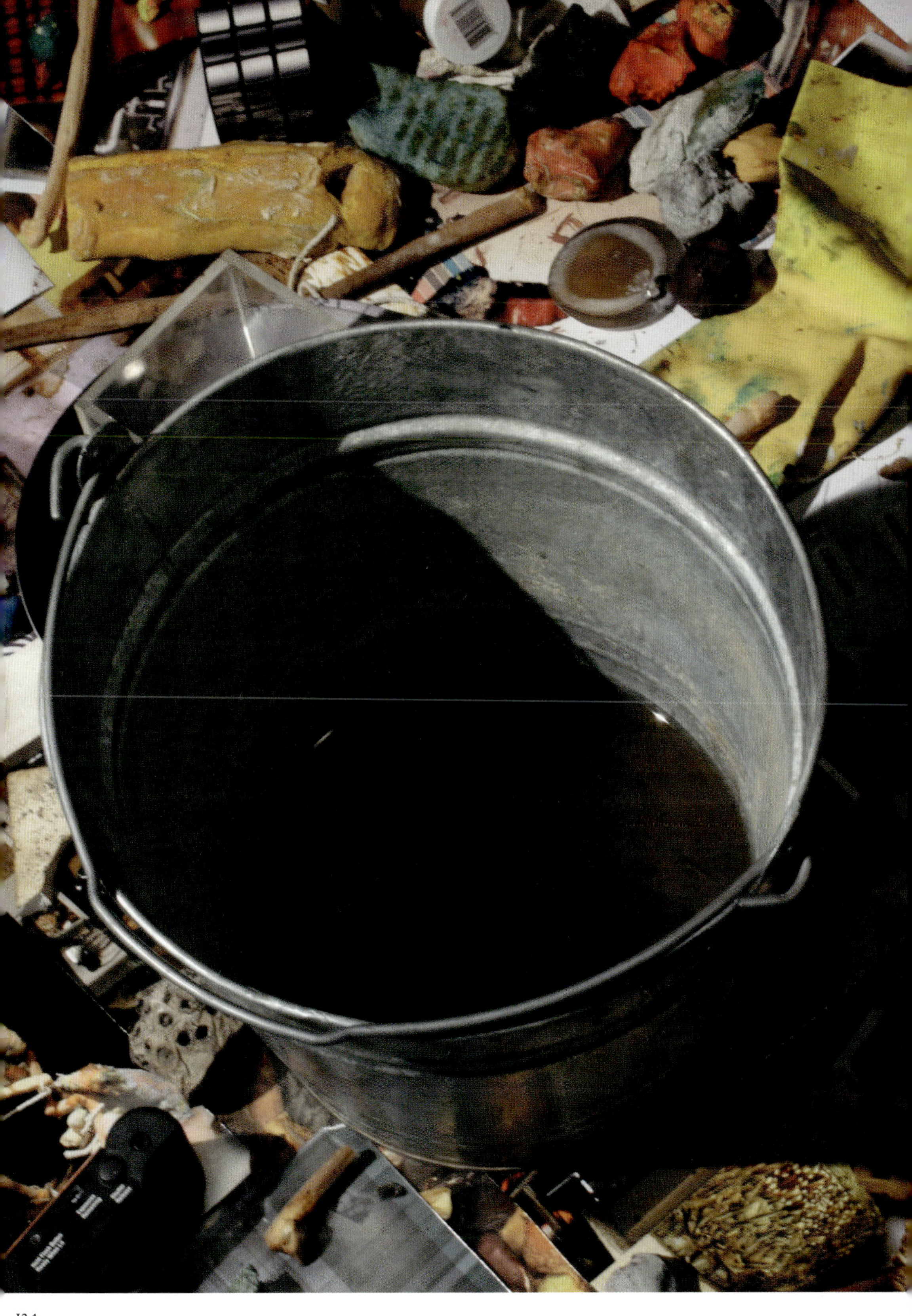

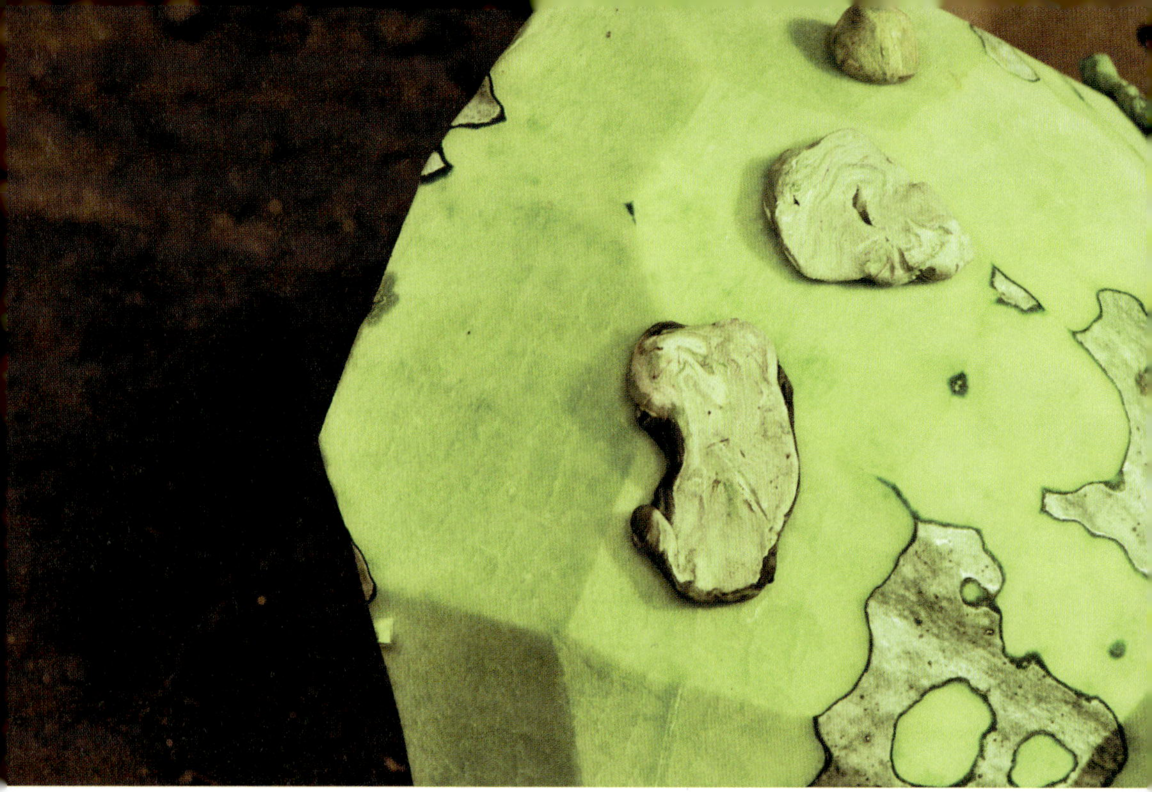

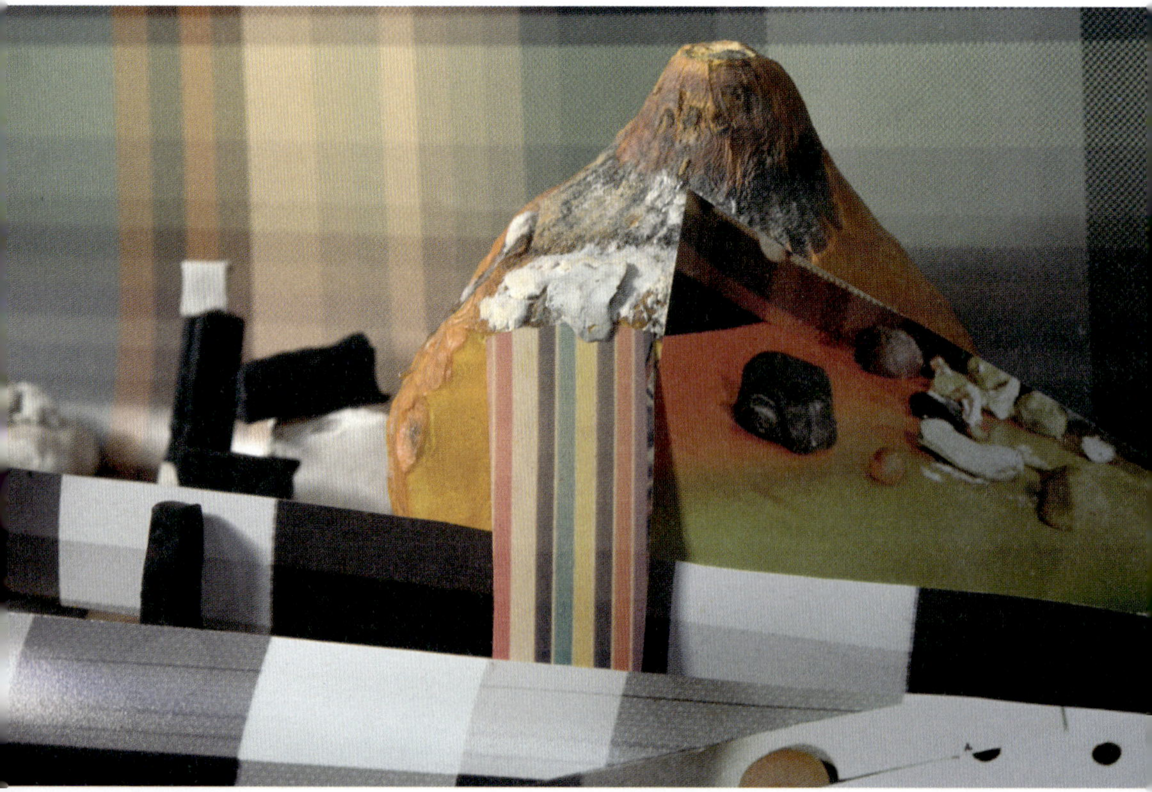

126 *Untitled #65, January 4, 2009,* 2009, from *Seed Stage,* pigment print, 14 x 21 inches. Collection of the Whitney Museum of American Art, New York; purchase, with funds from the Photography Committee and Henry Nias Foundation, 2009.28.65. Courtesy of the artist and Laurel Gitlen, New York.

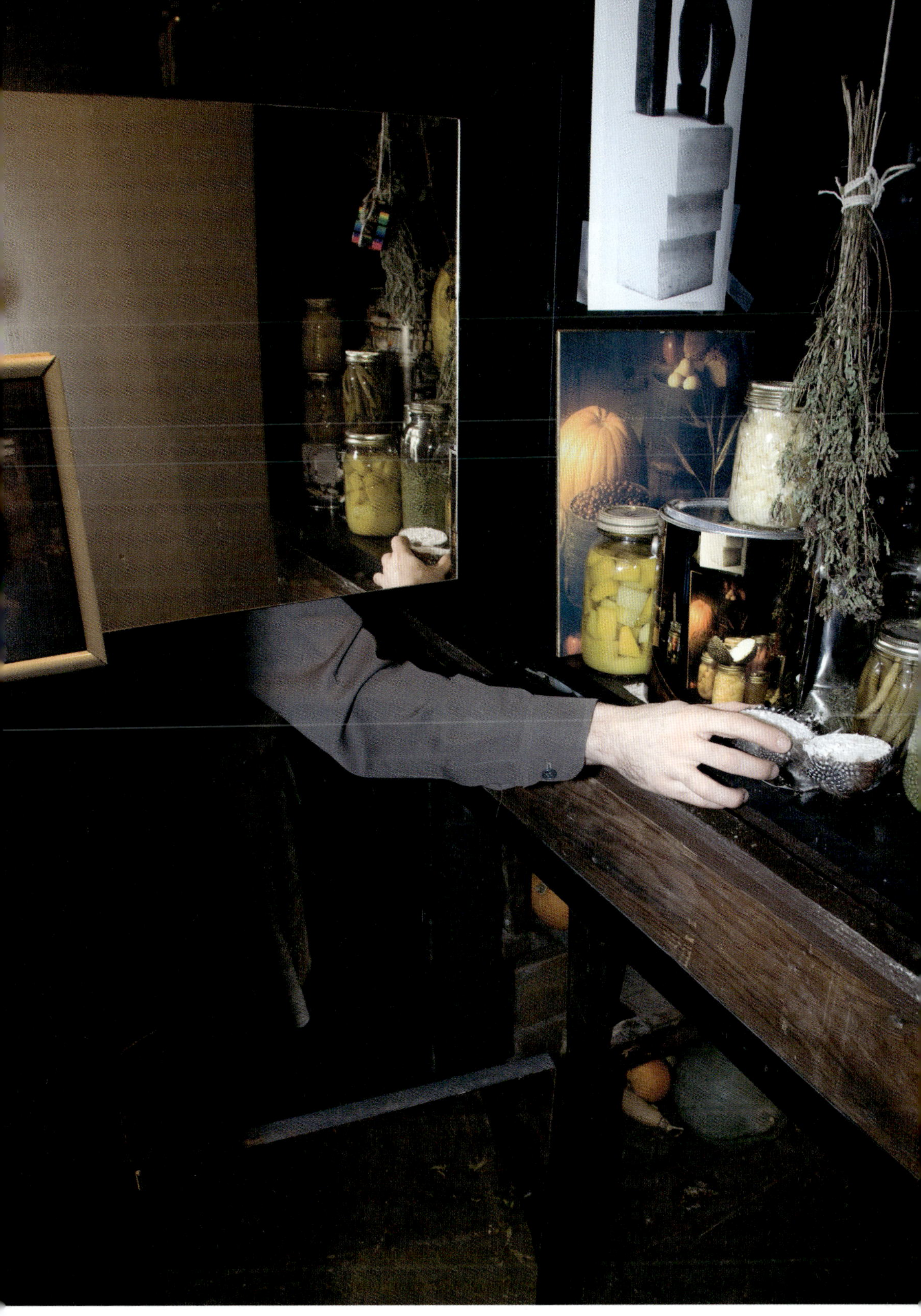

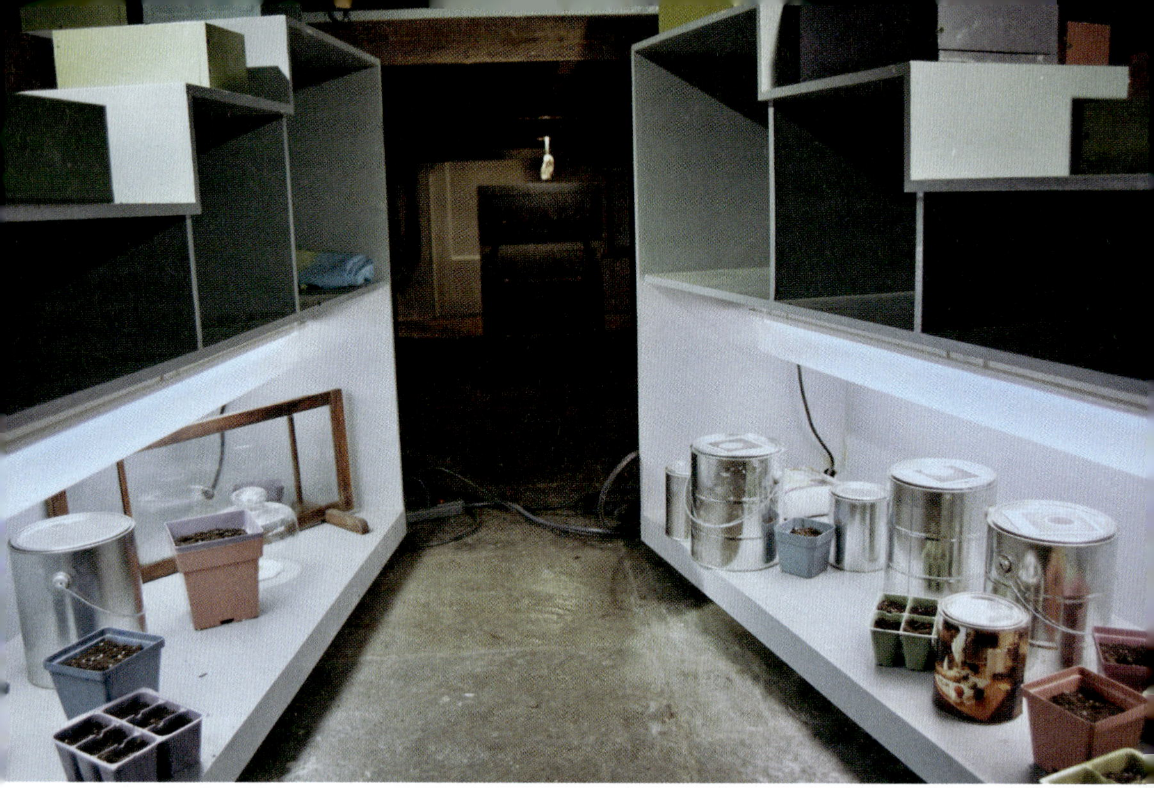

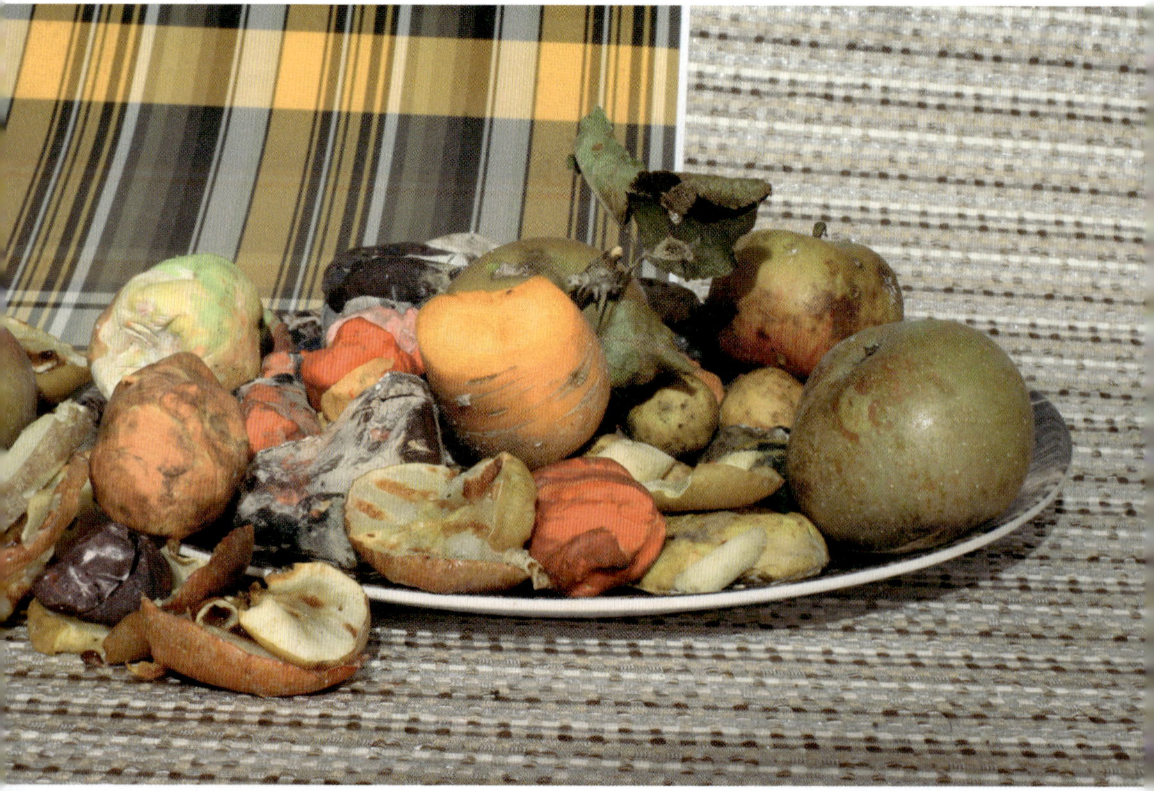

Untitled #4, October 3, 2008, 2008, from *Seed Stage,* pigment print, 36 1/2 x 53 1/4 inches. Collection of the Whitney Museum of American Art, New York; purchase, with funds from the Photography Committee and Henry Nias Foundation, 2009.28.4. Courtesy of the artist and Laurel Gitlen, New York.

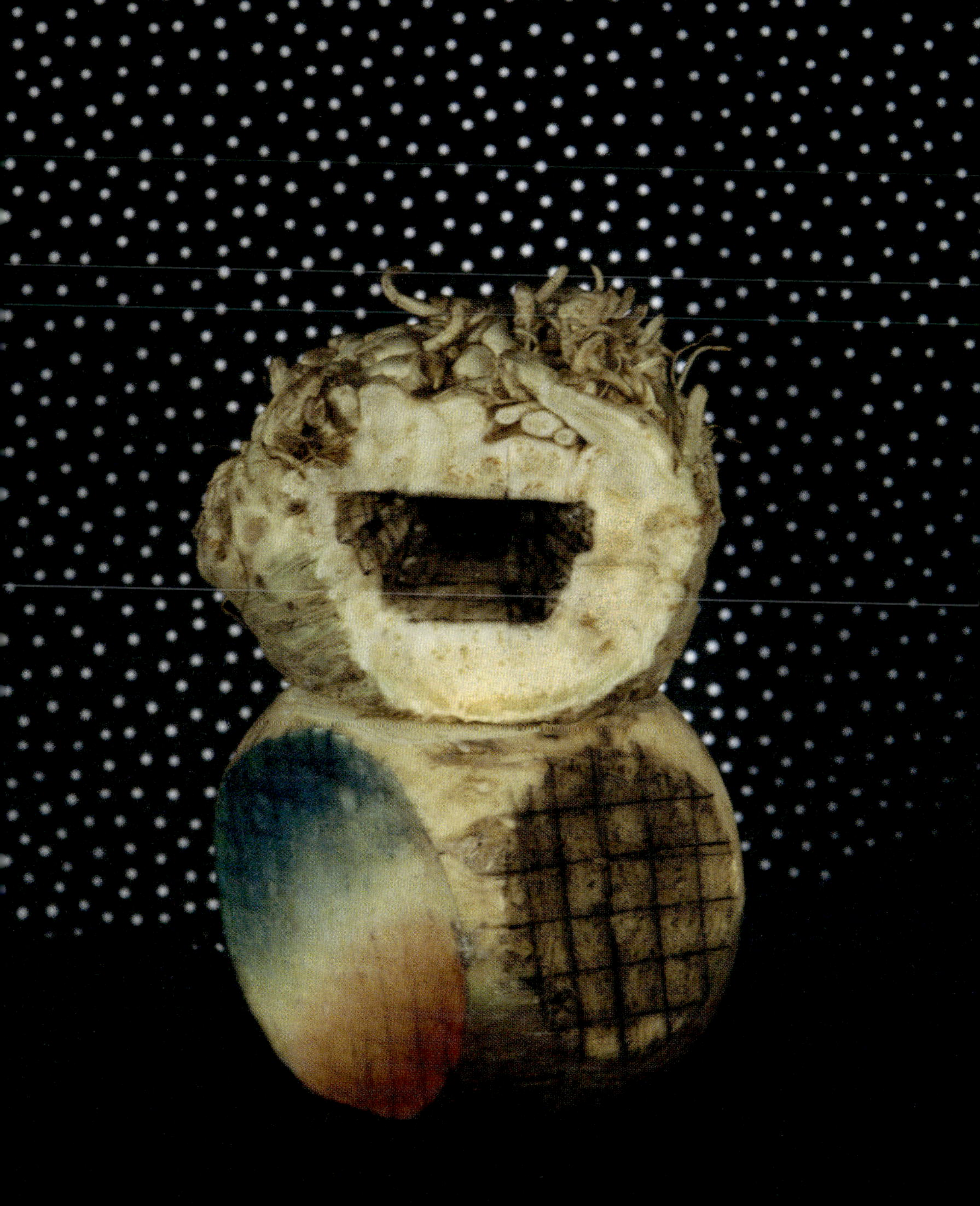

 Untitled #71, January 4, 2009, 2009, from *Seed Stage,* pigment print, 36 1/2 x 53 1/4 inches. Collection of the Whitney Museum of American Art, New York; purchase, with funds from the Photography Committee and Henry Nias Foundation, 2009.28.71. Courtesy of the artist and Laurel Gitlen, New York.

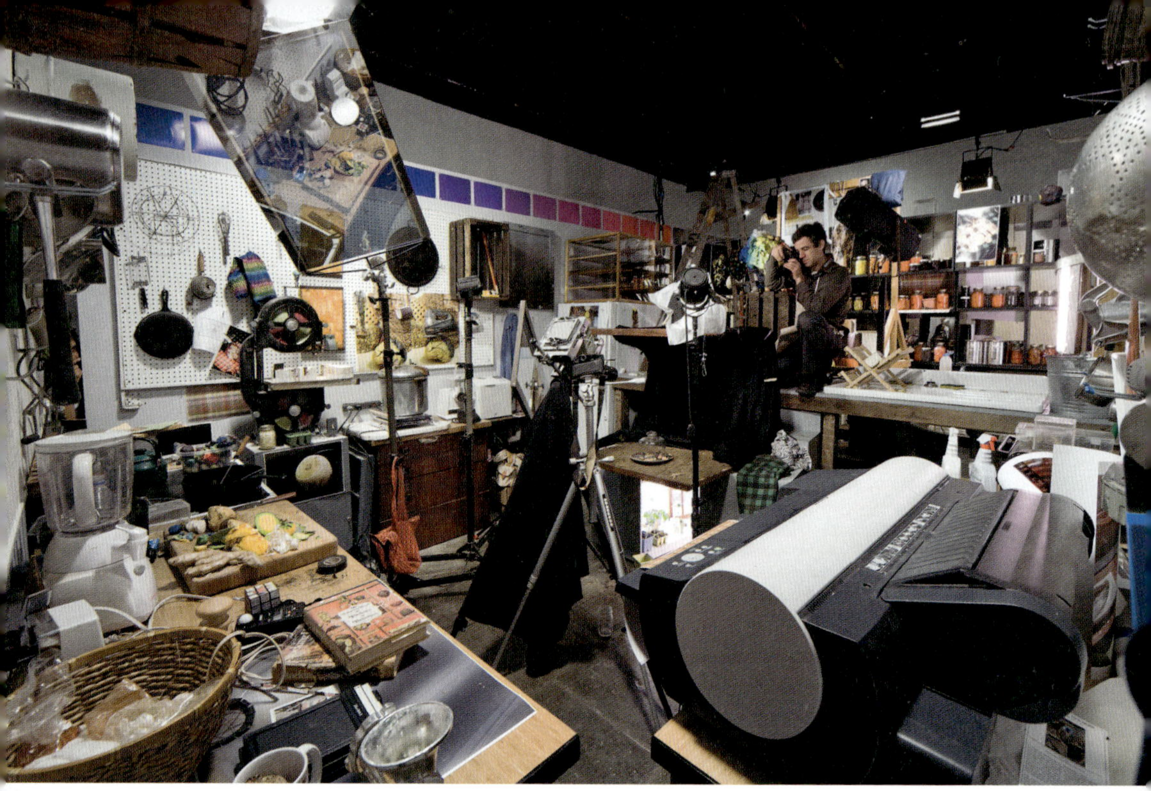

 Untitled #8, October 5, 2008, 2008, from *Seed Stage*, pigment print, 10 x 15 inches. Collection of the Whitney Museum of American Art, New York; purchase, with funds from the Photography Committee and Henry Nias Foundation, 2009.28.8. Courtesy of the artist and Laurel Gitlen, New York.

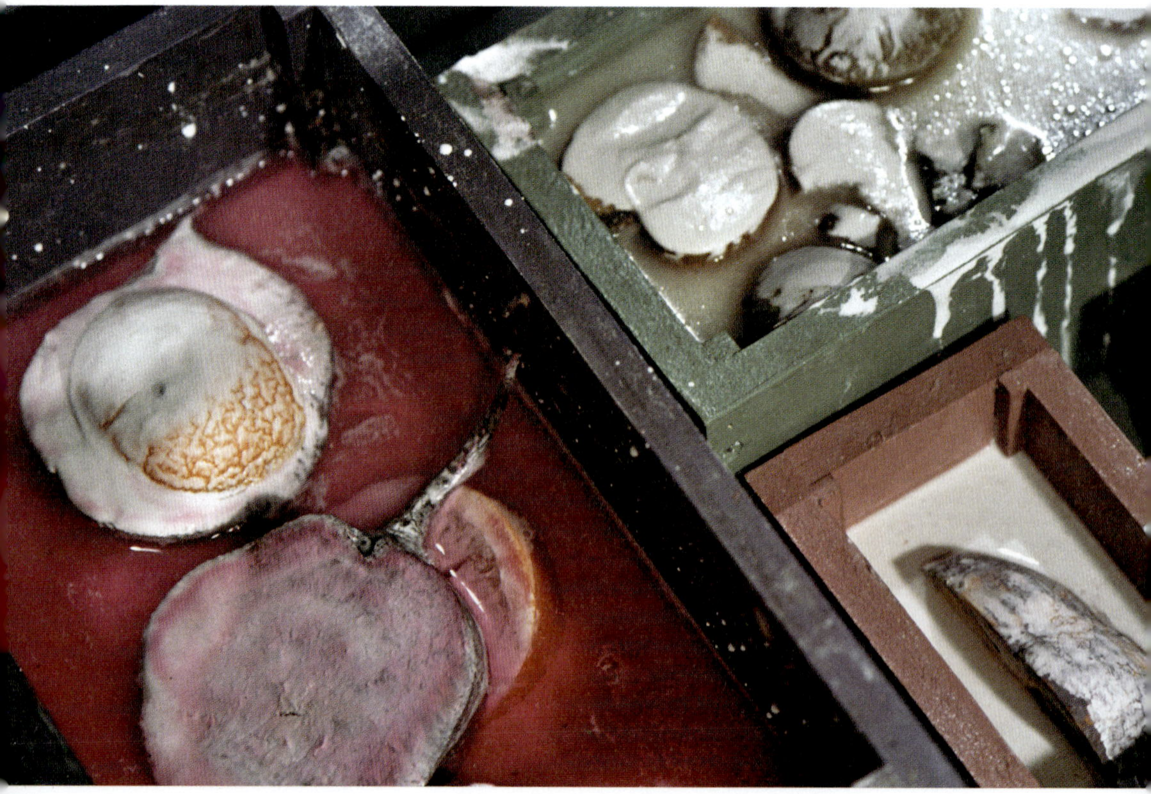

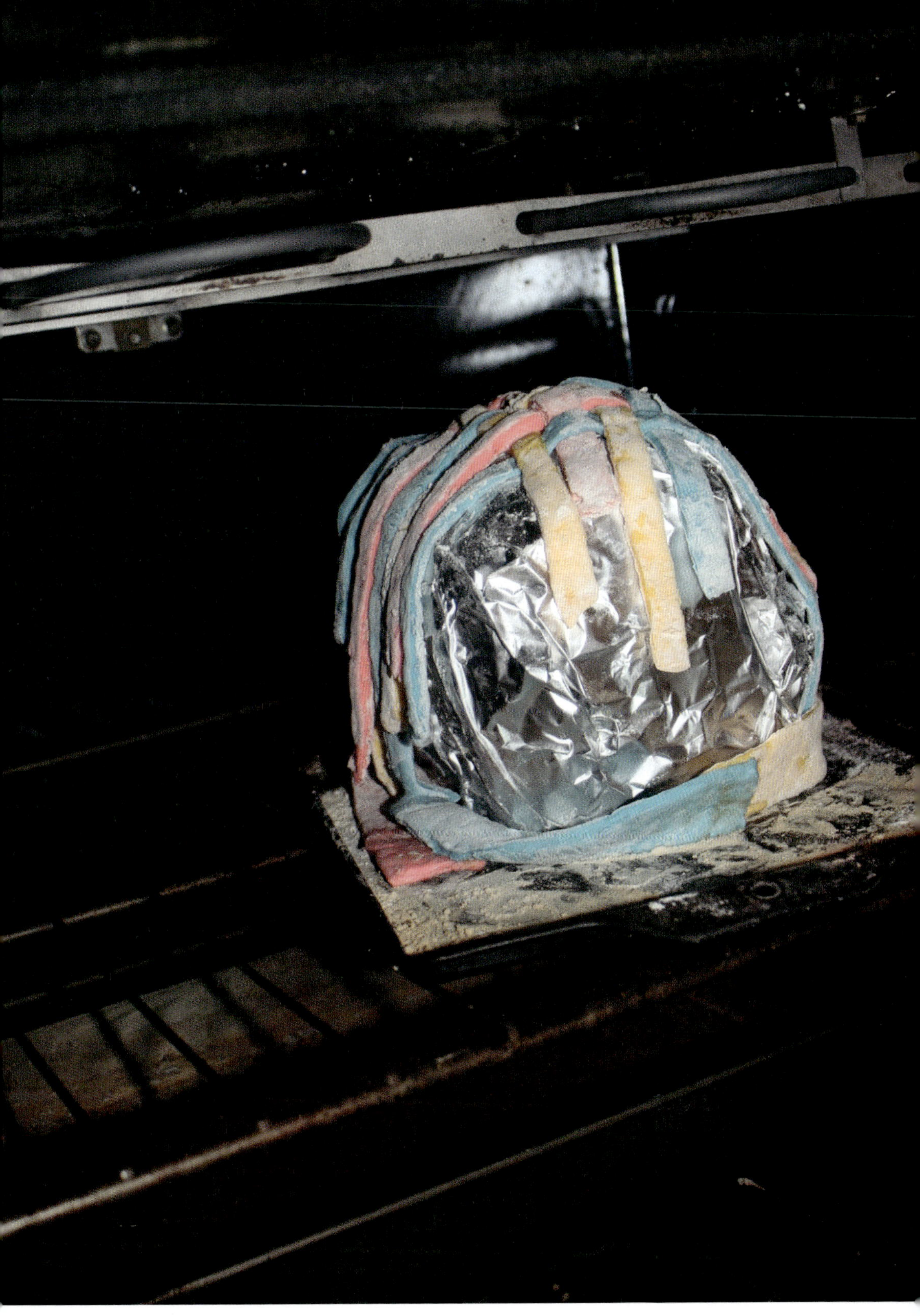

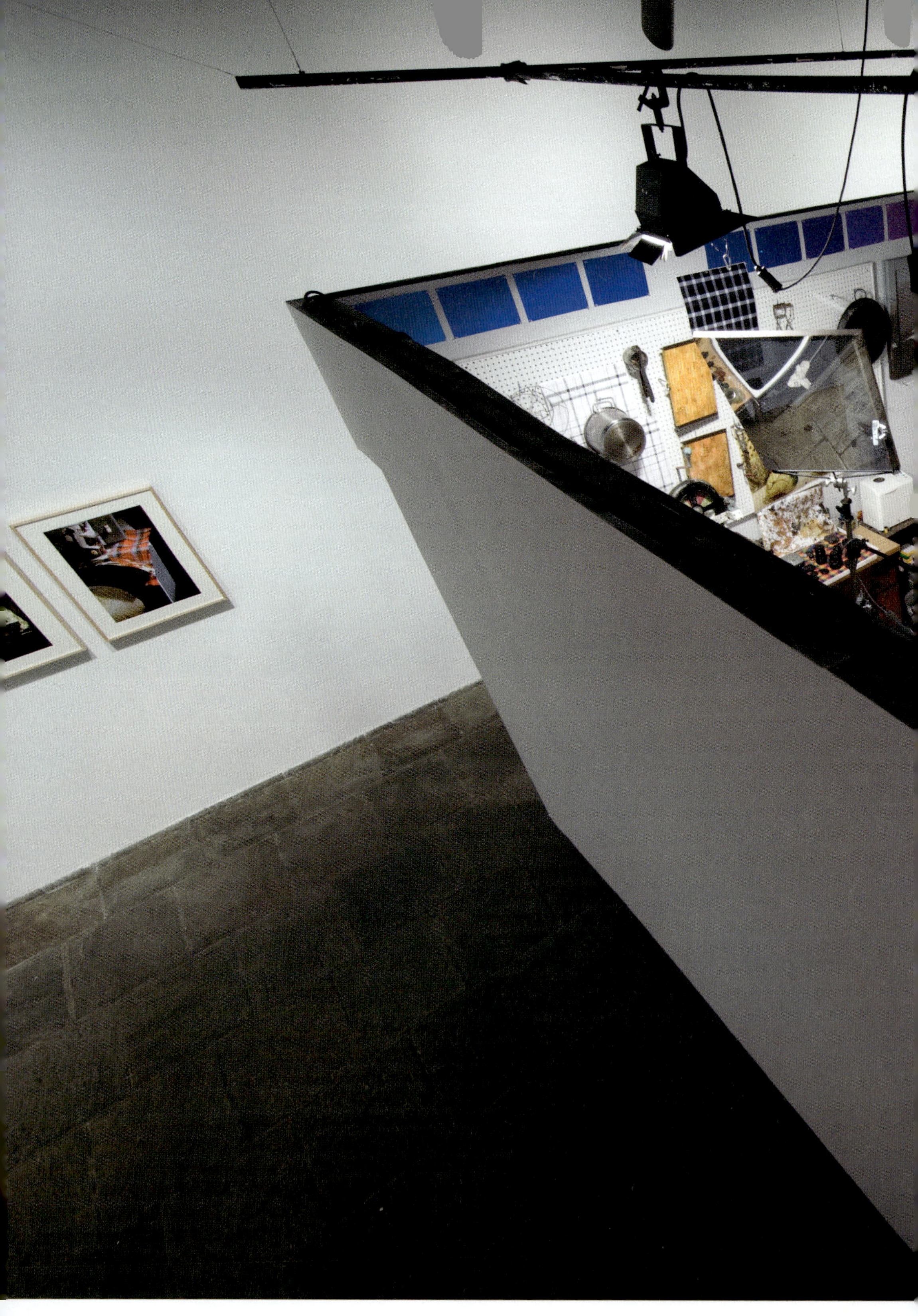

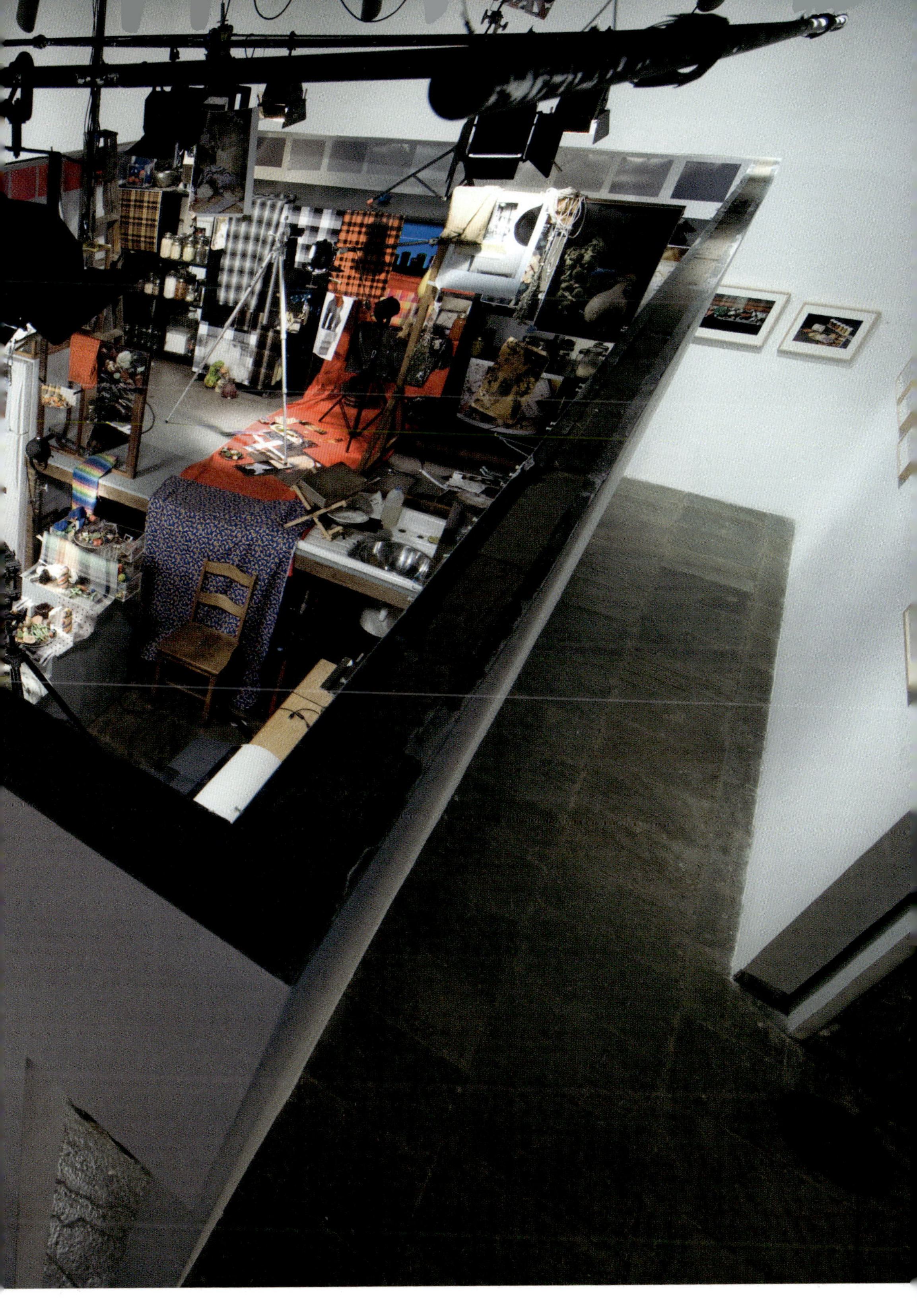

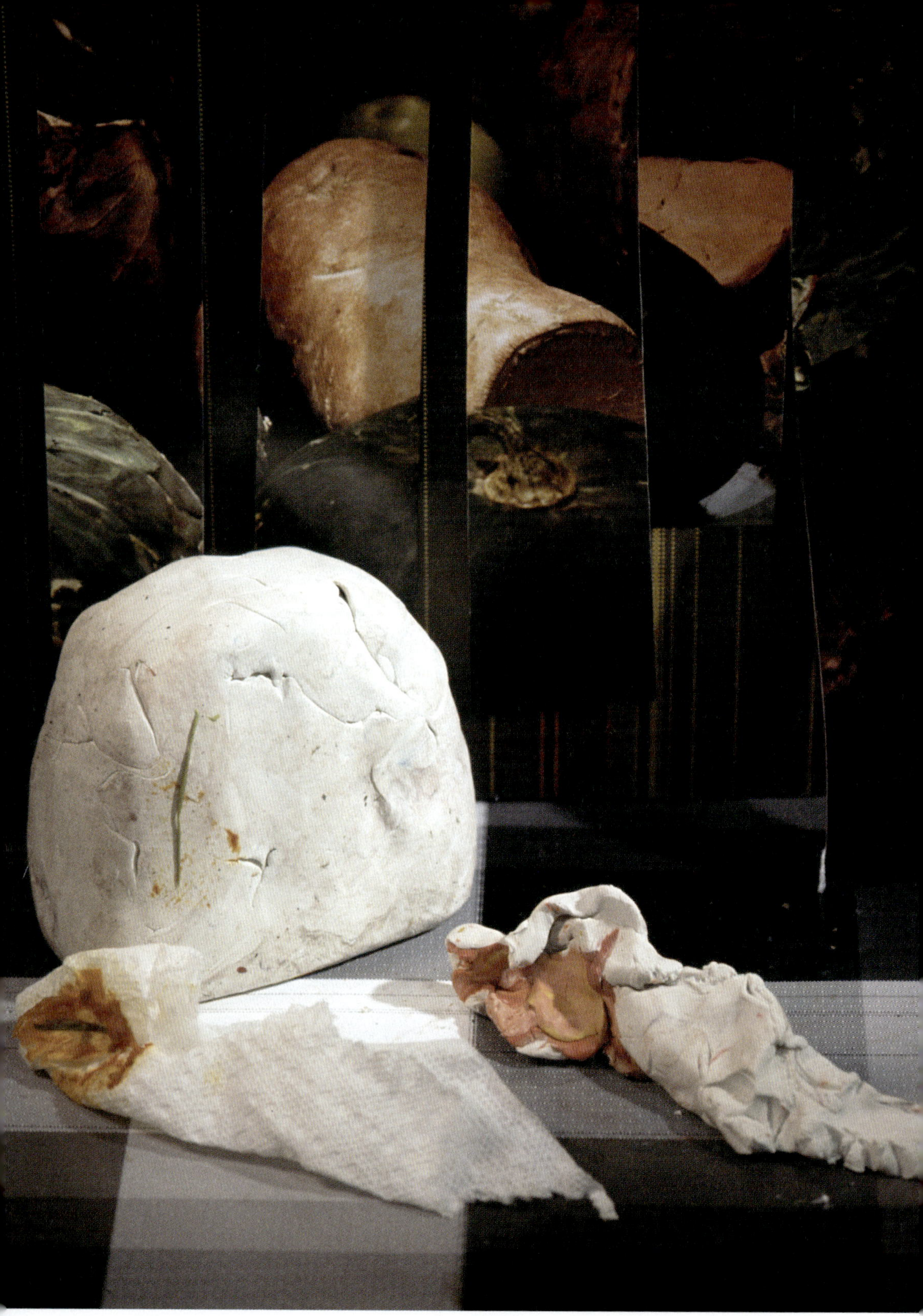

 Untitled #47, December 13, 2008, 2008, from *Seed Stage*, pigment print, 16 x 10 9/16 inches. Collection of the Whitney Museum of American Art, New York; purchase, with funds from the Photography Committee and Henry Nias Foundation, 2009.28.47. Courtesy of the artist and Laurel Gitlen, New York.

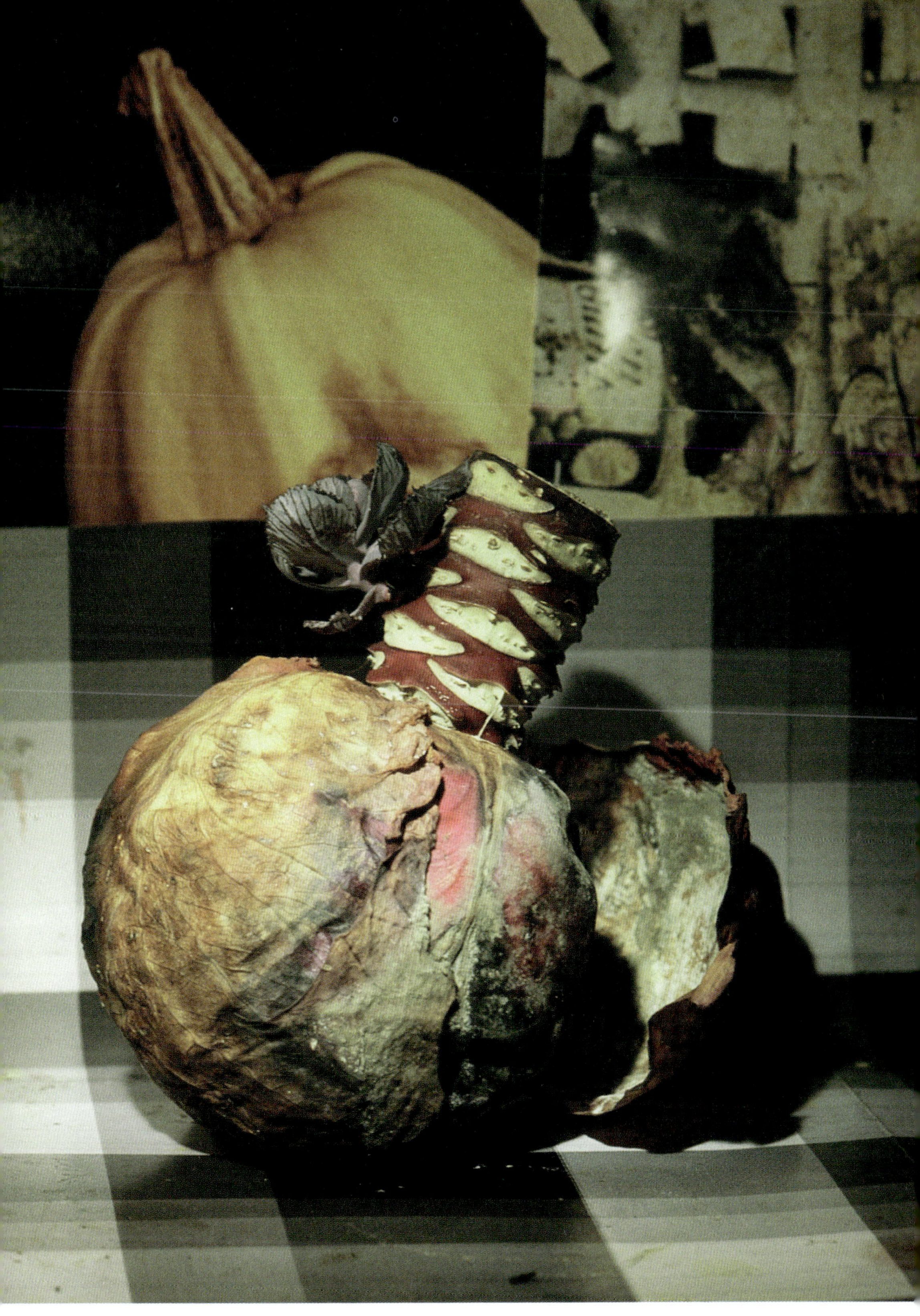

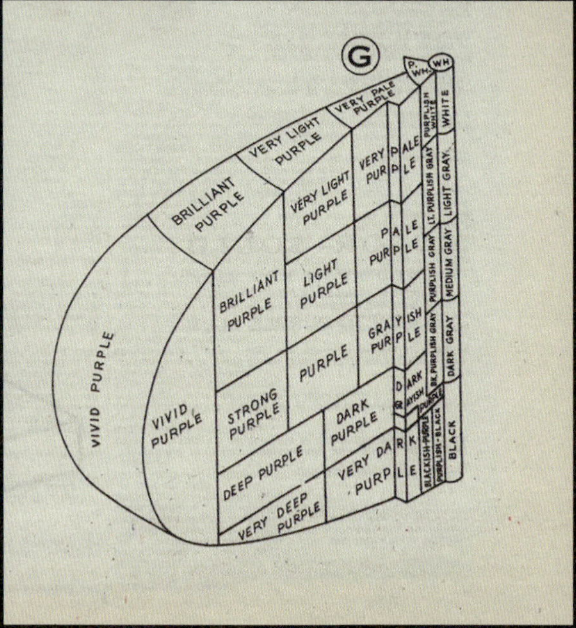

G
P. WH.
WH
VERY PALE PURPLE
VERY LIGHT PURPLE
PURPLISH WHITE
WHITE
BRILLIANT PURPLE
VERY LIGHT PURPLE
VERY PALE PURPLE
LT. PURPLISH GRAY
PURPLISH GRAY
LIGHT GRAY.
PALE PURPLE
BRILLIANT PURPLE
LIGHT PURPLE
MEDIUM GRAY
VIVID PURPLE
PURPLE
GRAYISH PURPLE
BK. PURPLISH GRAY
DARK GRAY
VIVID PURPLE
STRONG PURPLE
PURPLE
GRAYISH PURPLE
DARK GRAYISH PURPLE
DEEP PURPLE
DARK PURPLE
DARK GRAYISH PURPLE
BLACKISH PURPLE
PURPLISH BLACK
BLACK
VERY DARK PURPLE
VERY DEEP PURPLE

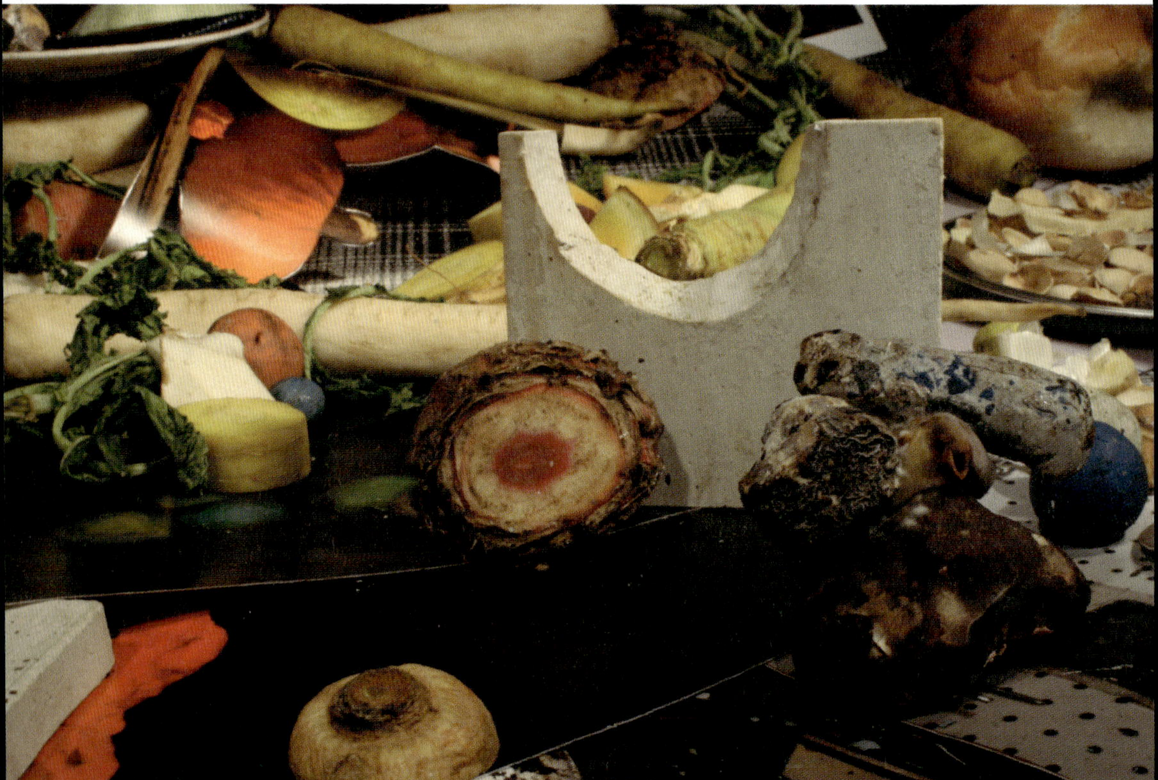

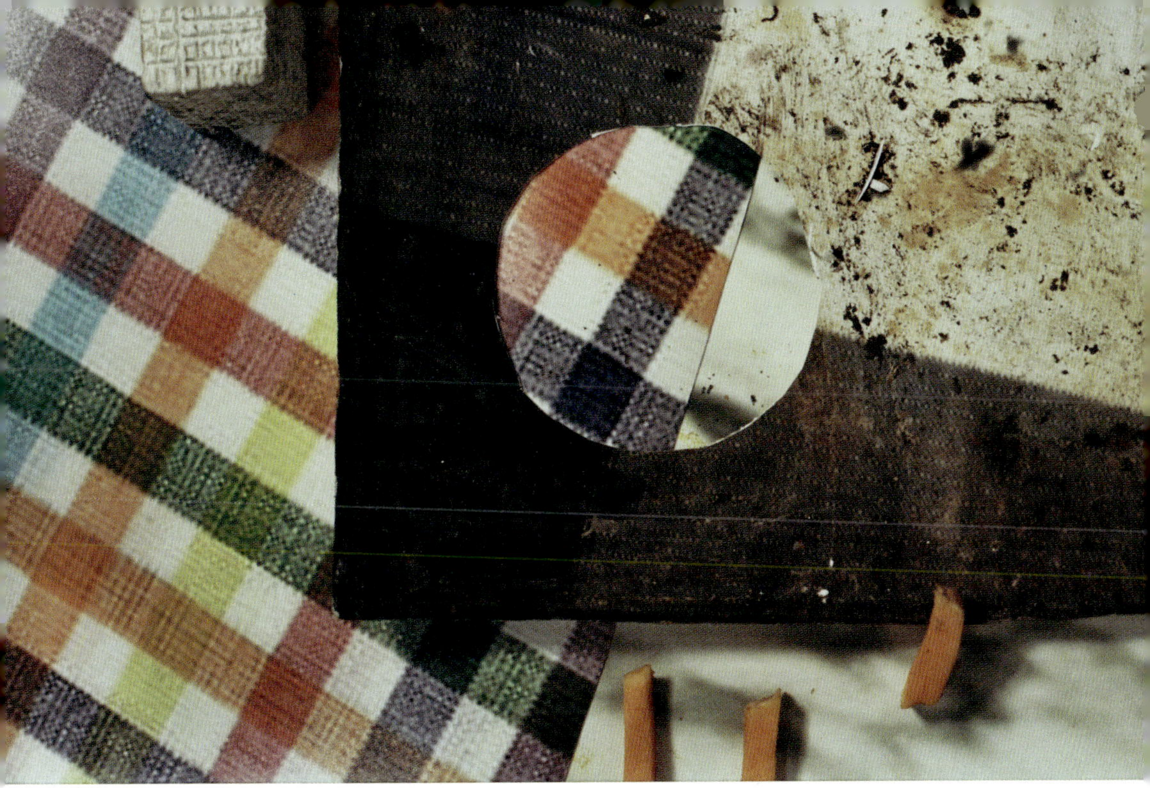

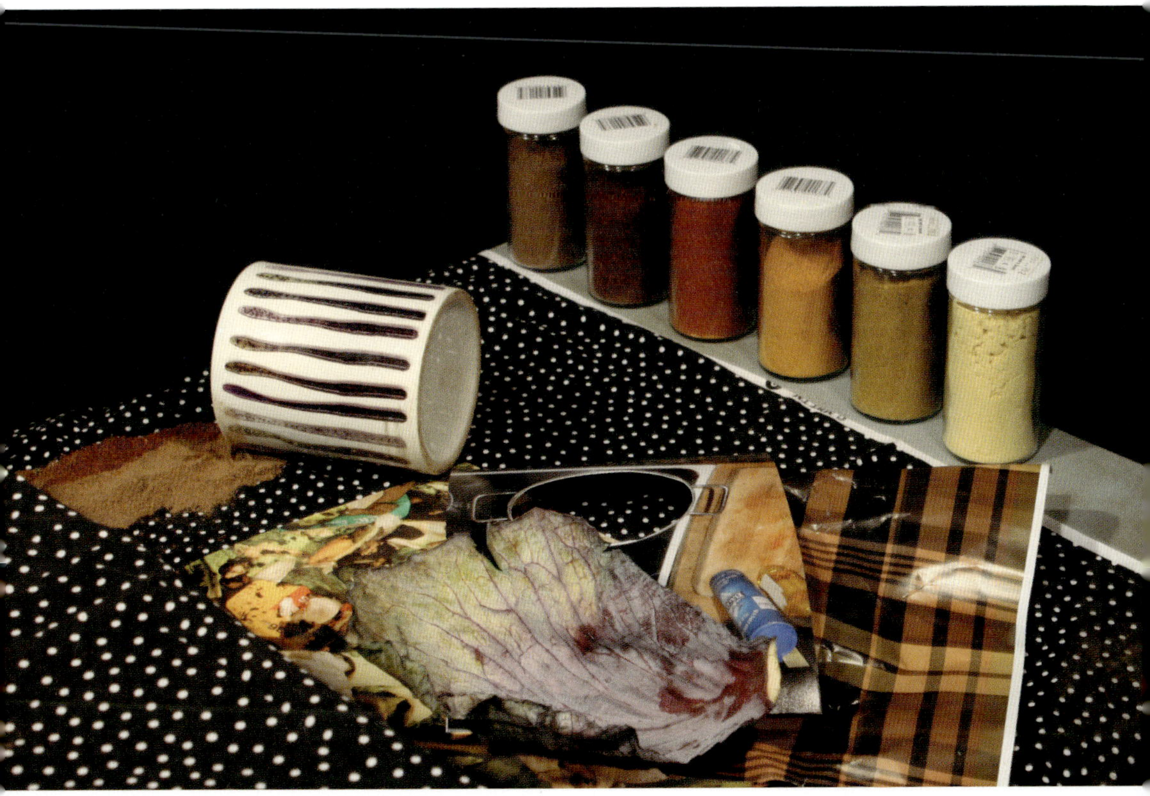

139

140 *Untitled #21, October 25, 2008*, 2008, from *Seed Stage*, pigment print, 8 5/8 x 13 inches. Collection of the Whitney Museum of American Art, New York; purchase, with funds from the Photography Committee and Henry Nias Foundation, 2009.28.21. Courtesy of the artist and Laurel Gitlen, New York.

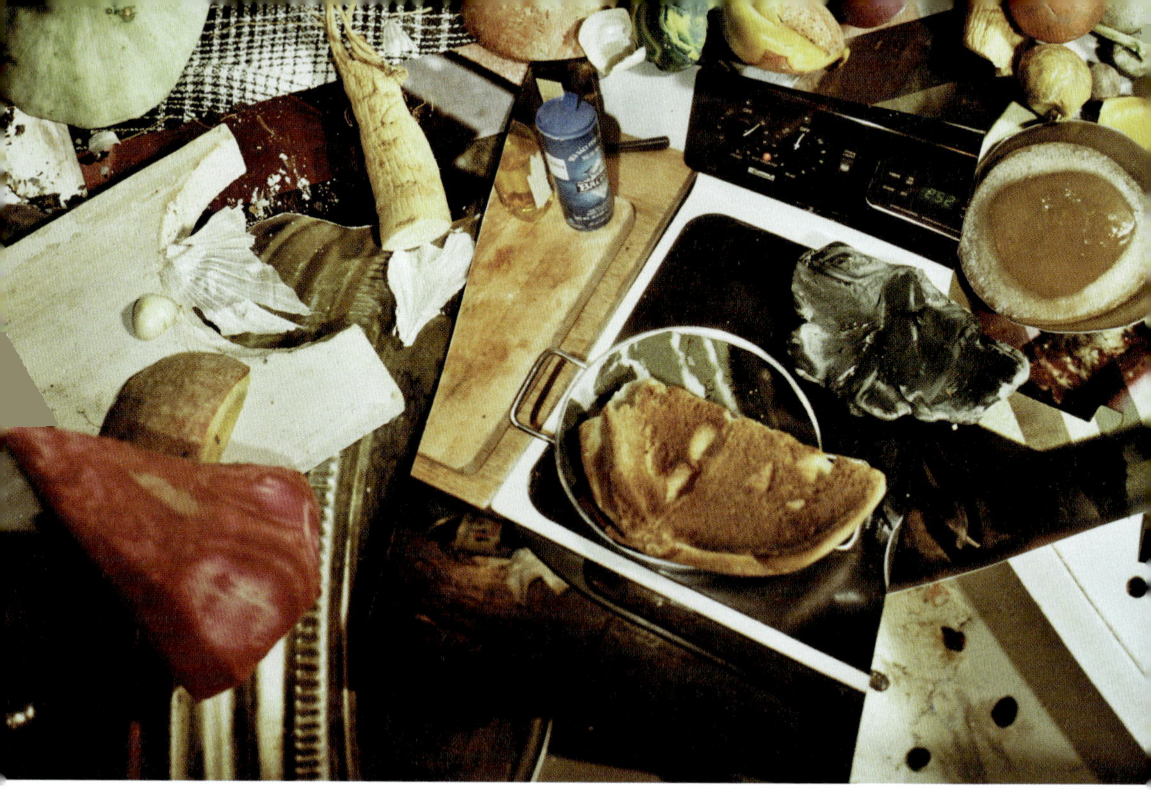

 Untitled #42, November 21, 2008, 2008, from *Seed Stage*, pigment print, 10 5/8 x 16 inches. Collection of the Whitney Museum of American Art, New York; purchase, with funds from the Photography Committee and Henry Nias Foundation, 2009.28.42. Courtesy of the artist and Laurel Gitlen, New York.

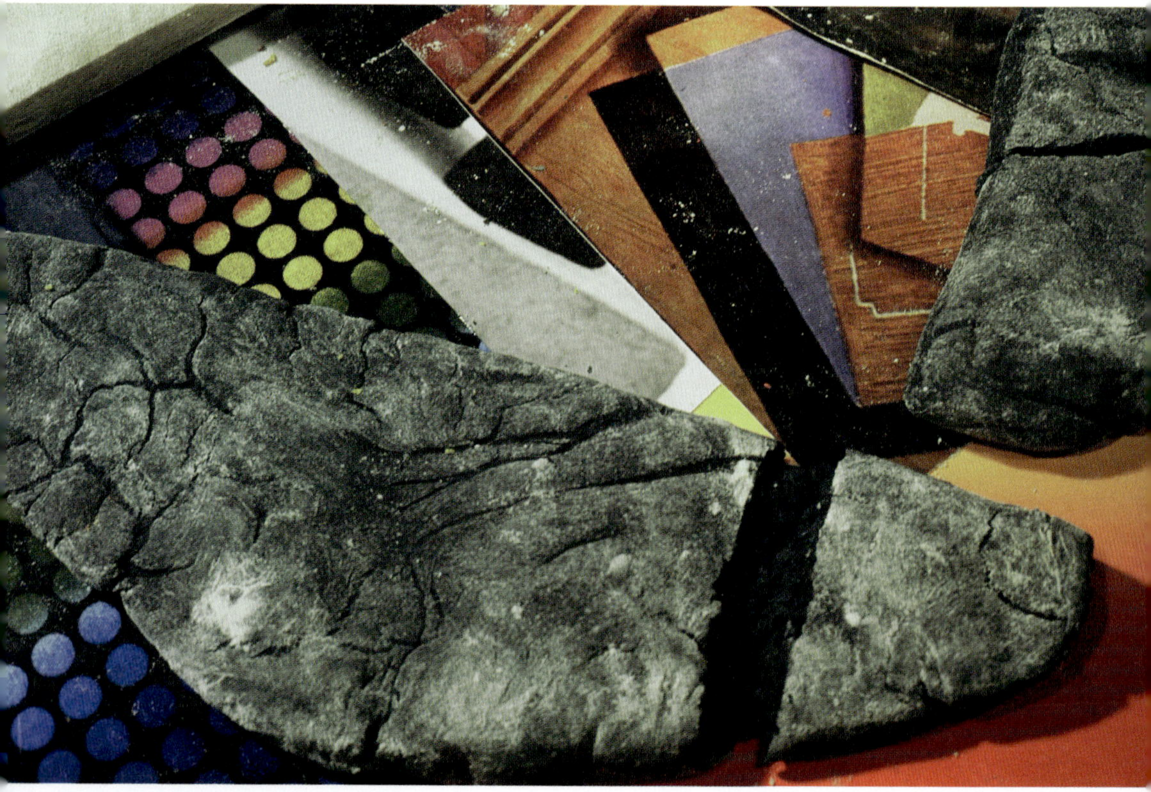

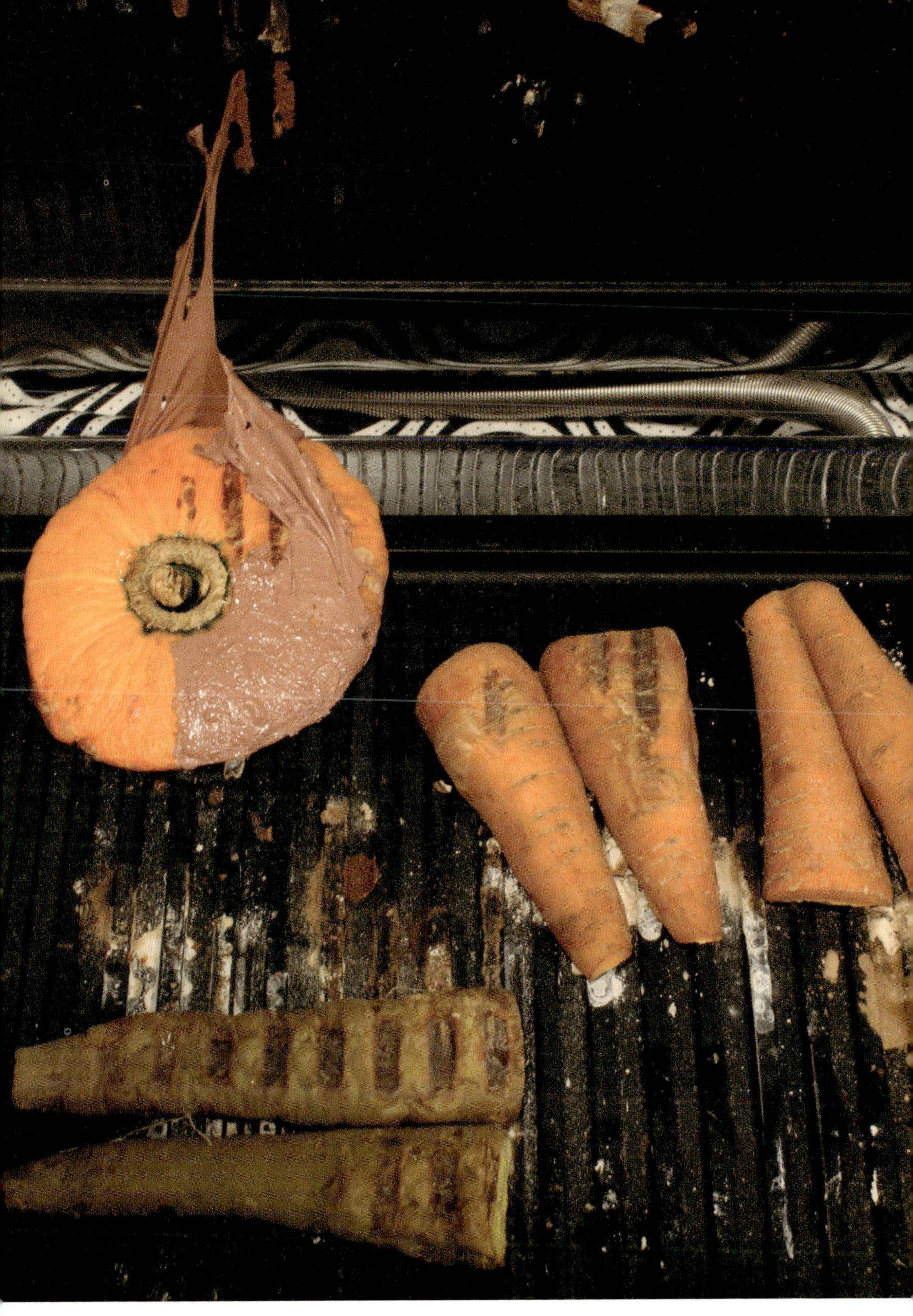

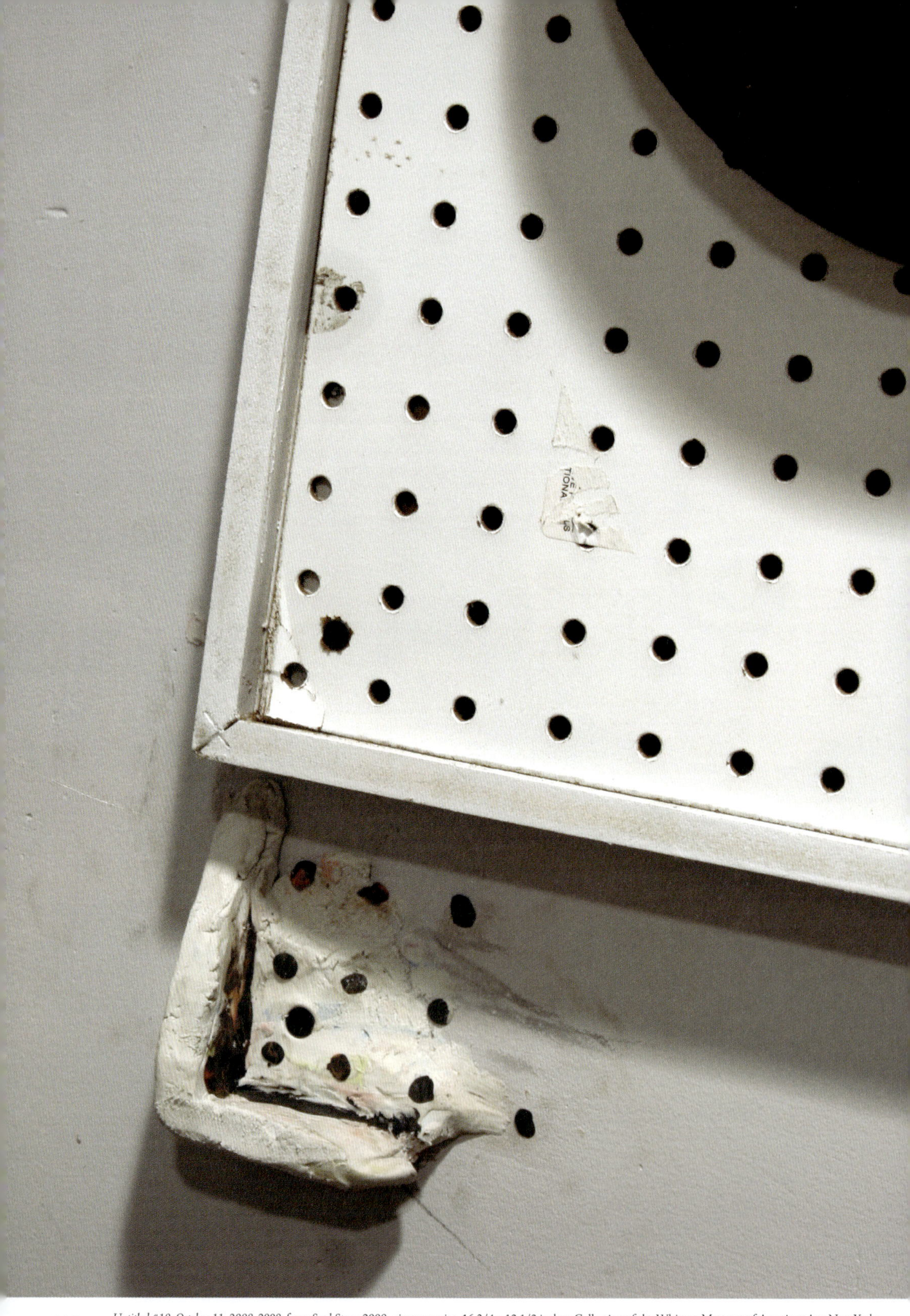

 Untitled #10, October 11, 2008, 2008, from *Seed Stage*, 2008, pigment print, 16 3/4 x 12 1/2 inches. Collection of the Whitney Museum of American Art, New York; purchase, with funds from the Photography Committee and Henry Nias Foundation, 2009.28.10. Courtesy of the artist and Laurel Gitlen, New York.

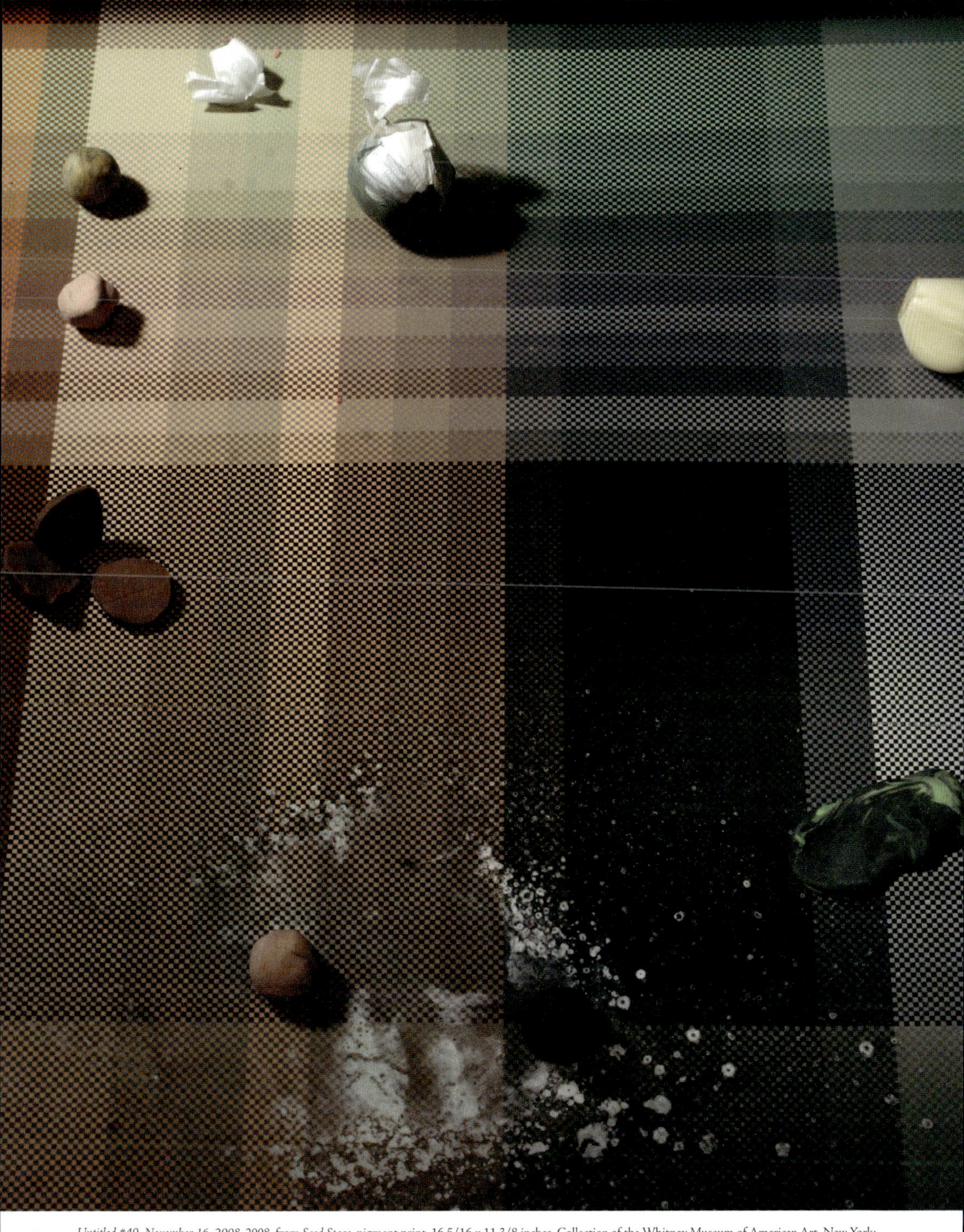

145   *Untitled #40, November 16, 2008*, 2008, from *Seed Stage*, pigment print, 16 5/16 x 11 3/8 inches. Collection of the Whitney Museum of American Art, New York; purchase, with funds from the Photography Committee and Henry Nias Foundation, 2009.28.40. Courtesy of the artist and Laurel Gitlen, New York.

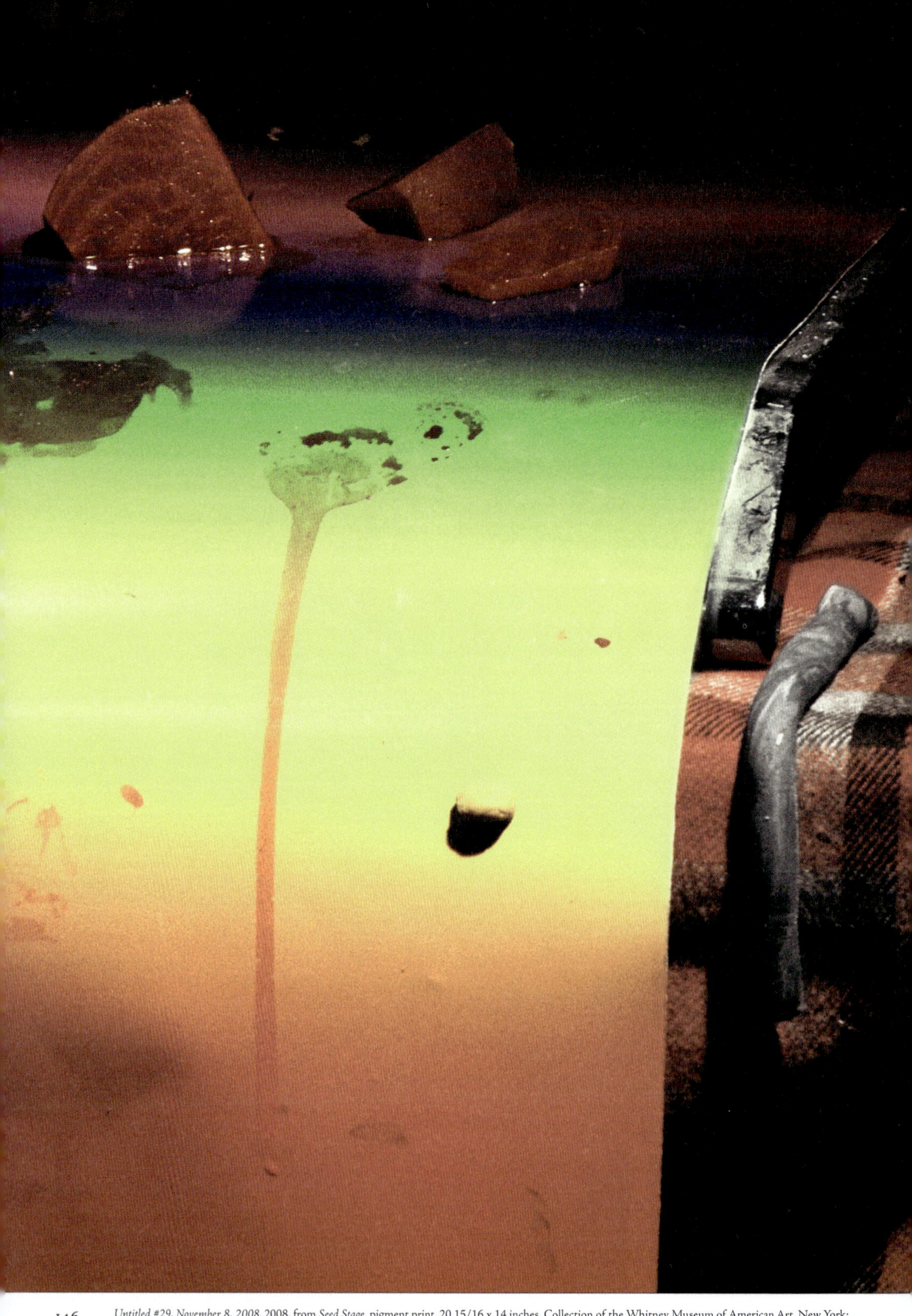

 Untitled #29, November 8, 2008, 2008, from *Seed Stage,* pigment print, 20 15/16 x 14 inches. Collection of the Whitney Museum of American Art, New York; purchase, with funds from the Photography Committee and Henry Nias Foundation, 2009.28.29. Courtesy of the artist and Laurel Gitlen, New York.

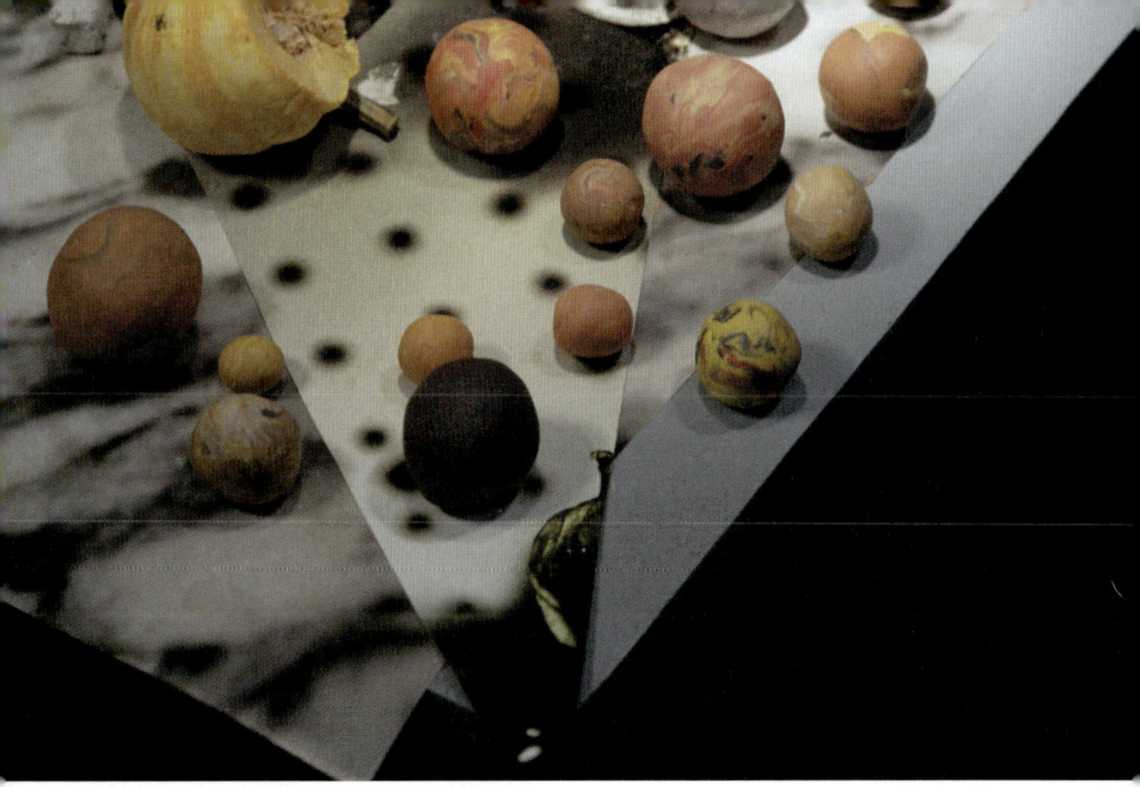

Untitled #58, January 2, 2009, 2009, from *Seed Stage*, pigment print, 14 x 20 15/16 inches. Collection of the Whitney Museum of American Art, New York; purchase, with funds from the Photography Committee and Henry Nias Foundation, 2009.28.58. Courtesy of the artist and Laurel Gitlen, New York.

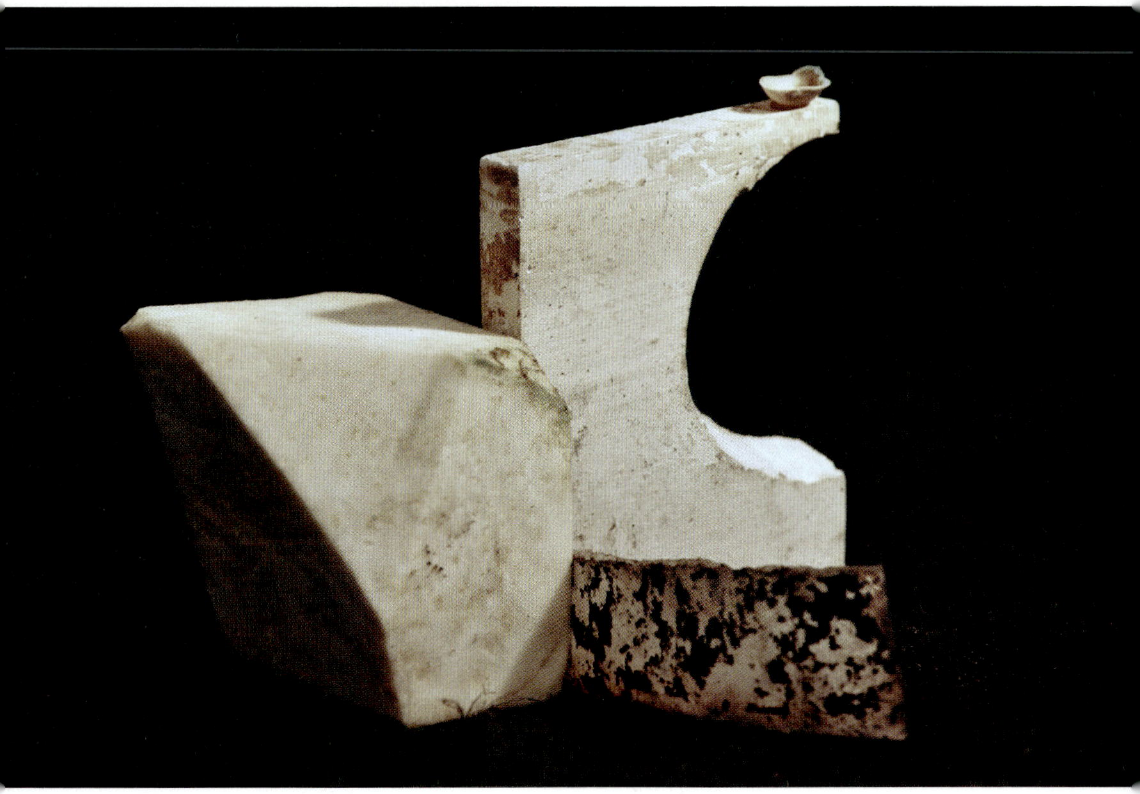

Untitled #18, October 19, 2008, 2008, from *Seed Stage*, pigment print, 10 5/8 x 16 inches. Collection of the Whitney Museum of American Art, New York; purchase, with funds from the Photography Committee and Henry Nias Foundation, 2009.28.18. Courtesy of the artist and Laurel Gitlen, New York.

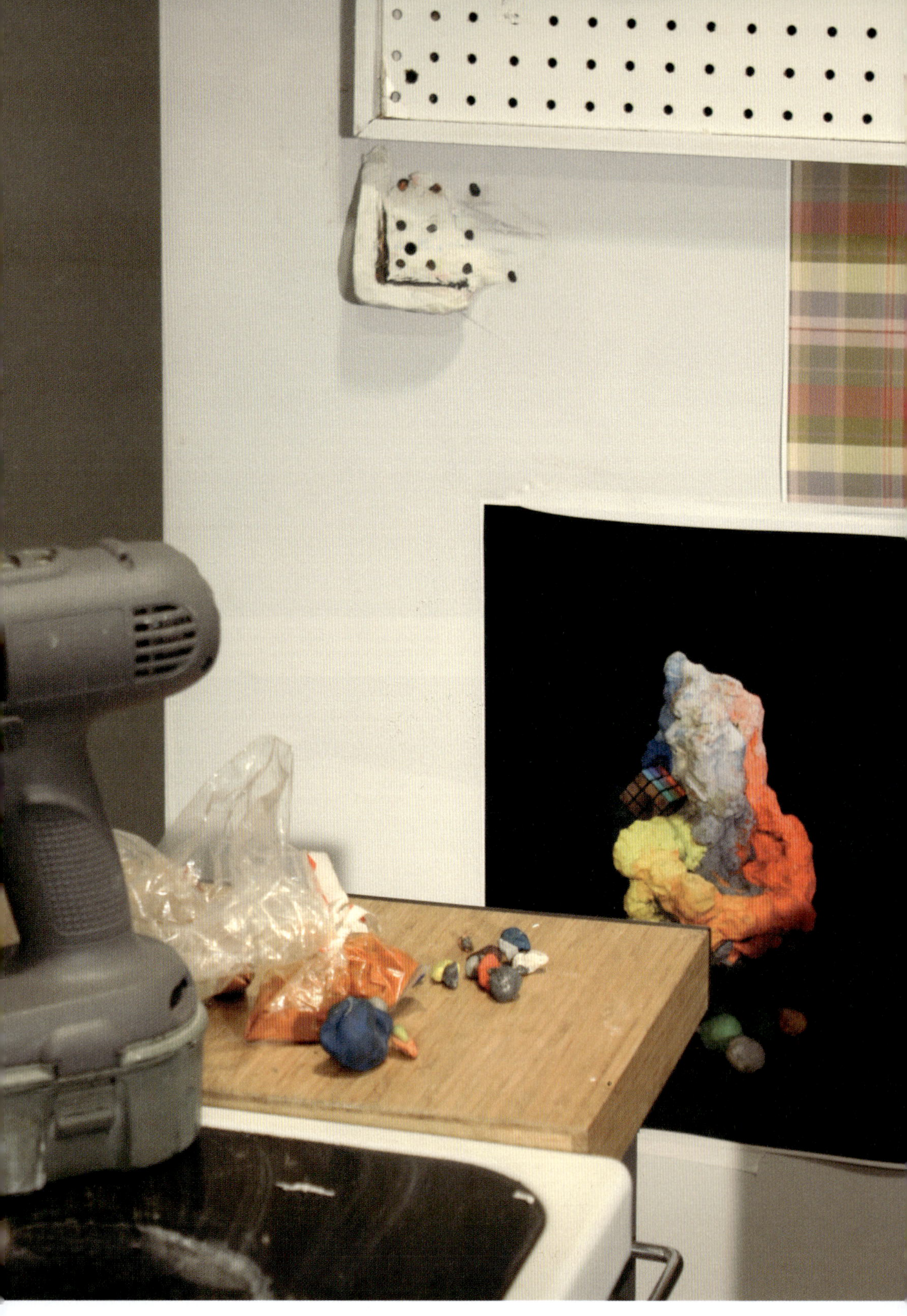

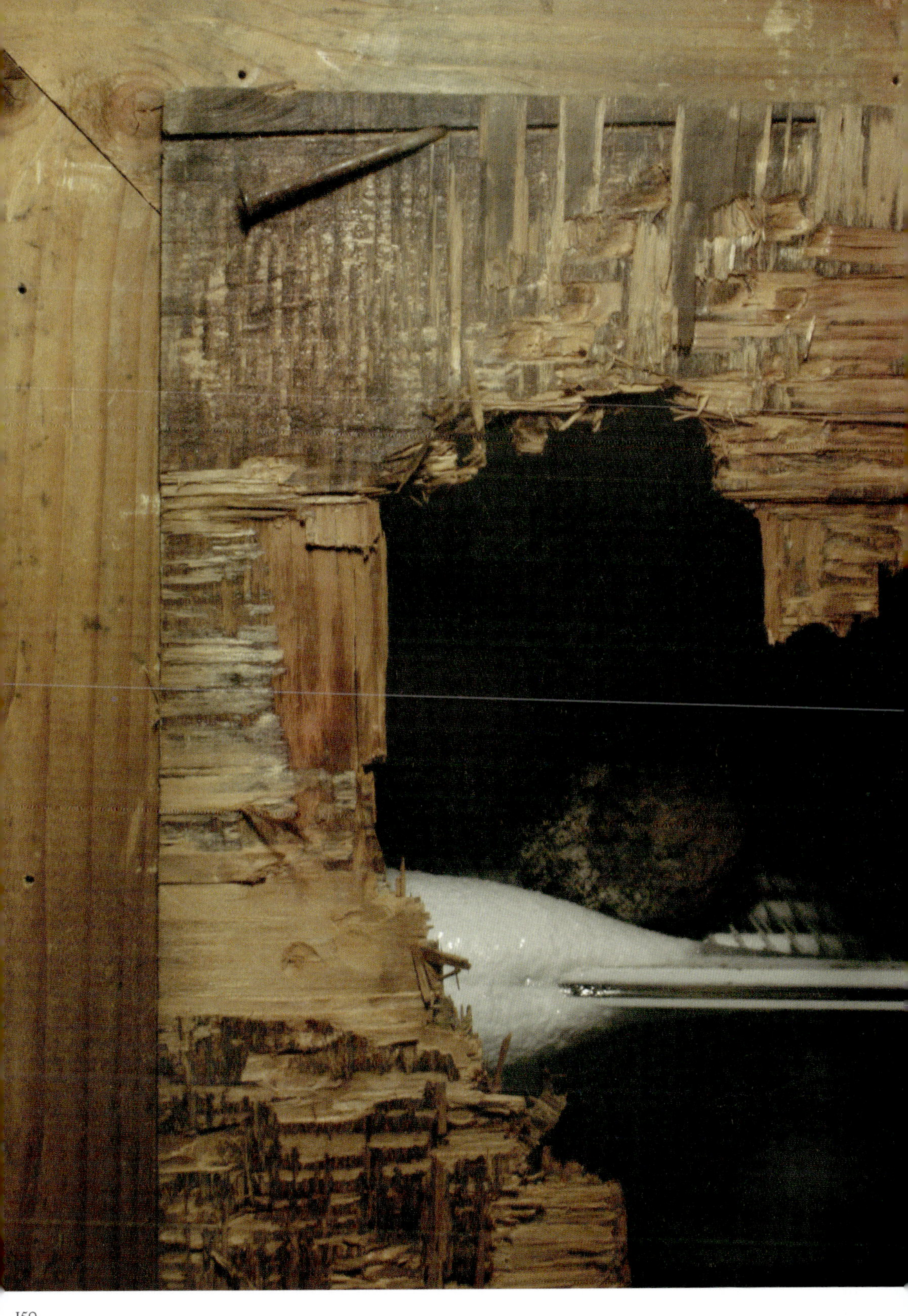

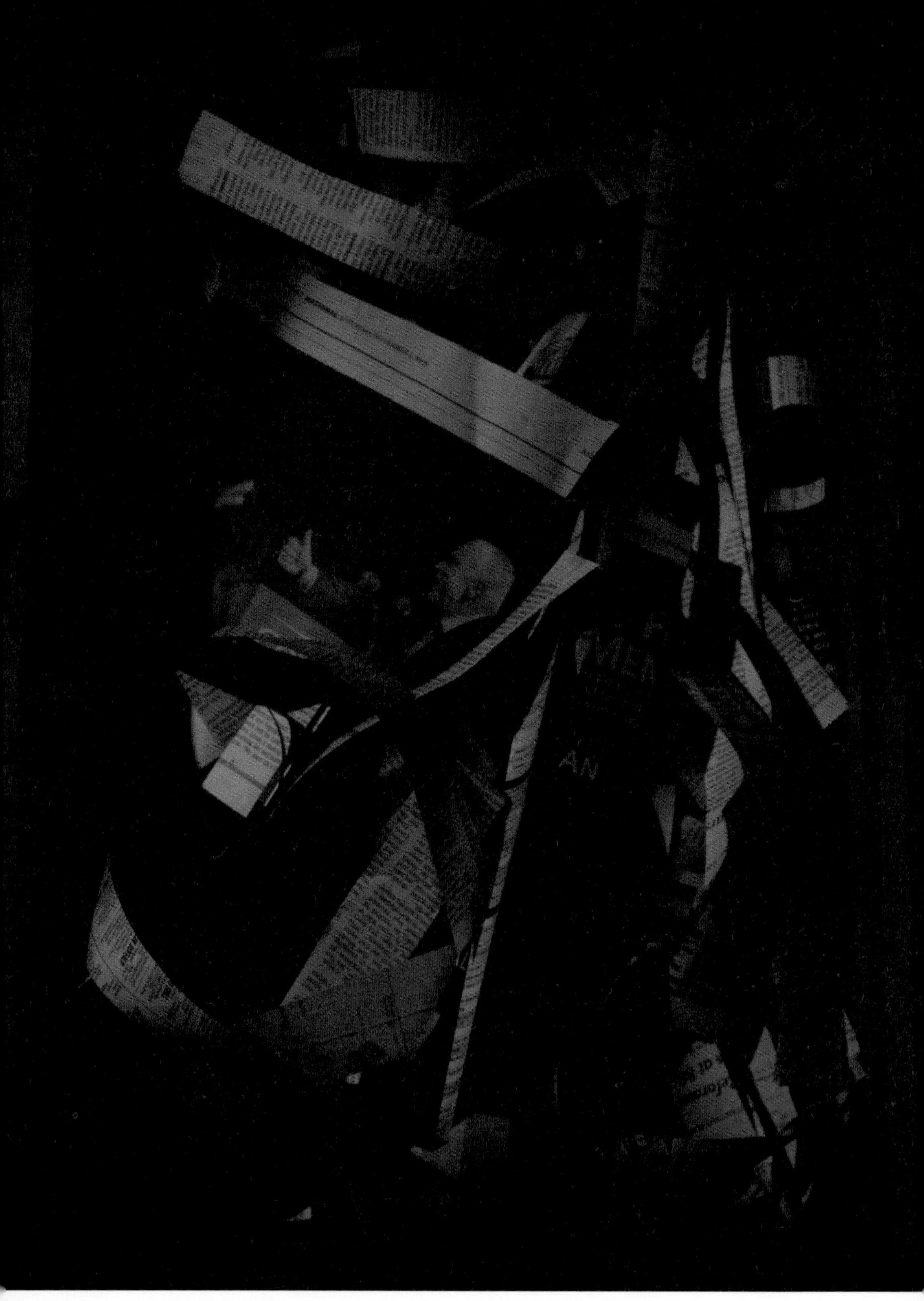

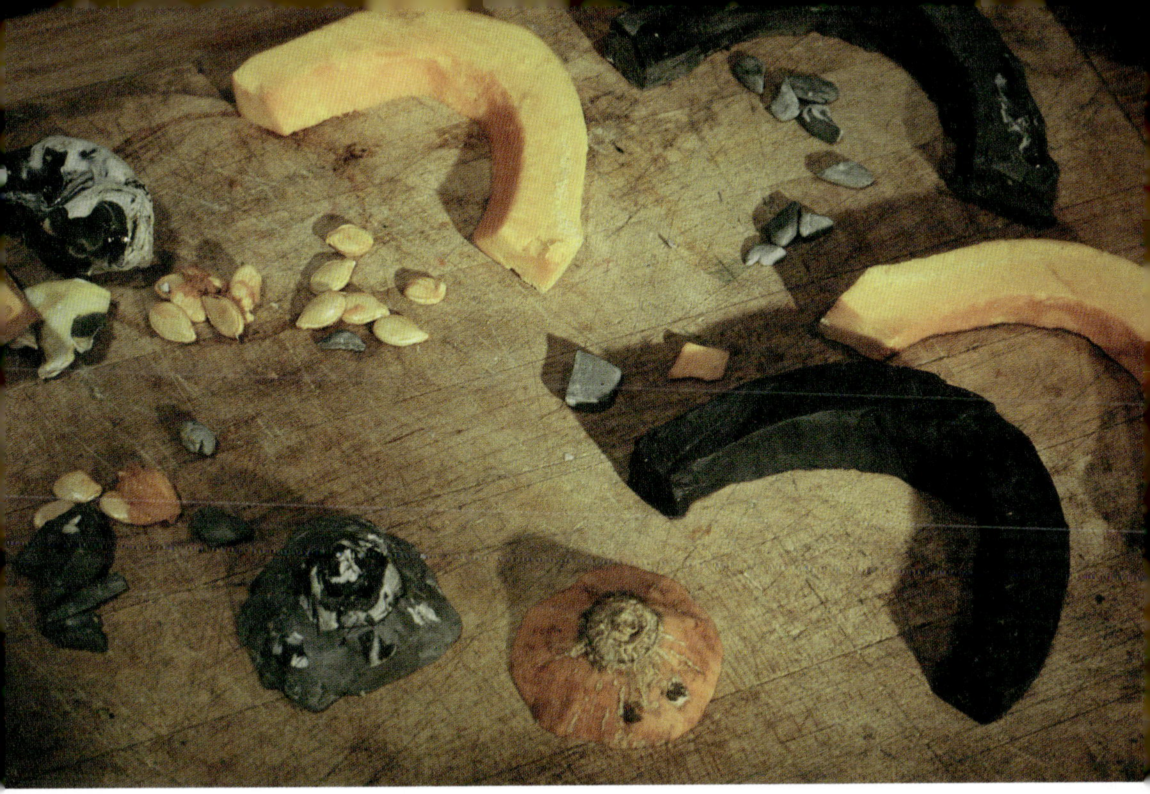

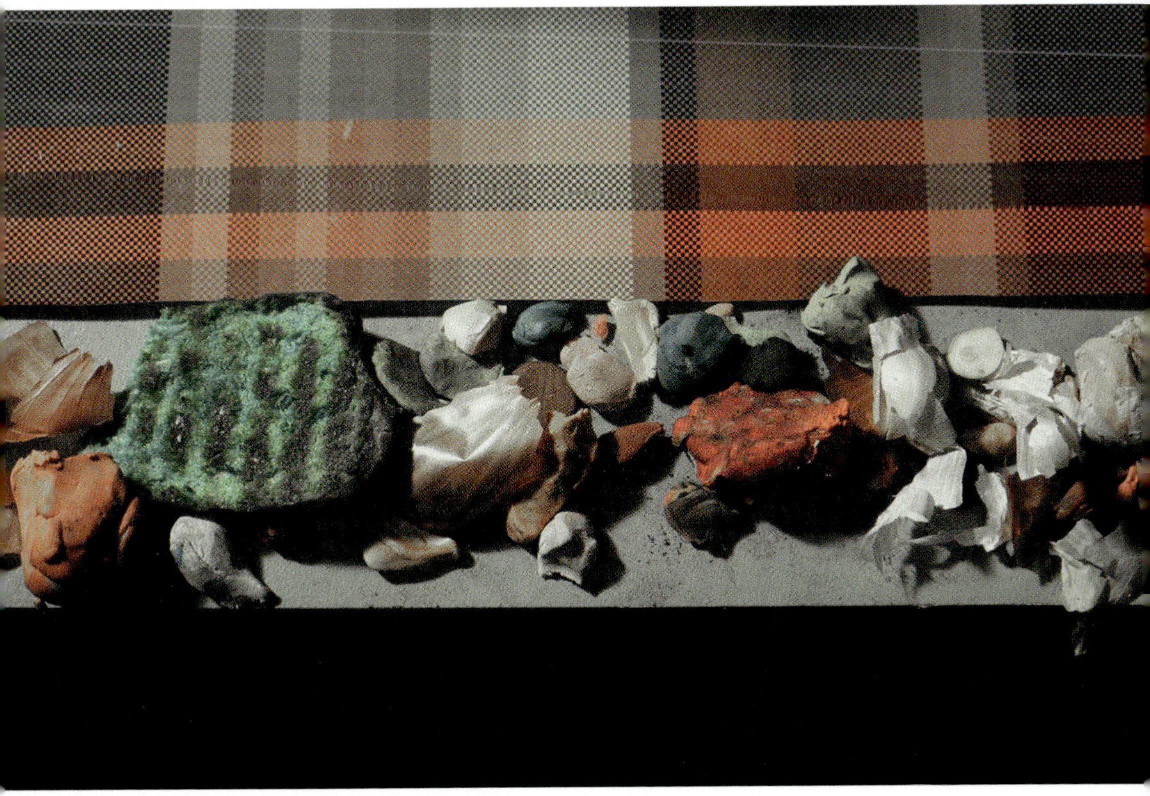

153 *Untitled #37, November 14, 2008*, 2008, from *Seed Stage*, pigment print, 11 x 16 inches. Collection of the Whitney Museum of American Art, New York; purchase, with funds from the Photography Committee and Henry Nias Foundation, 2009.28.37. Courtesy of the artist and Laurel Gitlen, New York.

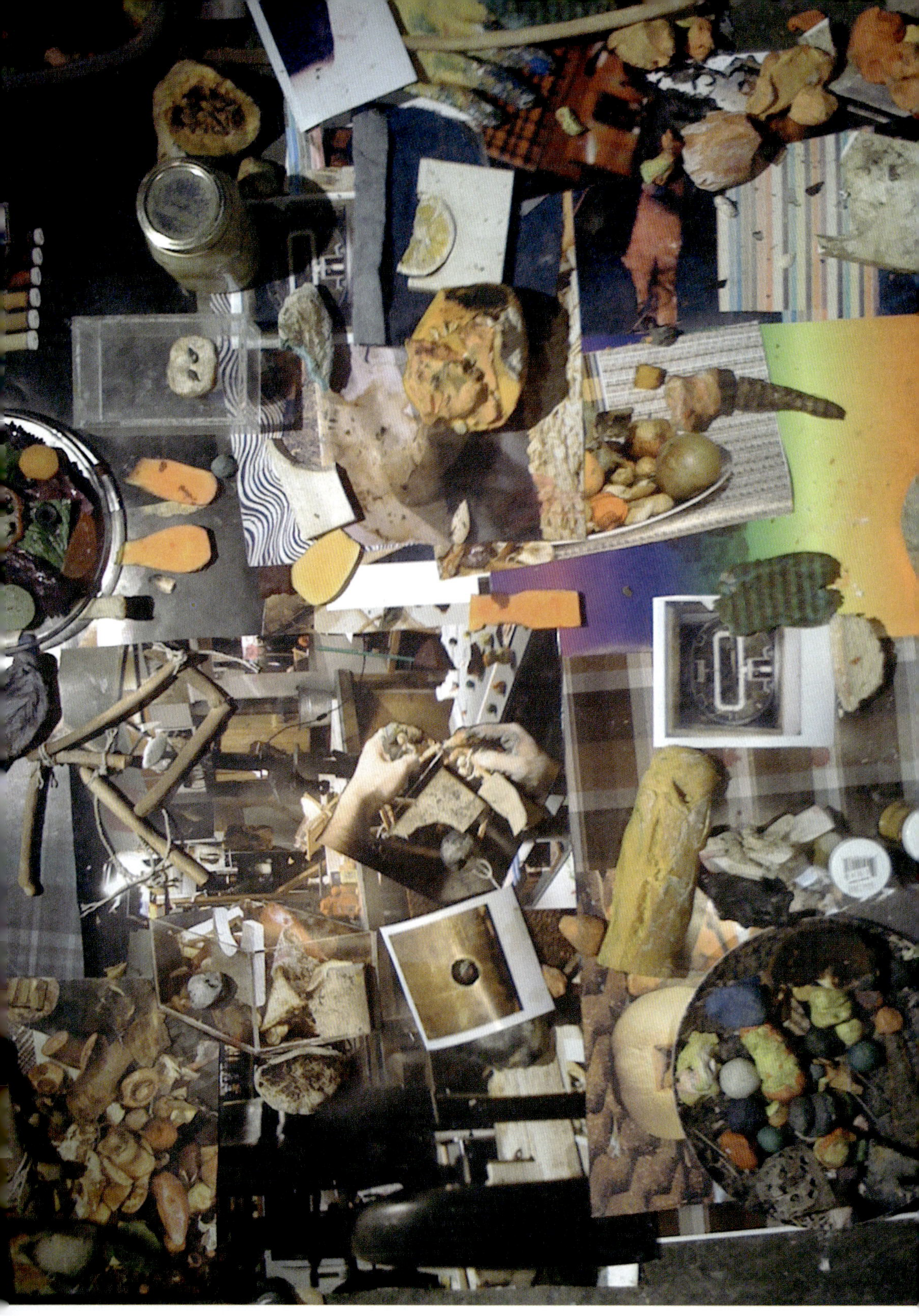

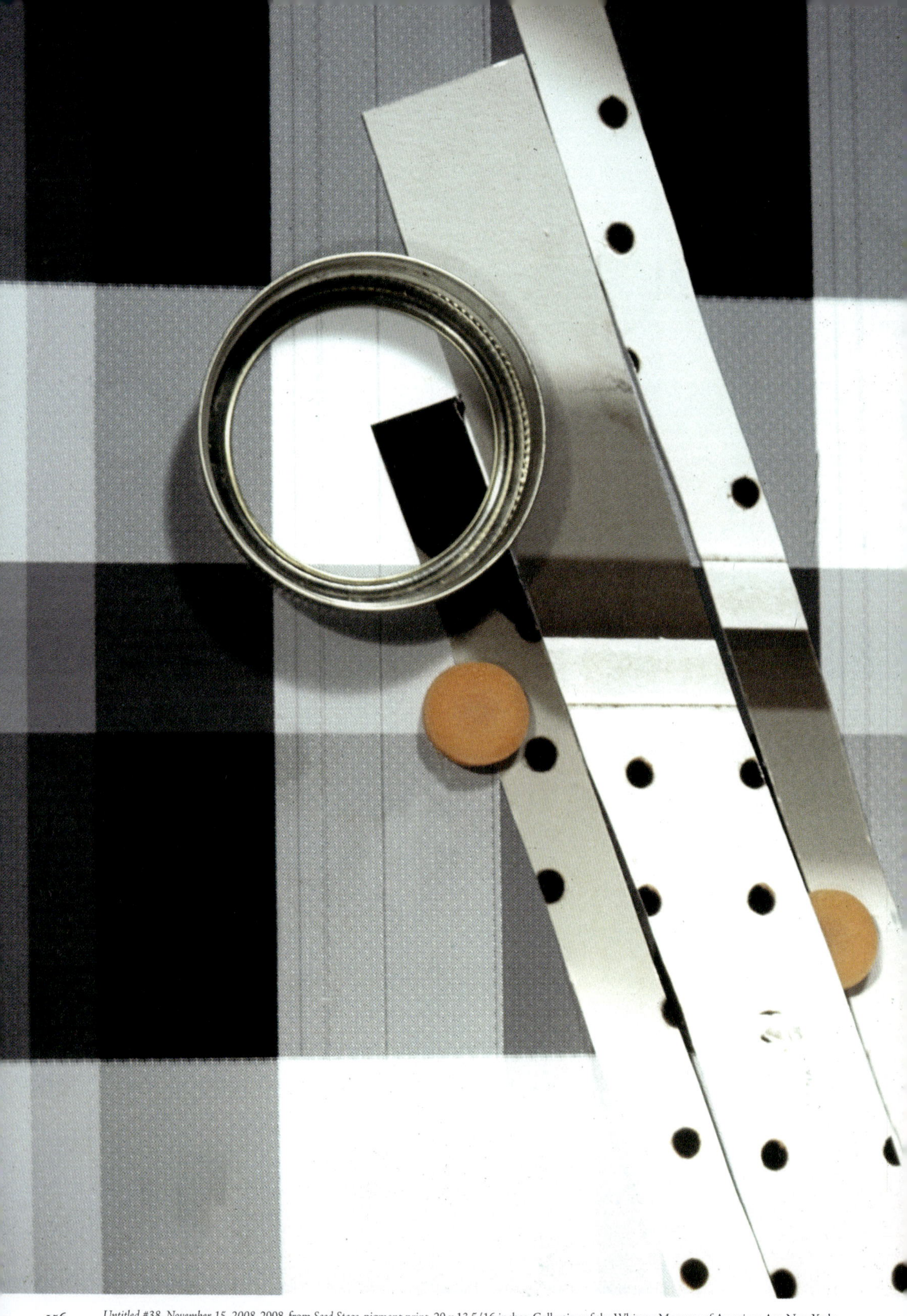

Untitled #38, November 15, 2008, 2008, from *Seed Stage*, pigment print, 20 x 13 5/16 inches. Collection of the Whitney Museum of American Art, New York; purchase, with funds from the Photography Committee and Henry Nias Foundation, 2009.28.38. Courtesy of the artist and Laurel Gitlen, New York.

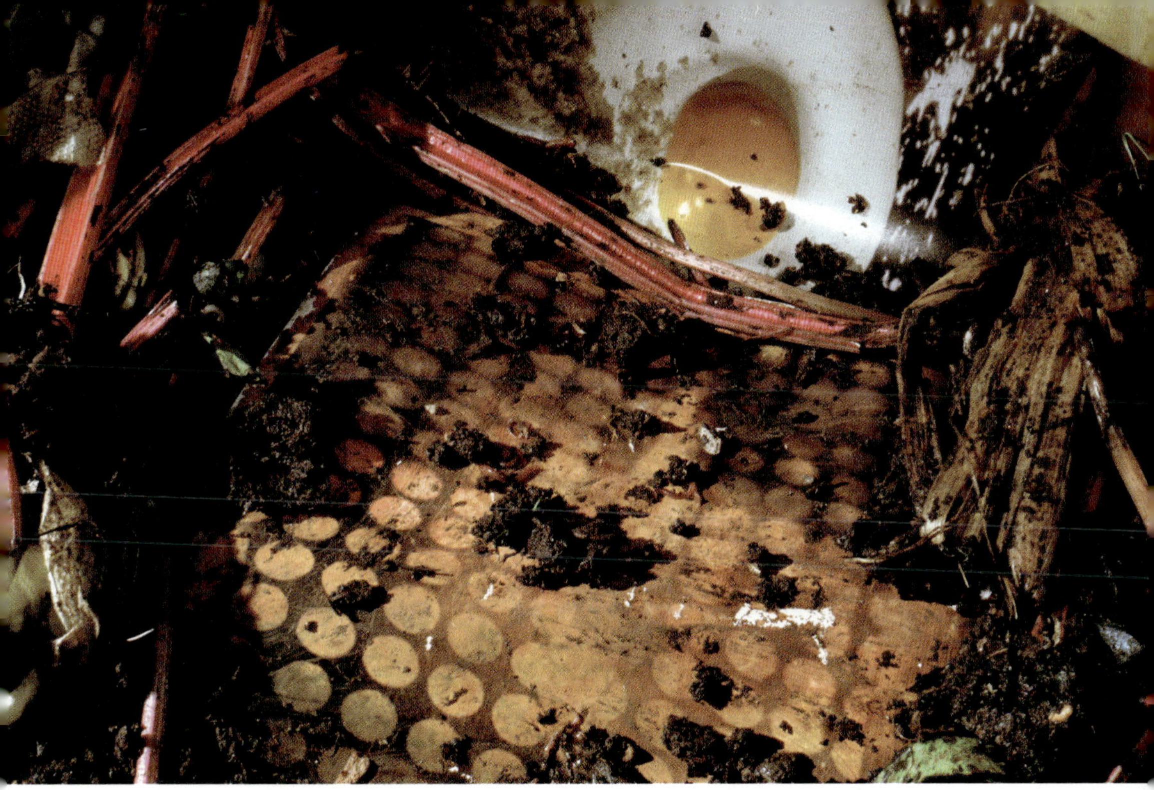

Untitled #6, October 5, 2008, 2008, from *Seed Stage*, pigment print, 12 1/4 x 16 3/4 inches. Collection of the Whitney Museum of American Art, New York; purchase, with funds from the Photography Committee and Henry Nias Foundation, 2009.28.6. Courtesy of the artist and Laurel Gitlen, New York.

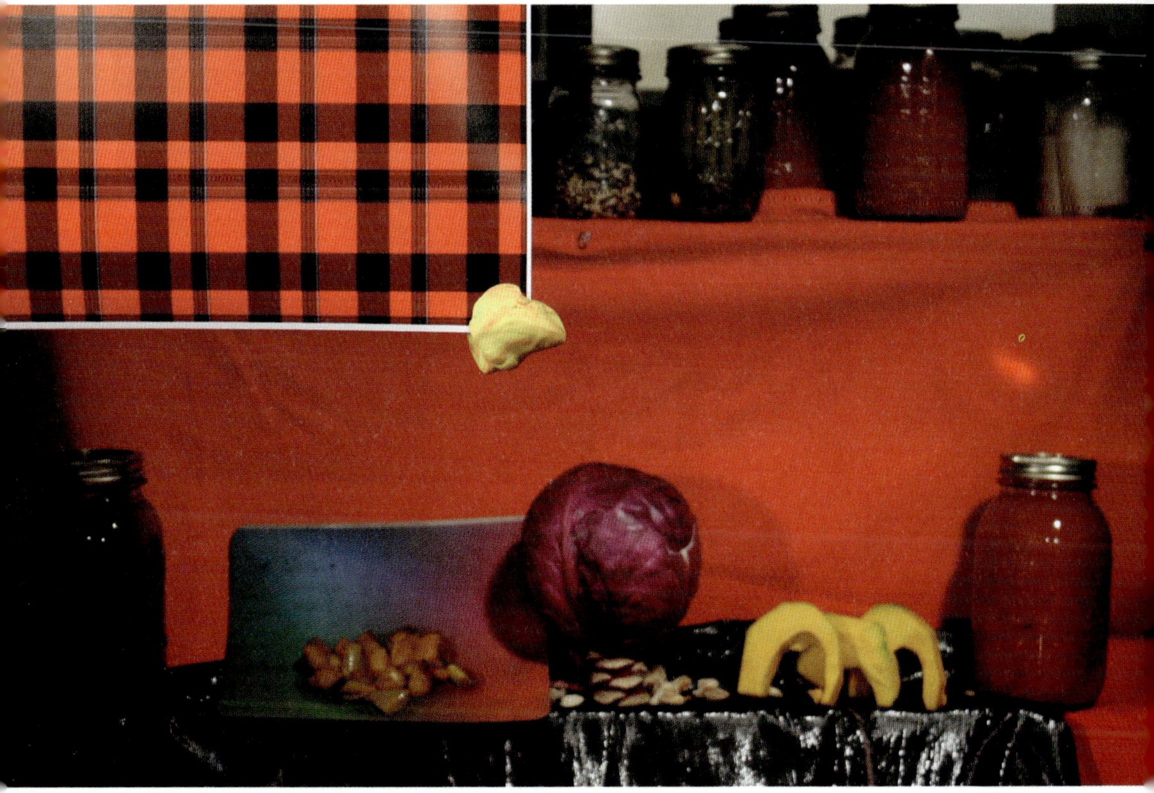

158   *Untitled #24, October 26, 2008*, 2008, from *Seed Stage*, pigment print, 10 5/8 x 16 inches. Collection of the Whitney Museum of American Art, New York; purchase, with funds from the Photography Committee and Henry Nias Foundation, 2009.28.24. Courtesy of the artist and Laurel Gitlen, New York.

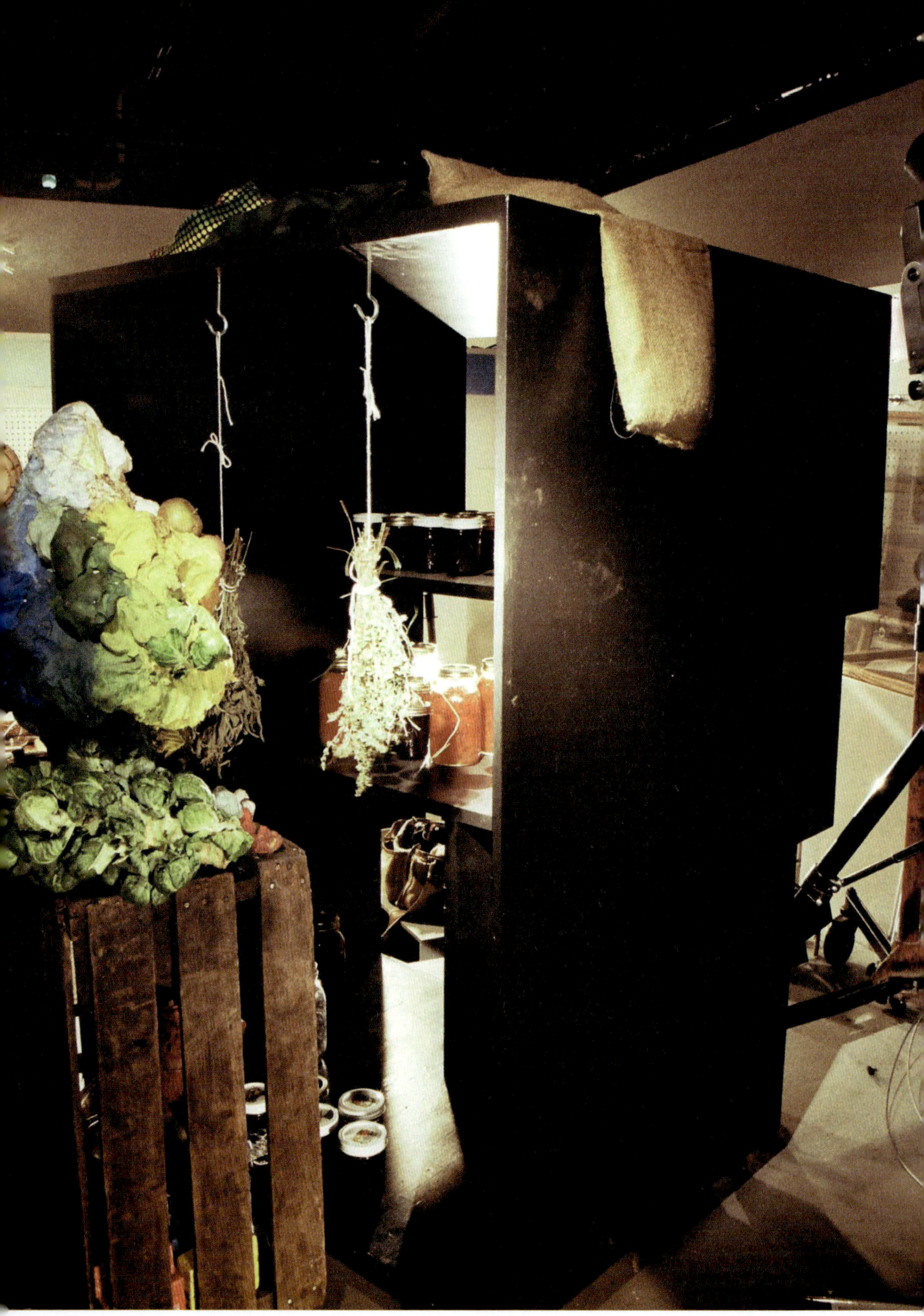

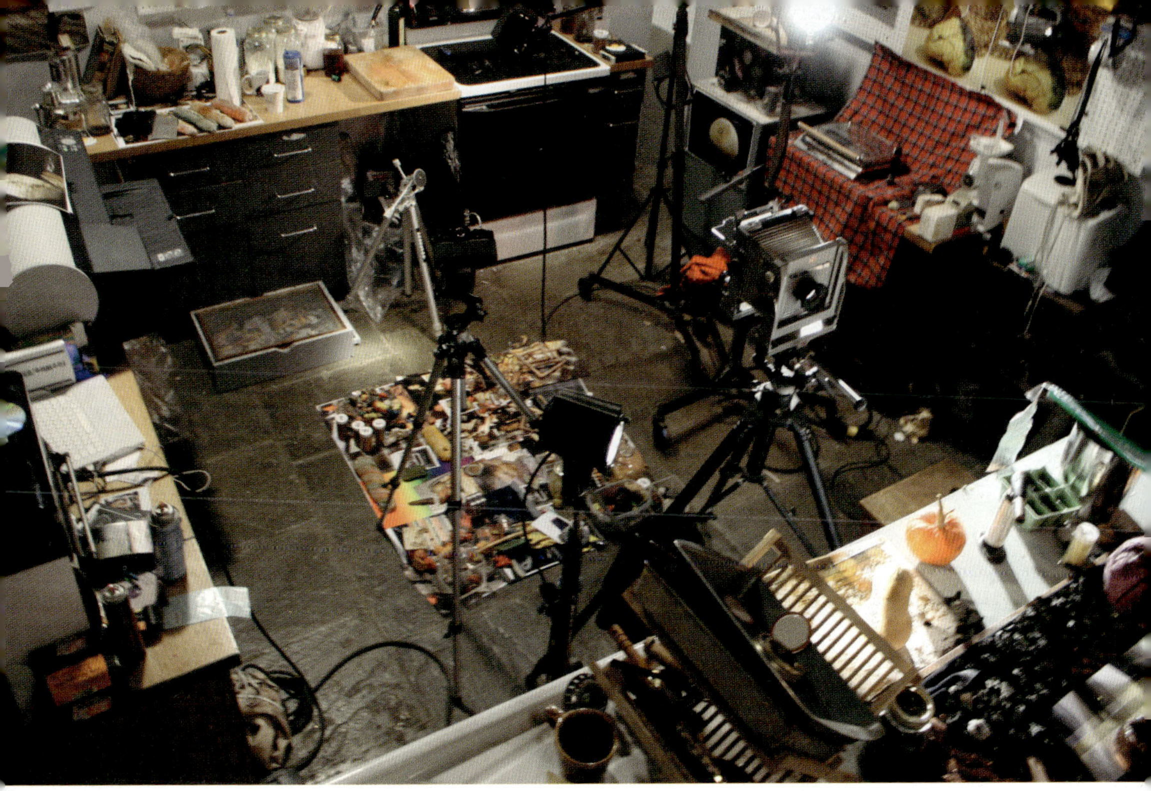

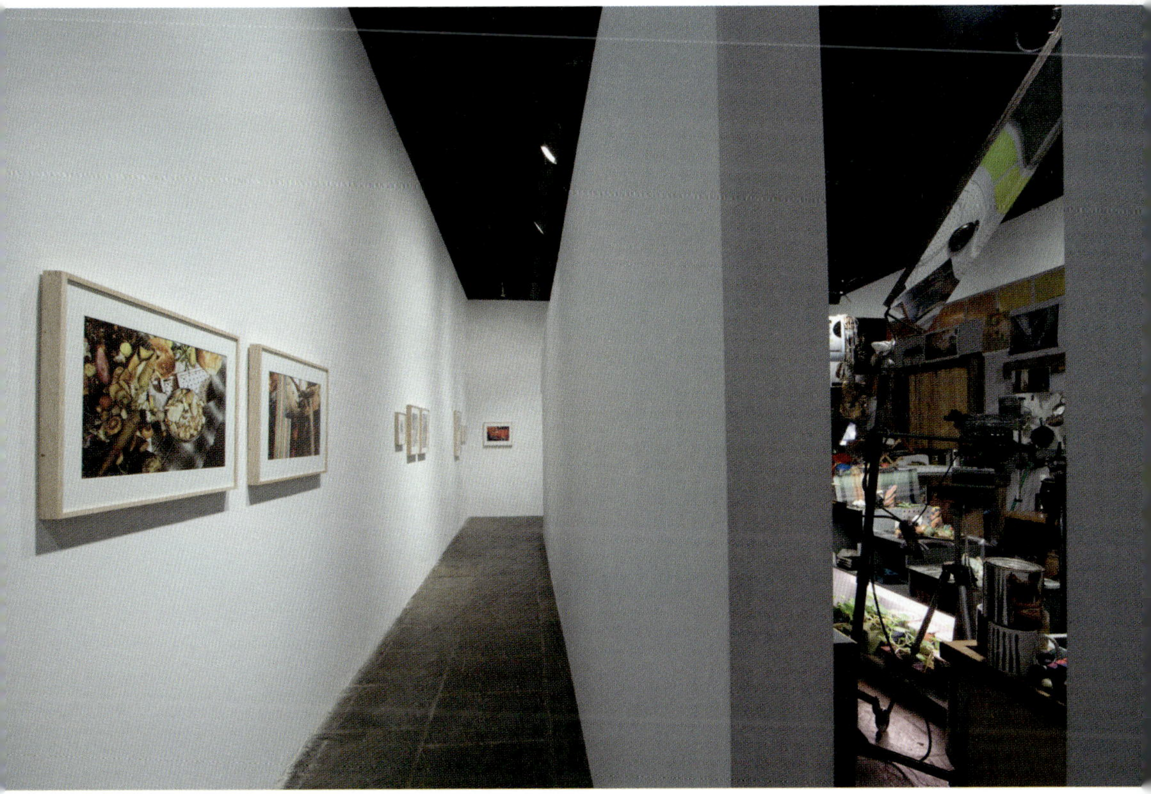

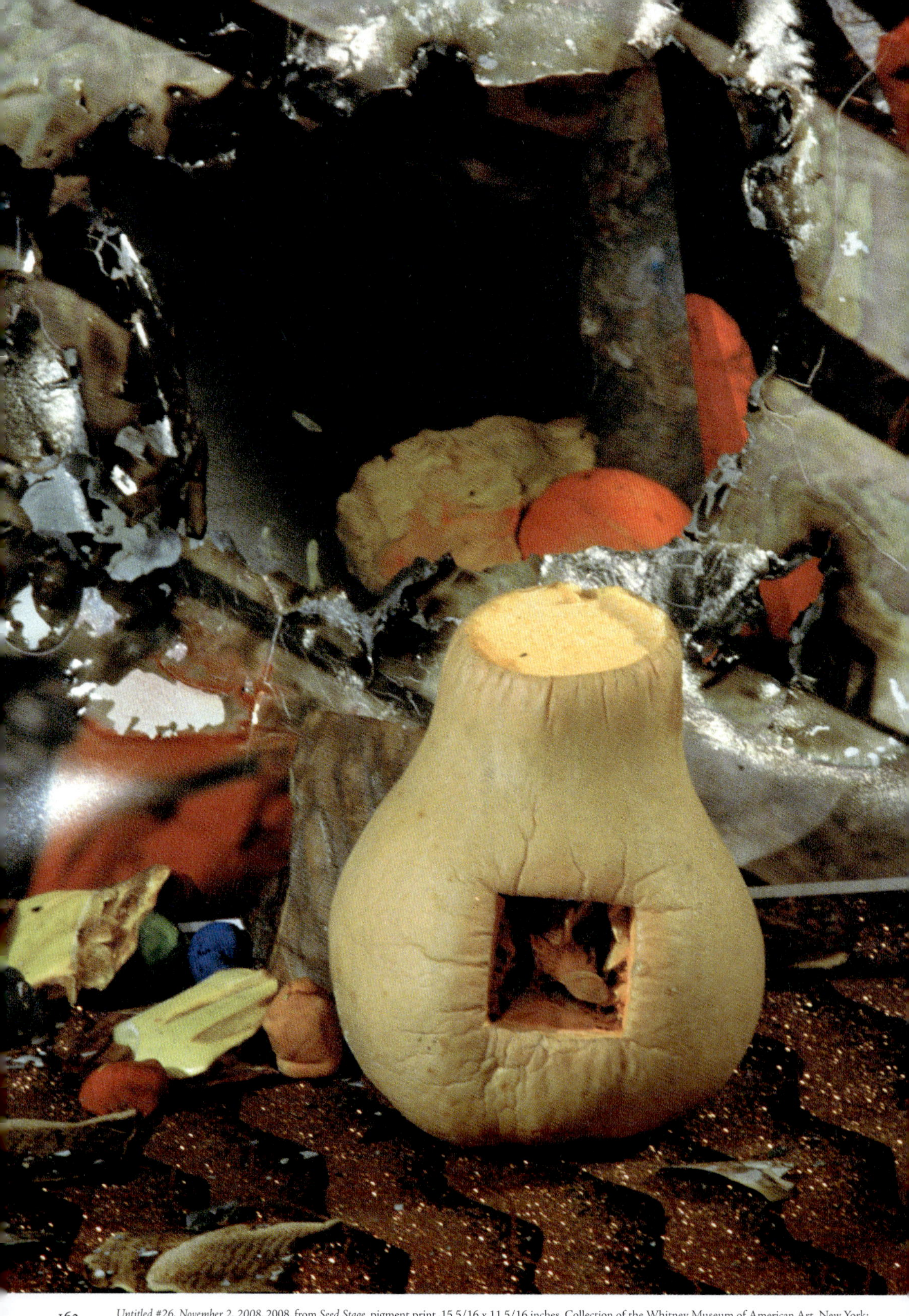

 Untitled #26, November 2, 2008, 2008, from *Seed Stage*, pigment print, 15 5/16 x 11 5/16 inches. Collection of the Whitney Museum of American Art, New York; purchase, with funds from the Photography Committee and Henry Nias Foundation, 2009.28.26. Courtesy of the artist and Laurel Gitlen, New York.

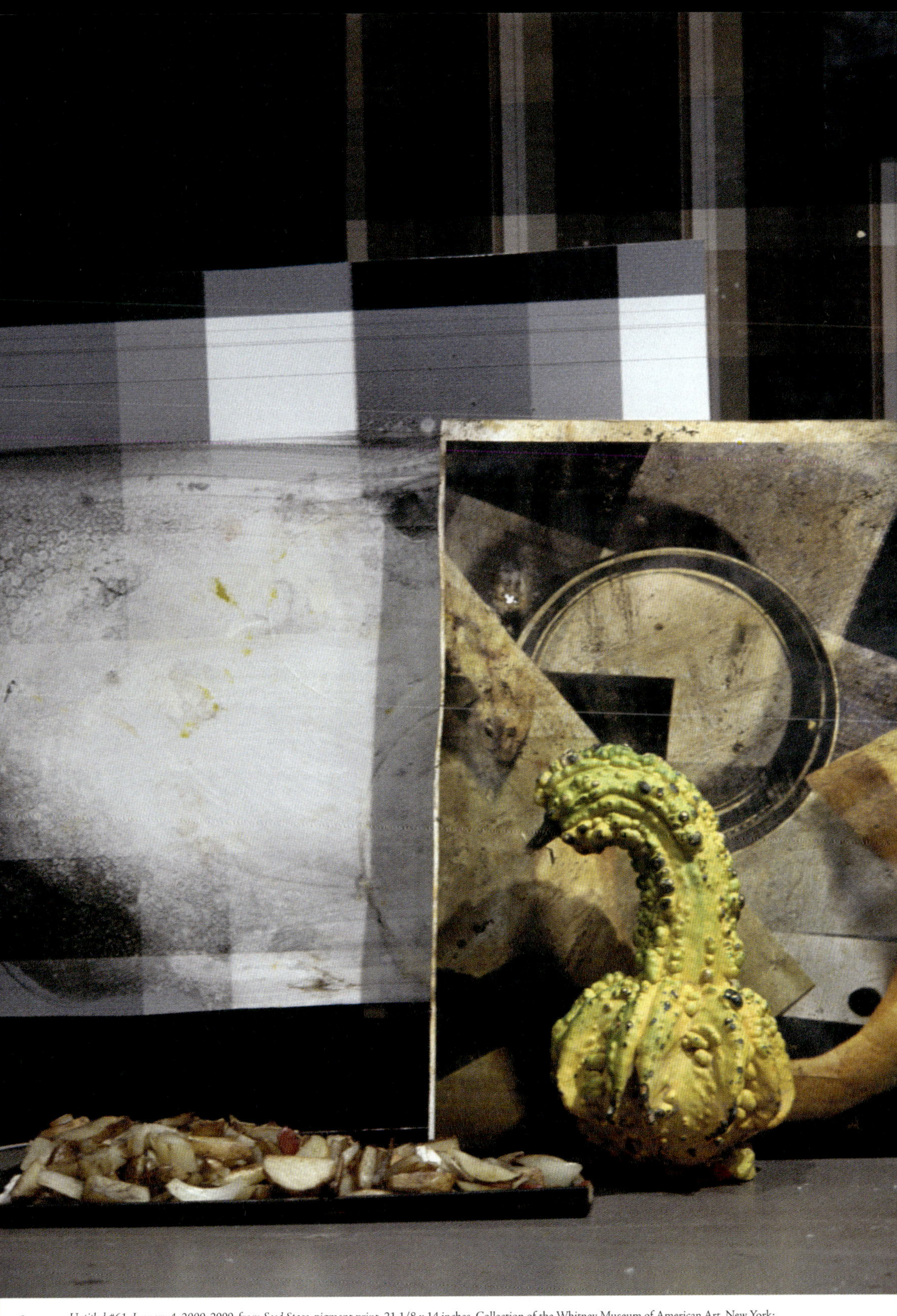

Untitled #61, January 4, 2009, 2009, from *Seed Stage*, pigment print, 21 1/8 x 14 inches. Collection of the Whitney Museum of American Art, New York; purchase, with funds from the Photography Committee and Henry Nias Foundation, 2009.28.61. Courtesy of the artist and Laurel Gitlen, New York.

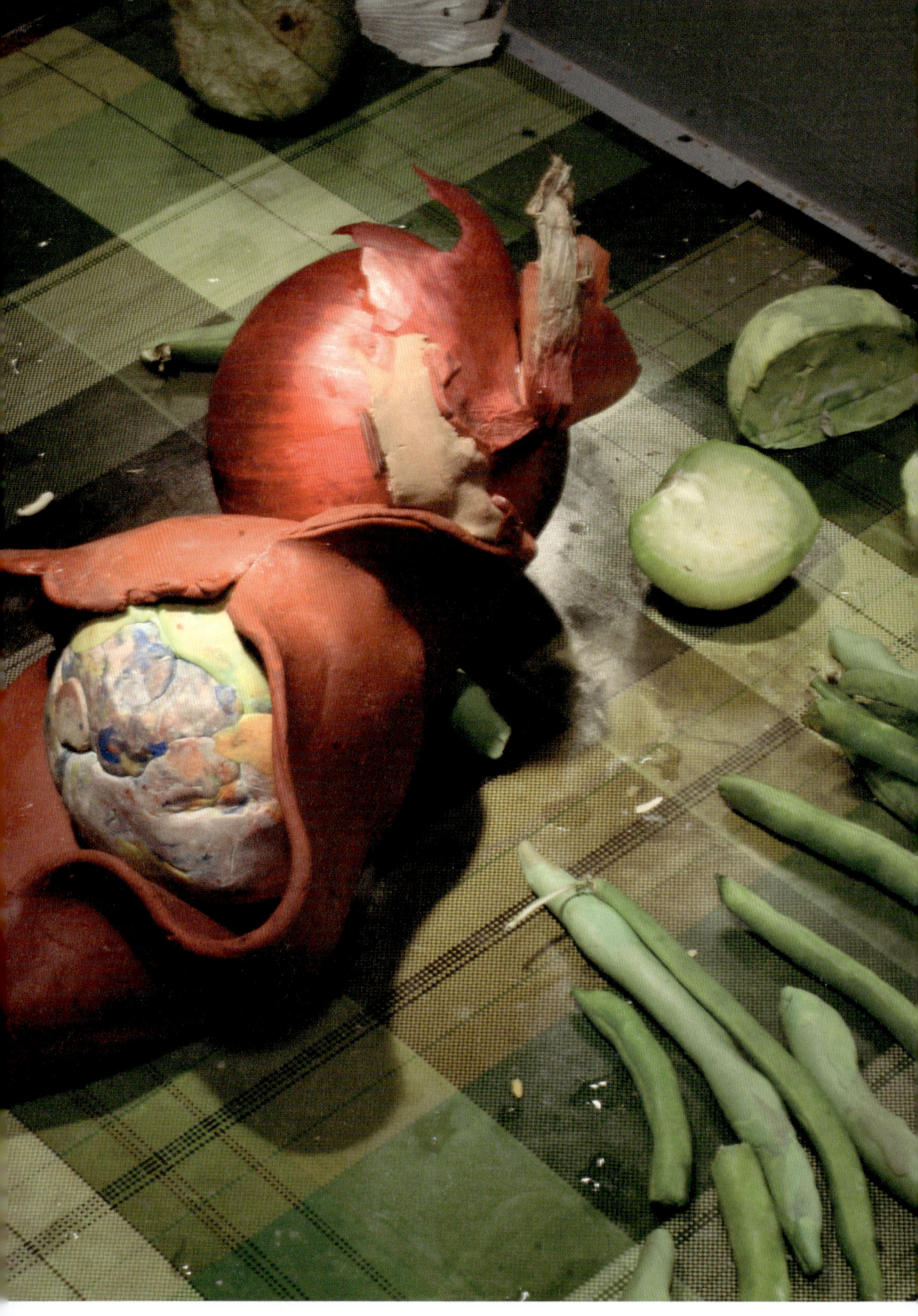

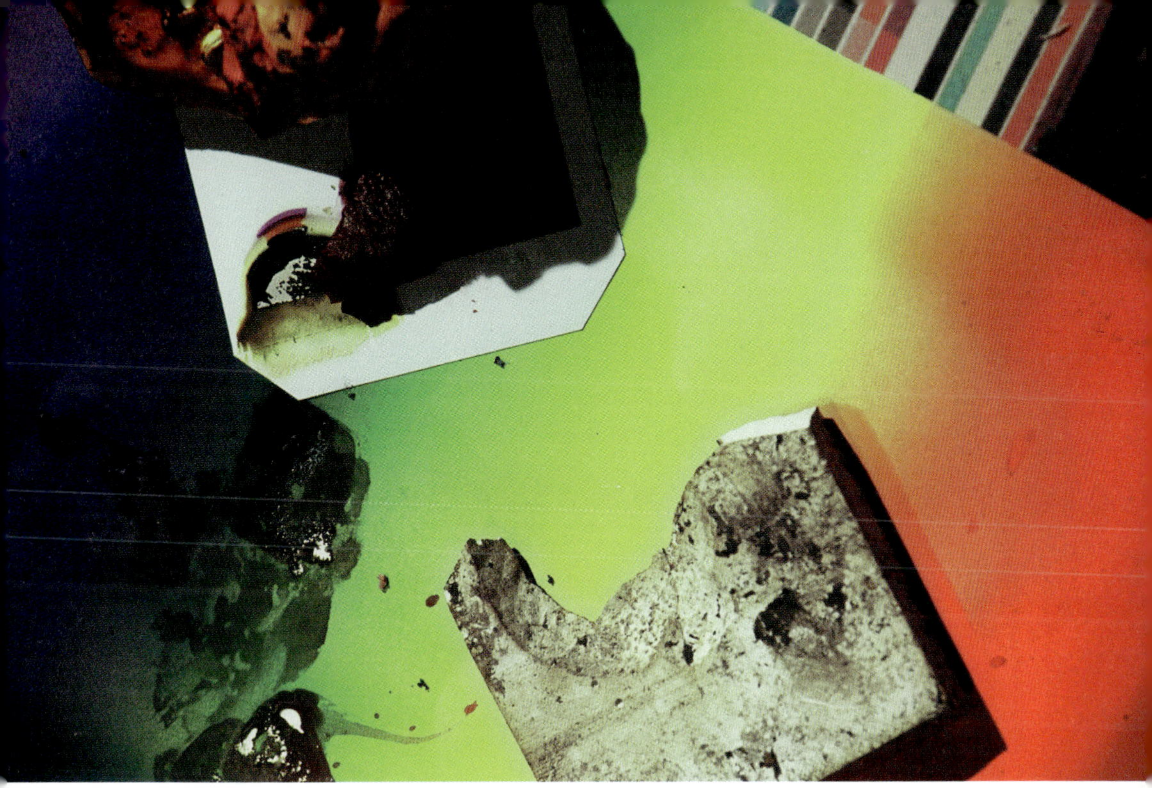

 Untitled #34, November 9, 2008, 2008, from *Seed Stage*, pigment print, 14 x 20 11/16 inches. Collection of the Whitney Museum of American Art, New York; purchase, with funds from the Photography Committee and Henry Nias Foundation, 2009.28.34. Courtesy of the artist and Laurel Gitlen, New York.

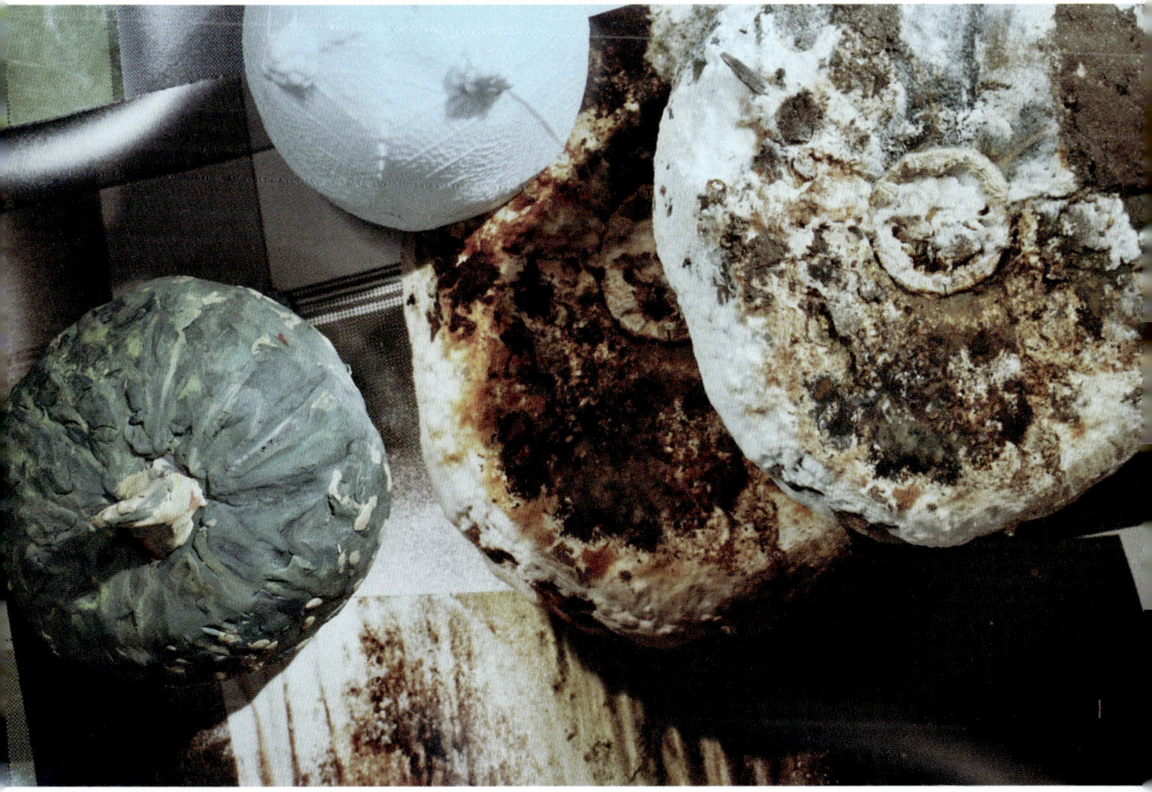

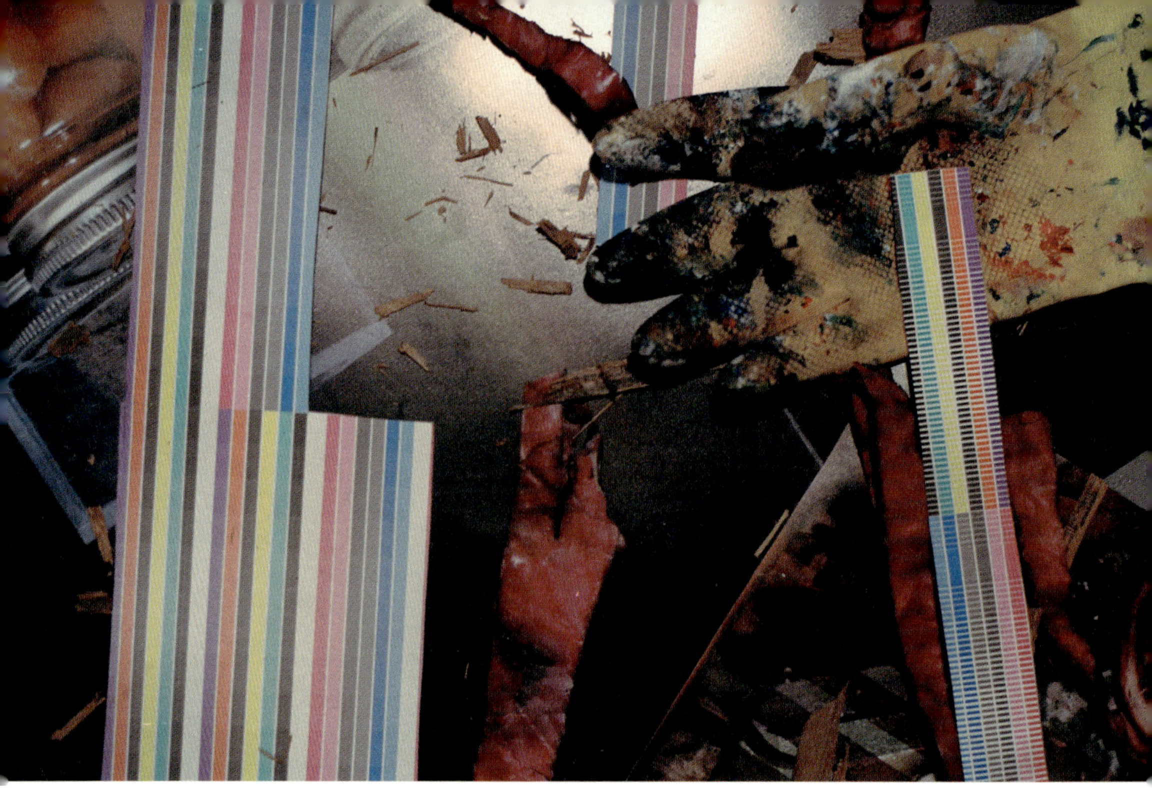

167   *Untitled #22, October 25, 2008, 2008, from Seed Stage*, pigment print, 14 x 20 7/16 inches. Collection of the Whitney Museum of American Art, New York; purchase, with funds from the Photography Committee and Henry Nias Foundation, 2009.28.22. Courtesy of the artist and Laurel Gitlen, New York.

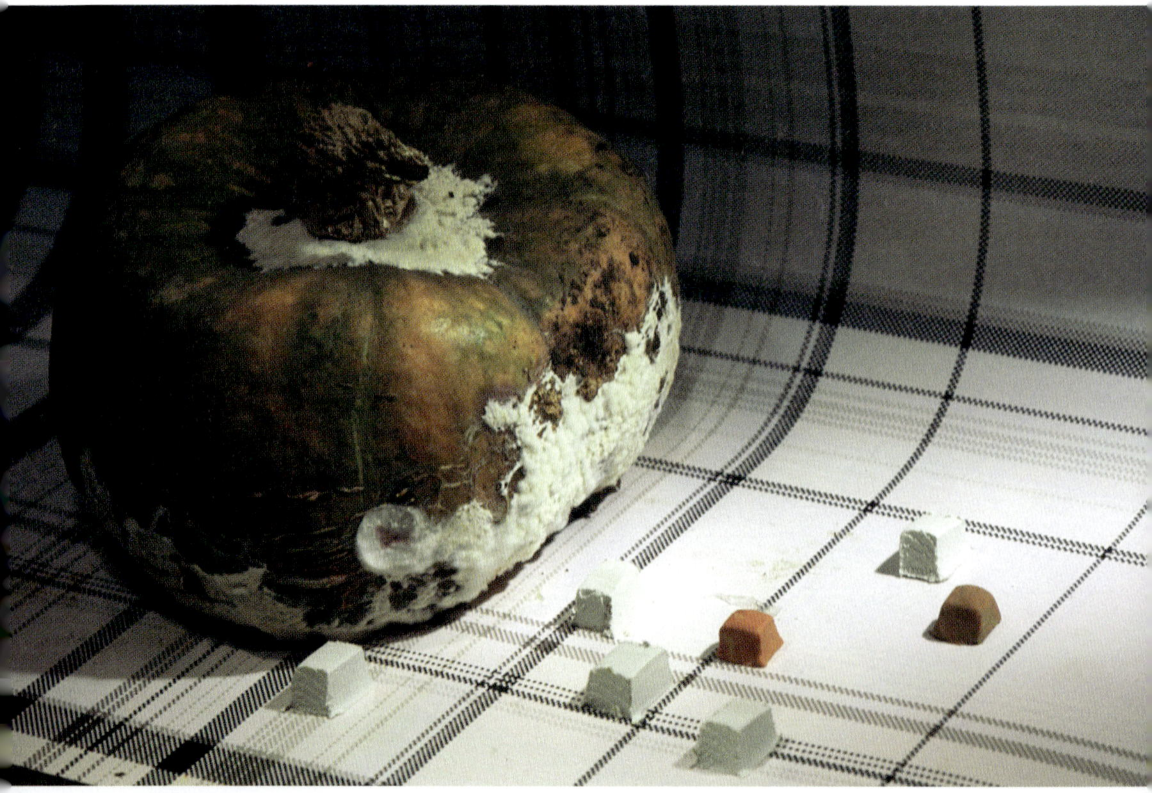

168   *Untitled #50, December 21, 2008, 2008, from Seed Stage*, pigment print, 14 x 21 inches. Collection of the Whitney Museum of American Art, New York; purchase, with funds from the Photography Committee and Henry Nias Foundation, 2009.28.50. Courtesy of the artist and Laurel Gitlen, New York.

Chapter 4, **Wall**

Wall
Western Bridge, Seattle, WA
March 25–April 3, 2010
Curated by Eric Fredericksen

Wall took place over eight days and consisted of the production of a video that tracked a hole in a wall being patched and then cut open again. Removing actual sections of drywall, plywood, and insulation from the gallery walls, Hewitt built a rectangular installation/workspace. In the video, printed photographic replicas of materials, tools, and the artist's hands appear alongside "original" versions of each. The materials from the walls of the institution were supplemented with tools, computers, cameras, and printers to create a fragmented cube surrounding the tabletop where the video was being produced. Viewers could watch the activities taking place on the worktable via a live feed on a wall outside the gallery room.

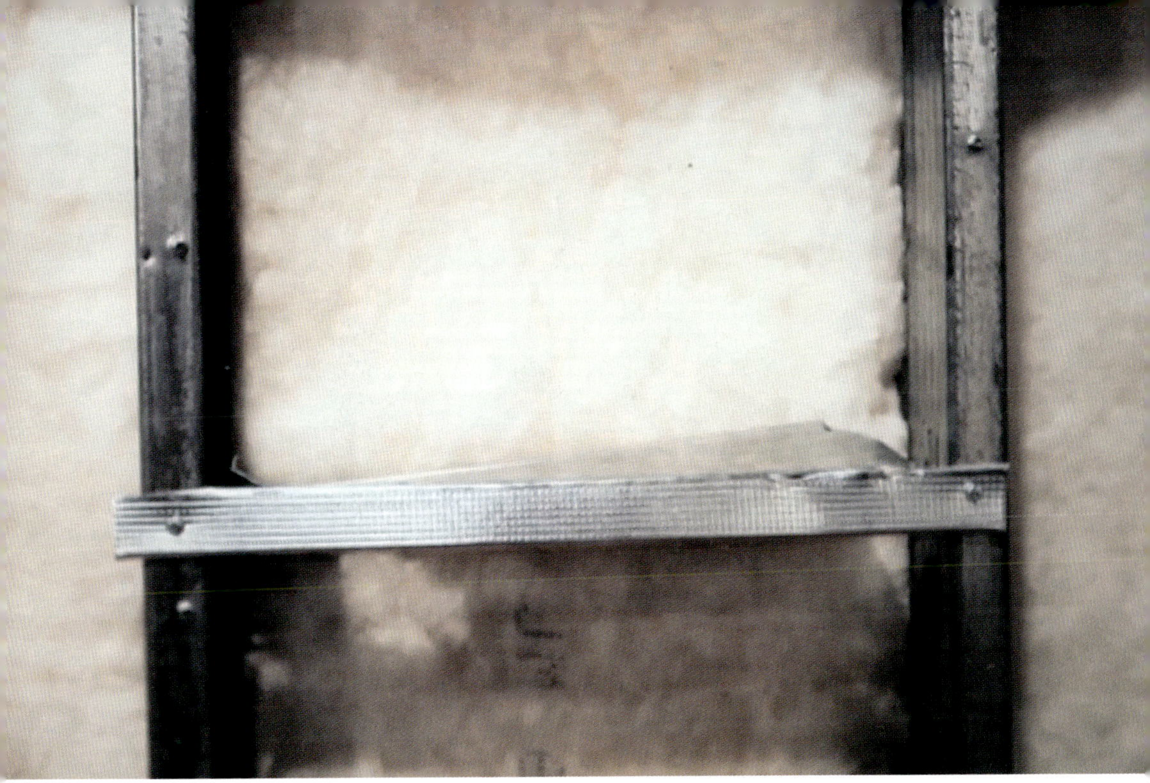

169   *Wall*, 2010, video still, video with sound, 72:00 minutes. Collection of William and Ruth True, Seattle. Courtesy of the artist and Laurel Gitlen, New York.

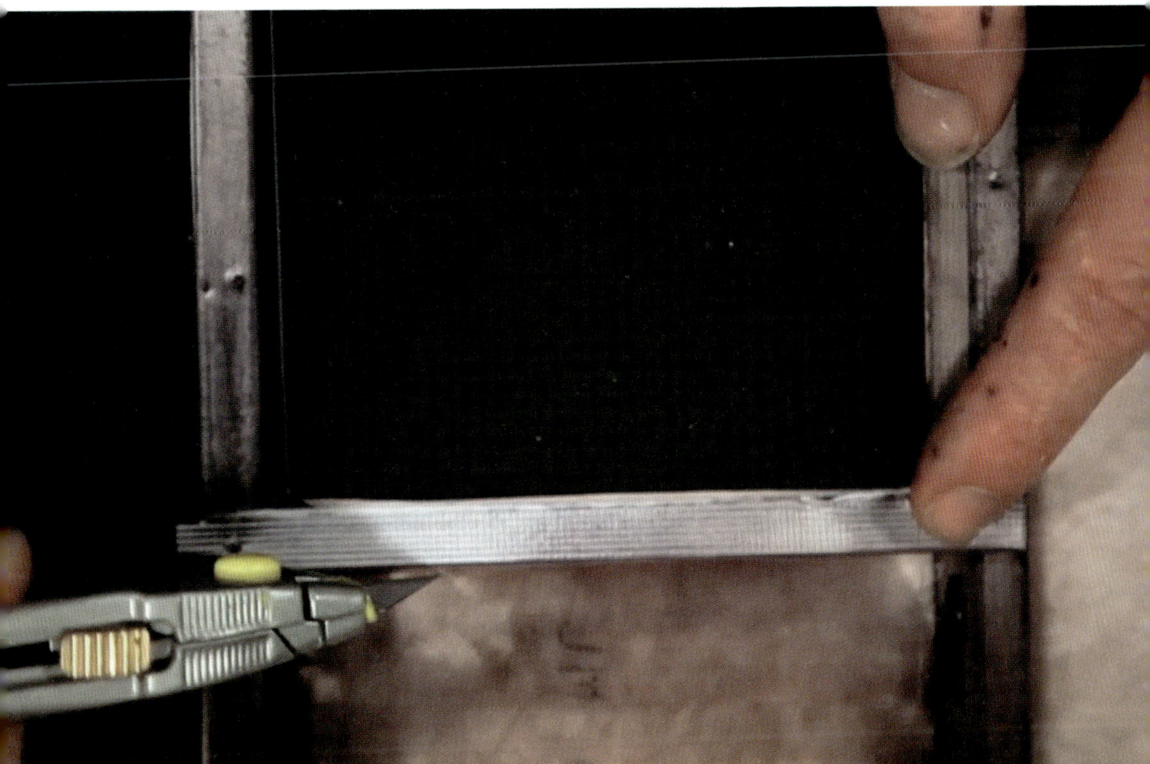

170   *Wall*, 2010, video still, video with sound, 72:00 minutes. Collection of William and Ruth True, Seattle. Courtesy of the artist and Laurel Gitlen, New York.

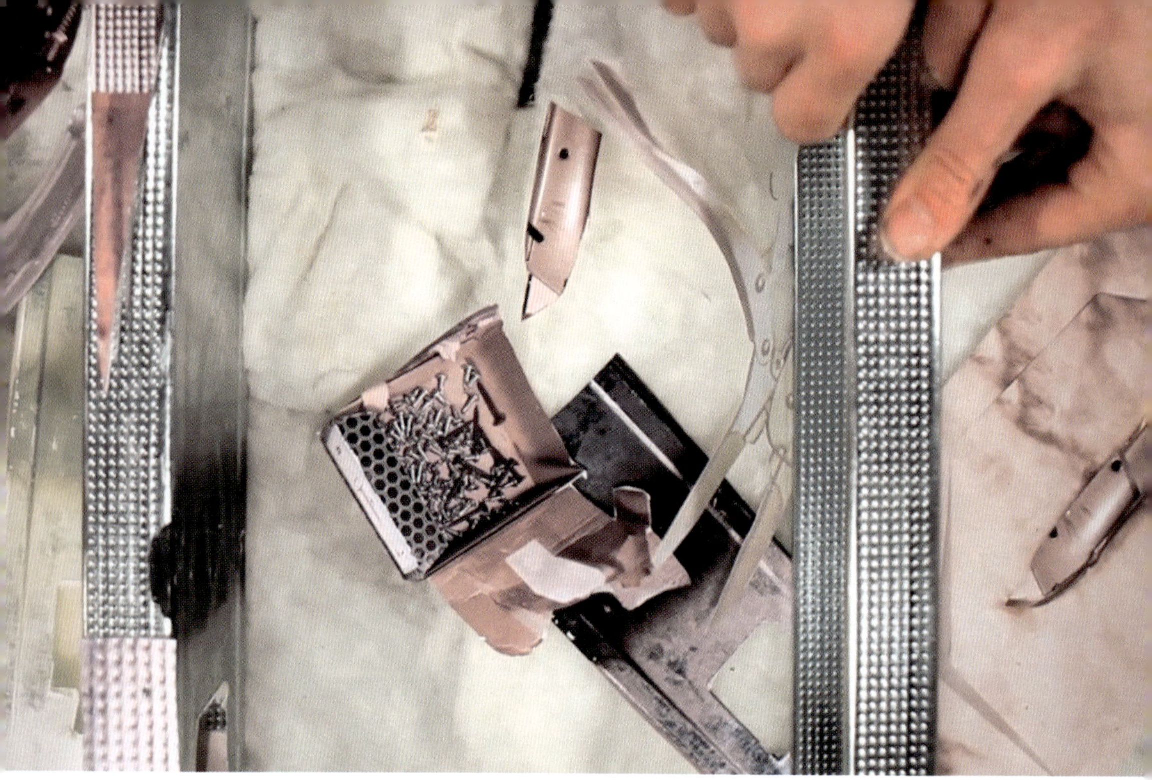

171   *Wall*, 2010, video still, video with sound, 72:00 minutes. Collection of William and Ruth True, Seattle. Courtesy of the artist and Laurel Gitlen, New York.

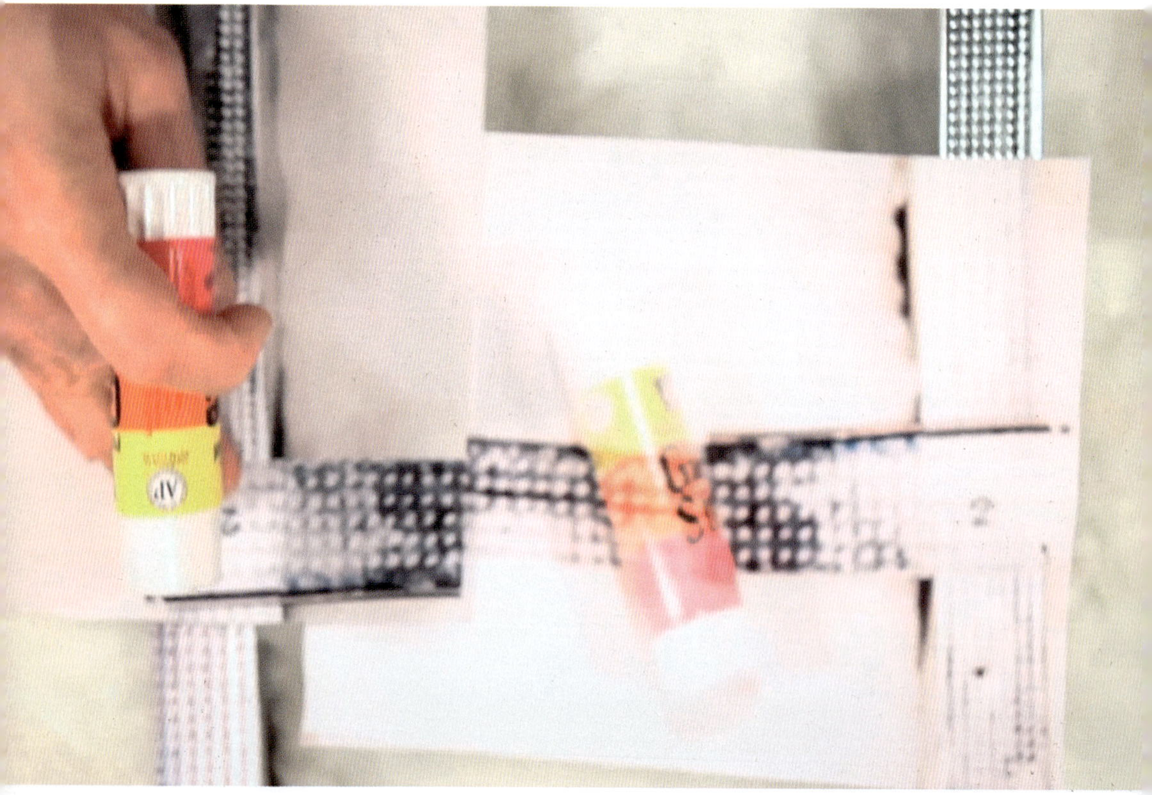

172   *Wall*, 2010, video still, video with sound, 72:00 minutes. Collection of William and Ruth True, Seattle. Courtesy of the artist and Laurel Gitlen, New York.

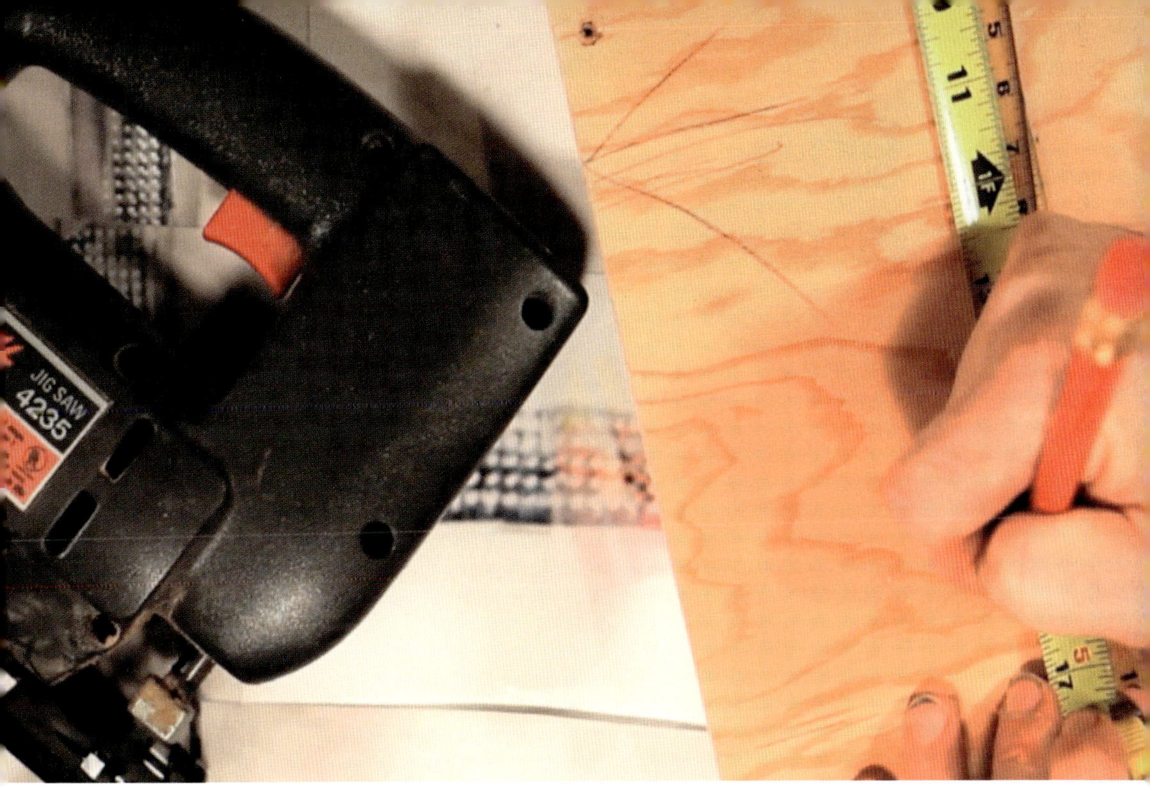

173   *Wall*, 2010, video still, video with sound, 72:00 minutes. Collection of William and Ruth True, Seattle. Courtesy of the artist and Laurel Gitlen, New York.

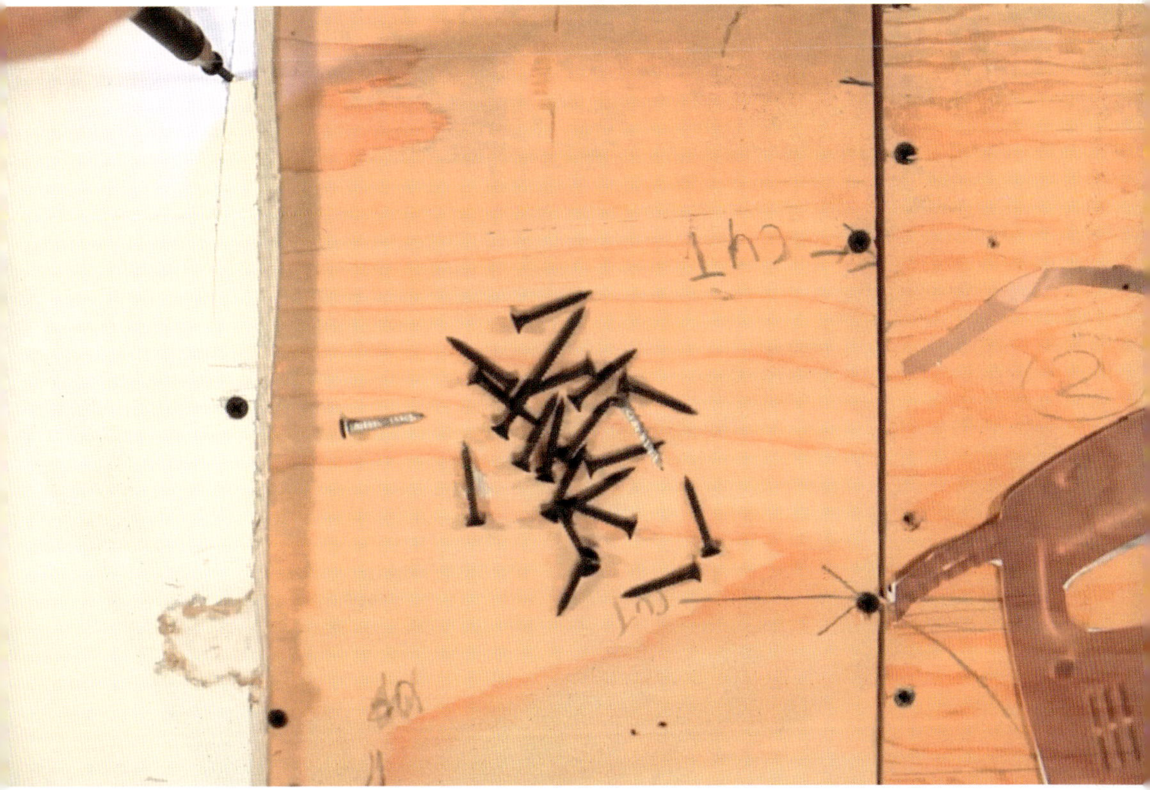

174   *Wall*, 2010, video still, video with sound, 72:00 minutes. Collection of William and Ruth True, Seattle. Courtesy of the artist and Laurel Gitlen, New York.

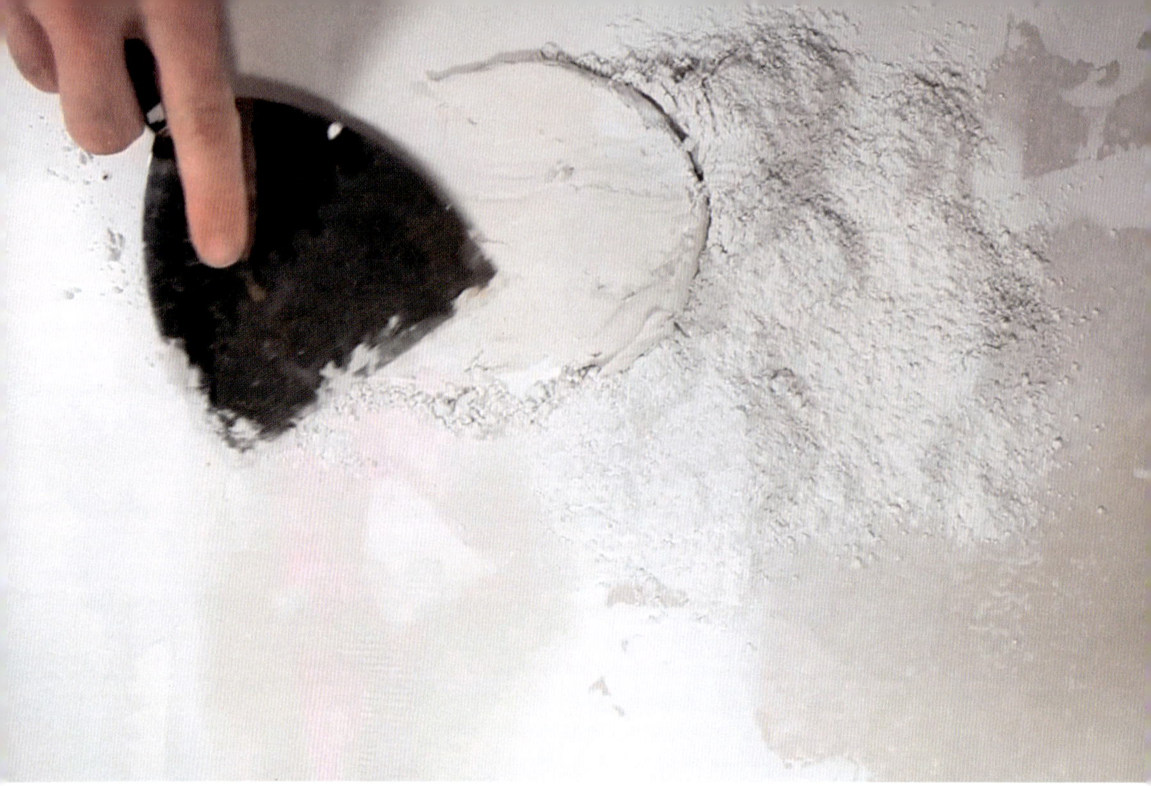

175   *Wall*, 2010, video still, video with sound, 72:00 minutes. Collection of William and Ruth True, Seattle. Courtesy of the artist and Laurel Gitlen, New York.

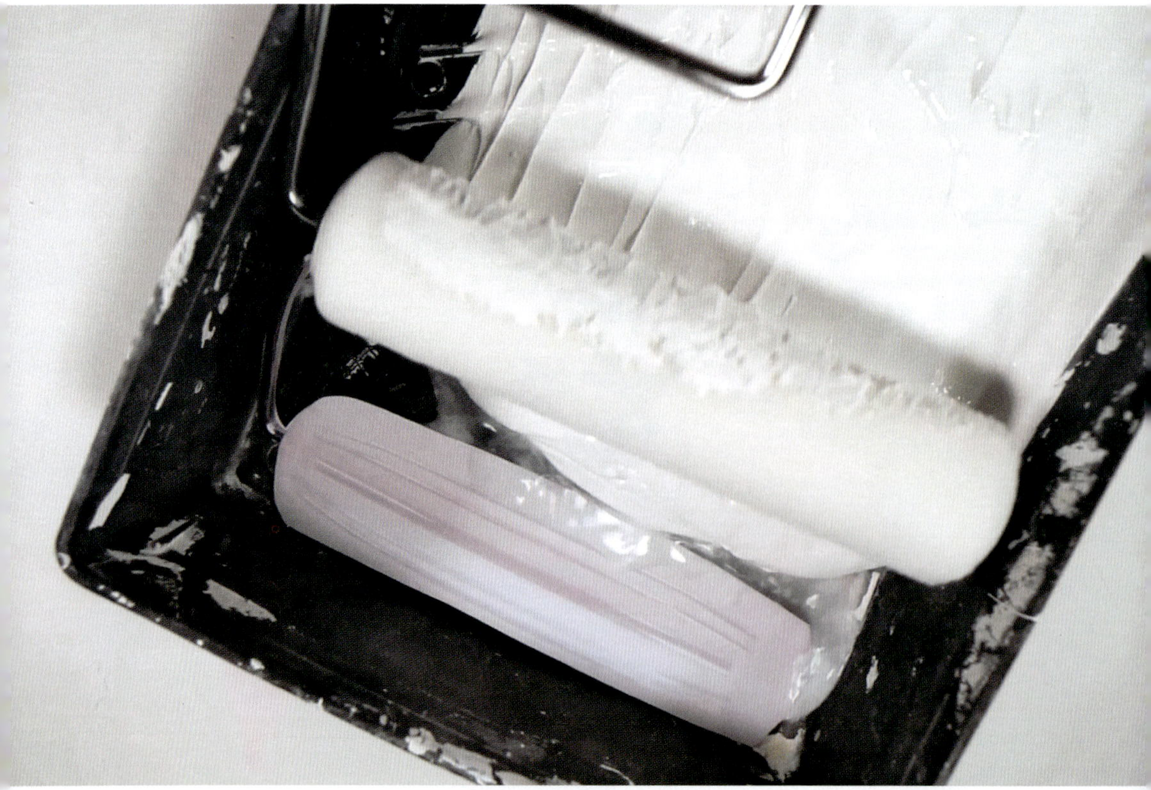

176   *Wall*, 2010, video still, video with sound, 72:00 minutes. Collection of William and Ruth True, Seattle. Courtesy of the artist and Laurel Gitlen, New York.

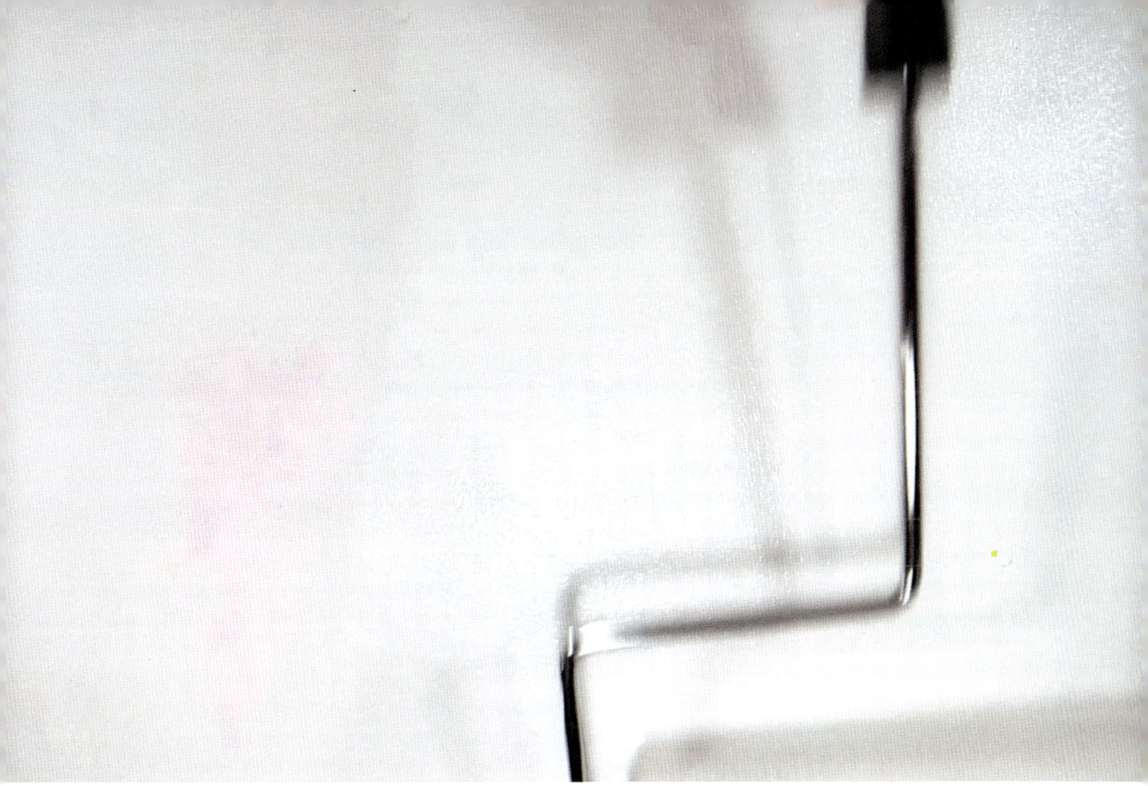

 Wall, 2010, video still, video with sound, 72:00 minutes. Collection of William and Ruth True, Seattle. Courtesy of the artist and Laurel Gitlen, New York.

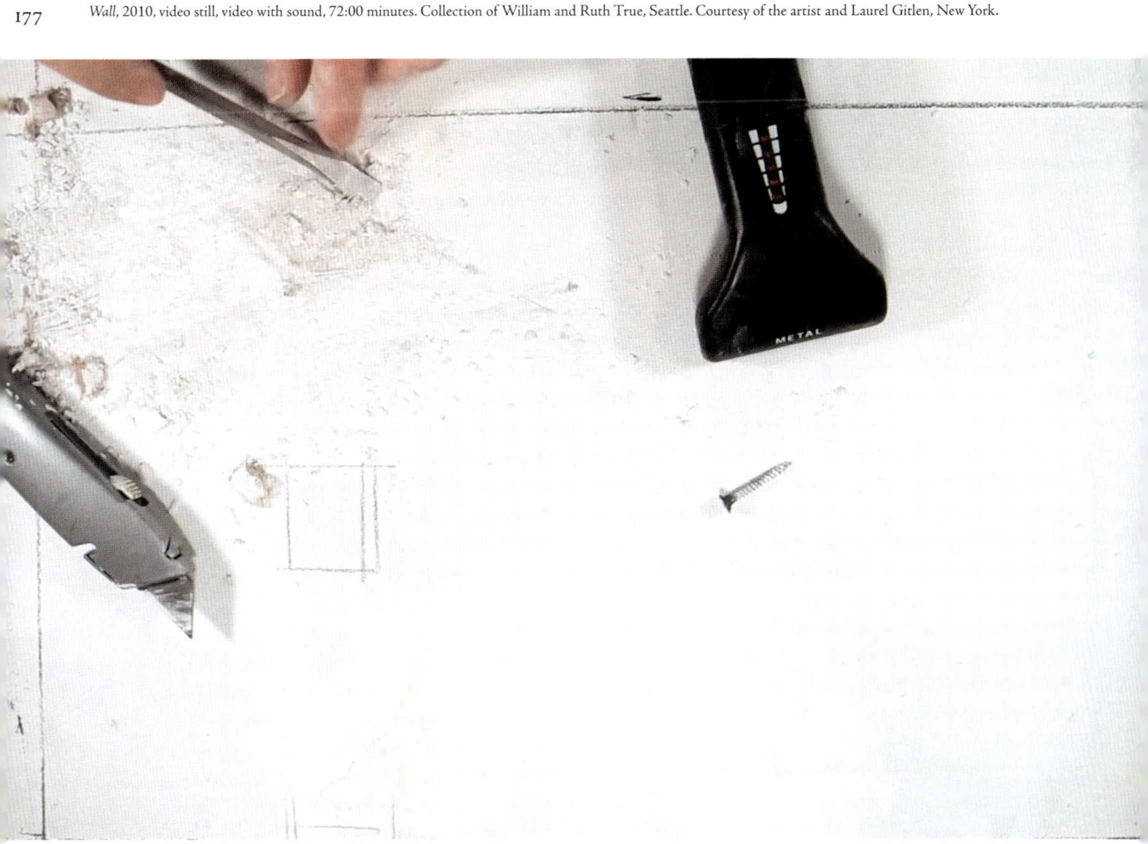

 Wall, 2010, video still, video with sound, 72:00 minutes. Collection of William and Ruth True, Seattle. Courtesy of the artist and Laurel Gitlen, New York.

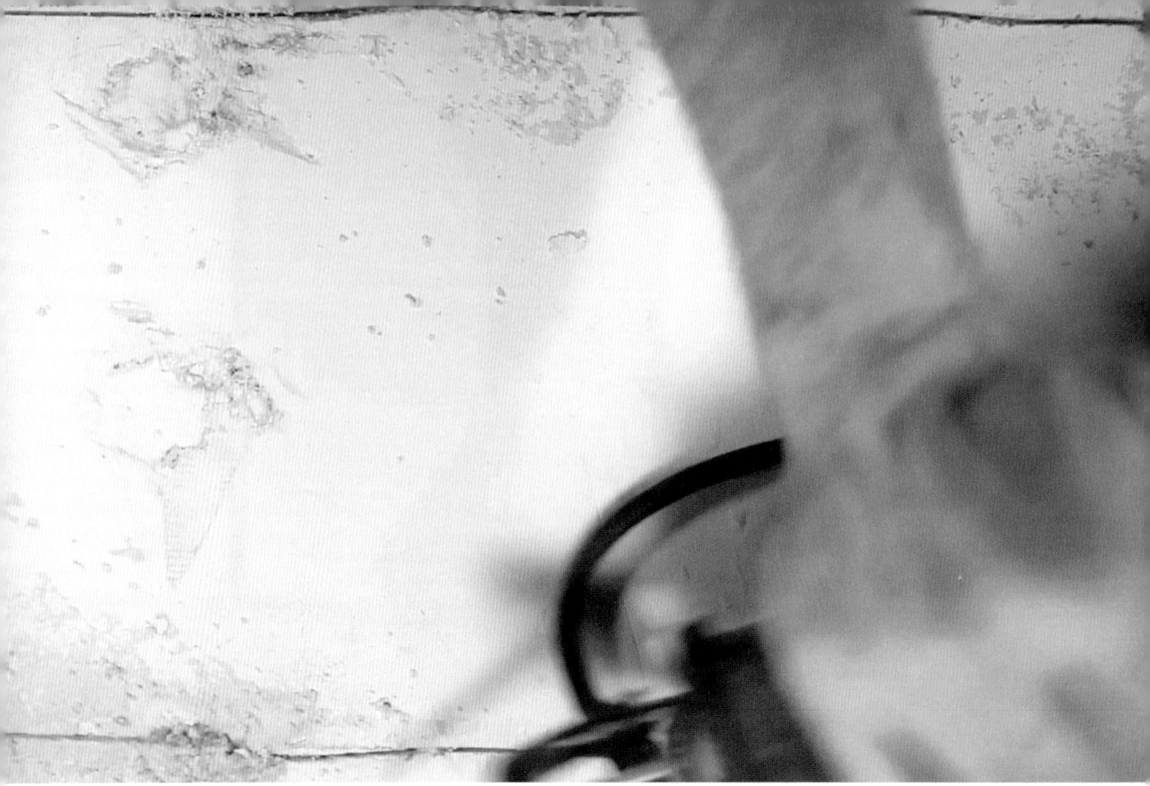

 Wall, 2010, video still, video with sound, 72:00 minutes. Collection of William and Ruth True, Seattle. Courtesy of the artist and Laurel Gitlen, New York.

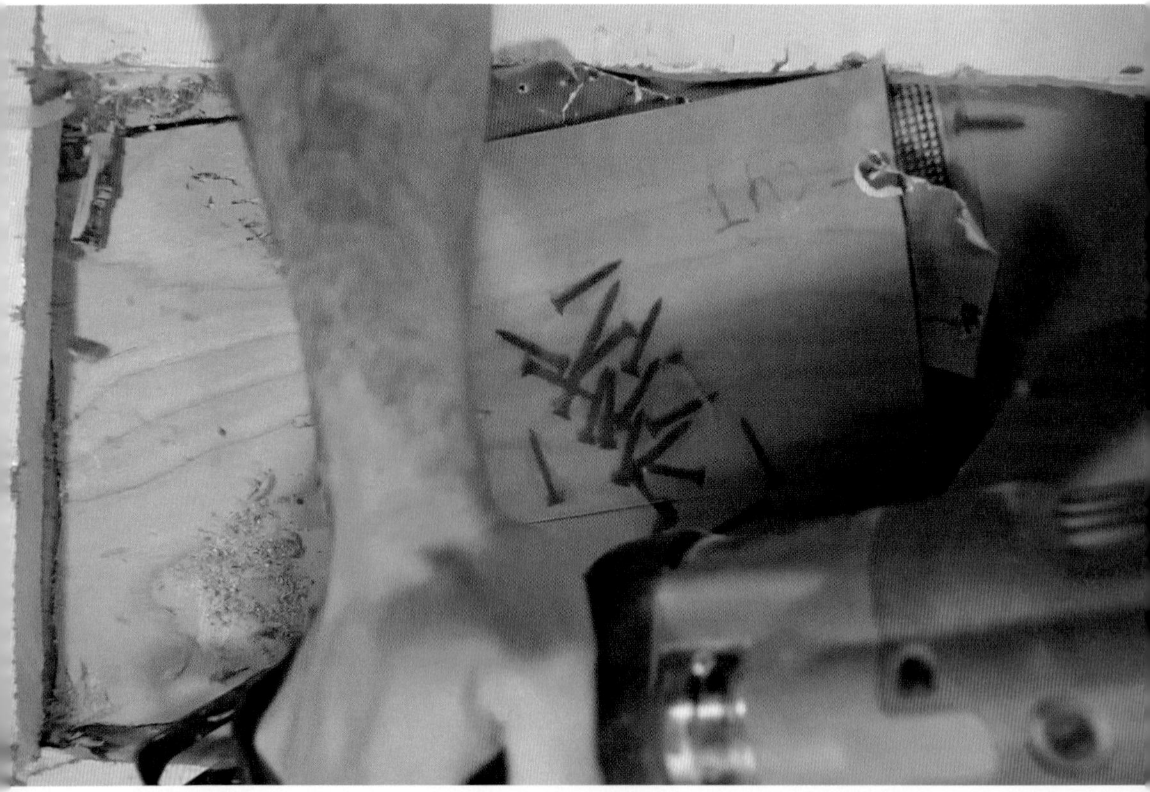

 Wall, 2010, video still, video with sound, 72:00 minutes. Collection of William and Ruth True, Seattle. Courtesy of the artist and Laurel Gitlen, New York.

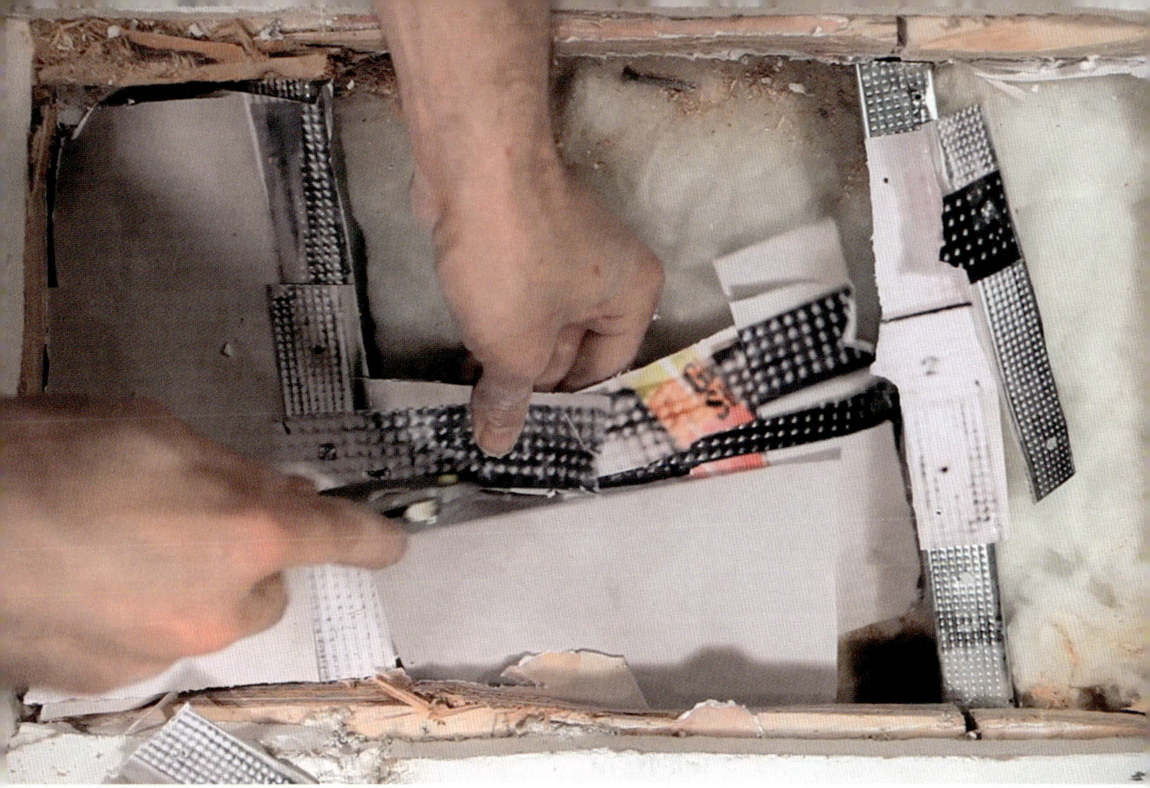

181   *Wall*, 2010, video still, video with sound, 72:00 minutes. Collection of William and Ruth True, Seattle. Courtesy of the artist and Laurel Gitlen, New York.

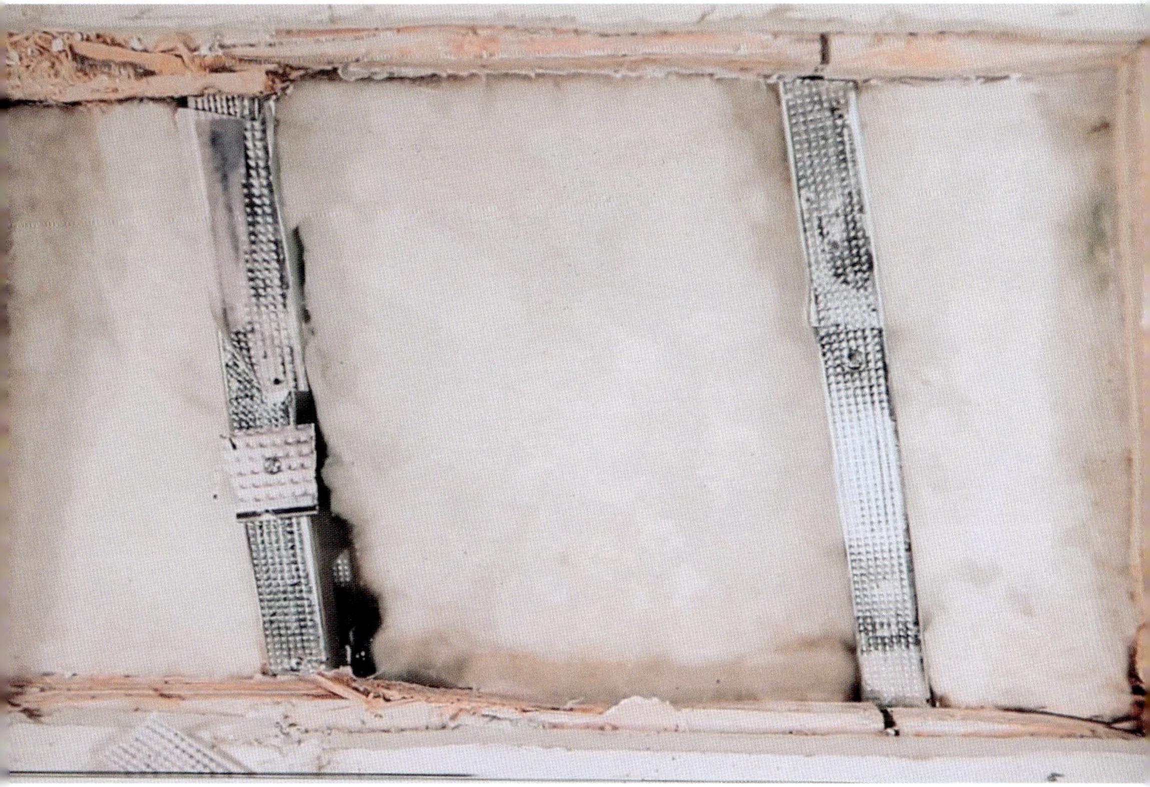

182   *Wall*, 2010, video still, video with sound, 72:00 minutes. Collection of William and Ruth True, Seattle. Courtesy of the artist and Laurel Gitlen, New York.

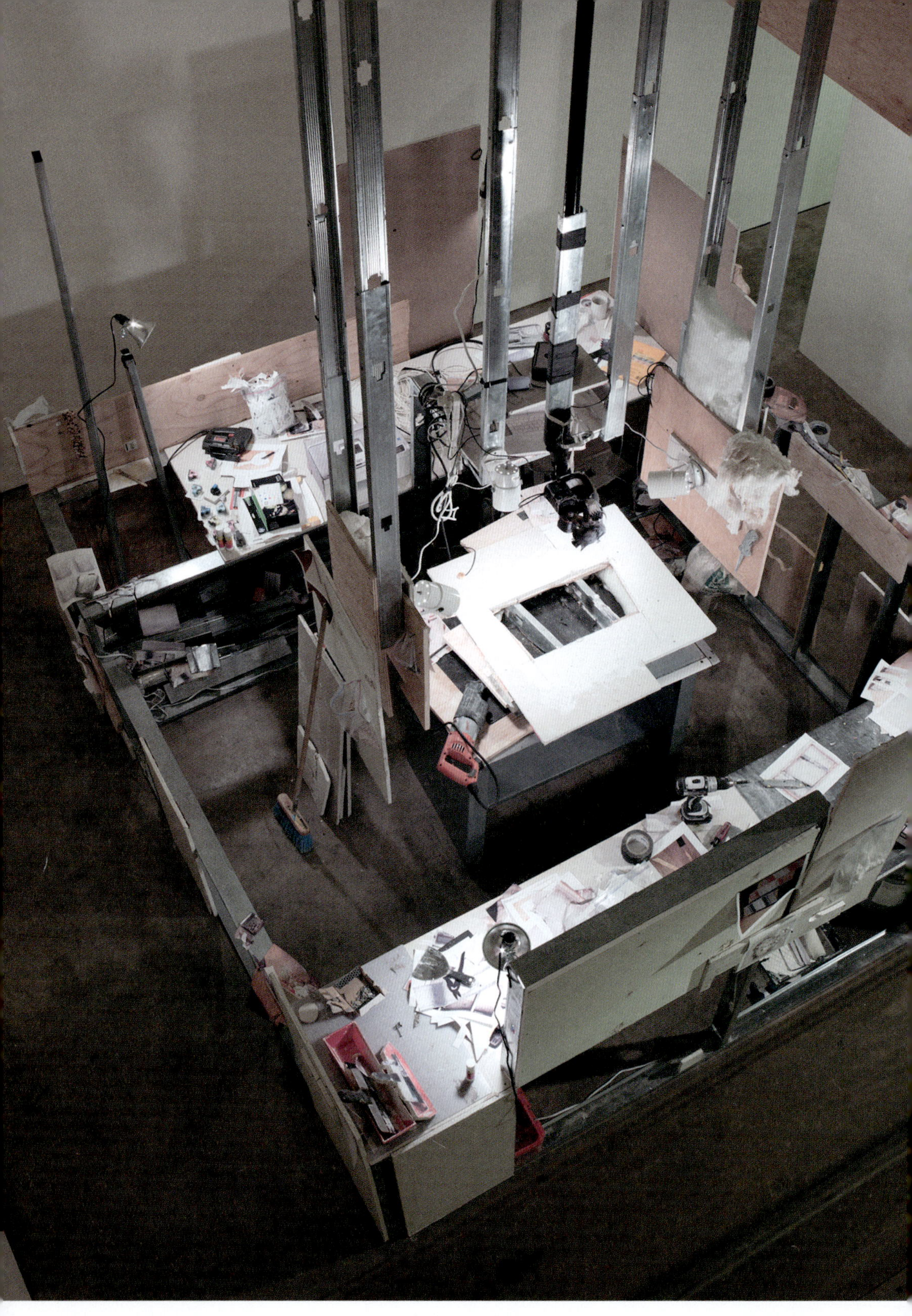

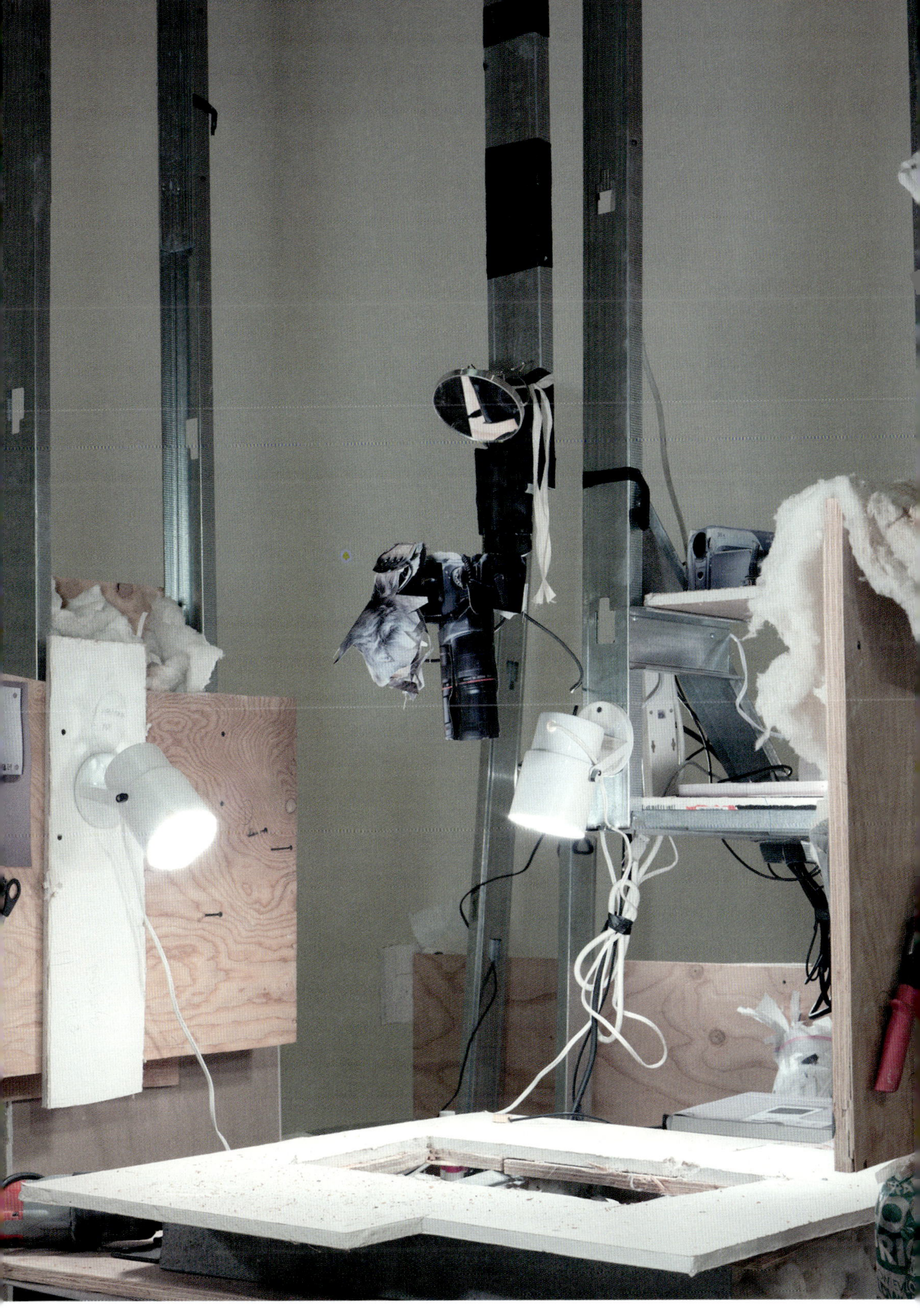

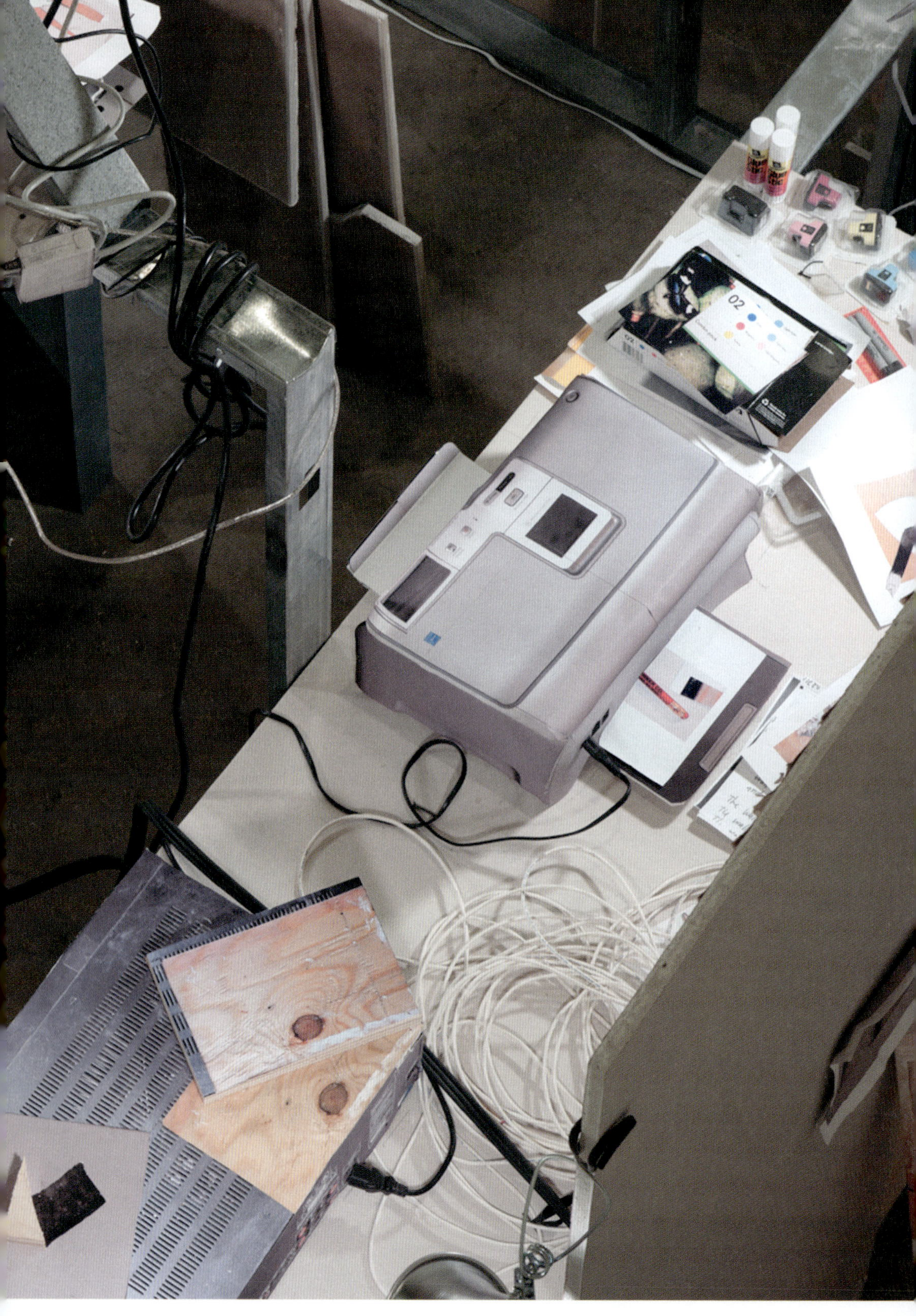

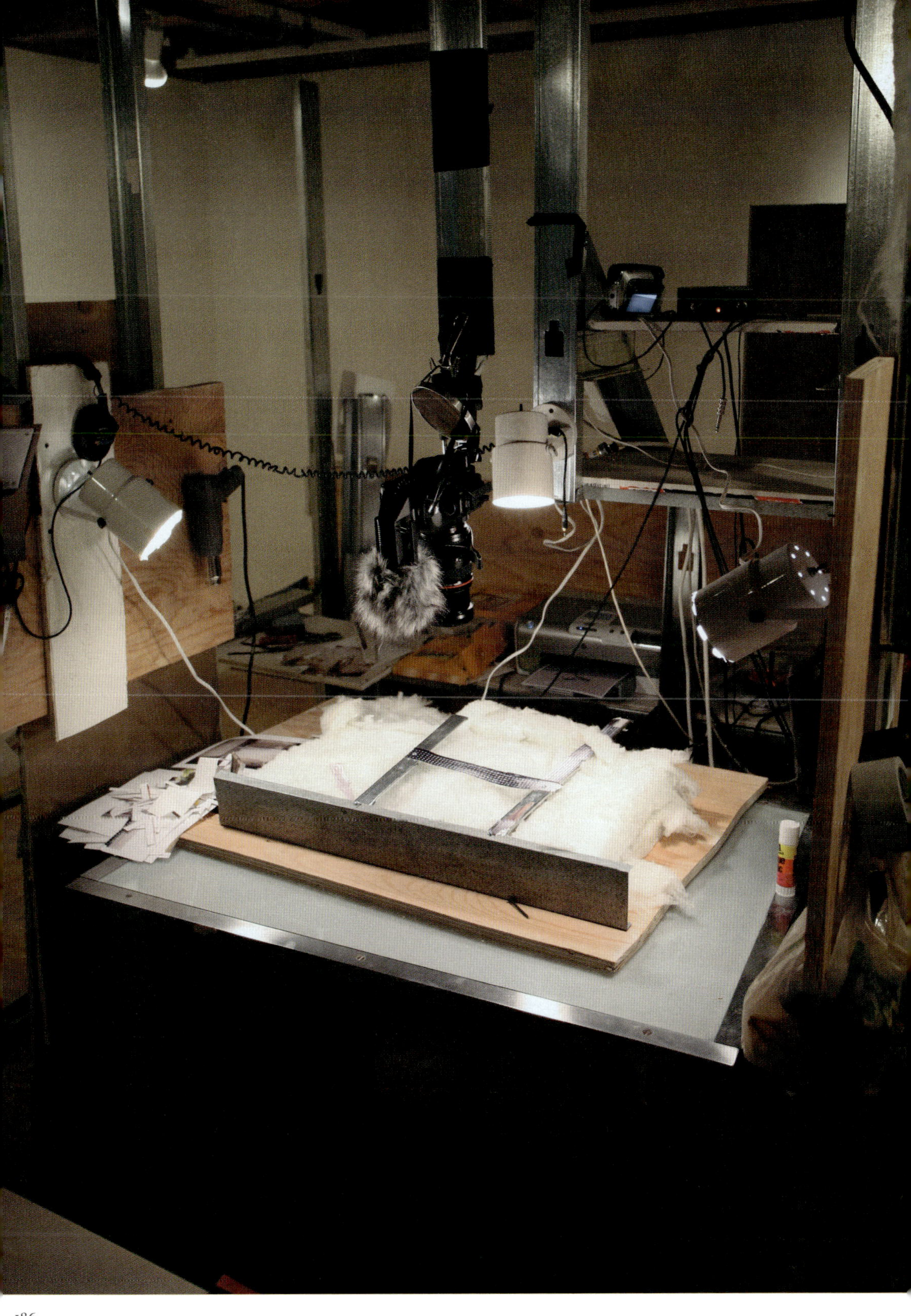

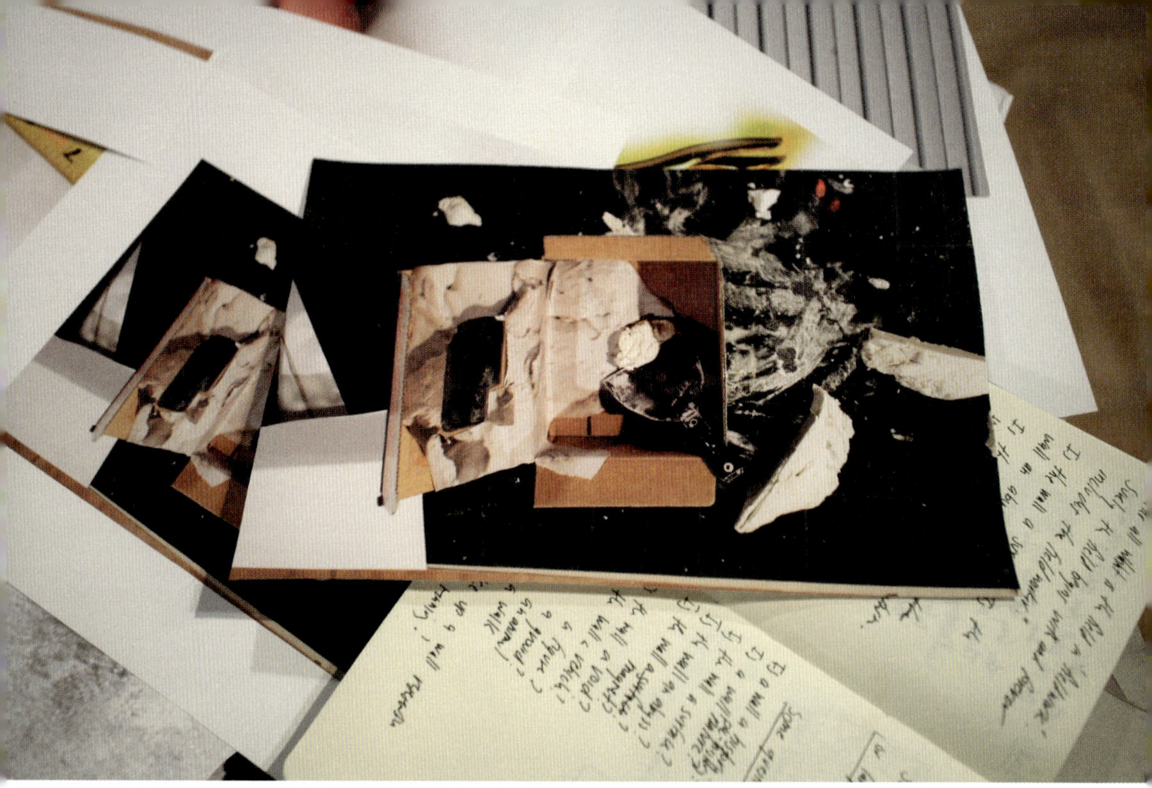

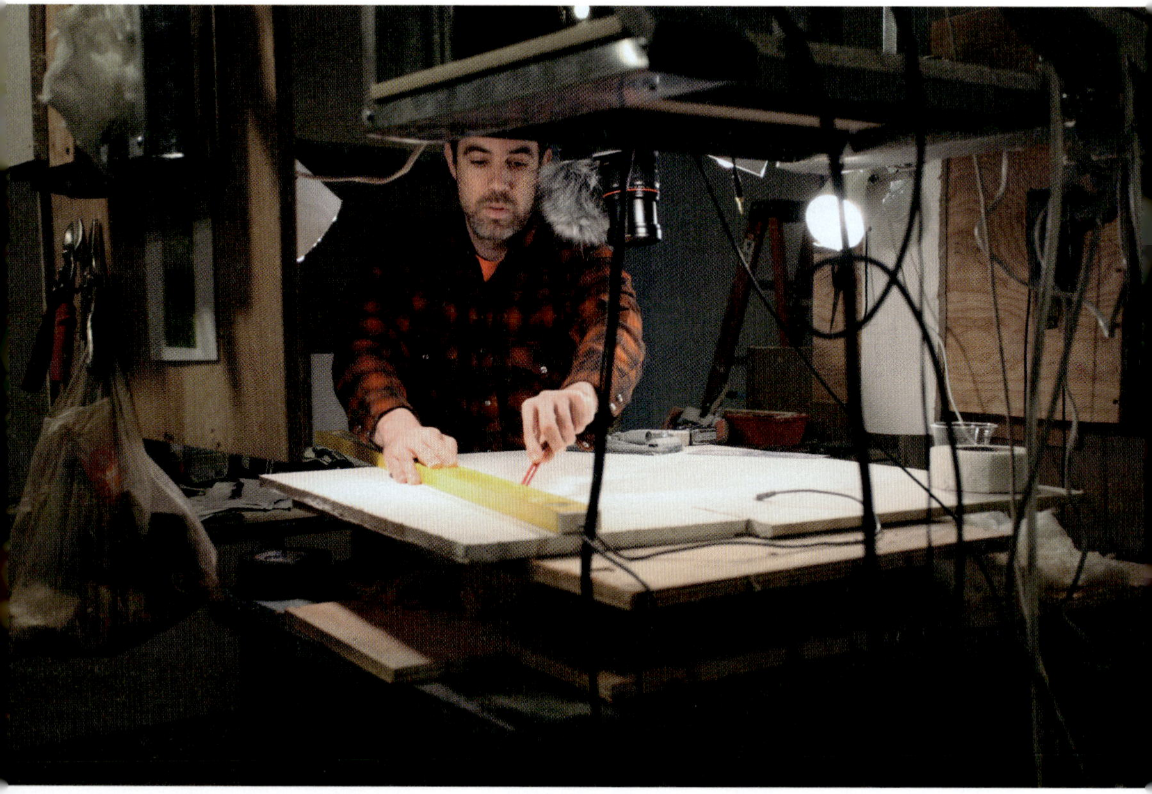

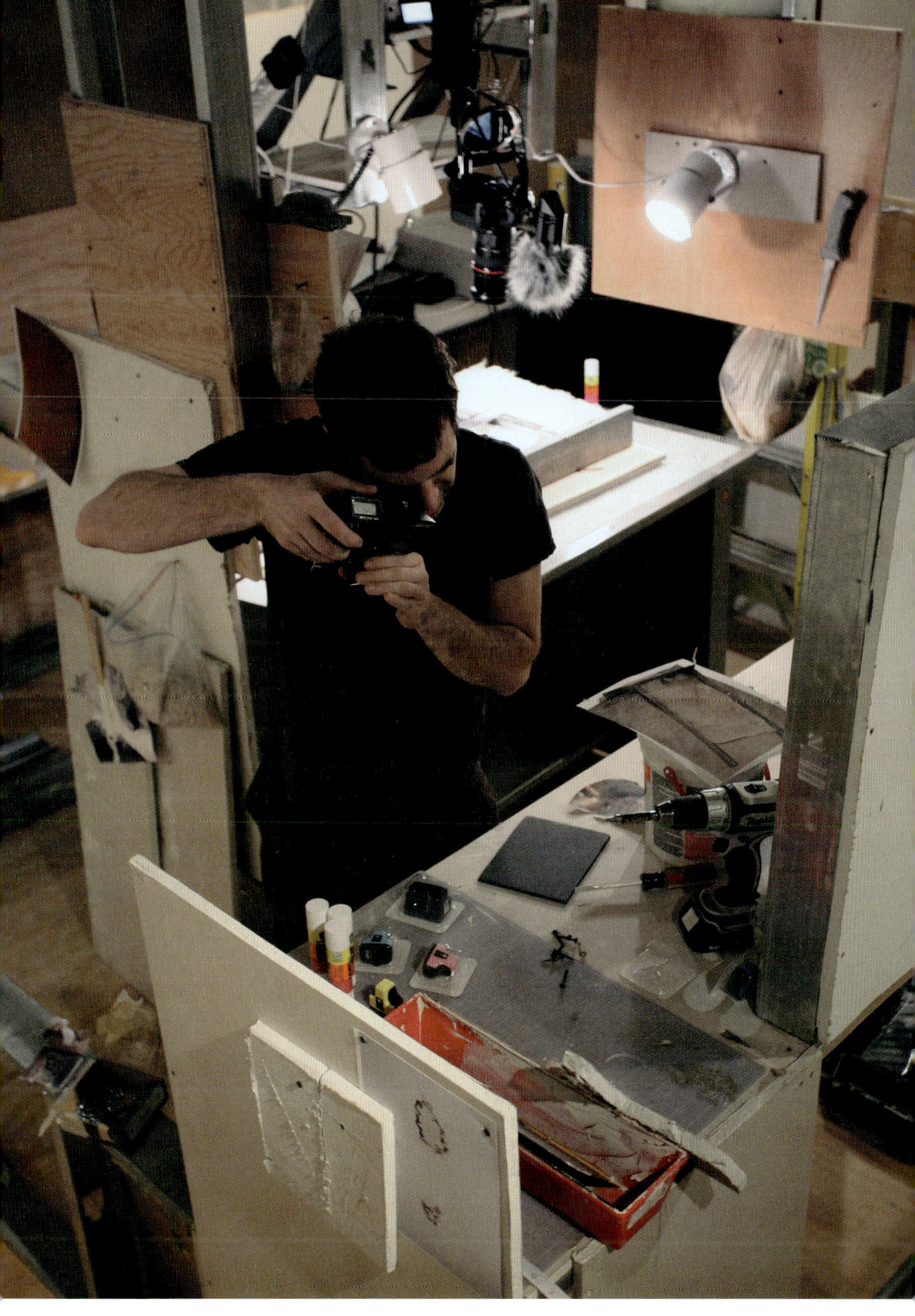

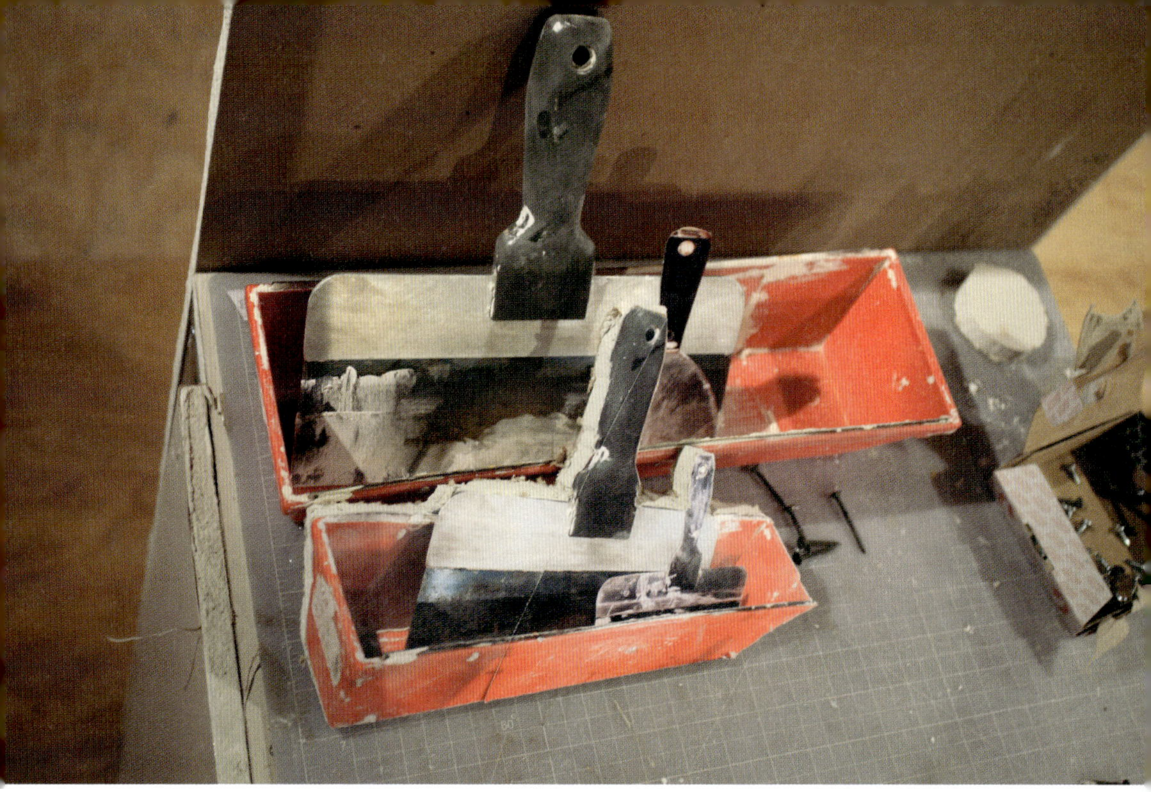

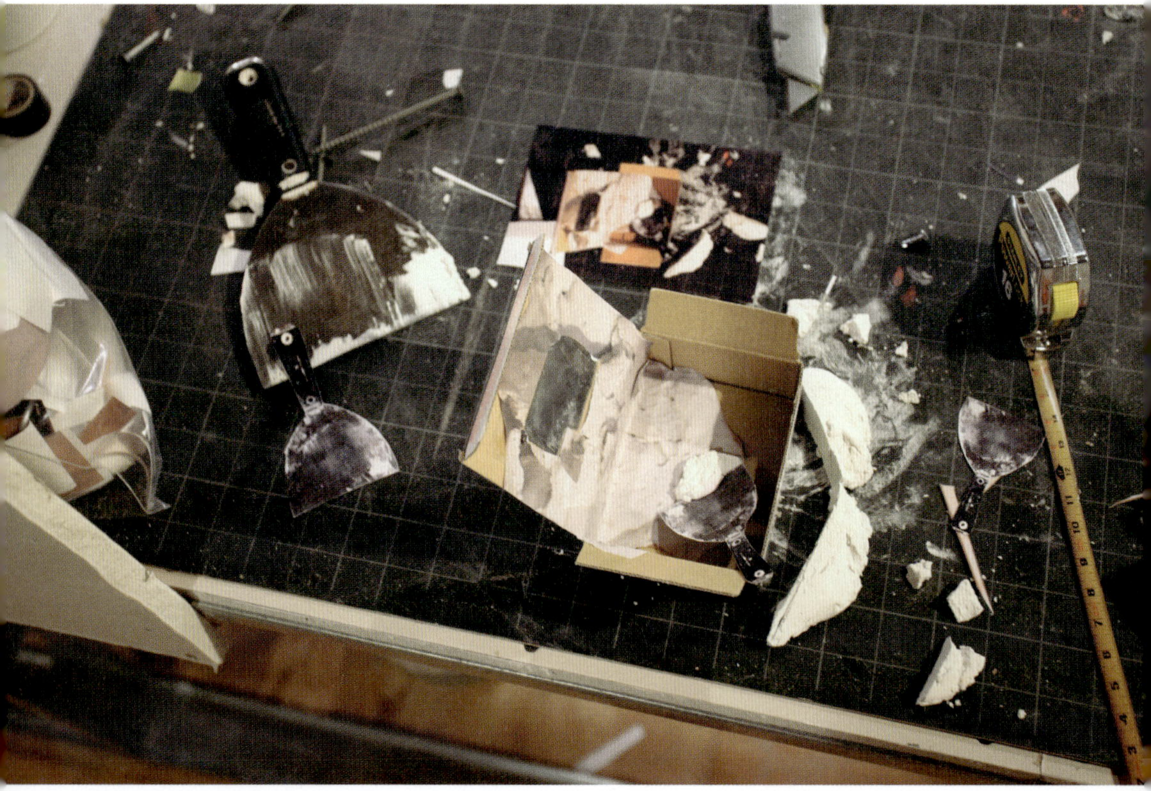

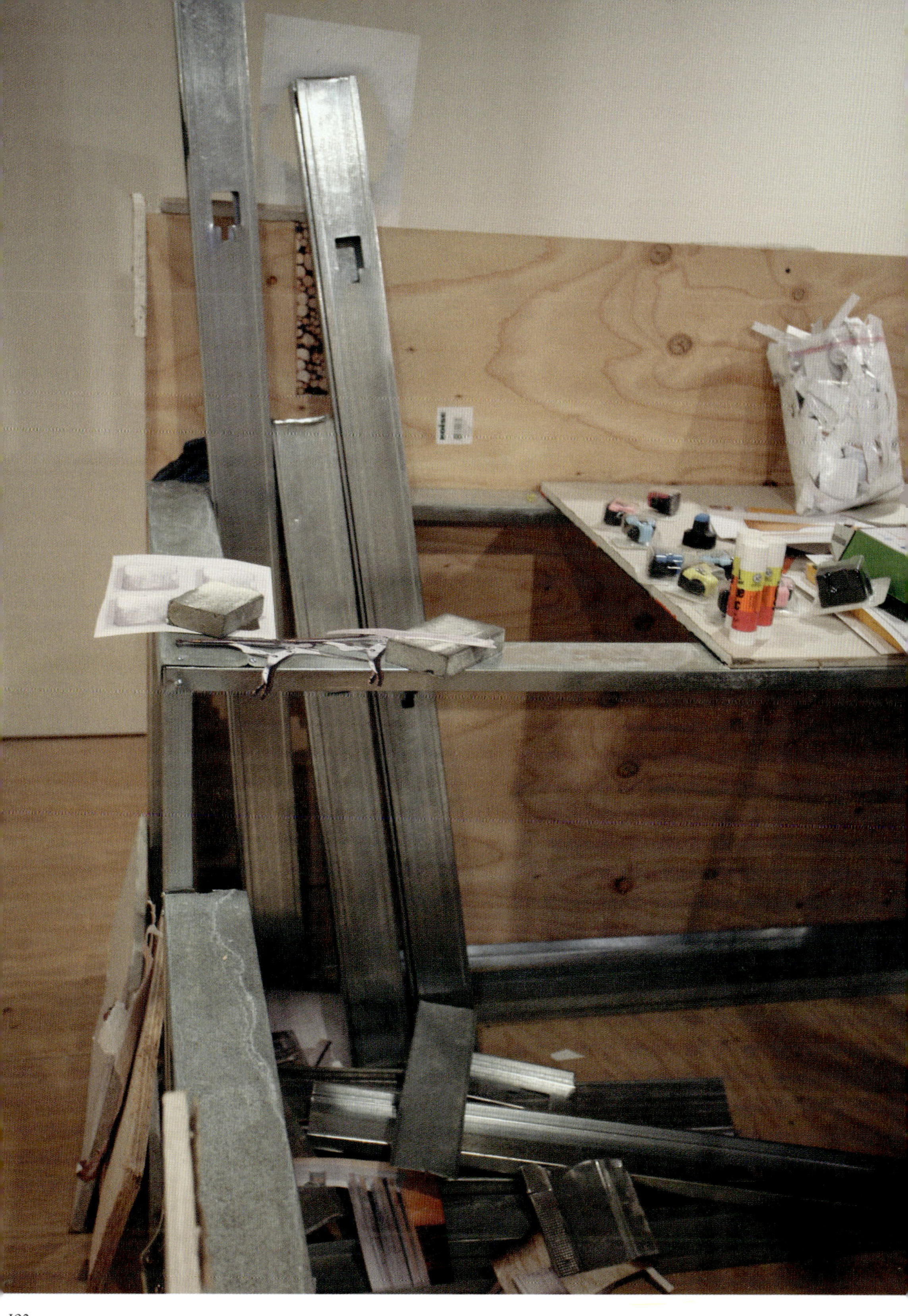

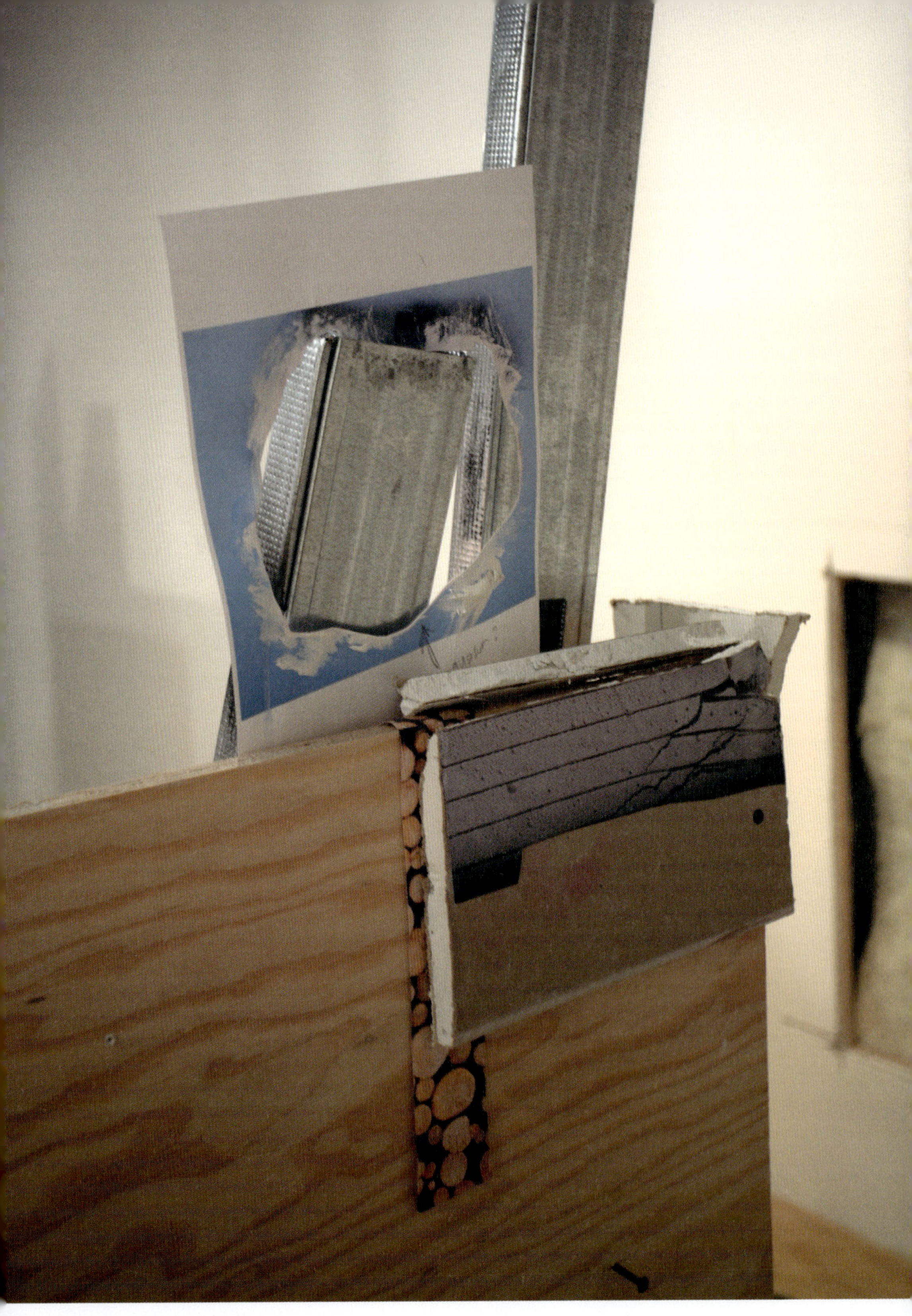

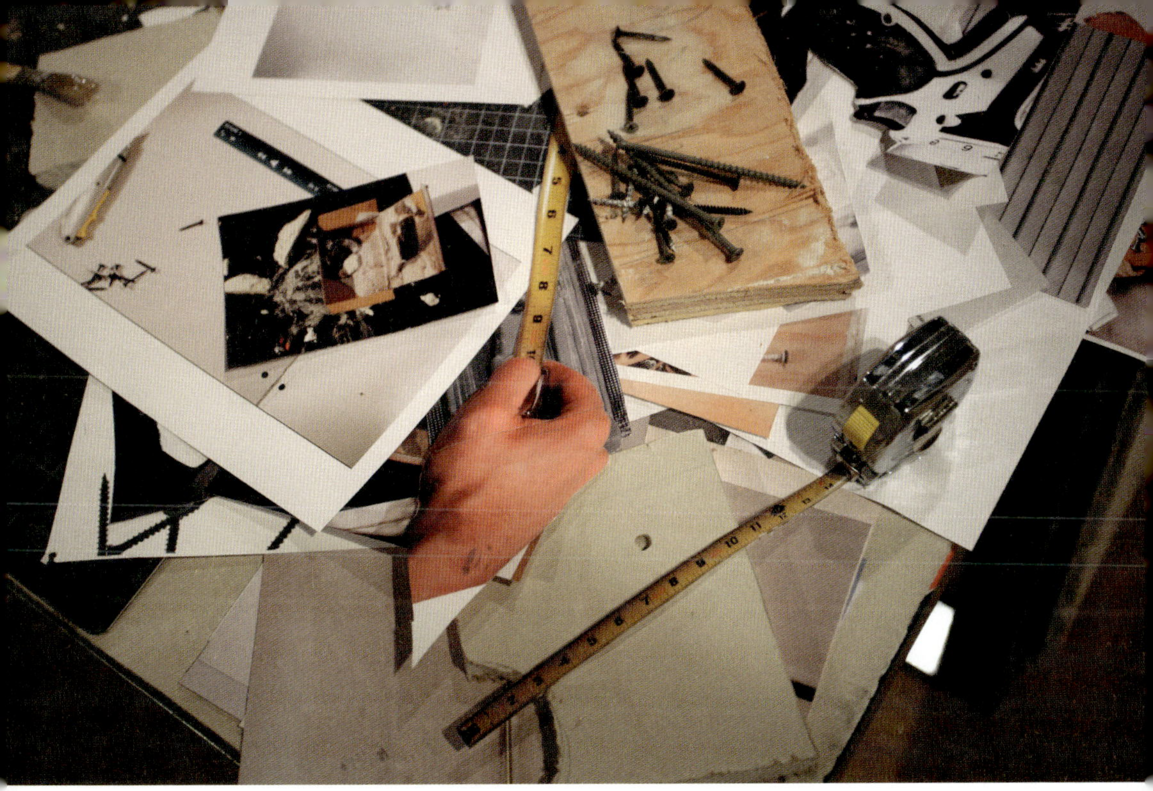

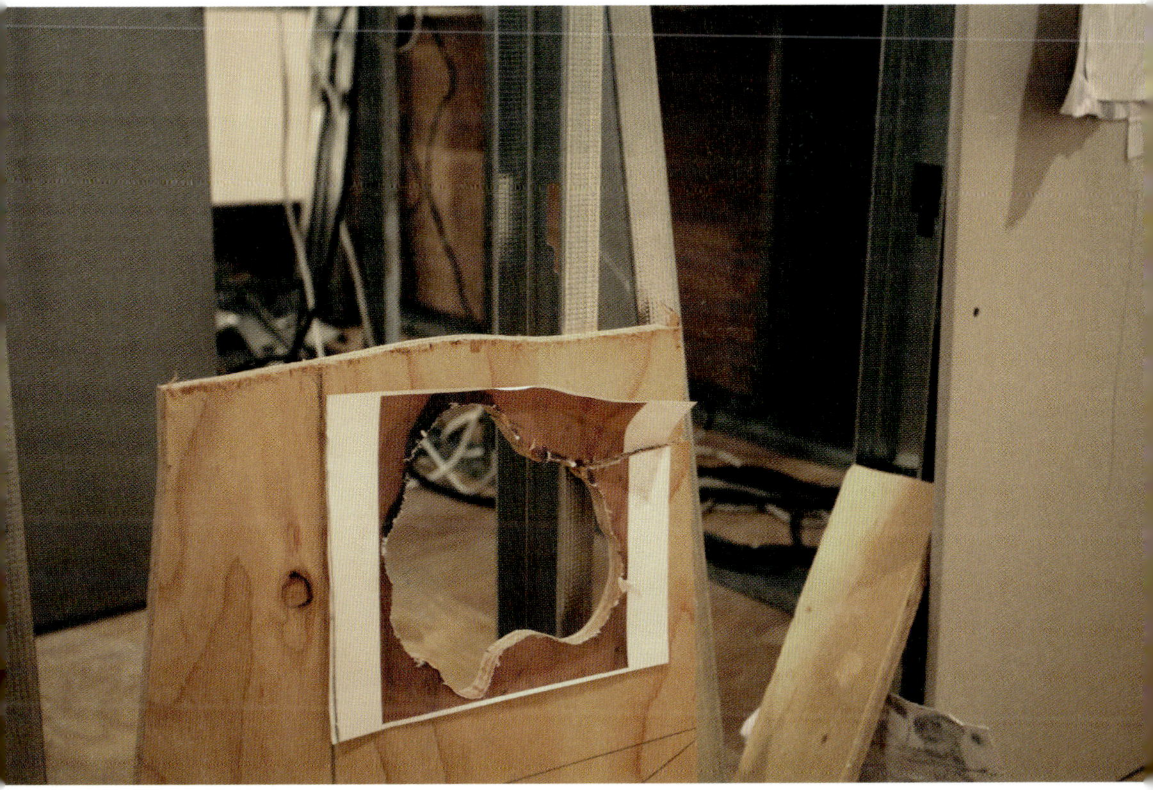

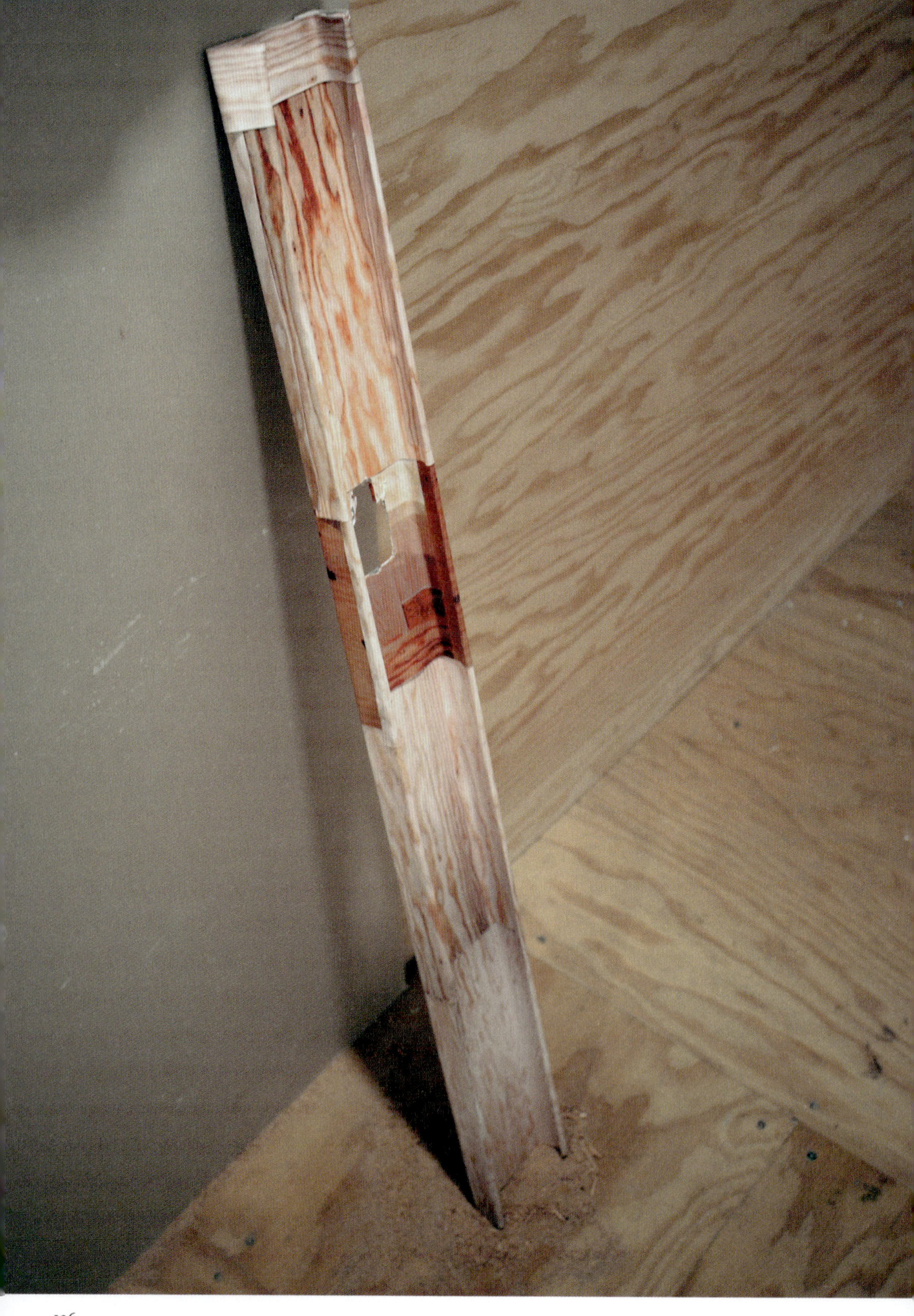

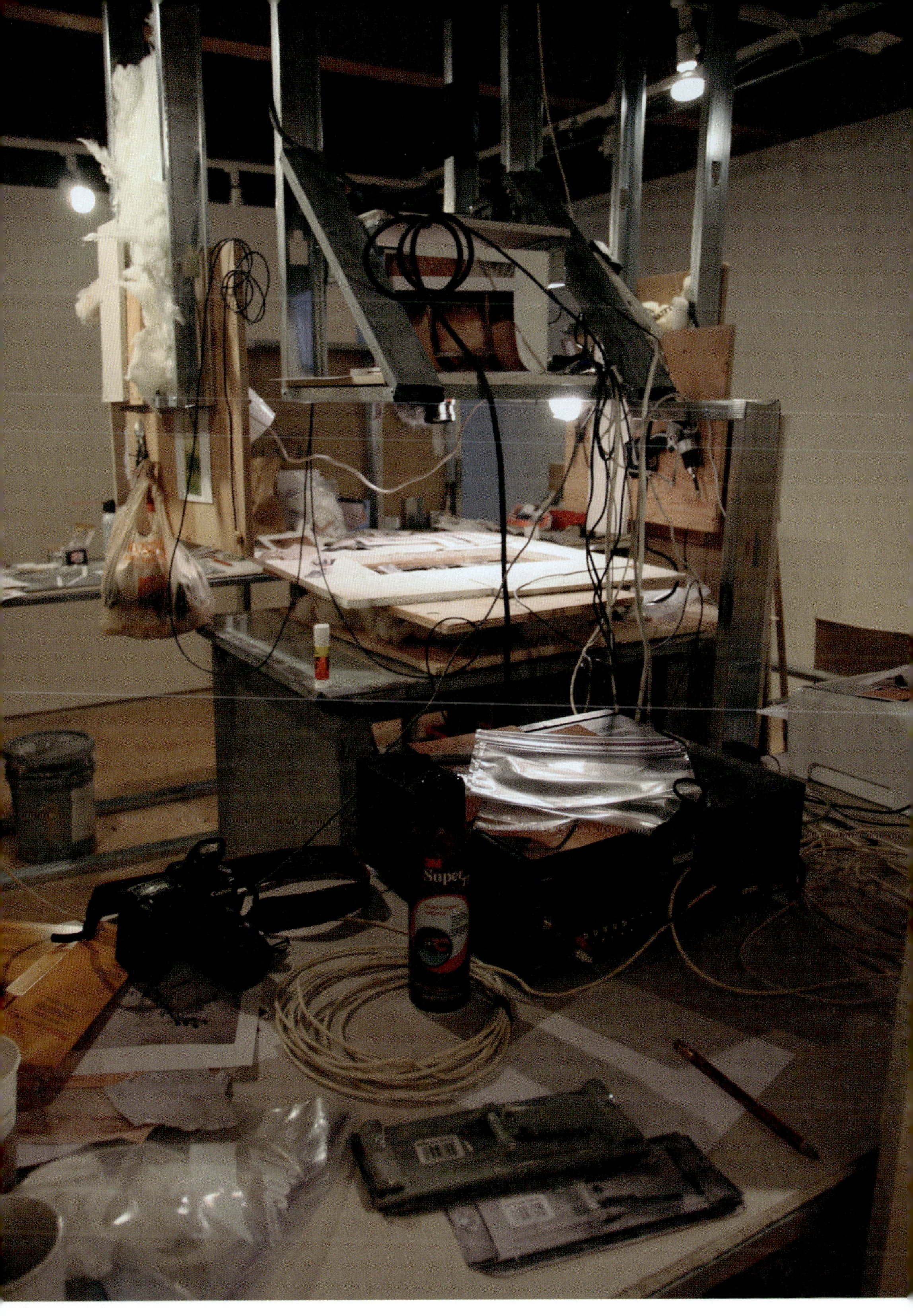

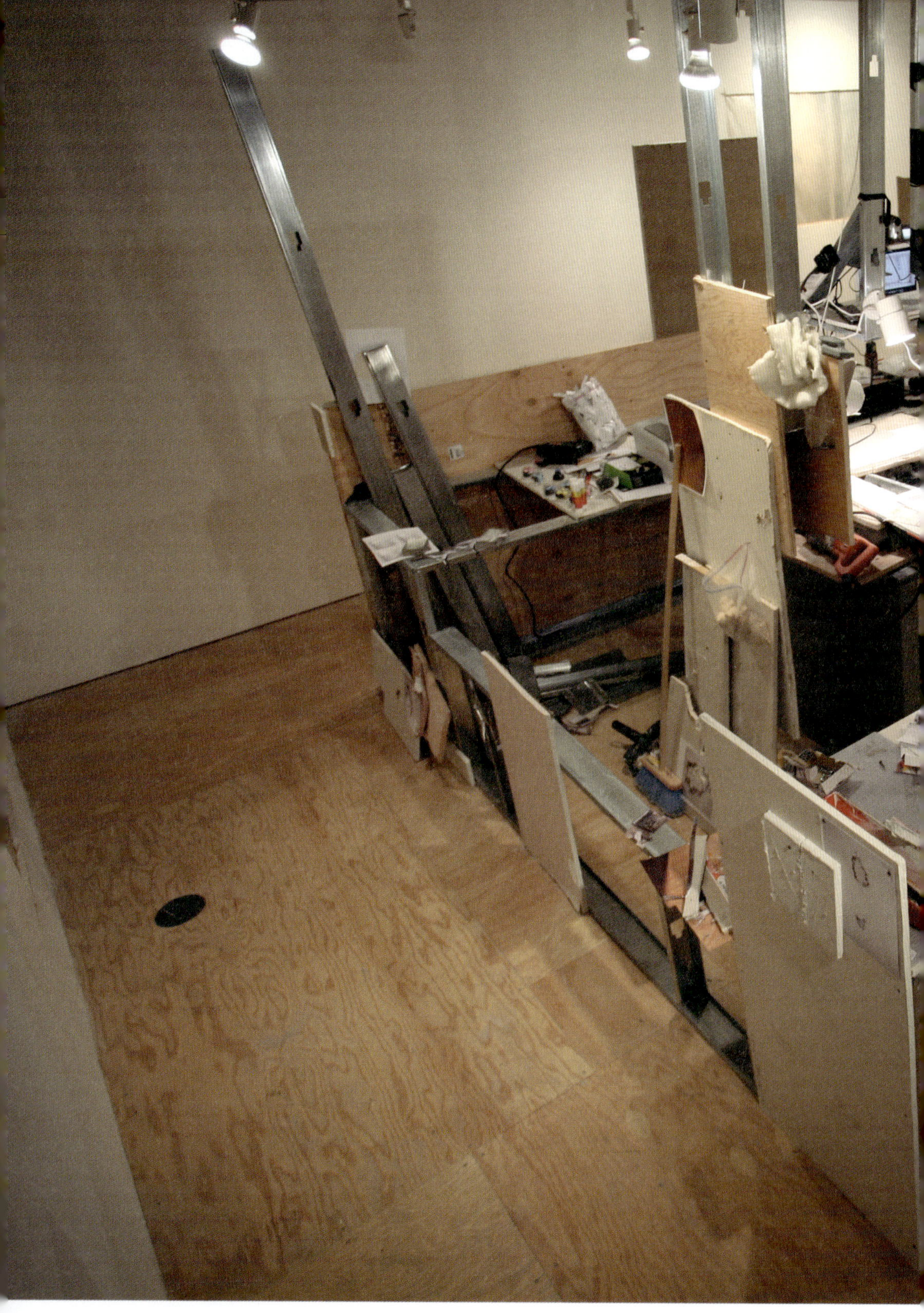

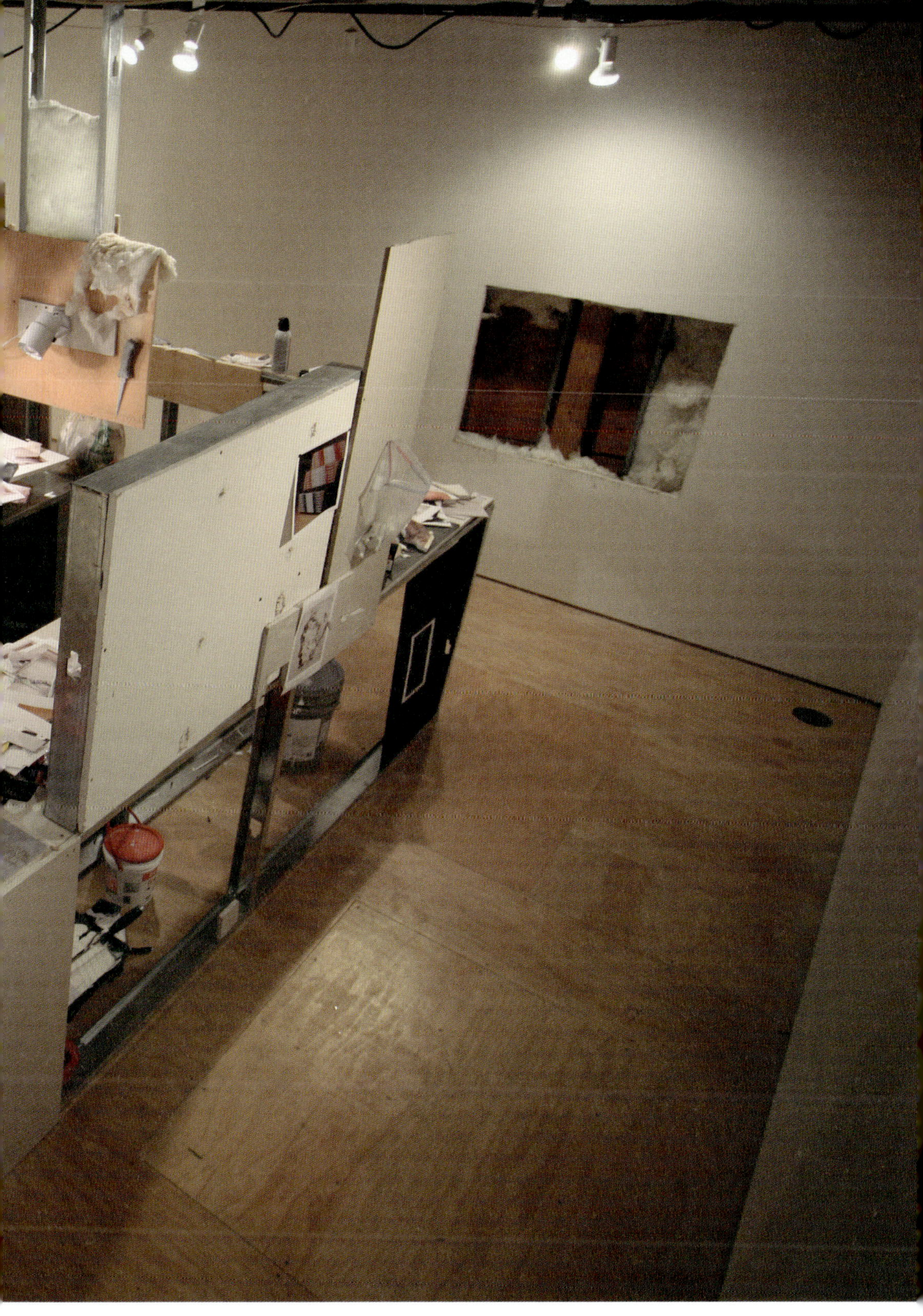

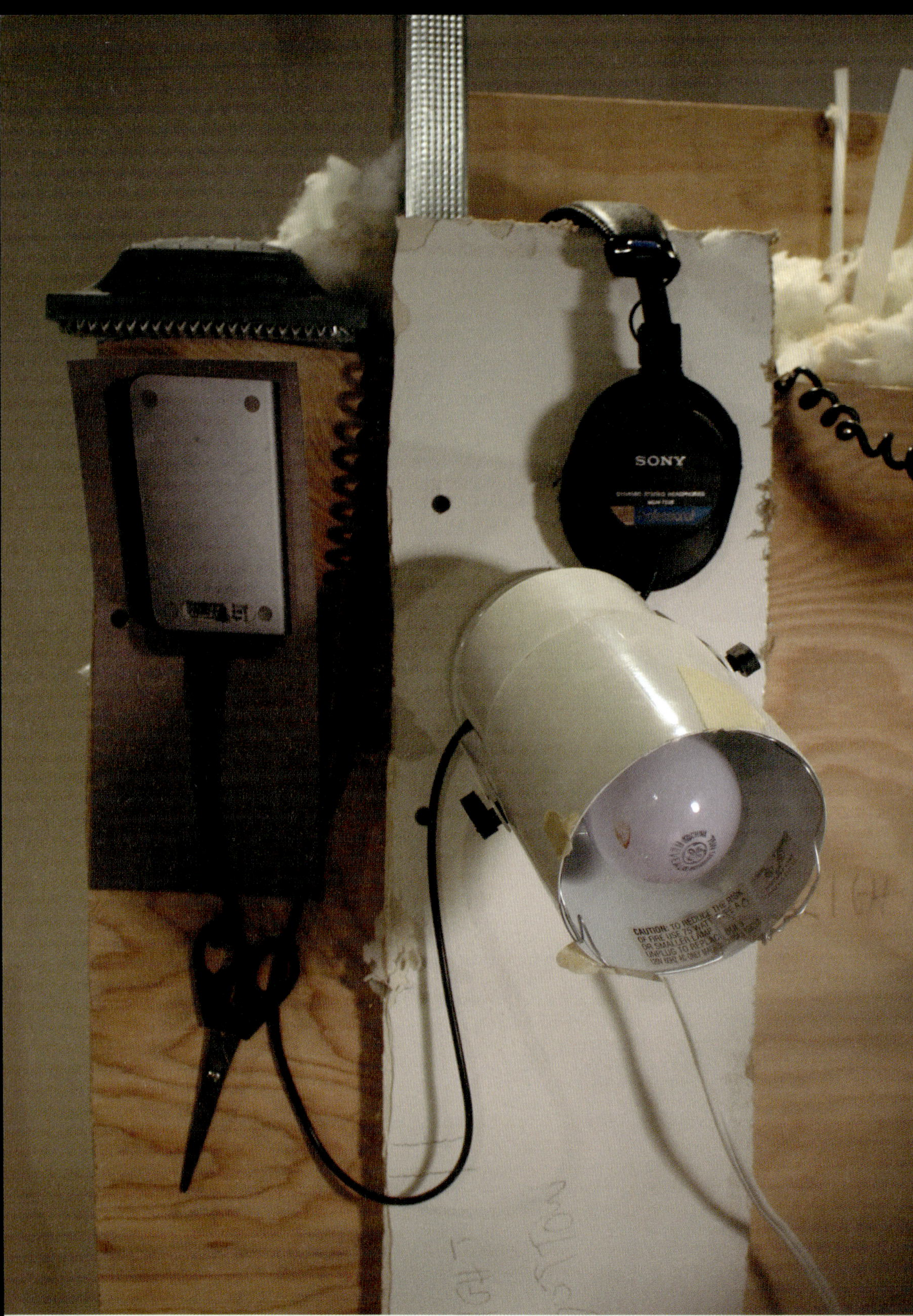

SONY
DYNAMIC STEREO HEADPHONES
MDR-7506
CAUTION: TO REDUCE THE RISK
OF FIRE USE 75 WATT
OR SMALLER LAMP

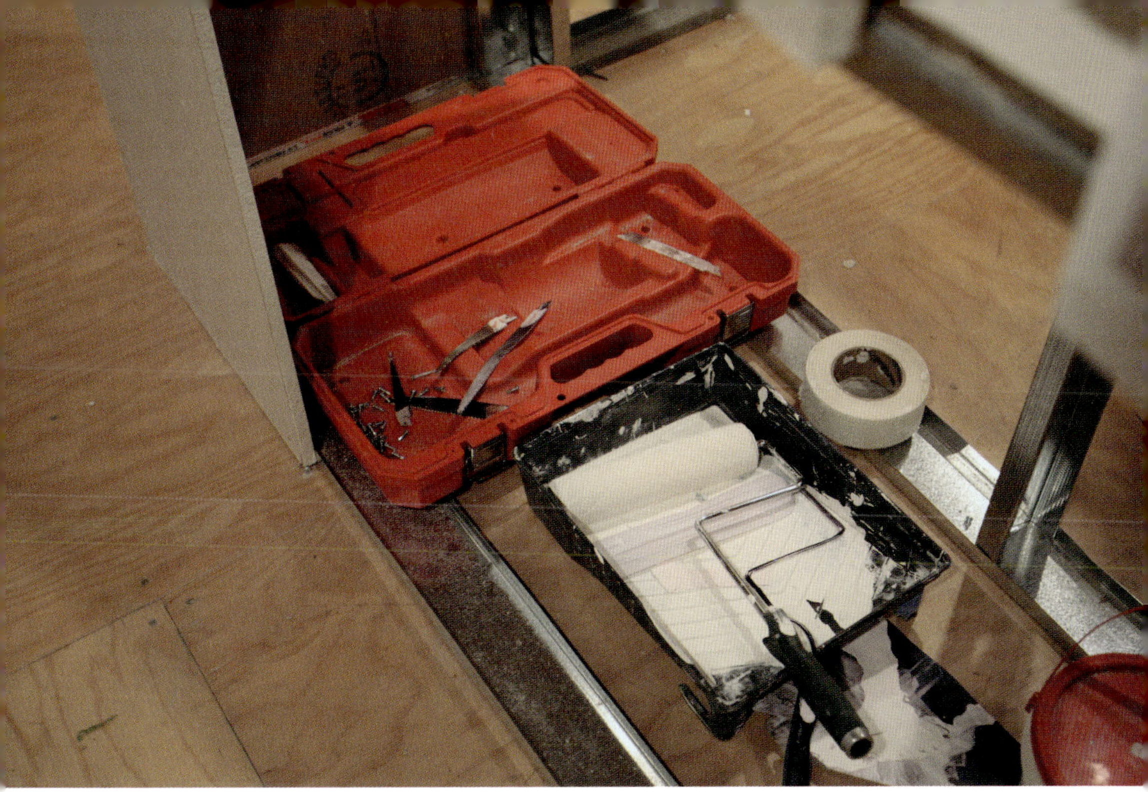

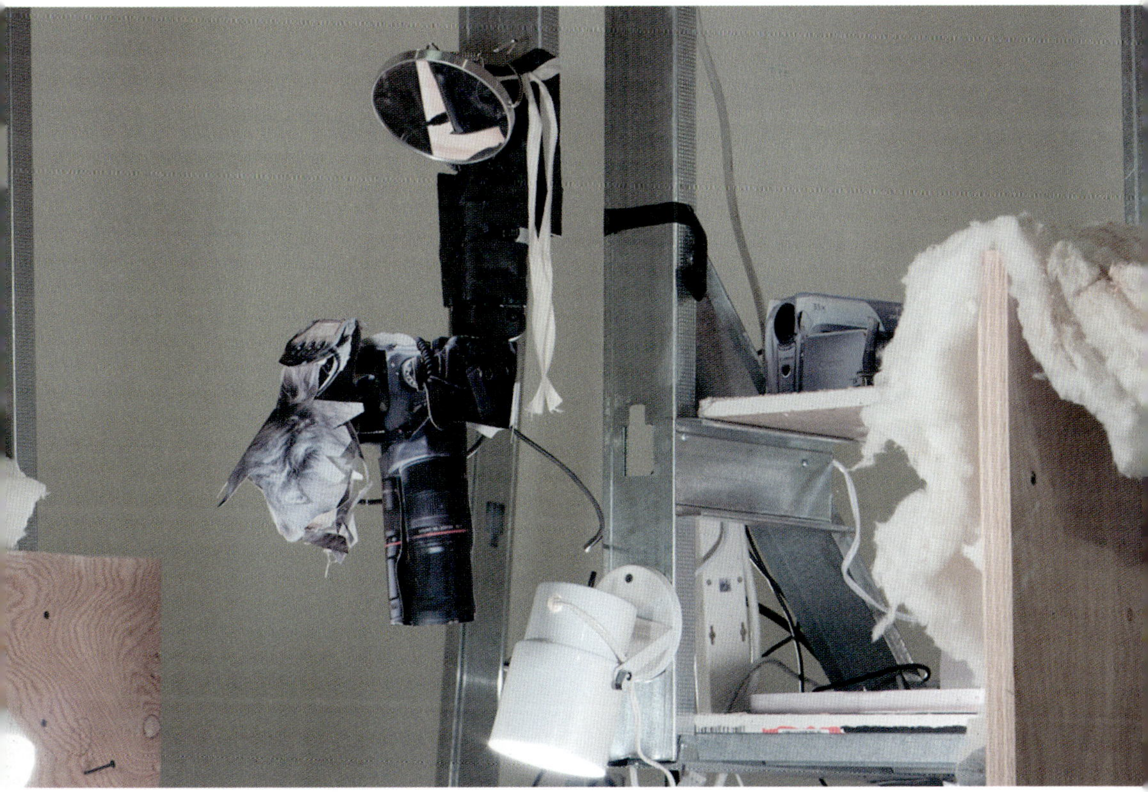

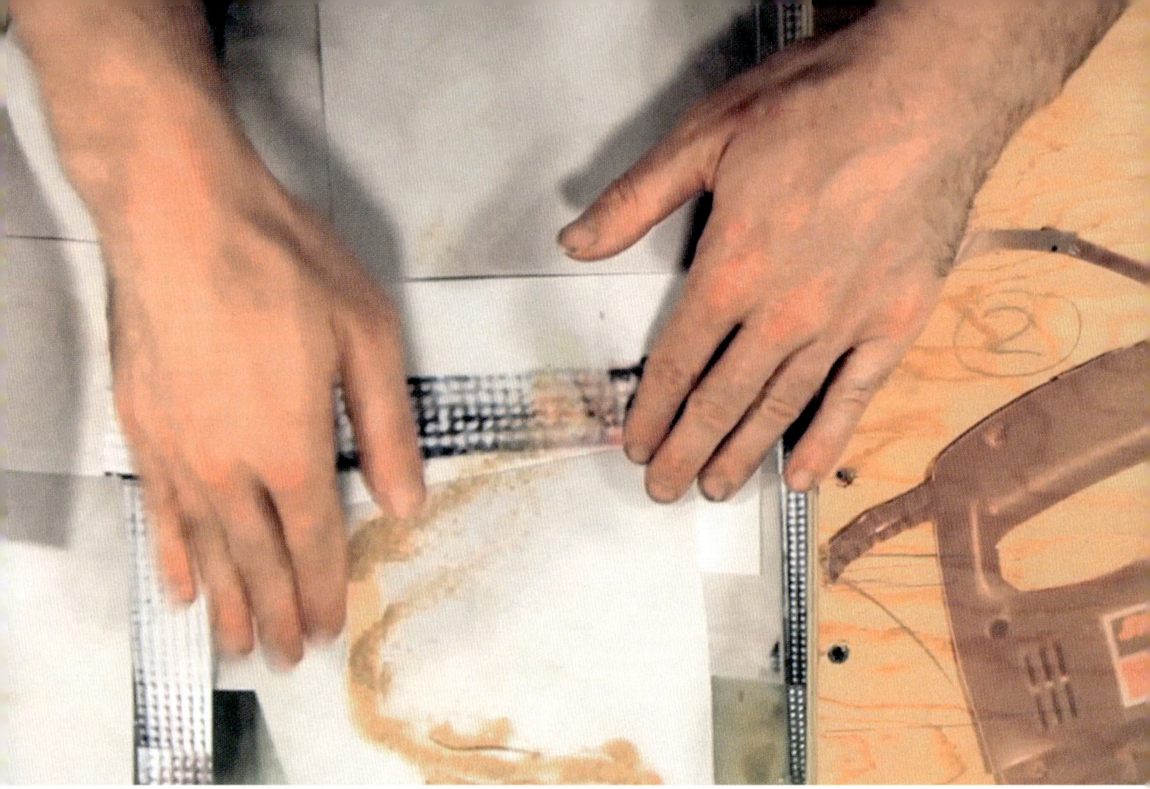

 Wall, 2010, video still, video with sound, 72:00 minutes. Collection of William and Ruth True, Seattle. Courtesy of the artist and Laurel Gitlen, New York.

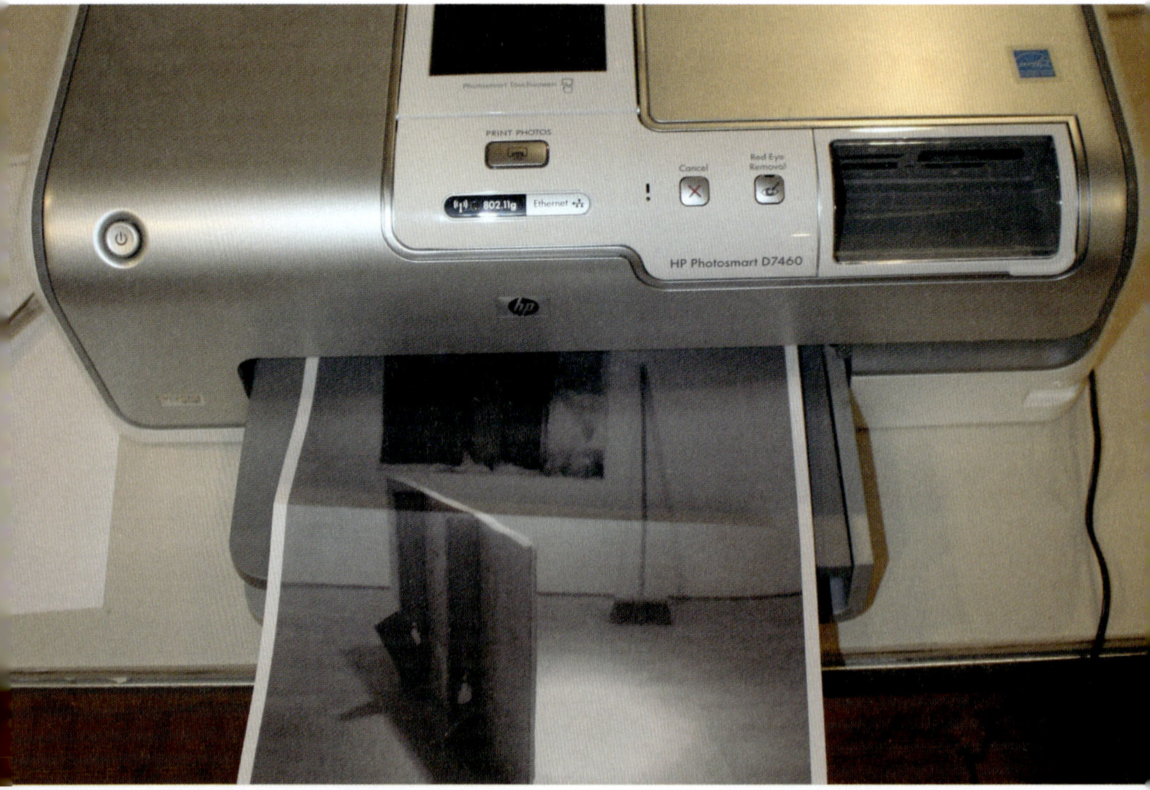

Chapter 5, Drying Flowers with Microwaves

For *Drying Flowers with Microwaves*, Hewitt created a series of large, formal still life photographs, working behind a tall white wall that bisected the gallery space. Viewers caught fleeting glimpses of the artist reflected in a series of mirrors elevated above this concealed area. Microwave ovens were used to preserve flowers and plants that were then integrated into arrangements to be photographed. Incorporating plants and objects from both Florida and Vermont (Hewitt's home state), the photographs connected to the Japanese flower-arranging tradition of ikebana and the history of Florida as a mythic fountain of youth.

Captions

205–214, 239, 240: *Drying Flowers with Microwaves*, 2010. Installation view, Dorsch Gallery. Courtesy Emerson Dorsch, Miami.
215, 223, 245: Set documentation of *Drying Flowers with Microwaves*, 2010. Courtesy of the artist.
216–218, 221, 224, 227, 229–231: Research photograph for *Drying Flowers with Microwaves*. Courtesy of the artist.
222, 228, 233–238, 244: Research image for *Drying Flowers with Microwaves*, found online. Courtesy of the artist.
232: Installation in progress, *Drying Flowers with Microwaves*, 2010. Dorsch Gallery, Miami. Courtesy of the artist.
242: Working image from *Drying Flowers with Microwaves*, 2010. Courtesy of the artist.

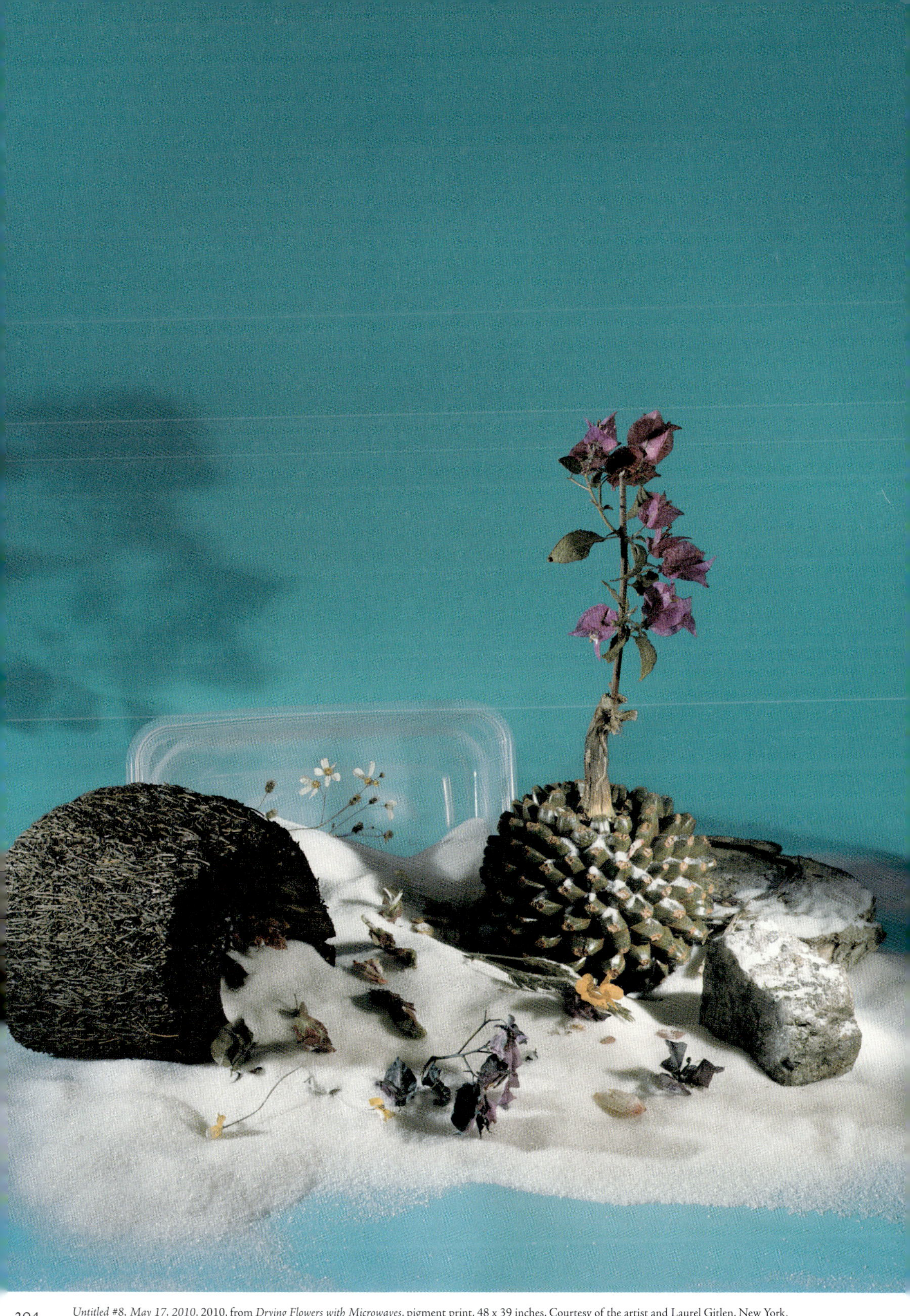

Untitled #8, May 17, 2010, 2010, from *Drying Flowers with Microwaves*, pigment print, 48 x 39 inches. Courtesy of the artist and Laurel Gitlen, New York.

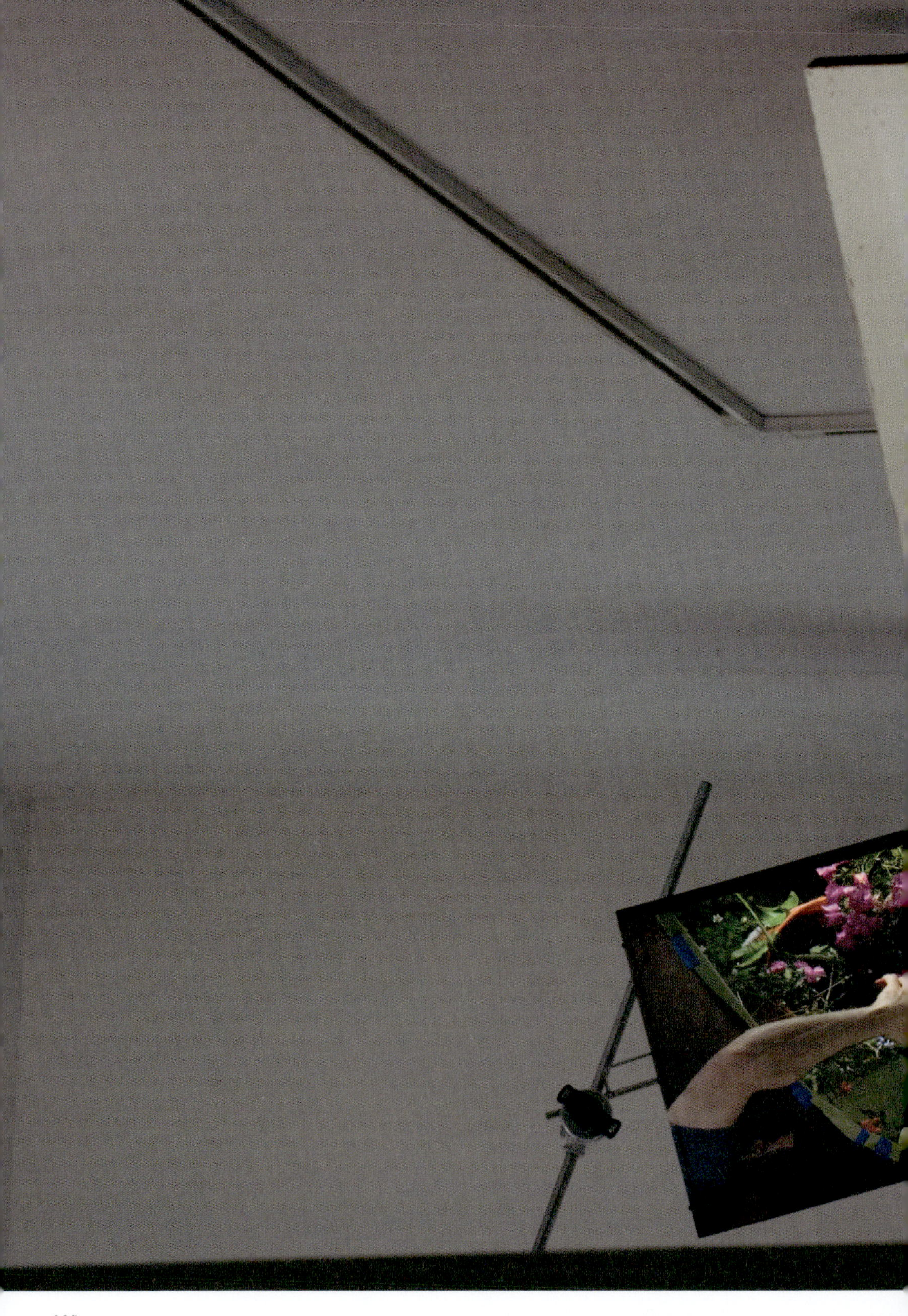

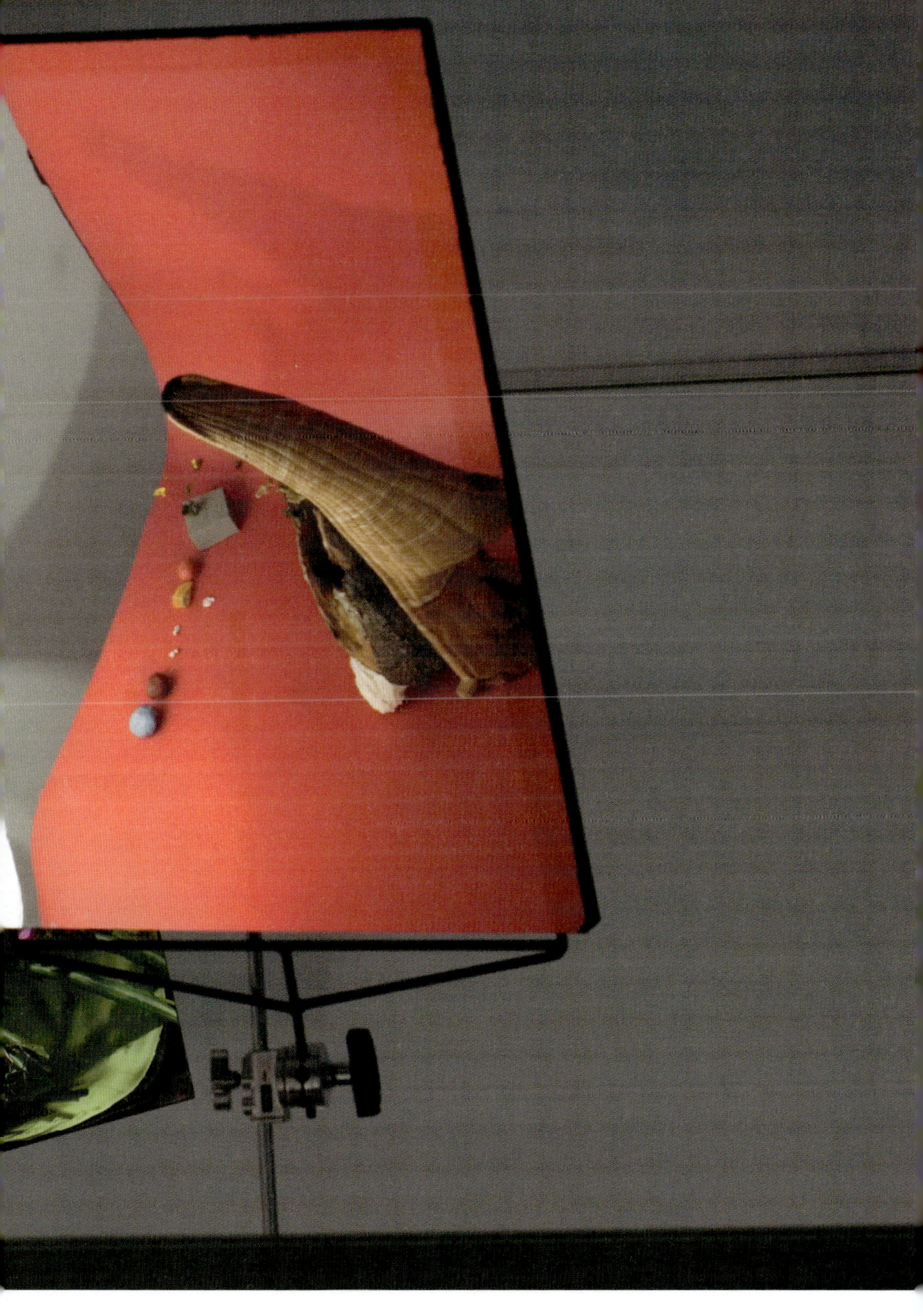

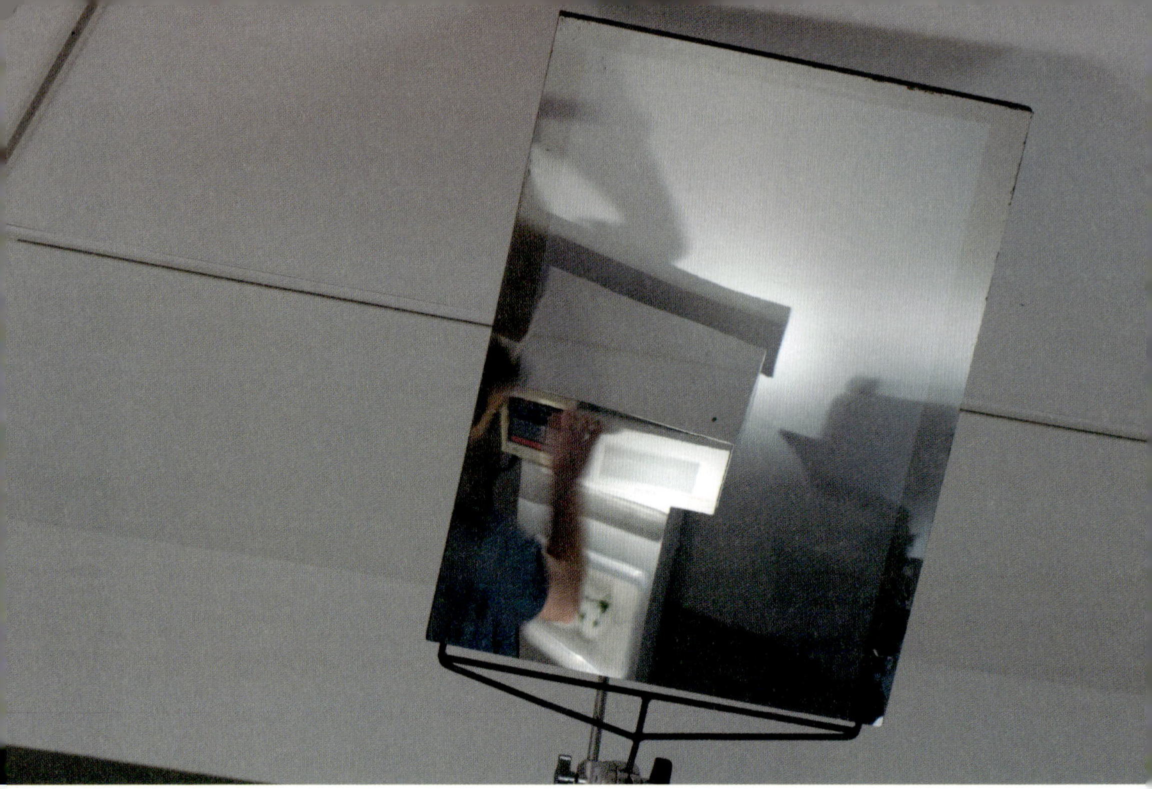

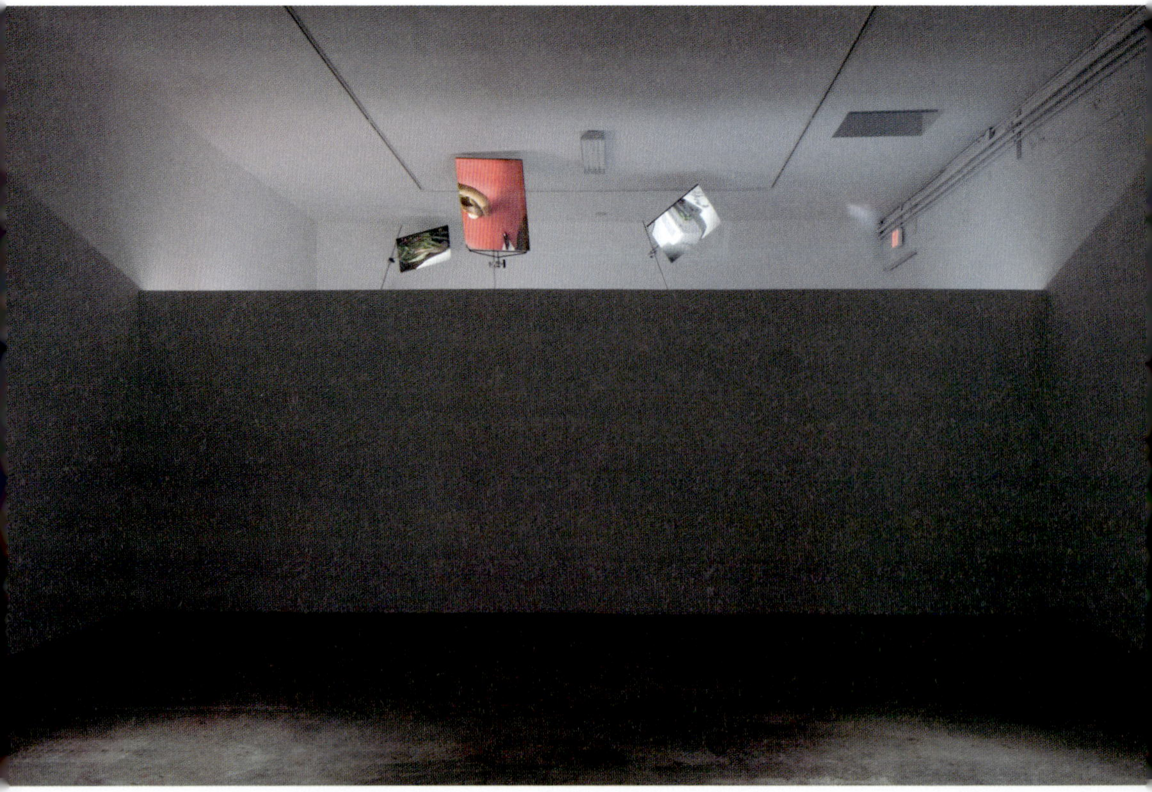

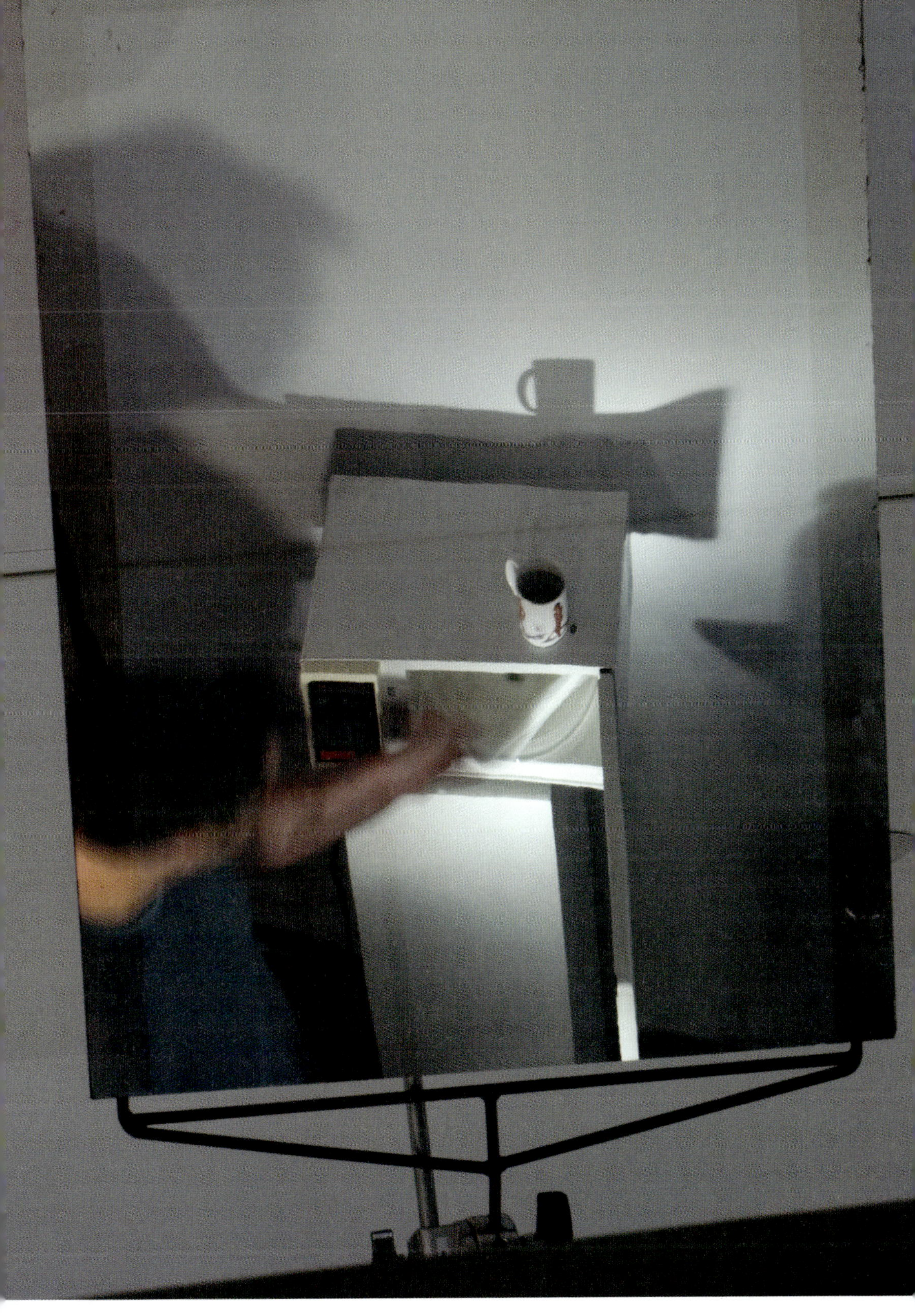

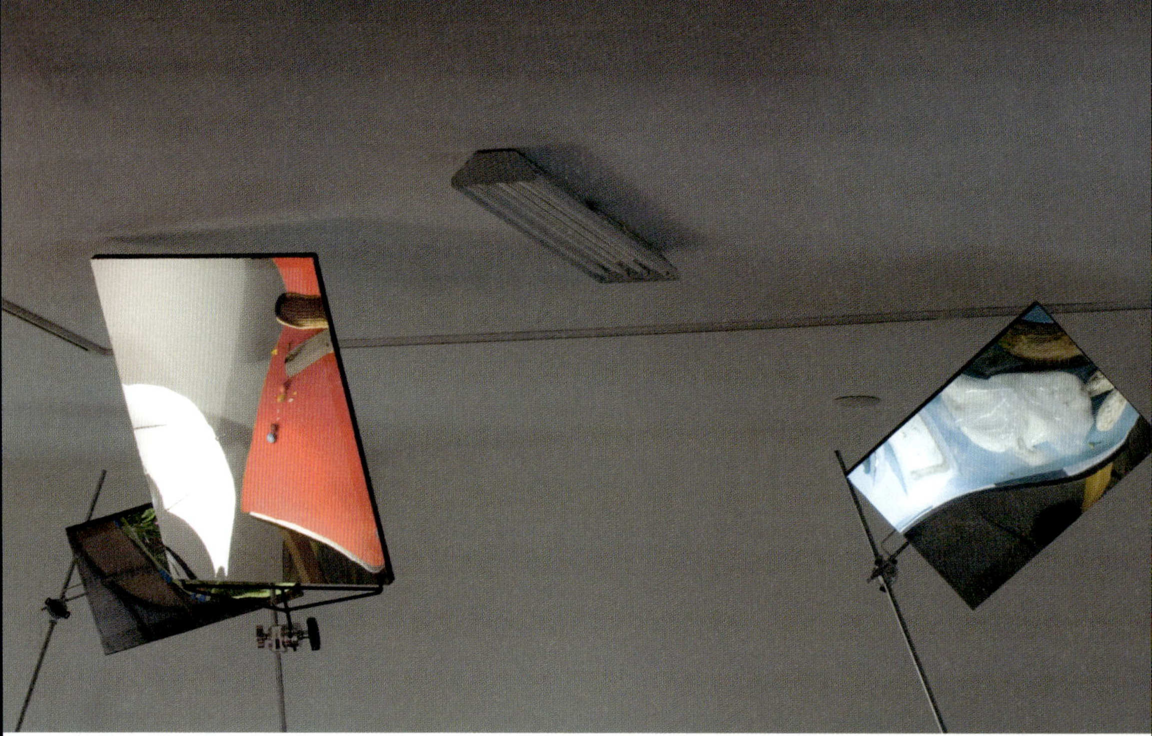

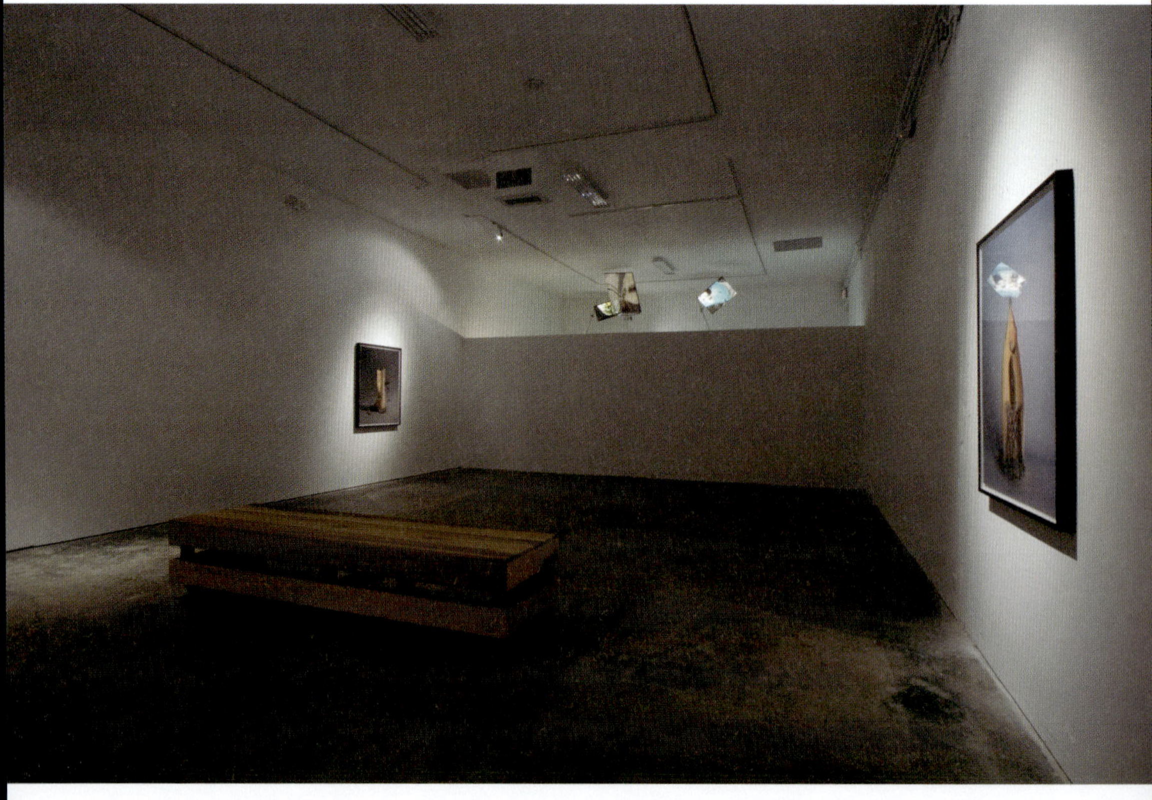

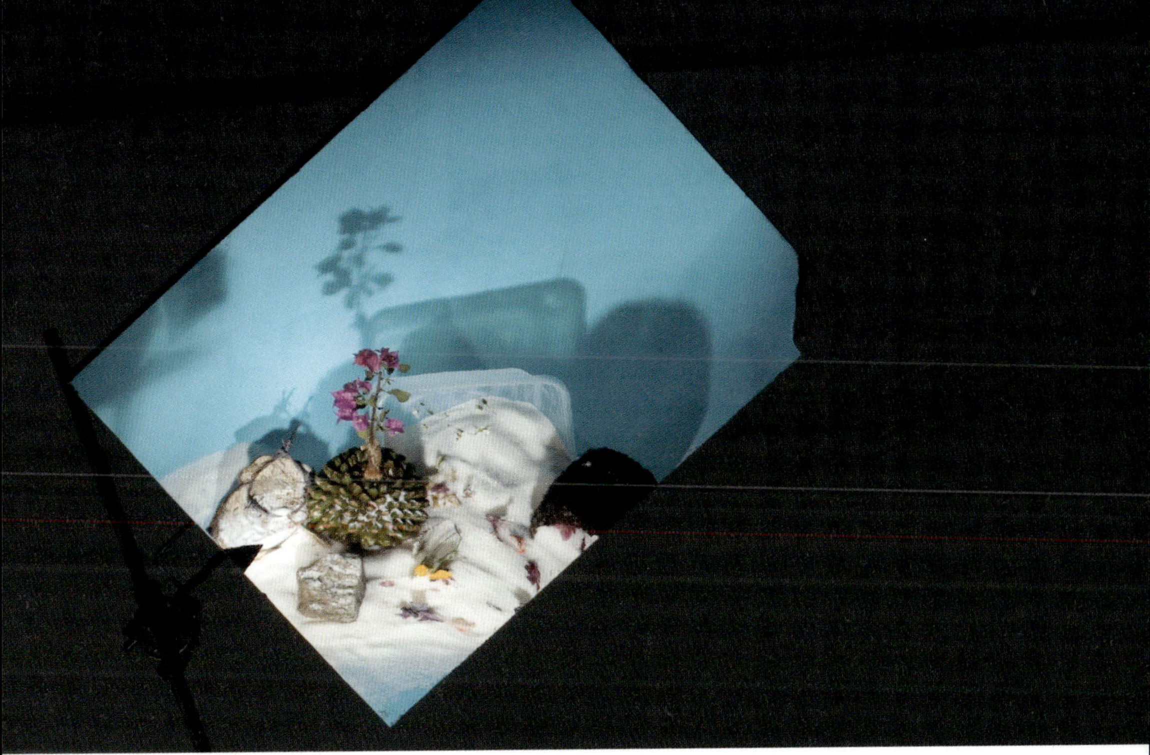

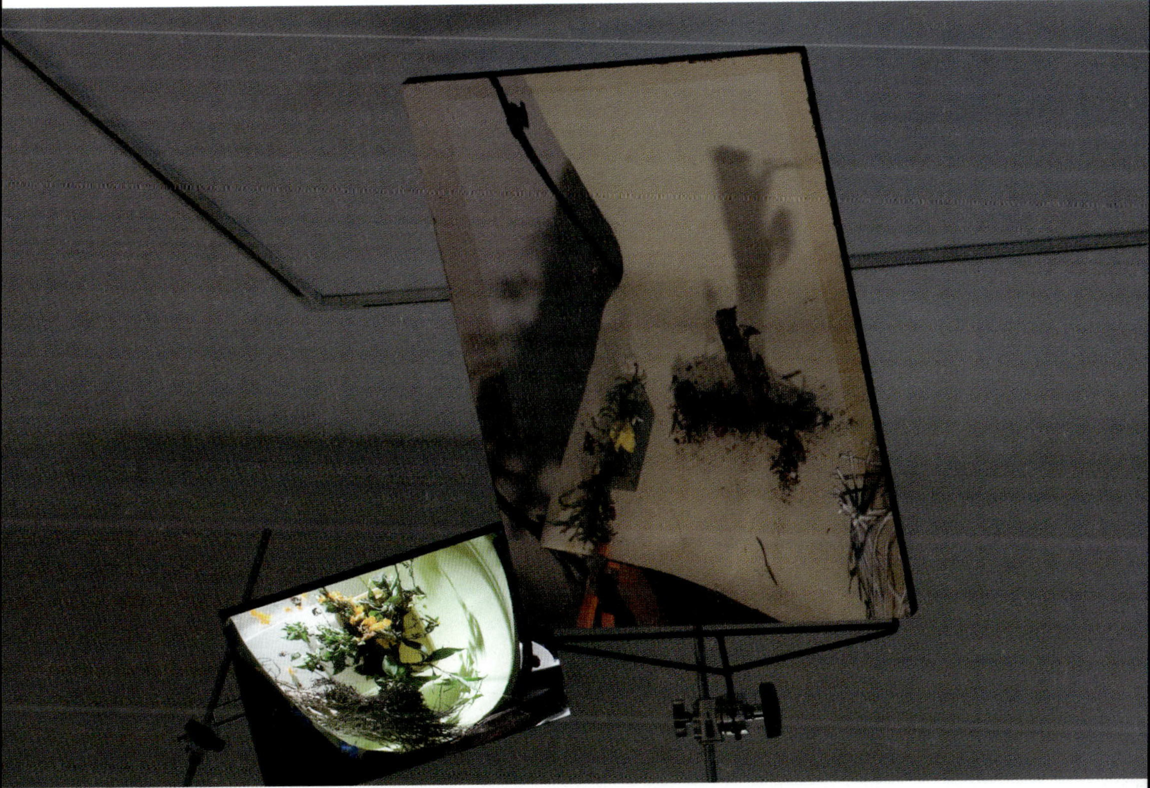

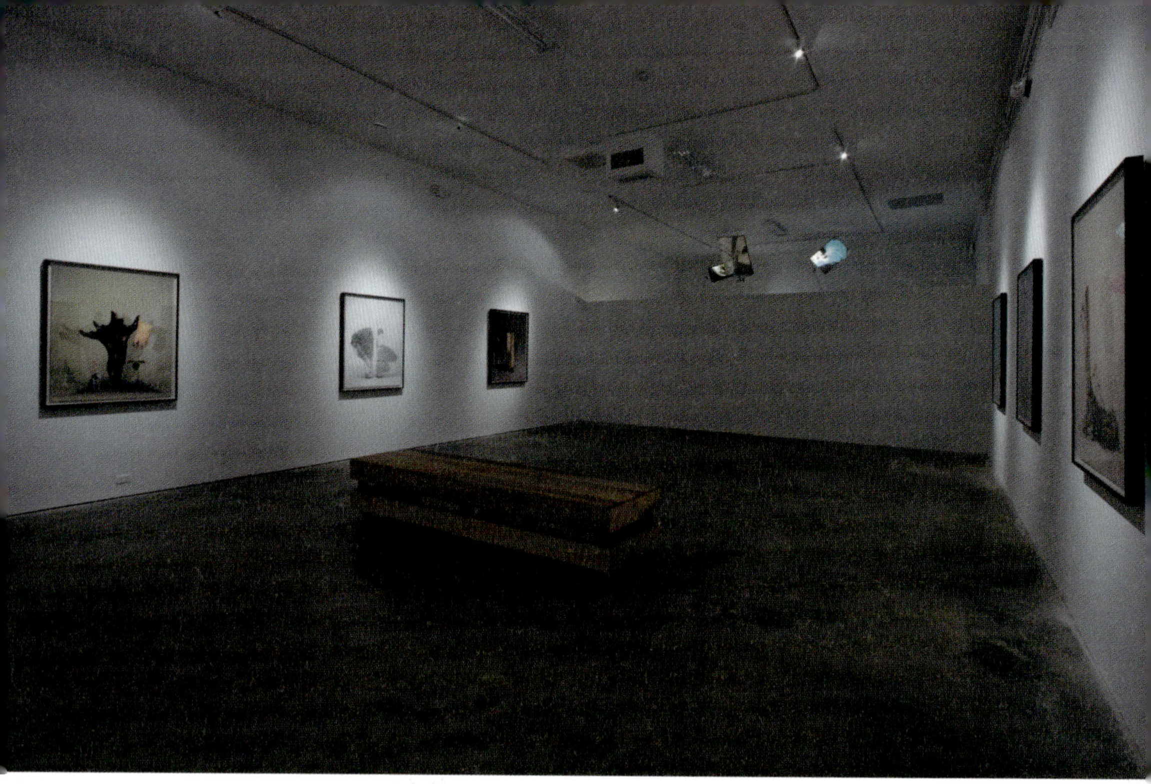

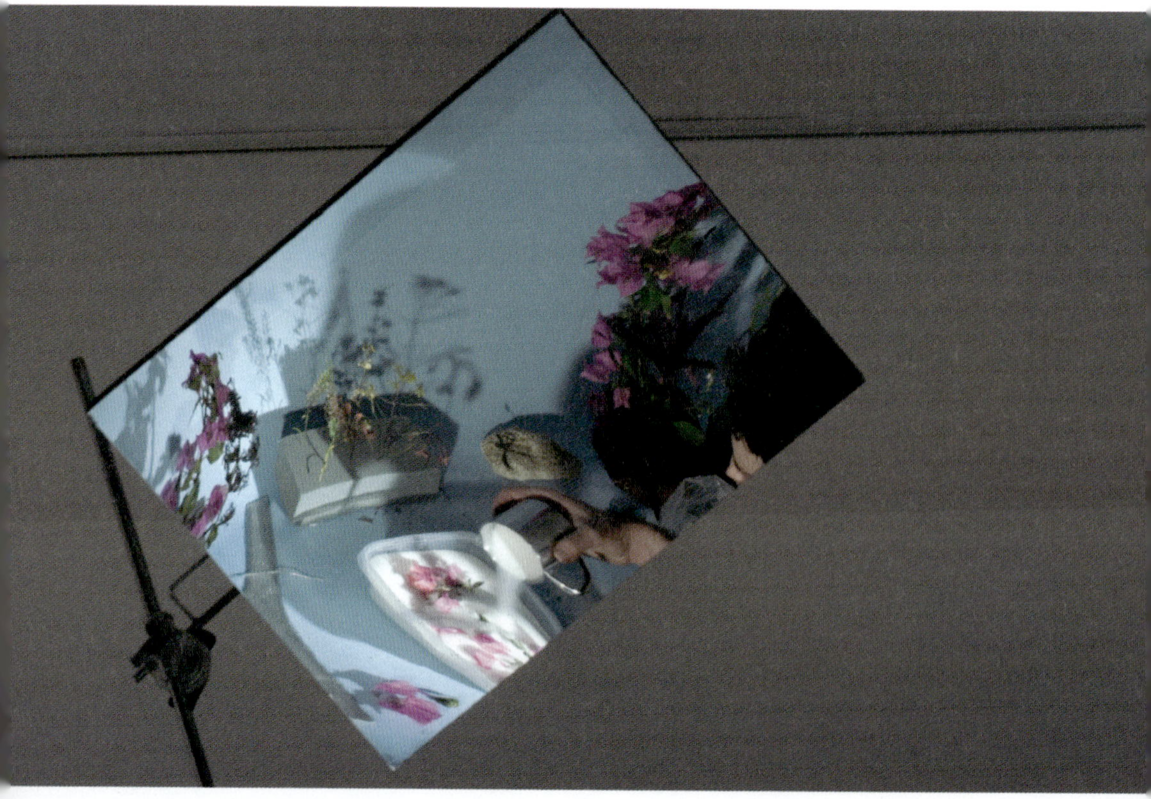

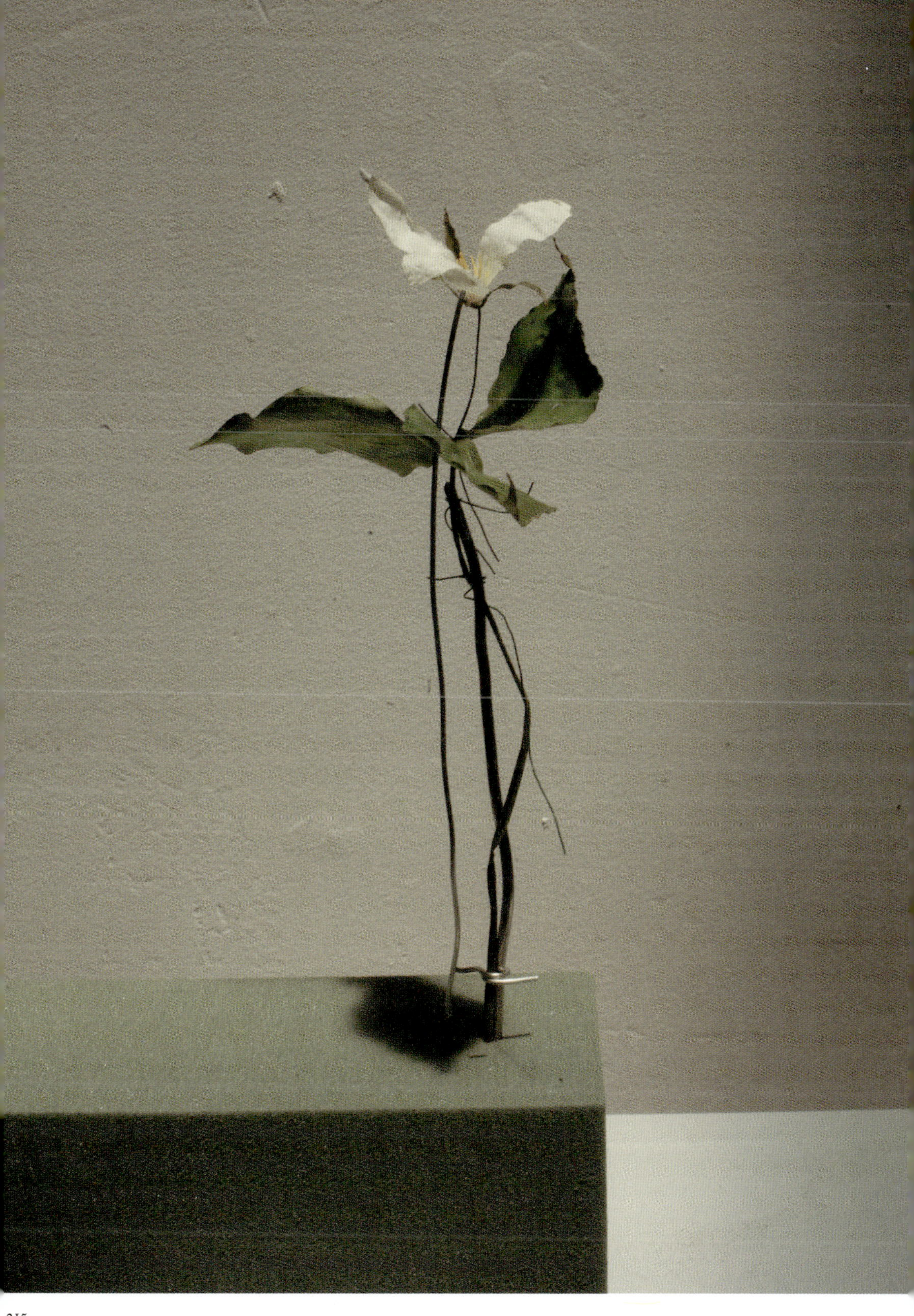

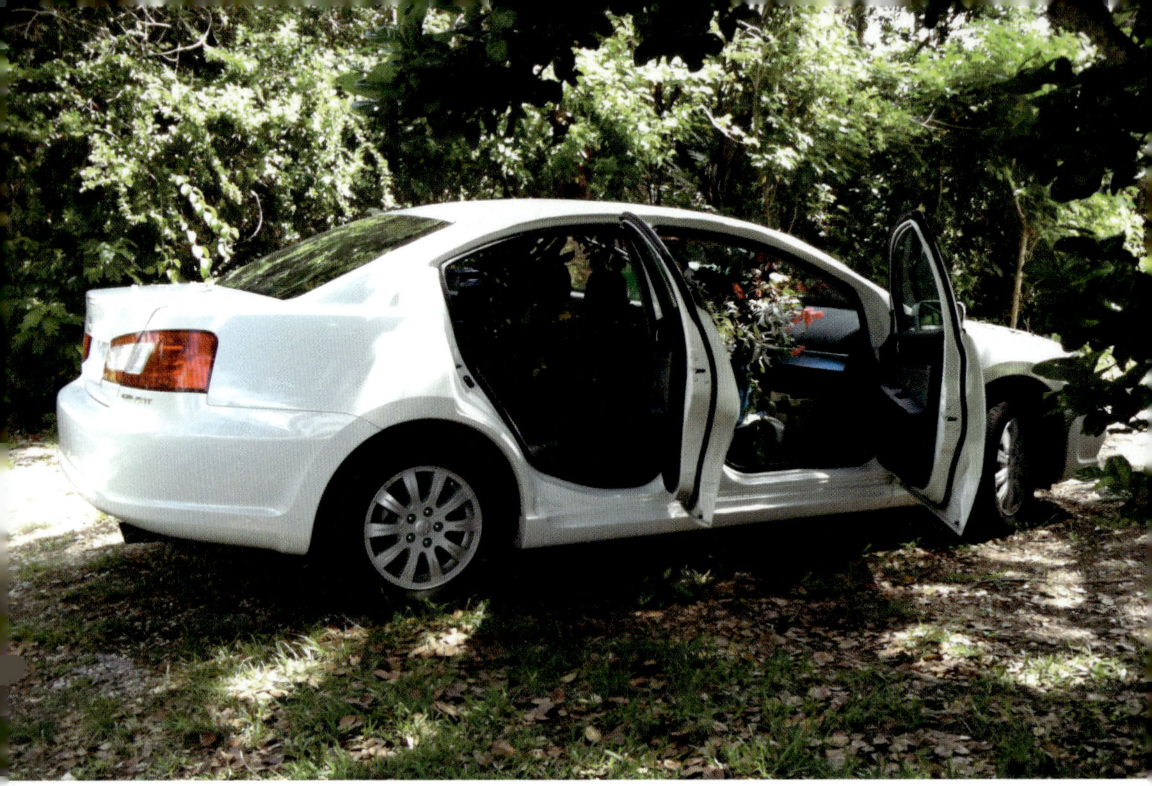

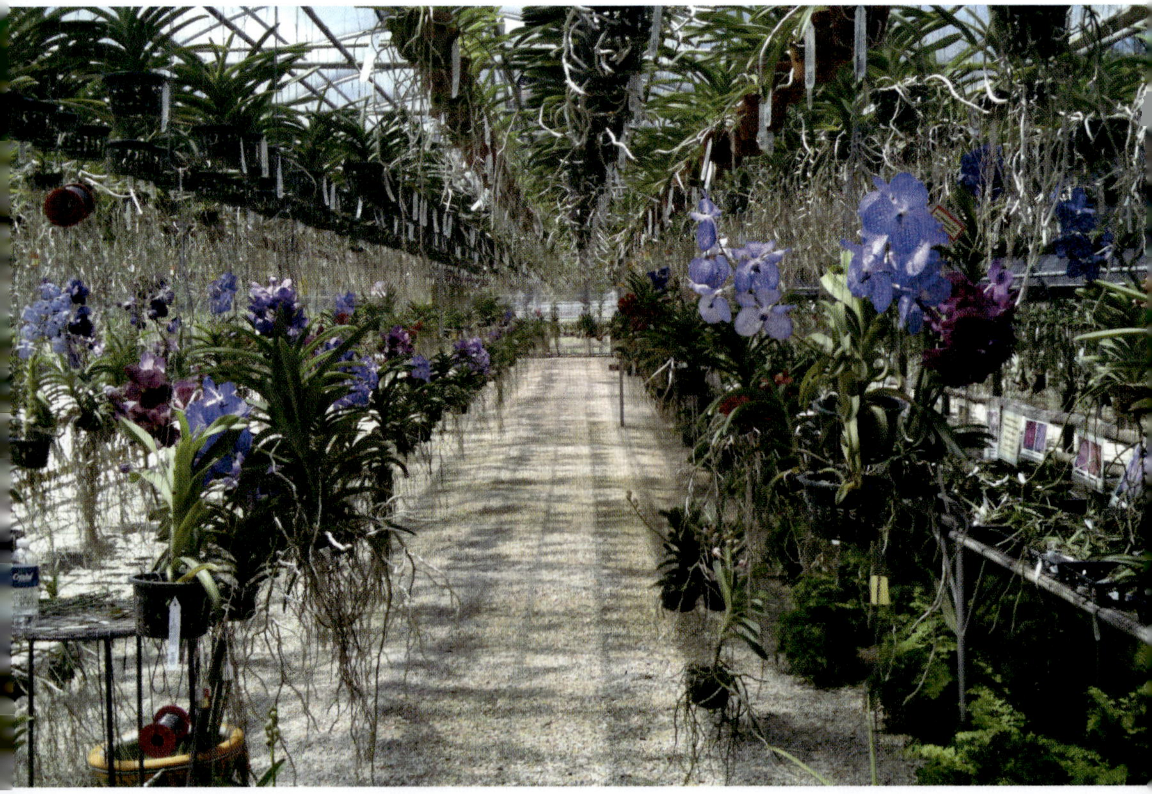

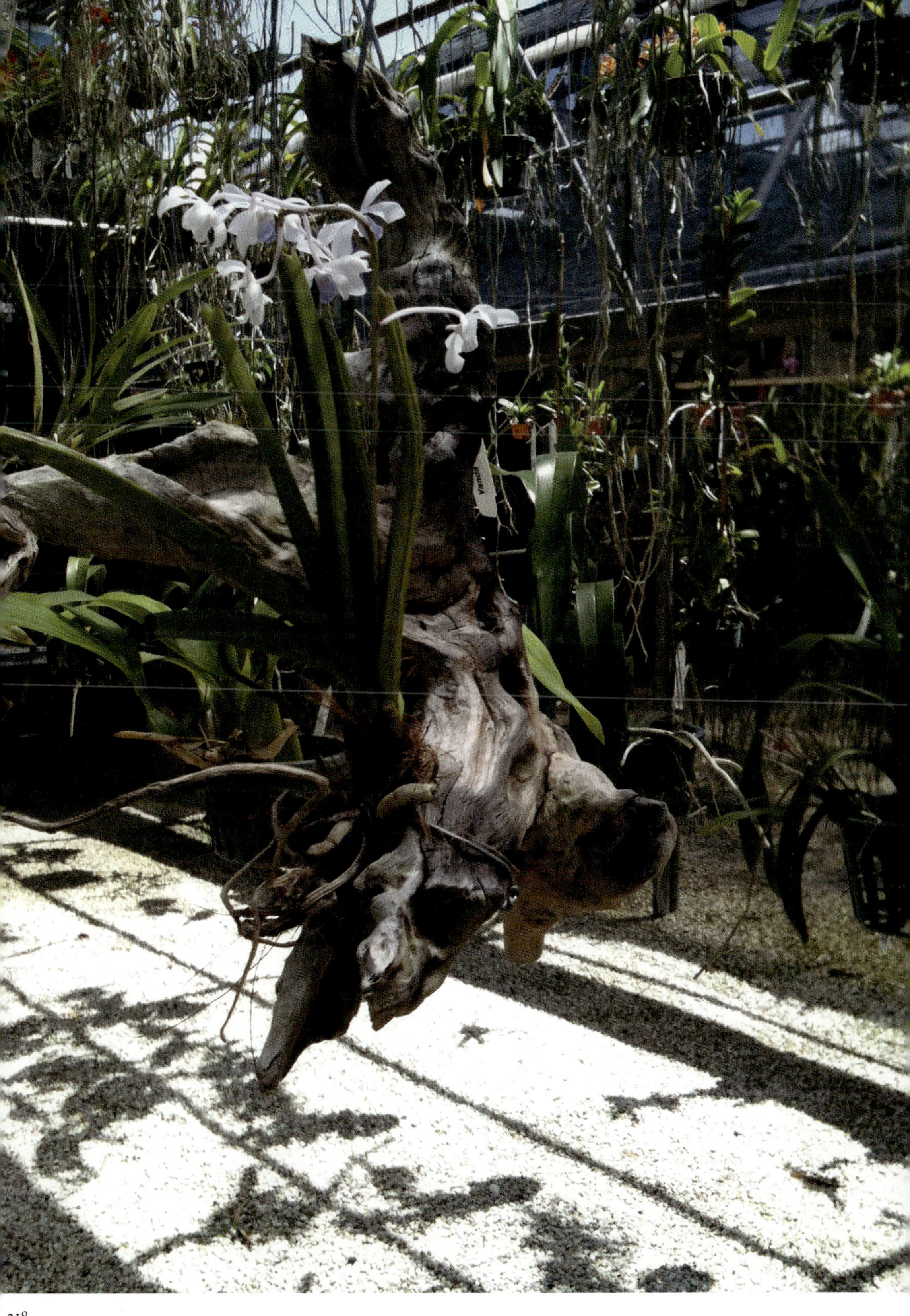

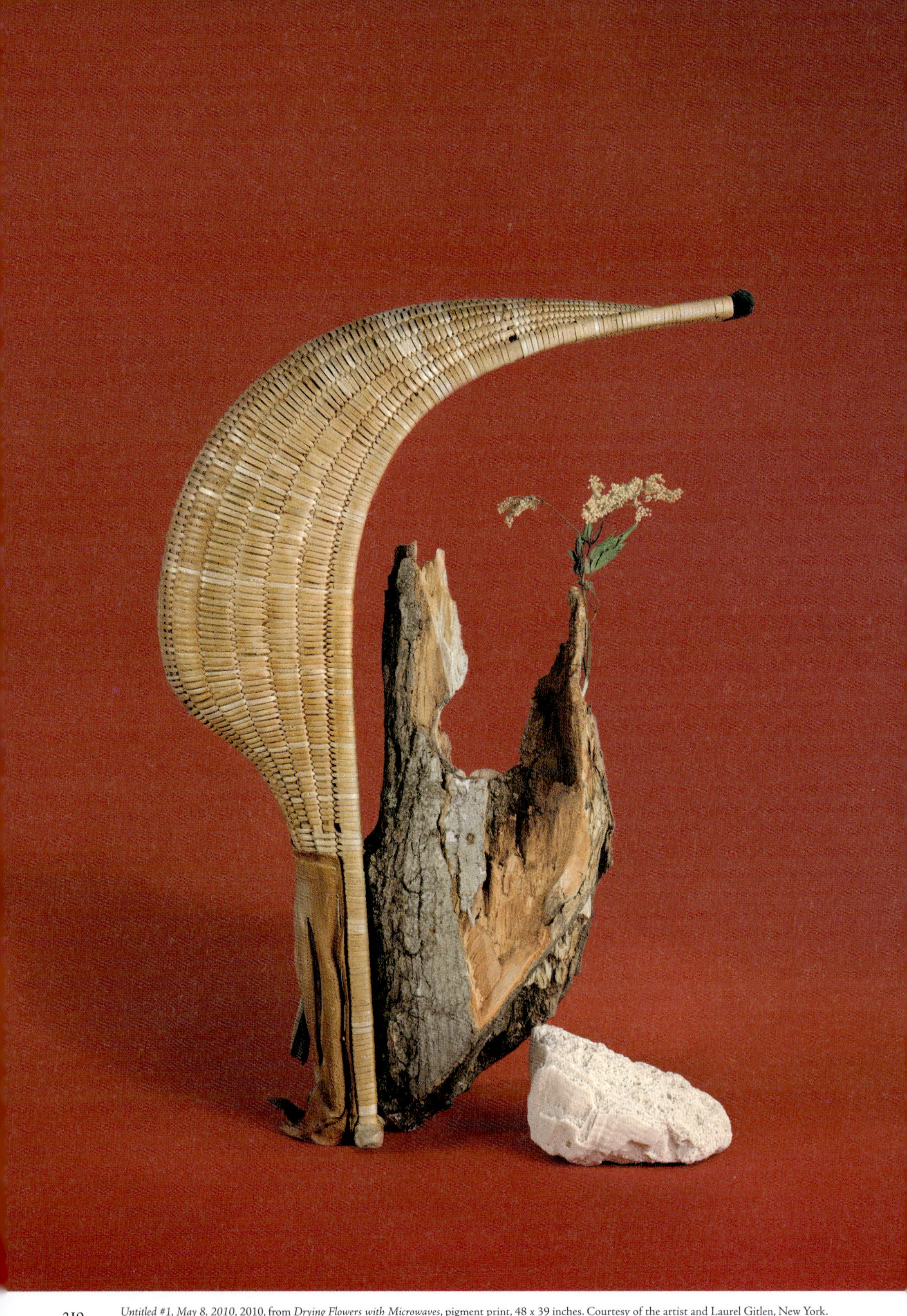

 Untitled #1, May 8, 2010, 2010, from *Drying Flowers with Microwaves*, pigment print, 48 x 39 inches. Courtesy of the artist and Laurel Gitlen, New York.

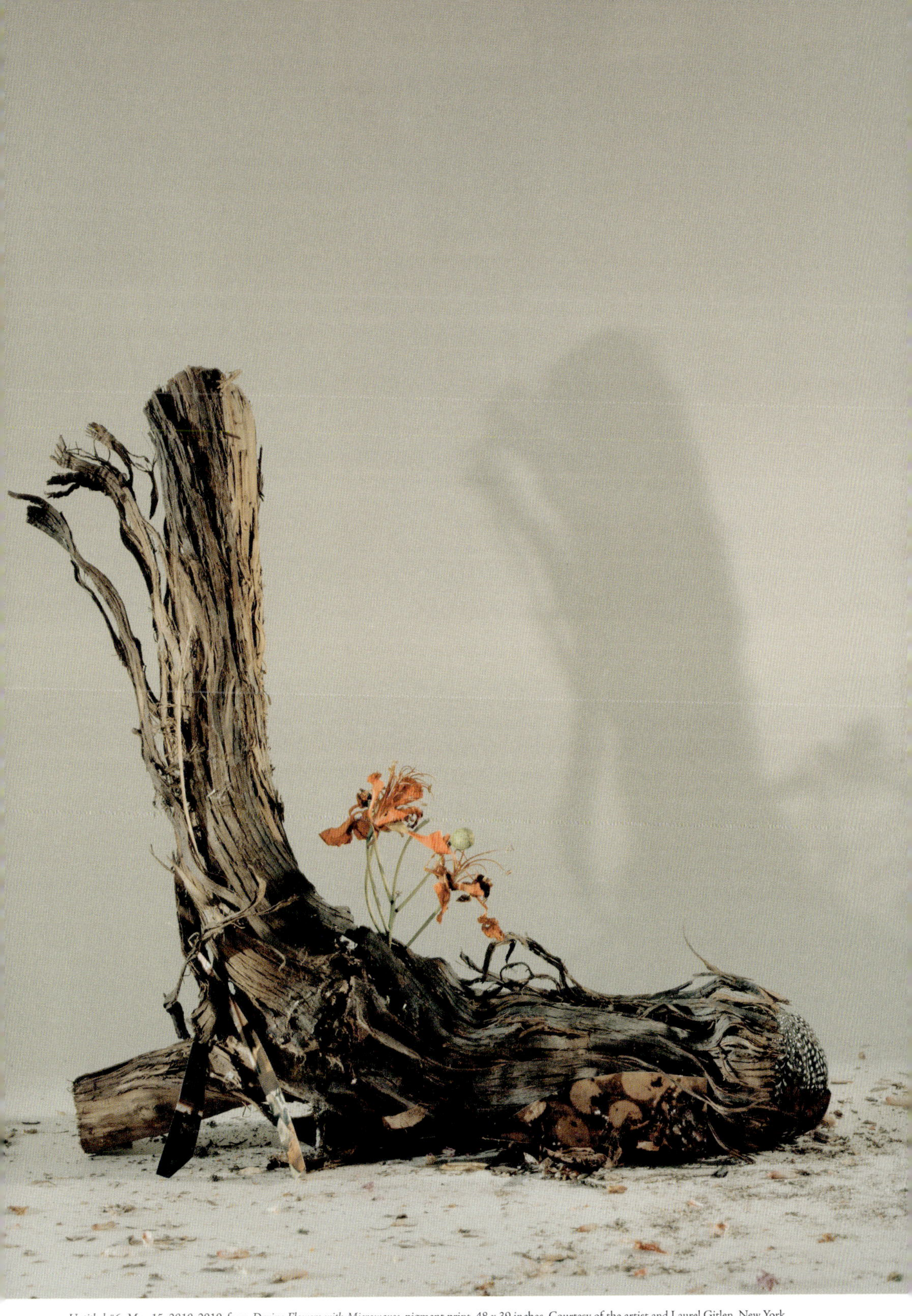

  Untitled #6, May 15, 2010, 2010, from *Drying Flowers with Microwaves*, pigment print, 48 x 39 inches. Courtesy of the artist and Laurel Gitlen, New York.

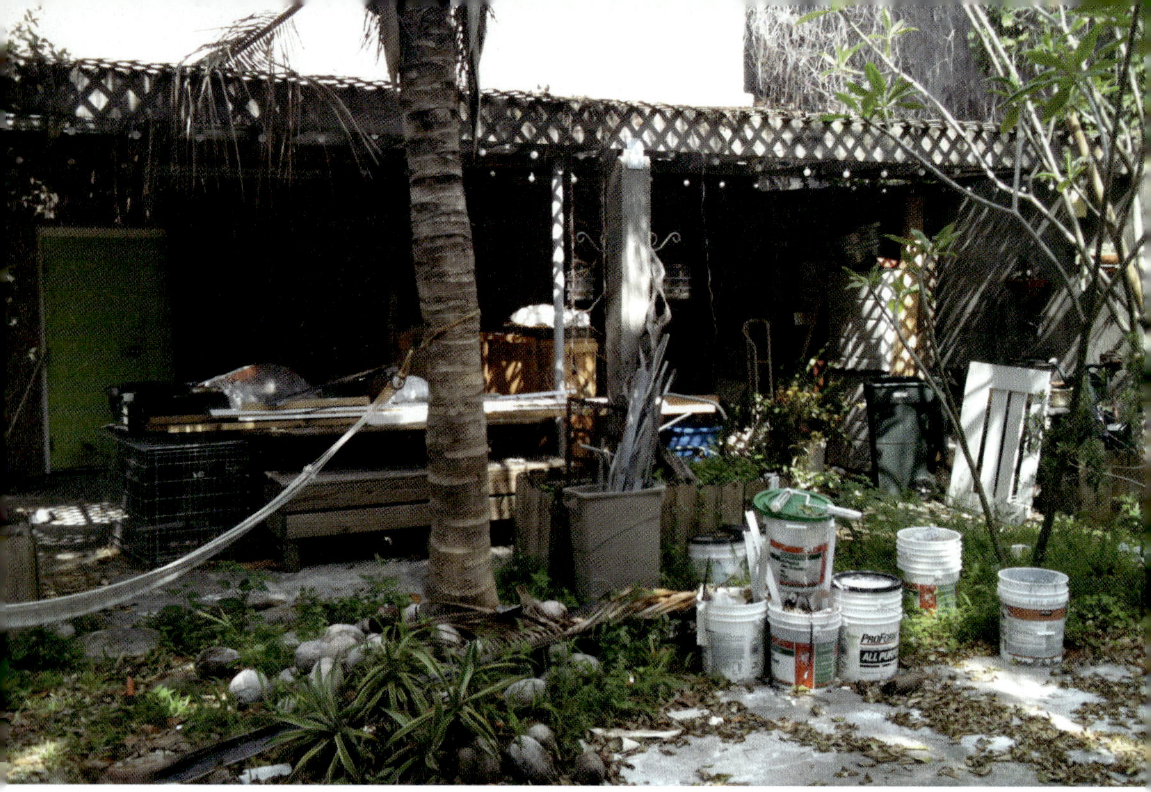

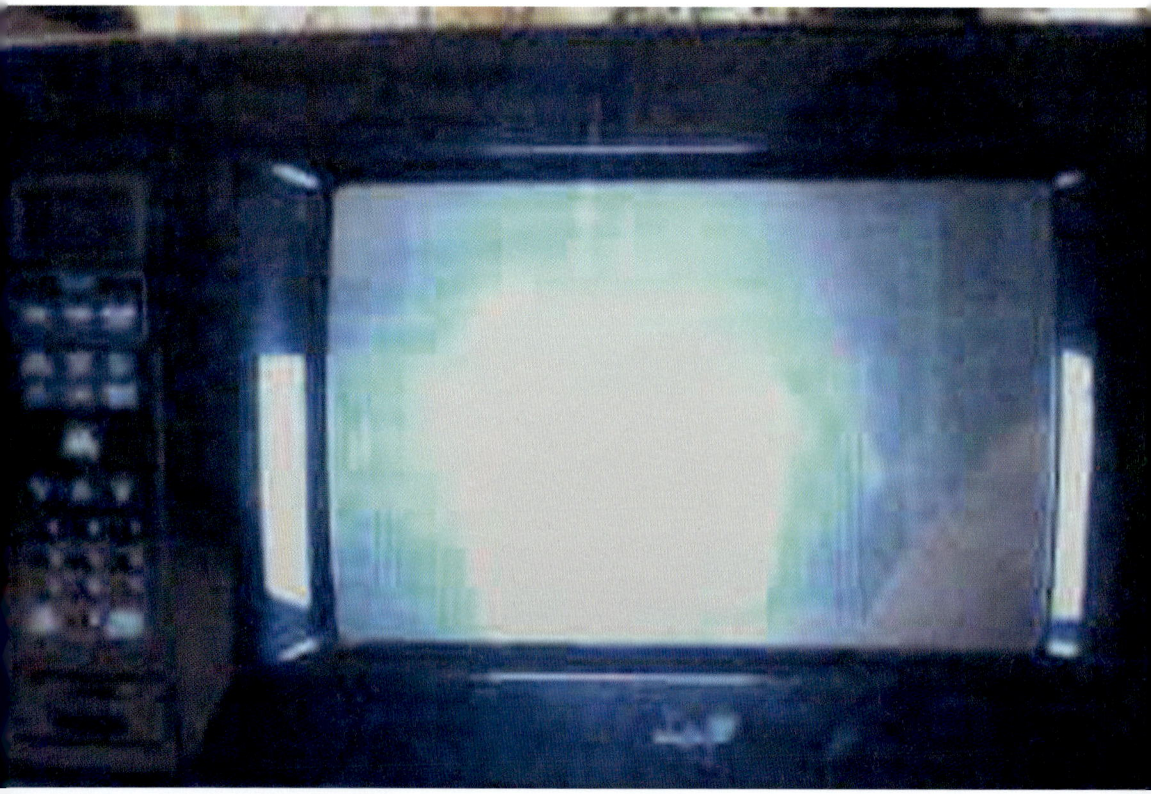

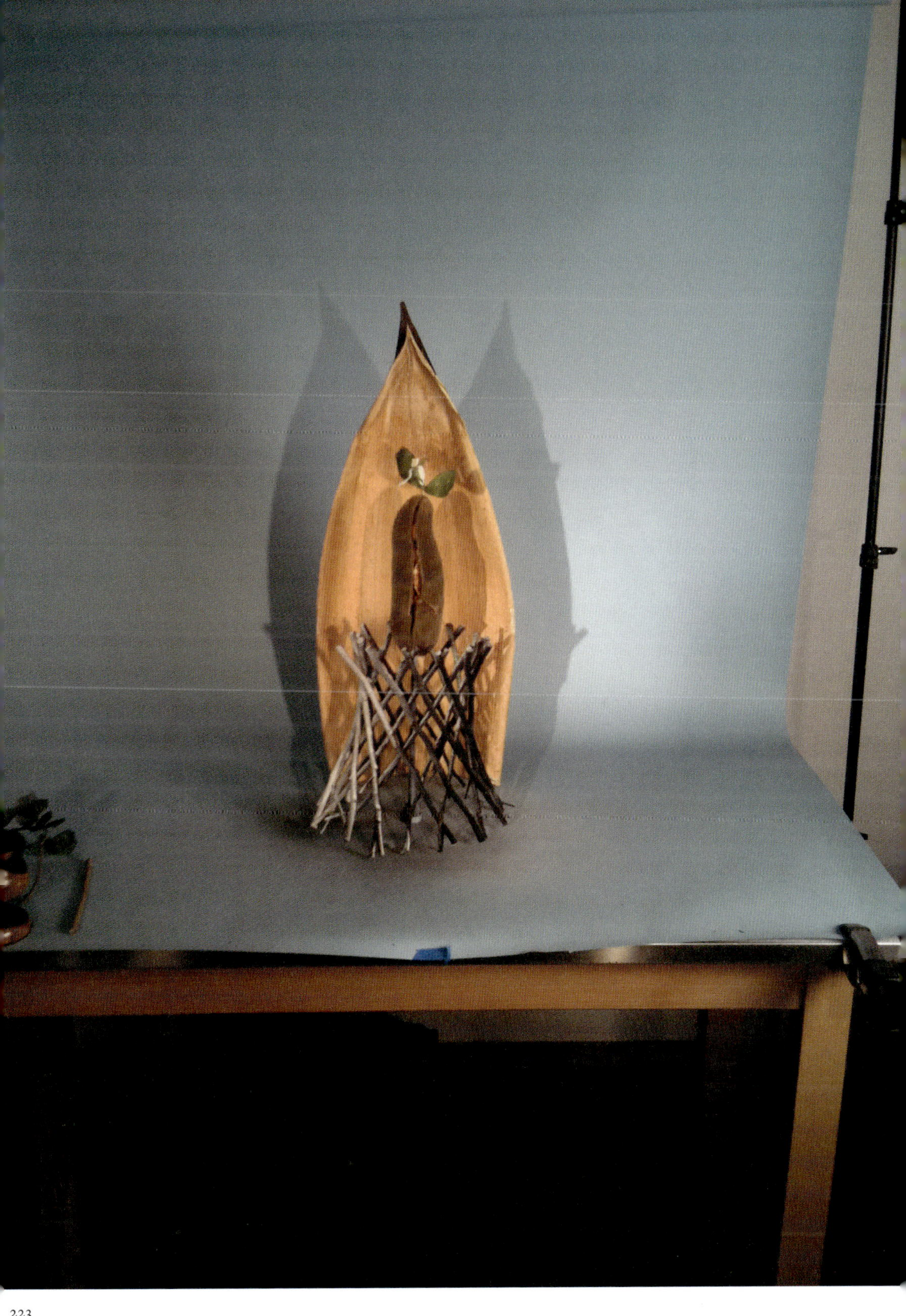

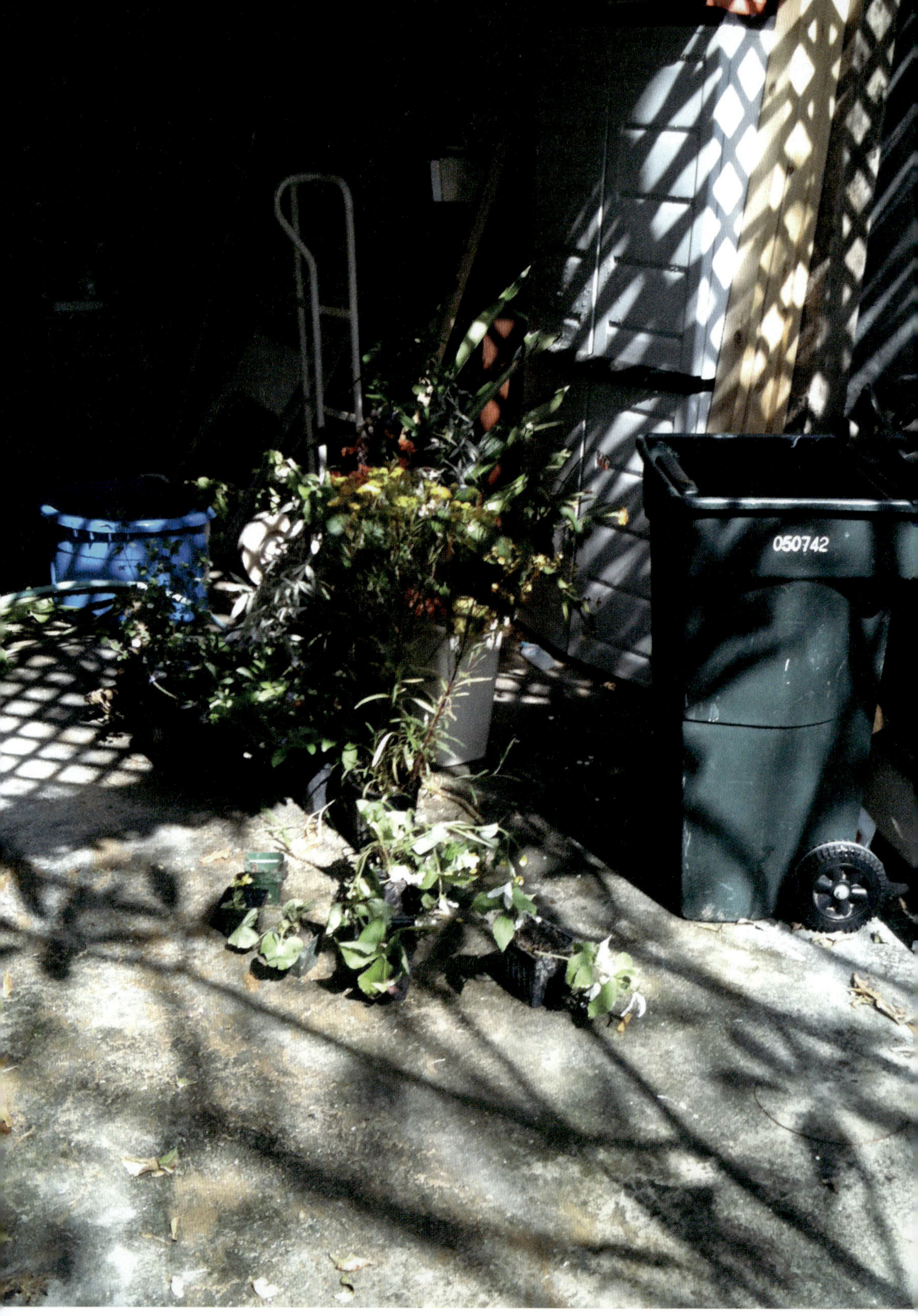

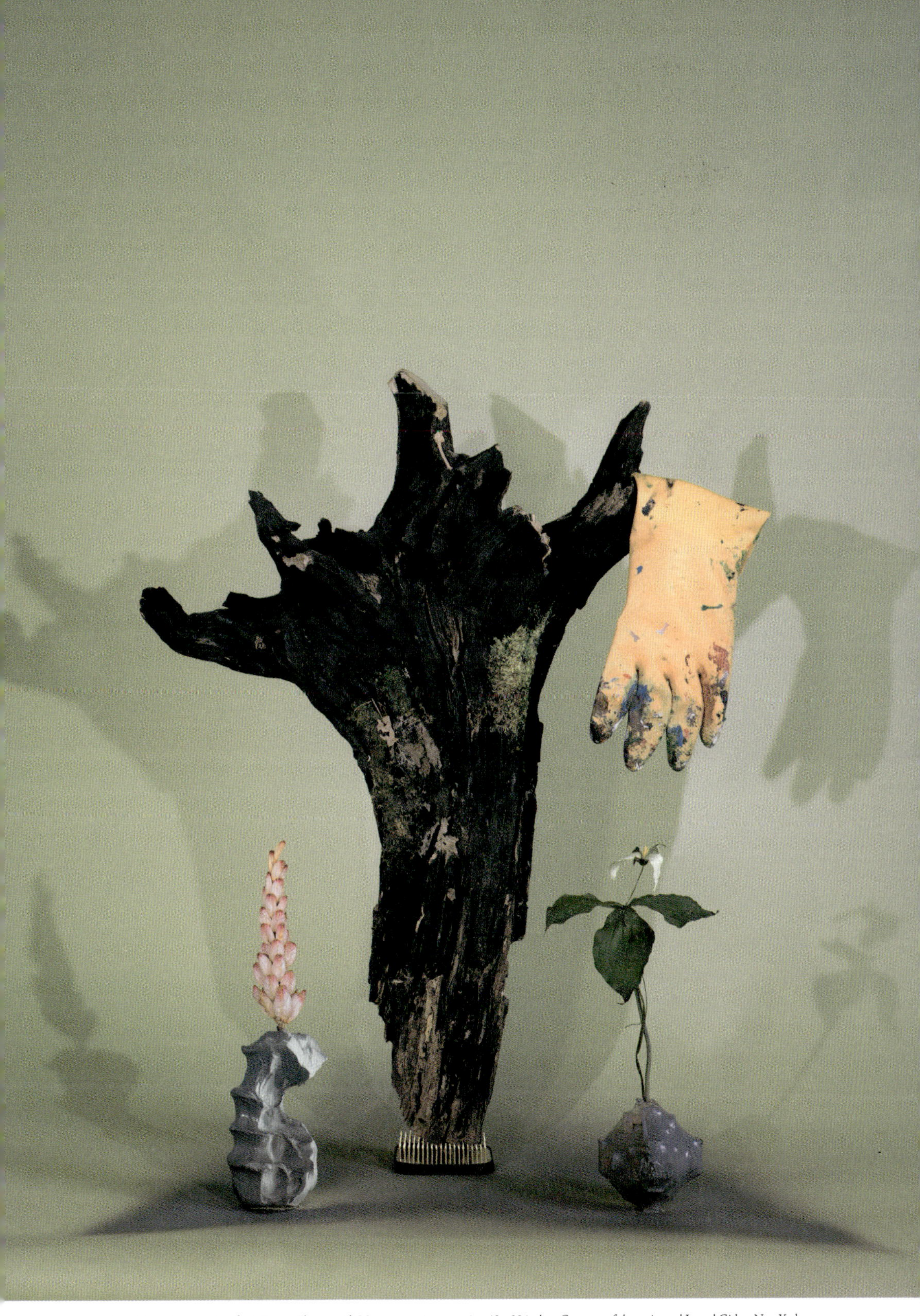

 Untitled #5, May 12, 2010, 2010, from *Drying Flowers with Microwaves*, pigment print, 48 x 39 inches. Courtesy of the artist and Laurel Gitlen, New York.

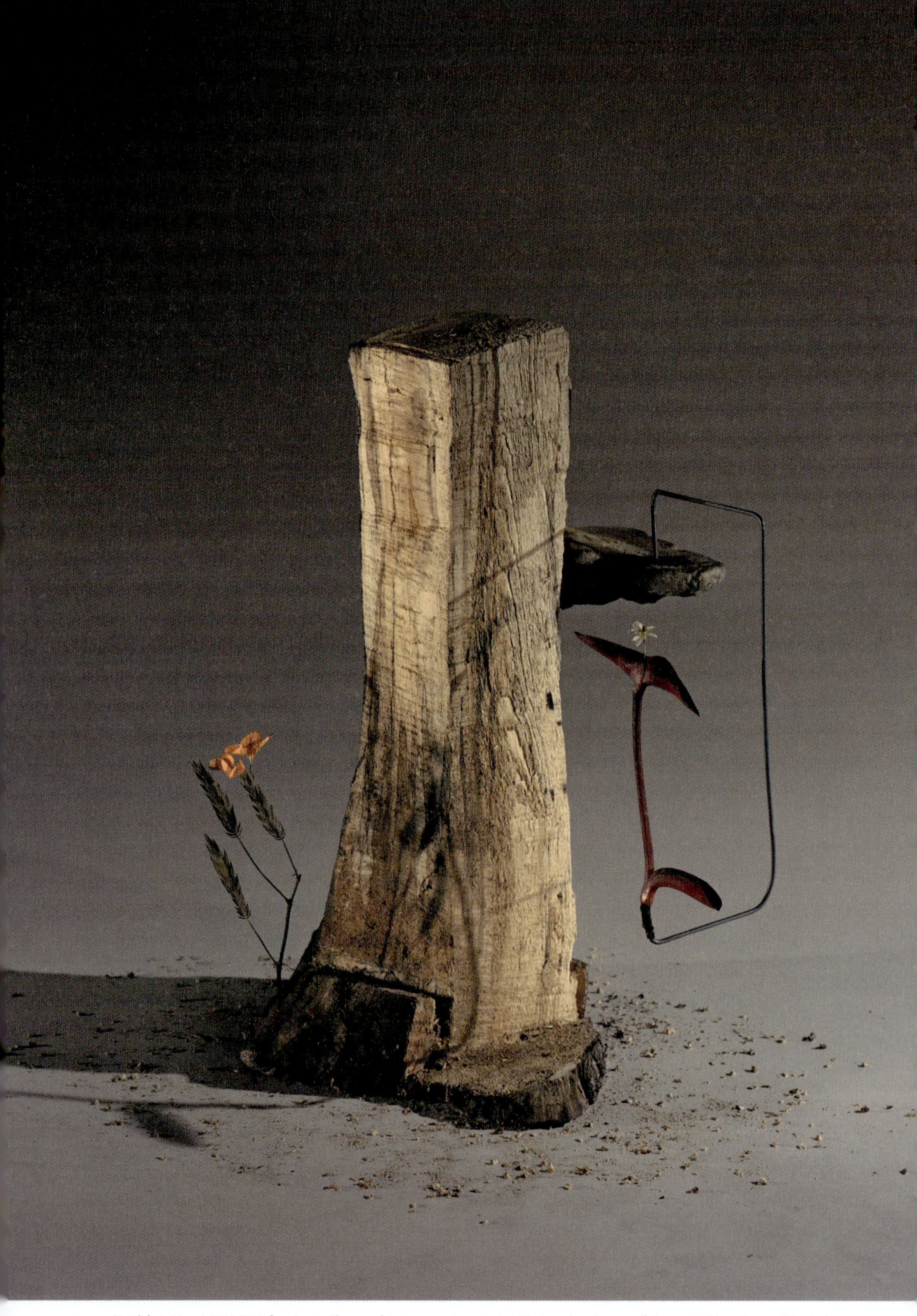

 Untitled #3, May 10, 2010, 2010, from *Drying Flowers with Microwaves*, pigment print, 48 x 39 inches. Courtesy of the artist and Laurel Gitlen, New York.

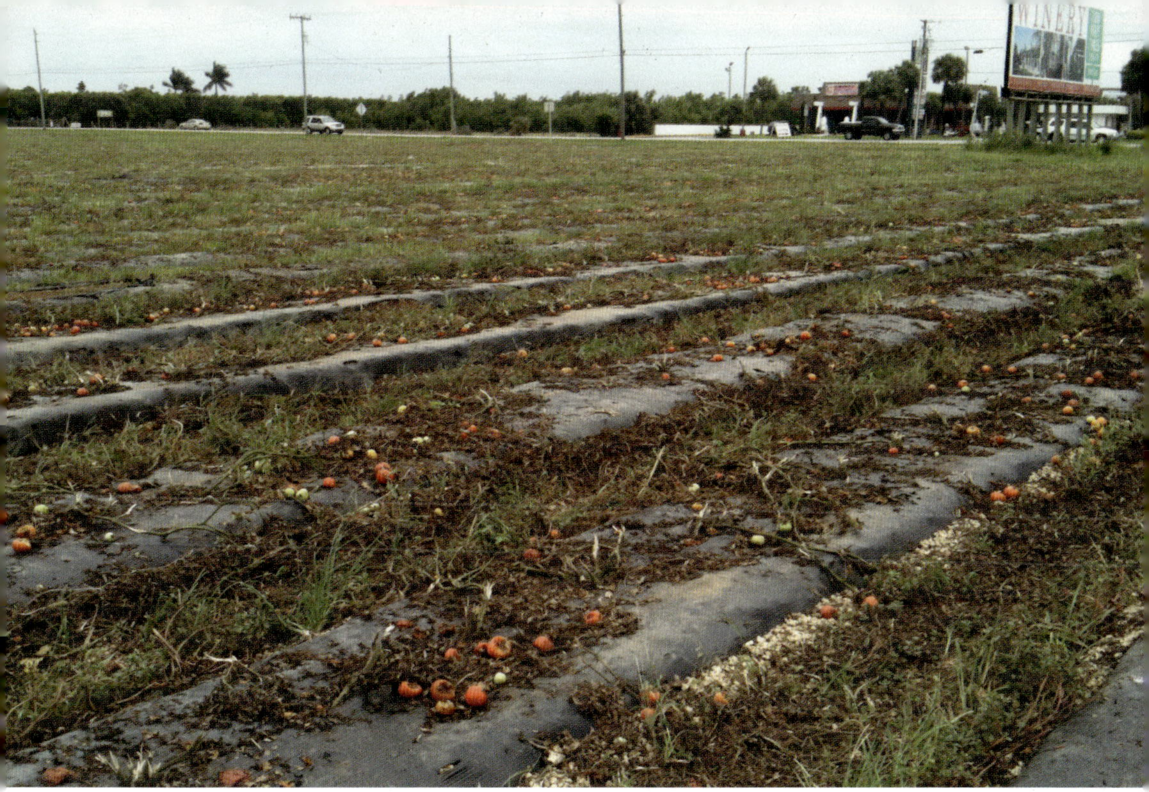

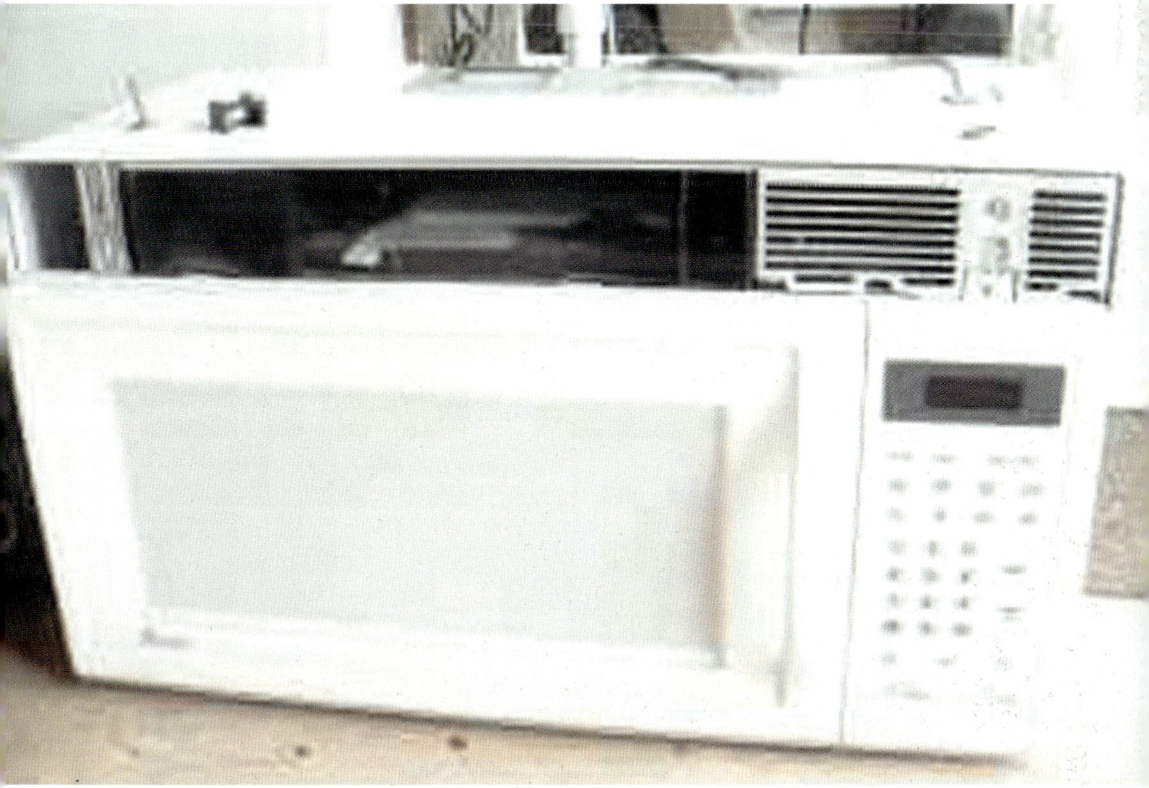

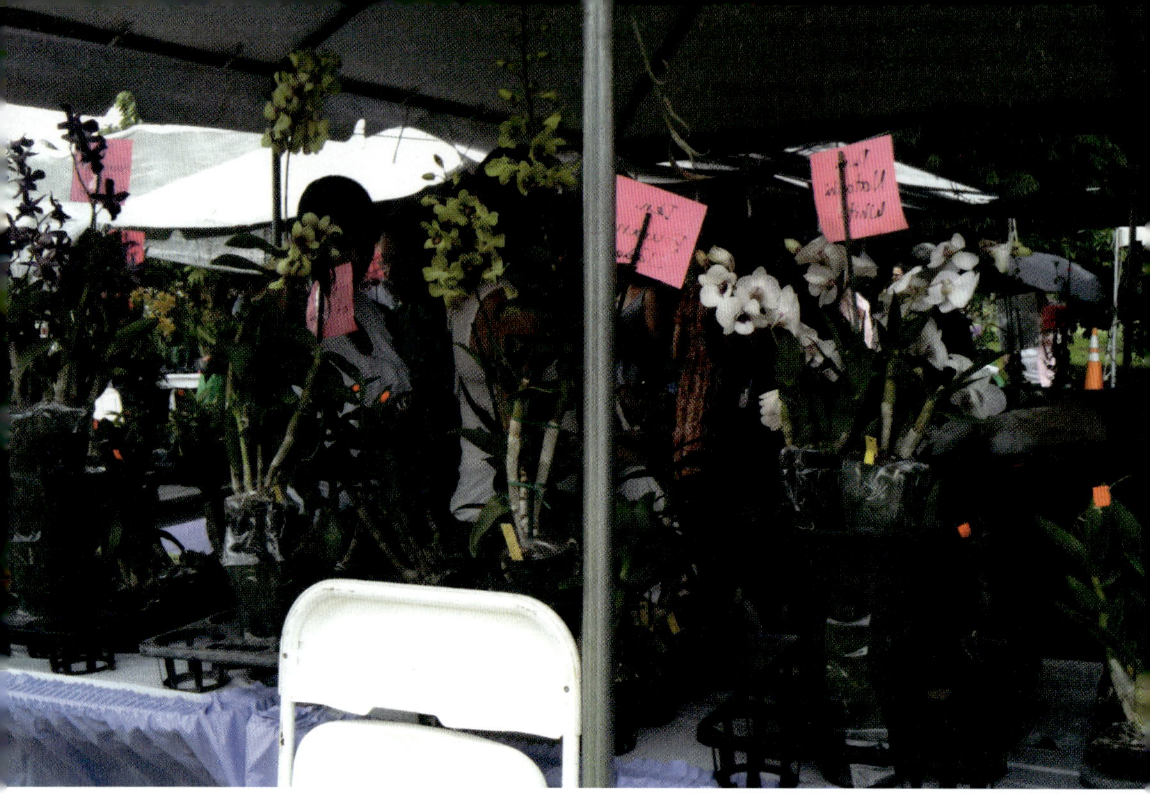

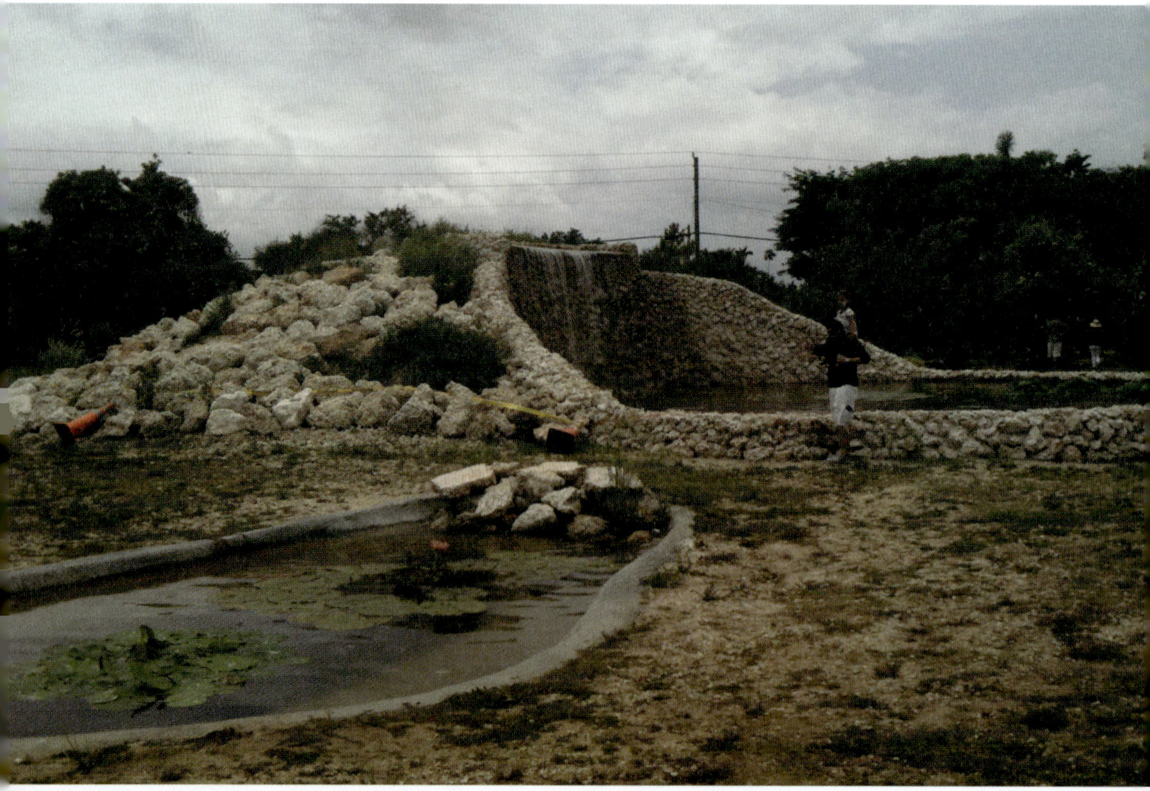

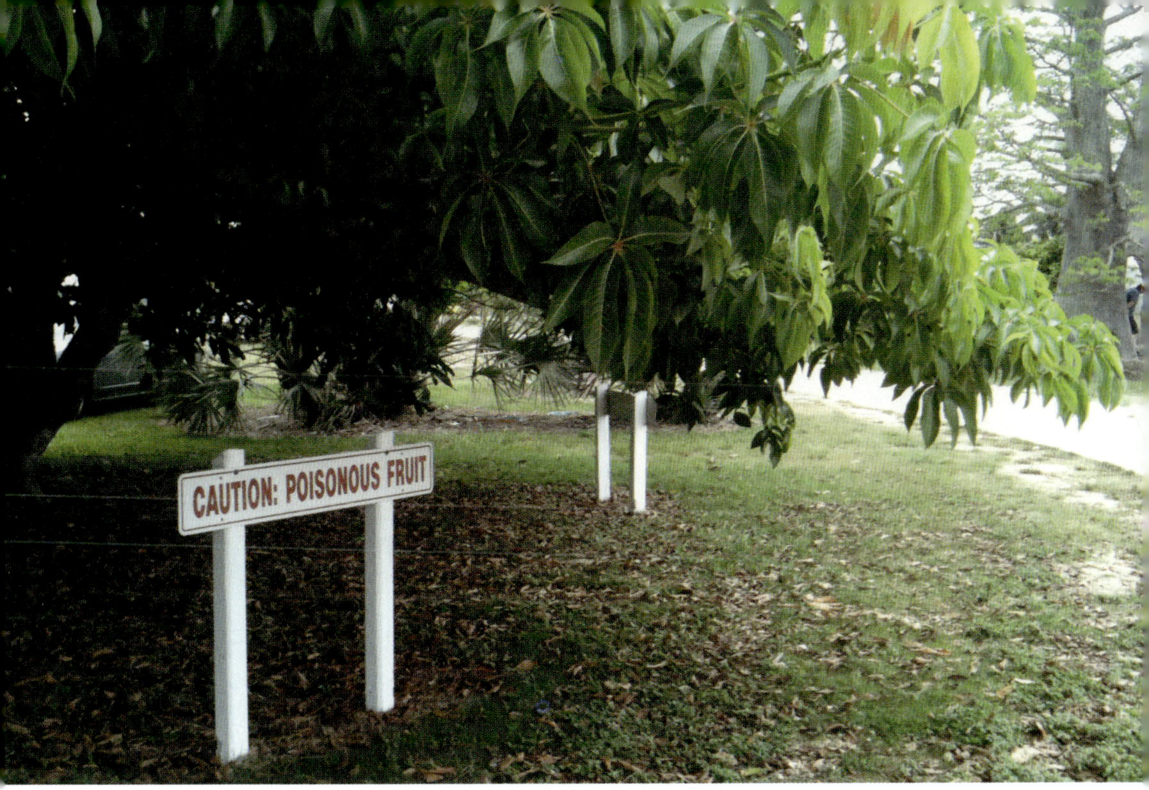

231

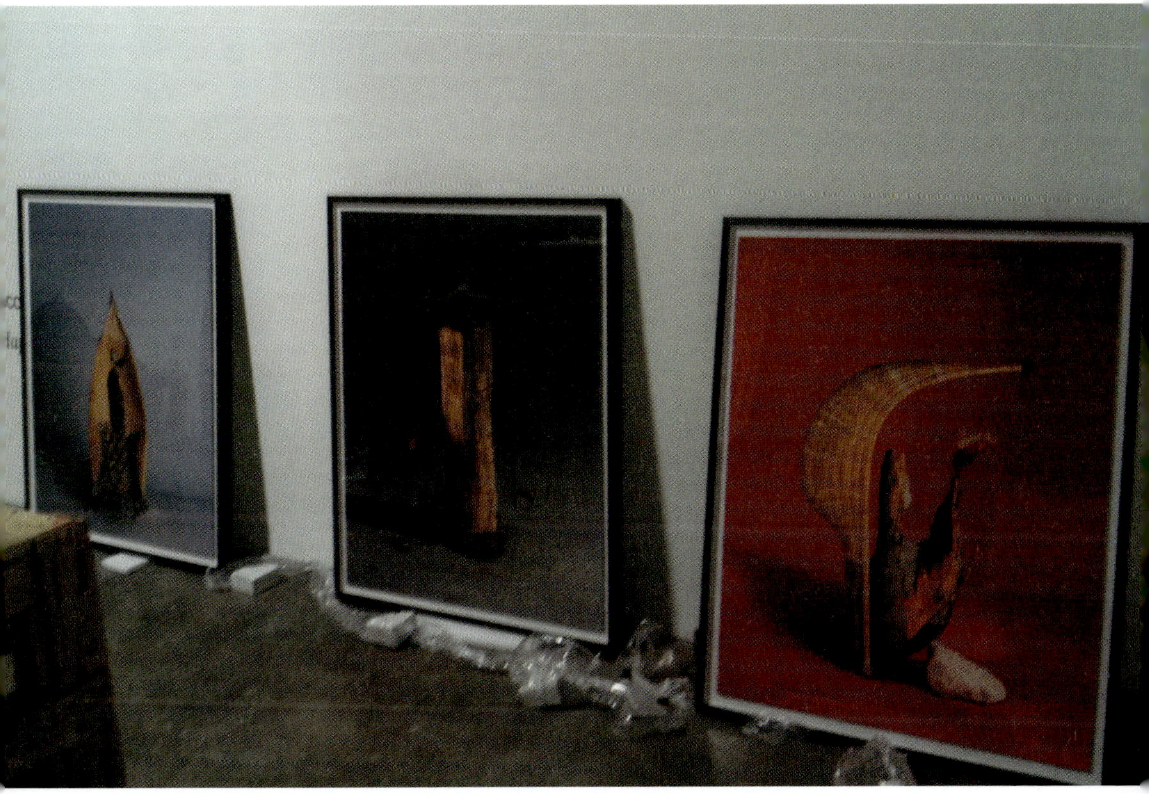

232

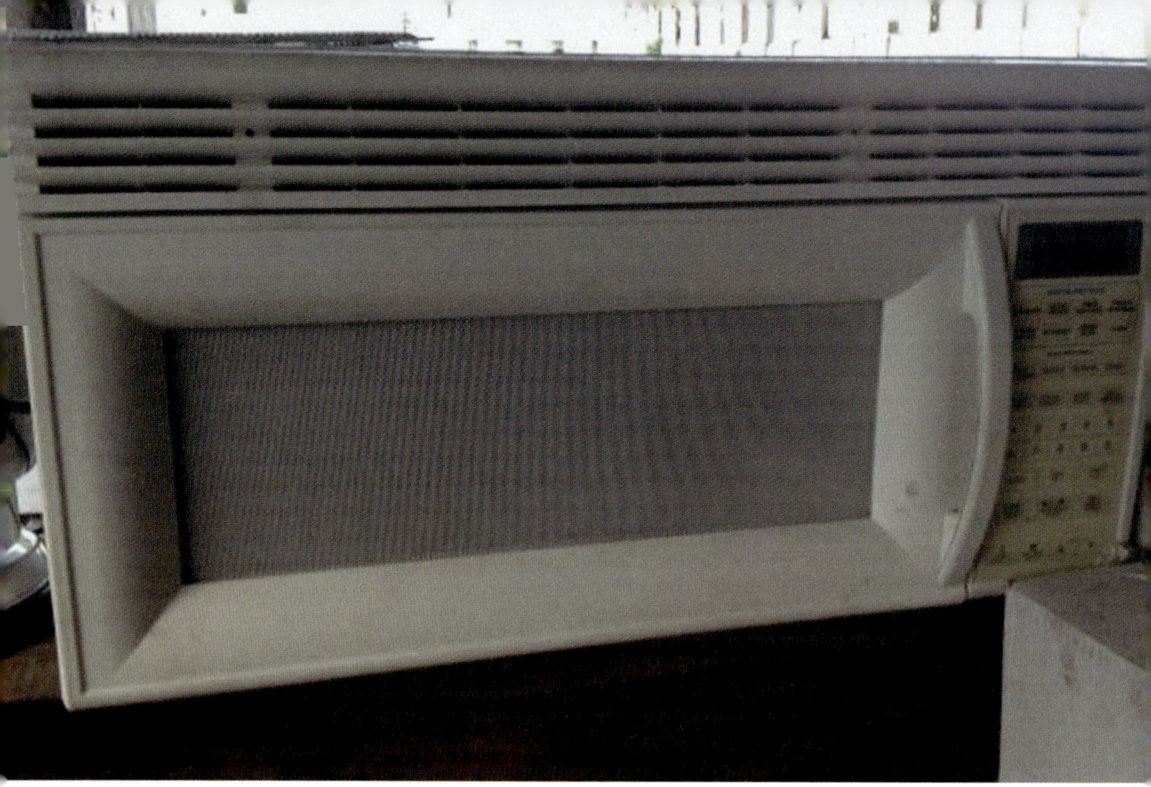

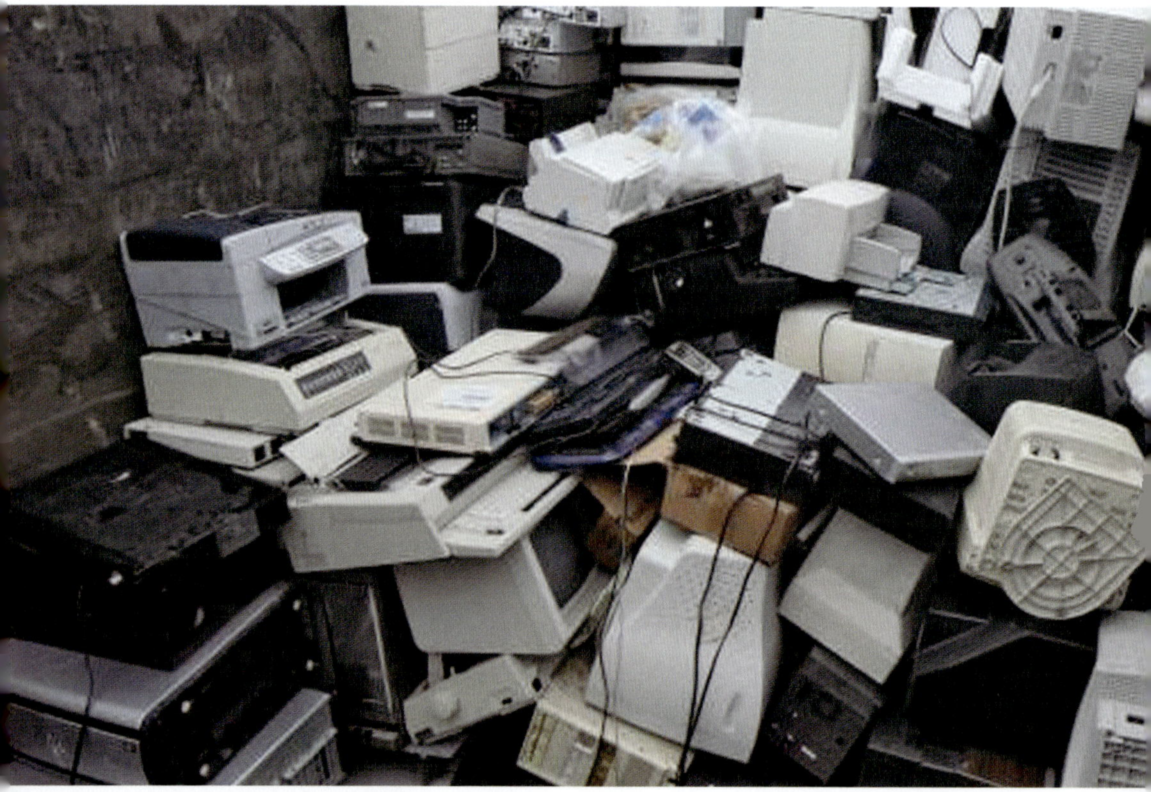

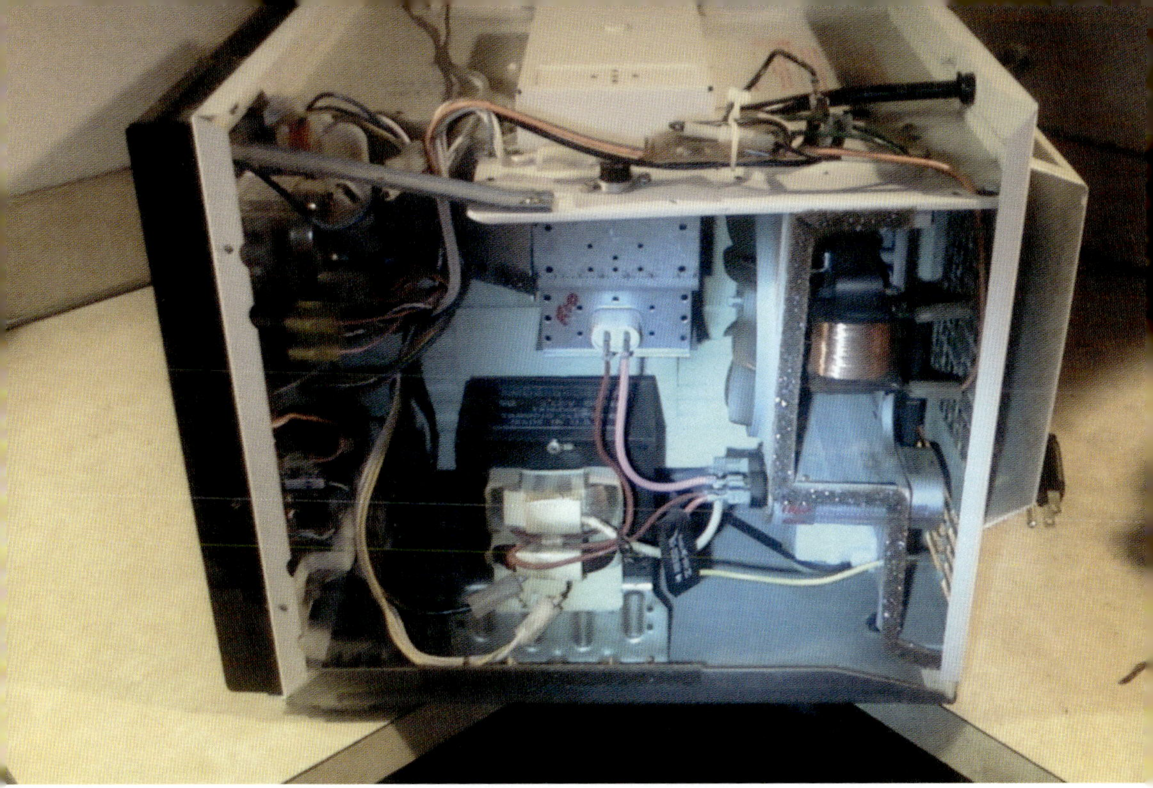

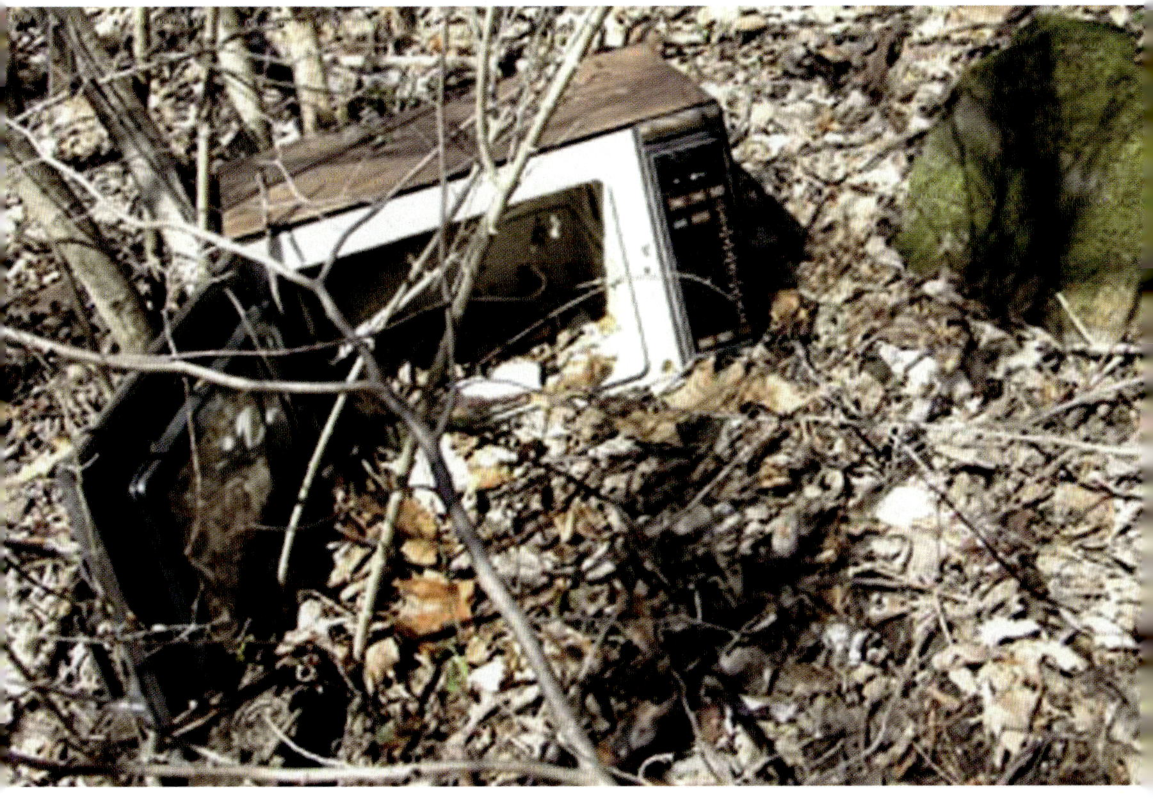

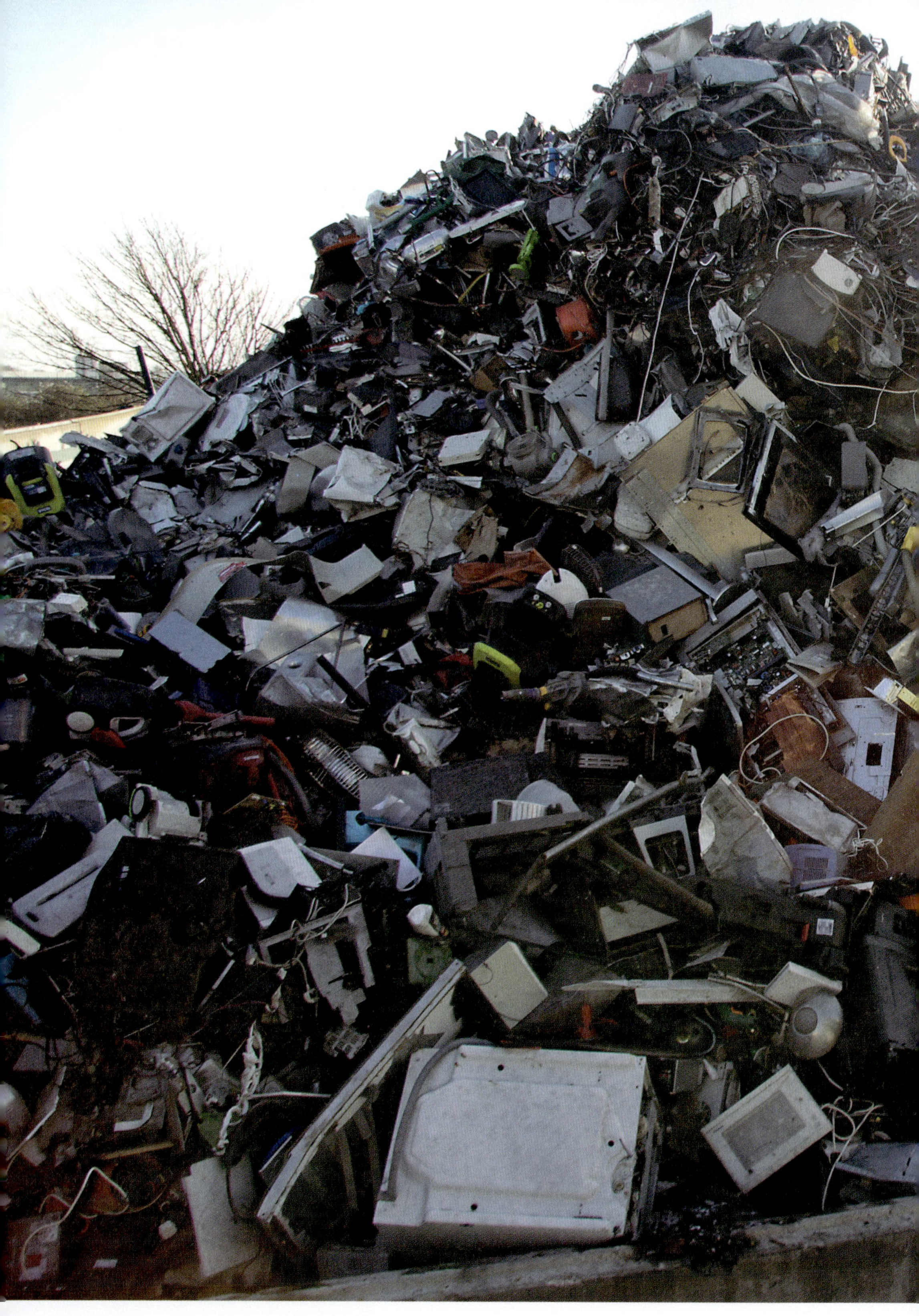

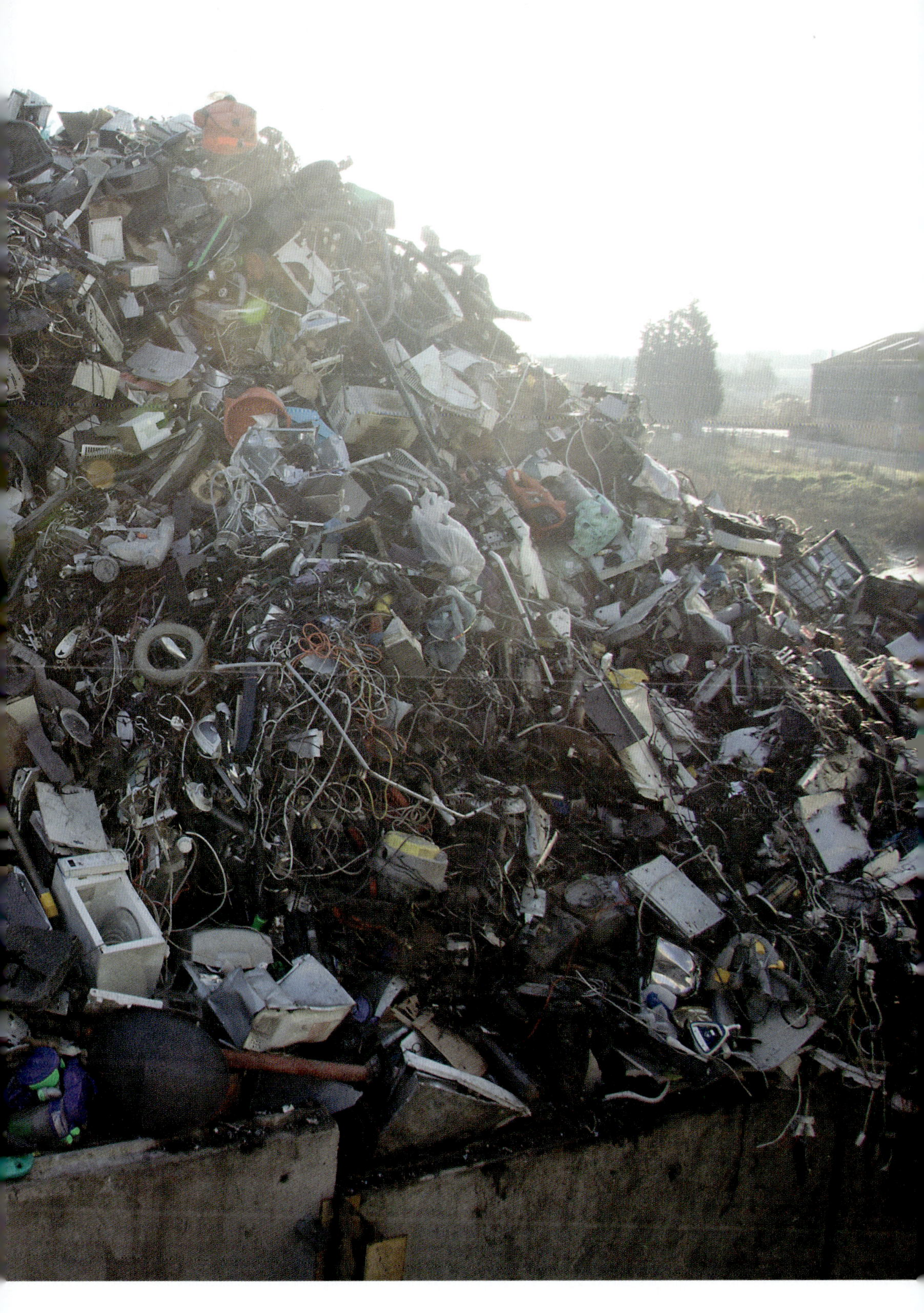

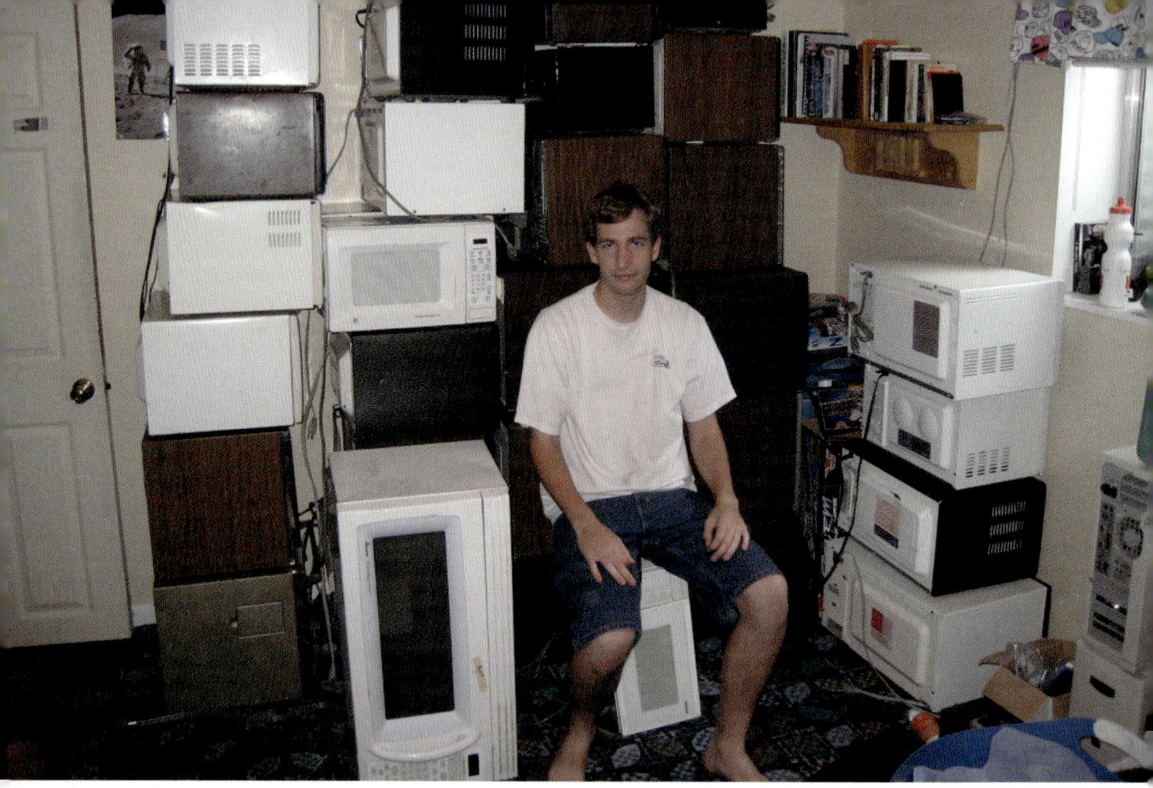

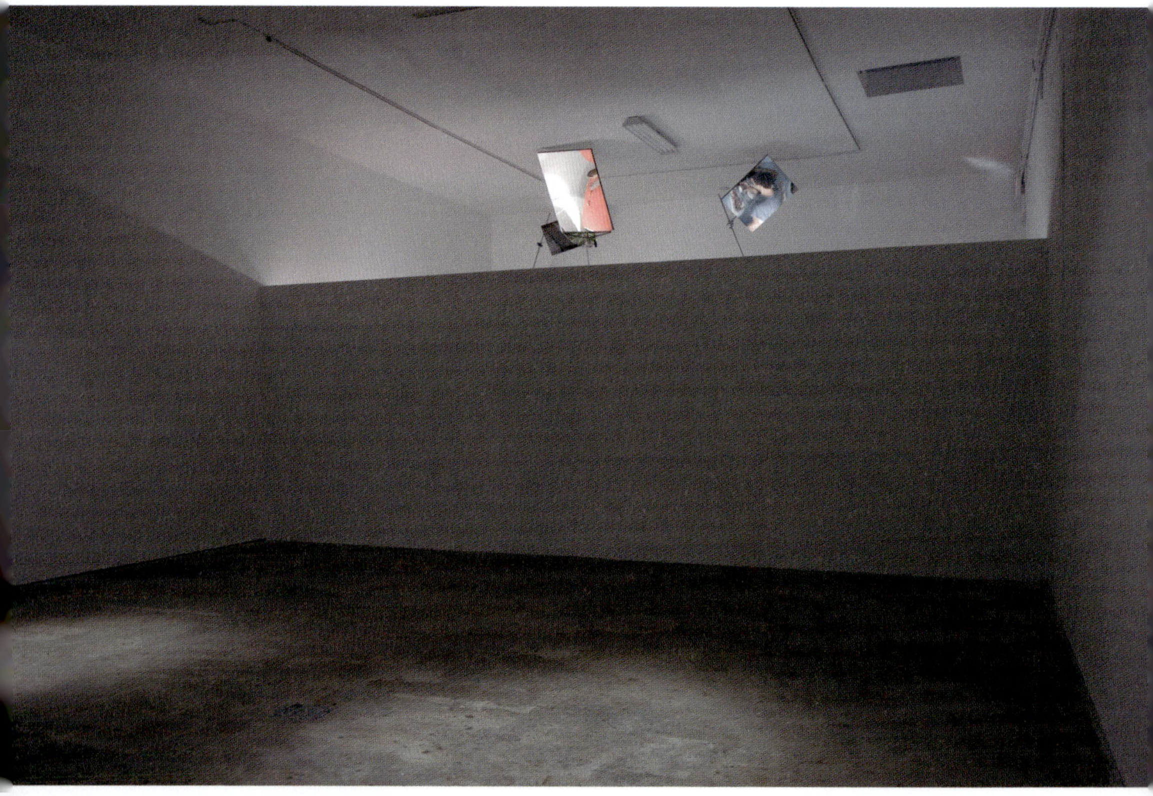

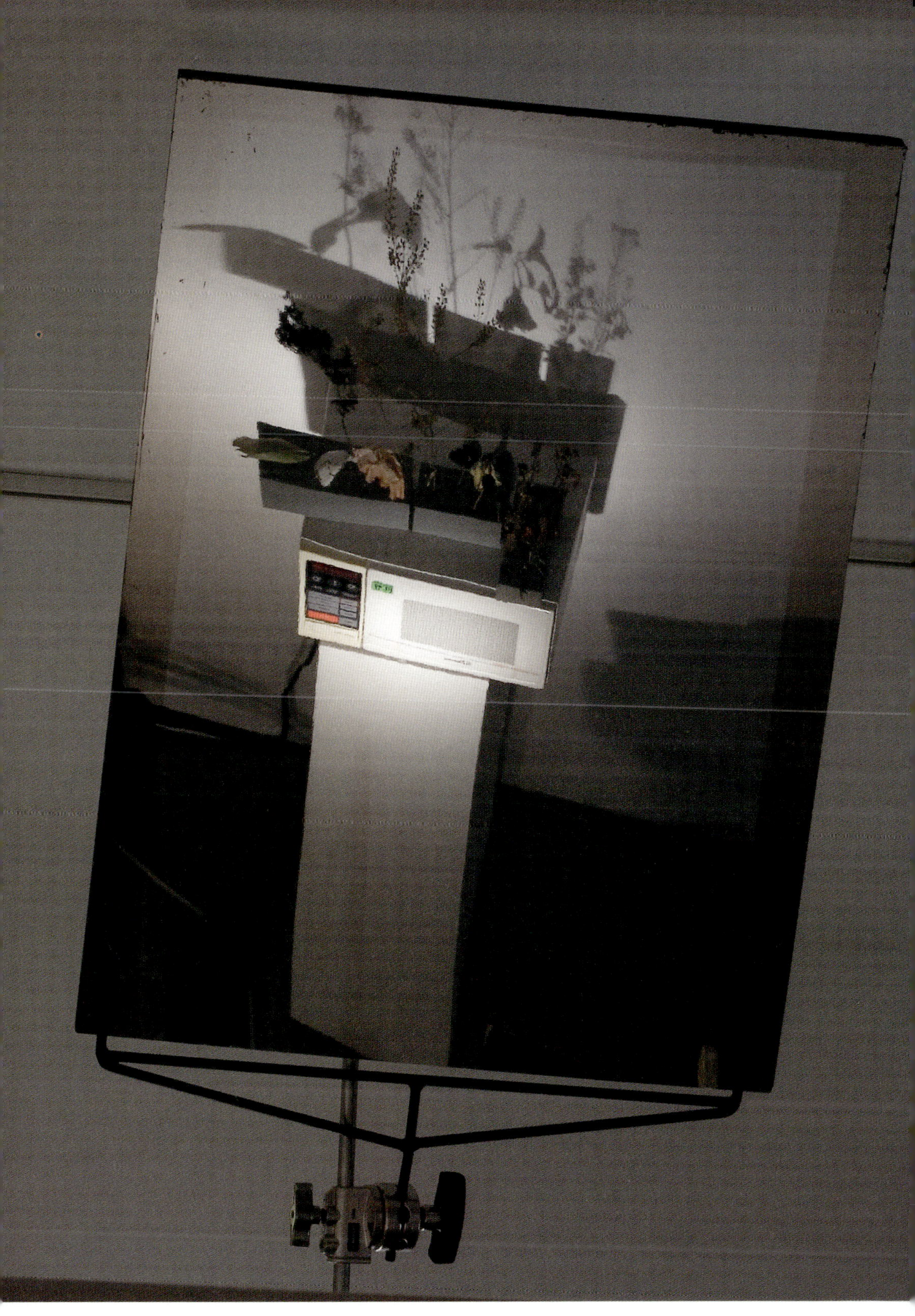

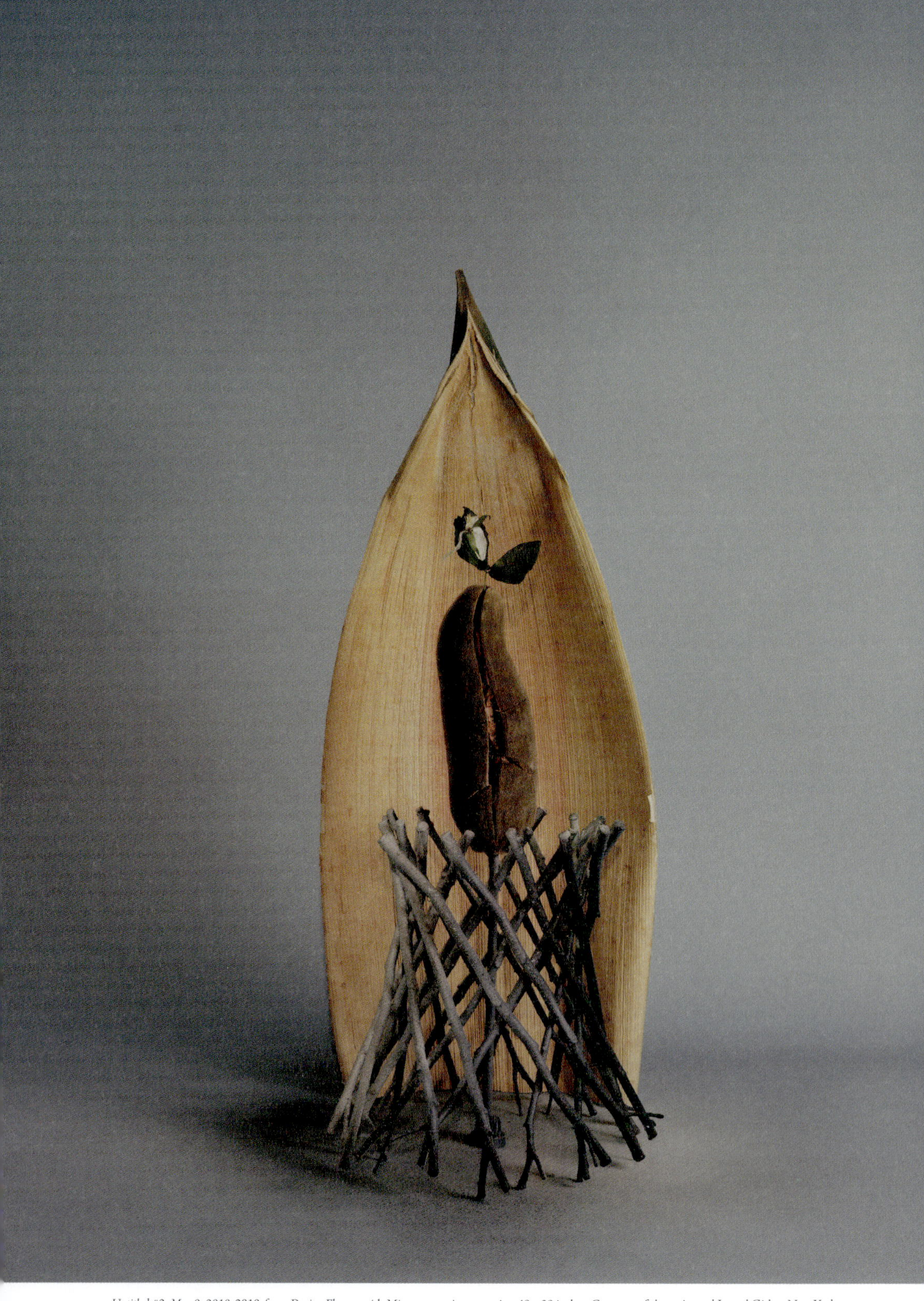

241 *Untitled #2, May 9, 2010*, 2010, from *Drying Flowers with Microwaves*, pigment print, 48 x 39 inches. Courtesy of the artist and Laurel Gitlen, New York.

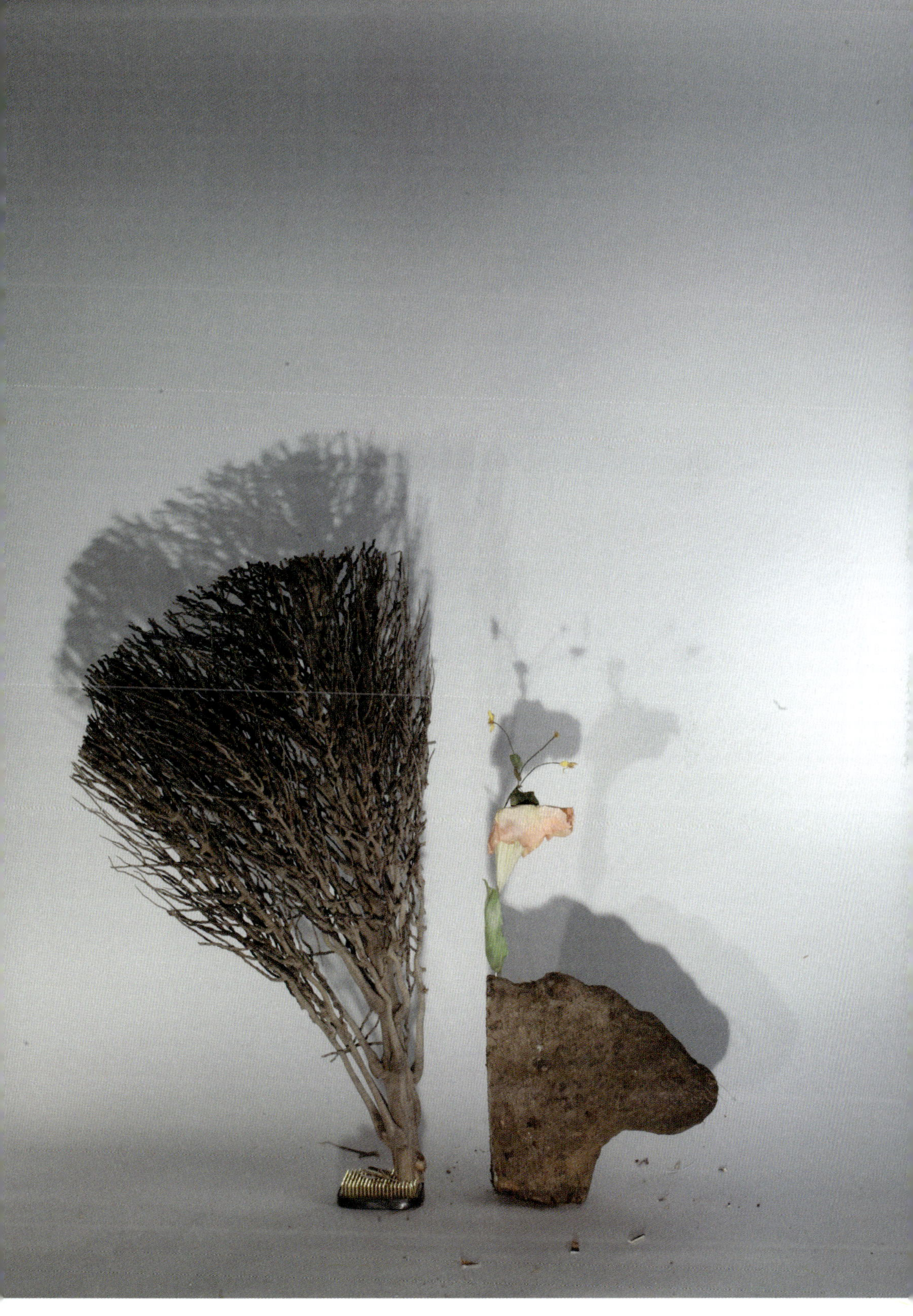

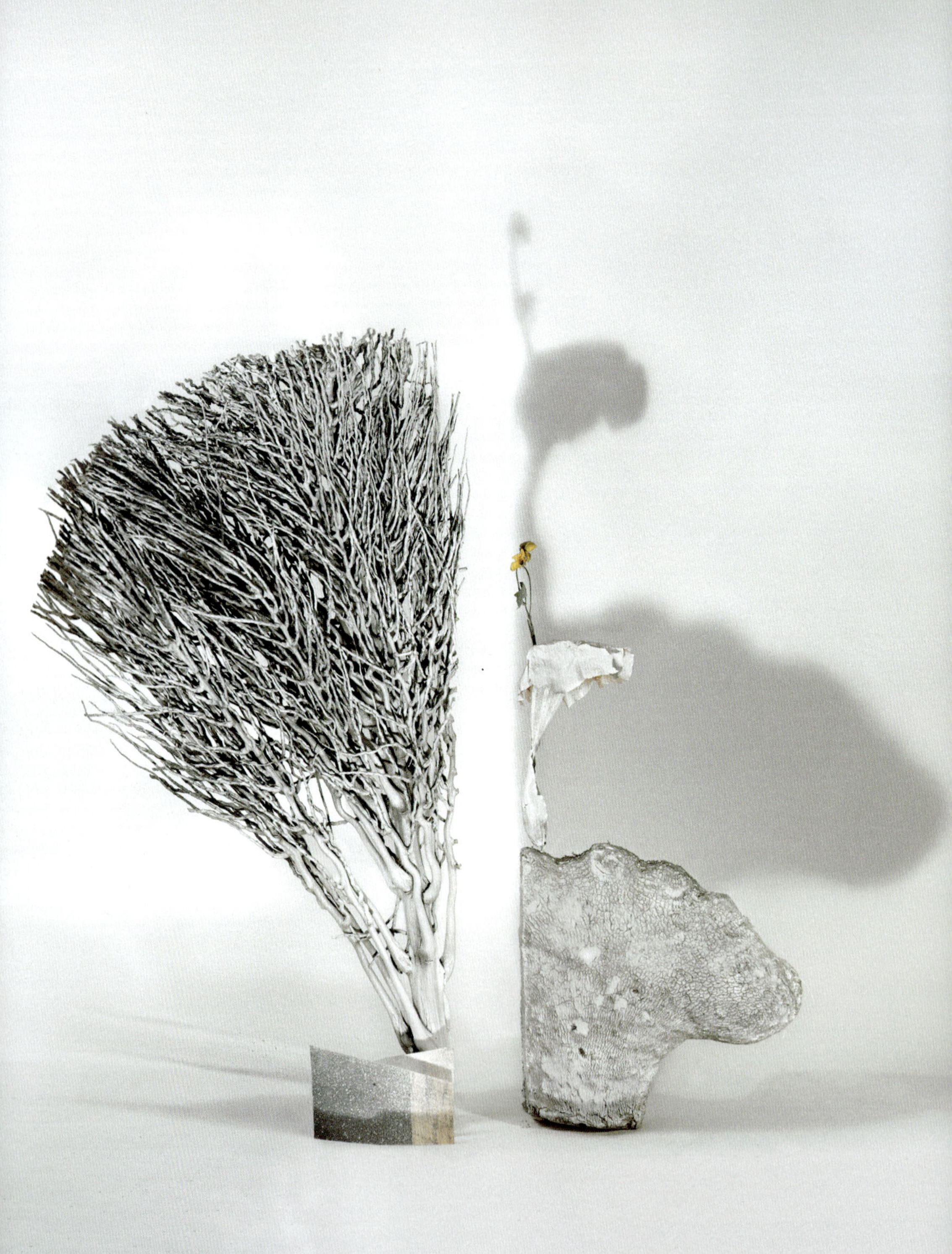

243   *Untitled #7, May 16, 2010*, 2010, from *Drying Flowers with Microwaves*, pigment print, 48 x 39 inches. Courtesy of the artist and Laurel Gitlen, New York.

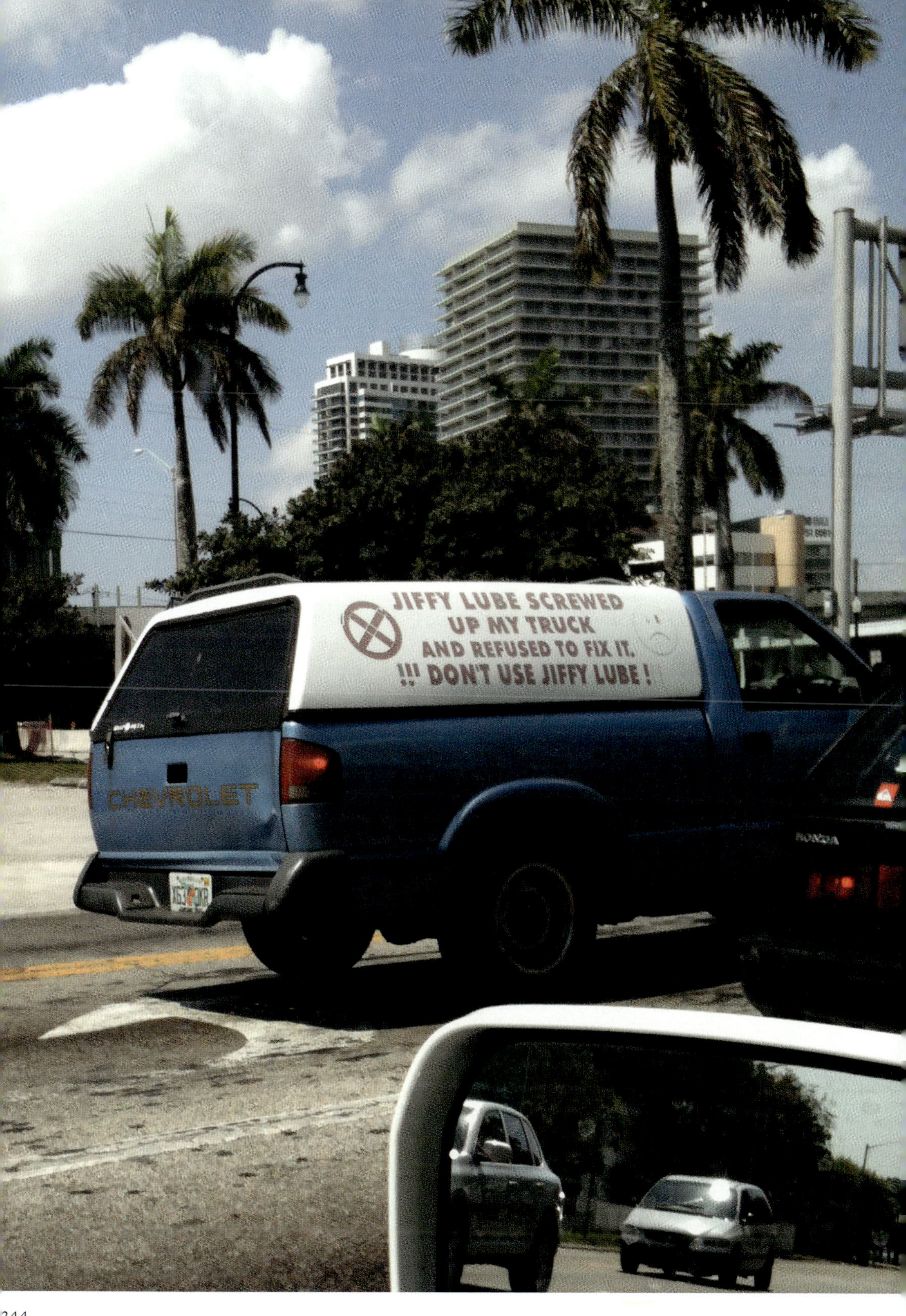

JIFFY LUBE SCREWED
UP MY TRUCK
AND REFUSED TO FIX IT.
!!! DON'T USE JIFFY LUBE !
CHEVROLET
HONDA

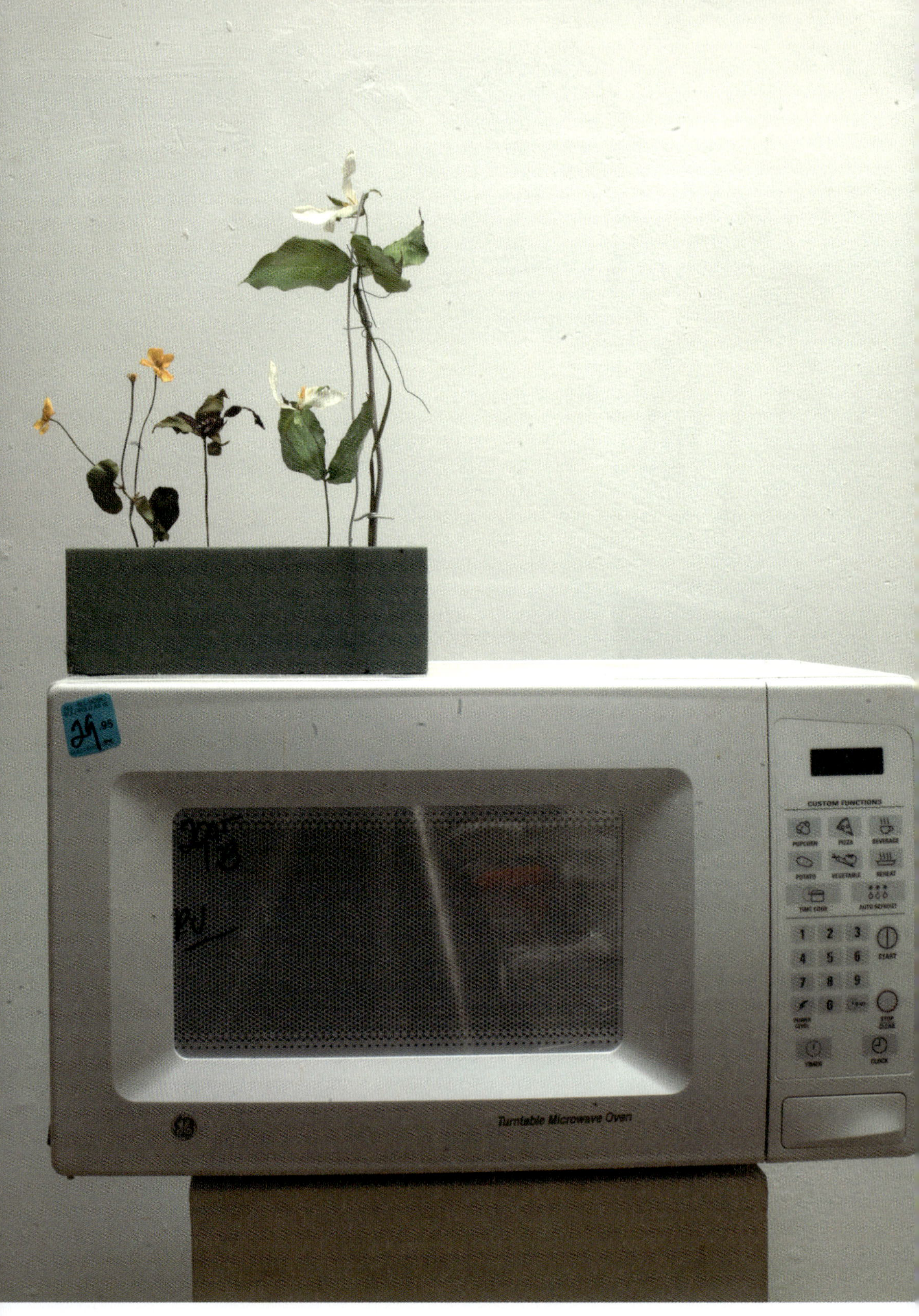

Chapter 6, **The Grey Flame and the Brown Light**

The Grey Flame and the Brown Light
BCA Center, Burlington, VT
July 2–September 4, 2010
Curated by Christopher Thompson

The Grey Flame and the Brown Light was inspired by one of philosopher Ludwig Wittgenstein's color logic problems, where he pondered the impossibility of a "brown light" or a "grey flame." In the gallery, Hewitt created a workspace on top of an excised section of Vermont forest floor, using the soil to undertake an investigation of the colors brown and grey. This space was covered with a roof of wooden slats, resembling a stage or gymnasium floor. Sections of this roof slid open, allowing Hewitt to elevate flatbed scanners, which were used to capture images of rocks, ash, sand, soil, and decaying vegetal matter. Each scan was compressed and averaged in Photoshop to create a single color, typically somewhere in the grey-to-brown range, and then saturated into a vibrant monochrome. These image files were printed on a digital pigment printer and then "shed" back onto the forest floor, where they slowly dissolved into the soil, to be later re-scanned and exhibited as prints.

Captions

246: Preparatory work for *The Grey Flame and the Brown Light*. Courtesy of the artist.
247, 248, 252, 255: Set documentation of *The Grey Flame and the Brown Light*, 2010. Courtesy of the artist.
250, 251, 253, 254, 266, 271, 277: *The Grey Flame and the Brown Light*, 2010. Installation view, BCA Center. Photo: Raychel Severence. Courtesy BCA Center, Burlington, VT.
253: Installation in progress, *The Grey Flame and the Brown Light*, 2010. Photo: Corin Hewitt. Courtesy of the artist.
256–259, 261, 268: Process image from *The Grey Flame and the Brown Light*, 2010. Courtesy of the artist.
265, 267: Still from live video feed in *The Grey Flame and the Brown Light*, 2010. Courtesy of the artist.
269: Research image for *The Grey Flame and the Brown Light*, found online. Courtesy of the artist.
261: Screen capture of work in progress for *The Grey Flame and the Brown Light*, 2010. Courtesy of the artist.
262–264, 270, 272, 273, 275, 278, 279: *The Grey Flame and the Brown Light*, 2010. Performance documentation. Photo: Raychel Severence. Courtesy BCA Center, Burlington, VT.

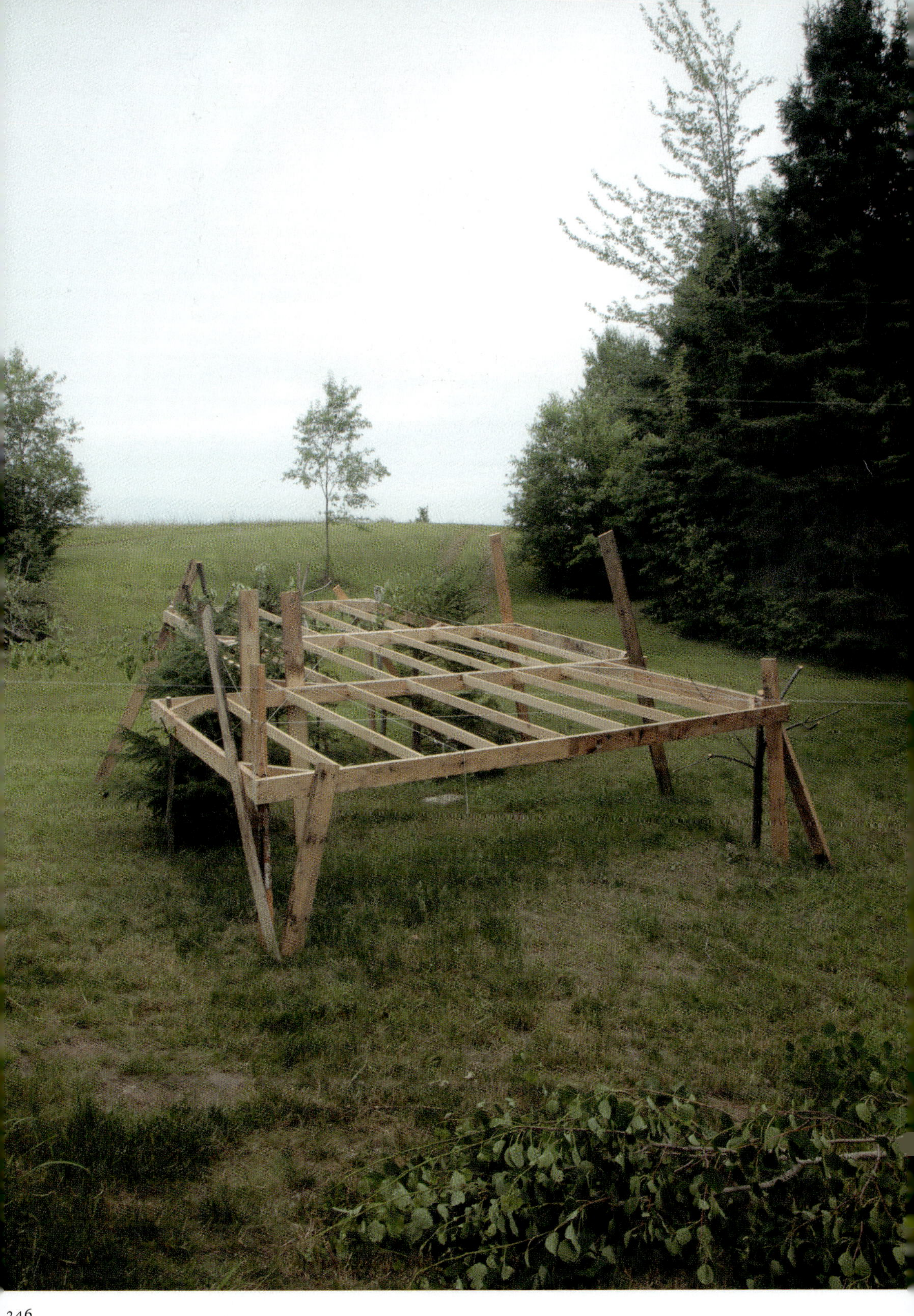

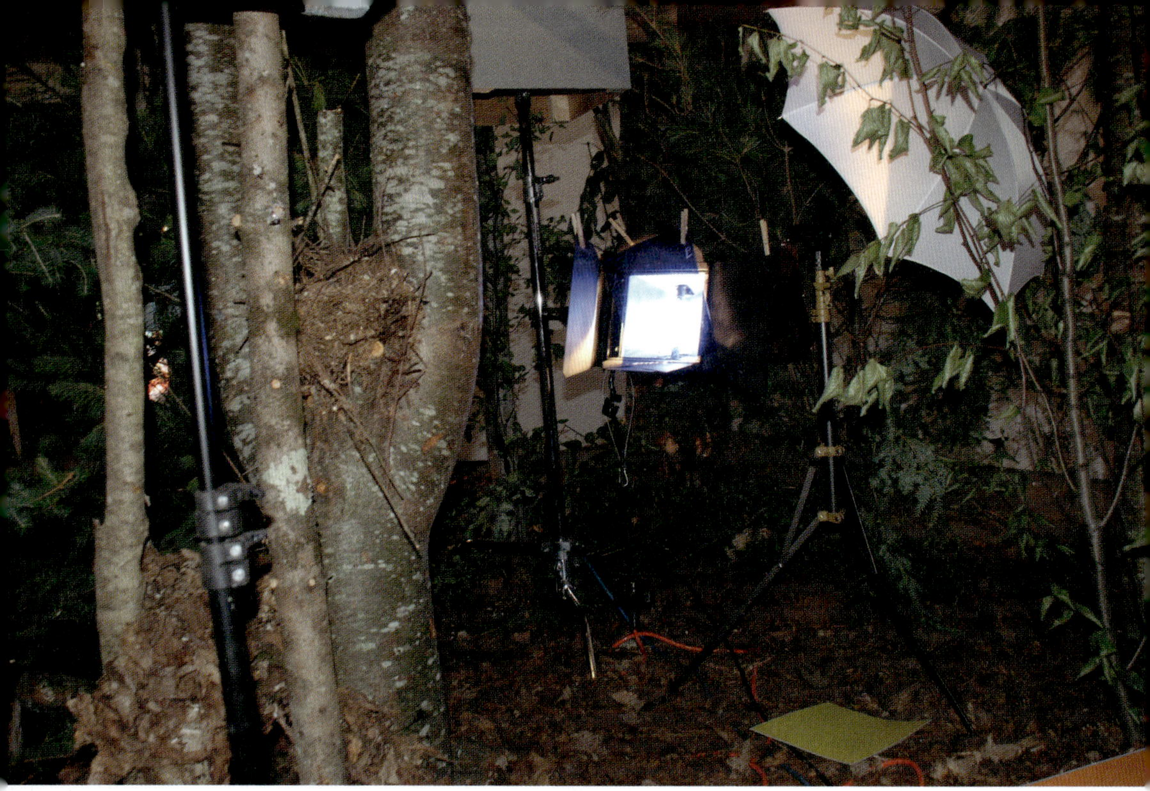

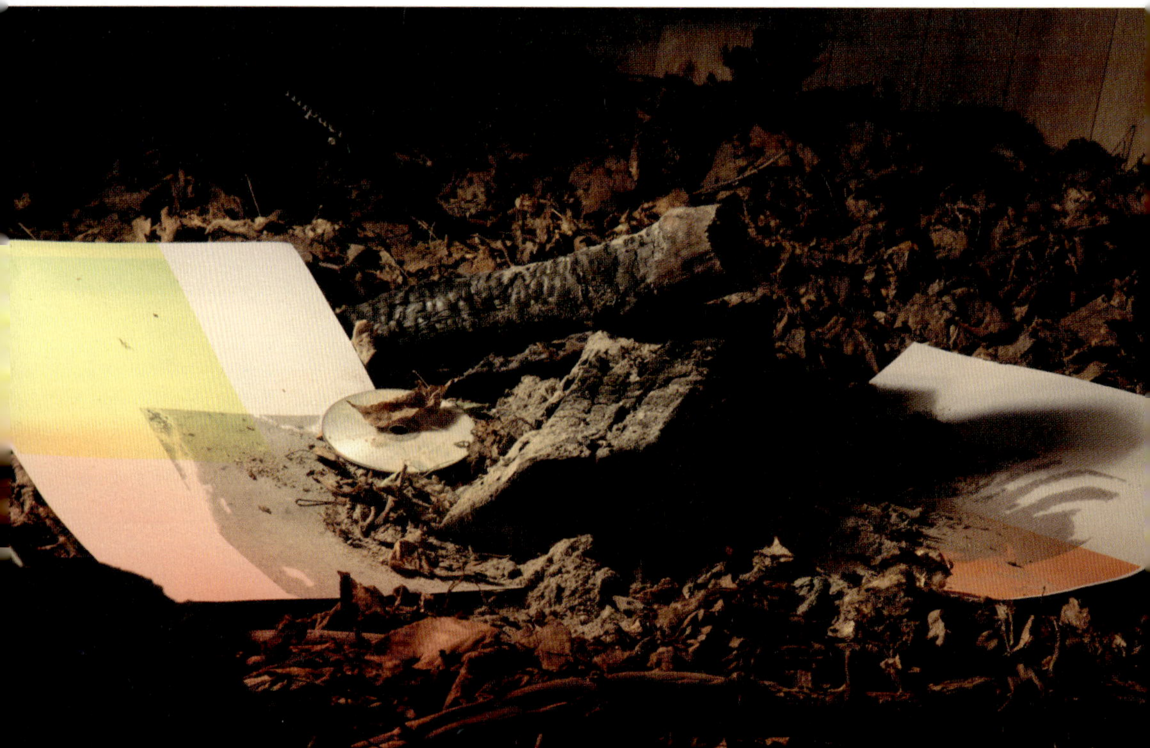

  Recomposed Monochrome (248, 246, 82), 2011, pigment print, 34 x 26 inches. Courtesy of the artist and Laurel Gitlen, New York.

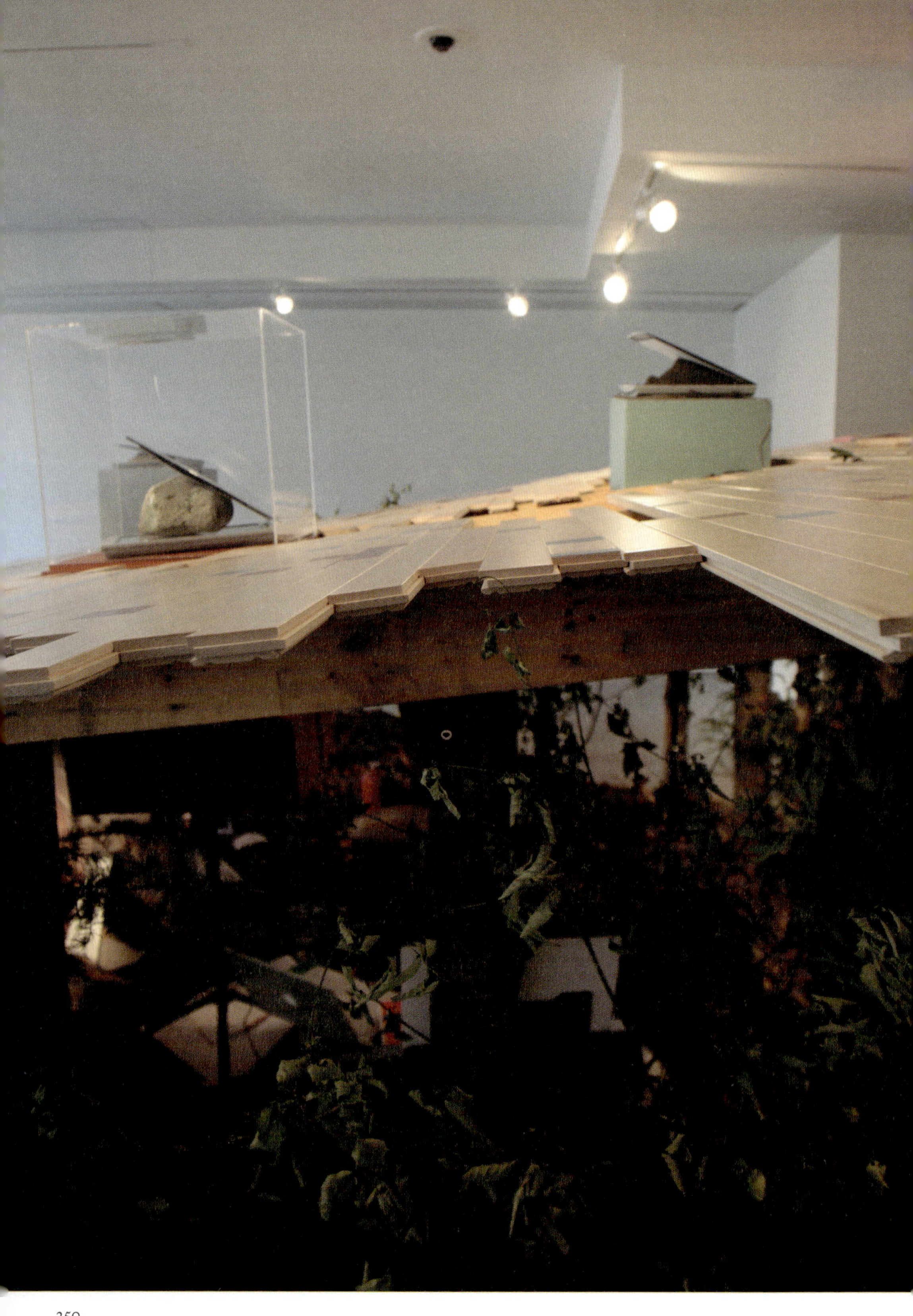

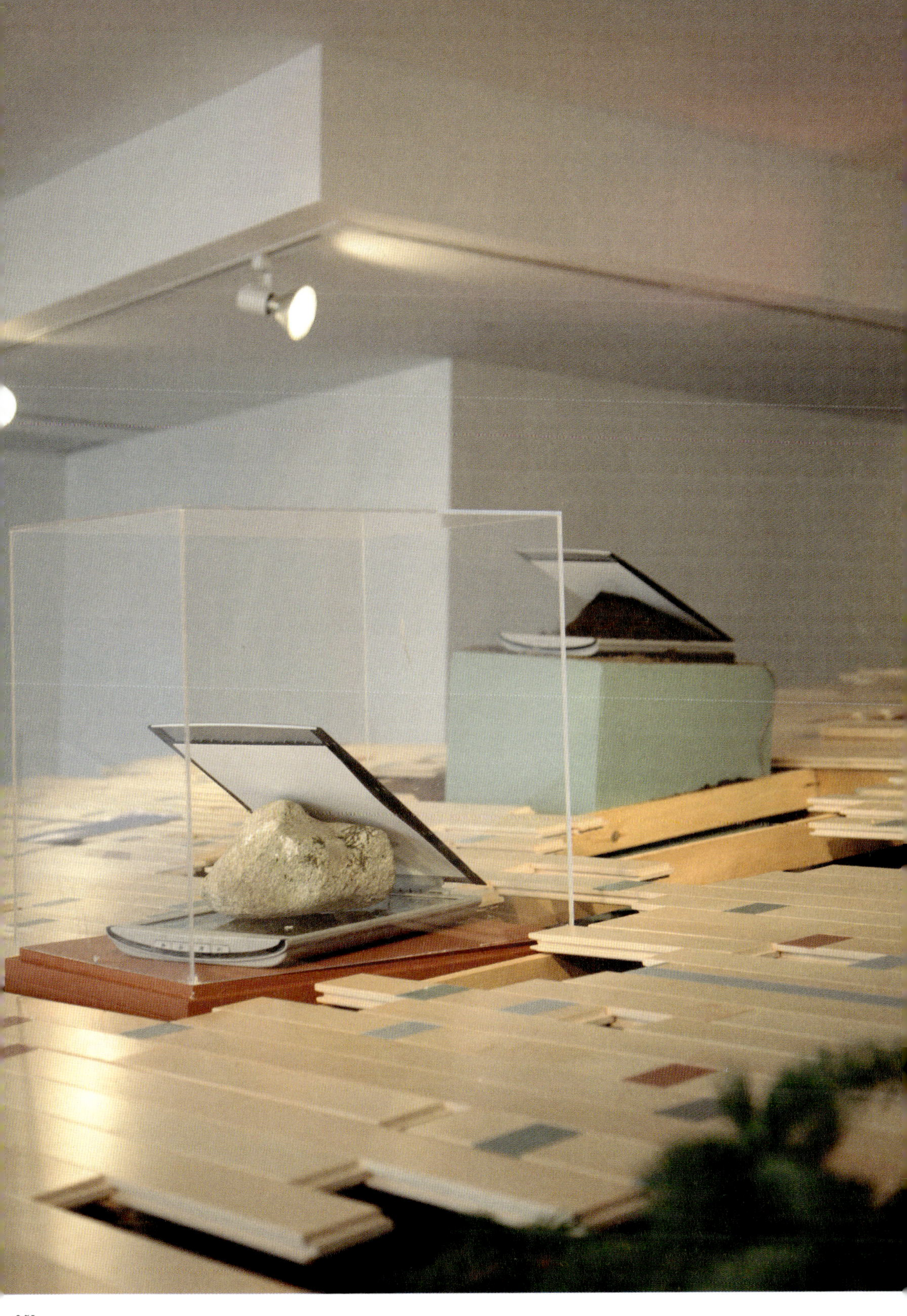

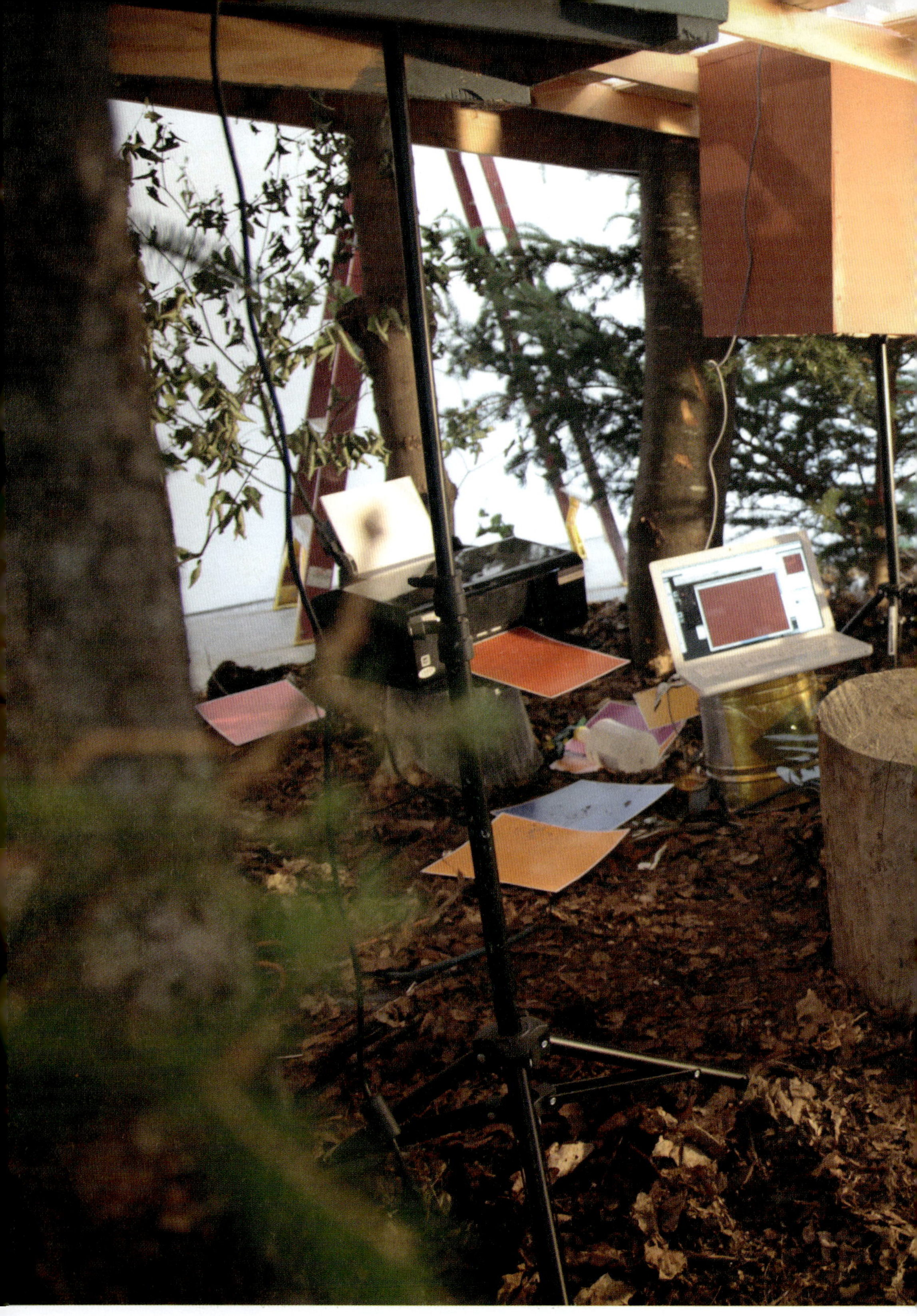

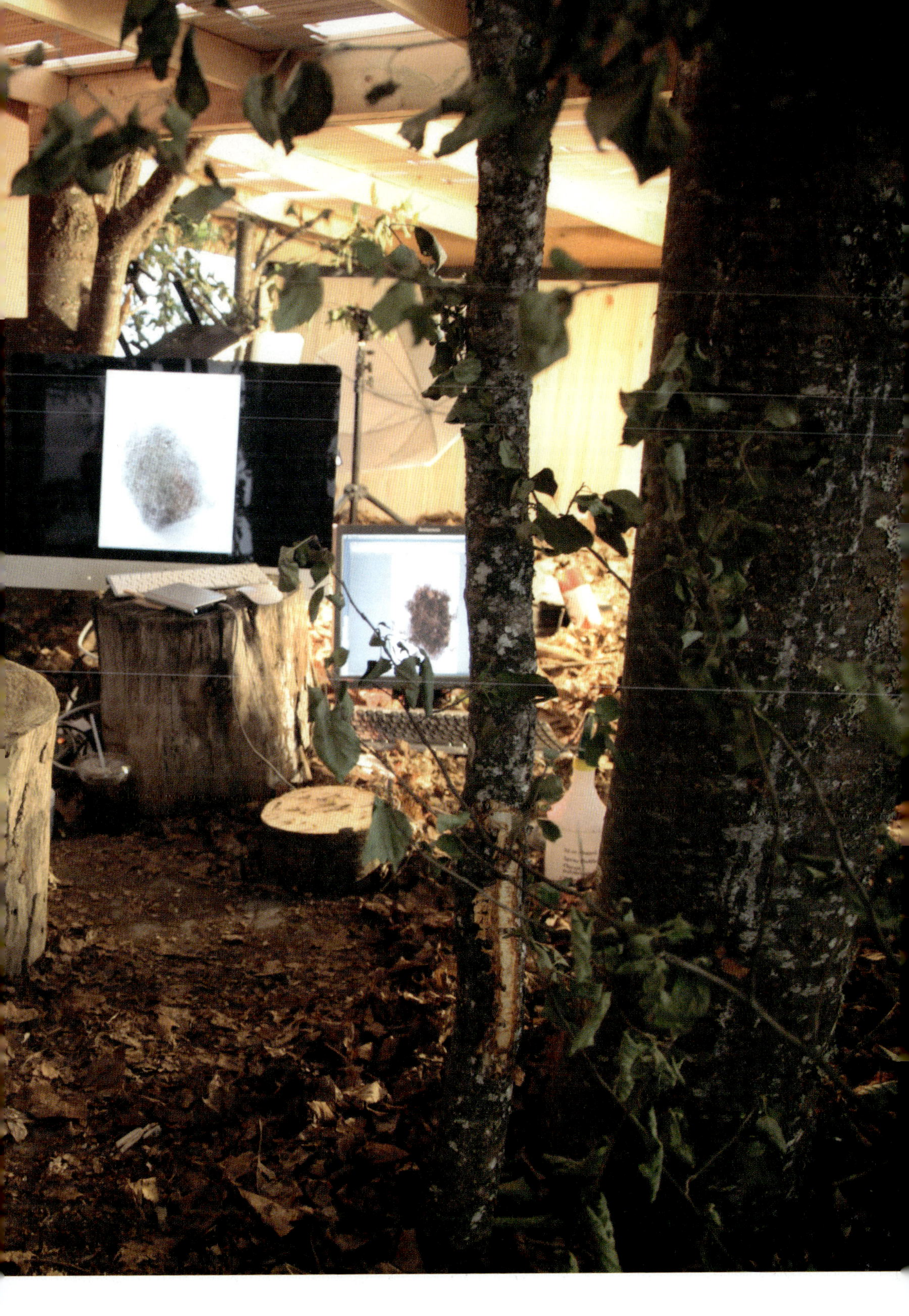

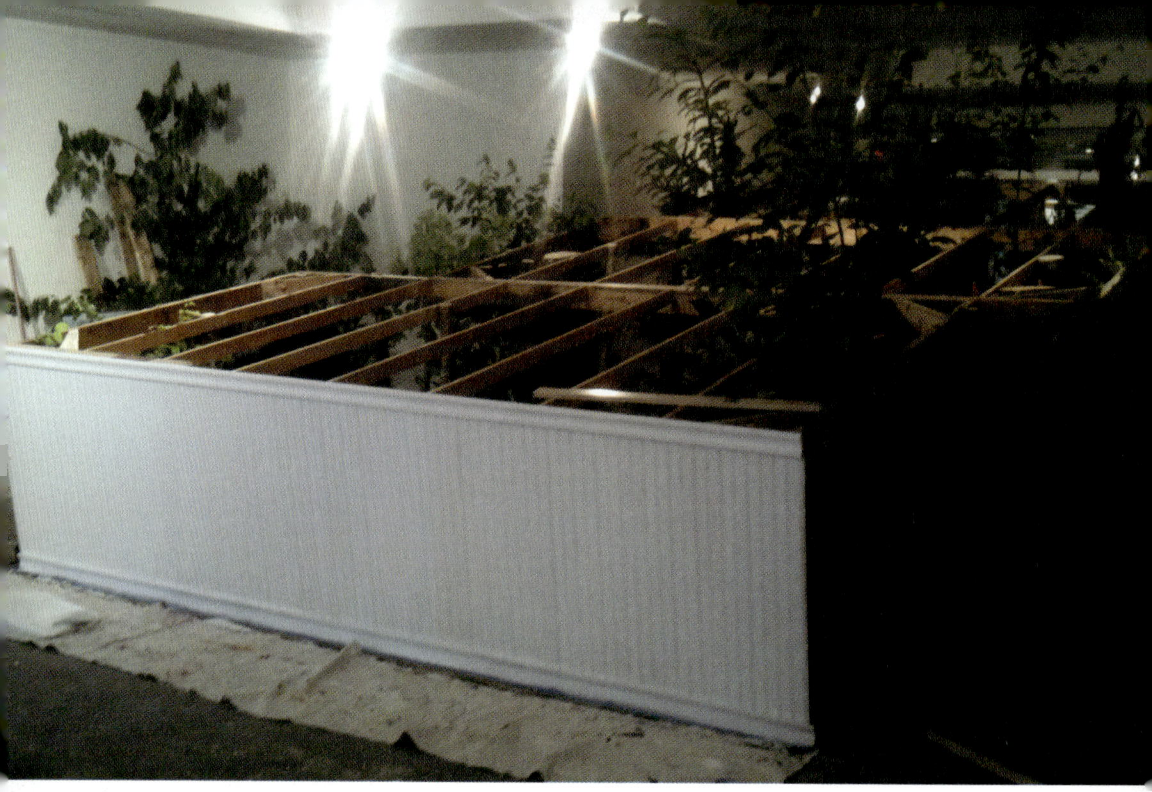

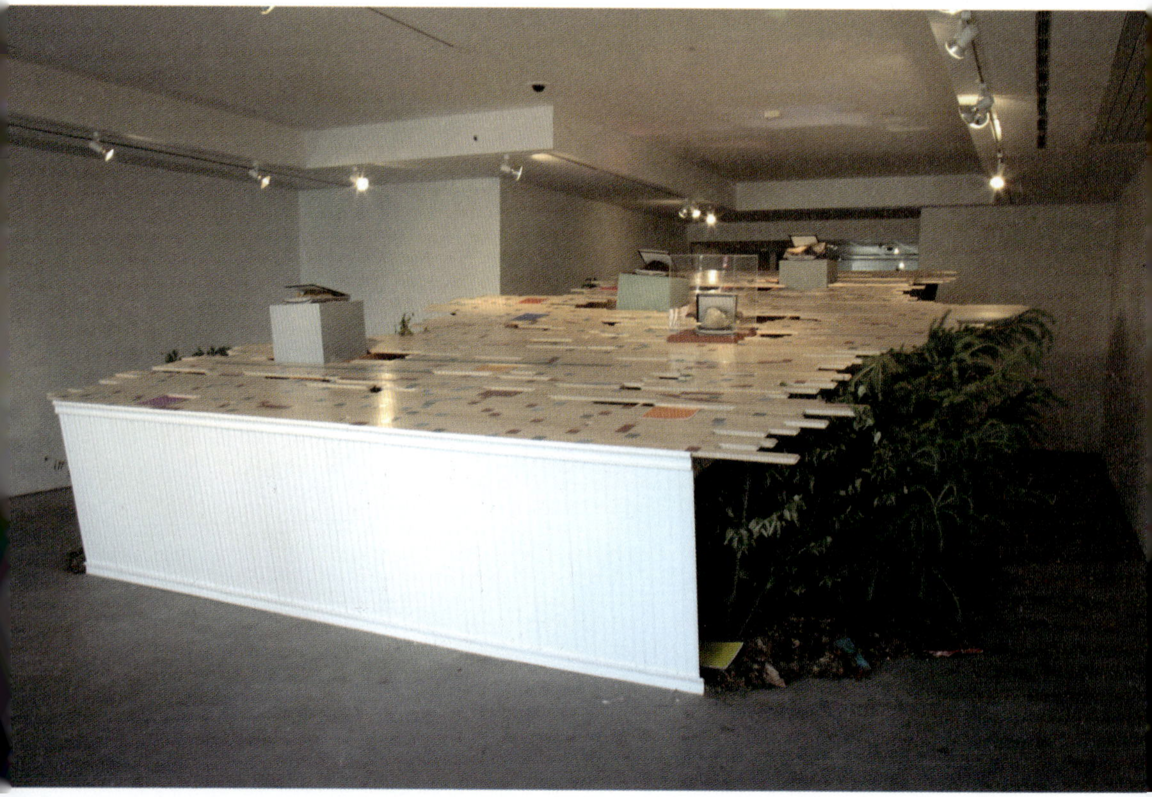

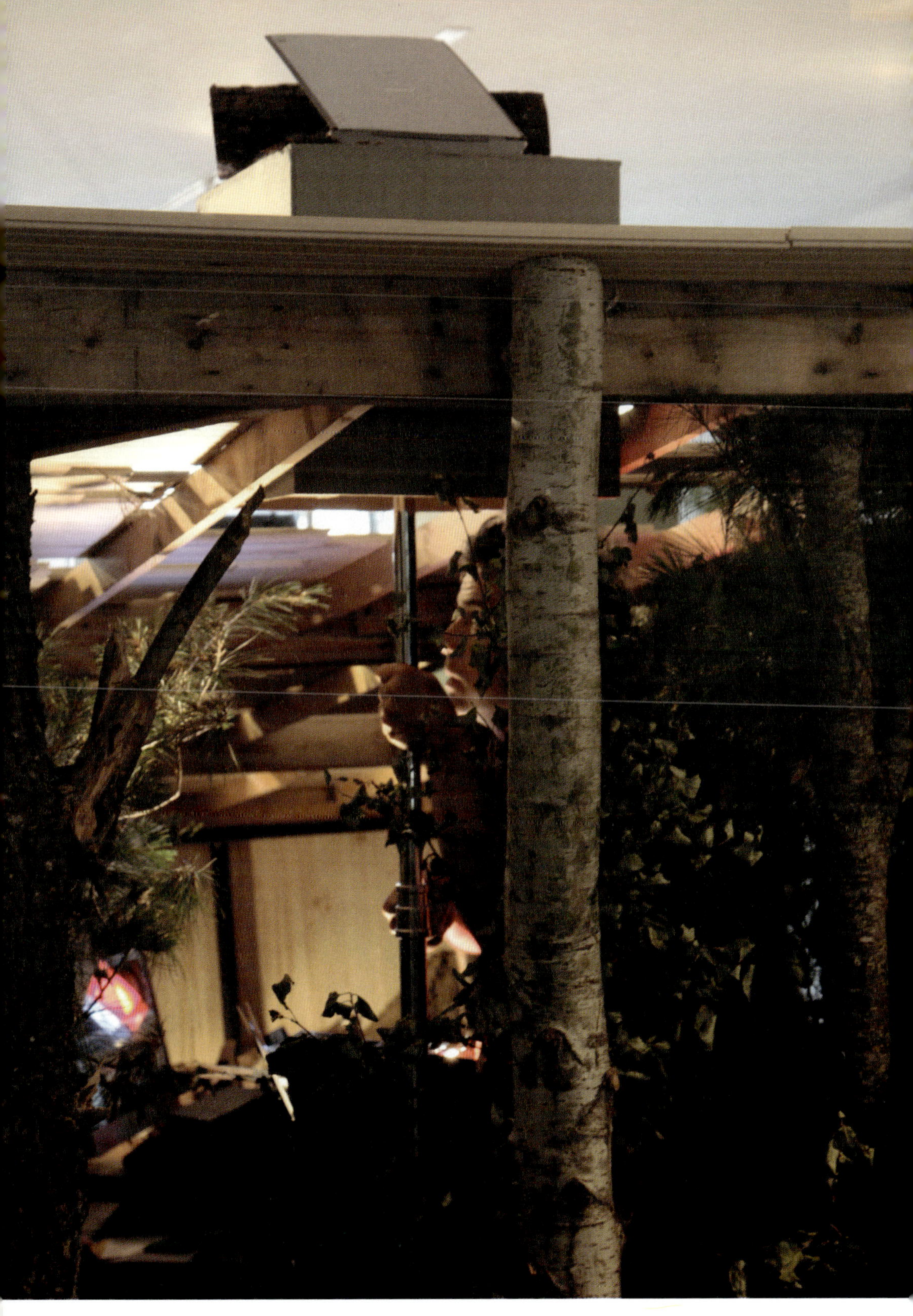

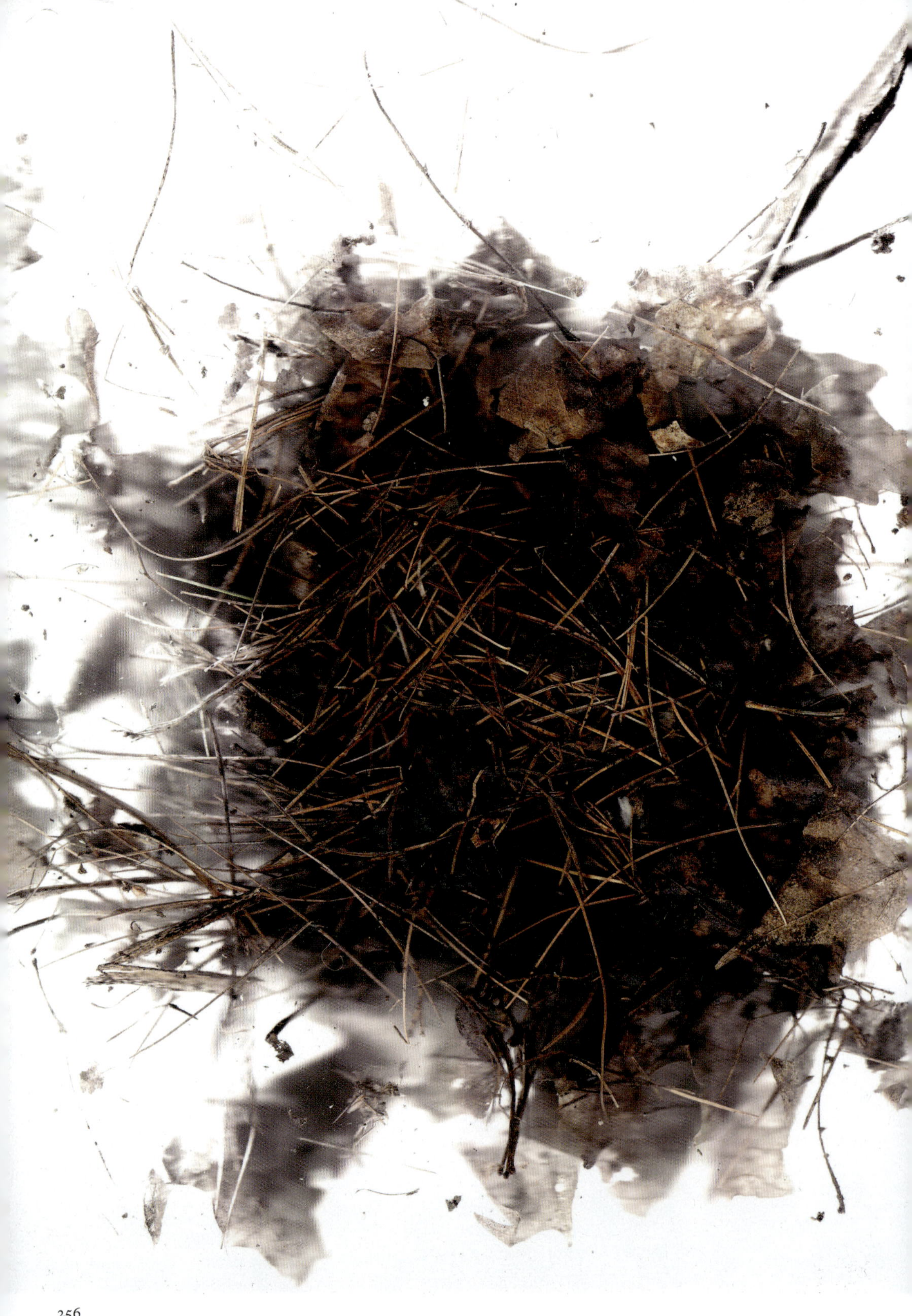

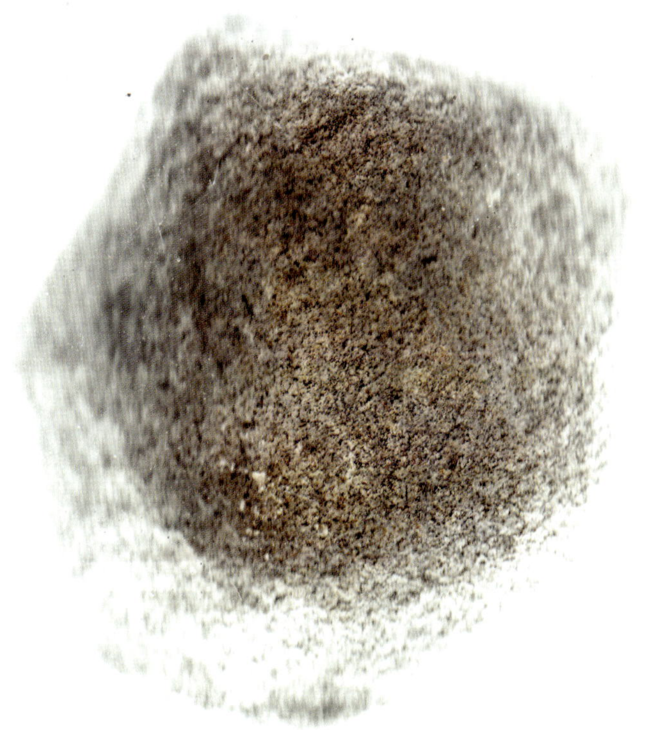

258

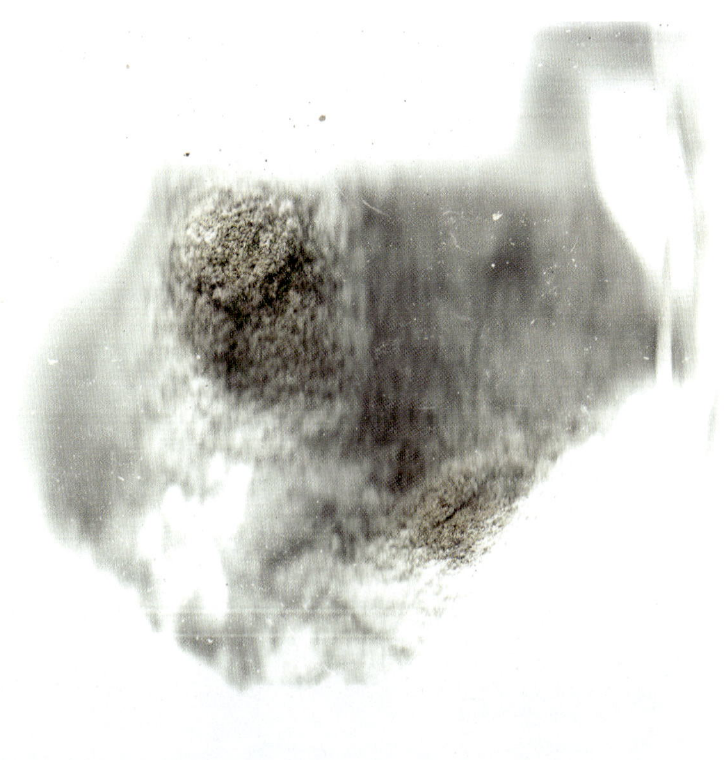

259

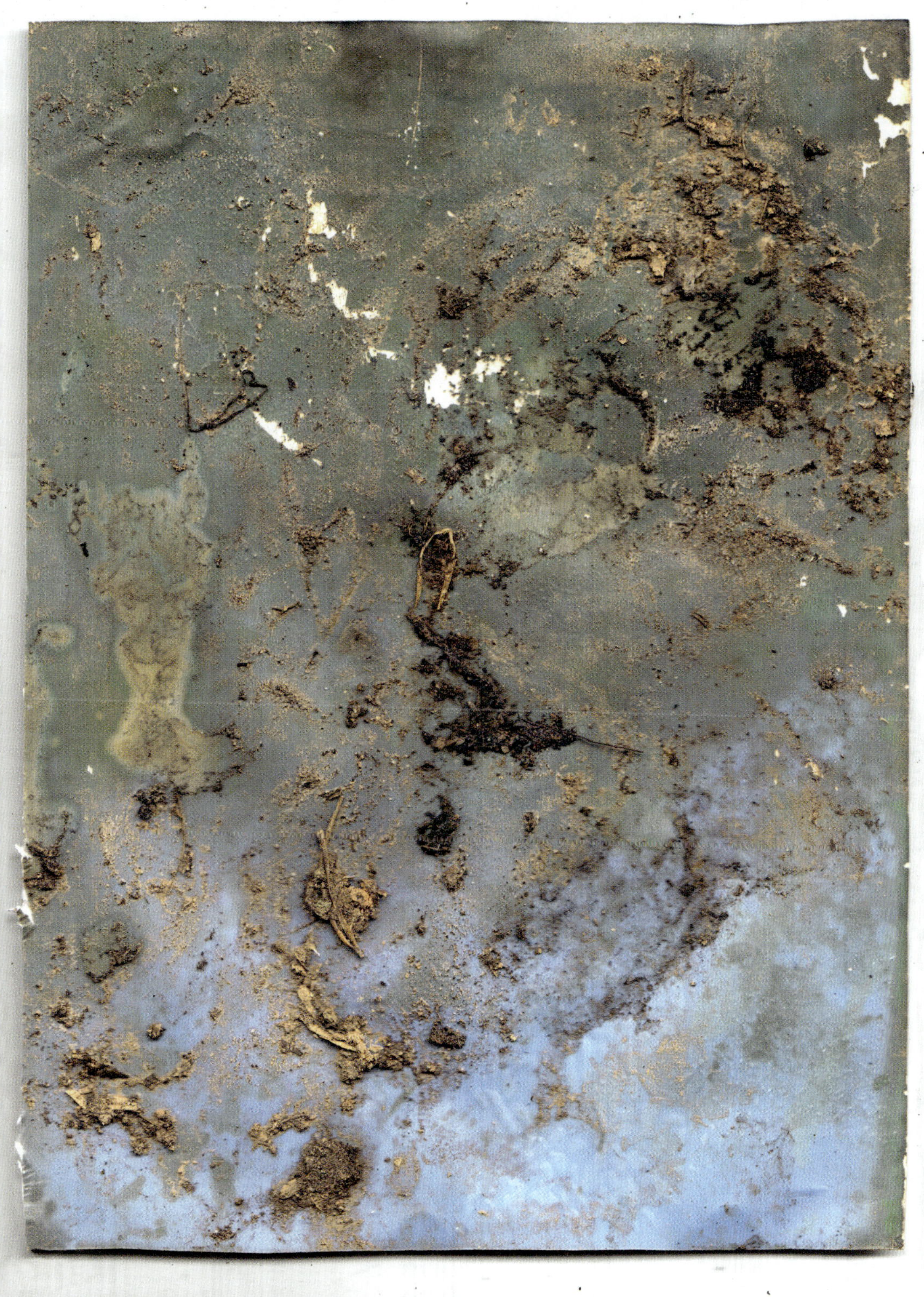

  Recomposed Monochrome (0, 188, 236), 2011, pigment print, 34 x 26 inches. Courtesy of the artist and Laurel Gitlen, New York.

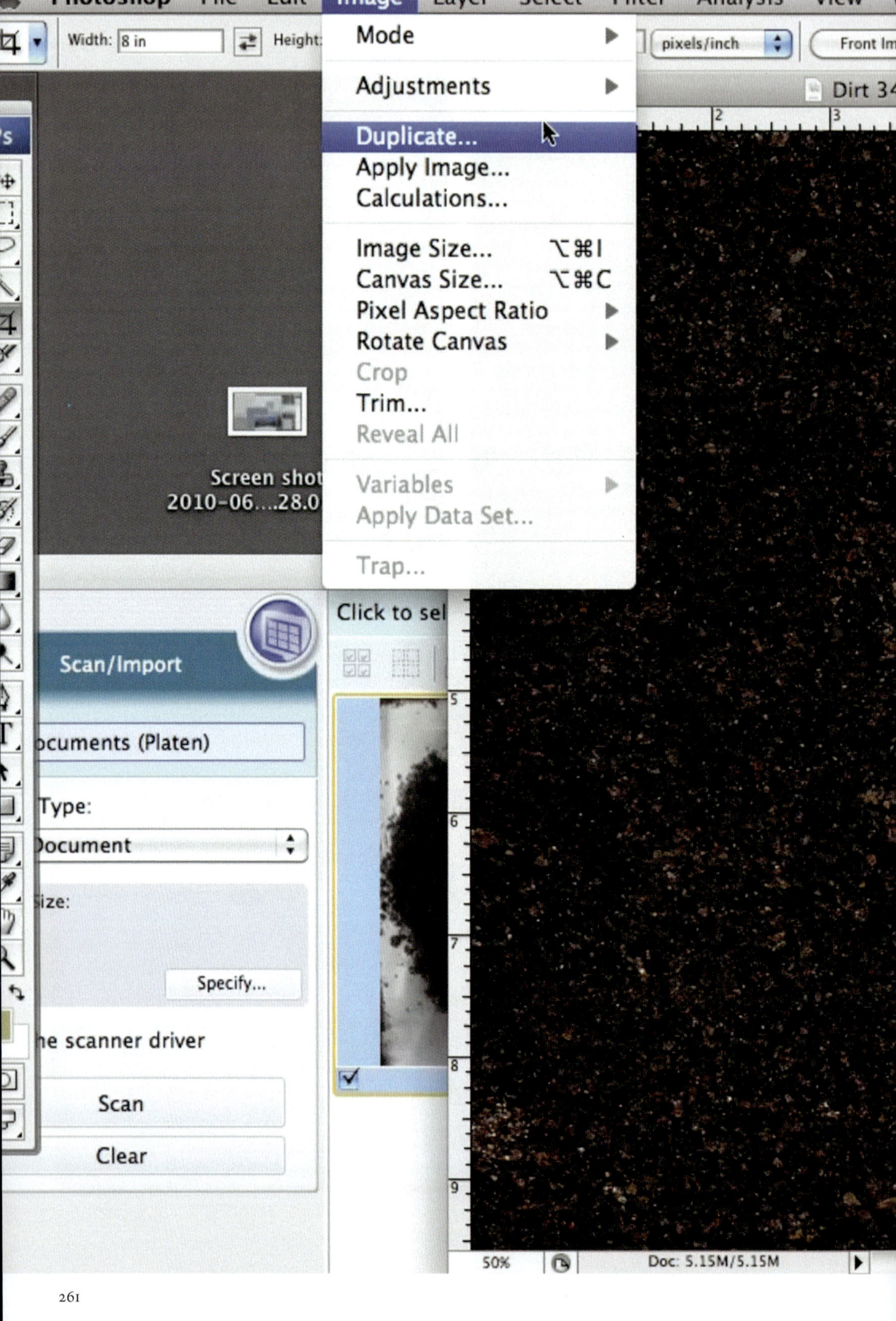

Photoshop   File   Edit   Image   Layer   Select   Filter   Analysis   View
Width: 8 in   Height: pixels/inch   Front Im
Mode
Adjustments
Duplicate...
Apply Image...
Calculations...
Image Size...   ⌥⌘I
Canvas Size...   ⌥⌘C
Pixel Aspect Ratio
Rotate Canvas
Crop
Trim...
Reveal All
Variables
Apply Data Set...
Trap...
Dirt 34
Screen shot
2010-06....28.0
Scan/Import
ocuments (Platen)
Type:
Document
ize:
Specify...
he scanner driver
Scan
Clear
Click to sel
50%
Doc: 5.15M/5.15M

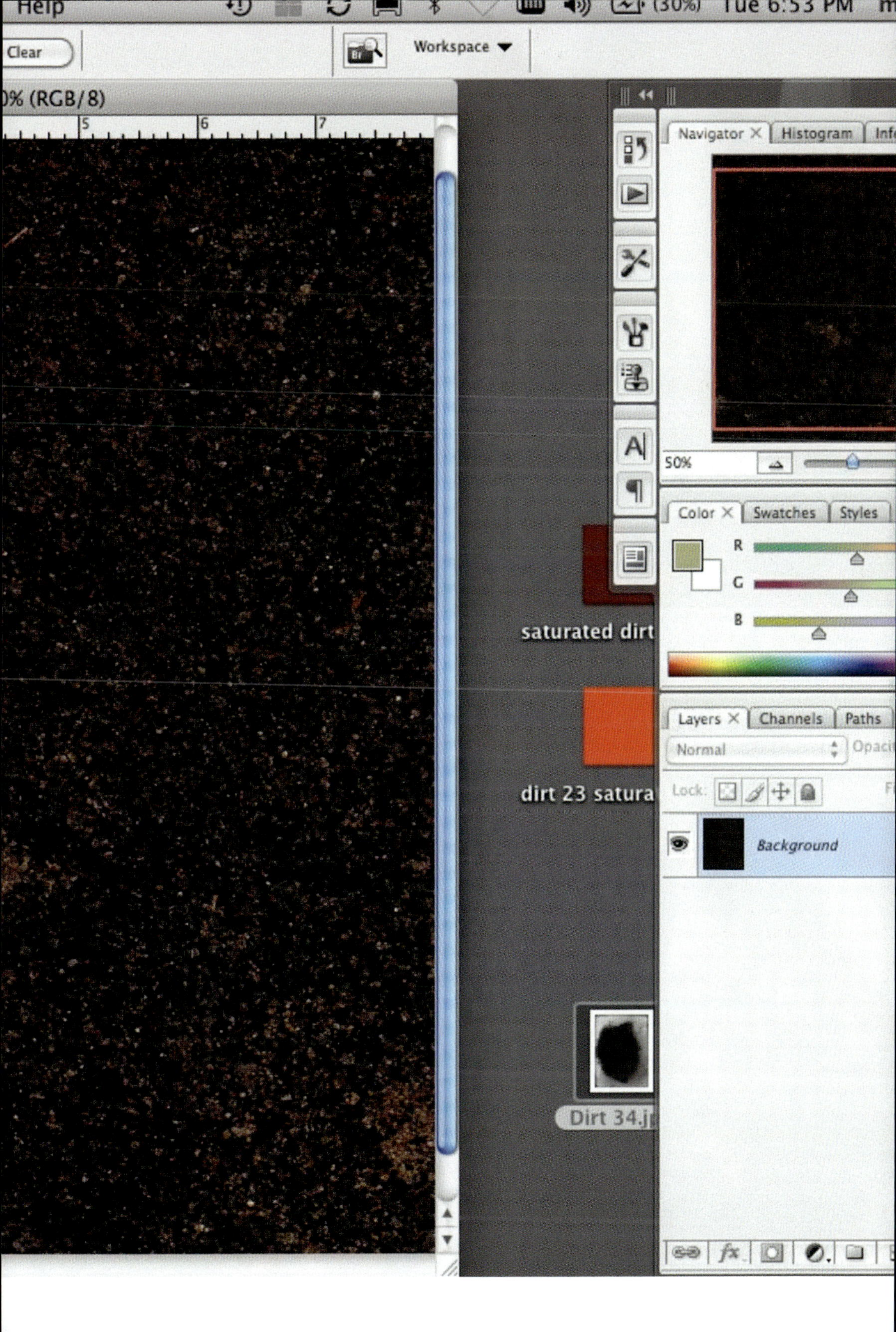

Help
Clear
Workspace
0% (RGB/8)
Navigator
Histogram
Inf
50%
Color
Swatches
Styles
R
G
B
saturated dirt
dirt 23 satura
Layers
Channels
Paths
Normal
Opaci
Lock:
F
Background
Dirt 34.j

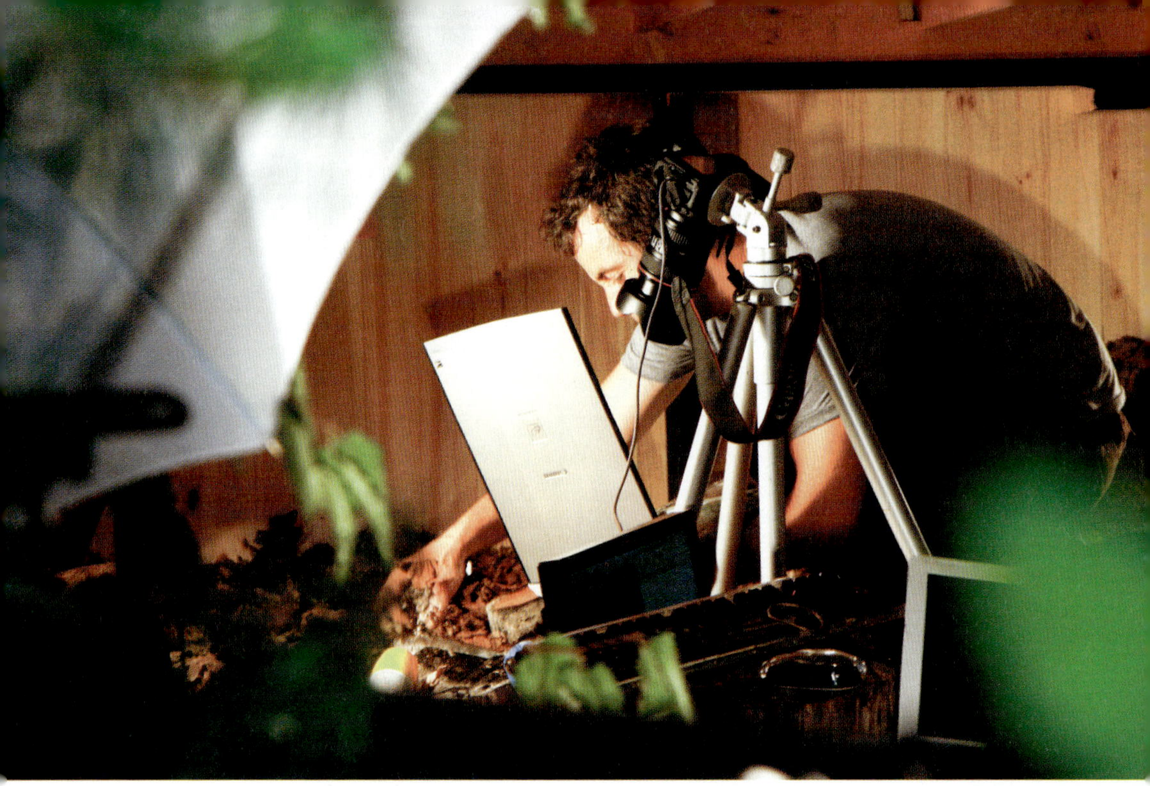

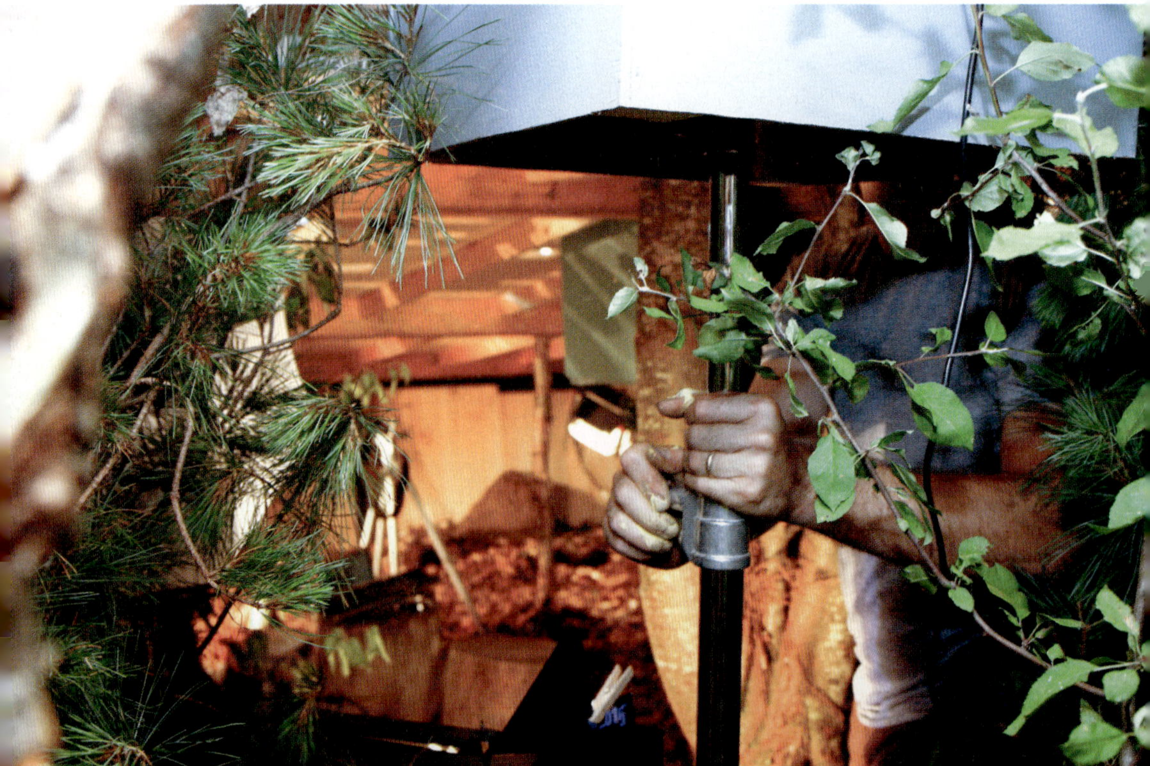

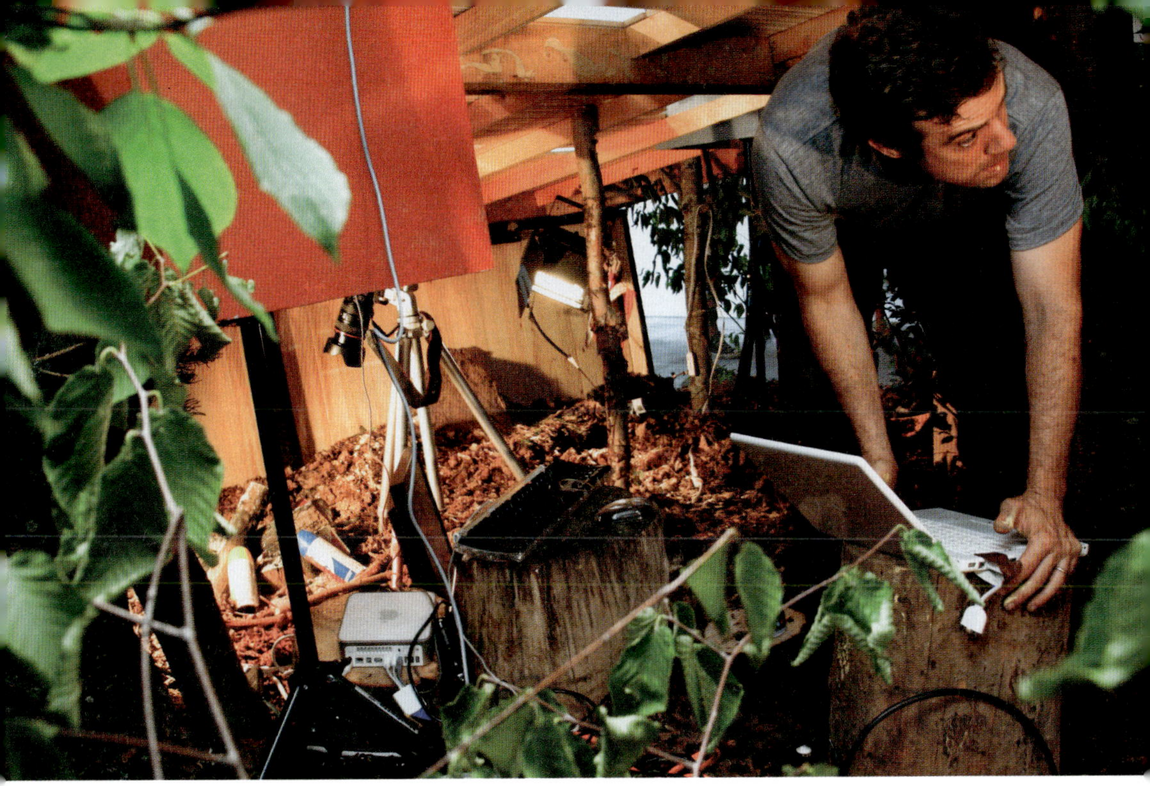

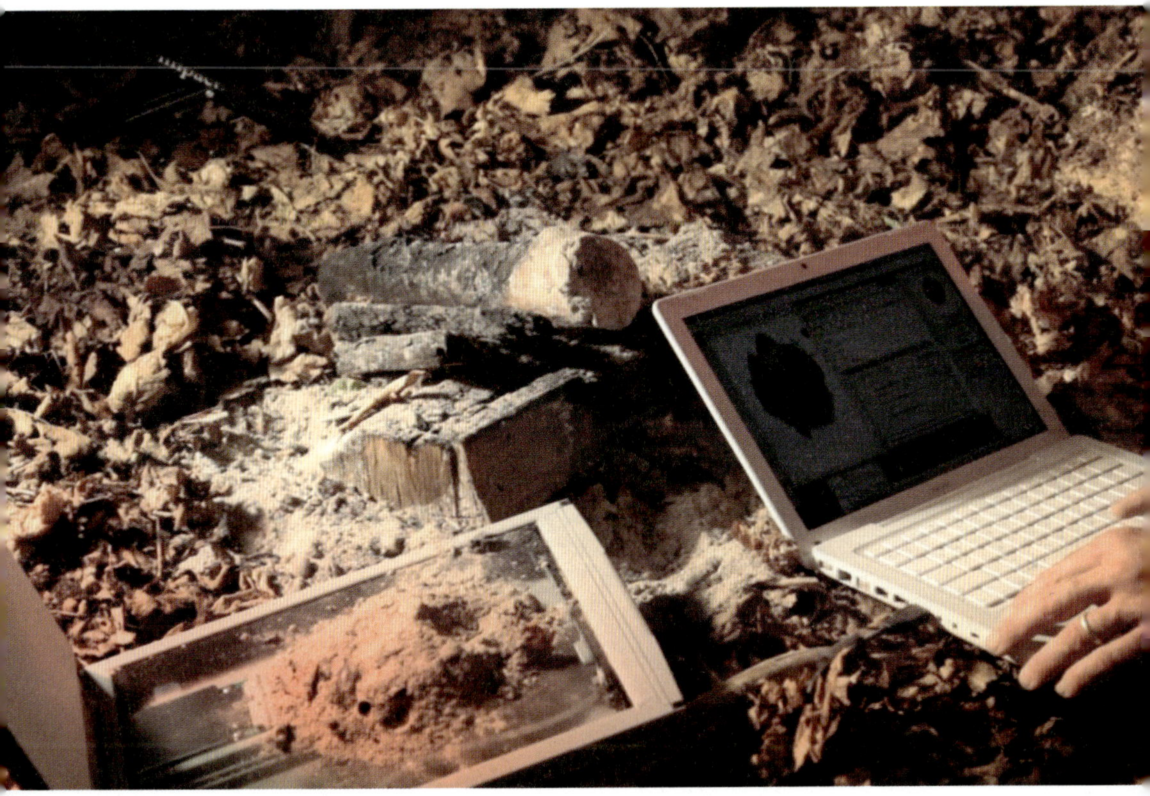

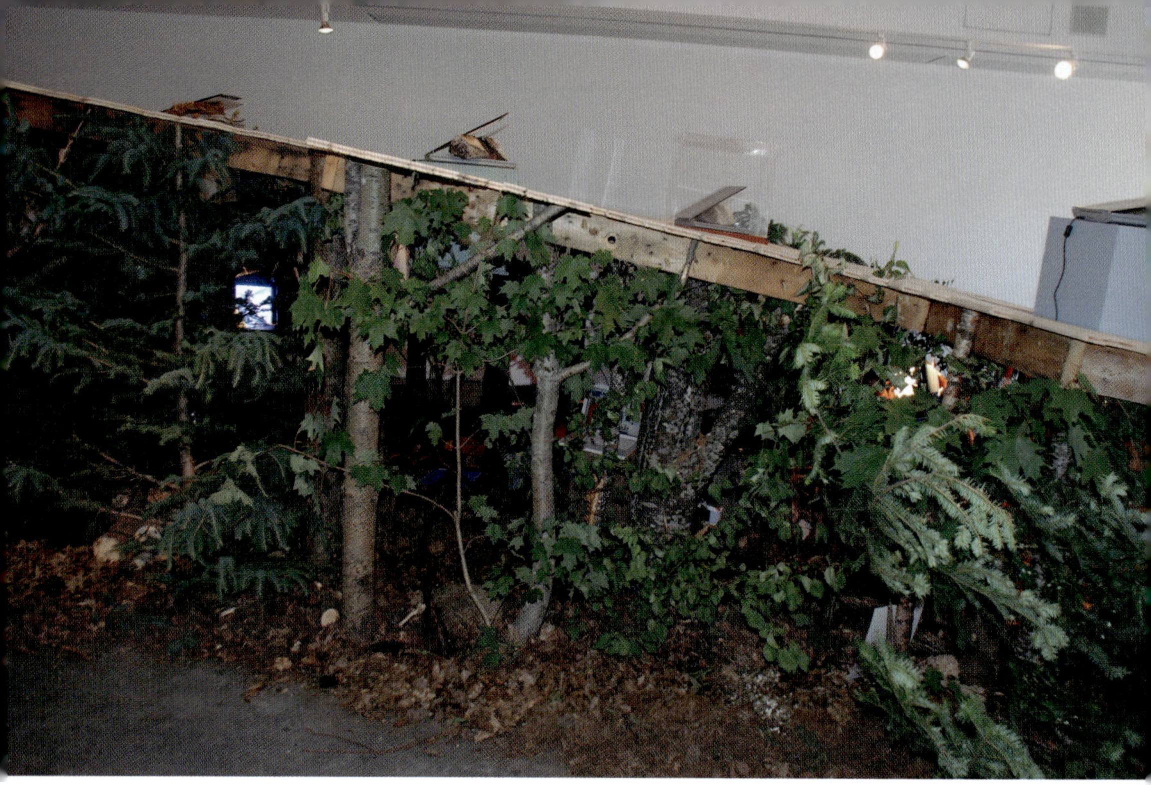

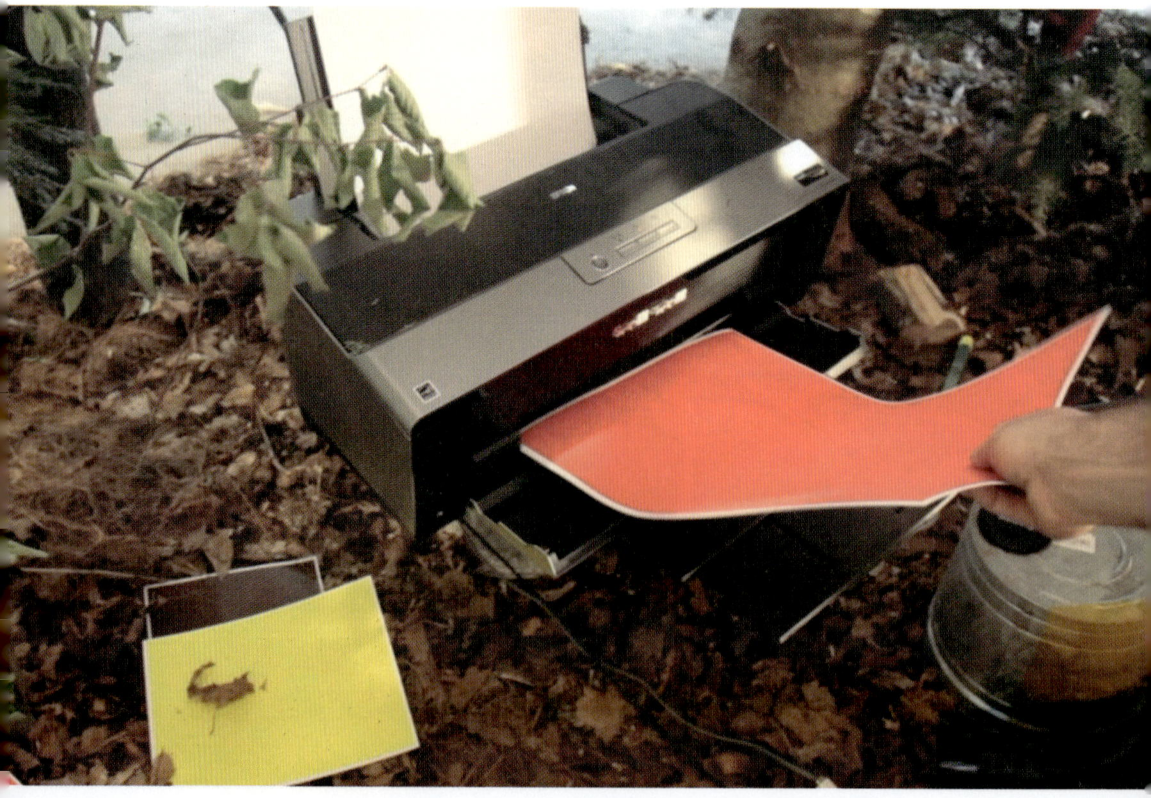

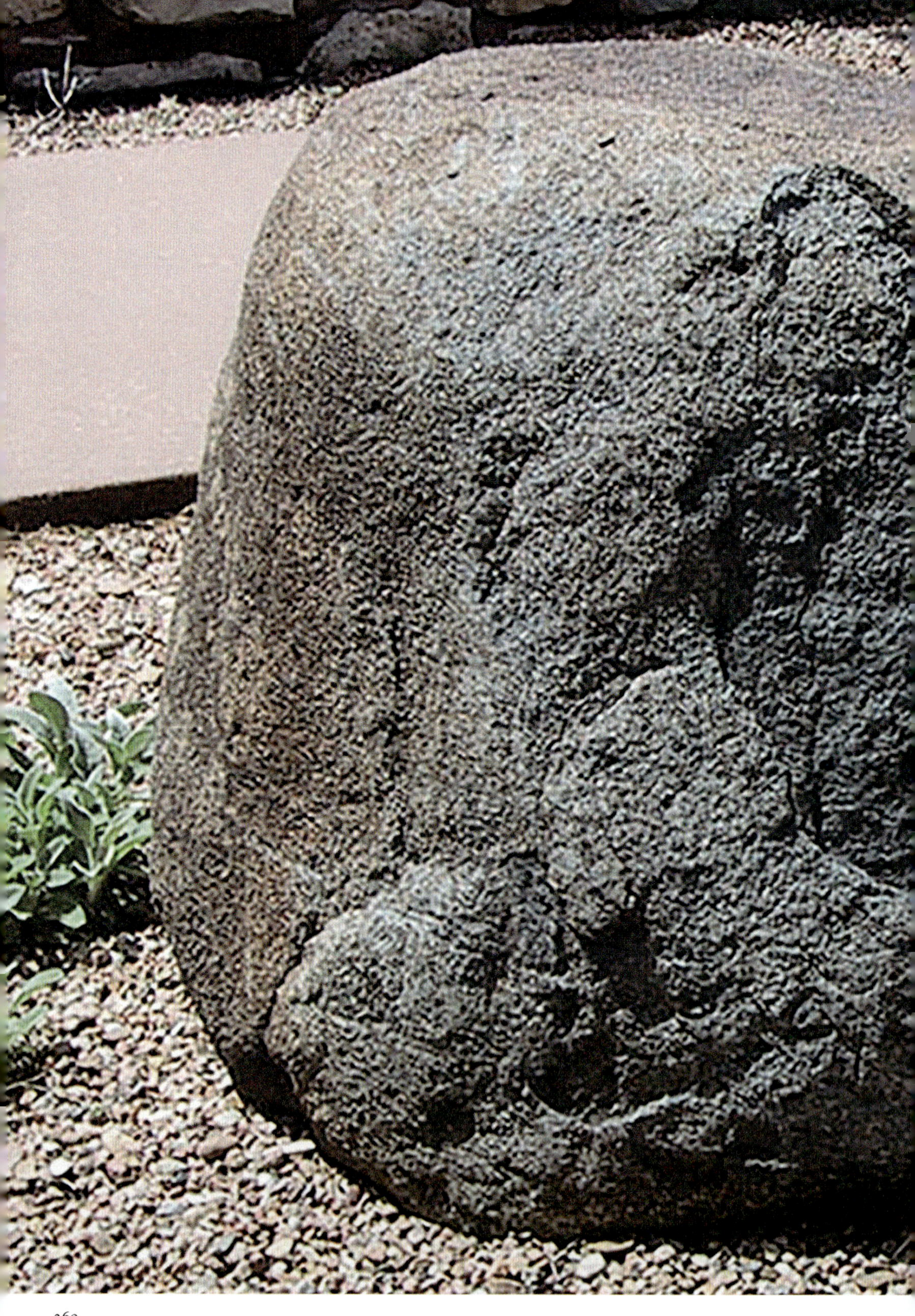

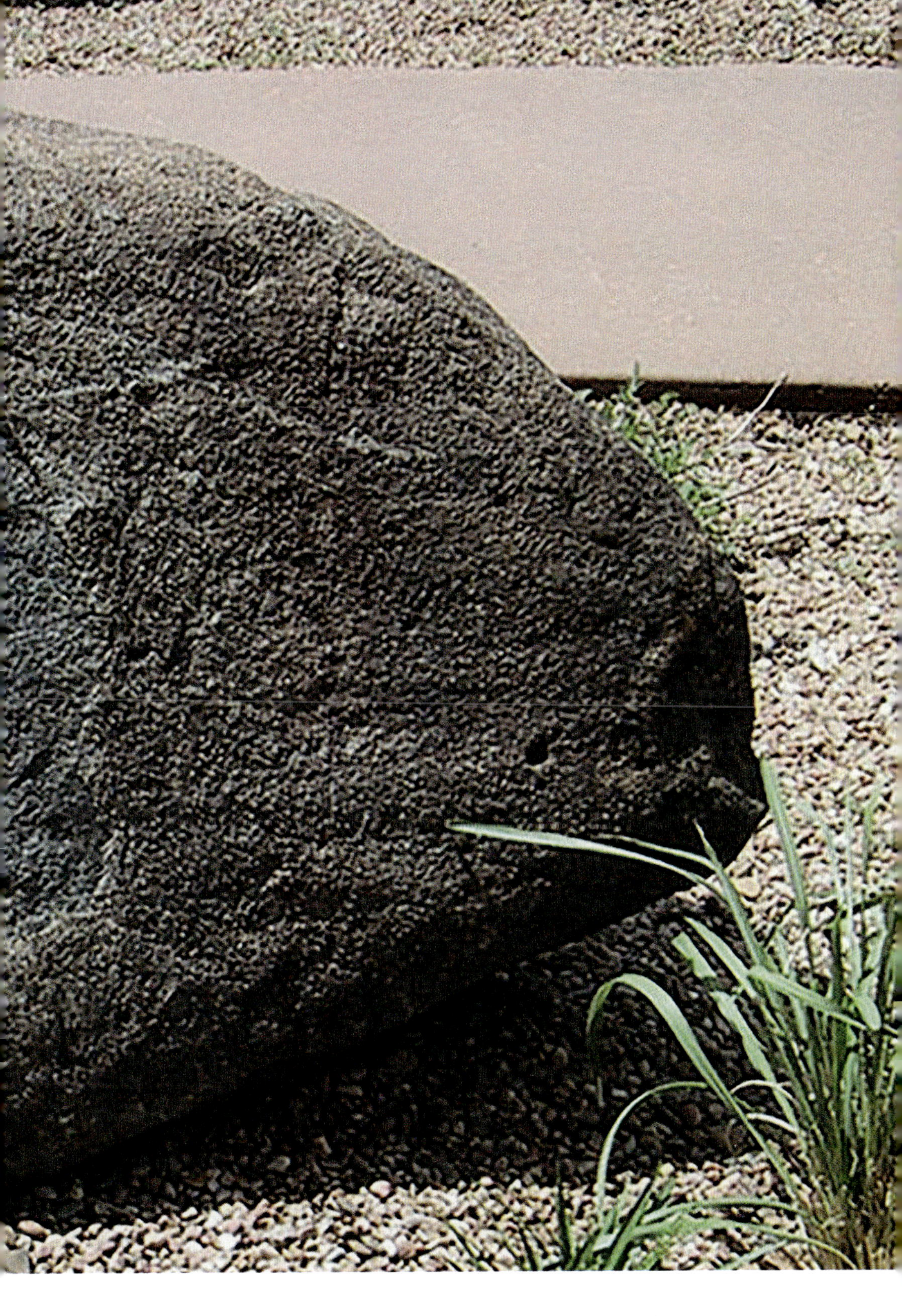

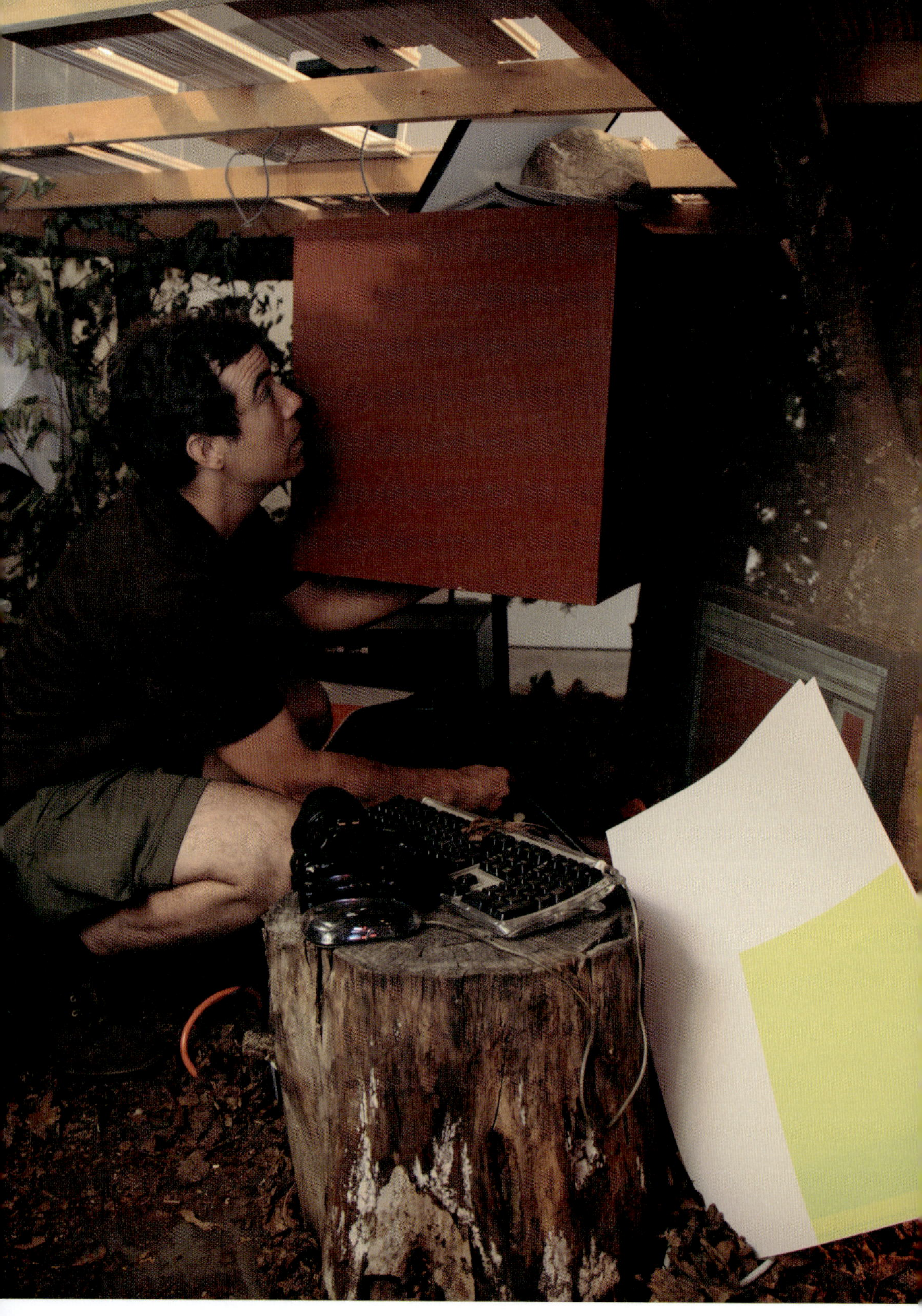

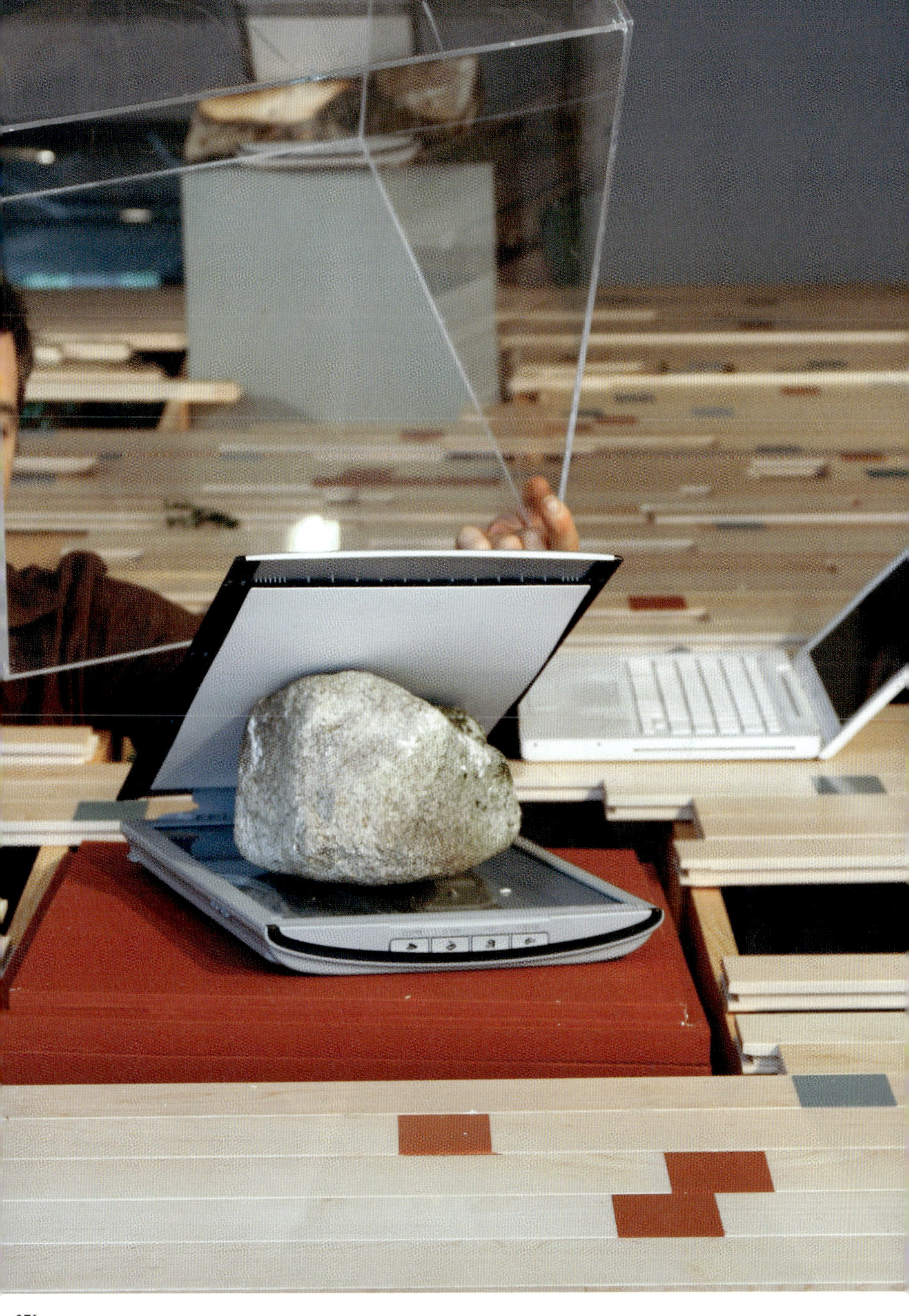

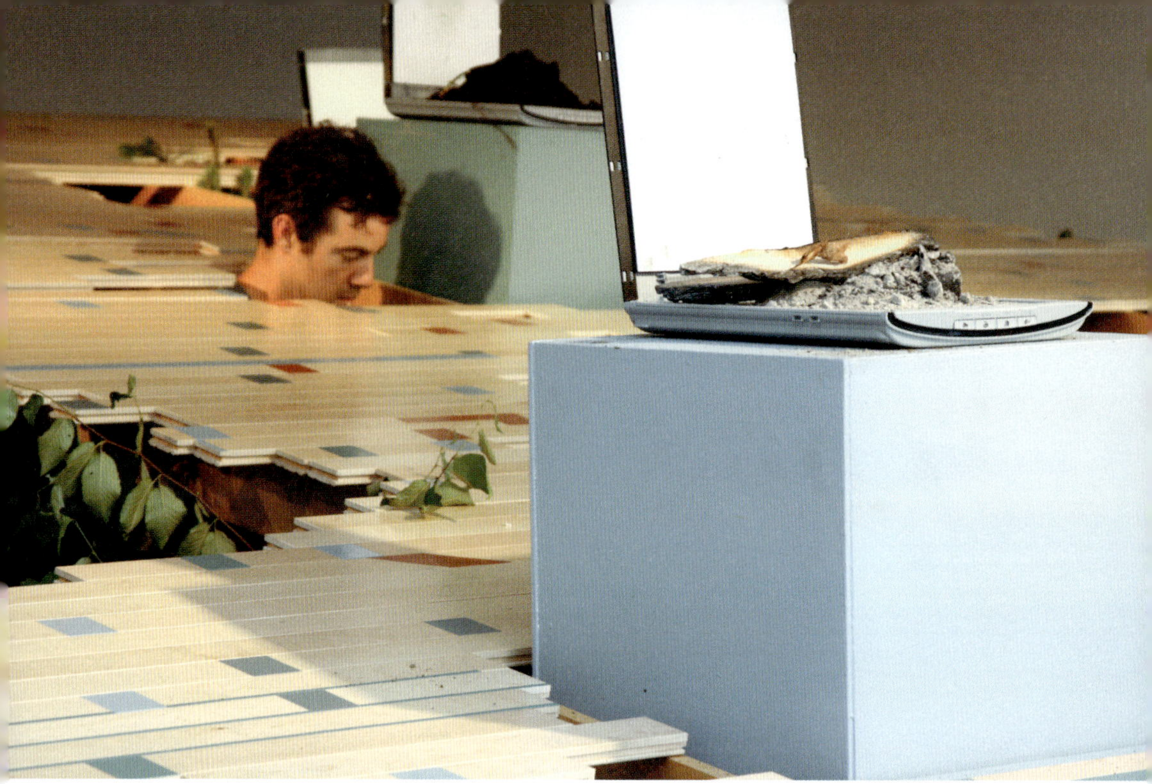

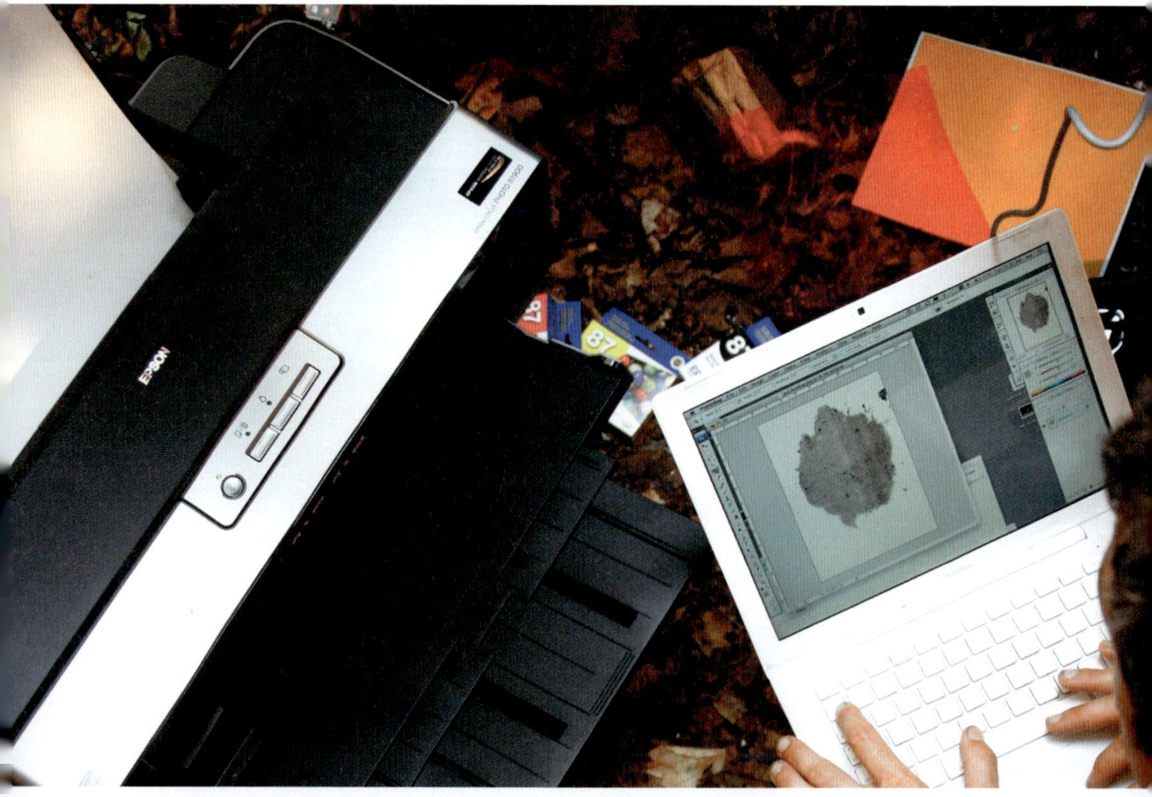

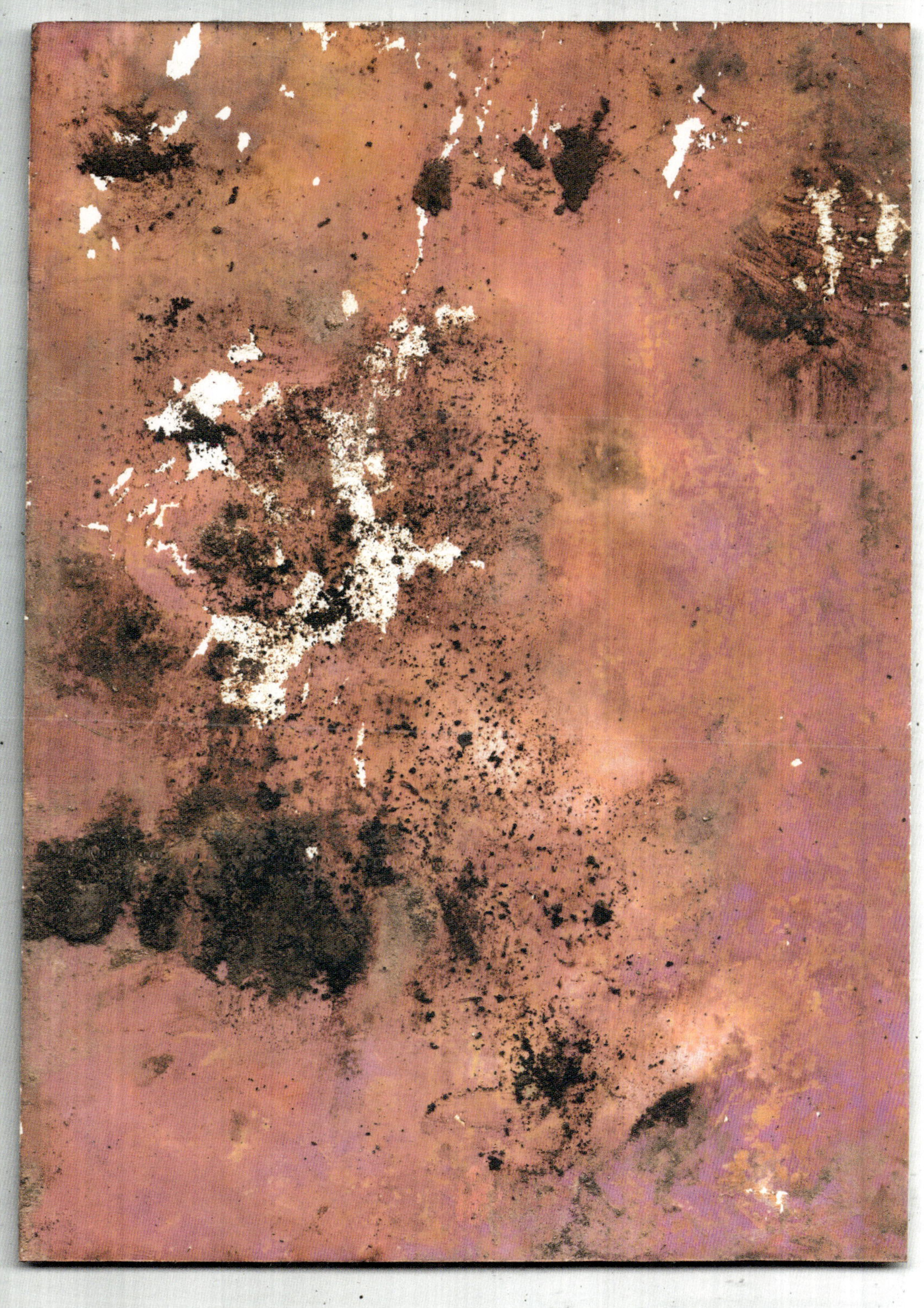

Recomposed Monochrome (216, 115, 177), 2011, pigment print, 36 x 24 inches. Courtesy of the artist and Laurel Gitlen, New York.

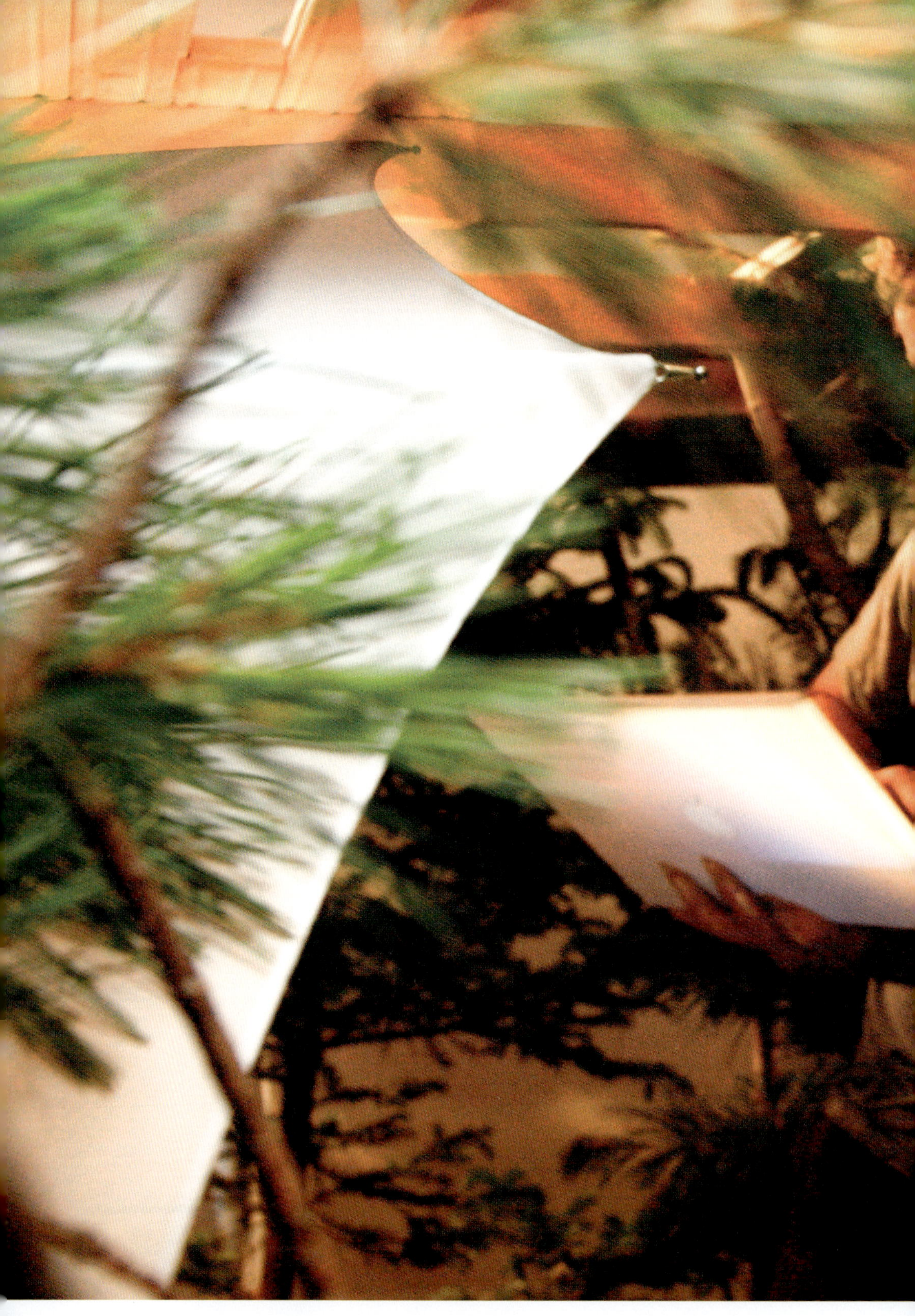

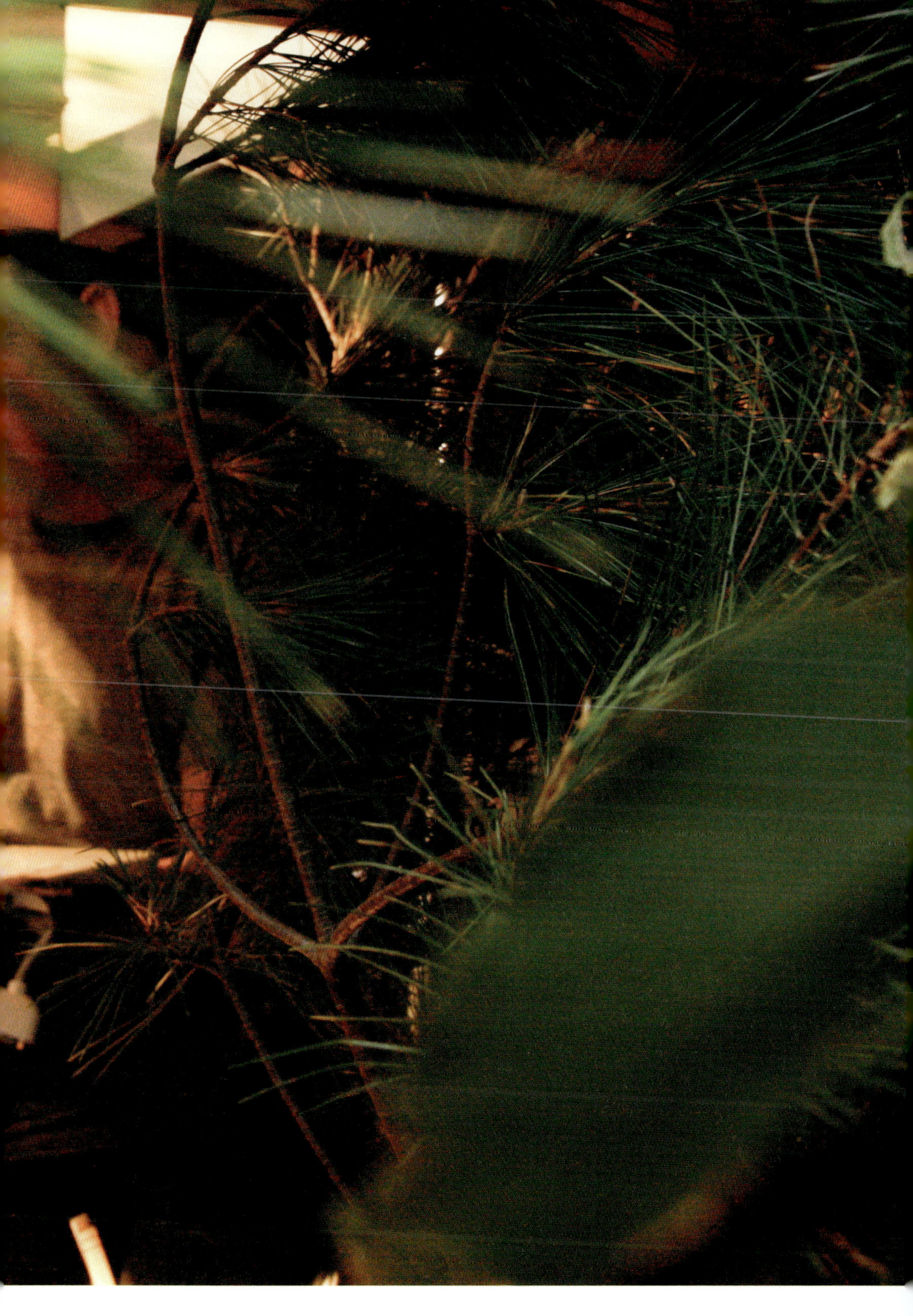

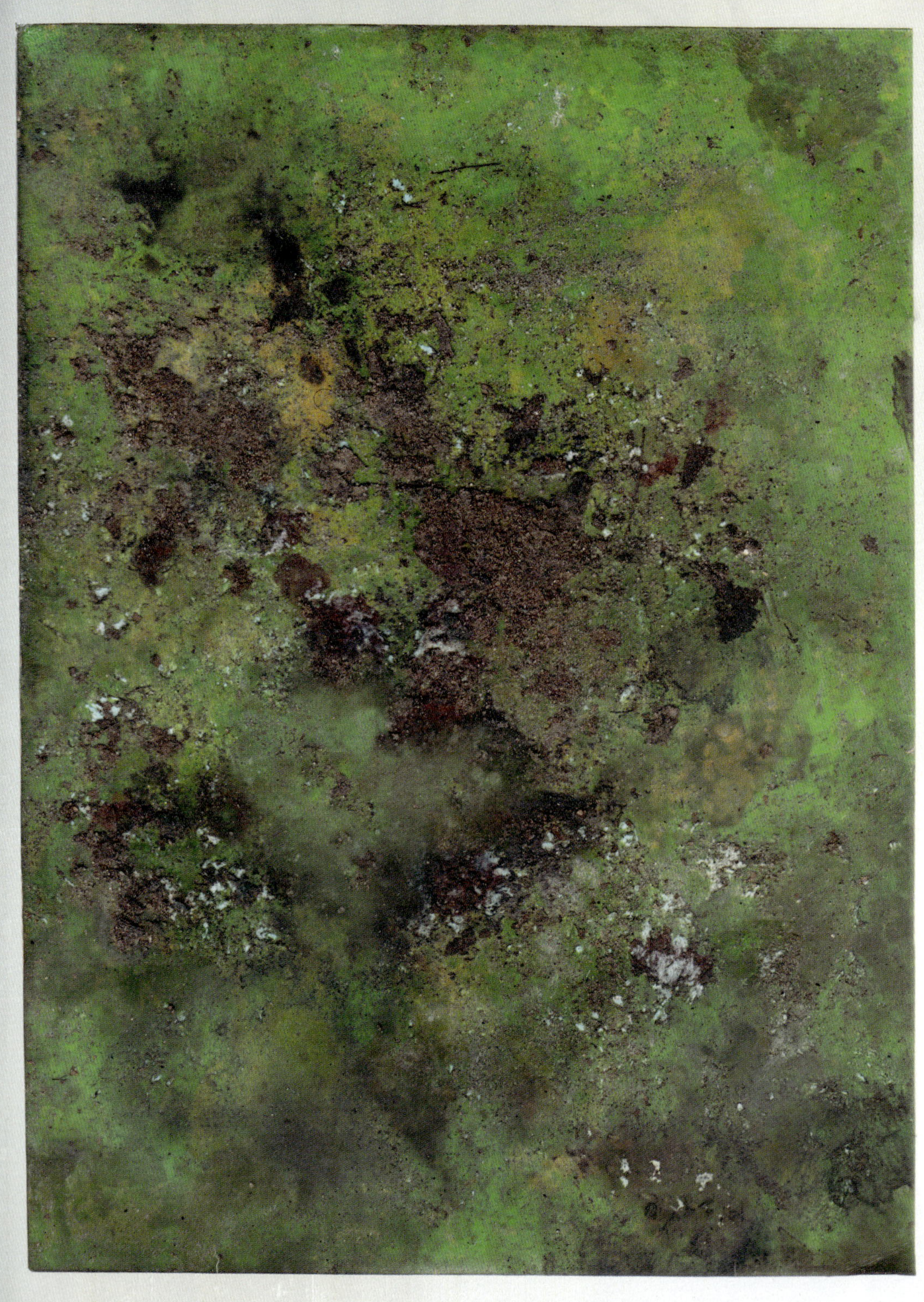

276   *Recomposed Monochrome (72, 124, 58)*, 2011, pigment print, 36 x 24 inches inches. Courtesy of the artist and Laurel Gitlen, New York.

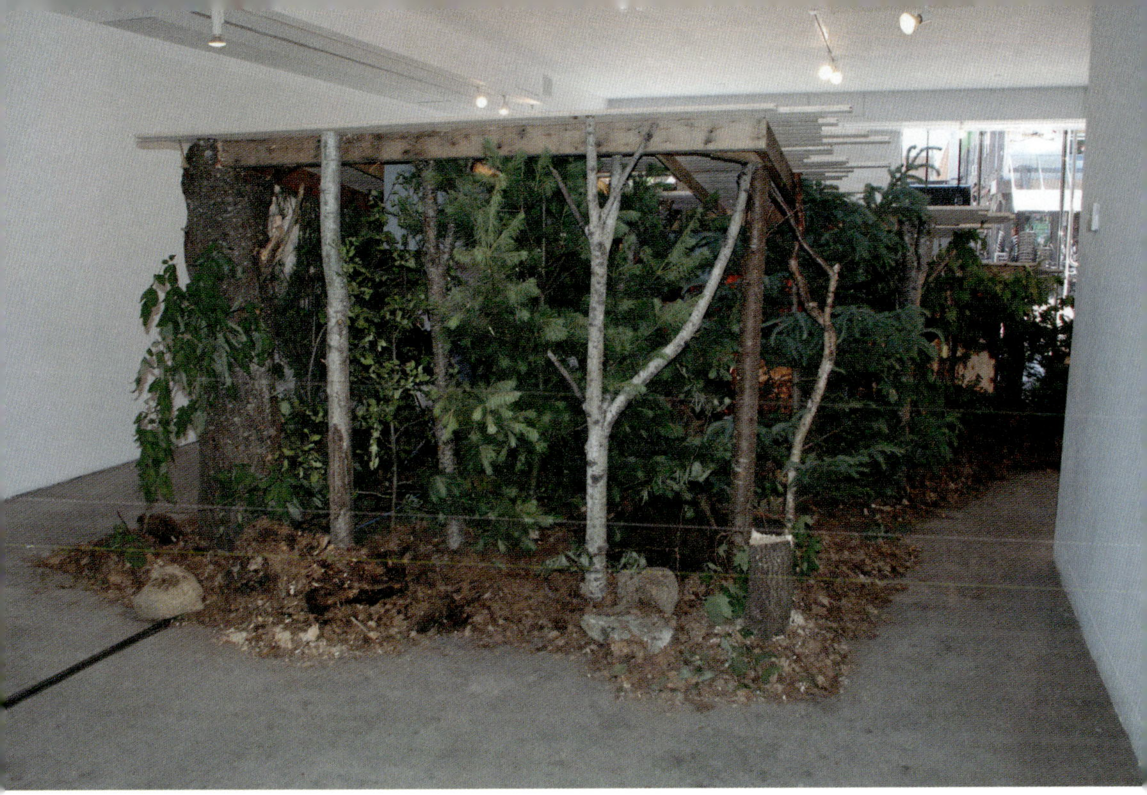

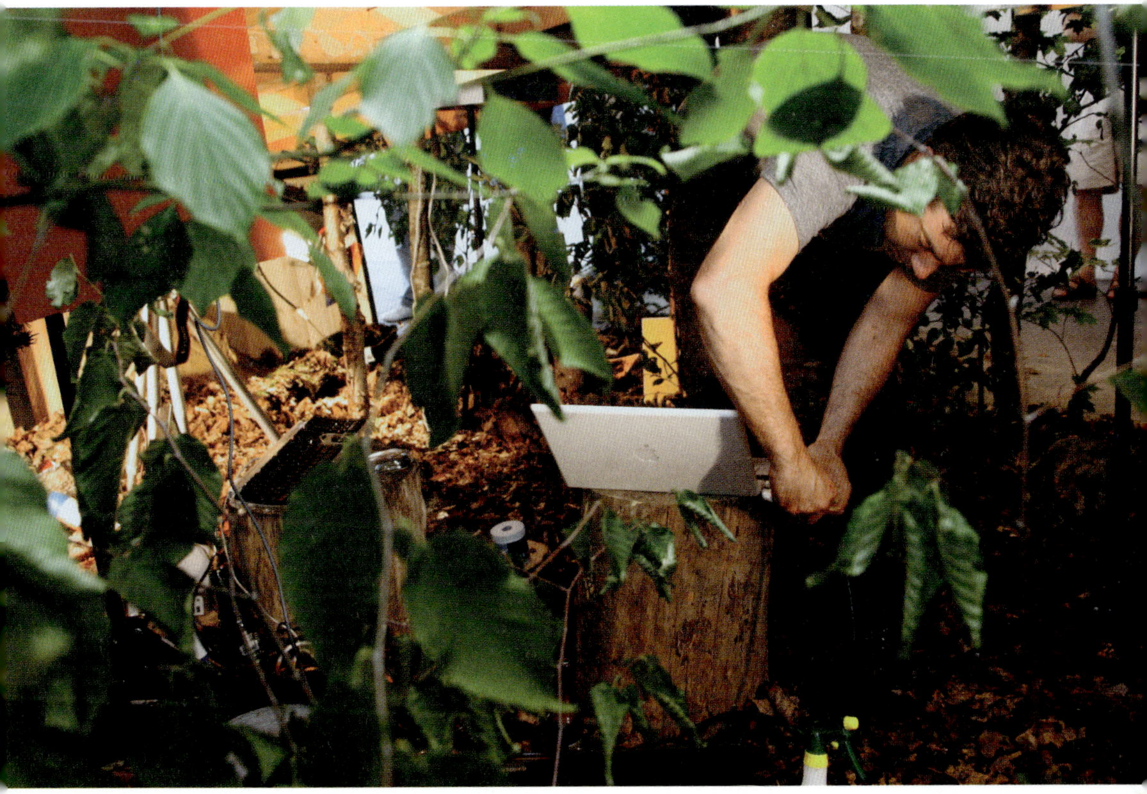

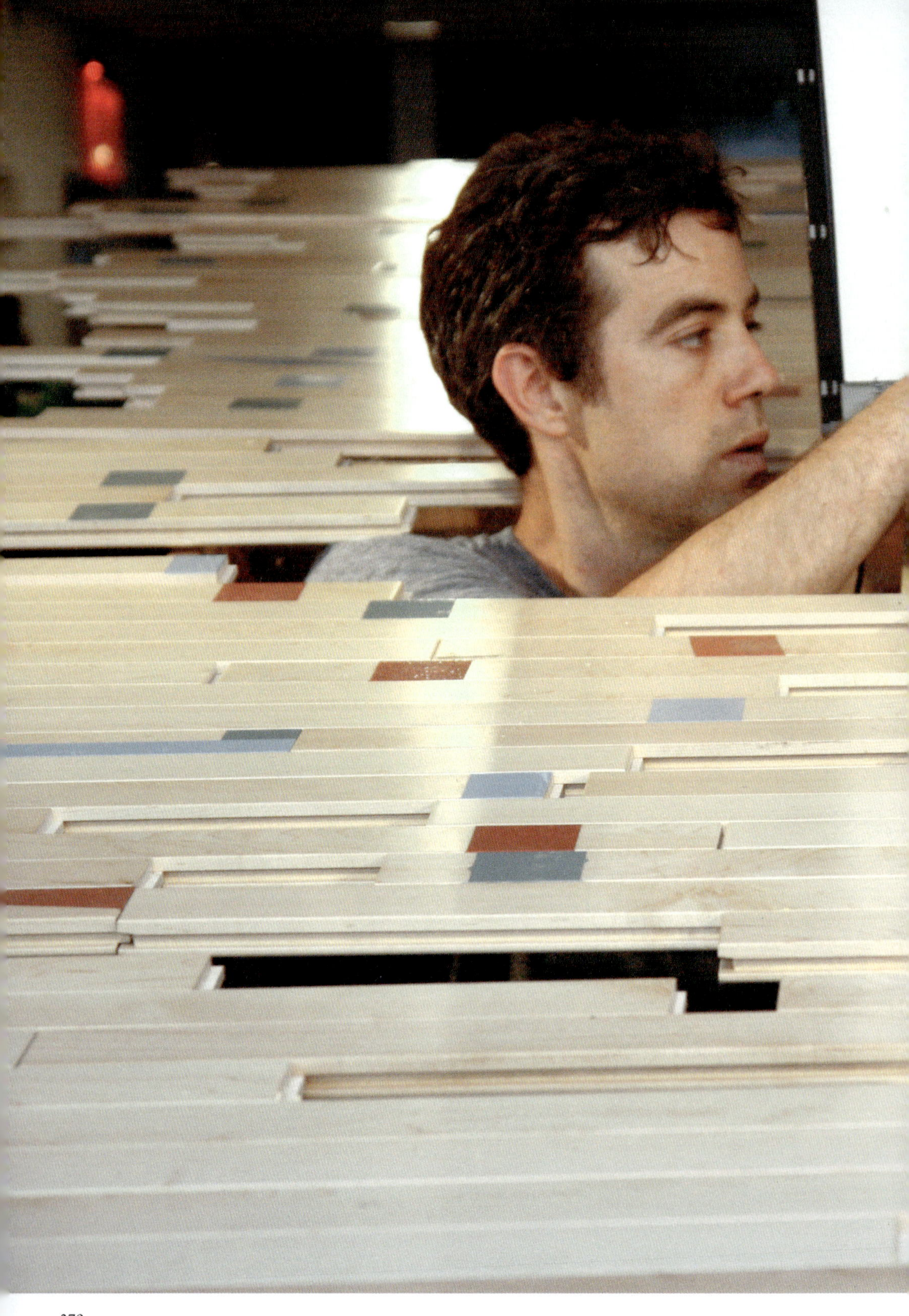

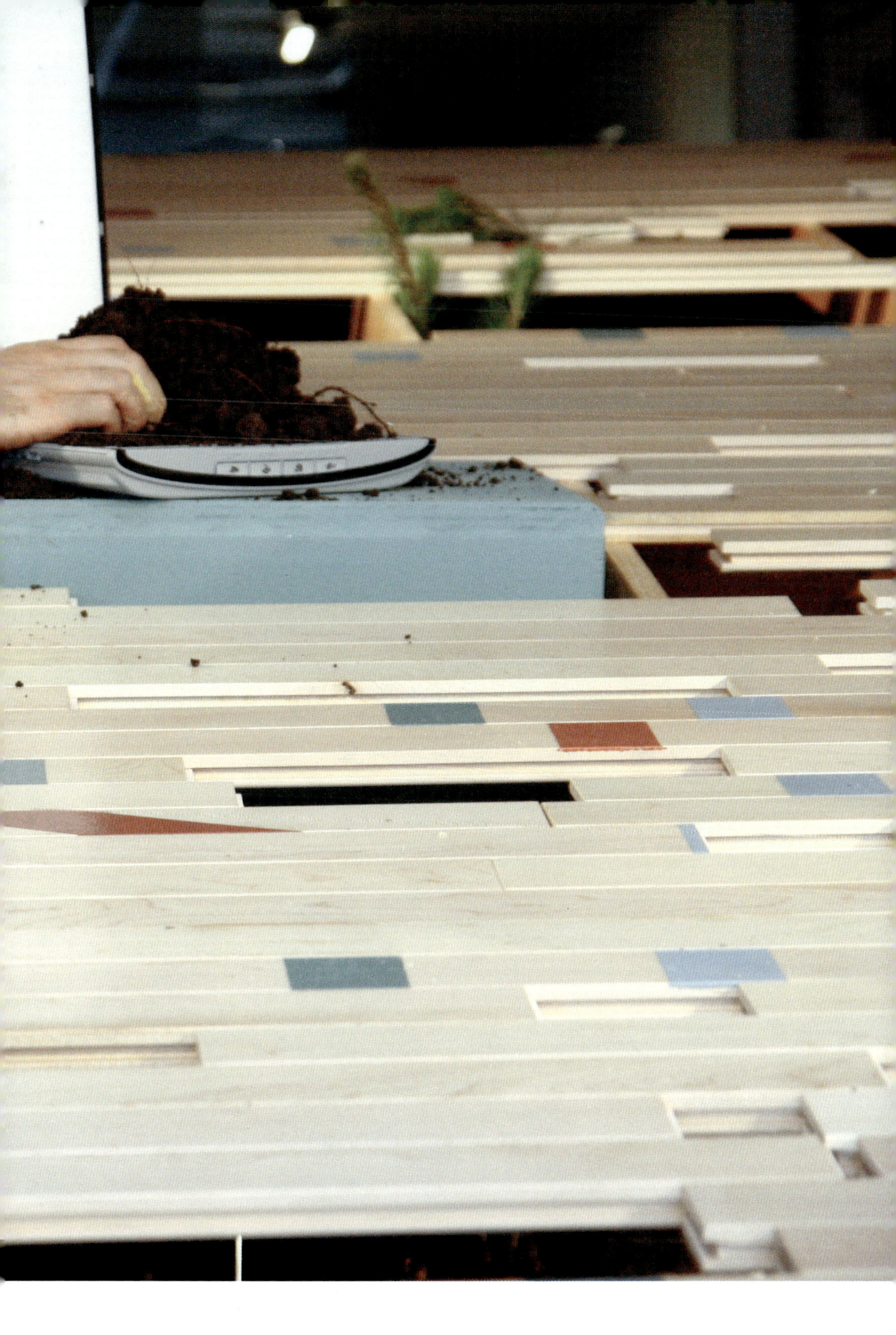

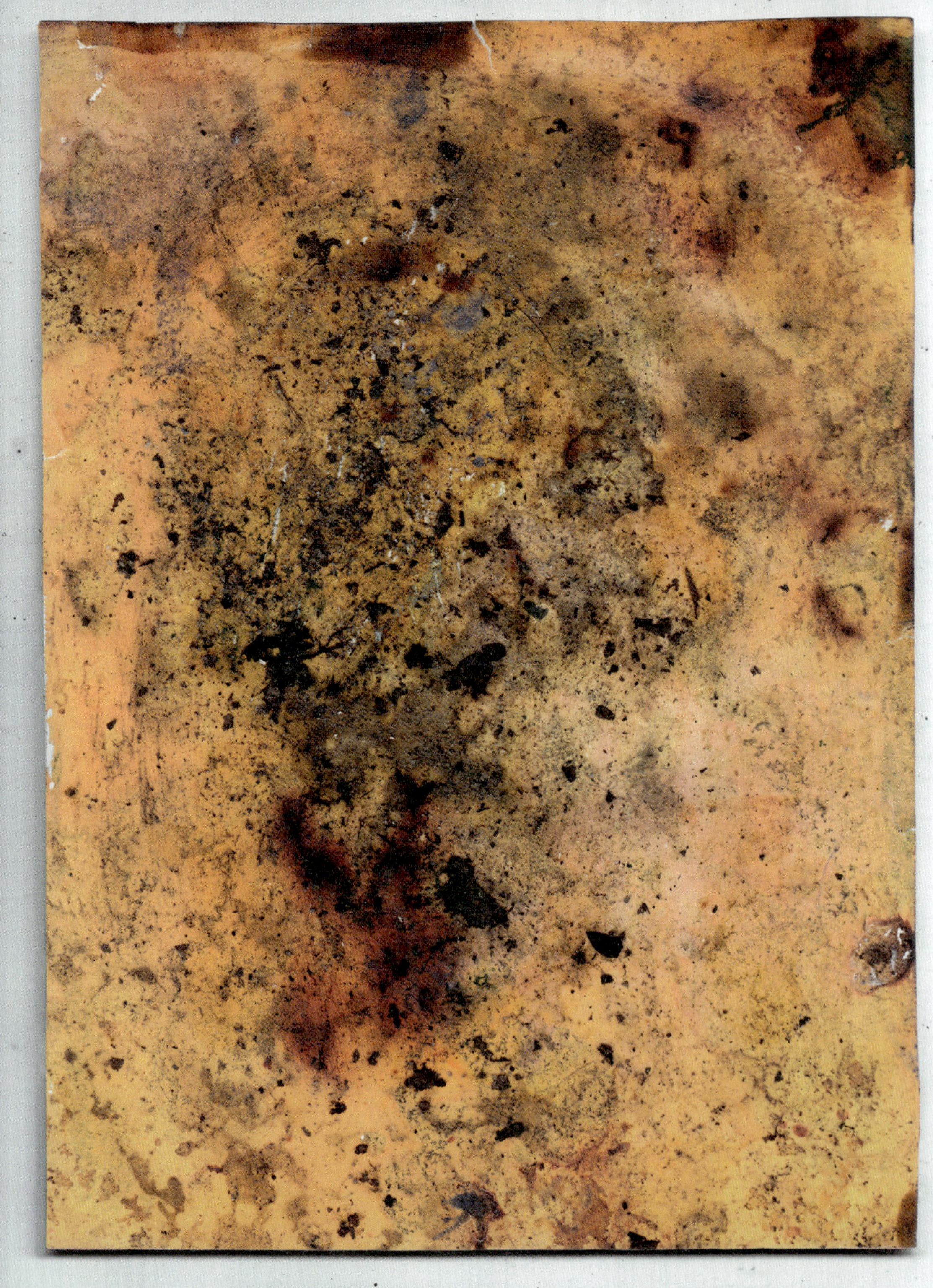

 Recomposed Monochrome (243, 170, 0), 2011, pigment print, 34 x 26 inches. Courtesy of the artist and Laurel Gitlen, New York.

Chapter 7, **The Hedge**

The Hedge
Museum of Contemporary Art Cleveland, OH
January 18–April 14, 2013
Curated by David Norr

For *The Hedge*, Hewitt designed a room-within-a-room, which created a hidden workspace lining the gallery. Cutouts in the walls of the interior room framed an array of layered elements, displayed as relief collage: photographs of Hewitt's studio in Richmond as backdrops or "grounds"; cast forms making up new wall-stud geometries; and an array of objects and replicas, including toast, crackers, makeup, rubber gloves, and flash drives. Over the course of the exhibition, Hewitt continued to change the backdrops and arrangements, replacing them with alternates and making slight adjustments, while intermittent sounds of labor, sometimes live and sometimes pre-recorded, emanated from behind the walls.

Captions

281, 285, 289-292, 294-297, 302, 310-315, 318, 320: Process image for *The Hedge*, 2013. Courtesy of the artist.
288: *The Hedge*, 2013. Installation view, MOCA Cleveland. Photo: Corin Hewitt. Courtesy of the artist.
293: Research material for *The Hedge*. Courtesy of the artist.
301: *The Hedge*, 2013. Installation view, MOCA Cleveland. Photo: Tim Safranek Photographics. Courtesy of MOCA Cleveland.
304, 305: *The Hedge*, 2013. Installation in progress. Photo: Rose Bouthillier. Courtesy of MOCA Cleveland.
316: Gallery model for *The Hedge*. Courtesy of the artist.
317: Corin Hewitt, *The Hedge*, 2013, installation in progress. Photo: Corin Hewitt. Courtesy of the artist.

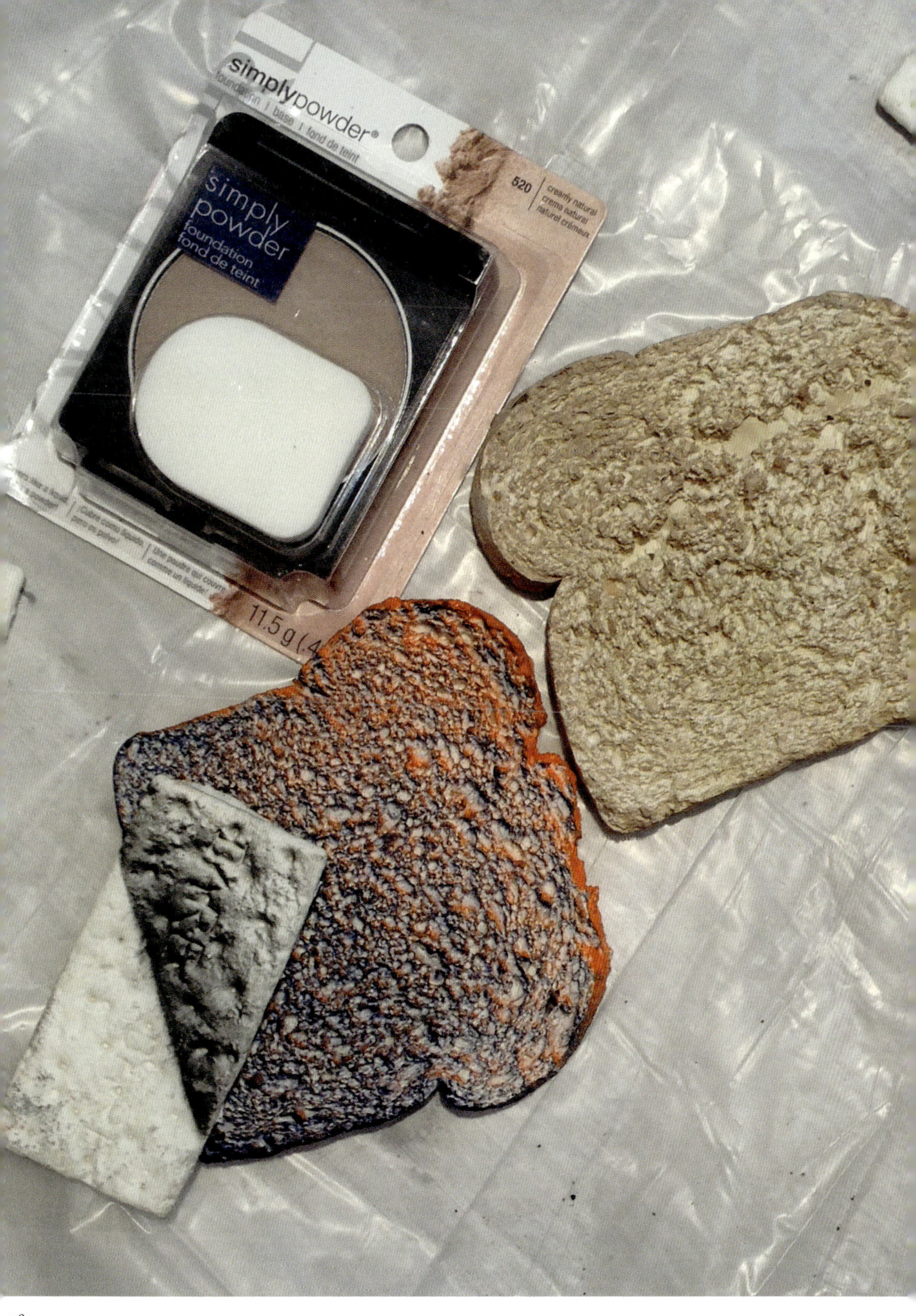

simplypowder
foundation | base | fond de teint
simply powder
foundation
fond de teint
520
creamy natural
crema natural
naturel crémeux
11.5 g (4

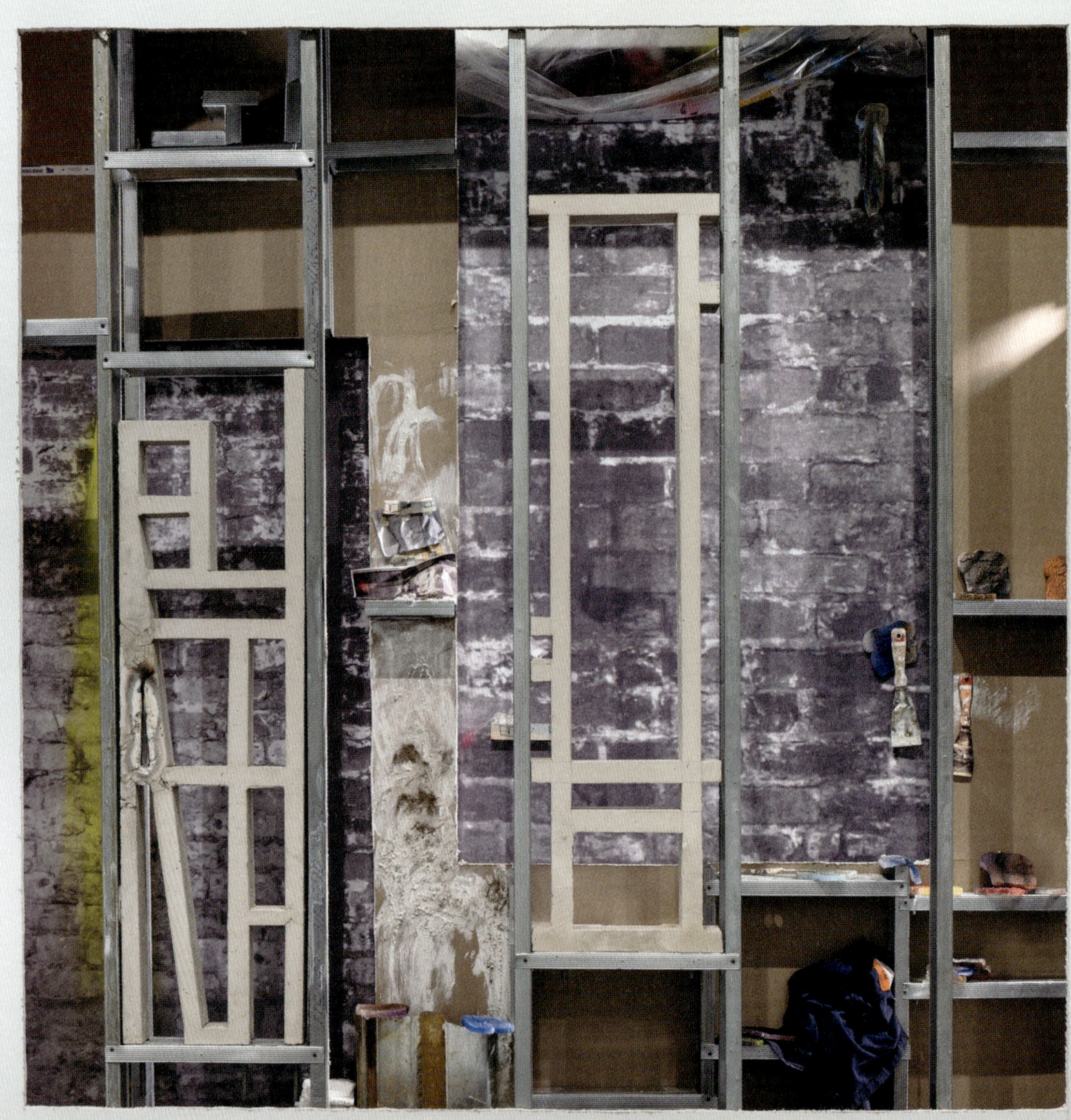

282   *Untitled #4*, 2013, from *The Hedge*, mixed media installation, 80 1/2 x 80 inches. Photo: Tim Safranek Photographics. Courtesy of MOCA Cleveland.

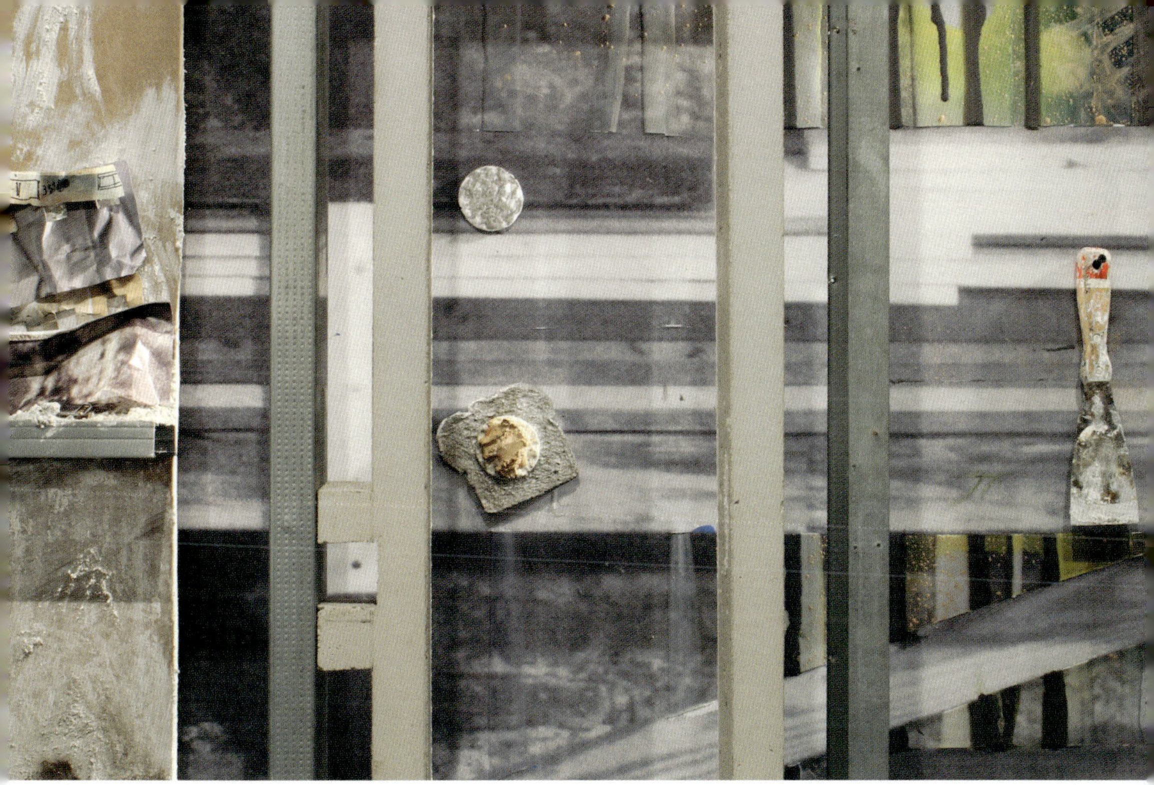

Untitled #4 (detail), 2013, from *The Hedge*, 2013, mixed media installation, 80 1/2 x 80 inches. Photo: Rose Bouthillier. Courtesy of MOCA Cleveland.

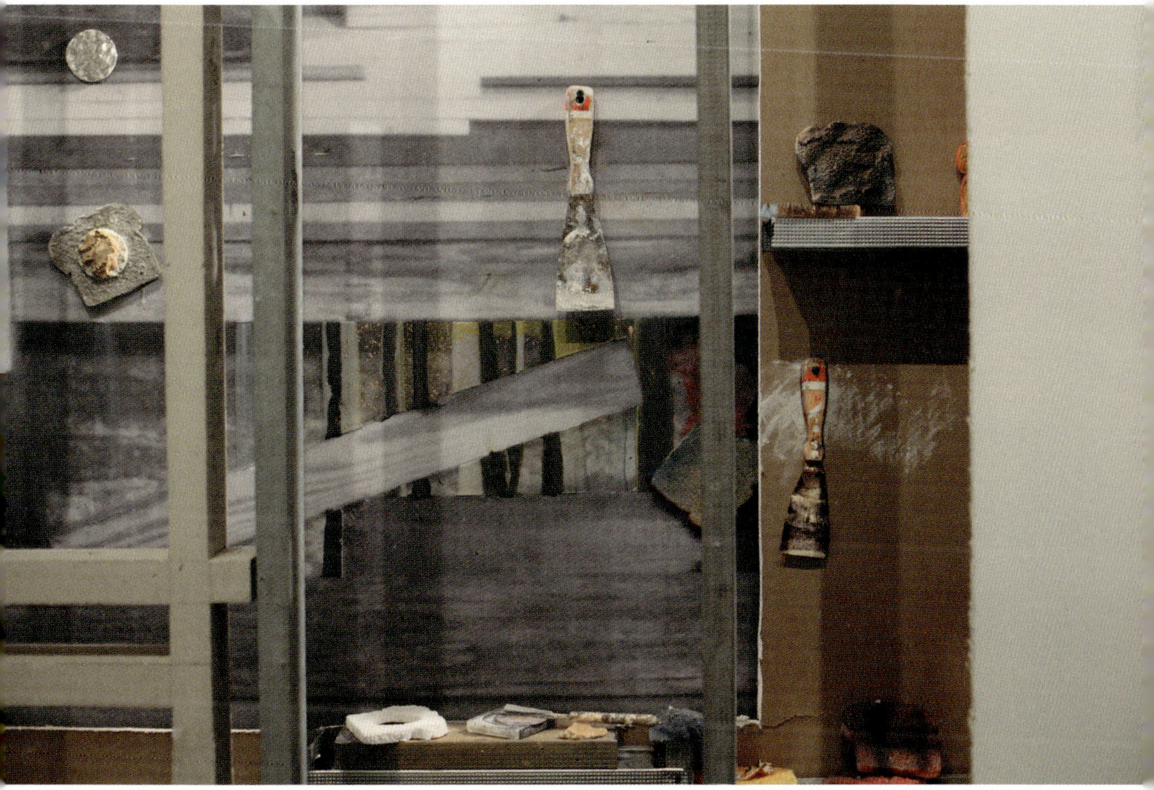

Untitled #4 (detail), 2013, from *The Hedge*, 2013, mixed media installation, 80 1/2 x 80 inches. Photo: Rose Bouthillier. Courtesy of MOCA Cleveland.

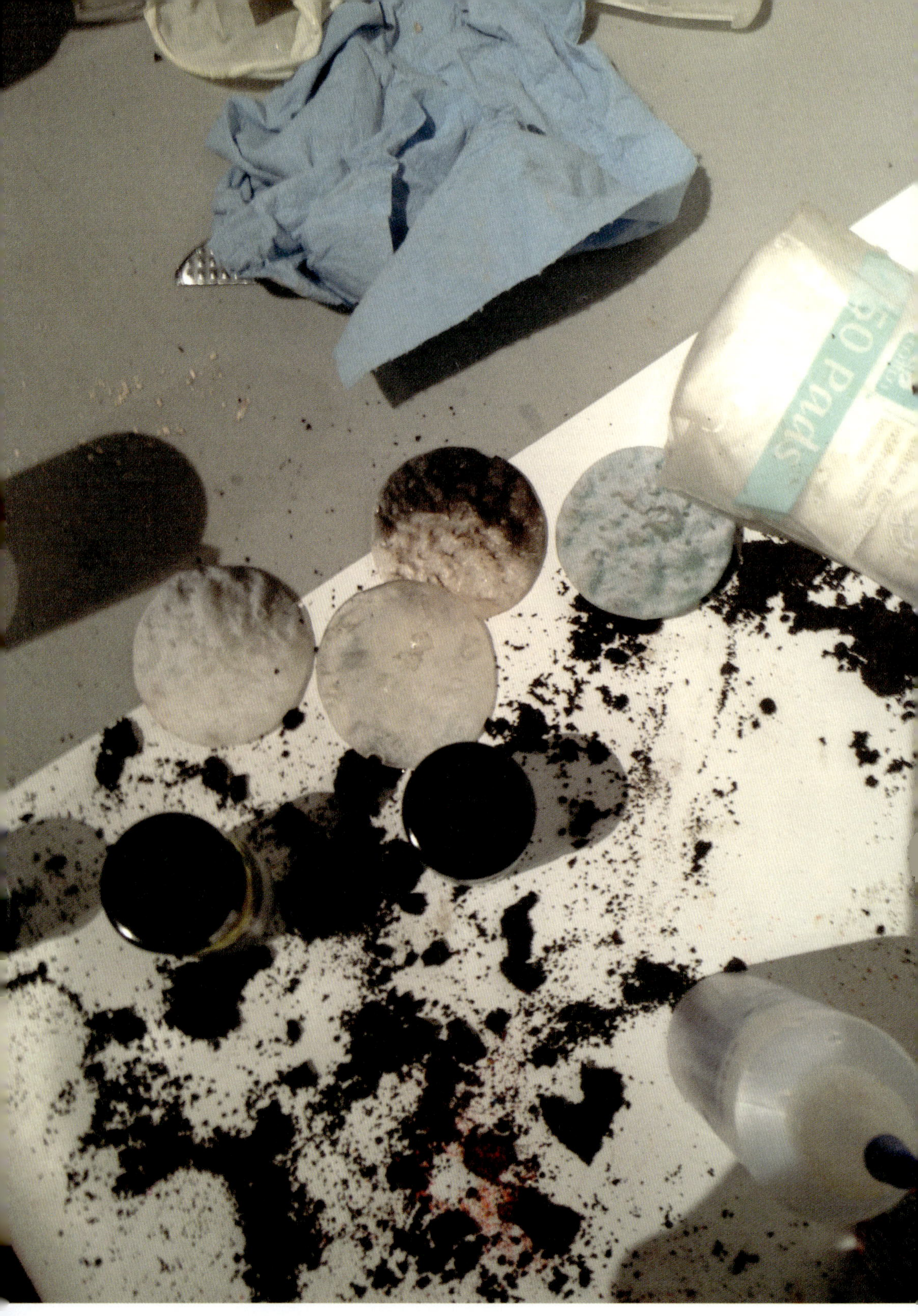

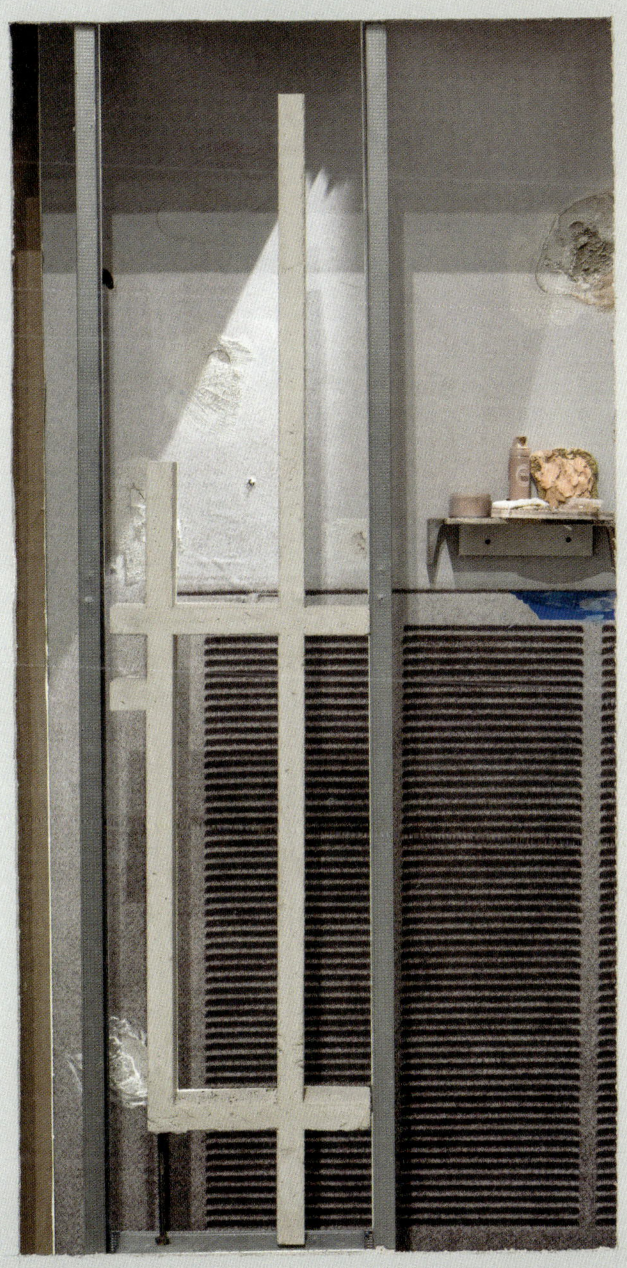

Untitled #3, 2013, from *The Hedge*, mixed media installation, 66 3/4 x 33 1/4 inches. Photo: Tim Safranek Photographics. Courtesy of MOCA Cleveland.

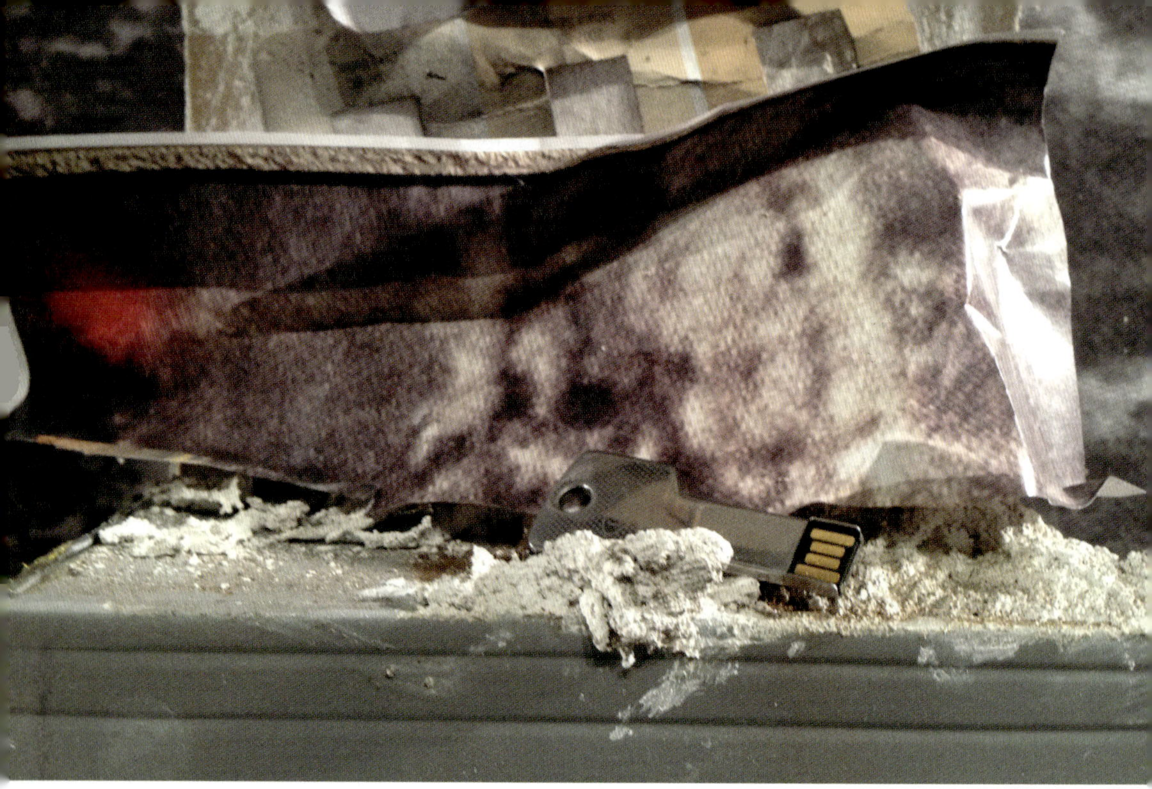

 Untitled #4 (detail), 2013, from *The Hedge*, mixed media installation, 80 1/2 x 80 inches. Photo: Corin Hewitt. Courtesy of the artist.

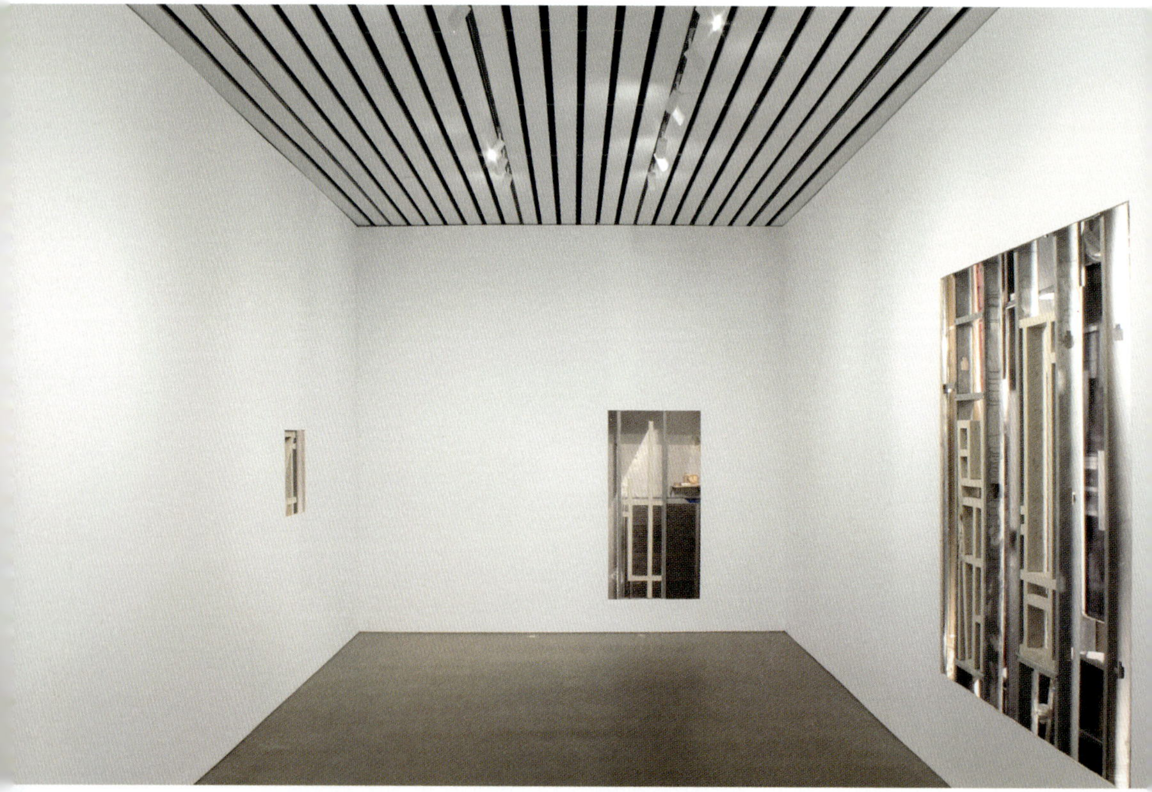

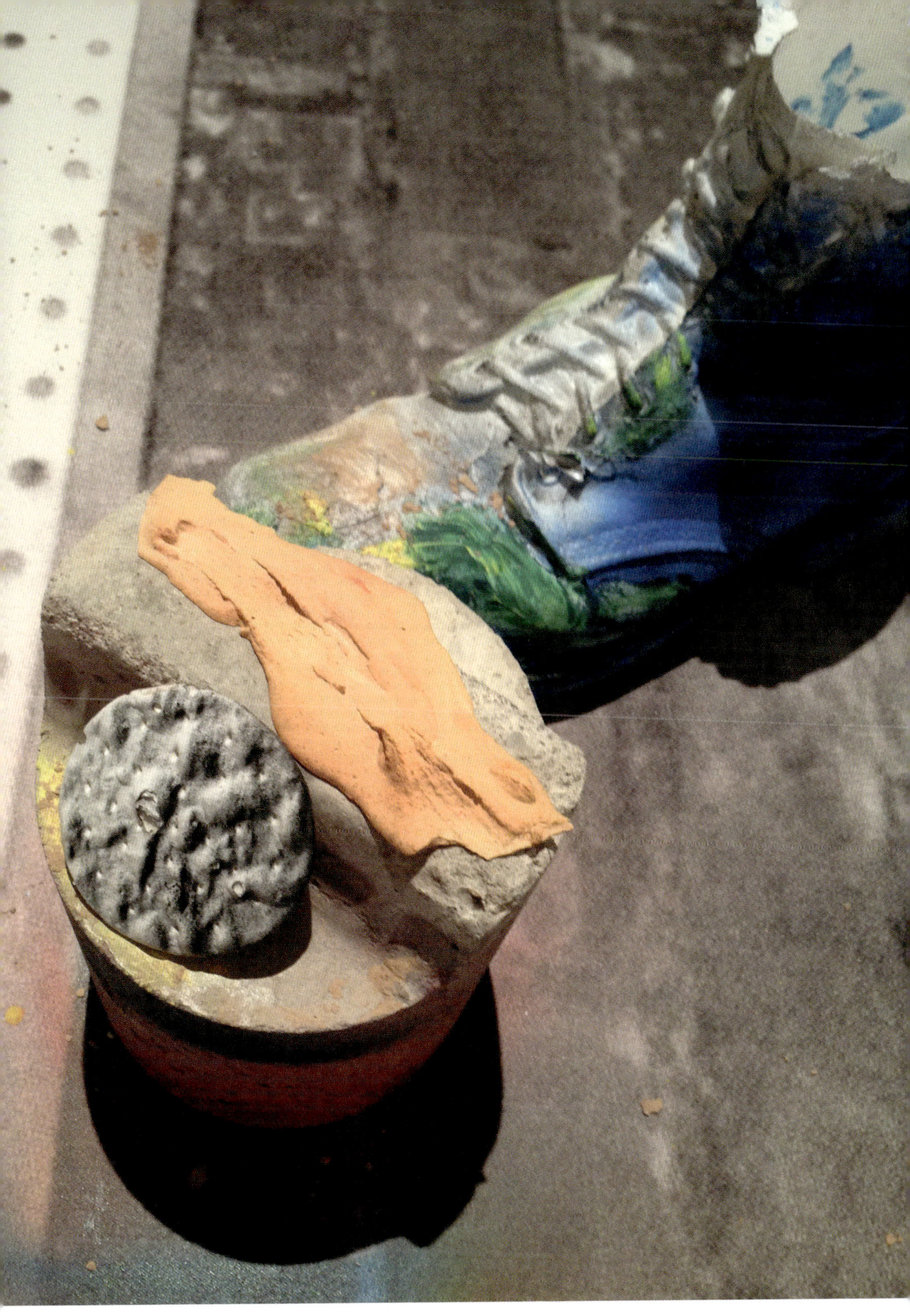

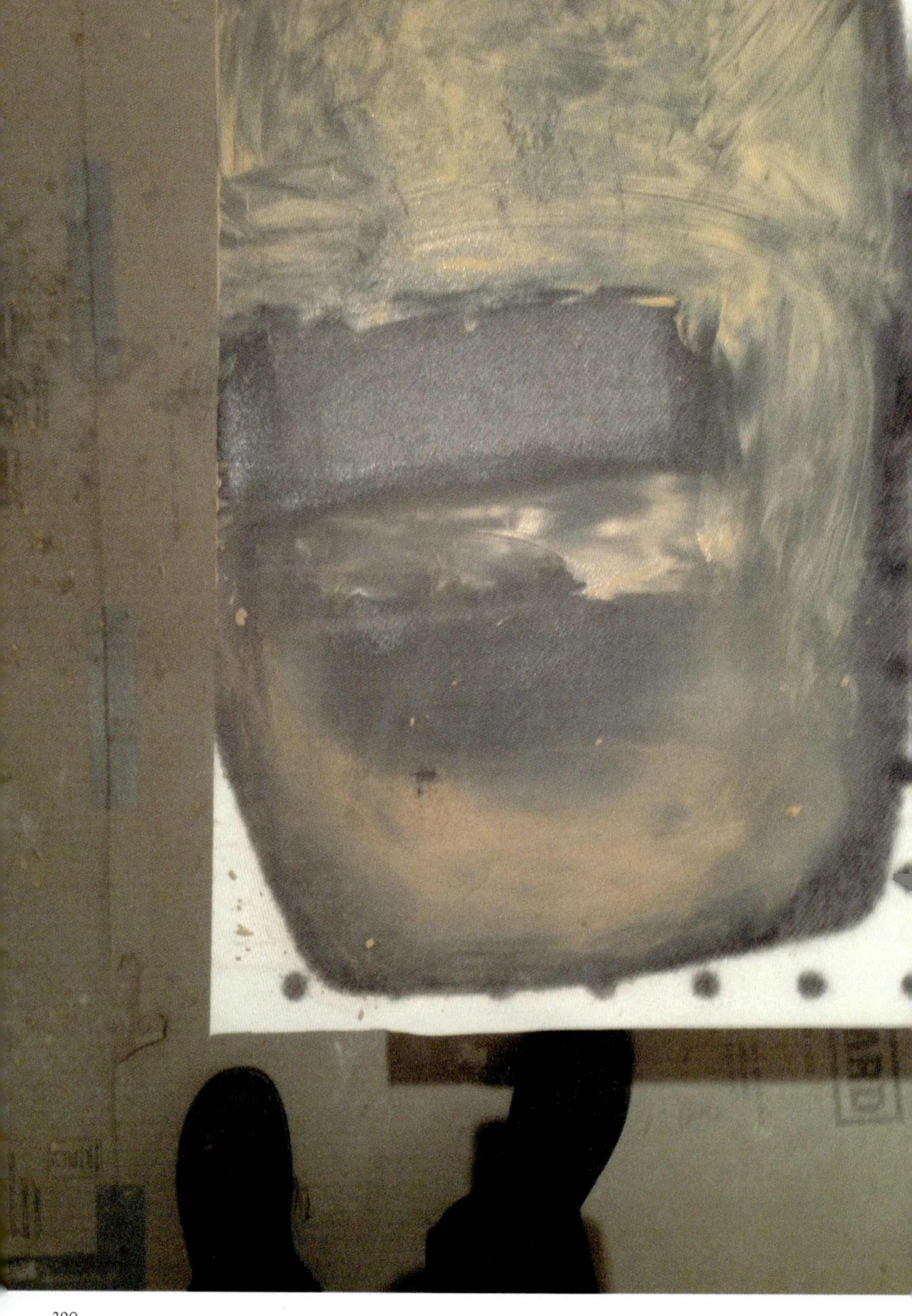

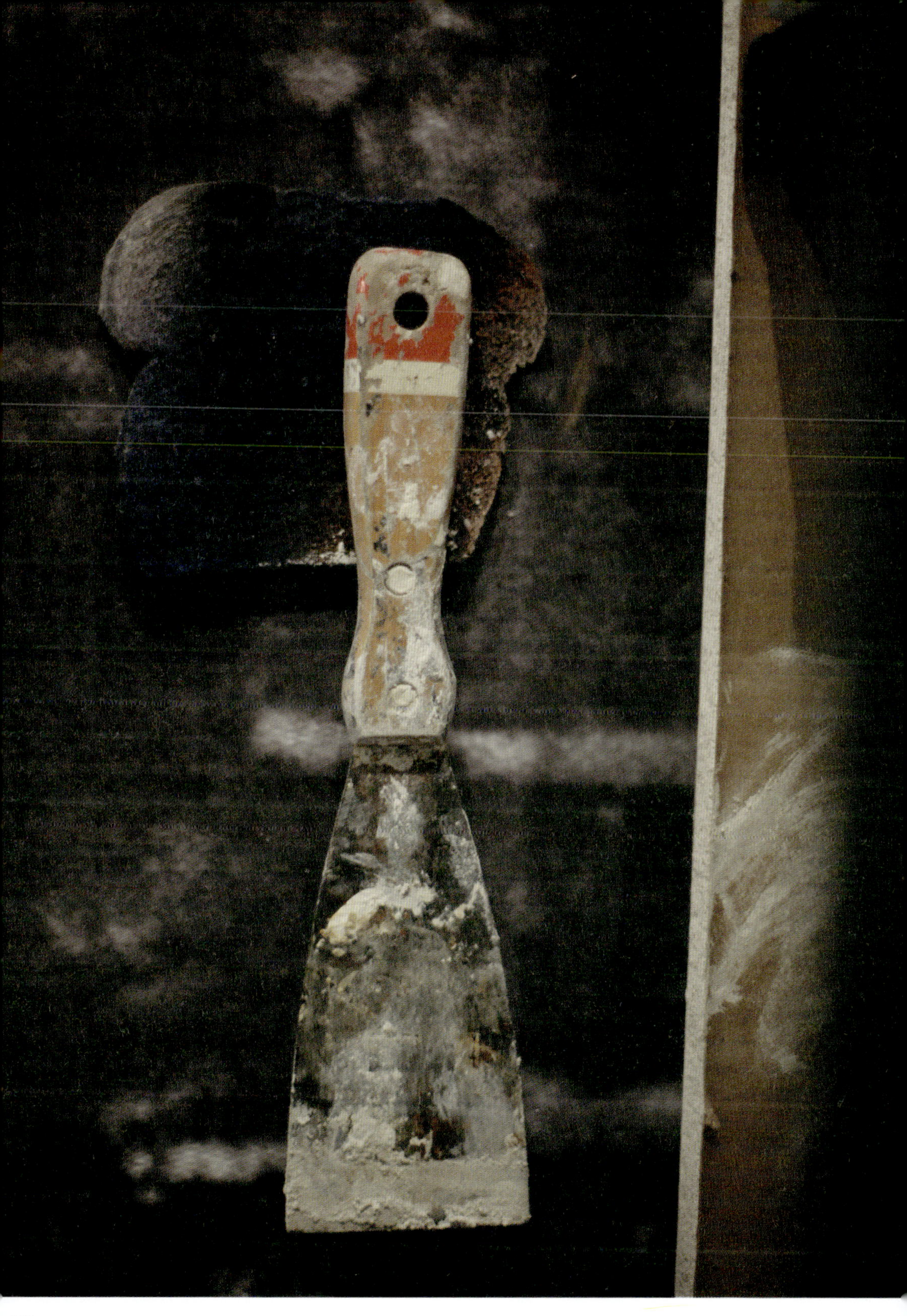

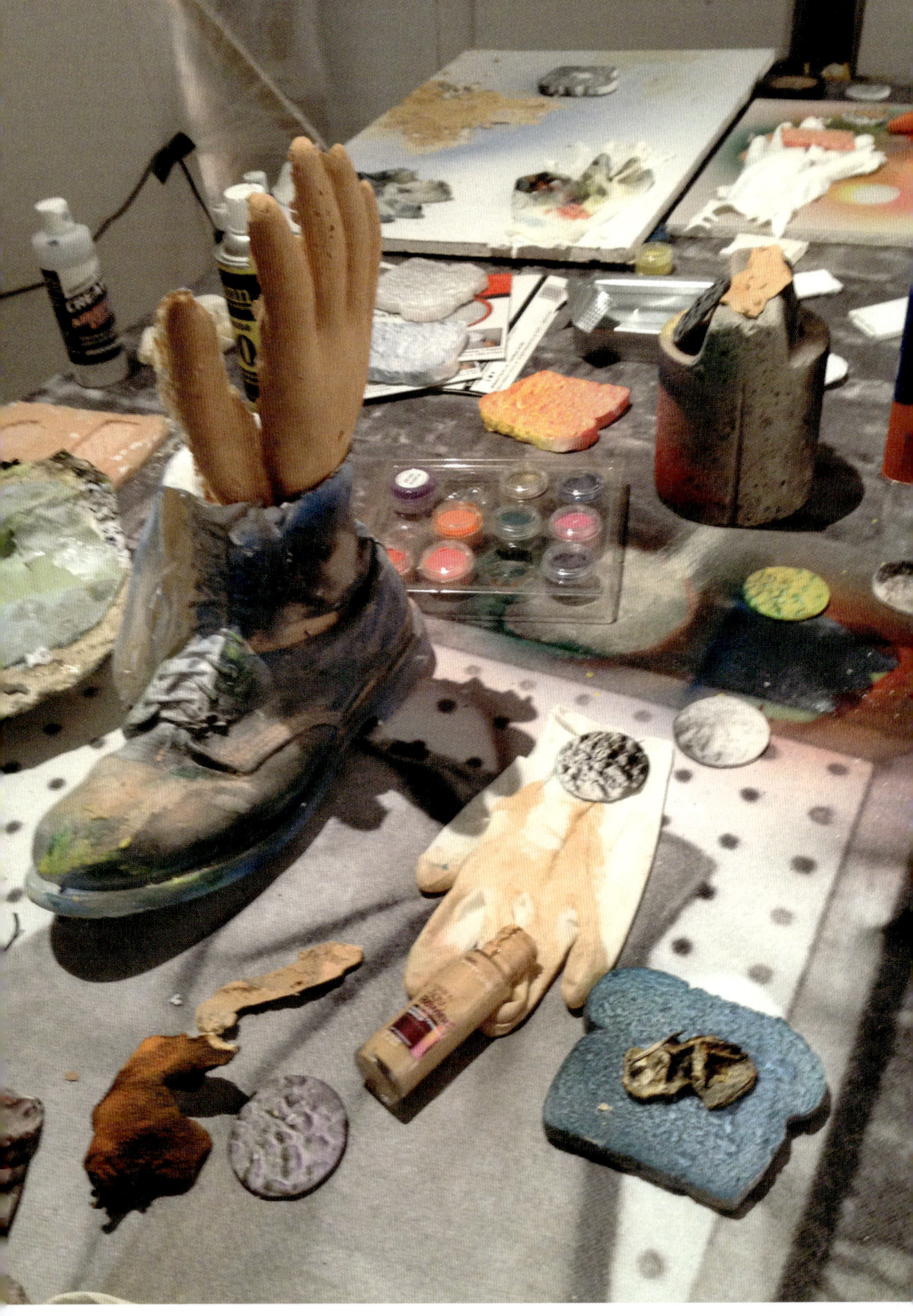

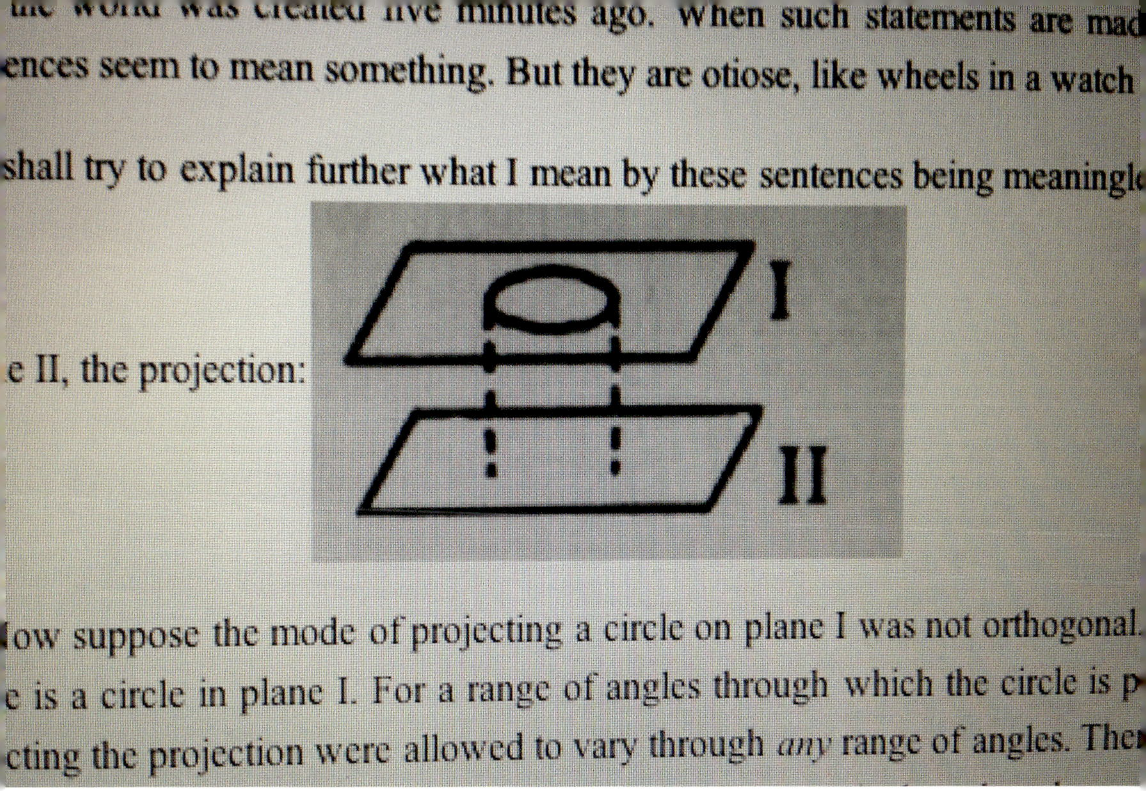

the world was created five minutes ago. When such statements are mad
ences seem to mean something. But they are otiose, like wheels in a watch

shall try to explain further what I mean by these sentences being meaningl

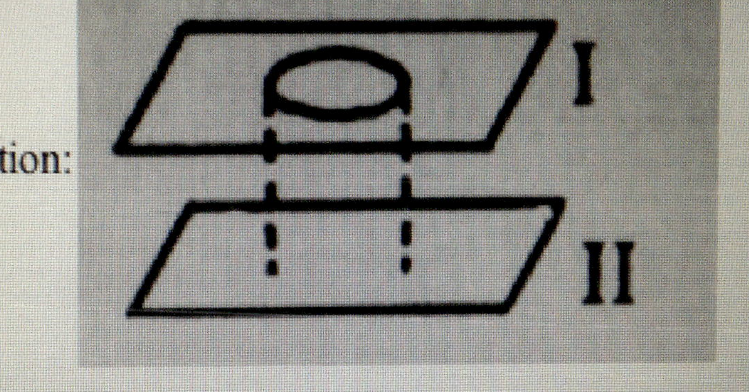

e II, the projection:

ow suppose the mode of projecting a circle on plane I was not orthogonal.
e is a circle in plane I. For a range of angles through which the circle is p
cting the projection were allowed to vary through *any* range of angles. The

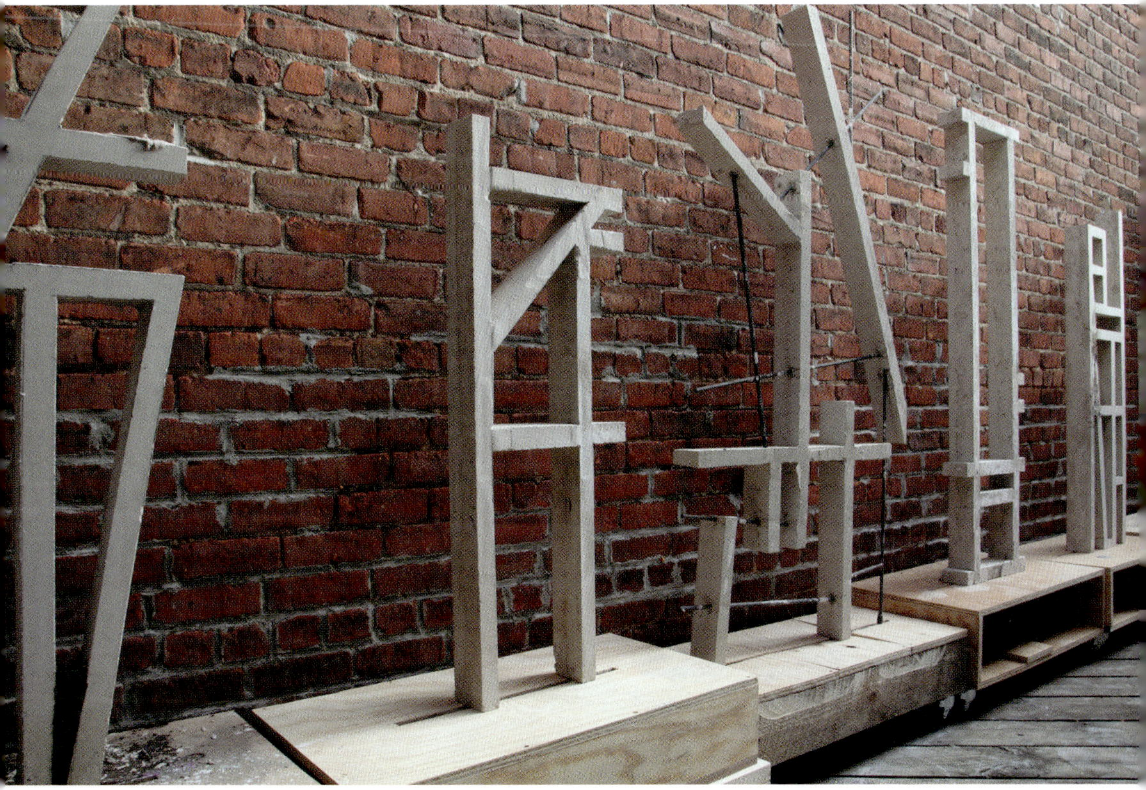

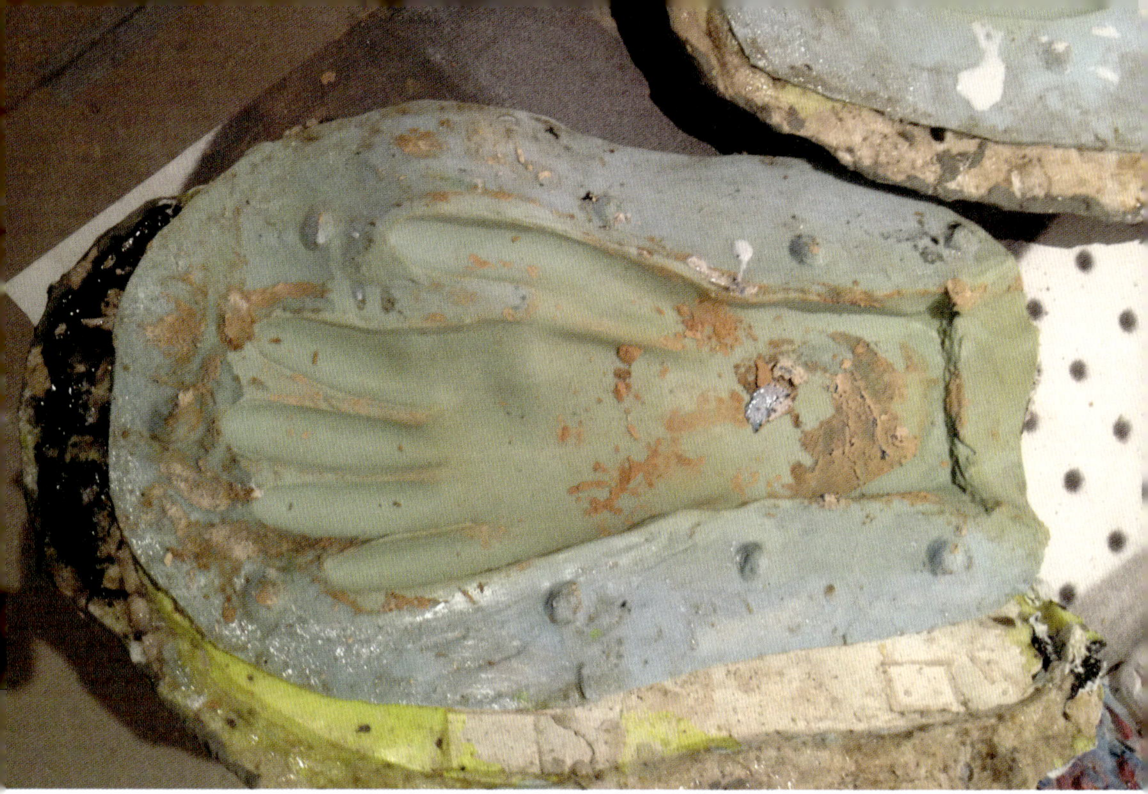

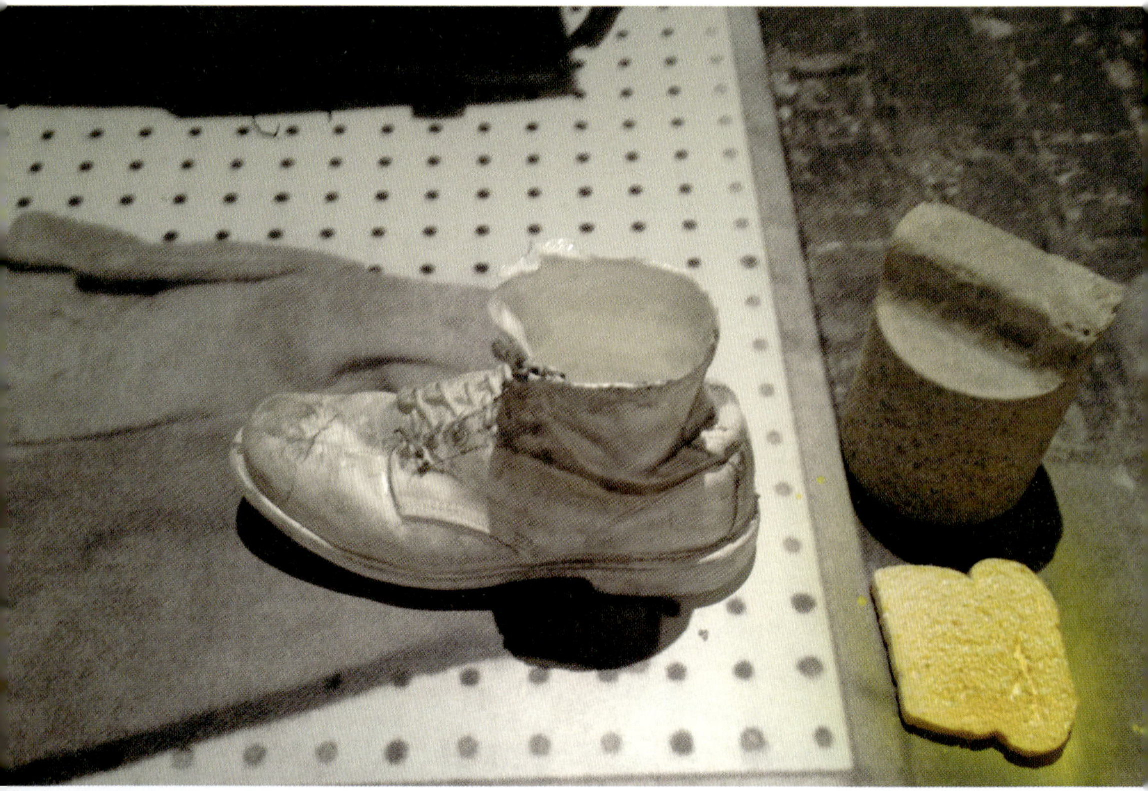

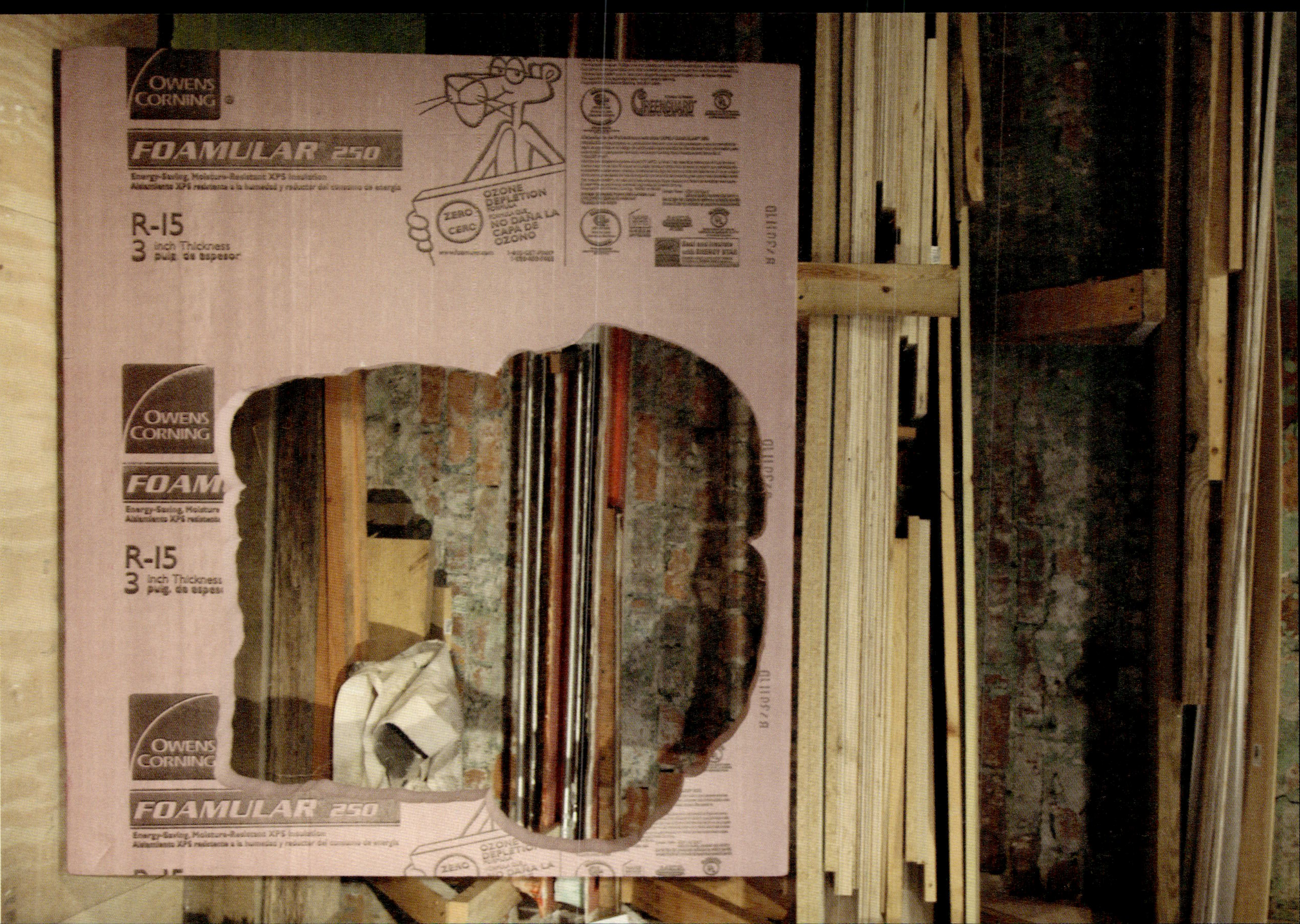

OWENS CORNING
FOAMULAR 250
Energy-Saving, Moisture-Resistant XPS Insulation
Aislamiento XPS resistente a la humedad y reductor del consumo de energía
R-15
3 inch Thickness
pulg. de espesor
OZONE DEPLETION
ZERO
CERO
NO DAÑA LA CAPA DE OZONO
GREENGUARD

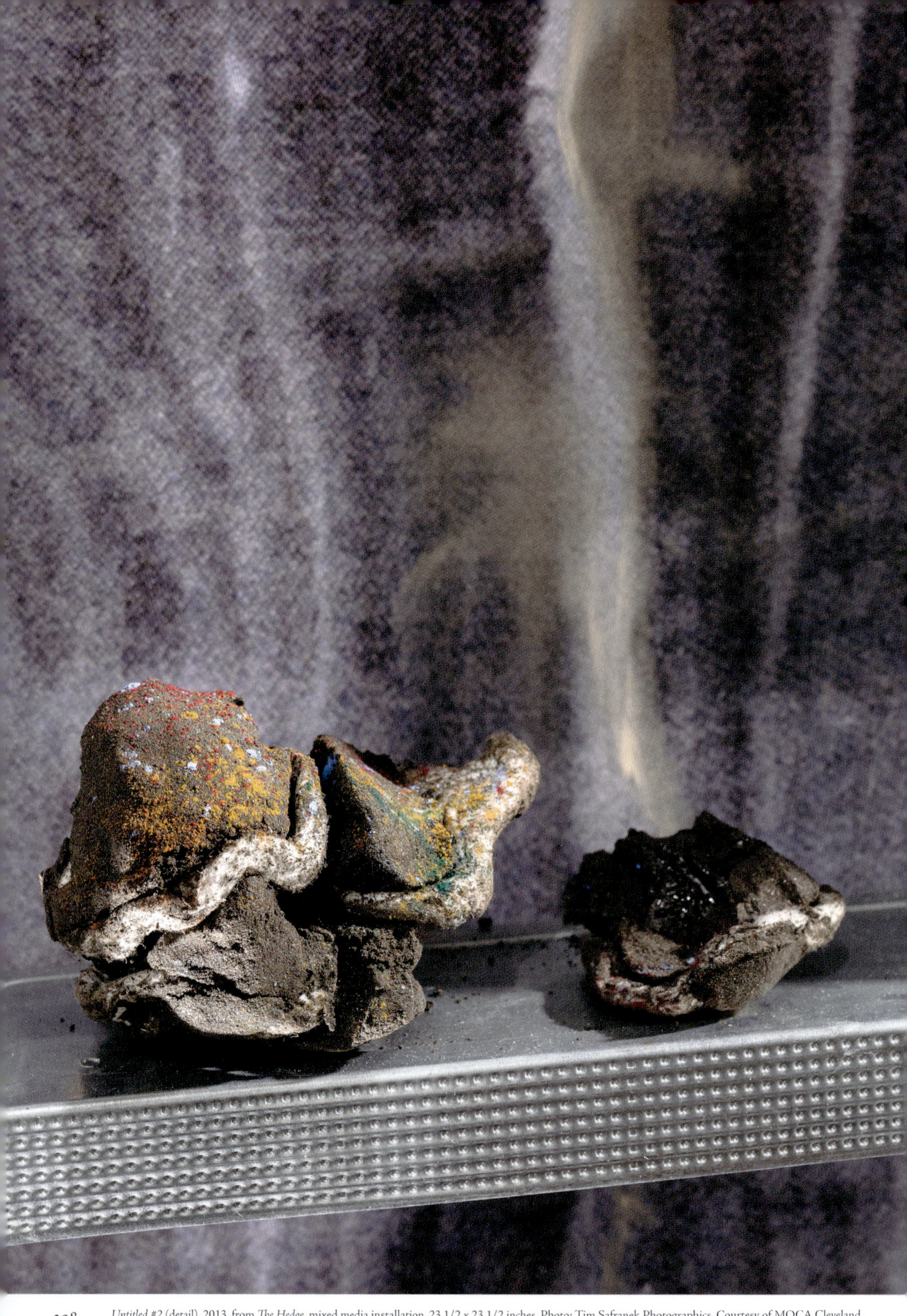

 Untitled #2 (detail), 2013, from *The Hedge*, mixed media installation, 23 1/2 x 23 1/2 inches. Photo: Tim Safranek Photographics. Courtesy of MOCA Cleveland.

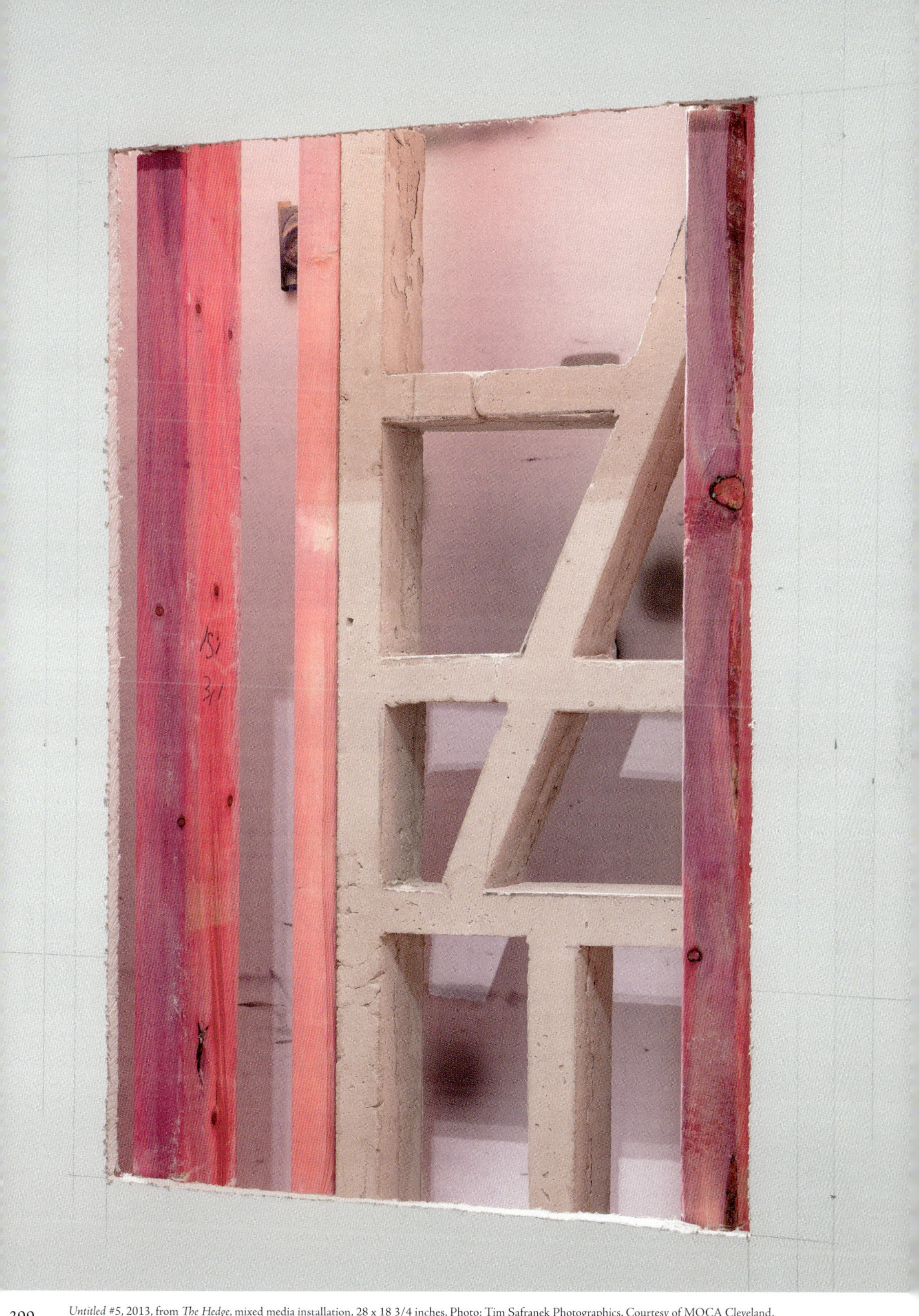

  Untitled #5, 2013, from *The Hedge*, mixed media installation, 28 x 18 3/4 inches. Photo: Tim Safranek Photographics. Courtesy of MOCA Cleveland.

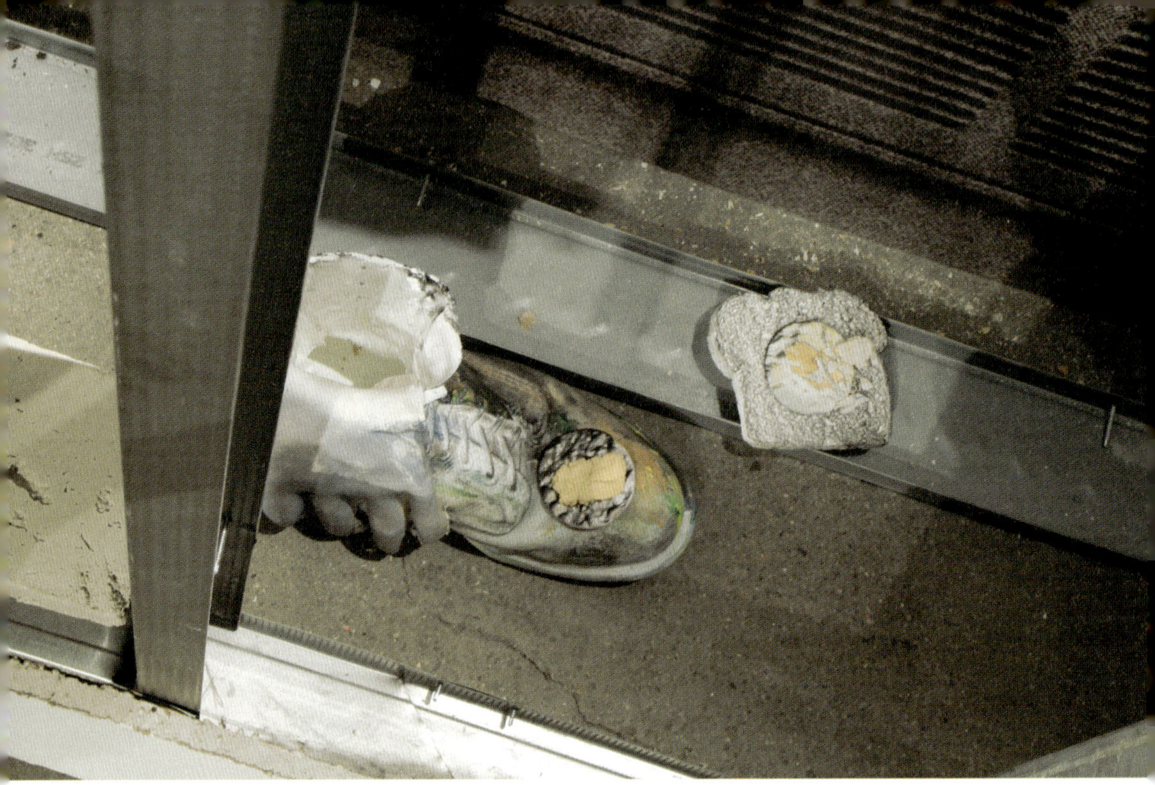

300   *Untitled #3* (detail), 2013, from *The Hedge*, mixed media installation, 66 3/4 x 33 1/4 inches. Photo: Rose Bouthillier. Courtesy of MOCA Cleveland.

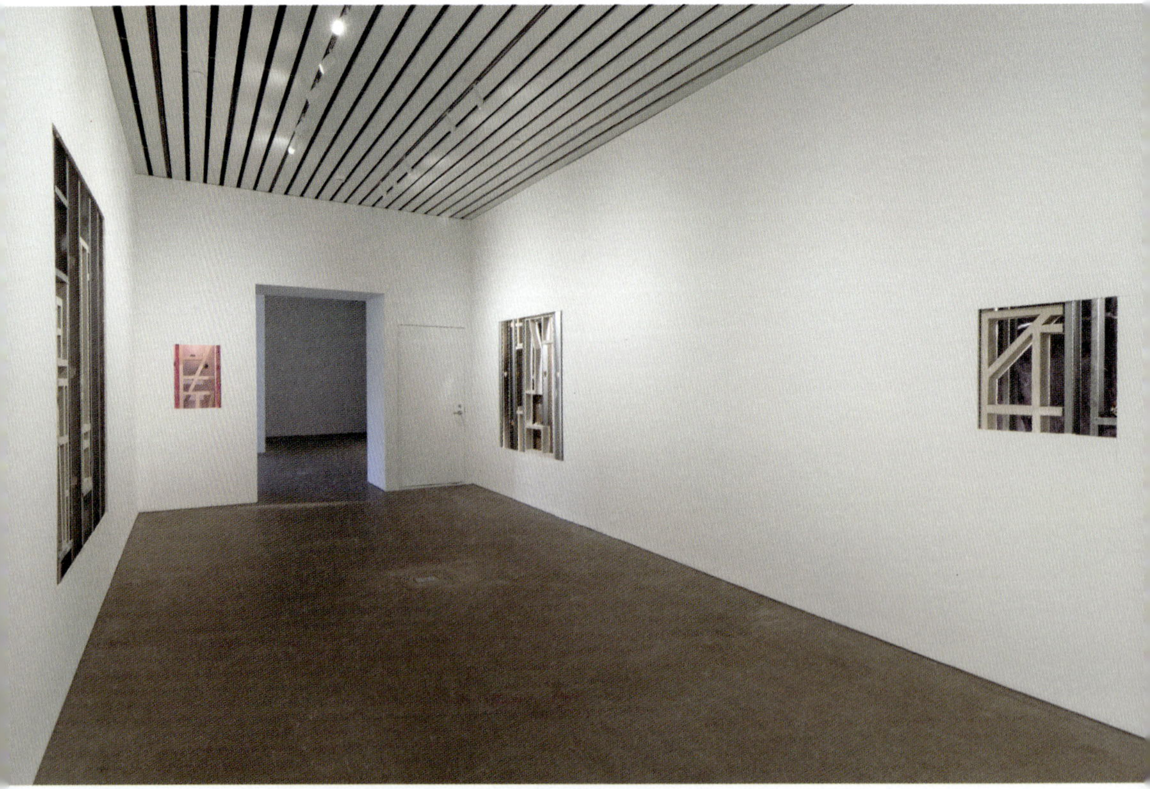

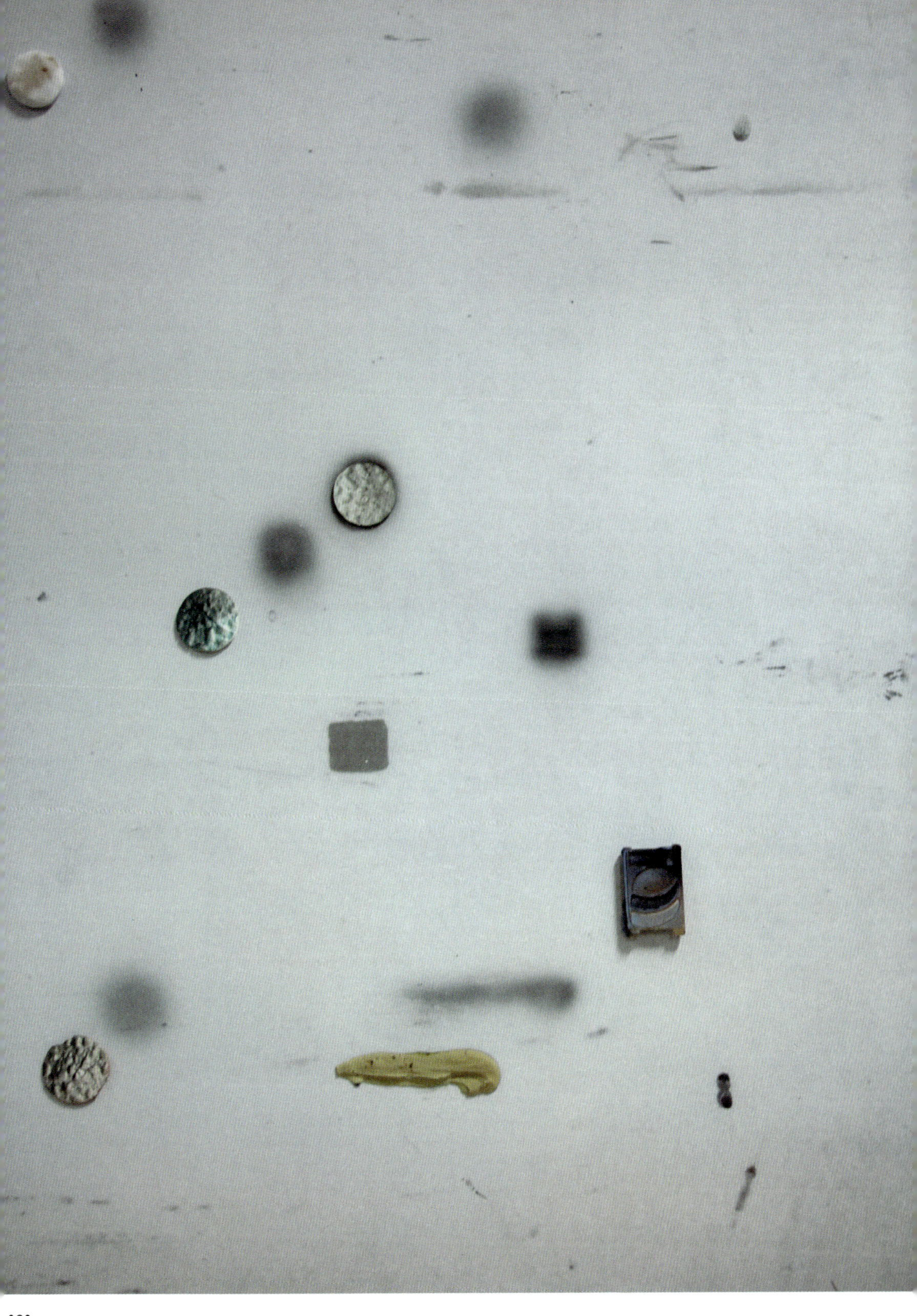

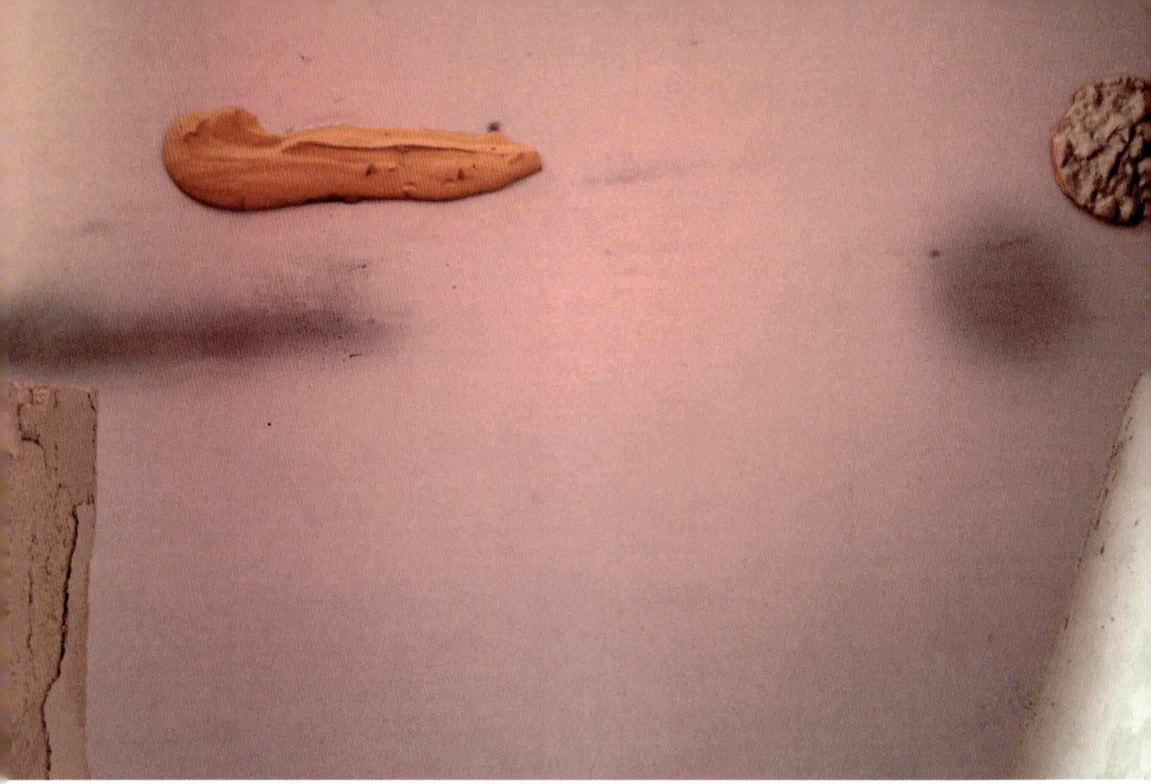

   Untitled #5 (detail), 2013, from *The Hedge*, mixed media installation, 28 x 18 3/4 inches. Photo: Corin Hewitt. Courtesy of the artist.

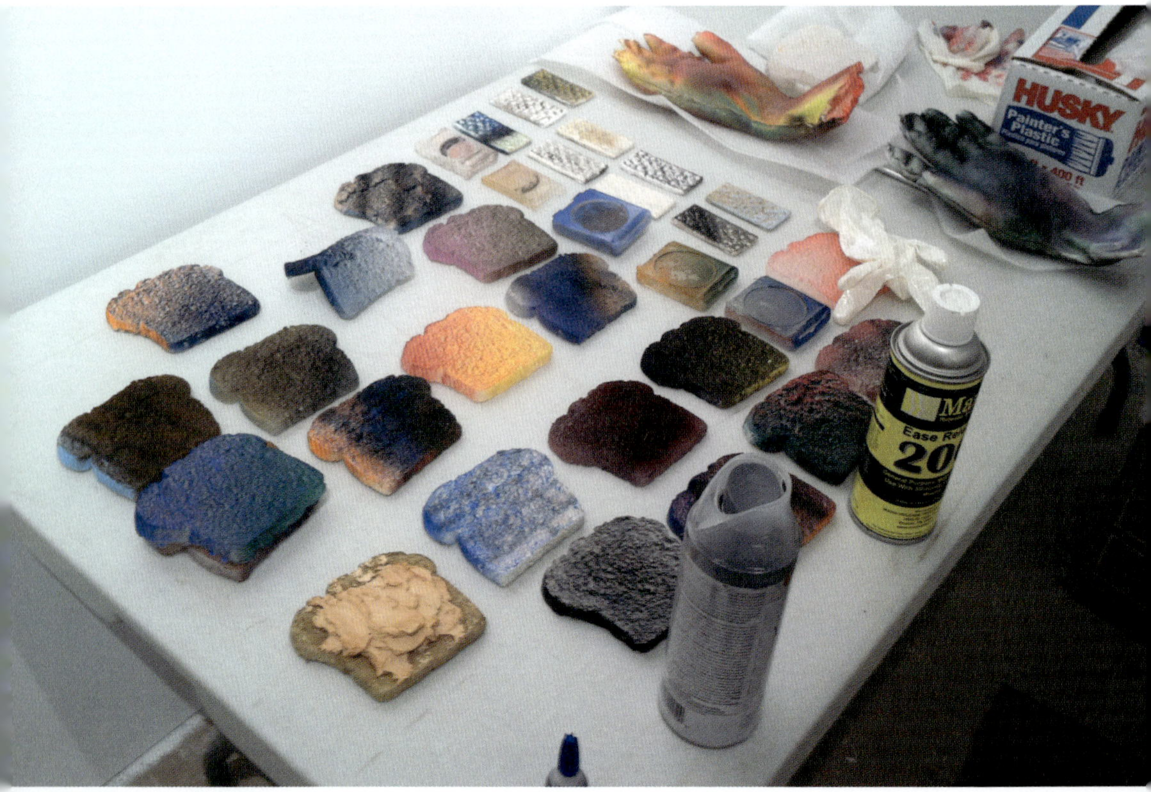

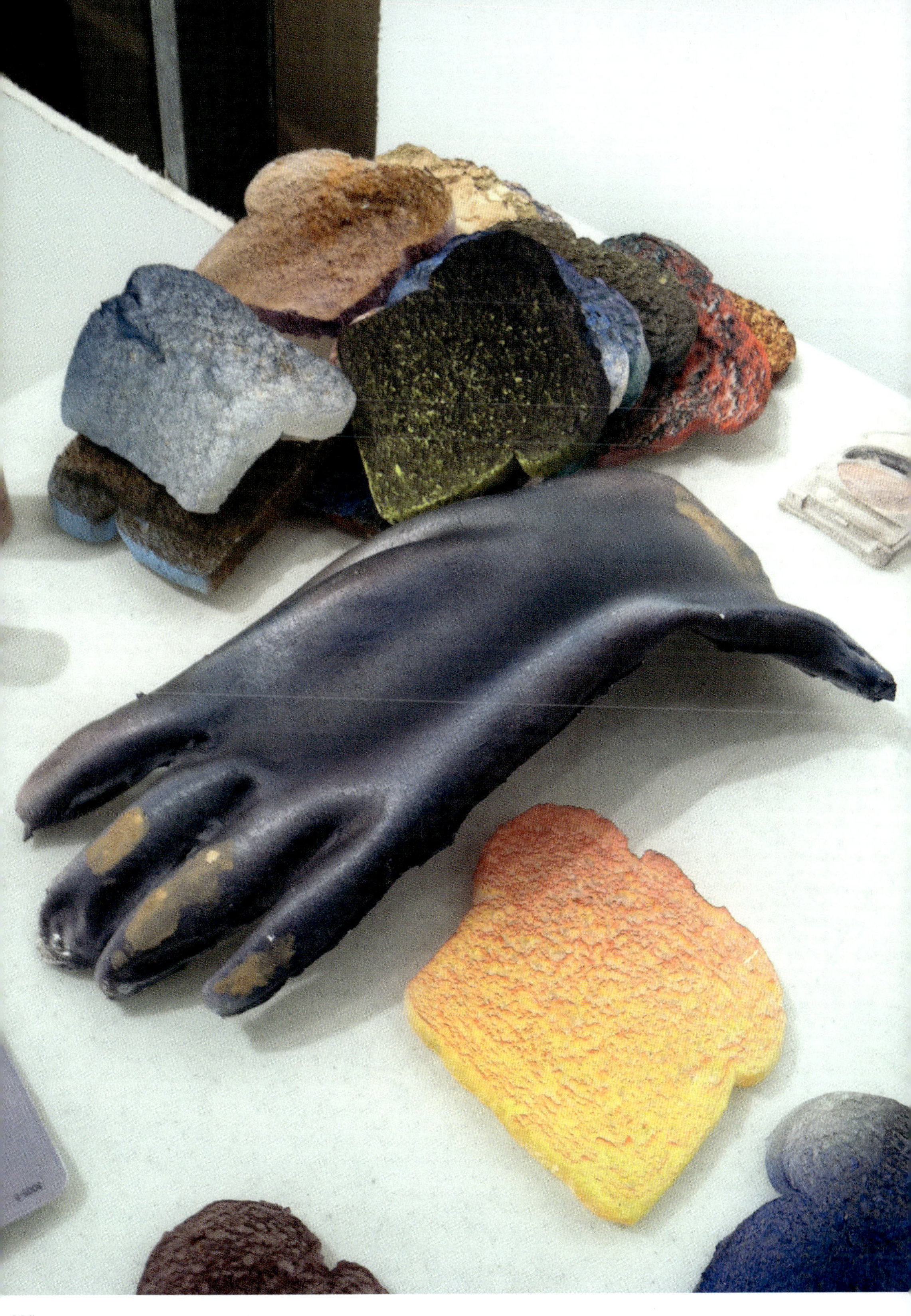

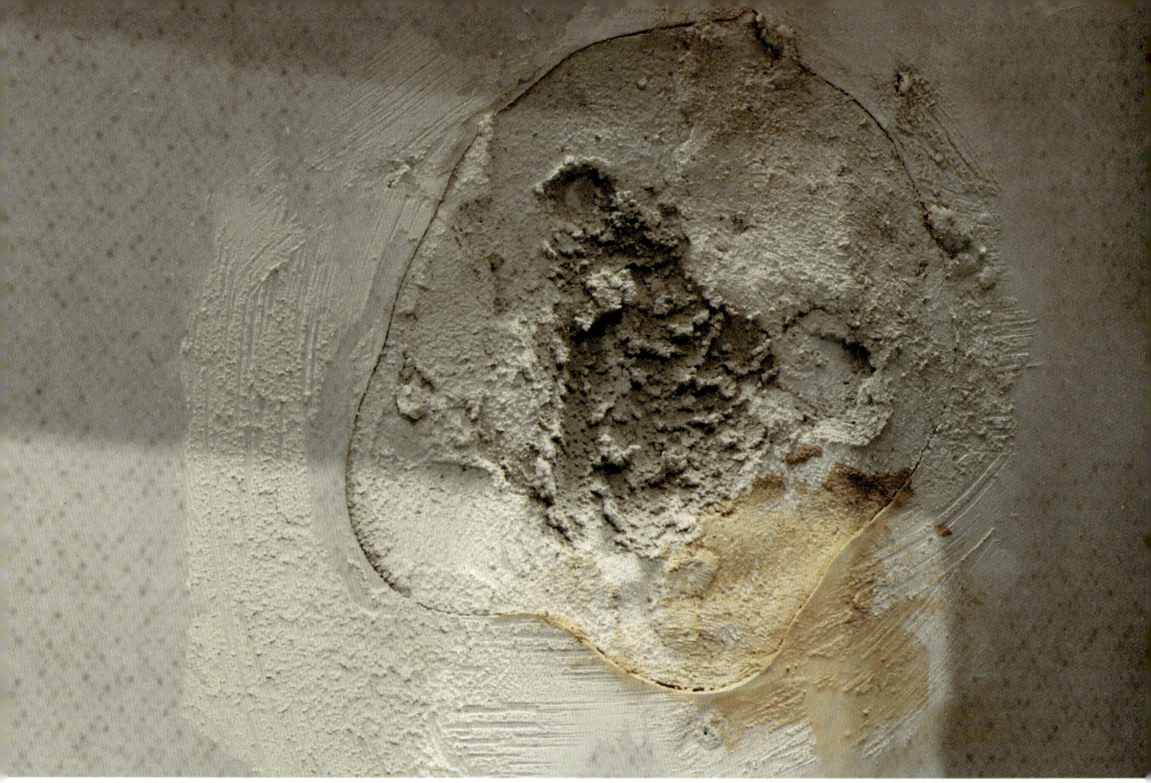

   Untitled #3 (detail), 2013, from *The Hedge*, mixed media installation, 66 3/4 x 33 1/4 inches. Photo: Rose Bouthillier. Courtesy of MOCA Cleveland.

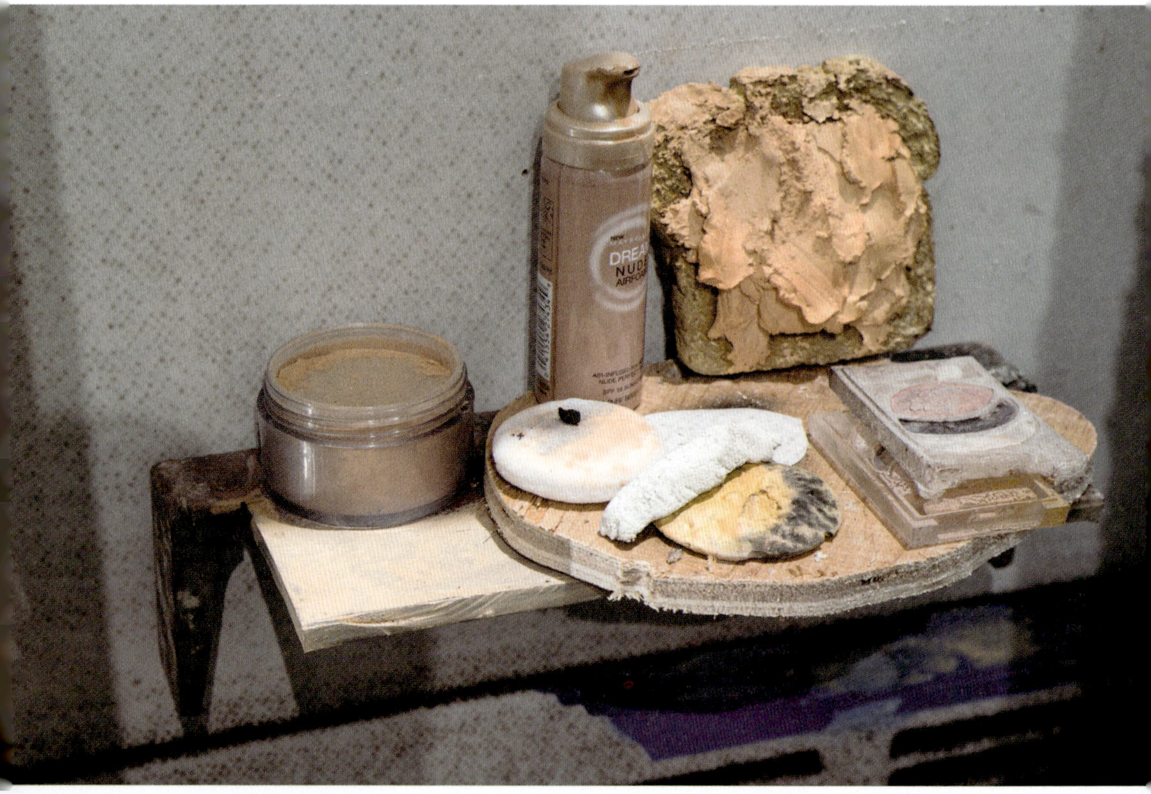

   Untitled #3 (detail), 2013, from *The Hedge*, mixed media installation, 66 3/4 x 33 1/4 inches. Photo: Rose Bouthillier. Courtesy of MOCA Cleveland.

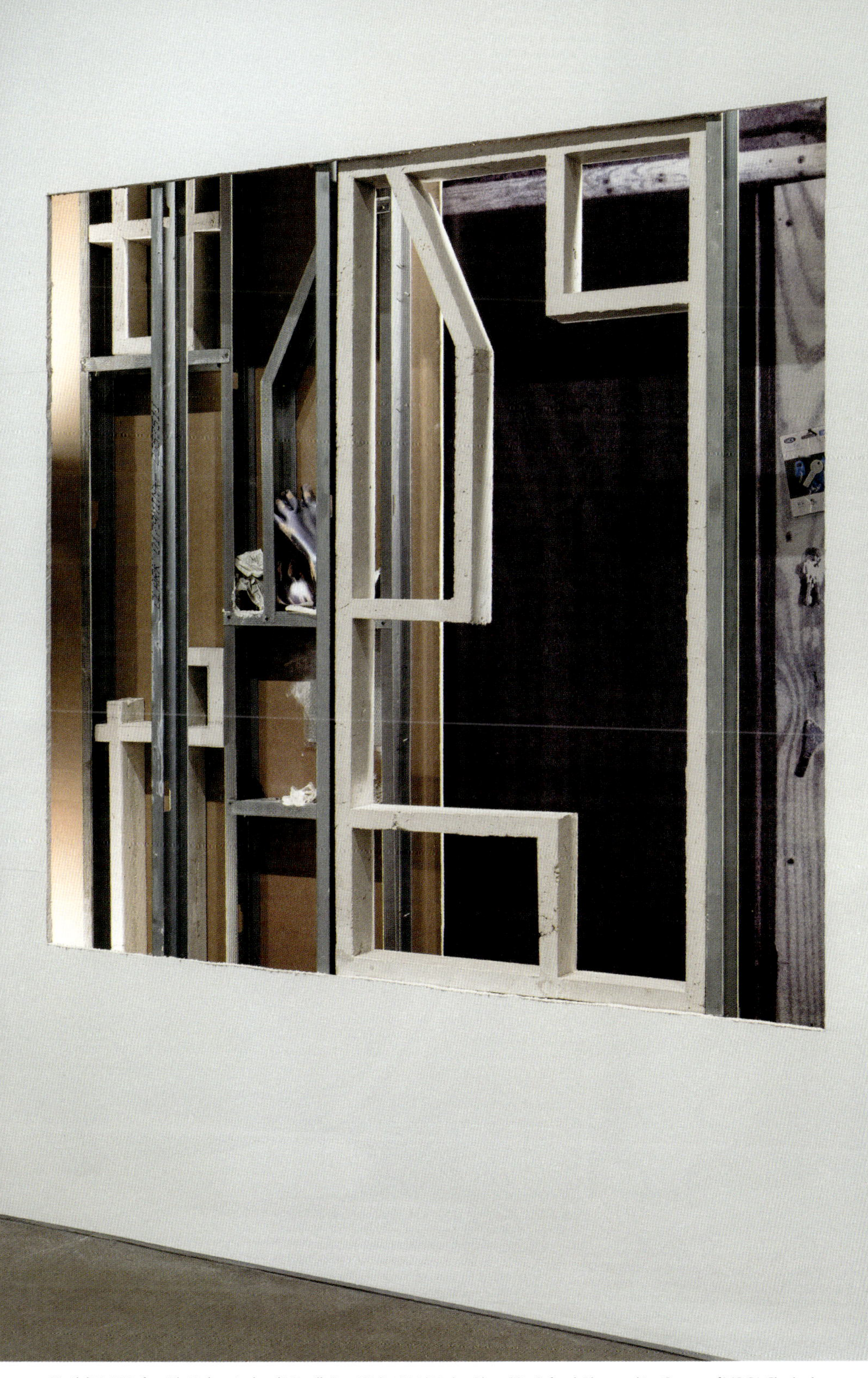

   Untitled #1, 2013, from *The Hedge*, mixed media installation, 60 1/2 x 67 1/2 inches. Photo: Tim Safranek Photographics. Courtesy of MOCA Cleveland.

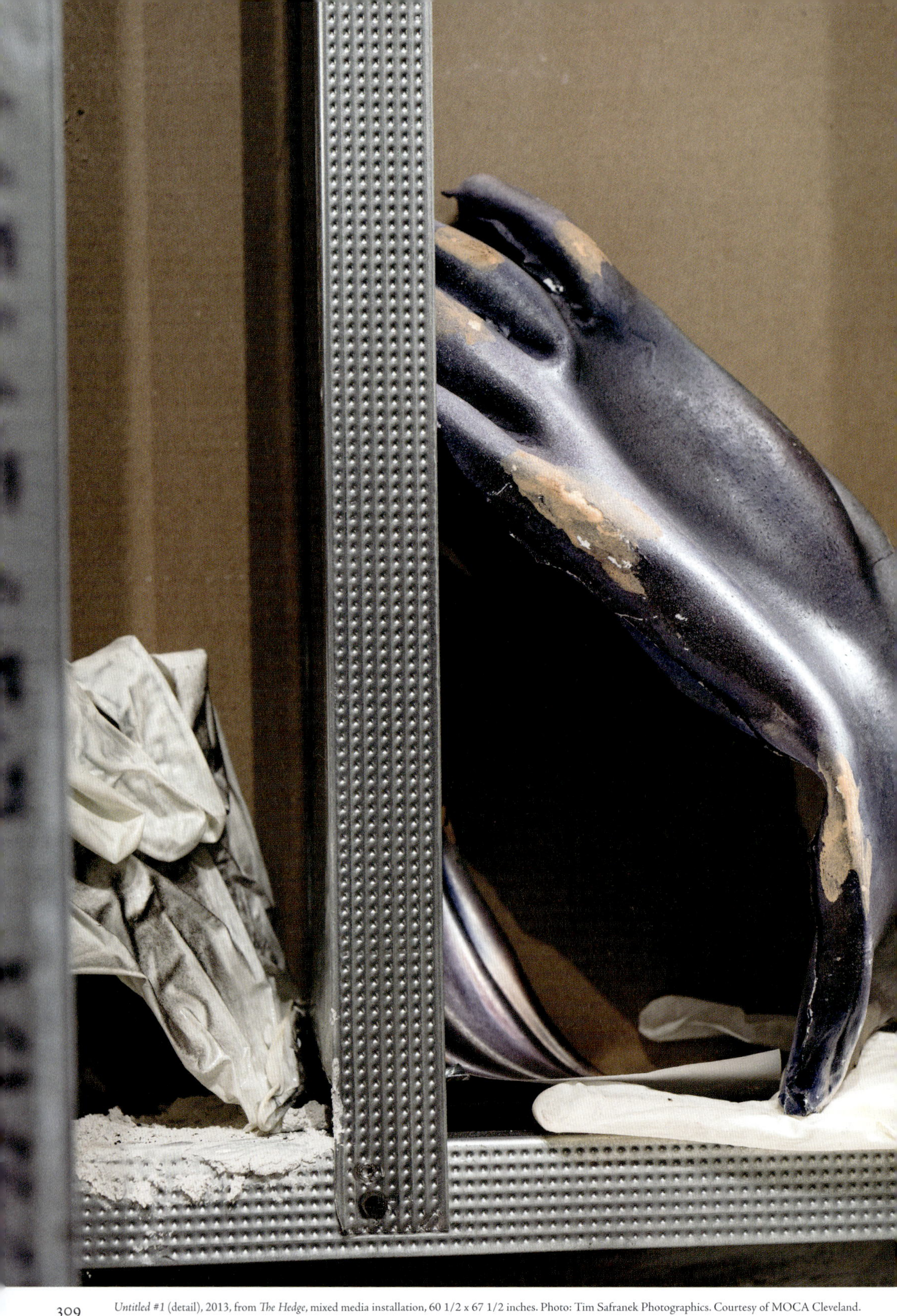

 Untitled #1 (detail), 2013, from *The Hedge*, mixed media installation, 60 1/2 x 67 1/2 inches. Photo: Tim Safranek Photographics. Courtesy of MOCA Cleveland.

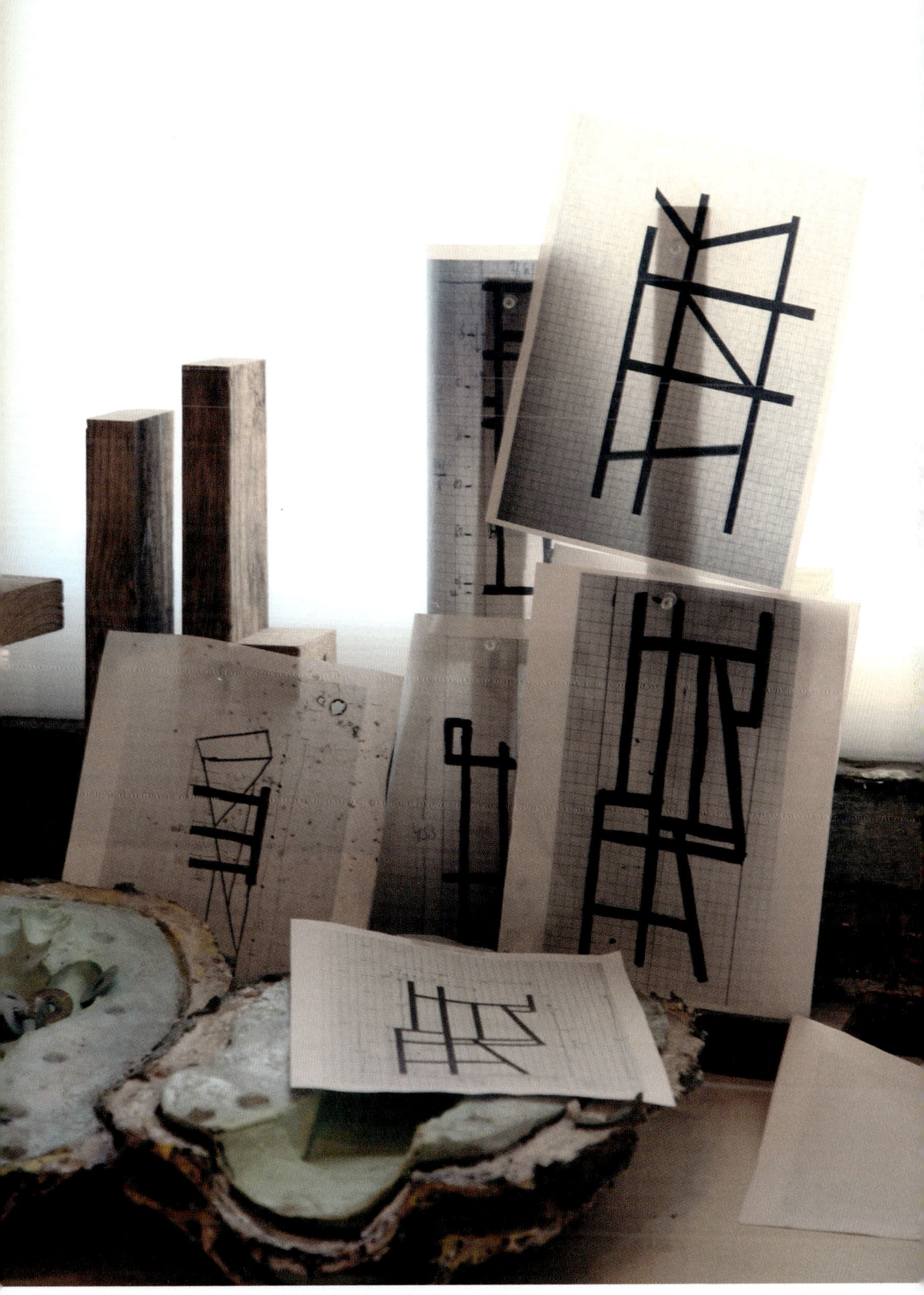

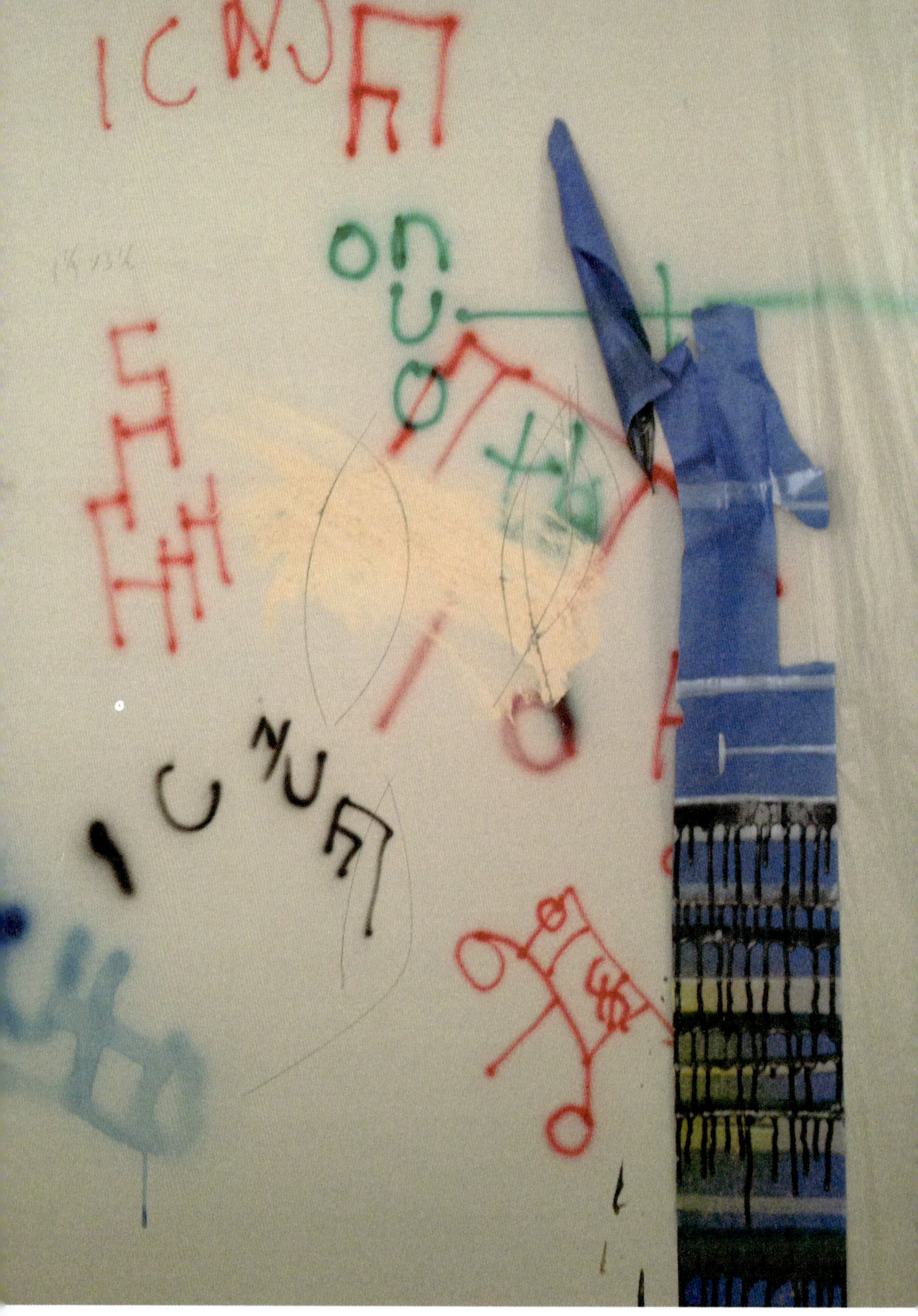

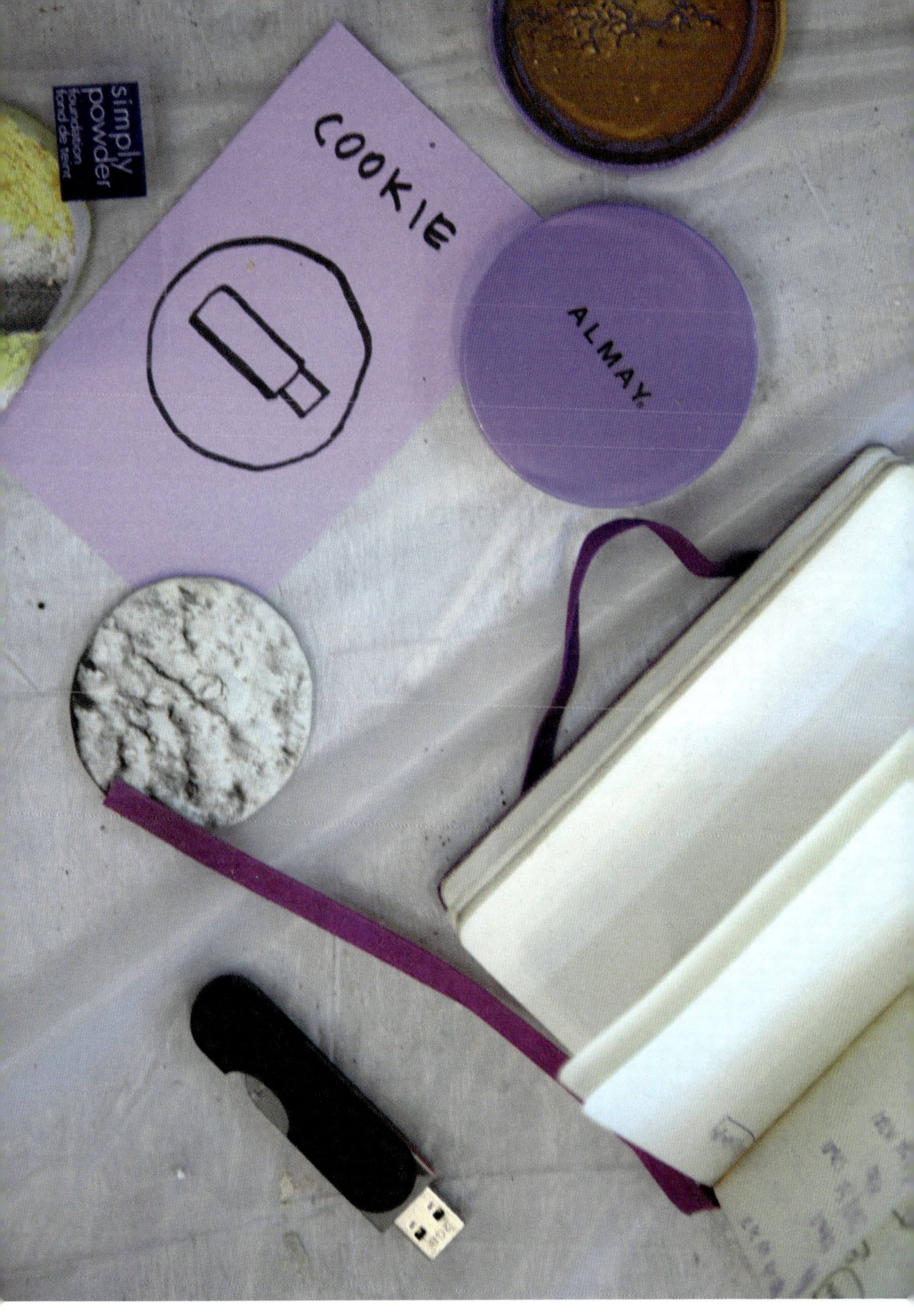

simply
powder
foundation
fond de teint
COOKIE
ALMAY

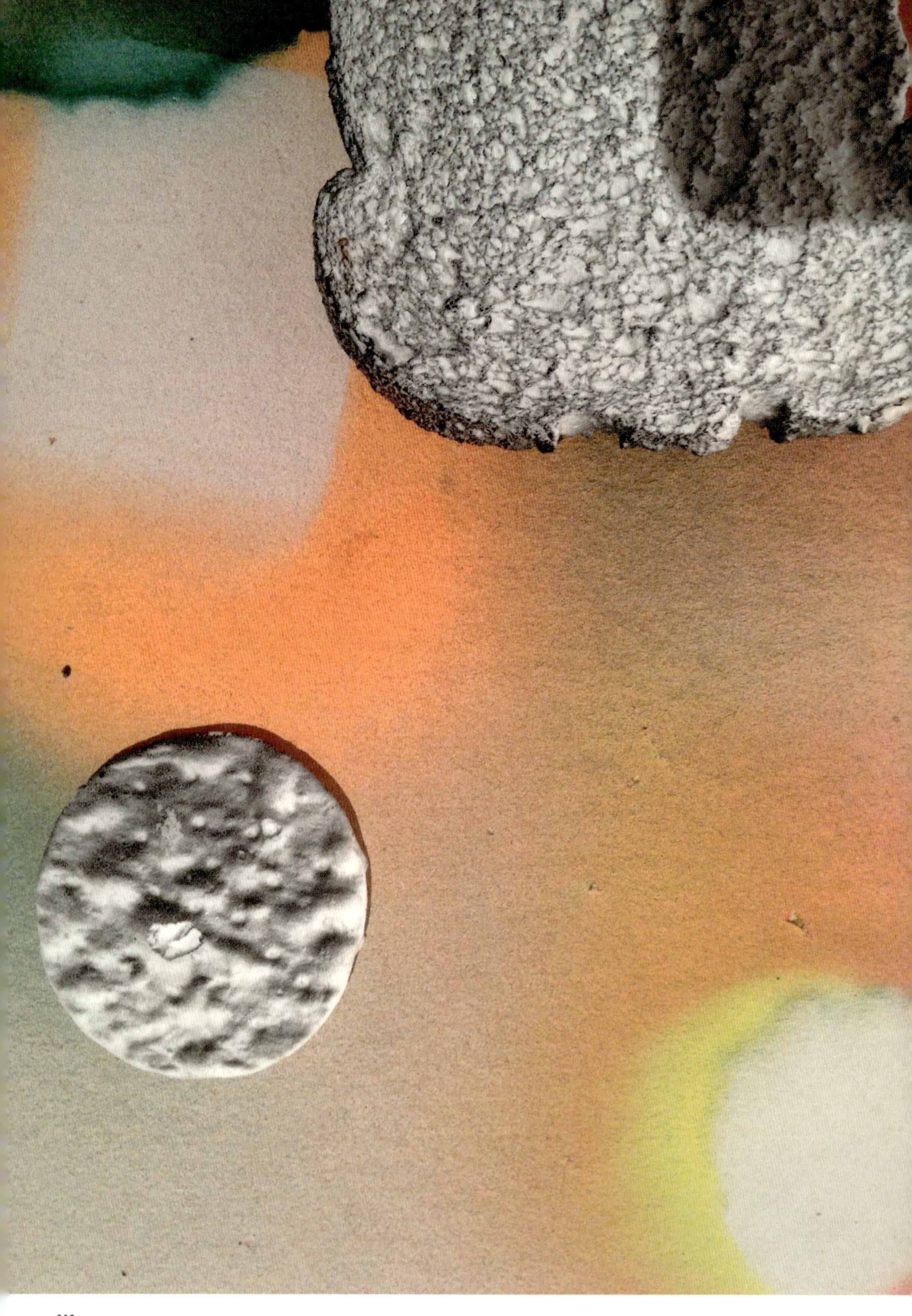

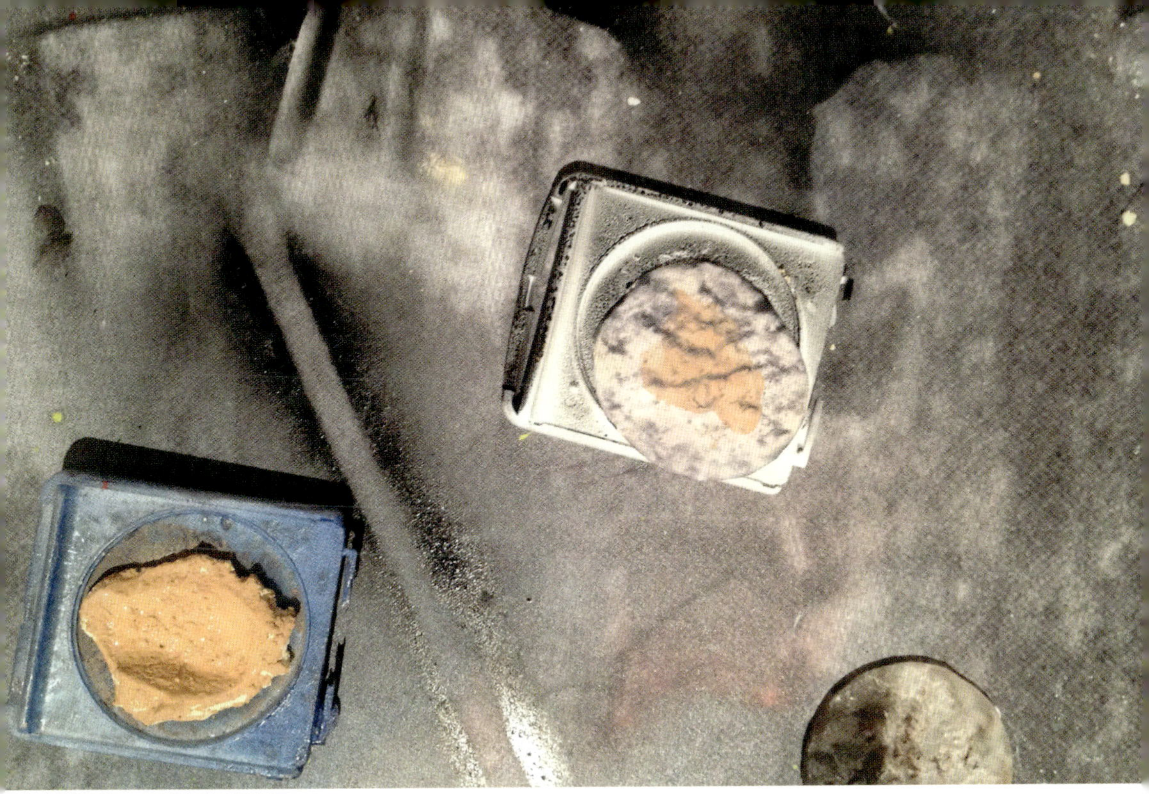

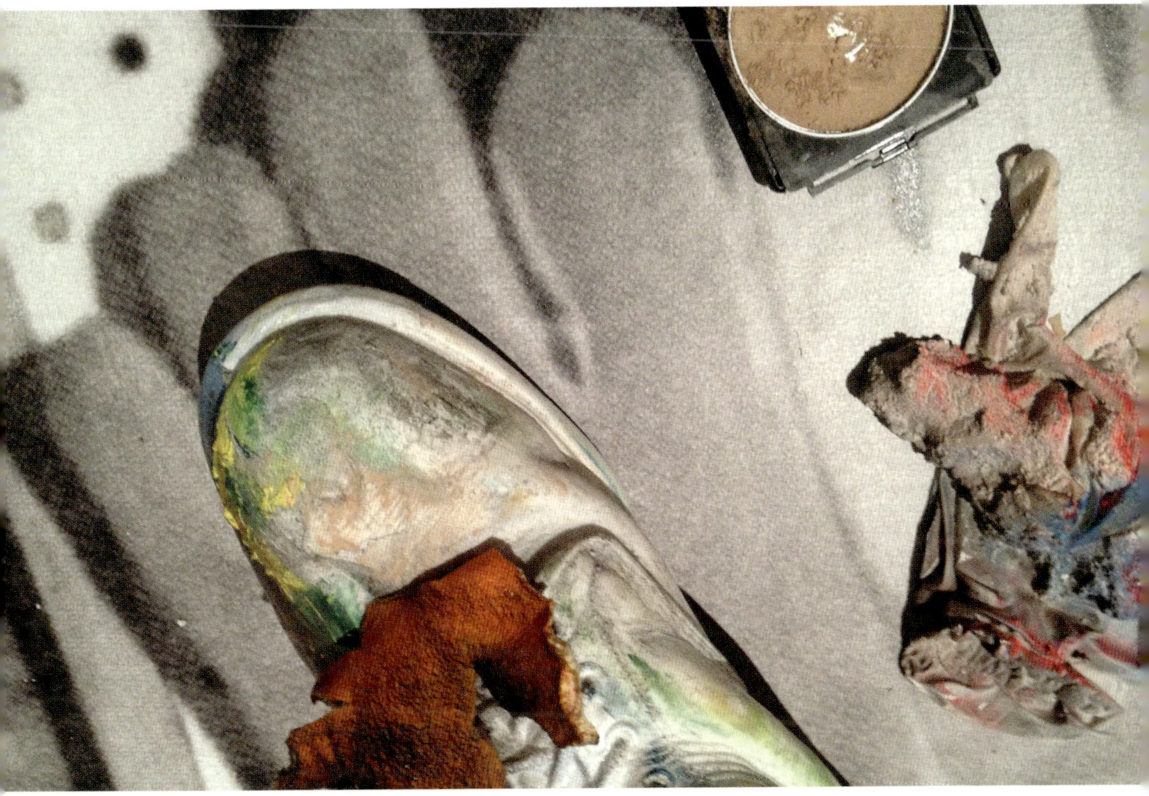

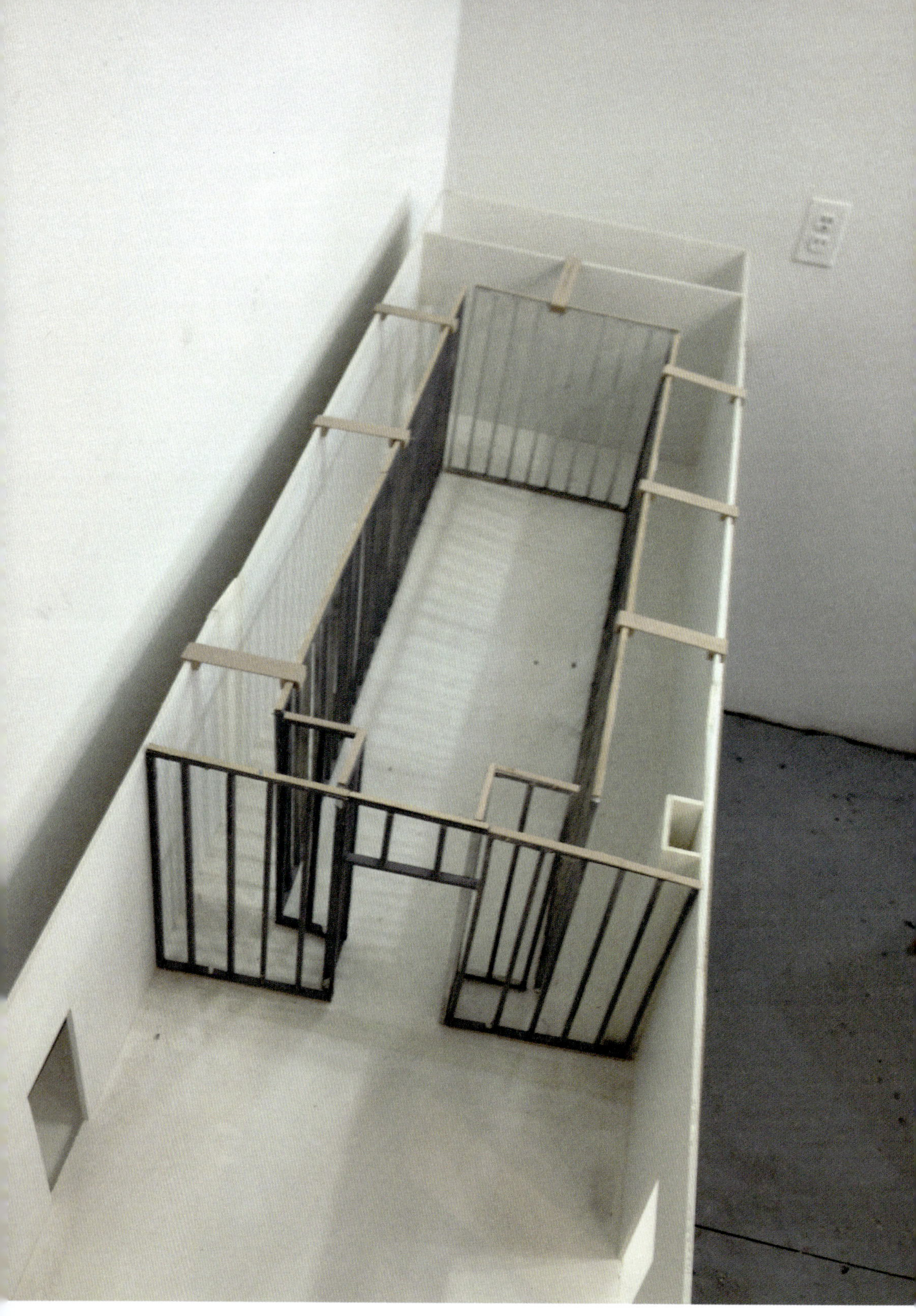

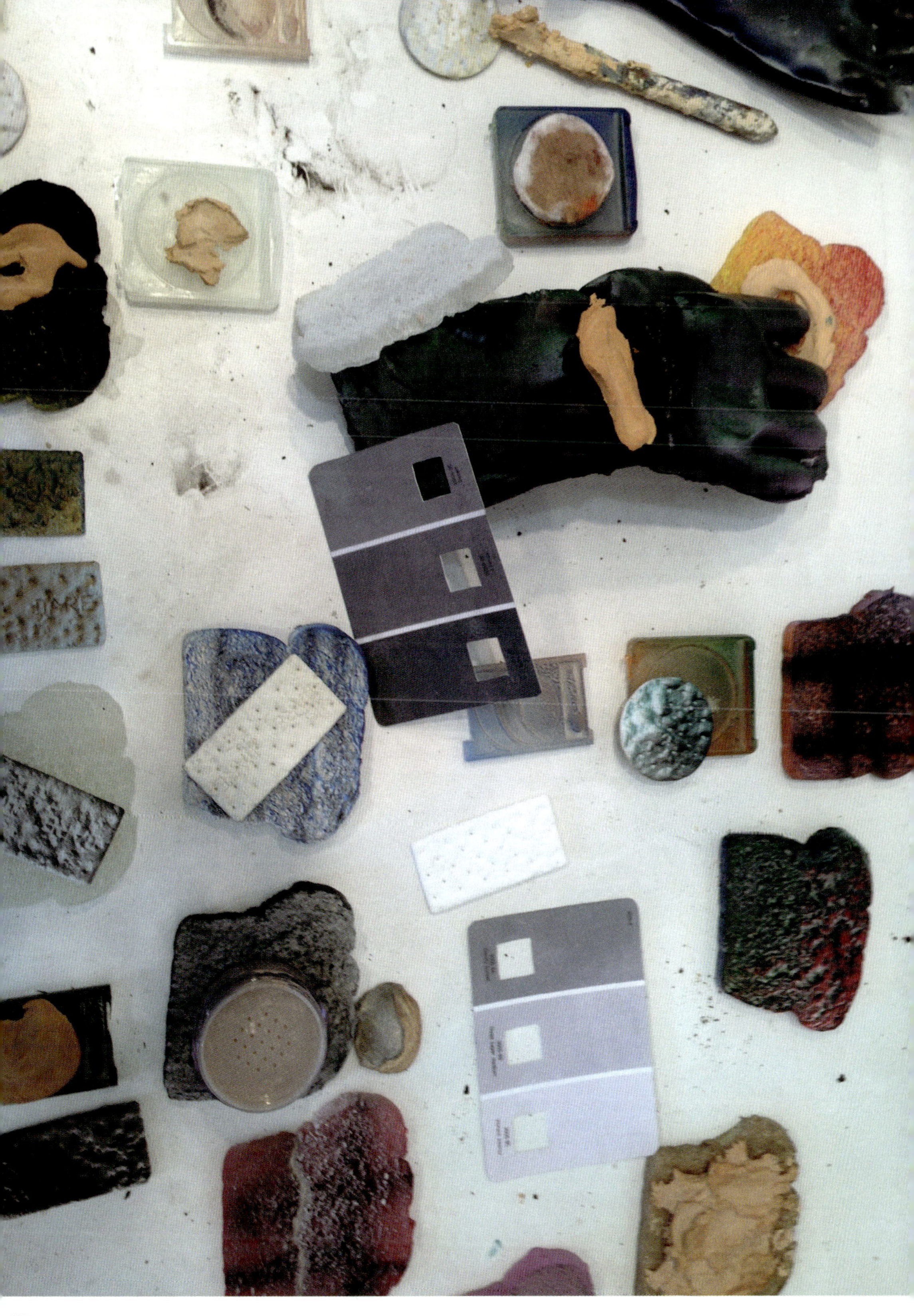

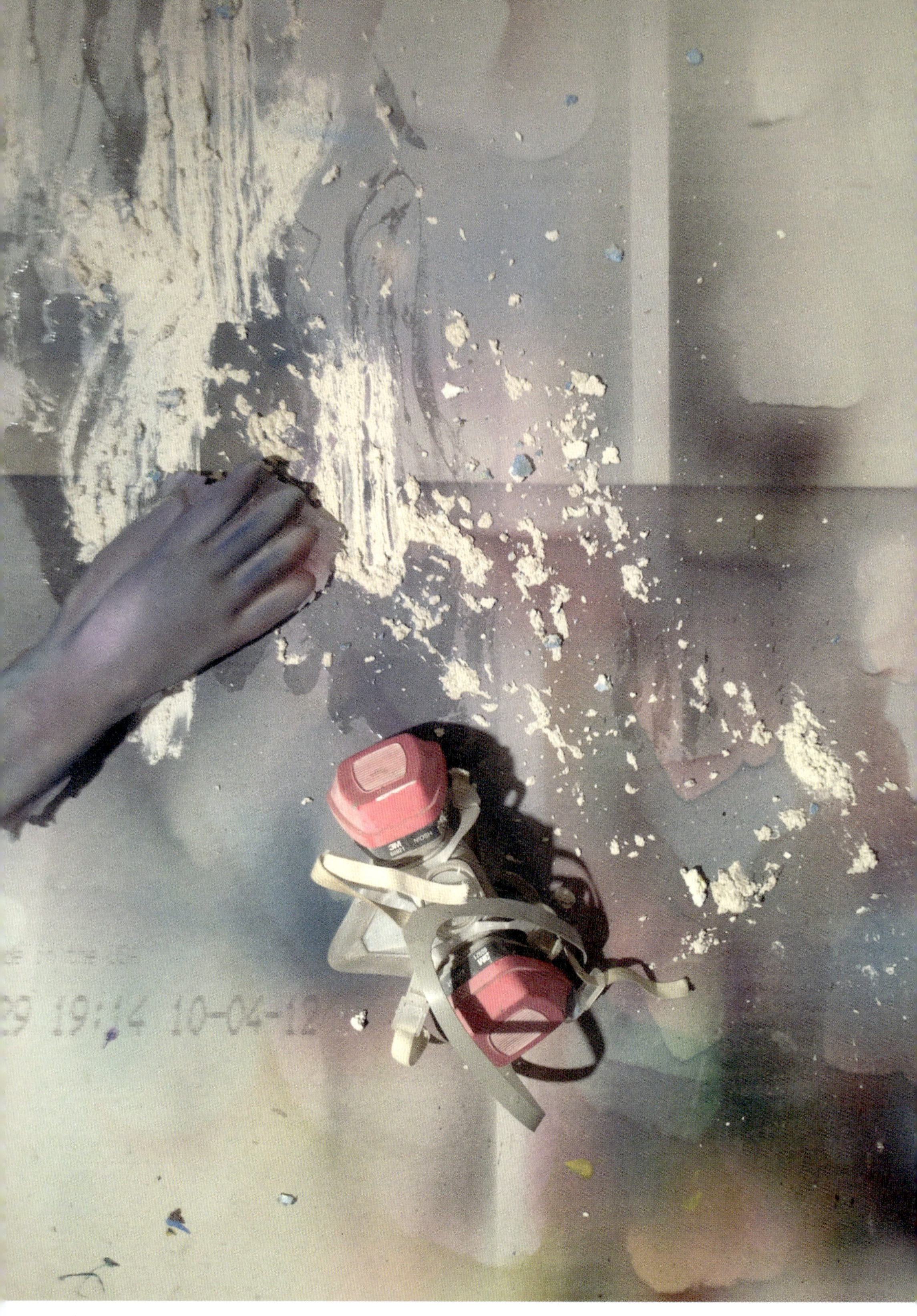

3M 6001 NIOSH
3M
9 19:14 10-04-12

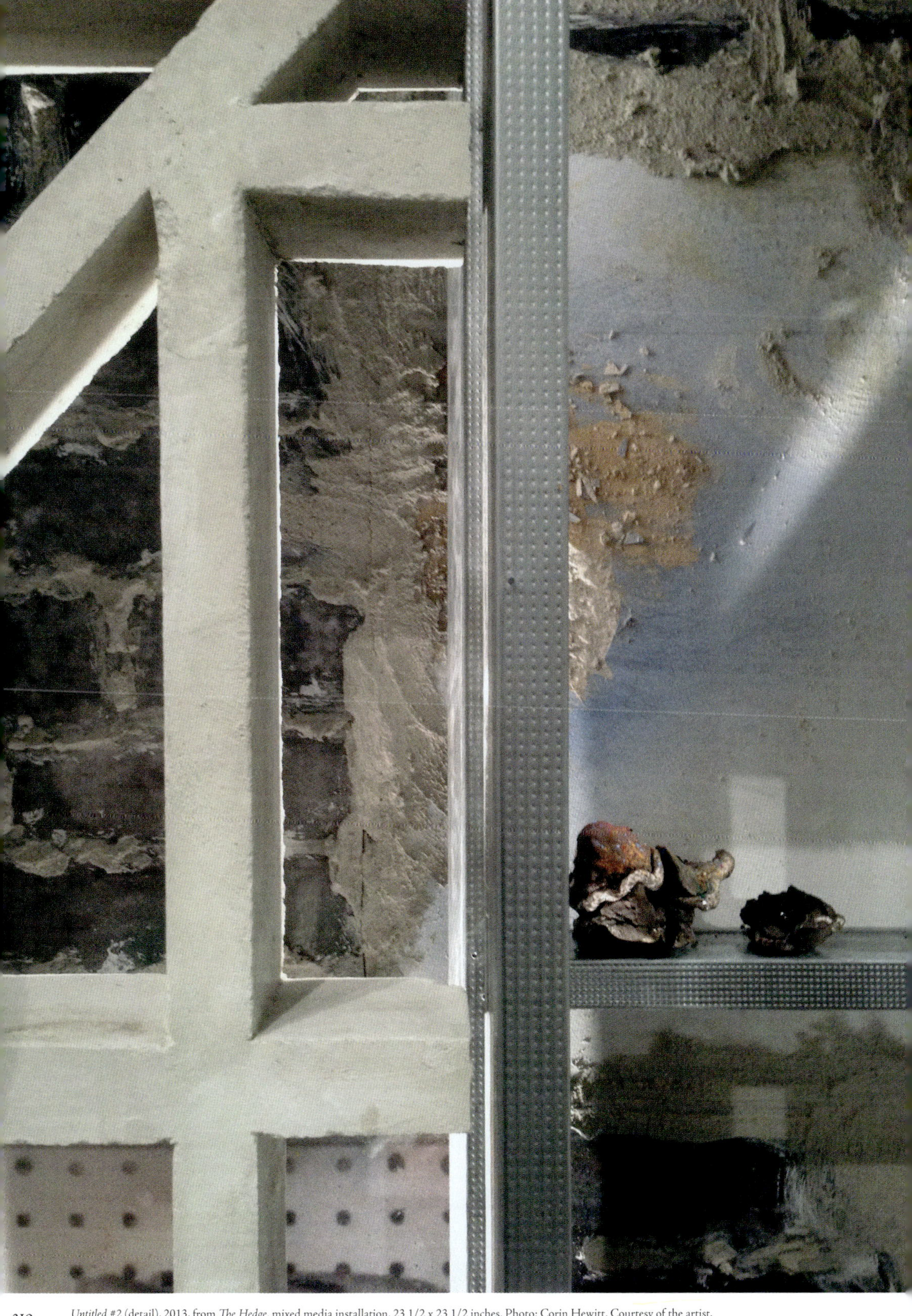

Untitled #2 (detail), 2013, from *The Hedge,* mixed media installation, 23 1/2 x 23 1/2 inches. Photo: Corin Hewitt. Courtesy of the artist.

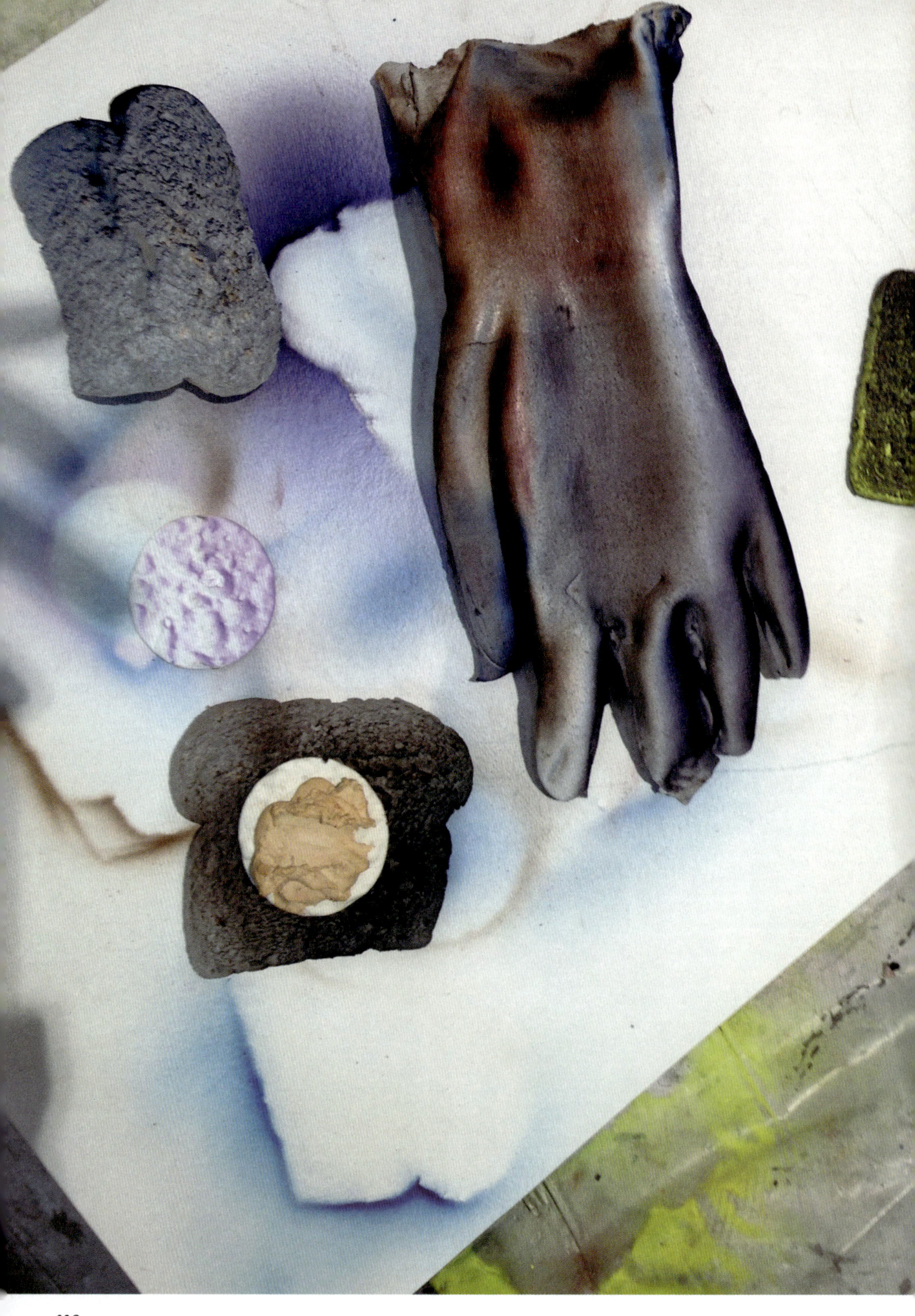